GAAP Guidebook

2018 Edition

Steven M. Bragg

For more information about AccountingTools® products, visit our Web site at www.accountingtools.com.

ISBN-13: 978-1-938910-99-9

Printed in the United States of America

Table of Contents

Preface

The accounting by businesses in the United States is largely governed by Generally Accepted Accounting Principles (GAAP). The source documents for GAAP cover multiple thousands of pages, so their heft alone makes them difficult to research. The *GAAP Guidebook* lightens the research chore by presenting the essential elements of GAAP in a single volume, with an emphasis on key accounting requirements and disclosures. These essential elements are closely supported by several hundred examples and tips.

Following an introduction to GAAP in Chapter 1, the *Guidebook* covers in Chapters 2 through 13 all aspects of the presentation of financial statements, including accounting changes and error corrections, earnings per share, interim reporting, and segment reporting. We then move on to the accounting for assets in Chapters 14 through 20, which encompasses receivables, investments, inventory, intangible assets, and fixed assets. Chapters 21 through 28 cover a broad range of liability and equity issues, while Chapters 29 through 35 address a number of income statement topics – revenue recognition, compensation expense, income taxes, and more. Finally, Chapters 36 through 46 delve into a number of major transaction types, including business combinations, consolidations, derivatives, fair value, foreign currency, leases, and subsequent events. The chapters include tips, podcast references, and a variety of illustrations.

You can find the answers to many accounting questions in the *Guidebook* that might otherwise require extensive research in the original GAAP source documents, such as:

- What is the proper presentation of a balance sheet?
- What does an indirect method statement of cash flows look like?
- How do I calculate diluted earnings per share?
- What information must be included in interim financial statements?
- How do I use a cost layering system to account for inventory?
- What is the process for testing intangible assets for impairment?
- How do I account for fixed assets acquired in a business combination?
- What is the correct accounting for a stock split?
- When can I recognize revenue?
- How do I account for a defined benefit pension plan?
- How do I account for a business combination?

The *GAAP Guidebook* is designed for both professionals and students. Professionals can use it as a handy reference tool that reduces research time, while students will find that it clarifies many of the more arcane accounting topics.

Centennial, Colorado
November 2017

About the Author

Steven Bragg, CPA, has been the chief financial officer or controller of four companies, as well as a consulting manager at Ernst & Young. He received a master's degree in finance from Bentley College, an MBA from Babson College and a Bachelor's degree in Economics from the University of Maine. He has been a two-time president of the Colorado Mountain Club and is an avid alpine skier, mountain biker, and certified master diver. Mr. Bragg resides in Centennial, Colorado. He has written the following books and courses:

7 Habits of Effective CEOs
7 Habits of Effective CFOs
7 Habits of Effective Controllers
Accountant Ethics [for multiple states]
Accountants' Guidebook
Accounting Changes and Error Corrections
Accounting Controls Guidebook
Accounting for Casinos and Gaming
Accounting for Derivatives and Hedges
Accounting for Earnings per Share
Accounting for Inventory
Accounting for Investments
Accounting for Intangible Assets
Accounting for Leases
Accounting for Managers
Accounting for Stock-Based Compensation
Accounting Procedures Guidebook
Agricultural Accounting
Behavioral Ethics
Bookkeeping Guidebook
Budgeting
Business Combinations and Consolidations
Business Insurance Fundamentals
Business Ratios
Business Valuation
Capital Budgeting
CFO Guidebook
Change Management
Closing the Books
Coaching and Mentoring
Conflict Management
Constraint Management
Construction Accounting
Corporate Cash Management
Corporate Finance

Cost Accounting (college textbook)
Cost Accounting Fundamentals
Cost Management Guidebook
Credit & Collection Guidebook
Crowdfunding
Developing and Managing Teams
Effective Collections
Employee Onboarding
Enterprise Risk Management
Fair Value Accounting
Financial Analysis
Financial Forecasting and Modeling
Fixed Asset Accounting
Foreign Currency Accounting
Fraud Examination
Fraud Schemes
GAAP Guidebook
Governmental Accounting
Health Care Accounting
Hospitality Accounting
How to Audit Cash
How to Audit Equity
How to Audit Fixed Assets
How to Audit for Fraud
How to Audit Inventory
How to Audit Liabilities
How to Audit Receivables
How to Run a Meeting
Human Resources Guidebook
IFRS Guidebook
Interpretation of Financial Statements
Inventory Management
Investor Relations Guidebook
Lean Accounting Guidebook
Mergers & Acquisitions

(continued)

Negotiation

New Controller Guidebook

Nonprofit Accounting

Partnership Accounting

Payables Management

Payroll Management

Performance Appraisals

Project Accounting

Project Management

Public Company Accounting

Purchasing Guidebook

Real Estate Accounting

Records Management

Recruiting and Hiring

Revenue Recognition

Sales and Use Tax Accounting

The MBA Guidebook

The Soft Close

The Statement of Cash Flows

The Year-End Close

Treasurer's Guidebook

Working Capital Management

On-Line Resources by Steven Bragg

Steven maintains the accountingtools.com web site, which contains continuing professional education courses, the Accounting Best Practices podcast, and over a thousand articles on accounting subjects.

Chapter 1
Introduction

Introduction

In this chapter, we provide an introduction to the nature of GAAP, and how to use this book and other source materials to research GAAP topics. We also provide brief descriptions of the accounting principles upon which much of the GAAP elsewhere in this book is based.

What is GAAP?

GAAP is short for Generally Accepted Accounting Principles. GAAP is a large group of accounting standards and common industry usage that have been developed over many years. GAAP is used by businesses to properly organize their financial information into accounting records and summarize it into financial statements, as well as disclose certain supporting information.

One of the reasons for using GAAP is so that anyone reading the financial statements of multiple companies has a reasonable basis for comparison, since all companies using GAAP have created their financial statements using the same set of rules.

GAAP covers a broad array of topics, which are aggregated into the following major categories:

- *Presentation.* Covers the proper formatting and presentation of the financial statements, and includes the following topic areas:
  - Presentation of financial statements
  - Balance sheet
  - Statement of shareholder equity
  - Comprehensive income
  - Income statement
  - Statement of cash flows
  - Notes to financial statements
  - Accounting changes and error corrections
  - Changing prices
  - Earnings per share
  - Interim reporting
  - Limited liability entities
  - Personal financial statements
  - Risks and uncertainties
  - Segment reporting

- *Assets*. Describes the accounting for the main types of assets, and includes the following topic areas:
  - o Cash and cash equivalents
  - o Receivables
  - o Investments – debt and equity securities
  - o Investments – equity method and joint ventures
  - o Investments – other
  - o Inventory
  - o Other assets and deferred costs
  - o Intangibles – goodwill and other
  - o Property, plant, and equipment

- *Liabilities*. Describes the accounting for the main types of liabilities, and includes the following topic areas:
  - o Liabilities
  - o Asset retirement and environmental obligations
  - o Exit or disposal cost obligations
  - o Deferred revenue
  - o Commitments
  - o Contingencies
  - o Guarantees
  - o Debt
  - o Distinguishing liabilities from equity

- *Equity*. Addresses the accounting issues related to equity in general, stock dividends and splits, equity-based payments to non-employees, spinoffs, and similar matters.
- *Revenue recognition*. Covers the accounting issues related to revenue in general, sales of products and services, multiple-element arrangements, the milestone method, construction-type contracts, gains and losses, agent considerations, customer payments, and similar matters.
- *Expenses*. Describes the accounting for a number of the more complex types of expenses, and includes the following topic areas:
  - o Cost of sales and services
  - o Compensation – general
  - o Compensation – nonretirement postemployment benefits
  - o Compensation – retirement benefits
  - o Compensation – stock compensation
  - o Other expenses
  - o Research and development
  - o Income taxes

- *Broad transactions*. Describes several transaction types that cannot be classified within one of the preceding areas, and which has broad applicability to many industries. The following topic areas are included:

- o Business combinations
- o Collaborative arrangements
- o Consolidation
- o Derivatives and hedging
- o Fair value assessment
- o Financial instruments
- o Foreign currency matters
- o Interest
- o Leases
- o Nonmonetary transactions
- o Related party disclosures
- o Reorganizations
- o Subsequent events
- o Transfers and servicing

- *Industry.* Includes accounting that is specific to certain industries, ranging from agriculture to software, and with a particular emphasis on the entertainment, financial services, and real estate industries.

GAAP is derived from the pronouncements of a series of government-sponsored accounting entities of which the Financial Accounting Standards Board (FASB) is the latest. The Securities and Exchange Commission also issues accounting pronouncements through its Accounting Staff Bulletins and other announcements that are applicable only to publicly-held companies, and which are considered to be part of GAAP. GAAP is codified into the Accounting Standards Codification, which is available on-line at asc.fasb.org in a rudimentary format and in a more easily searchable printed four-volume series.

GAAP is used primarily by businesses reporting their financial results in the United States. International Financial Reporting Standards, or IFRS, is the accounting framework used in most other countries. GAAP is much more rules-based than IFRS. IFRS focuses more on general principles than GAAP, which makes the IFRS body of work much smaller, cleaner, and easier to understand than GAAP.

There are several working groups that are gradually reducing the differences between the GAAP and IFRS accounting frameworks, so eventually there should be only minor differences in the reported results of a business if it switches between the two frameworks. The working groups are proceeding diligently, but there are still many issues to reconcile, so it may still require a number of years before the two accounting frameworks are in approximate alignment. There have been occasional statements that the two frameworks (and presumably their supporting organizations) will eventually be merged, but this has not yet occurred.

How this Book is Organized

This book is designed to provide a streamlined view of GAAP that can also be used for training purposes.

The GAAP source document is multiple thousands of pages long. Within those pages, GAAP follows a rigid format that provides for each topic a set of sections covering an overview, objectives, scope, glossary, recognition, measurement, presentation, disclosure, implementation guidance, relationships, and transition information. Because of the highly sub-divided nature of the presentation, it may be necessary to wade through a substantial amount of information before finding the specific guidance needed. The *GAAP Guidebook* condenses GAAP to provide only the information that the reader is most likely to need, and in far fewer sections. The book does so by focusing on recognition, measurement, and disclosures, while eliminating much of the implementation guidance that is less likely to be referenced by the mainstream user.

The chapter layout of the *GAAP Guidebook* is structured to closely adhere to the topic structure used in GAAP. Thus, the reader will find that the chapters listed in the table of contents are nearly the same as the GAAP topic list noted in the last section. This chapter format is not optimal, since some topics are scattered among several parts of GAAP. Nonetheless, we have chosen to use this chapter format so that GAAP topics can be more easily cross-referenced in the *Guidebook* to the Accounting Standards Codification for more detailed research.

A few other chapters are not provided, because the source GAAP contains so little information that there is no point in providing chapter coverage. Industry-specific GAAP is covered in separate books by the author that deal with these topics, such as *Agricultural Accounting*, *Construction Accounting*, *Hospitality Accounting*, *Nonprofit Accounting*, *Real Estate Accounting*, and *Accounting for Casinos and Gaming*.

How to Use this Book

There are multiple tools available in this book for researching GAAP topics. The primary challenge is simply locating the correct topic, since there are hundreds of them in the book. To make searching easier in the *Guidebook*, we have added dozens of sub-topics, which appear in the table of contents beneath the chapter titles. We have also endeavored to expand the index to the greatest extent possible, using alternative index terms. Several other sources of information are:

- *Podcast episodes*. The author manages the Accounting Best Practices podcast, which provides information about a variety of accounting topics, and which has been downloaded more than three million times. When there is a podcast episode relevant to a chapter, it is noted in a text box at the be-ginning of the chapter.
- *Tips*. A variety of accounting management tips are sprinkled throughout the book, usually immediately after a related GAAP topic.
- *Glossary*. The book contains a lengthy glossary of accounting terminology.

In addition, consider researching accounting topics on the accountingtools.com website. The site contains articles, blog posts, podcasts, and other information on thousands of accounting topics. Use of the site is completely free.

Accounting Principles

Almost all of this book contains descriptions of the accounting rules and disclosures required by GAAP. However, the other chapters do not address the general accounting principles that provide structure to the GAAP accounting framework. These accounting principles have been described somewhat in the Statements of Financial Accounting Concepts, as well as the standards of previous rule-setting bodies, and sometimes from common usage. The principles are:

- *Accrual principle*. The concept that accounting transactions should be recorded in the accounting periods when they actually occur, rather than in the periods when there are cash flows associated with them. This is the foundation of the accrual basis of accounting. It is important for the construction of financial statements that show what actually happened in an accounting period, rather than being artificially delayed or accelerated by the associated cash flows. For example, if the accrual principle is ignored, one would record an expense only when it is paid, which might incorporate a lengthy delay caused by the payment terms for the associated supplier invoice.

- *Conservatism principle*. The concept states that expenses and liabilities should be recorded as soon as possible, but revenues and assets are only recorded when it is certain that they will occur. This introduces a conservative slant to the financial statements that may yield lower reported profits, since revenue and asset recognition may be delayed for some time. This principle tends to encourage the recordation of losses earlier, rather than later. This concept can be taken too far, where a business persistently misstates its results to be worse than is realistically the case.

- *Consistency principle*. The concept that, once an accounting principle or method is adopted, it should continue to be used until a demonstrably better principle or method comes along. Not following the consistency principle means that a business could continually jump between different accounting treatments of its transactions that make its long-term financial results extremely difficult to discern.

- *Cost principle*. The concept that a business should only record its assets, liabilities, and equity investments at their original purchase costs. This principle is becoming less valid, as a host of accounting standards are heading in the direction of adjusting to fair value.

- *Economic entity principle*. The concept that the transactions of a business should be kept separate from those of its owners and other businesses. This prevents intermingling of assets and liabilities among multiple entities.

- *Full disclosure principle*. The concept that one should include in or alongside the financial statements of a business all of the information that may impact a reader's understanding of those financial statements. The accounting standards have greatly amplified upon this concept in specifying an enormous number of informational disclosures.

- *Going concern principle*. The concept that a business will remain in operation for the foreseeable future. This means that it would be justifiable to defer the recognition of some expenses, such as depreciation, until later periods. Otherwise, the accountant would have to recognize all expenses at once and not defer any of them.
- *Matching principle*. The concept that, when revenue is recorded, one should record all related expenses at the same time. Thus, inventory is charged to the cost of goods sold at the same time that revenue is recorded from the sale of those inventory items. This is a cornerstone of the accrual basis of accounting.
- *Materiality principle*. The concept that a transaction should be recorded in the accounting records if not doing so might have altered the decision making process of someone reading the company's financial statements. This is quite a vague concept that is difficult to quantify, which has led some of the more picayune controllers to record even the smallest transactions.
- *Monetary unit principle*. The concept that a business should only record transactions that can be stated in terms of a unit of currency. Thus, it is easy enough to record the purchase of a fixed asset, since it was bought for a specific price, whereas the value of the quality control system of a business is not recorded. This concept keeps a business from engaging in an excessive level of estimation in deriving the value of its assets and liabilities.
- *Reliability principle*. The concept that only those transactions that can be proven should be recorded. For example, a supplier invoice is solid evidence that an expense has been recorded. This concept is of prime interest to auditors, who are constantly in search of the evidence supporting transactions.
- *Revenue recognition principle*. The concept that revenue is only recognized when a business has substantially completed the earnings process. So many people have skirted around the fringes of this concept to commit reporting fraud that a variety of standard-setting bodies have developed a massive amount of information about what constitutes proper revenue recognition.
- *Time period principle*. The concept that a business should report the results of its operations over a standard period of time. This may qualify as the most glaringly obvious of all accounting principles, but is intended to create a standard set of comparable periods, which is useful for trend analysis.

When there is a question about GAAP that could result in several possible treatments of an accounting transaction or disclosure, it is sometimes useful to resolve the question by viewing the GAAP guidance in light of these accounting principles. Doing so may indicate that one solution more closely adheres to the general intent of the accounting framework, and so is a better solution.

Summary

The *GAAP Guidebook* is intended to be what the name implies – a guide to GAAP. We expect that it will be useful as a handy reference when there is a specific question about GAAP, not as a book to be read from cover to cover. The immense amount of material that was condensed into this book inevitably means that there is little room for many of the explanatory comments typically found in an introductory accounting textbook concerning why a particular accounting rule was established. Instead, we assume that you already have a working knowledge of the general structure of accounting, and only need clarification on a particular accounting issue. If more information is needed about how accounting works, rather than the rules stated in the *Guidebook*, consider buying the author's other books on accounting management, such as *Closing the Books* and *The New Controller Guidebook*. All of the author's books can be purchased at the accountingtools.com website.

Chapter 2
Presentation of Financial Statements

205 = GAAP codification area for the presentation of financial statements

Introduction

The presentation of financial statements in GAAP is a rather odd assemblage of two unrelated topics. One section describes the benefits of presenting comparative financial statements that span multiple periods, while a second section addresses the situations in which discontinued operations must be segregated within the financial statements, and related accounting issues. We cover both topics and their related disclosures in this chapter. The information in this chapter applies to business and not-for-profit entities.

Related Podcast Episode: Episode 185 of the Accounting Best Practices Podcast discusses going concern disclosures. It is available at: **www.accountingtools.com/podcasts** or **iTunes**

Related Chapters

See the following chapters for discussions of issues related to the presentation of financial statements:

- *Earnings per share*. Discusses how the earnings per share related to discontinued operations must be disclosed.
- *Foreign currency matters*. Covers how to translate financial statements that are stated in a foreign currency.
- *Segment reporting*. Covers the reporting of the operating segments of a publicly-held company.

Overview of the Presentation of Financial Statements

GAAP encourages the use of comparative financial statements, which are the side-by-side comparison of financial statements for two or more periods. By doing so, it is easier for the reader to discern the operational performance of a business. Ideally, comparative financial statements should include a pairing of the current year and at least one preceding year for the following reports:

- The balance sheet
- The income statement
- The statement of changes in equity

If financial statements are presented in a comparative format, the disclosures that accompany the financial statements should also include those for the prior years that are included in the comparative format, though only if they continue to be of significance.

Presentation Disclosures

It is entirely possible that the information aggregated into the line items in comparative financial statements will be aggregated differently from year to year. If so, disclose the nature of these changes.

If a company is publicly-held, its financial statement disclosures are also governed by a variety of requirements of the Securities and Exchange Commission (SEC), which include the following:

- *Identical notes.* If the same disclosure is required for several financial statements, it is not necessary to duplicate the disclosures, as long as the single disclosure is referenced in all applicable parts of the financial statements.
- *Materiality.* If GAAP states that a certain amount be reported, but that amount is immaterial, it does not have to be separately stated in the financial statements. It is also allowable to aggregate several of these immaterial amounts.
- *Order of data presentation.* The SEC does not express a preference for the order in which data is presented in financial statements (such as the most recent financial statements being positioned to the left when being shown in a comparative format). However, whatever ordering is adopted must be consistently applied throughout the financial statements.
- *Whole dollar presentation.* It is acceptable to present money amounts in whole dollars or multiples thereof (such as in thousands or millions of dollars).

Tip: If a business has any intention of eventually being publicly-held, it is useful to begin following SEC reporting guidelines as soon as possible, so that prior-period financial results will not have to be restated in the required SEC format at some later date.

Liquidation Basis of Accounting

Liquidation basis accounting is concerned with preparing the financial statements of a business in a different way if the liquidation of a business is considered to be imminent. *Imminent* refers to one of the following two conditions:

- *Liquidation plan.* A plan for liquidation has been approved, and is likely to be achieved.
- *Forced liquidation.* A third party is forcing the business into liquidation, and is likely to achieve this goal.

The accounting under the liquidation basis of accounting differs in several respects from normal accrual-basis accounting. The key differences are:

- Recognize any assets that had not previously been recognized, but which are expected to either be sold in liquidation or used to pay off liabilities. This means it is possible to recognize internally generated intangible assets – which would not normally be the case. The main point is to only recognize items if they are actually worth something in liquidation.
- It is allowable to recognize in aggregate those assets that had not been previously recognized, rather than individually.
- Accrue for the expected disposal costs of assets that will be liquidated. These costs should be presented in aggregate.
- Accrue for those income and expense items that will be earned or incurred through the end of the expected liquidation period. An example of such an income item is the expected profits from orders that have not yet been fulfilled. An example of such an expense item is wage and salary costs expected to be incurred. This should only be done when there is a reasonable basis upon which to make the estimates.

Tip: In liquidation accounting, assets are measured at the estimated amount for which they can be sold – which may or may not be their fair market value. If the liquidation is rushed, this could mean that the estimated selling price is less than fair market value.

It is not permissible to anticipate a release from a liability that has not yet occurred. Instead, continue to recognize the liability until such time as an actual release has been confirmed.

Do not discount disposal costs to their present value. Also, there is no discounting of accrued income. There is no real point in doing so, since the business will presumably be liquidated so soon that the amount of any discount would probably be immaterial.

What if a company does not liquidate just yet, and instead drags along for a few reporting periods? In each period, remeasure the assets and liabilities and adjust them in the accounting records to their liquidation values as necessary.

Under the liquidation basis of accounting, a business must issue two new statements, which are as follows:

- *The statement of net assets in liquidation.* Shows the net assets available for distribution at the end of the reporting period.
- *The statement of changes in net assets in liquidation.* Shows the changes in net assets during the reporting period.

Liquidation Basis Disclosures

When liquidation basis accounting is employed, the following minimum set of disclosures must be included in the financial statements:

- *Basis of presentation.* Note that the financial statements are prepared in accordance with the liquidation basis of accounting. Also disclose the circumstances under which the company shifted to the liquidation basis, and how the business has determined that liquidation is imminent.
- *Plan of liquidation.* Describe the manner in which the company expects to dispose of its assets, as well as those items not previously recognized as assets. Also note the manner in which liabilities are expected to be settled, and the date by which it is expected that the liquidation will have been completed.
- *Assumptions.* Describe the methods and assumptions used to determine the recorded amounts of assets and liabilities. Also note any subsequent changes to these methods and assumptions.
- *Accruals.* Note those costs and income items accrued in anticipation of liquidation, as well as the time periods over which these items are expected to be paid or earned.

Going Concern Disclosures

An organization is assumed to be a going concern, and so should prepare financial statements on that basis. If that is not the case, the entity instead prepares its financial statements using the liquidation basis of accounting, as described earlier in the Liquidation Basis of Accounting section. If situations arise that make an organization's ability to continue as a going concern unclear, management is required to disclose the situation.

The management team should evaluate whether there are substantial doubts about an entity's ability to continue as a going concern. This forward-looking evaluation should cover the one-year period after financial statements are issued or are available to be issued. Substantial doubt is considered to be present when conditions and events make it probable that the organization will not be able to meet its obligations as they become due for payment. Examples of such conditions and events are:

- Adverse financial ratios
- Adverse legislation
- An uninsured loss
- Debt restructurings to avoid default
- Denial of trade credit by suppliers
- Loan defaults
- Loss of a key customer
- Loss of a key patent or copyright
- Negative cash flows

- Operating losses
- Unprofitable long-term commitments
- Work stoppages

The outcome of this evaluation can be mitigated by the presence of management plans to mitigate the conditions, but only if it is probable that the plans can be implemented. Examples of such management plans are ones that cut expenses, or raise cash through the sale of assets, borrowing, or the sale of shares.

Even when management plans may mitigate the situation, a disclosure must still accompany the financial statements that describes the conditions or events triggering the doubt about being able to continue as a going concern, evaluates the significance of these events, and states management's plans to alleviate the situation.

If management's plans cannot alleviate the situation, then the disclosure must state that there is substantial doubt about the entity's ability to continue as a going concern within one year from the financial statement issuance date. Additional disclosures should include:

- The conditions or events causing there to be substantial doubt about the ability to continue as a going concern
- An evaluation by management of the significance of these conditions or events in regard to the ability of the business to meet its obligations
- The plans intended to mitigate the effects of the conditions or events

Discontinued Operations

GAAP requires special presentation treatment of the results of operations of a component of an entity that is either being held for sale or which has already been disposed of. It must be reported as a discontinued operation within the financial statements if the asset disposal represents a strategic shift that will have a major impact on the operations and financial results of a business. Examples of strategic shifts are the disposals of:

- A major equity method investment
- A major geographic region
- A major line of business

EXAMPLES

(1) Armadillo Industries plans to cancel one of its pressurized container products, due to a lack of sales. The product is part of a larger product group which management plans to continue to support. Since there is no strategic shift, there is no need to classify operations related to the single product as a discontinued operation.

(2) Upon further consideration, Armadillo decides to list the entire container product group for sale. This is a clear strategic shift, so Armadillo should classify it as a discontinued operation.

(3) Armadillo sells one of its product lines. Part of the sale agreement stipulates that the buyer will pay Armadillo a 5% royalty on any sales related to the product line for the next three years. Armadillo will have no continuing operational involvement in the product line. Since Armadillo will have no significant continuing involvement, the product line should be disclosed as a discontinued operation.

If the preceding condition is met, the organization must report the results of operations of the component for current and prior periods in a separate discontinued operations section of the income statement. The following information should be reported:

- The major classes of line items constituting the pretax profit or loss of the component for current and prior periods
- Either the total operating and investing cash flows of the component, or its significant noncash items (which someone could then use to estimate cash flows)
- If there is a noncontrolling interest, state the pretax profit or loss attributable to the parent

EXAMPLE

Armadillo Industries has decided to put its money-losing body armor division up for sale, which results in the following reporting in the lower part of its income statement:

Income from continuing operations before income taxes	$15,000,000	
Income taxes	5,250,000	
Income from continuing operations		$9,750,000
Discontinued operations (Note G)		
Loss from operations of discontinued body armor division (including loss on disposal of $1,200,000)	-6,000,000	
Income tax benefit	2,100,000	
Loss on discontinued operations		-3,900,000
Net income		$5,850,000

If there were adjustments for disposal-related amounts previously reported for discontinued operations, they should be classified separately within the discontinued operations section of the income statement in the current period. Examples of these adjustments are:

- *Benefit plan obligations.* Contingencies related to employee benefit plan obligations are settled, such as postemployment benefits. This type of adjustment is usually restricted to being classified within discontinued operations if it occurs no later than one year following the disposal transaction, unless delayed by circumstances beyond the control of the company.
- *Contingent liabilities.* Contingencies related to liabilities associated with a disposal transaction are subsequently resolved, such as site remediation liabilities retained by the seller.
- *Contingent terms.* Contingencies related to terms under which a disposal transaction was concluded are subsequently resolved, such as adjustments to the initial price paid.

Some companies tend to take advantage of the preceding rule regarding classifying subsequent adjustments within discontinued operations, by adopting a loose interpretation of whether an expense is really associated with a discontinued operation. By doing so, they shift expenses out of their income from operations. Auditors are aware of this issue and so may disallow some inclusions, so clearly document the reasons for classifying expenses within discontinued operations.

If the buyer of a discontinued operation assumes the debt associated with the operation, any interim interest expense incurred by the seller should be allocated to discontinued operations. If the general interest expense of the selling business cannot be directly associated with a discontinued operation, then allocate interest expense to the operation based on the following ratio:

$$\frac{\text{Assets to be sold or discontinued} - \text{Debt to be paid as a result of the disposal}}{\substack{\text{Total company net assets} + \text{Consolidated debt} - (\text{Debt assumed by buyer} \\ + \text{Debt to be paid as a result of the disposal} + \text{Debt directly attributed to other} \\ \text{company operations})}}$$

The allocation of interest should be consistently applied to all discontinued operations.

The treatment of general corporate overhead is not the same as interest expense. Instead, GAAP specifically does *not* allow the allocation of general corporate overhead to discontinued operations.

Discontinued Operations Disclosures

When there are assets being held for sale, or which have been sold, disclose the following information as part of the financial statements:

- The circumstances leading to the disposal or expected disposal
- The manner and timing of the disposal or expected disposal
- The carrying amounts of the major asset and liability classes included in the disposal group

- The gain or loss on disposal
- The amounts of revenue and pretax profit or loss reported as part of discontinued operations

If there is an expectation that a cluster of assets and related liabilities are to be sold as a group (known as a *disposal group*), separately state these assets and liabilities on the balance sheet. It is not allowed to present them as a single net amount on the balance sheet.

If the decision is made to alter the existing plan to sell a disposal group, disclose the facts and circumstances leading to the decision, and the effect on the results of operations for all periods presented.

If an operation is classified as a discontinued operation but continues to generate continuing indirect cash flows (such as interest income from seller-provided financing, and passive royalty interests in the operations of the disposed components), then disclose the following information:

- The activities causing the cash flows
- The time period over which the cash flows are expected to continue
- The reasons why the continuing cash flows are not the direct cash flows of the component

If there were adjustments for disposal-related amounts previously reported for discontinued operations, they should be classified separately within the discontinued operations section of the income statement in the current period.

If a business expects to have continuing involvement with a component that has been or is to be disposed of, disclose the intra-entity amounts recorded before the disposal transaction. Also disclose the types of involvement that the company will have with the component after the disposal transaction has been completed.

The SEC has stated that, if a business allocates interest expense to any discontinued operations, it must clearly disclose the related accounting policy and the amount of allocated interest expense.

Summary

The disclosure of information about discontinued operations can safely be described as onerous, if only because it requires restating information that is usually segregated in a different way within the income statement and balance sheet. Thus, some manual rewriting of at least the income statement will probably be required from the standard format automatically generated by a company's accounting software. Consequently, it makes sense to spend time evaluating whether there are any reasonable grounds for disqualifying a disposal from treatment as a discontinued operation. As an alternative, consider advising management not to engage in disposal activities anywhere near the end of the company's fiscal year, so that there are no proposed transactions worthy of consideration as discontinued operations.

Chapter 3
Balance Sheet

210 = GAAP codification area for the balance sheet

Introduction

In most organizations, the balance sheet is considered the second most important of the financial statements, after the income statement. A common financial reporting package is to issue the income statement and balance sheet, along with supporting materials. This does not comprise a complete set of financial statements, but it is considered sufficient for internal reporting purposes in many organizations.

In this chapter, we explore several possible formats for the balance sheet, and also describe how to create it. We also make note of the extensive additional reporting requirements imposed on the balance sheets of publicly-held companies.

Overview of the Balance Sheet

A balance sheet (also known as a statement of financial position) presents information about an entity's assets, liabilities, and shareholders' equity, where the compiled result must match this formula:

$$\text{Total assets} = \text{Total liabilities} + \text{Equity}$$

The balance sheet reports the aggregate effect of transactions as of a specific date. The balance sheet is used to assess an entity's liquidity and ability to pay its debts.

There is no specific requirement for the line items to be included in the balance sheet of a privately-held company (see the disclosures section for the much more extensive requirements for publicly-held businesses). The following line items, at a minimum, are normally included in the balance sheet:

Current Assets:

- Cash and cash equivalents
- Marketable securities
- Trade and other receivables
- Prepaid expenses
- Inventories

Non-Current Assets:

- Property, plant, and equipment
- Intangible assets
- Goodwill

Current Liabilities:

- Trade and other payables
- Customer deposits
- Cash collected on behalf of third parties
- Accrued expenses
- Current tax liabilities
- Current portion of loans payable
- Other financial liabilities

Non-Current Liabilities:

- Loans payable
- Deferred tax liabilities
- Long-term warranties
- Other non-current liabilities

Equity:

- Capital stock
- Additional paid-in capital
- Retained earnings

Items included in the current assets classification shall include all items to be sold or consumed within one year. However, if the operating cycle of a business is longer than one year, the classification can include any items that are sold or consumed within the operating cycle of the business. Classify all of the following as current assets:

- *Cash.* This is cash available for current operations, as well as any short-term, highly liquid investments that are readily convertible to known amounts of cash and which are so near their maturities that they present an insignificant risk of value changes. Do not include cash whose withdrawal is restricted, to be used for other than current operations, or segregated for the liquidation of long-term debts; such items should be classified as longer-term.
- *Marketable securities.* This includes those securities representing the investment of cash available for current operations, including trading securities.

- *Accounts receivable.* This includes trade accounts, notes, and acceptances that are receivable. Also, include receivables from officers, employees, affiliates, and others if they are collectible within a year. Do not include any receivable for which there is no expectation of collection within 12 months; such items should be classified as longer-term.
- *Prepaid expenses.* This includes prepayments for insurance, interest, rent, taxes, unused royalties, advertising services, and operating supplies.
- *Inventory.* This includes merchandise, raw materials, work-in-process, finished goods, operating supplies, and maintenance parts.

Items specifically excluded from the current assets classification are:

- Cash whose use is restricted for other than current operations
- Investments in securities where the intent is to gain control over or affiliate with another entity
- Receivables not expected to be collected within 12 months
- The cash surrender value of life insurance policies
- Land and other types of natural resources
- Depreciable assets
- Long-term prepayments that will not be charged to expense for several years

A liability should be classified as current when the company expects to settle it during its normal operating cycle or within 12 months after the reporting period, or if it is scheduled for settlement within 12 months. Classify all of the following as current liabilities:

- *Payables.* This is all accounts payable incurred in the acquisition of materials and supplies that are used to produce goods or services.
- *Customer deposits.* This is payments made in advance by customers for orders they have placed with the company, and which will be applied against the final billing of those orders. Do not include a long-term prepayment in this category.
- *Cash collected on behalf of third parties.* A company may be in an agency relationship with another business, where it collects cash on behalf of the other business and forwards the funds to the other entity. This situation would arise when goods are sold on consignment.
- *Accrued expenses.* This is accrued expenses for items directly related to the operating cycle, such as accruals for compensation, rentals, royalties, and various taxes.
- *Current tax liabilities.* This is taxes payable in the near term, such as liabilities to remit sales taxes and payroll taxes.
- *Current portion of loans payable.* This is debts maturing within the next 12 months.

Current liabilities include accruals for amounts that can only be determined approximately, such as bonuses, and where the payee to whom payment will be made cannot initially be designated, such as a warranty accrual.

Here is an example of a balance sheet which presents information as of the end of two fiscal years:

Lowry Locomotion
Balance Sheet
As of December 31, 20X2 and 20X1

(000s)	12/31/20X2	12/31/20x1
ASSETS		
Current assets		
Cash and cash equivalents	$270,000	$215,000
Trade receivables	147,000	139,000
Inventories	139,000	128,000
Other current assets	15,000	27,000
Total current assets	$571,000	$509,000
Non-current assets		
Property, plant, and equipment	551,000	529,000
Goodwill	82,000	82,000
Other intangible assets	143,000	143,000
Total non-current assets	$776,000	$754,000
Total assets	$1,347,000	$1,263,000
LIABILITIES AND EQUITY		
Current liabilities		
Trade and other payables	$217,000	$198,000
Short-term borrowings	133,000	202,000
Current portion of long-term borrowings	5,000	5,000
Current tax payable	26,000	23,000
Accrued expenses	9,000	13,000
Total current liabilities	$390,000	$441,000
Non-current liabilities		
Long-term debt	85,000	65,000

(000s)	12/31/20X2	12/31/20x1
Deferred taxes	19,000	17,000
Total non-current liabilities	$104,000	$82,000
Total liabilities	$494,000	$523,000
Shareholders' equity		
Capital	100,000	100,000
Additional paid-in capital	15,000	15,000
Retained earnings	738,000	625,000
Total equity	$853,000	$740,000
Total liabilities and equity	$1,347,000	$1,263,000

The Common Size Balance Sheet

A common size balance sheet presents not only the standard information contained in a balance sheet, but also a column that notes the same information as a percentage of the total assets (for asset line items) or as a percentage of total liabilities and shareholders' equity (for liability or shareholders' equity line items).

It is extremely useful to construct a common size balance sheet that itemizes the results as of the end of multiple time periods, so that trend lines can be constructed to ascertain changes over longer time periods. The common size balance sheet is also useful for comparing the proportions of assets, liabilities, and equity between different companies, particularly as part of an industry or acquisition analysis.

For example, if one were to compare the common size balance sheet of a company to that of a potential acquiree, and the acquiree had 40% of its assets invested in accounts receivable versus 20% by the company, this may indicate that aggressive collection activities might reduce the acquiree's receivables if the company were to acquire it.

The common size balance sheet is not required under GAAP. However, being a useful document for analysis purposes, it is commonly distributed within a company for review by management.

There is no mandatory format for a common size balance sheet, though percentages are nearly always placed to the right of the normal numerical results. If balance sheet results are being reported as of the end of many periods, it may be possible to dispense with numerical results entirely, in favor of just presenting the common size percentages.

EXAMPLE

Lowy Locomotion creates a common size balance sheet that contains the balance sheet as of the end of its fiscal year for each of the past two years, with common size percentages to the right:

Lowry Locomotion
Common Size Balance Sheet
As of 12/31/20x2 and 12/31/20x1

	($) 12/31/20x2	($) 12/31/20x1	(%) 12/31/20x2	(%) 12/31/20x1
Current assets				
Cash	$1,200	$900	7.6%	7.1%
Accounts receivable	4,800	3,600	30.4%	28.3%
Inventory	3,600	2,700	22.8%	21.3%
Total current assets	$9,600	$7,200	60.8%	56.7%
Total fixed assets	6,200	5,500	39.2%	43.3%
Total assets	$15,800	$12,700	100.0%	100.0%
Current liabilities				
Accounts payable	$2,400	$1,800	15.2%	14.2%
Accrued expenses	480	360	3.0%	2.8%
Short-term debt	800	600	5.1%	4.7%
Total current liabilities	$3,680	$2,760	23.3%	21.7%
Long-term debt	9,020	7,740	57.1%	60.9%
Total liabilities	$12,700	$10,500	80.4%	82.7%
Shareholders' equity	3,100	2,200	19.6%	17.3%
Total liabilities and equity	$15,800	$12,700	100.0%	100.0%

The Comparative Balance Sheet

A comparative balance sheet presents side-by-side information about an entity's assets, liabilities, and shareholders' equity as of multiple points in time. For example, a comparative balance sheet could present the balance sheet as of the end of each year for the past three years. Another variation is to present the balance sheet as of the end of each month for the past 12 months on a rolling basis. In both cases, the intent is to provide the reader with a series of snapshots of a company's financial condition over a period of time, which is useful for developing trend line analyses.

The comparative balance sheet is not required under GAAP for a privately-held company, but the Securities and Exchange Commission (SEC) does require it in numerous circumstances for the reports issued by publicly-held companies, particularly the annual Form 10-K and the quarterly Form 10-Q. The usual SEC requirement is to report a comparative balance sheet for the past two years, with additional requirements for quarterly reporting.

There is no standard format for a comparative balance sheet. It is somewhat more common to report the balance sheet as of the least recent period furthest to the right, though the reverse is the case when balance sheets are reported in a trailing twelve months format.

The following is a sample of a comparative balance sheet that contains the balance sheet as of the end of a company's fiscal year for each of the past three years:

Sample Comparative Balance Sheet

	as of 12/31/20X3	as of 12/31/20X2	as of 12/31/20X1
Current assets			
Cash	$1,200,000	$900,000	$750,000
Accounts receivable	4,800,000	3,600,000	3,000,000
Inventory	3,600,000	2,700,000	2,300,000
Total current assets	$9,600,000	$7,200,000	$6,050,000
Total fixed assets	6,200,000	5,500,000	5,000,000
Total assets	$15,800,000	$12,700,000	$11,050,000
Current liabilities			
Accounts payable	$2,400,000	$1,800,000	$1,500,000
Accrued expenses	480,000	360,000	300,000
Short-term debt	800,000	600,000	400,000
Total current liabilities	$3,680,000	$2,760,000	$2,200,000
Long-term debt	9,020,000	7,740,000	7,350,000
Total liabilities	$12,700,000	$10,500,000	$9,550,000
Shareholders' equity	3,100,000	2,200,000	1,500,000
Total liabilities and equity	$15,800,000	$12,700,000	$11,050,000

The sample comparative balance sheet reveals that the company has increased the size of its current assets over the past few years, but has also recently invested in a large amount of additional fixed assets that have likely been the cause of a significant boost in its long-term debt.

How to Construct the Balance Sheet

If an accounting software package is being used, it is quite easy to construct the balance sheet. Just access the report writing module, select the time period for which the balance sheet is to be printed, and print it. If the balance sheet is instead constructed manually, follow these steps:

1. Create the trial balance report.
2. List each account pertaining to the balance sheet in a separate column of the trial balance.
3. Add the difference between the revenue and expense line items on the trial balance to a separate line item in the equity section of the balance sheet.
4. Aggregate these line items into those to be reported in the balance sheet as a separate line item.
5. Shift the result into the preferred balance sheet format.

The following example illustrates the construction of a balance sheet.

EXAMPLE

The accounting software for Lowry Locomotion breaks down at the end of July, and the controller has to create the financial statements by hand. He has a copy of Lowry's trial balance, which is shown below. He transfers this information to an electronic spreadsheet, creates separate columns for accounts to include in the balance sheet, and copies those balances into these columns. This leaves a number of accounts related to the income statement, which he can ignore for the purposes of creating the balance sheet. However, he *does* include the net loss for the period in the "Current year profit" row, which is included in the equity section of the balance sheet.

Lowry Locomotion Extended Trial Balance

	Adjusted Trial Balance		Balance Sheet		Aggregation	
	Debit	Credit	Debit	Credit	Debit	Credit
Cash	$60,000		$60,000		$60,000	
Accounts receivable	230,000		230,000		230,000	
Inventory	300,000		300,000		300,000	
Fixed assets (net)	210,000		210,000		210,000	
Accounts payable		$90,000		$90,000		$165,000
Accrued liabilities		75,000		75,000		
Notes payable		420,000		420,000		420,000
Equity		350,000		350,000		215,000
Current year profit			135,000			

Balance Sheet

	Adjusted Trial Balance		Balance Sheet		Aggregation	
Revenue		450,000				
Cost of goods sold	290,000					
Salaries expense	225,000					
Payroll tax expense	20,000					
Rent expense	35,000					
Other expenses	15,000					
Totals	$1,385,000	$1,385,000	$935,000	$935,000	$800,000	$800,000

In the "Aggregation" columns of the extended trial balance, the controller has aggregated the liabilities for accounts payable and accrued liabilities in the accounts payable line, and aggregated equity and current year profit into the equity line. He then transfers this information into the following condensed balance sheet:

Lowry Locomotion
Balance Sheet
For the month ended July 31, 20X1

Assets	
Cash	$60,000
Accounts receivable	230,000
Inventory	300,000
Fixed Assets	210,000
Total assets	$800,000
Liabilities	
Accounts payable	$165,000
Notes payable	420,000
Total liabilities	$585,000
Equity	$215,000
Total liabilities and equity	$800,000

Offsetting

Offsetting is the practice of combining selected assets and liabilities on the balance sheet, so that only the net amount appears. In general, GAAP does not allow offsetting. Instead, the full amount of assets and liabilities are to be separately stated on the balance sheet; by doing so, readers gain a better understanding of the financial position of a business.

The one scenario in which offsetting is allowed is when there is a right of setoff, where a debtor has the right to apply debt owed to another party to a debt owed by the same other party to the debtor. For the purposes of offsetting, the right of setoff only applies when both of the following conditions have been met:

- The amounts owed between the two parties are determinable
- The business issuing the balance sheet has a legally enforceable right of setoff and intends to use it

If the preceding conditions are met, a company can offset the designated assets and liabilities on its balance sheet, and only report the net amount.

Treatment of Negative Cash

It is possible for a negative cash balance to appear on the balance sheet if a company has issued checks for more funds than it has in its checking account. If so, it is customary to move the amount of the overdrawn checks into a liability account, and set up the entry to automatically reverse, thereby immediately shifting the cash withdrawal back into the cash account at the beginning of the next reporting period. There are two options for which liability account to use to store the overdrawn amount, which are:

- *Separate account.* The more theoretically correct approach is to segregate the overdrawn amount in its own account, such as "overdrawn checks" or "checks paid exceeding cash." However, since this is likely to be a small account balance, it clutters the balance sheet with an extra line. Or, if smaller accounts are aggregated together on the balance sheet, it will not appear by itself on the balance sheet, and so conveys no real information to the user. If so, try the next option.
- *Accounts payable account.* Record the amount in the accounts payable account. If this is done, the accounts payable detail report will no longer exactly match the total account balance. However, as long as the entry automatically reverses, the overdrawn amount should not clutter up the account for long. This approach is especially appealing if overdrawn checks are a rarity.

Balance Sheet Disclosures

This entire chapter has been about the disclosure of a company's balance sheet, as defined by GAAP. In addition, the SEC has enumerated a number of additional disclosures regarding the reporting of the various line items stated in the balance sheet, which are as follows:

- *Cash.* Disclose the nature and amount of any cash that has been restricted in regard to its withdrawal or usage. Describe whether there are any compensating balance arrangements that are maintained in order to assure future credit availability.

- *Accounts receivable.* Separately state the amounts receivable from customers, related parties, underwriters/promoters/employees not in the ordinary course of business, and other parties.
- *Long-term contracts.* If the receivables line item includes amounts due under long-term contracts, disclose the following information:
    - Balances billed but not yet paid by customers under contractually-allowed retainage provisions. Also state the amounts to be collected by year, and the amounts to be collected after one year.
    - The sales value of performance and similar amounts not yet billed to customers, and the amounts expected to be collected after one year.
    - Billed or unbilled amounts for which realization is uncertain, and the amounts expected to be collected after one year.
- *Inventory.* State the amounts of the major classes of inventory, such as raw materials, work in process, and finished goods, as well as the basis under which the amounts were determined, such as the first in, first out method. If any general and administrative (G&A) expense was charged to inventory, state the aggregate amount of G&A incurred in each period and the amount remaining in inventory. If the LIFO method was used, state the excess of replacement cost over the LIFO inventory value, if the amount is material.
- *Other current assets.* State in separate line items or in the accompanying disclosures any amounts exceeding five percent of total current assets.
- *Accumulated depreciation.* Separately state the amount of any accumulated depreciation, depletion, and/or amortization.
- *Intangible assets.* Separately state each class of intangible assets in excess of five percent of total assets, along with the basis for the amount recorded. Disclose any significant changes in these line items. Separately state the amount of any accumulated amortization.
- *Other assets.* State in separate line items or in the accompanying disclosures any amounts exceeding five percent of total assets. Disclose any significant changes in these line items.
- *Deferred charges.* If there is a significant deferred charge, disclose the policy for the deferral and amortization of the charge.
- *Accounts payable.* Separately state the amounts payable to banks for borrowings, factors and other financial institutions for borrowings, the holders of commercial paper, trade creditors, related parties, underwriters/promoters/employees not in the ordinary course of business, and others.
- *Lines of credit.* The amounts and terms of unused lines of credit, as well as the weighted average interest rate on short-term borrowings outstanding.
- *Other current liabilities.* State in separate line items or in the accompanying disclosures any amounts exceeding five percent of total current liabilities.
- *Long-term debt.* Separately describe each type of debt, including the rate of interest, the date of maturity, any contingencies related to debt payment, the priority of the debt, and the basis of convertibility (if any). Also disclose the

amount and terms of any unused commitments for long-term financing arrangements.

- *Other liabilities*. State in separate line items or in the accompanying disclosures any amounts exceeding five percent of total liabilities.
- *Deferred credits*. Separately state deferred income taxes, deferred tax credits, and deferred income (if material).
- *Redeemable preferred stock*. State the title of each issuance of redeemable preferred stock, the carrying amount, and the redemption amount. If there are several issuances, it is acceptable to state them all in aggregate on the balance sheet and provide supporting details in the accompanying notes. Also state the number of these shares authorized and outstanding. Further, describe each issuance, including its redemption features, holder rights in the event of default, the effects if a redemption payment is not made, the aggregate redemption requirements in each of the next five years, and any changes in each issuance during the periods covered by the presented income statements.
- *Nonredeemable preferred stock*. If preferred stock is only redeemable at the option of the issuing company, state the title of each issuance and its dollar amount. Also state the number of these shares authorized and outstanding. Further, note any changes in each issuance during the periods covered by the presented income statements.
- *Common stock*. State the number of shares issued and outstanding for each class of common shares, as well as the dollar amount. Also indicate whether the shares are convertible. Further, note any changes in each issuance during the periods covered by the presented income statements.
- *Retained earnings*. Separately state the amounts of appropriated and unappropriated retained earnings.

The SEC also requires that, for all types of stock, disclosure be made of the dollar amount of shares subscribed but unissued, and any deduction for subscriptions receivable.

Please note that these SEC-mandated requirements are *only* applicable to the balance sheets of publicly-held companies.

Summary

Though a number of formats for the balance sheet were shown in this chapter, the most common one by far for internal reporting purposes is to present it only as of the end of the accounting period being reported – comparative balance sheets are usually only used by publicly-held companies or in situations where a business is specifically issuing financial statements meant to cover multiple reporting periods.

A better approach than single-period reporting is to configure the report writer in the accounting software to automatically issue a multi-period balance sheet that shows the balance sheet as of the end of each of the last 12 months. This gives management an excellent view of trends for key assets and liabilities. This format is superior to the single-period balance sheet, and should replace it where possible.

Chapter 4
Comprehensive Income

220 = GAAP codification area for comprehensive income

Introduction

Not all of the income-generating activity of a business appears in its income statement. Some items have experienced gains or losses, but have not yet been realized, and so do not appear in the income statement until some later date. To provide early warning to investors regarding potential gains and losses that may be realized in the future, we use the concept of comprehensive income. In this chapter, we define comprehensive income and show how it is disclosed. The guidance in this chapter applies to all entities, except those that have no items of other comprehensive income, and not-for-profit entities.

Related Podcast Episodes: Episodes 152 and 155 of the Accounting Best Practices Podcast discuss changes to other comprehensive income and the reporting of other comprehensive income reclassifications, respectively. They are available at: **www.accountingtools.com/podcasts** or **iTunes**

Related Chapters

See the Income Statement chapter for discussions of issues related to comprehensive income.

Overview of Comprehensive Income

The intent behind the concept of comprehensive income is to report on all changes in the equity of a business, other than those involving the owners of the business. Not all of these transactions appear in the income statement, so comprehensive income is needed to provide a more comprehensive view. Comprehensive income is comprised of net income and other comprehensive income. Net income is already adequately disclosed in the income statement. This means that other comprehensive income is the true focus of the comprehensive income topic. Other comprehensive income is comprised of the following items:

Foreign Currency Items

- Foreign currency translation adjustments
- Gains and losses on intra-company foreign currency transactions where settlement is not planned in the foreseeable future

Hedging Item

- Gains and losses on derivative instruments that are cash flow hedges
- Gains and losses on foreign currency translation adjustments that are net investment hedges in a foreign entity

Investment Items

- Unrealized holding gains and losses on available-for-sale debt securities
- Unrealized holding gains and losses resulting from the transfer of a debt security from the held-to-maturity classification to the available-for-sale classification
- Amounts recognized in other comprehensive income for debt securities classified as available-for-sale and held-to-maturity, if the impairment is not recognized in earnings
- Subsequent changes in the fair value of available-for-sale debt securities that had previously been written down as impaired

Postretirement Benefit Items

- Gains and losses from pension or postretirement benefits that have not been recognized as a component of net periodic benefit cost
- Prior service costs or credits associated with pension or postretirement benefits
- Transition assets or obligations linked to pension or postretirement benefits that have not been recognized as a component of net periodic benefit cost

Other

- Changes in fair value that are attributable to the credit risk of specific liabilities for which the fair value option has been selected

The following items are specifically excluded from other comprehensive income:

- Investments by owners
- Distributions to owners
- Any items that must be reported as direct adjustments to any non-income equity accounts, such as additional paid-in capital and retained earnings. Examples are:
  - Taxes not payable in cash
  - A reduction in equity related to an employee stock ownership plan
  - A net cash settlement resulting from a change in the value of a contract

If a business has a noncontrolling interest in another entity, it should report amounts for net income and comprehensive income attributable to the parent and the minority interest in the financial statements where comprehensive income is presented.

If the items initially stated in other comprehensive income are later displayed as part of net income (typically because the transactions have been settled), this is essentially a reclassification out of the other comprehensive income classification. Otherwise, the items will be double-counted within comprehensive income. For example, an unrealized gain on an investment is initially recorded within other comprehensive income and is then sold, at which point the gain is realized and shifted from other comprehensive income to net income. In short, there is a continual shifting of items from other comprehensive income to net income over time.

Comprehensive Income Disclosures

If a company has no items of other comprehensive income in any period presented, it can avoid reporting comprehensive income entirely. If it is necessary to present comprehensive income, it should be displayed with the same prominence as for other financial statements.

There is no specific format that GAAP requires for the reporting of other comprehensive income, though presenting it in a format modeled on that of the income statement is encouraged.

Items of comprehensive income must be reported in a financial statement for the period in which they are recognized. If this information is presented within a single continuous income statement, the presentation shall encompass the following:

- Net income and its components
- Other comprehensive income and its components
- Total comprehensive income

Comprehensive Income

EXAMPLE

Armadillo Industries presents the following statement of income and comprehensive income.

Armadillo Industries
Statement of Income and Comprehensive Income
For the Year Ended December 31, 20X2

Revenues		$250,000
Expenses		-200,000
Other gains and losses		10,000
Gain on sale of securities		5,000
Income from operations before tax		$65,000
Income tax expense		-20,000
Net income		$45,000
Other comprehensive income, net of tax		
Foreign currency translation adjustments		2,000
Unrealized holding gains arising during period		11,000
Defined benefit pension plans:		
Prior period service cost arising during period	-$4,000	
Net loss arising during period	-1,000	-5,000
Other comprehensive income		8,000
Comprehensive income, net of tax		$53,000

If comprehensive income is stated in two separate statements, they shall be presented consecutively. The presentation of other comprehensive income shall encompass the following:

- Begin with net income (optional)
- State the components of and total for other comprehensive income
- State the total for comprehensive income

EXAMPLE

Armadillo Industries presents the following separate statement of comprehensive income.

Armadillo Industries
Statement of Comprehensive Income
For the Year Ended December 31, 20X2

Net income		$45,000
Other comprehensive income, net of tax		
Foreign currency translation adjustments		2,000
Unrealized holding gains arising during period		11,000
Defined benefit pension plans:		
Prior period service cost arising during period	-$4,000	
Net loss arising during period	-1,000	-5,000
Other comprehensive income		8,000
Comprehensive income, net of tax		$53,000

A complete set of financial statements should include the following documents:

- Balance sheet
- Income statement
- Comprehensive income
- Statement of cash flows
- Investments by and distributions to owners during the period (usually contained within a retained earnings statement)

When there are reclassification adjustments from other comprehensive income to net income, these adjustments must be disclosed, either on the statement in which comprehensive income is reported, or in the accompanying notes.

In addition, the total of other comprehensive income for the reporting period must be stated in the balance sheet in a component of equity that is stated separately from retained earnings and additional paid-in capital. A suggested title for this line item is *accumulated other comprehensive income*.

Comprehensive Income

EXAMPLE

Armadillo Industries reports accumulated other comprehensive income within the equity section of its balance sheet as follows:

Equity:	
Common stock	$1,000,000
Paid-in capital	850,000
Retained earnings	4,200,000
Accumulated other comprehensive income	270,000
Total equity	$6,320,000

Another GAAP requirement is to present all changes in the accumulated balances for each component of other comprehensive income stated as a component of equity, either on the face of the financial statements or in the accompanying disclosures. This shall include a separate presentation for each component of other comprehensive income that reveals current period reclassifications out of accumulated other comprehensive income.

EXAMPLE

Armadillo Industries presents the following information about the changes in its accumulated other comprehensive income in the notes accompanying its financial statements:

	Foreign Currency Items	Unrealized Gains on Securities	Defined Benefit Pension Plans	Accumulated Other Comprehensive Income
Beginning balance	$10,000	$272,000	-$20,000	$262,000
Current period change	2,000	11,000	-5,000	8,000
Ending balance	$12,000	$283,000	-$25,000	$270,000

GAAP may require that certain amounts be reclassified out of accumulated other comprehensive income and into net income in their entirety. If so, a business must separately disclose information about these effects on net income for each material transfer from a component of accumulated other comprehensive income and into net income. This disclosure can be provided in one of two ways:

- *On the face of the income statement.* In this format, report the changes parenthetically on each impacted line item. Also parenthetically report the aggregate tax effect of these reclassifications on the tax expense line item.

- *Within the accompanying notes.* In this format, report the significant reclassifications for each component of accumulated other comprehensive income. Both before-tax and net-of-tax presentations are allowed.

There are two allowed methods for incorporating income tax effects into the presentation of other comprehensive income information. Either report items of other comprehensive income net of income tax effects, or show them before tax and then add an aggregate income tax expense or benefit line item that relates to all of the individual items presented.

EXAMPLE

Armadillo Industries includes the following disclosure in the notes accompanying its financial statements regarding the tax effects on each component of other comprehensive income:

	Before-tax Amount	Tax Expense or Benefit	Net of Tax Amount
Foreign currency translation adjustments	$2,700	-$700	$2,000
Unrealized holding gains arising during period	14,850	-$3,850	11,000
Defined benefit pension plans:			
Prior period service costs arising during period	-5,400	1,400	-4,000
Net loss arising during period	-1,350	350	-1,000
Other comprehensive income	$10,800	-$2,800	$8,000

Summary

It is entirely possible that a smaller business will have no need to present other comprehensive income information, since it does not deal with any of the items stated in the Overview section that are considered to fall into that category. Thus, interest in this chapter is likely to be confined to the accounting departments of larger corporations that regularly deal with hedging, foreign currency transactions, complex investments, and pensions.

Chapter 5
Income Statement

225 = GAAP codification area for the income statement

Introduction

In most organizations, the income statement is considered the most important of the financial statements, and may even be the only one of the financial statements that is produced. Given its importance, we spend extra time in this chapter addressing different income statement formats, and then walk through the steps needed to create an income statement. The guidance in this chapter applies to all entities.

Related Chapters

See the following chapters for discussions of issues related to the income statement:

- *Accounting changes and error corrections*. Covers how error corrections are stated in the income statement.
- *Comprehensive income*. Covers the components of comprehensive income and how to disclose this information.

Overview of the Income Statement

The income statement is an integral part of an entity's financial statements, and contains the results of its operations during an accounting period, showing revenues and expenses, and the resulting profit or loss.

There are two ways to present the income statement. One method is to present all items of revenue and expense for the reporting period in a statement of comprehensive income. Alternatively, this information can be split into an income statement and a statement of comprehensive income. Smaller companies tend to ignore the distinction and simply aggregate the information into a document that they call the income statement; this is sufficient for internal reporting, but auditors will require the expanded version before they certify the financial statements of a business.

There are no specific requirements for the line items to include in the income statement of a privately-held business, but the following line items are typically used, based on general practice:

- Revenue
- Tax expense
- Post-tax profit or loss for discontinued operations and their disposal
- Profit or loss

- Other comprehensive income, subdivided into each component thereof
- Total comprehensive income

A key additional item is to present an analysis of the expenses in profit or loss, using a classification based on their nature or functional area; the goal is to maximize the relevance and reliability of the presented information. If the decision is made to present expenses by their nature, the format looks similar to the following:

Sample Presentation by Nature of Items

Revenue		$xxx
Expenses		
Direct materials	$xxx	
Direct labor	xxx	
Salaries expense	xxx	
Payroll taxes	xxx	
Employee benefits	xxx	
Depreciation expense	xxx	
Telephone expense	xxx	
Other expenses	xxx	
Total expenses		$xxx
Profit before tax		$xxx

Alternatively, if expenses are presented by their functional area, the format looks similar to the following, where most expenses are aggregated at the department level.

Sample Presentation by Function of Items

Revenue	$xxx
Cost of goods sold	xxx
Gross profit	xxx
Administrative expenses	$xxx
Distribution expenses	xxx
Research and development expenses	xxx
Sales and marketing expenses	xxx
Other expenses	xxx
Total expenses	$xxx
Profit before tax	$xxx

Of the two methods, presenting expenses by their nature is easier, since it requires no allocation of expenses between functional areas. Conversely, the functional area presentation may be more relevant to users of the information, who can more easily see where resources are being consumed.

Consider adding additional headings, subtotals, and line items to the items noted above if doing so will increase the user's understanding of the entity's financial performance.

An example follows of an income statement that presents expenses by their nature, rather than by their function.

EXAMPLE

Lowry Locomotion presents its results in two separate statements by their nature, resulting in the following format, beginning with the income statement:

Lowry Locomotion
Income Statement
For the years ended December 31

(000s)	20x2	20x1
Revenue	$900,000	$850,000
Expenses		
Direct materials	$270,000	$255,000
Direct labor	90,000	85,000
Salaries	300,000	275,000
Payroll taxes	27,000	25,000
Depreciation expense	45,000	41,000
Telephone expense	30,000	20,000
Other expenses	23,000	22,000
Finance costs	29,000	23,000
Other income	-25,000	-20,000
Profit before tax	$111,000	$124,000
Income tax expense	38,000	43,000
Profit from continuing operations	$73,000	$81,000
Loss from discontinued operations	42,000	0
Profit	$31,000	$81,000

Lowry Locomotion then continues with the following statement of comprehensive income:

Lowry Locomotion
Statement of Comprehensive Income
For the years ended December 31

(000s)	20x2	20x1
Profit	$31,000	$81,000
Other comprehensive income		
Exchange differences on translating foreign operations	$5,000	$9,000
Available-for-sale financial assets	10,000	-2,000
Actuarial losses on defined benefit pension plan	-2,000	-12,000
Other comprehensive income, net of tax	$13,000	-$5,000
Total comprehensive income	$18,000	$76,000

The income statement formats shown in this section and through the remainder of the chapter are designed for typical for-profit organizations. Other methods of presentation have been developed for certain types of businesses, such as not-for-profit organizations, investment companies, and insurance entities.

The Single-Step Income Statement

The simplest format in which an income statement can be constructed is the single-step income statement. In this format, a single subtotal is presented for all revenue line items, and a single subtotal for all expense line items, with a net gain or loss appearing at the bottom of the report. A sample single-step income statement follows.

Sample Single-Step Income Statement

Revenues	<u>$1,000,000</u>
Expenses:	
Cost of goods sold	350,000
Advertising	30,000
Depreciation	20,000
Rent	40,000
Payroll taxes	28,000
Salaries and wages	400,000
Supplies	32,000
Travel and entertainment	<u>50,000</u>
Total expenses	<u>950,000</u>
Net income	<u>$50,000</u>

The single-step format is not heavily used, because it forces the reader of an income statement to separately summarize subsets of information within the income statement. For a more readable format, try the following multi-step approach.

The Multi-Step Income Statement

The multi-step income statement involves the use of multiple sub-totals within the income statement, which makes it easier for readers to aggregate selected types of information within the report. The usual subtotals are for the gross margin, operating expenses, and other income, which allow readers to determine how much the company earns just from its manufacturing activities (the gross margin), what it spends on supporting operations (the operating expense total) and which components of its results do not relate to its core activities (the other income total). A sample format for a multi-step income statement follows.

Sample Multi-Step Income Statement

Revenues	$1,000,000
Cost of goods sold	350,000
Gross margin	$650,000
Operating expenses	
Advertising	30,000
Depreciation	20,000
Rent	40,000
Payroll taxes	28,000
Salaries and wages	380,000
Supplies	32,000
Travel and entertainment	50,000
Total operating expenses	$580,000
Other income	
Interest income	-5,000
Interest expense	25,000
Total other income	$20,000
Net income	$50,000

The Condensed Income Statement

A condensed income statement is simply an income statement with many of the usual line items condensed down into a few lines. Typically, this means that all revenue line items are aggregated into a single line item, while the cost of goods sold appears as one line item, and all operating expenses appear in another line item. A typical format for a condensed income statement is:

Sample Condensed Income Statement

Revenues	$1,000,000
Cost of goods sold	350,000
Sales, general, and administrative expenses	580,000
Financing income and expenses	20,000
Net income	$50,000

A condensed income statement is typically issued to those external parties who are less interested in the precise sources of a company's revenues or what expenses it incurs, and more concerned with its overall performance. Thus, bankers and investors may be interested in receiving a condensed income statement.

The Contribution Margin Income Statement

A contribution margin income statement is an income statement in which all variable expenses are deducted from sales to arrive at a contribution margin, from which all fixed expenses are then subtracted to arrive at the net profit or loss for the period. This income statement format is a superior form of presentation, because the contribution margin clearly shows the amount available to cover fixed costs and generate a profit (or loss).

In essence, if there are no sales, a contribution margin income statement will have a zero contribution margin, with fixed costs clustered beneath the contribution margin line item. As sales increase, the contribution margin will increase in conjunction with sales, while fixed costs remain approximately the same.

A contribution margin income statement varies from a normal income statement in the following three ways:

- Fixed production costs are aggregated lower in the income statement, after the contribution margin;
- Variable selling and administrative expenses are grouped with variable production costs, so that they are a part of the calculation of the contribution margin; and
- The gross margin is replaced in the statement by the contribution margin.

Thus, the format of a contribution margin income statement is:

Sample Contribution Margin Income Statement

+	Revenues
-	Variable production expenses (such as materials, supplies, and variable overhead)
-	Variable selling and administrative expenses
=	Contribution margin
-	Fixed production expenses (including most overhead)
-	Fixed selling and administrative expenses
=	Net profit or loss

In many cases, direct labor is categorized as a fixed expense in the contribution margin income statement format, rather than a variable expense, because this cost does not always change in direct proportion to the amount of revenue generated.

Instead, management needs to keep a certain minimum staffing in the production area, which does not vary even if there are lower production volumes.

The key difference between gross margin and contribution margin is that fixed production costs are included in the cost of goods sold to calculate the gross margin, whereas they are not included in the same calculation for the contribution margin. This means that the contribution margin income statement is sorted based on the variability of the underlying cost information, rather than by the functional areas or expense categories found in a normal income statement.

It is useful to create an income statement in the contribution margin format in order to determine that proportion of expenses that truly varies directly with revenues. In many businesses, the contribution margin will be substantially higher than the gross margin, because such a large proportion of production costs are fixed and few of its selling and administrative expenses are variable.

The Multi-Period Income Statement

A variation on any of the preceding income statement formats is to present them over multiple periods, preferably over a trailing 12-month period. By doing so, readers of the income statement can see trends in the information, as well as spot changes in the trends that may require investigation. This is an excellent way to present the income statement, and is highly recommended. The following sample shows the layout of a multi-period income statement over a four-quarter period, with key items noted in bold font.

Sample Multi-Period Income Statement

	Quarter 1	Quarter 2	Quarter 3	Quarter 4
Revenues	$1,000,000	$1,100,000	$1,050,000	$1,200,000
Cost of goods sold	350,000	385,000	368,000	**480,000**
Gross margin	$650,000	$715,000	$682,000	$720,000
Operating expenses				
Advertising	30,000	0	**60,000**	30,000
Depreciation	20,000	21,000	22,000	24,000
Rent	40,000	40,000	**50,000**	50,000
Payroll taxes	28,000	28,000	28,000	26,000
Salaries and wages	380,000	385,000	385,000	370,000
Supplies	32,000	30,000	31,000	33,000
Travel and entertainment	50,000	45,000	40,000	60,000
Total operating expenses	$580,000	$549,000	$616,000	$593,000
Other income				
Interest income	-5,000	-5,000	-3,000	-1,000
Interest expense	25,000	25,000	30,000	**39,000**
Total other income	$20,000	$20,000	$27,000	$38,000
Net income	$50,000	$146,000	$39,000	$89,000

The report shown in the sample reveals several issues that might not have been visible if the report had only spanned a single period. These issues are:

- *Cost of goods sold.* This cost is consistently 35% of sales until Quarter 4, when it jumps to 40%.
- *Advertising.* There was no advertising cost in Quarter 2 and double the amount of the normal $30,000 quarterly expense in Quarter 3. The cause could be a missing supplier invoice in Quarter 2 that was received and recorded in Quarter 3.
- *Rent.* The rent increased by $10,000 in Quarter 3, which may indicate a scheduled increase in the rent agreement.
- *Interest expense.* The interest expense jumps in Quarter 3 and does so again in Quarter 4, while interest income declined over the same periods. This indicates a large increase in debt.

In short, the multi-period income statement is an excellent tool for spotting anomalies in the presented information from period to period.

How to Construct the Income Statement

If an accounting software package is being used, it is quite easy to construct an income statement. Just access the report writing module, select the time period for which the income statement is required, and print it.

> **Tip:** If the accountant is using a report writer to create an income statement in the accounting software, there is a good chance that the first draft of the report will be wrong, due to some accounts being missed or duplicated. To ensure that the income statement is correct, compare it to the default income statement report that is usually provided with the accounting software, or compare the net profit or loss on the report to the current year earnings figure listed in the equity section of the balance sheet. If there is a discrepancy, the income statement is incorrect.

The situation is more complex if the decision is made to create an income statement by hand. This involves the following steps:

1. Create the trial balance report.
2. List each account pertaining to the income statement in a separate column of the trial balance.
3. Aggregate these line items into those to be stated in the income statement as a separate line item.
4. Shift the result into the preferred income statement format.

The following example illustrates the construction of an income statement.

EXAMPLE

The accounting software for Lowry Locomotion breaks down at the end of July, and the controller has to create the financial statements by hand. He has a copy of Lowry's trial balance, which is shown below. He transfers this information to an electronic spreadsheet, creates separate columns for accounts to include in the income statement, and copies those balances into these columns. This leaves a number of accounts related to the balance sheet, which he can ignore for the purposes of creating the income statement.

Lowry Locomotion Extended Trial Balance

	Adjusted Trial Balance		Income Statement		Aggregation	
	Debit	Credit	Debit	Credit	Debit	Credit
Cash	$60,000					
Accounts receivable	230,000					
Inventory	300,000					
Fixed assets (net)	210,000					
Accounts payable		$90,000				
Accrued liabilities		75,000				
Notes payable		420,000				
Equity		350,000				
Revenue		450,000		$450,000		$450,000
Cost of goods sold	290,000		$290,000		$290,000	
Salaries expense	225,000		225,000		245,000	
Payroll tax expense	20,000		20,000			
Rent expense	35,000		35,000			
Other expenses	15,000		15,000		50,000	
Totals	$1,385,000	$1,385,000	$585,000	$450,000	$585,000	$450,000

In the "Aggregation" columns of the extended trial balance, the controller has aggregated the expenses for salaries and payroll taxes into the salaries expense line, and aggregated the rent expense and other expenses into the other expenses line. He then transfers this information into the following condensed income statement.

Lowry Locomotion
Income Statement
For the month ended July 31, 20X1

Revenue	$450,000
Cost of goods sold	290,000
Salaries expenses	245,000
Other expenses	50,000
Net loss	-$135,000

Income Statement Disclosures

The GAAP requirements for the specific line items to be included in an income statement are remarkably vague. However, the requirements of the Securities and Exchange Commission (SEC) for the income statements issued by publicly-held companies are not vague at all. The SEC requires that the following information be included in an income statement (we do not include the somewhat different requirements for a public utility):

Revenue Items

- Net sales of tangible products
- Income from rentals
- Revenues from services
- Other revenues

If any one of the preceding revenue items is not more than 10 percent of the sum of all revenue items, it can be combined with another revenue item. If so, the related expense items must also be combined.

Cost of Goods Sold Items

- Cost of tangible goods sold (a merchandising business can include the costs of occupancy and buying in this classification)
- Expenses applicable to rental income
- Cost of services
- Expenses applicable to other revenues

Other Expense Items

- Selling, general and administrative expenses
- Provision for doubtful accounts
- Other general expenses

Non-Operating Other Items

- Non-operating income. Separately state, either within the income statement or in the attached disclosures, the amounts earned from dividends, interest on securities holdings, net profits on securities holdings, and miscellaneous other income. If there are material amounts in the miscellaneous other income line item, either state the nature of the transactions separately in the income statement or within the attached disclosures.
- Interest and amortization of debt discount and expense
- Non-operating expenses. Separately state, either within the income statement or in the attached disclosures, the amounts of net losses on securities and miscellaneous income deductions. If there are material amounts in the miscellaneous income deductions line item, either state the nature of the transactions separately in the income statement or within the attached disclosures.

Income or Loss Items

- Income or loss before income tax expense
- Income tax expense
- Equity in the earnings of unconsolidated subsidiaries
- Income or loss from continuing operations
- Discontinued operations
- Cumulative effects of changes in accounting principles
- Net income or loss
- Net income attributable to a non-controlling interest
- Net income attributable to a controlling interest
- Earnings per share information (see the Earnings per Share chapter)

If there is a recovery due to business interruption insurance, disclose the nature of the event resulting in losses, the aggregate amount of business interruption insurance recoveries in the period, and the income statement line item in which the recoveries are located.

Summary

Of the income statement formats presented in this chapter, the most commonly used is the sample shown for the multi-step income statement. This format reveals expenses by nature, not by department. It is customary to create additional department-level statements that break down the expenditures for individual departments, so that department managers can see the results of the entire business on the income statement, and then review the results pertaining only to their departments on a separate document. The sales manager may also want to see additional detail for the types of revenue generated.

The contribution margin income statement certainly makes theoretical sense, but is rarely used, because outside users of financial statements are more accustomed to seeing a gross margin format on the income statement. Thus, if it is to be used, prepare a contribution margin income statement for internal consumption and have a second, more traditional version available to distribute outside of the company.

Chapter 6
Statement of Cash Flows

230 = GAAP codification area for the statement of cash flows

Introduction

The statement of cash flows is the least used of the financial statements, and may not be issued at all for internal financial reporting purposes. The recipients of financial statements seem to be mostly concerned with the profit information on the income statement, and to a lesser degree with the financial position information on the balance sheet. Nonetheless, the cash flows on the statement of cash flows can provide valuable information, especially when combined with the other elements of the financial statements. At a minimum, be prepared to construct a statement of cash flows for the annual financial statements, which will presumably be issued outside of the company.

This chapter addresses the two formats used for the statement of cash flows, as well as how to assemble the information needed for the statement.

Overview of the Statement of Cash Flows

The statement of cash flows contains information about the flows of cash into and out of a company; in particular, it shows the extent of those company activities that generate and use cash and cash equivalents. It is particularly useful for assessing the differences between net income and the related cash receipts and payments. The following general requirements apply to the statement of cash flows:

- *Cash balance matching.* The beginning and ending amounts of cash and cash equivalents shown in the statement of cash flows should match the amounts of cash and cash equivalents shown in the balance sheet for the same dates.
- *Classifications.* Report net cash provided or used in the categories of operating, investing, and financing activities.
- *Format.* Entities are encouraged to use the direct method of report presentation (see the next section).
- *Reconciliation.* There shall be a reconciliation of the net income of a business to its net cash flow from operating activities, which shall report all major classes of reconciling items in separate line items. If the direct method is used (see the next section), the reconciliation shall be provided in a separate schedule. If the indirect method is used (see the Indirect Method section), the reconciliation can be integrated into the statement of cash flows, or provided as a separate schedule.

The primary activities reported on the statement of cash flows are:

- *Operating activities.* These are an entity's primary revenue-producing activities. Examples of cash inflows from operating activities are cash receipts from the sale of goods or services, accounts receivable, lawsuit settlements, and supplier refunds. Examples of cash outflows for operating activities are for payments to employees and suppliers, fines, lawsuit settlements, cash payments to lenders for interest, contributions to charity, cash refunds to customers, and the settlement of asset retirement obligations.
- *Investing activities.* These generally involve the acquisition and disposal of available-for-sale securities. Examples of cash inflows from investing activities are cash receipts from the sale or collection of loans, the sale of securities issued by other entities, the sale of long-term assets, and the proceeds from insurance settlements related to damaged property. Examples of cash outflows from investing activities are cash payments for loans made to other entities, the purchase of the debt or equity of other entities, and the purchase of fixed assets (including capitalized interest).
- *Financing activities.* These are the activities resulting in alterations to the amount of contributed equity and an entity's borrowings. Examples of cash inflows from financing activities are cash receipts from the sale of an entity's own equity instruments or from issuing debt, and proceeds from derivative instruments. Examples of cash outflows from financing activities are cash outlays for dividends, share repurchases, payments for debt issuance costs, and the pay down of outstanding debt.

Some types of cash flows could be classified as being in more than one of the preceding classifications. If so, the designated classification should be based on the activity most likely to provide the majority of cash flows for an item.

EXAMPLE

Mole Industries has a rent-to-purchase feature on its line of trench digging equipment, where customers can initially rent the equipment and then apply the rental payments to an outright purchase. The rental of equipment could be considered an investing activity. However, since the company earns the bulk of its cash flow from the sale of equipment, the cash flows are placed within the operating activities classification.

Tip: Create a policy regarding how certain items are to be classified within the statement of cash flows. Otherwise, there may be some variation from period to period in categorizing items as cash equivalents or investments.

In general, hedging activities are to be classified according to their nature, even if they are paired with another activity as a hedge. Thus, cash received from a loan should be classified as a financing activity, even if the loan is intended to hedge an investment. The exception is transactions accounted for as fair value hedges or cash flow hedges; in these cases, the hedging transactions are included in the classifications of the items with which they are being paired for hedging purposes. If the hedge accounting is discontinued, then subsequent cash flows of a hedging activity are to be classified according to their nature.

The *direct method* or the *indirect method* can be used to present the statement of cash flows. These methods are described in the following sections.

The Direct Method

The direct method of presenting the statement of cash flows shows specific cash flows in the operating activities section of the report. GAAP requires that the following classes of operating cash receipts and payments be included in the report:

- Cash collected from customers
- Interest and dividends received
- Other operating cash receipts
- Cash paid to employees and suppliers
- Interest paid
- Income taxes paid
- Other operating cash payments

GAAP also requires that the cash inflows and the cash outflows for investing and financing activities be reported separately within the statement of cash flows. Thus, cash payments for the purchase of fixed assets must be reported on a separate line item from cash receipts from the sale of fixed assets.

The format of the direct method appears in the following example.

EXAMPLE

Lowry Locomotion constructs the following statement of cash flows using the direct method:

Lowry Locomotion
Statement of Cash Flows
For the year ended 12/31/20X1

Cash flows from operating activities		
Cash receipts from customers	$45,800,000	
Cash paid to suppliers	-29,800,000	
Cash paid to employees	-11,200,000	
Cash generated from operations	4,800,000	
Interest paid	-310,000	
Income taxes paid	-1,700,000	
Net cash from operating activities		$2,790,000
Cash flows from investing activities		
Purchase of fixed assets	-580,000	
Proceeds from sale of equipment	110,000	
Net cash used in investing activities		-470,000
Cash flows from financing activities		
Proceeds from issuance of common stock	1,000,000	
Proceeds from issuance of long-term debt	500,000	
Principal payments under capital lease obligation	-10,000	
Dividends paid	-450,000	
Net cash used in financing activities		1,040,000
Net increase in cash and cash equivalents		3,360,000
Cash and cash equivalents at beginning of period		1,640,000
Cash and cash equivalents at end of period		$5,000,000

Reconciliation of net income to net cash provided by operating activities:

Net income		$2,665,000
Adjustments to reconcile net income to net cash provided by operating activities:		
Depreciation and amortization	$125,000	
Provision for losses on accounts receivable	15,000	
Gain on sale of equipment	-155,000	
Increase in interest and income taxes payable	32,000	
Increase in deferred taxes	90,000	
Increase in other liabilities	18,000	
Total adjustments		125,000
Net cash provided by operating activities		$2,790,000

The standard-setting bodies encourage the use of the direct method, but it is rarely used, for the excellent reason that the information in it is difficult to assemble; companies simply do not collect and store information in the manner required for this format. Instead, they use the indirect method, which is described in the following section.

The Indirect Method

Under the indirect method of presenting the statement of cash flows, the presentation begins with net income or loss, with subsequent additions to or deductions from that amount for non-cash revenue and expense items, resulting in cash generated from operating activities. This means that the effects of the deferral or accrual of expenses in the income statement must be removed, as well as such non-cash expenses as depreciation and amortization, so that cash flows can be more readily observed.

The format of the indirect method appears in the following example.

Statement of Cash Flows

EXAMPLE

Lowry Locomotion constructs the following statement of cash flows using the indirect method:

Lowry Locomotion
Statement of Cash Flows
For the year ended 12/31/20X2

Cash flows from operating activities		
Net income		$3,000,000
Adjustments for:		
Depreciation and amortization	$125,000	
Provision for losses on accounts receivable	20,000	
Gain on sale of facility	-65,000	
		80,000
Increase in trade receivables	-250,000	
Decrease in inventories	325,000	
Decrease in trade payables	-50,000	
		25,000
Cash generated from operations		3,105,000
Cash flows from investing activities		
Purchase of fixed assets	-500,000	
Proceeds from sale of equipment	35,000	
Net cash used in investing activities		-465,000
Cash flows from financing activities		
Proceeds from issuance of common stock	150,000	
Proceeds from issuance of long-term debt	175,000	
Dividends paid	-45,000	
Net cash used in financing activities		280,000
Net increase in cash and cash equivalents		2,920,000
Cash and cash equivalents at beginning of period		2,080,000
Cash and cash equivalents at end of period		$5,000,000

The indirect method is very popular, because the information required for it is relatively easily assembled from the accounts that a business normally maintains.

How to Prepare the Statement of Cash Flows

The most commonly-used format for the statement of cash flows is the indirect method (as described in the preceding section). The general layout of an indirect method statement of cash flows is shown below, along with an explanation of the source of the information in the statement.

Company Name
Statement of Cash Flows
For the year ended 12/31/20XX

Line Item	Derivation
Cash flows from operating activities	
Net income	From the net income line on the income statement
Adjustment for:	
Depreciation and amortization	From the corresponding line items in the income statement
Provision for losses on accounts receivable	From the change in the allowance for doubtful accounts in the period
Gain/loss on sale of facility	From the gain/loss accounts in the income statement
Increase/decrease in trade receivables	Change in trade receivables during the period, from the balance sheet
Increase/decrease in inventories	Change in inventories during the period, from the balance sheet
Increase/decrease in trade payables	Change in trade payables during the period, from the balance sheet
Cash generated from operations	Summary of the preceding items in this section
Cash flows from investing activities	
Purchase of fixed assets	Itemized in the fixed asset accounts during the period
Proceeds from sale of fixed assets	Itemized in the fixed asset accounts during the period
Net cash used in investing activities	Summary of the preceding items in this section
Cash flows from financing activities	
Proceeds from issuance of common stock	Net increase in the common stock and additional paid-in capital accounts during the period
Proceeds from issuance of long-term debt	Itemized in the long-term debt account during the period
Dividends paid	Itemized in the retained earnings account during the period

Statement of Cash Flows

Line Item	Derivation
Net cash used in financing activities	Summary of the preceding items in this section
Net change in cash and cash equivalents	Summary of all preceding subtotals

A less commonly-used format for the statement of cash flows is the direct method. The general layout of this version is shown below, along with an explanation of the source of the information in the statement.

Company Name
Statement of Cash Flows
For the year ended 12/31/20XX

Line Item	Derivation
Cash flows from operating activities	
Cash receipts from customers	Summary of the cash receipts journal for the period
Cash paid to suppliers	Summary of the cash disbursements journal for the period (less the financing and income tax payments noted below)
Cash paid to employees	Summary of the payroll journal for the period
Cash generated from operations	Summary of the preceding items in this section
Interest paid	Itemized in the cash disbursements journal
Income taxes paid	Itemized in the cash disbursements journal
Net cash from operating activities	Summary of the preceding items in this section
Cash flows from investing activities	
Purchase of fixed assets	Itemized in the fixed asset accounts during the period
Proceeds from sale of fixed assets	Itemized in the fixed asset accounts during the period
Net cash used in investing activities	Summary of the preceding items in this section
Cash flows from financing activities	
Proceeds from issuance of common stock	Net increase in the common stock and additional paid-in capital accounts during the period
Proceeds from issuance of long-term debt	Itemized in the long-term debt account during the period

Line Item	Derivation
Principal payment under capital leases	Itemized in the capital leases liability account during the period
Dividends paid	Itemized in the retained earnings account during the period
Net cash used in financing activities	Summary of the preceding items in this section
Net change in cash and cash equivalents	Summary of all preceding subtotals

As can be seen from the explanations for either the indirect or direct methods, the statement of cash flows is more difficult to create than the income statement and balance sheet. In fact, a complete statement may require a substantial supporting spreadsheet that shows the details for each line item in the statement.

If the company's accounting software contains a template for the statement of cash flows, then use it. The information may not be aggregated quite correctly, and it may not contain all of the line items required for the statement, but it *will* produce most of the information needed, and is much easier to modify than the alternative of creating the statement entirely by hand.

Disclosures for the Statement of Cash Flows

The following disclosures are required by GAAP, and are associated with the statement of cash flows:

- *Cash equivalents*. If the company has a policy regarding which items are treated as cash equivalents, disclose the policy. Note that a change to this policy is considered a change in accounting principle, which would require the restatement of any prior-period financial statements that are presented alongside the current-period financial statements.
- *Interest and income taxes paid*. State the amounts of interest paid and income taxes paid during the period, but only if the indirect method of presentation is used.
- *Noncash investing and financing activities*. Disclose all investing and financing activities during the period that affect assets or liabilities, but which did not result in changes in cash during the period. Examples of such activities are:
  - o   The conversion of debt to equity
  - o   The exchange of assets or liabilities
  - o   Obtaining an asset in exchange for incurring a lease obligation
  - o   Receiving an asset as a gift

EXAMPLE

Lowry Locomotion discloses the following information in its financial statements:

> For purposes of deriving the statement of cash flows, Lowry considers all highly liquid debt instruments purchased with a maturity of one month or less to be cash equivalents.
>
> During the year, Lowry paid $100,000 in interest expense, net of capitalized interest. Also, Lowry paid $460,000 in income taxes during the same period.
>
> Lowry incurred a capital lease obligation of $350,000 when it leased new production equipment.
>
> During the year, investors converted $1,000,000 of convertible debt to 100,000 shares of Lowry's common stock.

Tip: GAAP specifically prohibits the reporting of cash flow per share.

Summary

The statement of cash flows is a useful ancillary statement that sometimes accompanies the income statement and balance sheet for internal reporting, but which is nearly always included in financial statements issued to outside parties. The report can be difficult to assemble, unless it is available as an accounting software template, which is why it tends to be treated as an occasional add-on to the other elements of the financial statements. If it is to be used, we strongly recommend using the indirect method instead of the direct method, since the information required for the direct method of presentation is not easily gathered from the accounting records.

Chapter 7
Notes to Financial Statements

235 = GAAP codification area for notes to financial statements

Introduction

The notes that accompany financial statements comprise an important part of the full package of information imparted by financial statements. While there are many types of disclosures to include in financial statement notes, this section of GAAP is primarily concerned with the presentation of the key accounting policies used by management to record financial information. The chapter also discusses the substantially more detailed requirements of the Securities and Exchange Commission (SEC), which only apply to publicly-held companies. The guidance in this chapter applies to all entities.

Overview of Notes to Financial Statements

A description of all significant accounting policies of the business must be included in the notes that accompany the financial statements. Even in cases where only one or a few of the financial statements are released, the accountant should still include in the accompanying notes those accounting policies that most directly pertain to the statements being released.

Tip: If the company has not changed its accounting policies since its last fiscal year, and the financial statements are both unaudited and being released for an interim period, it is acceptable to not include accounting policies in the accompanying disclosures.

The accounting policies that should be disclosed by a business are those that materially affect its financial position, cash flows, or results of operations, and explain the appropriateness of those principles concerning revenue recognition and cost allocations to current and future periods. GAAP specifically requires that disclosure be made if an accounting principle involves an unusual application of GAAP, a selection among several valid alternatives, or principles peculiar to the company's industry.

The following are examples of situations where the related accounting policies should be disclosed:

- The basis of consolidation
- The method used to assign costs to inventory
- The methods used to depreciate or amortize fixed assets

- The recognition of profit on long-term construction contracts
- The recognition of revenue

Tip: It is not necessary to repeat the same policy disclosure several times within the financial statements. If the same disclosure is required several times, simply reference a single disclosure as needed.

The disclosure of accounting policies is preferred in a separate summary of accounting policies that precede the notes to the financial statements, or within the first of the notes to the financial statements.

As usual, the SEC requires significantly more detailed disclosure by publicly-held companies than the more general guidance expressed in GAAP. If a business is publicly-held, the SEC requires the following disclosures in the financial statements, not all of which relate to accounting policies:

- *Asset restrictions.* State any restrictions on the transfer of funds to the parent by its subsidiaries as dividends, loans, or advances, as well as the amounts of these restricted net assets at the end of the last fiscal year. There are qualifications on when the disclosure is required.
- *Debt changes.* Describe significant changes in the authorized or issued amounts of bonds, mortgages, and similar debt.
- *Defaults.* Describe any defaults on the payment of principal or interest, or any covenant breaches. If acceleration of the obligation has been waived, state the waiver period and the amount of the related default.
- *Dividend restrictions.* Describe significant restrictions on the payment of dividends, as well as the amount of retained earnings or net income that are restricted or free from restrictions. Also note the amount of retained earnings representing the undistributed earnings of >50% ownership interests under the equity method.
- *Income tax expense.* Disclose the components of income before income tax, and the components of income tax, which should include taxes currently payable and the net tax effects of timing differences. Also separately note the income tax amounts applicable to United States federal income taxes, foreign income taxes, and other income taxes (not required if the foreign or other taxes are less than 5% of income before taxes). Also reconcile the total income tax expense to the amount computed by multiplying the statutory tax rate by income before tax.
- *Liens.* State the assets subject to liens, the approximate amounts, and the obligations being collateralized.
- *Policies for derivatives.* Describe the policies used for derivative financial instruments ("derivatives"), and the methods for applying those policies, as well as the types of derivatives accounted for under each method, the criteria needed to qualify for each accounting method (and the alternative used if the criteria are not met), the methods used to account for the termination of

derivatives designated as hedges and under a variety of other circumstances, and when derivatives are to be reported in the financial statements.

- *Preferred shares.* Show the aggregate amount of preferences in the event of an involuntary liquidation in the equity section of the balance sheet. Also note any restriction on retained earnings if the aggregate preferences of preferred stock exceed their par value.

- *Related party transactions.* Identify related party transactions and state them on the balance sheet, income statement, or statement of cash flows, as applicable. Also, disclose any intercompany profits or losses resulting from transactions with related parties, and which have not been eliminated from the financial statements.

- *Repurchase agreements.* If the assets sold under repurchase agreements exceed 10% of total assets, separately disclose in the balance sheet the total liabilities incurred related to the repurchase agreements, as well as (in tabular format) the types of securities sold and their maturity terms, their carrying amounts and market values, and the repurchase liability. If the amount at risk under these agreements with a counterparty is greater than 10% of stockholders' equity, state the names of the counterparties, the amount at risk with each one, and the weighted average maturity of the agreements with each one.

- *Reverse repurchase agreements.* If the carrying amount of repurchase agreements exceeds 10% of total assets, separately disclose the amount in the balance sheet; also state in a footnote the policy for taking possession of assets bought under resale agreements, and the nature of any provisions to ensure that the market value of the assets is sufficient to protect the company if the counterparty were to default. If the amount at risk under these agreements exceeds 10% of stockholders' equity, state the names of the counterparties, the amount at risk with each one, and the weighted average maturity of the agreements with each one.

- *Subsidiary information.* Summarize the assets, liabilities, and results of operations for unconsolidated subsidiaries.

- *Warrants.* Describe and aggregate the amount of the securities called for by warrants or similar rights, the date from which they can be exercised, and the price at which they are exercisable.

If a publicly-held company chooses to issue condensed financial information rather than a complete set of financial statements, the SEC does not require that detailed footnote disclosures accompany the condensed information. However, disclosures must still be included for material contingencies, long-term obligations, and guarantees, along with a five-year schedule that summarizes debt maturities. The company must also separately disclose the amount of cash dividends paid to the parent company in each of the past three years by its consolidated subsidiaries, unconsolidated subsidiaries, and >50% owned persons accounted for under the equity method.

Summary

The disclosure of accounting policies as required by GAAP is usually quite static from period to period, and so requires only a cursory review to ensure that the policies have not changed since the last financial statements were issued. The SEC requirements are much more detailed, and will likely require considerably more updating when financial statements are issued.

Chapter 8
Accounting Changes and Error Corrections

250 = GAAP codification area for accounting changes and error corrections

Introduction

From time to time, a company will find that it must change its accounting to reflect a change in accounting principle or estimate, or it may locate an accounting error that must be corrected. In this chapter, we address the rules for both situations and how to disclose them, as well as for several related situations. The guidance in this chapter applies to all entities.

Related Chapters

See the Interim Reporting chapter for discussions of how to deal with the prior application of accounting changes to prior interim periods.

Changes in Accounting Principle

There is an assumption in GAAP that, once an accounting principle has been adopted by a business, the principle shall be consistently applied in recording transactions and events from that point forward. Consistent application is a cornerstone of accounting, since it allows the readers of financial statements to compare the results of multiple accounting periods. Given how important it is to maintain consistency in the application of accounting principles, a business should only change an accounting principle in one of the two following situations:

- The change is required by an update to GAAP
- The use of an alternative principle is preferable

Tip: Thoroughly document the reason for any change in accounting principle, since it will likely be reviewed by the company's auditors.

Whenever there is a change in accounting principle, retrospective application of the new principle to prior accounting periods is required, unless it is impracticable to do so. If it is impracticable to retroactively apply changes to prior interim periods of the current fiscal year, then the change in accounting principle can only be made as of the start of a subsequent fiscal year.

Tip: Where possible, companies are encouraged to adopt changes in accounting principle as of the first interim period of a fiscal year.

The activities required for retrospective application are:

1. Alter the carrying amounts of assets and liabilities for the cumulative effect of the change in principle as of the beginning of the first accounting period presented.
2. Adjust the beginning balance of retained earnings to offset the change noted in the first step.
3. Adjust the financial statements for each prior period presented to reflect the impact of the new accounting principle.

If it is impracticable to make these changes, then do so as of the earliest reported periods for which it is practicable to do so. It is considered impracticable to make a retrospective change when any of the following conditions apply:

- *Assumptions.* Making a retrospective application calls for assumptions about what management intended to do in prior periods, and those assumptions cannot be independently substantiated.
- *Efforts made.* The company has made every reasonable effort to do so.
- *Estimates.* Estimates are required, which are impossible to provide due to the lack of information about the circumstances in the earlier periods.

When making prior period adjustments due to a change in accounting principle, do so only for the direct effects of the change. A direct effect is one that is *required* to switch accounting principles.

EXAMPLE

Armadillo Industries changes from the last in, first out method of inventory accounting to the first in, first out method. Doing so calls for an increase in the ending inventory in the preceding period, which in turn increases net profits for that period. Altering the inventory balance is a direct effect of the change in principle.

An indirect effect of the change in principle would be a change in the corporate accrual for profit sharing in the prior period. Since it is an indirect effect, Armadillo does not record the change.

Changes in Accounting Estimate

A change in accounting estimate occurs when there is an adjustment to the carrying amount of an asset or liability, or the subsequent accounting for it. Examples of changes in accounting estimate are changes in:

- The allowance for doubtful accounts
- The reserve for obsolete inventory
- Changes in the useful life of depreciable assets

- Changes in the salvage values of depreciable assets
- Changes in the amount of expected warranty obligations

Changes in accounting estimate occur relatively frequently, and so would require a major amount of effort to make an ongoing series of retroactive changes to prior financial statements. Instead, GAAP only requires that changes in accounting estimate be accounted for in the period of change and thereafter. Thus, no retrospective change is required or allowed.

Changes in Reporting Entity

There are situations where a change in the entities included in consolidated financial statements effectively means that there is a change in reporting entity. If so, apply the change retrospectively to all of the periods being reported. The result should be the consistent presentation of financial information for the same reporting entity for all periods, including interim periods.

Correction of an Error in Previously Issued Financial Statements

From time to time, financial statements will be inadvertently issued that contain one or more errors. When such an error is discovered, the prior period financial statements to which the error applies must be restated. Restatement requires the following steps:

1. Alter the carrying amounts of assets and liabilities for the cumulative effect of the error as of the beginning of the first accounting period presented.
2. Adjust the beginning balance of retained earnings to offset the change noted in the first step.
3. Adjust the financial statements for each prior period presented to reflect the impact of the error.

Corrections Related to Prior Interim Periods

GAAP specifies several situations in which the financial statements of prior interim periods of the current fiscal year should be adjusted. These adjustments are for the following:

- Adjustment or settlement of litigation
- Income taxes
- Renegotiation proceedings
- Utility revenue under rate-making processes

Adjustments for these items are only necessary if all of the following criteria apply:

- The effect of the change is material to income from continuing operations, or its trend
- The adjustments are directly related to the prior interim periods
- The adjustment amount could not be reasonably estimated prior to the current interim period, but can now be estimated

If an adjustment occurs in any interim period other than the first period, use the following steps to account for it:

1. Include any portion of the adjustment that relates to current business activities in the current interim period.
2. Restate prior interim periods of the current fiscal year to include that portion of the item that relates to the business activities in those periods.
3. Restate the first interim period of the current fiscal year to include that portion of the item that relates to the business activities in prior fiscal years.

The Materiality of an Error

When an accounting error is discovered, determine whether it is material enough to report. To do so, compare its effect to the full-year estimated income or the full-year earnings trend. If it is not material, there is no need to disclose it. However, if the error is material in relation to the estimated income or earnings trend for an interim period, disclose the error in the financial statements for that interim period.

Accounting Changes and Error Corrections Disclosures

There are a number of variations on the disclosures required for the various types of accounting changes and error corrections, so we address each one within the following sub-sections.

Change in Accounting Principle

When there is a change in accounting principle, disclose all of the following items in the period in which the change takes place:

- *Nature of the change*. The nature of the change and why the new principle is preferable.
- *Application method*. State the method used to apply the change, including:
  - The information being adjusted
  - The effect of the change on income from continuing operations, net income, any other affected financial statement line items, and any affected per-share amounts

- o The cumulative effect of the change on retained earnings in the balance sheet as of the beginning of the earliest period presented
- o The reasons why retrospective application is impracticable (if this is the case), and the alternative method used to report the change

- *Indirect effects.* If the election has been made to recognize the indirect effects of a change in principle, disclose the effects, the amounts recognized in the current period, any applicable per-share amounts, and the same information for all prior periods presented (unless impracticable to do so).

These disclosures are required for all interim and annual financial statements that are reported.

When a new accounting principle is adopted, disclose the effect of the change on income from continuing operations, net income, and any related per-share amounts for all remaining interim periods in the current fiscal year.

Change in Accounting Estimate

If there is a change in estimate that will affect several future periods, disclose the effect on income from continuing operations, net income, and any related per-share amounts. This disclosure is not needed for ongoing changes in estimate that arise in the ordinary course of business, such as changes in reserves. In effect, this disclosure is only required if the change is material. If there is not an immediate material effect, but a material effect is expected in later periods, provide a description of the change in estimate.

Change in Reporting Entity

In those rare cases where there has been a change in reporting entity, disclose the nature of and reason for the change. In addition, report the effect of the change on net income, other comprehensive income, and any related per-share amounts for all periods presented. If there is not an immediate material effect, but a material effect is expected in later periods, state the nature of and reason for the change in the period in which the change occurred.

Error Corrections

When the financial statements are restated to correct an error, disclose the following information:

- A statement that the previously issued financial statements have been restated, and describe the error
- The effect of the error correction on financial statement line items and per-share amounts for each period presented

- The cumulative effect of the error correction on retained earnings as of the beginning of the earliest period presented
- The before-tax and after-tax effect on net income for each prior period reported. If the results of only one period are reported, indicate the effect on net income for the immediately preceding period

If there is an error correction related to prior interim periods of the current fiscal year, disclose the effect on income from continuing operations, net income, and related per-share amounts for all of the prior interim periods of the current fiscal year, as well as the restated results for these line items.

Historical Summaries

If a business issues historical summaries of its results for a number of prior years, be sure to adjust these summaries for any errors found in affected years, and disclose the changes alongside the summaries.

EXAMPLE

Armadillo Industries provides the following disclosure regarding a change in its method of accounting for the valuation of its inventory:

On January 1, 20X1, Armadillo changed its method for valuing inventory to the weighted-average method. The company had previously used the LIFO method to value its inventory. The new method was adopted because management felt that having very old inventory layers misrepresented the value of the company's reported inventory. The company's comparative financial statements for previous years have been adjusted to apply the new method retrospectively.

The following financial statement line items for fiscal years 20X1 and 20X0 were affected by this change in accounting principle:

20X1 Income Statement

	As Computed under LIFO	As Reported under Weighted Average	Effect of Change
Sales	$1,000,000	$1,000,000	$0
Cost of goods sold	600,000	580,000	20,000
Selling, general and administrative expenses	375,000	375,000	0
Income before taxes	25,000	45,000	20,000
Income taxes	9,000	16,000	-7,000
Net income	$16,000	$29,000	$13,000

20X0 Income Statement

	As Originally Reported	As Adjusted	Effect of Change
Sales	$900,000	$900,000	$0
Cost of goods sold	540,000	525,000	15,000
Selling, general and administrative expenses	350,000	350,000	0
Income before taxes	10,000	25,000	15,000
Income taxes	3,000	9,000	-6,000
Net income	$7,000	$16,000	$9,000

20X1 Balance Sheet

	As Computed under LIFO	As Reported under Weighted Average	Effect of Change
Cash	$100,000	$100,000	$0
Accounts receivable	350,000	350,000	0
Inventory	400,000	420,000	20,000
Total assets	$850,000	$870,000	$20,000
Accounts payable	$125,000	$125,000	$0
Income tax liability	9,000	16,000	7,000
Paid-in capital	500,000	500,000	0
Retained earnings	216,000	229,000	13,000
Total liabilities and stockholders' equity	$850,000	$870,000	$20,000

20X0 Balance Sheet

	As Originally Reported	As Adjusted	Effect of Change
Cash	$80,000	$80,000	$0
Accounts receivable	320,000	320,000	0
Inventory	360,000	375,000	15,000
Total assets	$760,000	$775,000	$15,000
Accounts payable	$100,000	$100,000	$0
Income tax liability	3,000	9,000	6,000
Paid-in capital	500,000	500,000	0
Retained earnings	157,000	166,000	9,000
Total liabilities and stockholders' equity	$760,000	$775,000	$15,000

Summary

Retrospective changes can require detailed detective work, judgment, and thorough documentation of the changes made. Given the amount of labor involved, it is cost-effective to find justifiable reasons for not making retrospective changes. Two valid methods for doing so are to question the materiality of the necessary changes, or to find reasons to instead treat issues as changes in accounting estimate.

If retrospective application is completely unavoidable, it may make sense to have the company's auditors review proposed retrospective changes in advance. Doing so minimizes the risk that an issue will be discovered by the auditors during the annual audit, which will require additional retrospective changes.

Chapter 9
Changing Prices

255 = GAAP codification area for changing prices

Introduction

The guidance in this chapter addresses the problem of how inflationary environments impact the reported results and financial position of a business. GAAP provides an extensive array of reporting requirements for those companies whose operations are located in areas where there is strong inflationary pressure. If one were to follow the GAAP guidance (which is not mandatory), the result would be supplemental reporting that restates elements of the financial statements to show how the reporting entity would have fared if there had been no inflation. In this chapter, we address the many detailed reporting requirements related to changing prices, and provide a sample report.

The guidance in this chapter applies to all business entities that use GAAP to prepare financial statements that are stated in U.S. dollars, as well as foreign entities that prepare financial statements in the currency of the country where its operations are located, and foreign entities that operate in countries experiencing hyperinflation.

Overview of Changing Prices

When there is a significant amount of price inflation or deflation, the impact on the financial statements of a company operating in that environment can be so severe that the value of the information in the statements declines to the point of being nearly useless. Consequently, it is acceptable under GAAP to issue price-level adjusted financial statements under the following circumstances:

- The financial statements are denominated in a foreign currency; and
- The financial statements are for businesses operating in countries with highly inflationary economies; and
- The financial statements are intended for readers in the United States.

In the following sub-sections, we address how to measure the various items that are to be disclosed.

Inventory and Fixed Assets

When deriving the current cost of inventory and fixed assets, use the following measurements:

- *Inventory.* Use the current cost or lower recoverable amount at the measurement date. Current cost is considered the current cost of purchasing the inventory items. If turnover is rapid and no appreciable amounts of depreciation are allocated to inventory, the cost of goods sold as measured with last in, first out (LIFO) costing can be considered a reasonable approximation for current cost (if the effect of LIFO liquidations are excluded).
- *Fixed assets.* Use the current cost or lower recoverable amount at the measurement date, for the remaining service potential of these assets. Current cost is considered the current cost of acquiring the same service potential as the existing fixed assets.
- *Partial contracts.* If there is a partially-completed contract, use the current cost or lower recoverable amount for those resources allocated to the project at the date of their use on the contract or commitment to the contract.

Current costs can be obtained, for example, from price indexes, current invoice prices, vendor price lists, or standard manufacturing costs. Current costs are assumed to be based on the manufacture or purchase of assets in a location that minimizes the total landed cost of inventory and/or fixed assets.

It is also acceptable to use historical costs that are adjusted by a price index, rather than using current costs. This option may be the most cost-effective alternative, since a price index is one of the simplest ways to generate information about changing prices.

If current costs are derived for assets located in foreign locations, and those costs are denominated in a foreign currency, translate the amounts into the company's functional currency at the current exchange rate.

Specialized Assets

Derive the current cost of mineral resources either at their current market buying prices, or at the current cost required to find and develop the necessary mineral reserves. It is generally easiest to use historical costs that are adjusted by a price index. The same approach is applicable to timberlands, income-producing real estate, and motion picture films.

Recoverable Amounts

It may be necessary to measure the recoverable amount of an asset. If so, this information can be derived from value in use (i.e., discounted future cash flows) or the current market value of the asset. The value in use option is better if there is no intent to immediately sell the asset. Only use current market value if there is a plan to immediately sell the asset. If there is a choice between measuring assets at their current cost or recoverable amount, and the recoverable amount appears to be materially and permanently lower than the current cost, then measure the assets at their recoverable amount.

If a business is subject to price controls, it may be reasonable to measure recoverable amounts at their historical costs. Recoverable amounts may even be lower than historical costs. However, if there is an expectation that the replacement of the service potential of the assets will be undertaken at some point, then measure the cost of goods sold, depreciation, amortization, and depletion at their current cost-current purchasing power amounts.

Income from Continuing Operations

The measurement of income from continuing operations on a current cost basis requires the following steps:

- Measure the cost of goods sold as of the date sold, using either its current cost or lower recoverable amount, or when those resources are used on or at least committed to a designated contract.
- Measure depreciation, amortization, and depletion based on either the average current cost of the service potential of the underlying fixed assets or their lower recoverable amount during the usage period.

It is allowable to measure all other revenue and expense items, as well as income taxes, at the amounts stated in the company's income statement.

Restatement of Current Cost Information

If a business does not have significant foreign operations, or if it uses the U.S. dollar as the functional currency for all of its significant foreign operations, use the consumer price index for all urban consumers (CPIUC) to convert its current costs into units of constant purchasing power.

If operations are measured in a foreign functional currency, measure the effects of inflation on its current cost information either by applying the CPIUC to its results following translation, or by applying a measure of the change in purchasing power for that currency prior to translation. Whichever method is used, apply it consistently for all operations measured in foreign functional currencies.

If a measure of the change in purchasing power for a currency is not available when the financial statements are being constructed, it is allowable for management to estimate the change in the general price level.

Translation Adjustments

If there is an election to translate results into the U.S. dollar from a foreign currency and then apply the CPIUC, then state the aggregate translation adjustment net of income taxes that were allocated to the translation adjustment in the company's financial statements. Alternatively, if the election is made to translate results by applying a measure of the change in purchasing power for a currency prior to translation, then state the aggregate translation adjustment net of:

- The income taxes that were allocated to the translation adjustment in the company's financial statements; and
- The aggregate parity adjustment. This is the amount required to measure net assets as of the end of the year in either average-for-the-year dollars or end-of-the-year dollars. The choice is based on whether income from continuing operations is based on average-for-the year or end-of-the-year functional currency units.

Purchasing Power Gains and Losses

The purchasing power gain or loss resulting from net monetary assets is the net gain or loss resulting from the restatement in units of constant purchasing power of the changes in the balances and transactions in monetary assets and liabilities. If the purchasing power gain or loss from net monetary assets is based on translating foreign currency results by first applying a measure of the change in purchasing power for the foreign currency and then translating it into U.S. dollars, then translate the purchasing power gain or loss into its U.S. dollar equivalent using the average exchange rate for the period.

Monetary assets are considered to be cash, time deposits, foreign currencies, trading investments, accounts receivable and notes receivable, the allowance for doubtful accounts, loans to employees, long-term receivables, refundable deposits, the cash surrender value of life insurance, advances to suppliers, deferred tax assets, and deferred life insurance policy acquisition costs.

Monetary liabilities are considered to be accounts payable, notes payable, accrued expenses payable, cash dividends payable, advances from customers, refundable deposits, long-term debt and related premiums and discounts, deferred tax liabilities, life insurance policy reserves, property and casualty insurance loss reserves, deposit liabilities of financial institutions, and capital stock subject to mandatory redemption.

Restatement Steps

In essence, the restatement steps required to convert historical cost information into current cost-constant purchasing power information are as follows:

1. Review the contents of inventory at the beginning and end of the year, as well as the cost of goods sold, to determine when costs were incurred.
2. Restate both inventory and the cost of goods sold, so that they are presented at current cost.
3. Review fixed assets to determine when they were acquired.
4. Restate fixed assets, depreciation, amortization, and depletion, so that they are presented at current cost.
5. Determine the aggregate amount of net monetary items at the beginning and end of the reporting period, as well as the net change in these items during the period.

6. Calculate the purchasing power gain or loss on the net monetary items.
7. Calculate the change in current cost for both inventory and fixed assets, as well as the effect of changes in the general price level.

Changing Prices Disclosures

The disclosures stated in this section are encouraged by GAAP, but not required.

Five-Year Summary

Disclose all of the following information for each of the most recent five years, and present it as supplemental information to the annual financial statements. The following information is not needed in interim financial statements, nor is it needed at a business segment level.

Disclosure Item	Cost Basis
Net sales	
Income from continuing operations	Current cost
Purchasing power gain or loss on net monetary items	
Change in current cost or lower recoverable amount of inventory and fixed assets, net of inflation	
Aggregate foreign currency translation adjustment	Current cost
Net assets at year end	Current cost
Income per common share from continuing operations	Current cost
Cash dividends declared per common share	
Market price per common share at year end	

The information shown in this five-year summary should be stated using one of the following pricing methodologies:

- In annual-average or end-of-year units of constant purchasing power.
- In dollars with the purchasing power equivalent of dollars of the base period of the CPIUC. If this pricing methodology is used, state the level of the CPIUC used for each of the five years. The CPIUC may have to be extrapolated, if it has not been published by the time the annual report is prepared.

If the business has a significant foreign operation that is measured in a currency other than the U.S. dollar, disclose whether inflationary adjustments to its current cost information are based on the CPIUC or on a functional currency general price level index.

If the company is presenting consolidated results, then this five-year summary should also be presented on a consolidated basis.

Finally, accompany the five-year summary with a discussion of the significance of changing prices on the business, along with an explanation of any specific items disclosed in the summary.

EXAMPLE

Armadillo Industries presents the following five-year summary of supplemental information related to changing prices as part of the disclosures that accompany its annual financial statements:

Five-year Comparison of Selected Financial Data
Adjusted for Effects of Changing Prices
In Thousands of Average 20X5 Dollars, except for Per Share Amounts

	20X5	20X4	20X3	20X2	20X1
Net sales and other operating revenues	$363,000	$342,000	$330,000	$309,000	$294,000
Income from continuing operations	18,000	16,000	4,000	23,000	10,000
Gain from decline in purchasing power of net amounts owed	14,000	9,000	2,000	17,000	7,000
Excess of increase in specific prices of inventory and fixed assets over the increase in the general price level	23,000	18,000	1,000	29,000	3,000
Foreign currency translation adjustment	-2,900	3,400	-5,800	-3,200	-1,500
Net assets at year-end	111,000	101,000	90,000	83,500	72,000
Per share information:					
Income from continuing operations	$4.00	$3.56	$0.89	$5.11	$2.22
Cash dividends declared	2.00	1.75	--	1.50	1.25
Market price at year-end	36	32	8	46	20

Other Current Year Disclosures

If income from continuing operations on a current cost-constant purchasing power basis differs significantly from income from continuing operations, then disclose the following additional information:

- *Current cost components.* Components of income from continuing operations on a current cost basis, either in the form of notes to the five-year summary, as a reconciliation from the primary income statement, or in a separate income statement format. No matter which format is used, the cost of goods sold, depreciation, amortization, and depletion (if any) should be separately stated.
- *Depreciation, current cost.* Any differences between asset depreciation, useful lives, and salvage values when calculating current cost-current purchasing power depreciation.
- *Depreciation, primary.* The methods and any estimates used to calculate depreciation in the financial statements.

- *Fixed asset cost change*. The change in current cost or lower recoverable amount both before and after adjusting for inflation effects on inventory and fixed assets.
- *Information sources*. The types of information used to calculate current costs for inventory, fixed assets, the cost of goods sold, depreciation, amortization, and depletion.
- *Purchasing power gains and losses*. The purchasing power net gain or loss for net monetary items, the change in the current cost or lower recoverable amount of inventory and fixed assets (net of inflation), and any translation adjustment.
- *Year-end figures*. The year-end amount of the current cost or lower recoverable amount for inventory and fixed assets.

Other Disclosures for Mineral Resources Assets

If a business has mineral reserves other than oil and gas, disclose all of the following information for each of the five preceding years:

- *Market prices*. The average market price for each significant mineral product.
- *Product quantities*. The estimated quantity of each mineral that can be recovered in significant quantities if the reserves contain mineral products.
- *Production quantities*. The quantities of each mineral product extracted each year, as well as the quantities milled.
- *Reserves ownership*. The quantities of proved or proved and probable mineral reserves that were purchased or sold in place during the year.
- *Reserves*. Estimates of proved or proved and probable mineral reserves at year-end.

When calculating quantities for these disclosures, include the quantities attributable to both the parent entity and its subsidiaries, if the disclosure is on a consolidated basis. If there is an investment in another entity under the equity method, do not include the quantities attributable to the investee; however, if the investor's share of these reserves is significant, report the information separately.

Summary

Though the guidance for changing prices is well-intentioned, it can also be quite difficult to compile and present the recommended information. Accordingly, consider the cost of these reporting suggestions and the resulting improvement in the value of the information provided to the readers of the company's financial statements. In many cases, the cost-benefit tradeoff will lean heavily in favor of not reporting the effects of changing prices. The reporting is most likely to be of use when a significant proportion of company operations are located in a country experiencing high levels of price inflation.

We have given somewhat limited coverage of this topic, in the expectation that most businesses will find that the reporting requirements are excessively onerous, and so will opt to not report the information contained within this chapter.

Chapter 10
Earnings per Share

260 = GAAP codification area for earnings per share

Introduction

If a company is publicly-held, two types of earnings per share information are to be reported within the financial statements. In this chapter, we describe how to calculate both basic and diluted earnings per share, as well as how to present this information within the financial statements. The information presented in this chapter only applies to entities with publicly-held common stock or potential common stock.

Basic Earnings per Share

Basic earnings per share is the amount of a company's profit or loss for a reporting period that is available to the shares of its common stock that are outstanding during a reporting period. If a business only has common stock in its capital structure, it presents only its basic earnings per share for income from continuing operations and net income. This information is reported on its income statement.

The formula for basic earnings per share is:

$$\frac{\text{Profit or loss attributable to common equity holders of the parent business}}{\text{Weighted average number of common shares outstanding during the period}}$$

In addition, subdivide this calculation into:

- The profit or loss from continuing operations attributable to the parent company
- The total profit or loss attributable to the parent company

When calculating basic earnings per share, incorporate into the numerator an adjustment for dividends. Deduct from the profit or loss the after-tax amount of any dividends declared on non-cumulative preferred stock, as well as the after-tax amount of any preferred stock dividends, even if the dividends are not declared; this does not include any dividends paid or declared during the current period that relate to previous periods.

Also, incorporate the following adjustments into the denominator of the basic earnings per share calculation:

- *Contingent stock.* If there is contingently issuable stock, treat it as though it were outstanding as of the date when there are no circumstances under which the shares would *not* be issued.
- *Weighted-average shares.* Use the weighted-average number of shares during the period in the denominator. This is done by adjusting the number of shares outstanding at the beginning of the reporting period for common shares repurchased or issued in the period. This adjustment is based on the proportion of the days in the reporting period that the shares are outstanding.

EXAMPLE

Lowry Locomotion earns a profit of $1,000,000 net of taxes in Year 1. In addition, Lowry owes $200,000 in dividends to the holders of its cumulative preferred stock. Lowry calculates the numerator of its basic earnings per share as follows:

$$\$1,000,000 \text{ Profit} - \$200,000 \text{ Dividends} = \underline{\$800,000}$$

Lowry had 4,000,000 common shares outstanding at the beginning of Year 1. In addition, it sold 200,000 shares on April 1 and 400,000 shares on October 1. It also issued 500,000 shares on July 1 to the owners of a newly-acquired subsidiary. Finally, it bought back 60,000 shares on December 1. Lowry calculates the weighted-average number of common shares outstanding as follows:

Date	Shares	Weighting (Months)	Weighted Average
January 1	4,000,000	12/12	4,000,000
April 1	200,000	9/12	150,000
July 1	500,000	6/12	250,000
October 1	400,000	3/12	100,000
December 1	-60,000	1/12	-5,000
			4,495,000

Lowry's basic earnings per share is:

$800,000 adjusted profits ÷ 4,495,000 weighted-average shares = $0.18 per share

Diluted Earnings per Share

Diluted earnings per share is the profit for a reporting period per share of common stock outstanding during that period; it includes the number of shares that would have been outstanding during the period if the company had issued common shares for all potential dilutive common stock outstanding during the period.

If a company has more types of stock than common stock in its capital structure, it must present both basic earnings per share and diluted earnings per share information; this presentation must be for both income from continuing operations and net income. This information is reported on the company's income statement.

To calculate diluted earnings per share, include the effects of all dilutive potential common shares. This means that the number of shares outstanding is increased by the weighted average number of additional common shares that would have been outstanding if the company had converted all dilutive potential common stock to common stock. This dilution may affect the profit or loss in the numerator of the dilutive earnings per share calculation. The formula is:

$$\frac{\text{(Profit or loss attributable to common equity holders of parent company}}{\text{(Weighted average number of common shares outstanding during the period}}$$

(Profit or loss attributable to common equity holders of parent company
+ After-tax interest on convertible debt + Convertible preferred dividends)
(Weighted average number of common shares outstanding during the period
+ All dilutive potential common stock)

It may be necessary to make two adjustments to the *numerator* of this calculation. They are:

- *Interest expense.* Eliminate any interest expense associated with dilutive potential common stock, since there is an assumption that these shares are converted to common stock. The conversion would eliminate the company's liability for the interest expense.
- *Dividends.* Adjust for the after-tax impact of dividends or other types of dilutive potential common shares.

It may be necessary to make additional adjustments to the *denominator* of this calculation. They are:

- *Anti-dilutive shares.* If there are any contingent stock issuances that would have an anti-dilutive impact on earnings per share, do not include them in the calculation. This situation arises when a business experiences a loss, because including the dilutive shares in the calculation would reduce the loss per share.
- *Dilutive shares.* If there is potentially dilutive common stock, add all of it to the denominator of the diluted earnings per share calculation. Unless there is more specific information available, assume that these shares are issued at the beginning of the reporting period.
- *Dilutive securities termination.* If a conversion option lapses during the reporting period for dilutive convertible securities, or if the related debt is extinguished during the reporting period, the effect of these securities should still be included in the denominator of the diluted earnings per share calculation for the period during which they were outstanding.

In addition to these adjustments to the denominator, also apply all of the adjustments to the denominator already noted for basic earnings per share.

> **Tip:** The rules related to diluted earnings per share appear complex, but they are founded upon one principle – that the accountant is trying to establish the absolute worst-case scenario to arrive at the smallest possible amount of earnings per share. If this person is faced with an unusual situation involving the calculation of diluted earnings per share and is not sure what to do, that rule will likely apply.

In addition to the issues just noted, here are a number of additional situations that could impact the calculation of diluted earnings per share:

- *Most advantageous exercise price.* When the number of potential shares that could be issued is calculated, do so using the most advantageous conversion rate from the perspective of the person or entity holding the security to be converted.
- *Settlement assumption.* If there is an open contract that could be settled in common stock or cash, assume that it will be settled in common stock, but only if the effect is dilutive. The presumption of settlement in stock can be overcome if there is a reasonable basis for expecting that settlement will be partially or entirely in cash.
- *Effects of convertible instruments.* If there are convertible instruments outstanding, include their dilutive effect if they dilute earnings per share. Consider convertible preferred stock to be anti-dilutive when the dividend on any converted shares is greater than basic earnings per share. Similarly, convertible debt is considered anti-dilutive when the interest expense on any converted shares exceeds basic earnings per share. The following example illustrates the concept.

EXAMPLE

Lowry Locomotion earns a net profit of $2 million, and it has 5 million common shares outstanding. In addition, there is a $1 million convertible loan that has an eight percent interest rate. The loan may potentially convert into 500,000 of Lowry's common shares. Lowry's incremental tax rate is 35 percent.

Lowry's basic earnings per share is $2,000,000 ÷ 5,000,000 shares, or $0.40/share. The following calculation shows the compilation of Lowry's diluted earnings per share:

Net profit	$2,000,000
+ Interest saved on $1,000,000 loan at 8%	80,000
- Reduced tax savings on foregone interest expense	-28,000
= Adjusted net earnings	$2,052,000
Common shares outstanding	5,000,000
+ Potential converted shares	500,000
= Adjusted shares outstanding	5,500,000
Diluted earnings per share ($2,052,000 ÷ 5,500,000)	**$0.37/share**

- *Option exercise.* If there are any dilutive options and warrants, assume that they are exercised at their exercise price. Then, convert the proceeds into the total number of shares that the holders would have purchased, using the average market price during the reporting period. Then use in the diluted earnings per share calculation the difference between the number of shares assumed to have been issued and the number of shares assumed to have been purchased. The following example illustrates the concept.

EXAMPLE

Lowry Locomotion earns a net profit of $200,000, and it has 5,000,000 common shares outstanding that sell on the open market for an average of $12 per share. In addition, there are 300,000 options outstanding that can be converted to Lowry's common stock at $10 each.

Lowry's basic earnings per share is $200,000 ÷ 5,000,000 common shares, or $0.04 per share.

Lowry's controller wants to calculate the amount of diluted earnings per share. To do so, he follows these steps:

1. *Calculate the number of shares that would have been issued at the market price.* Thus, he multiplies the 300,000 options by the average exercise price of $10 to arrive at a total of $3,000,000 paid to exercise the options by their holders.
2. *Divide the amount paid to exercise the options by the market price to determine the number of shares that could be purchased.* Thus, he divides the $3,000,000 paid to exercise the options by the $12 average market price to arrive at 250,000 shares that could have been purchased with the proceeds from the options.

3. *Subtract the number of shares that could have been purchased from the number of options exercised.* Thus, he subtracts the 250,000 shares potentially purchased from the 300,000 options to arrive at a difference of 50,000 shares.
4. *Add the incremental number of shares to the shares already outstanding.* Thus, he adds the 50,000 incremental shares to the existing 5,000,000 to arrive at 5,050,000 diluted shares.

Based on this information, the controller arrives at diluted earnings per share of $0.0396, for which the calculation is:

$$\$200,000 \text{ Net profit} \div 5,050,000 \text{ Common shares}$$

- *Put options.* If there are purchased put options, only include them in the diluted earnings per share calculation if the exercise price is higher than the average market price during the reporting period.
- *Written put options.* If there is a written put option that requires a business to repurchase its own stock, include it in the computation of diluted earnings per share, but only if the effect is dilutive. If the exercise price of such a put option is above the average market price of the company's stock during the reporting period, this is considered to be "in the money," and the dilutive effect is to be calculated using the following method, which is called the *reverse treasury stock method*:

    1. Assume that enough shares were issued by the company at the beginning of the period at the average market price to raise sufficient funds to satisfy the put option contract.
    2. Assume that these proceeds are used to buy back the required number of shares.
    3. Include in the denominator of the diluted earnings per share calculation the difference between the numbers of shares issued and purchased in steps 1 and 2.

EXAMPLE

A third party exercises a written put option that requires Armadillo Industries to repurchase 1,000 shares from the third party at an exercise price of $30. The current market price is $20. Armadillo uses the following steps to compute the impact of the written put option on its diluted earnings per share calculation:

1. Armadillo assumes that it has issued 1,500 shares at $20.
2. The company assumes that the "issuance" of 1,500 shares is used to meet the repurchase obligation of $30,000.
3. The difference between the 1,500 shares issued and the 1,000 shares repurchased is added to the denominator of Armadillo's diluted earnings per share calculation.

- *Call options*. If there are purchased call options, only include them in the diluted earnings per share calculation if the exercise price is lower than the market price.

> **Tip:** There is only a dilutive effect on the diluted earnings per share calculation when the average market price is greater than the exercise prices of any options or warrants.

- *Contingent shares in general*. Treat common stock that is contingently issuable as though it was outstanding as of the beginning of the reporting period, but only if the conditions have been met that would require the company to issue the shares. If the conditions were not met by the end of the period, then include in the calculation, as of the beginning of the period, any shares that would be issuable if the end of the reporting period were the end of the contingency period, and the result would be dilutive.
- *Contingent shares dependency*. If there is a contingent share issuance that is dependent upon the future market price of the company's common stock, include the shares in the diluted earnings per share calculation, based on the market price at the end of the reporting period; however, only include the issuance if the effect is dilutive. If the shares have a contingency feature, do not include them in the calculation until the contingency has been met.
- *Issuances based on future earnings and stock price*. There may be contingent stock issuances that are based on future earnings and the future price of a company's stock. If so, the number of shares to include in diluted earnings per share should be based on the earnings to date and the current market price as of the end of each reporting period. If both earnings and share price targets must be reached in order to trigger a stock issuance and both targets are not met, then do not include any related contingently issuable shares in the diluted earnings per share calculation.
- *Compensation in shares*. If employees are awarded shares that have not vested or stock options as forms of compensation, then treat these grants as options when calculating diluted earnings per share. Consider these grants to be outstanding on the grant date, rather than any later vesting date.

Always calculate the number of potential dilutive common shares independently for each reporting period presented in the financial statements.

Treasury Stock and Reverse Treasury Stock Methods

The preceding section addressed the calculation of diluted earnings per share. The dilutive effects of certain types of securities are dealt with using the treasury stock method or the reverse treasury stock method. These calculations are noted in the following sub-sections.

Treasury Stock Method

When an organization has outstanding call options or warrants, their dilutive effects are calculated using the treasury stock method. This method employs the following sequence of assumptions and calculations:

1. Assume that options and warrants are exercised at the beginning of the reporting period. If they were actually exercised later in the reporting period, use the actual date of exercise.
2. The proceeds garnered by the presumed option or warrant exercise are assumed to be used to purchase common stock at the average market price during the reporting period.
3. The difference between the number of shares assumed to have been issued and the number of shares assumed to have been purchased is then added to the denominator of the computation of diluted earnings per share.

In Step 2 of the process, the average market price during a quarterly reporting period is based on the average market prices during all three months of the reporting period. A simple average of weekly or monthly closing market prices is usually sufficient for this calculation. When prices fluctuate considerably, it might instead be necessary to use an average of the high and low prices for the reporting period.

When the year-to-date average pricing is determined, it is based on the year-to-date weighted average number of incremental shares included in each quarterly earnings per share computation.

The treasury stock method will only have a dilutive effect when the average market price of the common stock in the period is greater than the exercise price of the options or warrants.

The following example illustrates the concept.

EXAMPLE

Lowry Locomotion earns a net profit of $200,000, and it has 5,000,000 common shares outstanding that sell on the open market for an average of $12 per share. In addition, there are 300,000 options outstanding that can be converted to Lowry's common stock at $10 each.

Lowry's basic earnings per share is $200,000 ÷ 5,000,000 common shares, or $0.0400 per share.

Lowry's controller wants to calculate the amount of diluted earnings per share. To do so, he follows these steps:

1. *Calculate the number of shares that would have been issued at the market price.* Thus, he multiplies the 300,000 options by the average exercise price of $10 to arrive at a total of $3,000,000 paid to exercise the options by their holders.
2. *Divide the amount paid to exercise the options by the market price to determine the number of shares that could be purchased.* Thus, he divides the $3,000,000 paid to exercise the options by the $12 average market price to arrive at 250,000 shares that could have been purchased with the proceeds from the options.

3. *Subtract the number of shares that could have been purchased from the number of options exercised.* Thus, he subtracts the 250,000 shares potentially purchased from the 300,000 options to arrive at a difference of 50,000 shares.
4. *Add the incremental number of shares to the shares already outstanding.* Thus, he adds the 50,000 incremental shares to the existing 5,000,000 to arrive at 5,050,000 diluted shares.

Based on this information, the controller arrives at diluted earnings per share of $0.0396, for which the calculation is:

$200,000 Net profit ÷ 5,050,000 Common shares

This method may also be used when a business has issued the following instruments:

- Nonvested stock granted to employees
- Stock purchase contracts
- Partially paid stock subscriptions

Reverse Treasury Stock Method

A business may be party to a contract that requires it to buy back its own stock from a shareholder. This type of arrangement is called a put option. If the effect of a put option is dilutive (which occurs when the exercise price is higher than the average market price in a reporting period), it must be included in the diluted earnings per share calculation. The calculation of the effect of a put option is measured using the reverse treasury stock method, which involves the following steps:

1. Assume that enough shares were issued by the company at the beginning of the period at the average market price to raise sufficient funds to satisfy the put option contract.
2. Assume that these proceeds are used to buy back the required number of shares.
3. Include in the denominator of the diluted earnings per share calculation the difference between the numbers of shares issued and purchased in steps 1 and 2.

EXAMPLE

A third party exercises a written put option that requires Armadillo Industries to repurchase 1,000 shares from the third party at an exercise price of $30. The current market price is $20. Armadillo uses the following steps to compute the impact of the written put option on its diluted earnings per share calculation:

1. Armadillo assumes that it has issued 1,500 shares at $20.
2. The company assumes that the "issuance" of 1,500 shares is used to meet the repurchase obligation of $30,000.
3. The difference between the 1,500 shares issued and the 1,000 shares repurchased is added to the denominator of Armadillo's diluted earnings per share calculation.

Disclosure of Earnings per Share

The basic and diluted earnings per share information is normally listed at the bottom of the income statement, and is included for every period in the income statement. Also, if diluted earnings per share are reported in *any* of the periods included in a company's income statement, it must be reported for *all* of the periods included in the statement. The following sample illustrates the concept.

Sample Presentation of Earnings per Share

Earnings per Share	20x3	20x2	20x1
From continuing operations			
Basic earnings per share	$1.05	$0.95	$0.85
Diluted earnings per share	1.00	0.90	0.80
From discontinued operations			
Basic earnings per share	$0.20	$0.17	$0.14
Diluted earnings per share	0.15	0.08	0.07
From total operations			
Basic earnings per share	$1.25	$1.12	$0.99
Diluted earnings per share	1.15	0.98	0.87

Note that, if the company reports a discontinued operation, it must present the basic and diluted earnings per share amounts for this item. The information can be included either as part of the income statement or in the accompanying notes. The preceding sample presentation includes a disclosure for earnings per share from discontinued operations.

Tip: If the amounts of basic and diluted earnings per share are the same, it is allowable to have a dual presentation of the information in a single line item on the income statement.

In addition to the earnings per share reporting format just noted, a company is also required to report the following information:

- *Reconciliation.* State the differences between the numerators and denominators of the basic and diluted earnings per share calculations for income from continuing operations.
- *Preferred dividends effect.* State the effect of preferred dividends on the computation of income available to common stockholders for basic earnings per share.

- *Potential effects.* Describe the terms and conditions of any securities not included in the computation of diluted earnings per share due to their antidilutive effects, but which could potentially dilute basic earnings per share in the future.

SAMPLE DISCLOSURE

For the years ended December 31, 20X4, 20X3 and 20X2, there were approximately 9 million, 12 million and 29 million, respectively, of outstanding stock awards that were not included in the computation of diluted earnings per share because their effect was antidilutive.

- *Subsequent events.* Describe any transactions occurring after the latest reporting period but before the issuance of financial statements that would have a material impact on the number of common or potential common shares if they had occurred prior to the end of the reporting period.

Summary

It will have been evident from the discussions of earnings per share that the computation of diluted earnings per share can be quite complex if there is a correspondingly complex equity structure. In such a situation, it is quite likely that diluted earnings per share will be incorrectly calculated. To improve the accuracy of the calculation, create an electronic spreadsheet that incorporates all of the necessary factors impacting diluted earnings per share. Further, save the calculation for each reporting period on a separate page of the spreadsheet; by doing so, there will be an excellent record of how these calculations were managed in the past.

Chapter 11
Interim Reporting

270 = GAAP codification area for interim reporting

Introduction

If a company is publicly-held, the Securities and Exchange Commission (SEC) requires that the business file a variety of quarterly information on the Form 10-Q. This information is a reduced set of the requirements for the more comprehensive annual Form 10-K. The requirement to issue these additional financial statements may appear to be simple enough, but one must consider whether to report information assuming that quarterly results are stand-alone documents, or part of the full-year results of the business. This chapter discusses the disparities that these different viewpoints can cause in the financial statements, as well as how to report changes in accounting principle and estimate.

Related Chapters

See the following chapters for discussions of issues related to interim reporting:

- *Accounting Changes and Error Corrections*. Covers changes in accounting principle and changes in accounting estimate.
- *Inventory*. Covers the gross profit method for estimating ending inventory, as well as LIFO layer liquidation and the lower of cost or market rule as applied in interim periods.

Overview of Interim Reporting

A business will periodically create financial statements for shorter periods than the fiscal year, which are known as *interim periods*. The most common examples of interim periods are monthly or quarterly financial statements, though any period of less than a full fiscal year can be considered an interim period. The concepts related to interim periods are most commonly applicable to the financial statements of publicly-held companies, since they are required to issue quarterly financial statements that must be reviewed by their outside auditors; these financials must account for certain activities in a consistent manner, as well as prevent readers from being misled about the results of the business on an ongoing basis.

General Interim Reporting Rule

The general rule for interim period reporting is that the same accounting principles and practices be applied to interim reports that are used for the preparation of annual financial statements. The following bullet points illustrate revenues and expenses that follow the general rule, and therefore do not change for interim reporting:

- *Revenue*. Revenue is recognized in the same manner that is used for annual reporting, with no exceptions.
- *Costs associated with revenue*. If a cost is typically assigned to a specific sale (such as cost of goods sold items), expense recognition is the same as is used for annual reporting.
- *Direct expenditures*. If an expense is incurred in a period and relates to that period, it is recorded as an expense in that period. An example is salaries expense.
- *Accruals for estimated expenditures*. If there is an estimated expenditure to be made at a later date but which relates to the current period, it is recorded as an expense in the current period. An example is accrued wages.
- *Depreciation and amortization*. If there is a fixed asset, depreciation (for tangible assets) or amortization (for intangible assets) is ratably charged to all periods in its useful life.

In addition, there are cases where a company is accustomed to only making a year-end adjustment, such as to its reserves for doubtful accounts, obsolete inventory, and/or warranty claims, as well as for year-end bonuses. Where possible, these adjustments should be made in the interim periods, thereby reducing the amount of any residual adjustments still required in the year-end financial statements.

Variations from the Interim Reporting Rule

There are other cases in which the treatment of certain transactions will vary for interim periods. The following rules should be applied in these cases:

- *Expense allocation*. Non-product expenses should be allocated among interim periods based on time expired, usage, or benefits received. In most cases, this means that expenses will simply be charged to expense in the current period, with no allocation to other interim periods. However, it could result in spreading expense recognition over several months or quarters.
- *Arbitrary assignments*. It is not allowable to make arbitrary assignments of costs to certain interim periods.
- *Gains and losses*. Gains and losses that arise in an interim period shall be recognized at once, and not be deferred to any later interim periods.

EXAMPLE

Armadillo Industries incurs an annual property tax charge of $60,000. Also, Armadillo has historically earned an annual volume discount of $30,000 per year, based on its full-year purchases from a major supplier.

Since the property tax charge is applicable to all months in the year, the controller accrues a $5,000 monthly charge for this expense. Similarly, the volume discount relates back to volume purchases throughout the year, not just the last month of the year, in which the discount is retroactively awarded. Accordingly, the controller creates a monthly credit of $2,500 to reflect the expected year-end volume discount of $30,000.

The concepts of recognizing expenses are more thoroughly discussed in the next two sections, which address the integral view and the discrete view of how to handle interim expense recognition.

There are several specific areas in which the accounting for interim reporting can differ from what is used for annual reporting. In particular:

- *Estimated inventory*. It is acceptable to use the gross profit method or other methods (see the Inventory chapter) to estimate the cost of goods sold during interim periods. This is allowed in order to reduce the amount of time required to derive the cost of goods sold using a formal count of the ending inventory.
- *LIFO layers*. If a company uses the last in, first out (LIFO) method of calculating inventory (see the Inventory chapter), existing inventory cost layers may be liquidated during an interim period. If such a cost layer is expected to be replaced by the end of the fiscal year, the cost of sales for the interim period can include the expected replacement cost of that LIFO cost layer.
- *Lower of cost or market*. If there is a reduction in the market value of inventory, the difference between the market value and its cost should be charged to expense in an interim period (see the lower of cost or market rule in the Inventory chapter). However, it is allowable to offset the full amount of these losses with any market value gains in subsequent periods within the same fiscal year on the same inventory items. Alternatively, it is allowable to avoid recognizing these losses in an interim period if there are seasonal price fluctuations that are expected to result in an offsetting increase in market prices by the end of the year.
- *Purchase price and volume variances*. If a company uses a standard costing system to assign costs to its inventory items, it is acceptable to defer the recognition of any variances from standard cost in interim periods, if it has already been planned that these variances will have been absorbed by the end of the fiscal year. However, if there are unexpected purchase price or volume variances, recognize them in the interim period in which they occur.

EXAMPLE

Pianoforte International writes down the value of its mahogany wood holdings, due to a crash in world mahogany prices. The amount of the first-quarter write down is $100,000. By year-end, the market price has stabilized at a higher level, allowing Pianoforte to reverse $62,000 of the original write down and report the change in its fiscal year-end results.

Changes in Accounting Principle in Interim Periods

An accounting principle is an acceptable method for recording and reporting an accounting transaction. There is a change in accounting principle when:

- There are several accounting principles that apply to a situation, and the entity switches to a principle that has not been used in the past; or
- When the accounting principle that formerly applied to the situation is no longer generally accepted; or
- There is a change in the method of applying the principle.

Only change an accounting principle when doing so is required by GAAP, or one can justify that it is preferable to use the new principle. If the election is made to proceed with a change in accounting principle, apply it retrospectively to all prior periods, including all interim reporting, unless it is impractical to do so. To complete a retrospective application of a change in accounting principle, follow these steps:

1. Include the cumulative effect of the change on periods prior to those presented in the carrying amount of assets and liabilities as of the beginning of the first period in which financial statements are being presented; and
2. Enter an offsetting amount in the beginning retained earnings balance of the first period in which financial statements are being presented; and
3. Adjust all presented financial statements to reflect the change to the new accounting principle.

From a reporting perspective, a change in accounting principle requires disclosure of the change in principle from those applied in the comparable interim period of the prior annual period, as well as the preceding interim periods in the current fiscal year, and in the annual report for the prior fiscal year.

Changes in Accounting Estimate in Interim Periods

There is a change in accounting estimate when there is a change that affects the carrying amount of an existing asset or liability, or that alters the subsequent accounting for existing or future assets or liabilities. A change in estimate arises from the appearance of new information that alters the existing situation.

Changes in estimate are a normal part of accounting, and an expected part of the ongoing process of reviewing the current status and future benefits and obligations related to assets and liabilities. All of the following are situations where there is likely to be a change in accounting estimate:

- Allowance for doubtful accounts
- Reserve for obsolete inventory
- Changes in the useful life of depreciable assets
- Changes in the salvage values of depreciable assets
- Changes in the amount of expected warranty obligations
- Changes in the estimated effective annual tax rate

When there is a change in estimate, always account for it in the period of change. There is *no* need to restate earlier financial statements; thus, there is no need to restate any prior-period interim reporting. There should be disclosure in the current and subsequent interim periods of the effect on earnings of the change in estimate, if material in relation to any of the reporting periods presented. This disclosure should continue to be made for as long as necessary, to avoid any misleading comparisons between periods.

Tip: Where possible, adopt accounting changes during the first interim period of a fiscal year. Doing so eliminates any comparability problems between the interim periods for the remainder of the fiscal year.

Error Correction in Interim Periods

When determining the materiality of an error, relate the amount to the estimated profit for the entire fiscal year and the effect on the earnings trend, rather than for the current interim period. Otherwise, a disproportionate number of error corrections will be separately reported within the financial statements.

If an error correction is considered material at the interim period level but not for the full fiscal year, disclose the error in the interim report.

EXAMPLE

Armadillo Industries has profits of $1,000,000 in its first quarter, and expects to generate $4,000,000 of profits for the entire fiscal year. The company has historically considered materiality to be 5% of its profits. In the first quarter, the accounting department uncovers a $100,000 error. Though this amount is 10% of first-quarter profits, it is only 2.5% of full-year expected profits. Given the minimal impact on full-year profits, Armadillo does not have to segregate this information for reporting purposes in its first quarter interim reporting, though it must still disclose the information.

Adjustments to Prior Interim Periods

If an item impacting a company's profits occurs during an interim period other than the first interim period of the fiscal year, and some portion or all of it is an adjustment relating to a prior interim period of the current fiscal year, report the item as follows:

- Include that portion of the item that relates to the current interim period in the results of the current interim period
- Restate the results of prior interim periods to include that portion of the item relating to each interim period
- If there are any portions of the item relating to activities in prior fiscal years, include the change in a restatement of the first interim period of the current fiscal year

The Integral View

Under the integral view of producing interim reports, assume that the results reported in interim financial statements are an integral part of the full-year financial results (hence the name of this concept). This viewpoint produces the following accounting issues:

- *Accrue expenses not arising in the period.* If an expense will be paid later in the year that is incurred at least partially in the reporting period, accrue some portion of the expense in the reporting period. Here are several examples:

  o *Advertising.* If advertising is paid for in advance that is scheduled to occur over multiple time periods, recognize the expense over the entire range of time periods. Also, if there are clear benefits from an initial advertising expenditure that extend beyond the interim period in which the expenditure was made, expense recognition can be deferred to later periods (this concept may be difficult to prove to the auditors).

  o *Bonuses.* If there are bonus plans that may result in bonus payments later in the year, accrue the expense in all accounting periods. Only accrue this expense if it is possible to reasonably estimate the amount of the bonus, which may not always be possible during the earlier months covered by a performance contract.

  o *Contingencies.* If there are contingent liabilities that will be resolved later in the year, and which are both probable and reasonably estimated, then accrue the related expense.

  o *Profit sharing.* If employees are paid a percentage of company profits at year-end, and the amount can be reasonably estimated, then accrue the expense throughout the year as a proportion of the profits recognized in each period.

  o *Property taxes.* A local government entity issues an invoice to the company at some point during the year for property taxes. These taxes are intended to cover the entire year, so accrue a portion of the expense in each reporting period.

- *Tax rate.* A company is usually subject to a graduated income tax rate that incrementally escalates through the year as the business generates more profit. Under the integral view, use the expected tax rate for the entire year in every reporting period, rather than the incremental tax rate that applies only to the profits earned for the year to date.

EXAMPLE

The board of directors of Lowry Locomotion approves a senior management bonus plan for the upcoming year that could potentially pay the senior management team a maximum of $240,000. It initially seems probable that the full amount will be paid, but by the third quarter it appears more likely that the maximum amount to be paid will be $180,000. In addition, the company pays $60,000 in advance for a full year of advertising in *Locomotive Times* magazine. Lowry recognizes these expenses as follows:

	Quarter 1	Quarter 2	Quarter 3	Quarter 4	Full Year
Bonus expense	$60,000	$60,000	$30,000	$30,000	$180,000
Advertising	15,000	15,000	15,000	15,000	60,000

The accounting staff spreads the recognition of the full amount of the projected bonus over the year, but then reduces its recognition of the remaining expense starting in the third quarter, to adjust for the lowered bonus payout expectation.

The accounting staff initially records the $60,000 advertising expense as a prepaid expense, and recognizes it ratably over all four quarters of the year, which matches the time period over which the related advertisements are run by *Locomotive Times*.

One problem with the integral view is that it tends to result in a significant number of expense accruals. Since these accruals are usually based on estimates, it is entirely possible that adjustments should be made to the accruals later in the year, as the company obtains more precise information about the expenses that are being accrued. Some of these adjustments could be substantial, and may materially affect the reported results in later periods.

The Discrete View

Under the discrete view of producing interim reports, assume that the results reported for a specific interim period are *not* associated with the revenues and expenses arising during other reporting periods. Under this view, record the entire impact of a transaction within the reporting period, rather than ratably over the entire year. The following are examples of the situations that can arise under the discrete method:

- *Reduced accruals.* A substantially smaller number of accruals are likely under the discrete method, since the assumption is that one should not anticipate the recordation of transactions that have not yet arisen.
- *Gains and losses.* Do not spread the recognition of a gain or loss across multiple periods. If this were to be done, it would allow a company to spread a loss over multiple periods, thereby making the loss look smaller on a per-period basis than it really is.

Comparison of the Integral and Discrete Views

The integral view is clearly the better method from a theoretical perspective, since the causes of some transactions can span an entire year. For example, a manager may be awarded a bonus at the end of December, but he probably had to achieve specific results throughout the year to earn it. Otherwise, if a business were to adopt the discrete view, interim reporting would yield exceedingly varied results, with some periods revealing inordinately high or low profitability.

However, consider adopting the integral view from the perspective of accounting efficiency; that is, it is very time-consuming to maintain a mass of revenue and expense accruals, their ongoing adjustments, and documentation of the reasons for them throughout a year. Instead, use the integral view only for the more material transactions that are anticipated, and use the discrete view for smaller transactions. Thus, the accountant could accrue the expense for property taxes throughout the year if the amount is significant, or simply record it in the month when the invoice is received, if the amount is small.

Disclosures for Interim Reporting

The level of financial reporting contained within the interim reports of publicly-held companies is lower than the requirements for annual financial statements, which is necessary in order to release interim reports on an accelerated schedule. To prevent an excessive reduction in the level of reporting, GAAP requires the following minimum content in the financial statements:

- *Financial statement items*. Includes sales, provision for income taxes, net income, and comprehensive income.
- *Earnings per share*. Includes both basic and diluted earnings per share.

The following additional disclosures are specific to interim reports:

- *Cost of goods sold derivation*. If a different method is used during an interim period than at year-end to derive the cost of goods sold, this different method must be disclosed, as well as any significant adjustments resulting from a reconciliation with the annual physical inventory count.
- *Expenses charged wholly within current period*. If there are costs wholly charged to expense within an interim period, and for which there are no comparable expenses in the corresponding interim period of the preceding year, the nature and amount of the expense should be disclosed.
- *Prior period adjustment*. If there is a material retroactive prior period adjustment made during any interim period, disclosure must be made of the effect on net income and earnings per share of any prior period included in the report, as well as on retained earnings.
- *Seasonality*. When there are seasonal variations in a business, disclose the seasonal nature of its activities, thereby avoiding confusion about unusually high or low results in an interim period. It may also be necessary to supple-

ment interim reports with financial results for the 12-month periods ended at the interim date for the current and preceding years.

In addition, GAAP requires that the following standard disclosures found in annual reports also be addressed in interim reports. See the relevant GAAP chapters of this book for the specifics of these disclosures:

- Asset and liability fair value information
- Business combinations (involves pro forma disclosure of the financial statements for the current and preceding year to reflect the combined results of the businesses)
- Changes in accounting estimate
- Changes in accounting principle
- Contingent items (the significance of which is judged in relation to the annual financial statements)
- Defined benefit pension plan disclosures
- Derivative instrument information
- Disposals of a material component of the business, or material items considered unusual or infrequent
- Financial instrument fair value information
- Investments in debt and equity securities
- Other-than-temporary impairments
- Segment information
- Significant changes in financial position
- Significant changes in the provision for income taxes

> **Tip:** The Securities and Exchange Commission allows line items in the balance sheet to be aggregated if a line item is less than 10% of total assets and the amount has not changed by more than 25% since the end of the preceding fiscal year. The same concept applies to the income statement, except that the thresholds are 15% of average net income for the last three fiscal years (not including loss years) and the change limit is 20% from the corresponding interim period of the preceding fiscal year. For the statement of cash flows, the threshold is 10% of the average of net cash flows from operating activities for the last three years.

The SEC requires that the disclosures in interim reports not be misleading. This means that a material change from any disclosure in the most recent annual report should be noted in the next interim report. However, even if there is no significant change in a material contingency, the matter must continue to be disclosed until resolved.

Finally, the SEC requires that quarterly filings with it must include the following financial statements:

- A balance sheet as of the end of the most recent fiscal quarter
- A balance sheet as of the end of the preceding fiscal year

- An income statement for the most recent fiscal quarter and for the corresponding prior-year period
- An income statement for the fiscal year-to-date and for the corresponding prior-year period
- A statement of cash flows for the fiscal year-to-date
- A statement of cash flows for the corresponding prior-year periods

Summary

When creating interim financial reports, judiciously apply the integral and discrete views to the statements – that is, the integral method is more accurate, but the discrete view is more efficient; and a key factor in closing the books for an interim period is that there is less time than usual in which to complete all closing activities. In short, restrict the integral view to material transactions, and apply the discrete view to all other transactions.

Chapter 12
Risks and Uncertainties

275 = GAAP codification area for risks and uncertainties

Introduction

The information contained within the financial statements of a business are largely quantitative, and describe its historical results. However, the readers of financial statements may want to use them to judge the financial health and future prospects of a business, which requires additional information about the risks and uncertainties to which the company is subjected. In this chapter, we address the types of risks and uncertainties that should be reported in a company's financial statements.

The guidance in this chapter only applies to the financial statements for the most recent fiscal period presented, not for any prior periods that may also be provided for comparative purposes.

Related Chapter

See the Contingencies chapter for an additional discussion of risks and uncertainties.

Overview of Risks and Uncertainties

The focus of GAAP on risks and uncertainties involves sorting through the multitude of potential problems that a company faces, to focus and report upon the subset of issues that financial statement readers should be aware of in the near term. The areas of risk and uncertainty that may require reporting fall into any of the following three areas:

- *Concentrations*. This is the concentration of a company's business in certain portions of its operations that may cause vulnerabilities. Examples of these risks are concentrations of business transactions with suppliers or customers, revenue concentrations with certain products, concentrations in the available sources of supply, the availability of licenses, and concentrations by geographic region.
- *Estimates*. This is the estimates used to prepare a company's financial statements. Examples of such estimates are inventory obsolescence, asset impairment, estimates of lawsuit settlements, contingent liabilities, and the allowance for doubtful accounts.
- *Operations*. This is the nature of the operations conducted by a business, including its activities in certain geographic regions.

GAAP specifies that the disclosures associated with risks and uncertainties are *not* associated with risks and uncertainties in the following areas:

- Internal control deficiencies
- Personnel
- Possible catastrophes
- Proposed changes in accounting principles
- Proposed changes in regulations imposed by a government

Risks and Uncertainties Disclosures

GAAP requires that a business disclose its risks and uncertainties as of the date of its financial statements for the following areas:

- *Nature of operations.* Describe a company's major products or services, its primary markets, and the locations of those markets. If there are operations in more than one line of business, indicate the relative importance of each line of business and the basis for the comparison (such as by profits, assets, or revenues).

EXAMPLE

Armadillo Industries makes the following disclosure regarding the nature of its operations:

The company is a multinational manufacturing business. Armadillo's principal lines of business are the manufacture of body armor, metal plating for the protection of vehicles, and high-pressure containers, all of which are roughly the same in size, based on both assets and sales. The principal markets for the body armor products are police and military organizations in North America and Europe. Metal plating for vehicle protection is sold primarily in South America, while sales of high-pressure containers are sold primarily to government organizations worldwide.

- *Use of estimates to prepare financial statements.* State that the creation of financial statements requires the use of estimates by the preparers.

EXAMPLE

Armadillo Industries makes the following disclosure regarding its use of estimates to prepare financial statements:

The preparation of financial statements in accordance with Generally Accepted Accounting Principles requires management to make estimates and assumptions that affect the reported amounts of assets and liabilities and disclosure of contingent assets and liabilities at the date of the financial statements and the reported amounts of revenues and expenses during the reporting period. Actual results could differ from those estimates.

- *Significant estimates.* If it is reasonably possible that an estimate will change in the near term and the effect on the financial statements will be material, discuss the extent to which the estimates may change in the near term, and how the effect of those changes may be material. In particular, describe the use of estimates in determining the carrying amounts of assets or liabilities, or in the disclosure of contingencies. Also, state that it is at least reasonably possible that a change in estimate will occur in the near term.

EXAMPLE

Armadillo Industries makes the following disclosure regarding significant estimates:

Armadillo currently buys molybdenum, a key component in its high-pressure containers, from one supplier. Although there are a limited number of molybdenum suppliers, management believes that other suppliers could provide sufficient quantities on comparable terms. However, changing suppliers could delay manufacturing processes, resulting in a possible loss of sales that would have an adverse impact on operating results.

- *Vulnerabilities caused by concentrations.* Disclose concentrations if a concentration exists that makes the business vulnerable to the risk of a severe impact in the near term, and it is reasonably possible that the severe impact will occur. It is always considered reasonably possible that a customer will be lost in the near term, and that there will be disruptions of company operations outside of its home country. The disclosure should encompass the general nature of the risk. In addition, the following more specific disclosures are required:
  - *Labor unions.* If labor unions are present, disclose the percentage of employees covered by a collective bargaining agreement, and the percentage covered by such an agreement that will expire within one year.
  - *Geographic concentrations.* Disclose the carrying amounts of net assets by geographic region.

EXAMPLE

Armadillo Industries makes the following disclosure regarding a vulnerability related to a geographic region:

Included in Armadillo's December 31, 20X1 balance sheet is approximately $50 million of assets related to the company's body armor manufacturing facility in Italy.

The decision to disclose an estimate is based on the materiality of what using a different estimate would have had on the financial statements, rather than on the size of the existing estimate (which may be so small that it is considered immaterial).

There may be some overlap in the topics described in these four areas, which may call for combining certain discussions to avoid repetition. Also, if the required information is already presented elsewhere in the financial statements, there is no need to repeat it.

Summary

It is permissible to report additional risks and uncertainties beyond those required by GAAP. However, doing so may mean that there is an obligation to continue reporting those additional risks and obligations in future periods, just to be consistent with the reporting in past periods. Consequently, consider the long-term workload of continually monitoring and reporting upon additional risks and uncertainties before making additional disclosures.

Chapter 13
Segment Reporting

---

280 = GAAP codification area for segment reporting

Introduction

If a company is publicly-held, it needs to report segment information, which is part of the disclosures attached to the financial statements. This information is supposedly needed to give the readers of the financial statements more insights into the operations and prospects of a business, as well as to allow them to make more informed judgments about a public entity as a whole. In this chapter, we describe how to determine which business segments to report separately, and how to report that information. The information provided in this chapter does not apply to the following:

- Nonpublic entities
- Not-for-profit entities
- Subsidiaries, unless publicly-held and their financial statements are issued separately
- Joint ventures, unless publicly-held and their financial statements are issued separately

Overview of Segment Reporting

An operating segment is a component of a public entity, and which possesses the following characteristics:

- *Business activities*. It has business activities that can generate revenues and cause expenses to be incurred. This can include revenues and expenses generated by transactions with other operating segments of the same public entity. It can also include activities that do not yet include revenues, such as a start-up business.
- *Results reviewed*. The chief operating decision maker of the public entity regularly reviews its operating results, with the intent of assessing its performance and making decisions about allocating resources to it.
- *Financial results*. Financial results specific to it are available.

Generally, an operating segment has a manager who is accountable to the chief operating decision maker, and who maintains regular contact with that person, though it is also possible that the chief operating decision maker directly manages one or more operating segments.

If a company has a matrix form of organization, where some managers are responsible for geographic regions and others are responsible for products and services, the results of the products and services are considered to be operating segments.

Some parts of a business are not considered to be reportable business segments under the following circumstances:

- *Corporate overhead.* The corporate group does not usually earn outside revenues, and so is not considered a segment.
- *Post-retirement benefit plans.* A benefit plan can earn income from investments, but it has no operating activities, and so is not considered a segment.
- *One-time events.* If an otherwise-insignificant segment has a one-time event that boosts it into the ranks of reportable segments, do not report it, since there is no long-term expectation for it to remain a reportable segment.

The primary issue with segment reporting is determining which business segments to report. The rules for this selection process are quite specific. Report segment information if a business segment passes any one of the following three tests:

1. *Revenue.* The revenue of the segment is at least 10% of the consolidated revenue of the entire business; or
2. *Profit or loss.* The absolute amount of the profit or loss of the segment is at least 10% of the greater of the combined profits of all the operating segments reporting a profit, or of the combined losses of all operating segments reporting a loss (see the following example for a demonstration of this concept); or
3. *Assets.* The assets of the segment are at least 10% of the combined assets of all the operating segments of the business.

If the preceding tests are run and the accountant arrives at a group of reportable segments whose combined revenues are not at least 75% of the consolidated revenue of the entire business, then add more segments until the 75% threshold is surpassed.

If there is a business segment that used to qualify as a reportable segment and does not currently qualify, but for which there is an expectation of qualification in the future, continue to treat it as a reportable segment.

If there are operating segments that have similar economic characteristics, their results can be aggregated into a single operating segment, but only if they are similar in all of the following areas:

- The nature of their products and services
- The nature of their systems of production
- The nature of their regulatory environments (if applicable)
- Their types of customers
- Their distribution systems

The number of restrictions on this type of reporting makes it unlikely that one would be able to aggregate reportable segments.

After all of the segment testing has been completed, it is possible that there will be a few residual segments that do not qualify for separate reporting. If so, combine the information for these segments into an "other" category and include it in the segment report for the entity. Be sure to describe the sources of revenue included in this "other" category.

Finally, if an operating segment does not meet any of the preceding criteria, it can still be treated as a reportable segment if management decides that information about the segment may be of use to readers of the company's financial statements.

Tip: The variety of methods available for segment testing makes it possible that there will be quite a large number of reportable segments. If so, it can be burdensome to create a report for so many segments, and it may be confusing for the readers of the company's financial statements. Consequently, consider limiting the number of reportable segments to ten; aggregate the information for additional segments for reporting purposes.

EXAMPLE

Lowry Locomotion has six business segments whose results it reports internally. Lowry's controller needs to test the various segments to see which ones qualify as being reportable. He collects the following information:

Segment	(000s) Revenue	(000s) Profit	(000s) Loss	(000s) Assets
Diesel locomotives	$120,000	$10,000	$--	$320,000
Electric locomotives	85,000	8,000	--	180,000
Maglev cars	29,000	--	-21,000	90,000
Passenger cars	200,000	32,000		500,000
Toy trains	15,000	--	-4,000	4,000
Trolley cars	62,000	--	-11,000	55,000
	$511,000	$50,000	-$36,000	$1,149,000

In the table, the total profit exceeds the total loss, so the controller uses the total profit for the 10% profit test. The controller then lists the same table again, but now with the losses column removed and with test thresholds at the top of the table that are used to determine which segments are reported. An "X" mark below a test threshold indicates that a segment is reportable. In addition, the controller adds a new column on the right side of the table, which is used to calculate the total revenue for the reportable segments.

Segment	(000s) Revenue	(000s) Profit	(000s) Assets	75% Revenue Test
Reportable threshold (10%)	**$51,100**	**$5,000**	**$114,900**	
Diesel locomotives	X	X	X	$120,000
Electric locomotives	X	X	X	85,000
Maglev cars				
Passenger cars	X	X	X	200,000
Toy trains				
Trolley cars	X			62,000
			Total	$467,000

This analysis shows that the diesel locomotive, electric locomotive, passenger car, and trolley car segments are reportable, and that the combined revenue of these reportable segments easily exceeds the 75% reporting threshold. Consequently, the company does not need to separately report information for any additional segments.

Segment Disclosure

This section contains the disclosures for various aspects of segment reporting that are required under GAAP. At the end of each set of requirements is a sample disclosure containing the more common elements of the requirements.

Segment Disclosure

The key requirement of segment reporting is that the revenue, profit or loss, and assets of each segment be separately reported for any period for which an income statement is presented. In addition, reconcile this segment information back to the company's consolidated results, which requires the inclusion of any adjusting items. Also disclose the methods by which the determination was made for which segments to report. The essential information to include in a segment report includes:

- The types of products and services sold by each segment
- The basis of organization (such as by geographic region or product line)
- Revenues from external customers
- Revenues from inter-company transactions
- Interest income
- Interest expense
- Depreciation, depletion, and amortization expense
- Material expense items
- Income tax expense or income
- Other material non-cash items
- Profit or loss

If an operating segment only has minimal financial operations, it is not necessary to report any information about interest income or interest expense.

The following two items must also be reported if they are included in the determination of segment assets, or are routinely provided to the chief operating decision maker:

- Equity method interests in other entities.
- The total expenditure for additions to fixed assets. Expenditures for most other long-term assets are excluded from this requirement.

The preceding disclosures should be presented along with the following reconciliations, which should be separately identified and described:

Category	Reconciliation
Revenues	Total company revenues to reportable segment revenues
Profit or loss	Total consolidated income before income taxes, and discontinued operations to reportable segment profit or loss
Assets	Consolidated assets to reportable segment assets
Other items	Consolidated amounts to reportable segment amounts for every other significant item of disclosed segment information

If an operating segment qualifies for the first time as being reportable, also report the usual segment information for it in any prior period segment data that may be presented for comparison purposes, even if the segment was not reportable in the prior period. An exemption is allowed for this prior period reporting if the required information is not available, or if it would be excessively expensive to collect the information.

The operating segment information reported should be the same information reported to the chief operating decision maker for purposes of assessing segment performance and allocating resources. This may result in a difference between the information reported at the segment level and in the public entity's consolidated financial results. If so, disclose the differences between the two figures. This may include a discussion of any policies for the allocation of costs that have been centrally incurred, or the allocation of jointly-used assets.

The following additional items should also be included in the disclosure of operating segment information:

- The basis of accounting for any inter-segment transactions.
- Any changes in the methods used to measure segment profit or loss from the prior period, and the effect of those changes on the reported amount of segment profit or loss.
- A discussion of any asymmetrical allocations, such as the allocation of depreciation expense to a segment without a corresponding allocation of assets.

If a business is reporting condensed financial statements for interim periods, it must disclose the following information for each reportable segment:

- Revenues from external customers for the current quarter and year-to-date, with comparable information for the preceding year
- Revenues from inter-company transactions for the current quarter and year-to-date, with comparable information for the preceding year
- Profit or loss for the current quarter and year-to-date, with comparable information for the preceding year
- Total assets for which there has been a material change from the last annual disclosure
- A description of any differences in the basis of segmentation from the last annual disclosure, or in the method of measuring segment profit or loss
- A reconciliation of the aggregate segment profit or loss to the consolidated income before income taxes, and discontinued operations for the public company

If a public entity alters its internal structure to such an extent that the composition of its operating segments is changed, restate its reported results for earlier periods, as well as interim periods, to match the results and financial position of the new internal structure. This requirement is waived if it is impracticable to obtain the required information. The result may be the restatement of some information, but not all of the segment information. If an entity does alter its internal structure, it should disclose whether there has also been a restatement of its segment information for earlier periods. If the entity does not change its prior period information, it must report segment information in the current period under both the old basis and new basis of segmentation, unless it is impracticable to do so.

EXAMPLE

The controller of Lowry Locomotion produces the following segment report for the segments identified in the preceding example:

(000s)	Diesel	Electric	Passenger	Trolley	Other	Consolidated
Revenues	$120,000	$85,000	$200,000	$62,000	$44,000	$511,000
Interest income	11,000	8,000	28,000	8,000	2,000	57,000
Interest expense	--	--	--	11,000	39,000	50,000
Depreciation	32,000	18,000	50,000	6,000	10,000	116,000
Income taxes	4,000	3,000	10,000	-3,000	-7,000	7,000
Profit	10,000	8,000	32,000	-11,000	-25,000	14,000
Assets	320,000	180,000	500,000	55,000	94,000	1,149,000

Products, Services, and Customer Disclosure

A publicly-held entity must report the sales garnered from external customers for each product and service or group thereof, unless it is impracticable to compile this information.

The entity must also describe the extent of its reliance on its major customers. In particular, if revenues from a single customer exceed 10% of the entity's revenues, this fact must be disclosed, along with the total revenues garnered from each of these customers and the names of the segments in which these revenues were earned.

It is not necessary to disclose the name of a major customer.

If there is a group of customers under common control (such as different departments of the federal government), the revenues from this group should be reported in aggregate as though the revenues were generated from a single customer.

EXAMPLE

Armadillo Industries reports the following information about its major customers:

Revenues from one customer of Armadillo's home security segment represented approximately 12% of the company's consolidated revenues in 20X2, and 11% of consolidated revenues in 20X1.

Geographic Area Disclosure

A publicly-held entity must disclose the following geographic information, unless it is impracticable to compile:

- *Revenues*. All revenues generated from external customers, and attributable to the entity's home country, and all revenues attributable to foreign countries. Foreign-country revenues by individual country shall be stated if these country-level sales are material. There must also be disclosure of the basis under which revenues are attributed to individual countries.
- *Assets*. All long-lived assets (for which the definition essentially restricts reporting to fixed assets) that are attributable to the entity's home country, and all such assets attributable to foreign countries. Foreign-country assets by individual country shall be stated if these assets are material.

It is also acceptable to include in this reporting subtotals of geographic information by groups of countries.

Geographic area reporting is waived if providing it is impracticable. If so, the entity must disclose the fact.

EXAMPLE

Armadillo Industries reports the following geographic information about its operations:

	Revenues	Long-Lived Assets
United States	$27,000,000	$13,000,000
Mexico	23,000,000	11,000,000
Chile	14,000,000	7,000,000
Other foreign countries	8,000,000	2,000,000
Total	$72,000,000	$33,000,000

Summary

The determination of whether a business has segments is, to a large extent, based upon whether information is tracked internally at the segment level. Thus, if a company's accounting systems are sufficiently primitive, or if management is sufficiently disinterested to not review information about business segments, it is entirely possible that even a publicly-held company will have no reportable business segments.

If there *are* a number of reportable segments, consider using the report writing software in the accounting system to create a standard report that automatically generates the entire segment report for the disclosures. By using this approach, no time will be wasted manually compiling the information, and the accounting staff will avoid running the risk of making a mistake while doing so. However, if the reportable segments change over time, modify the report structure to match the new group of segments.

Chapter 14
Receivables

Introduction

Receivables are a key part of the accounting for any business that grants credit to its customers. Receivables can take many forms, including trade receivables, loans, notes, and other types of financial instruments. Receivables may also be transferred between parties, such as when a business has a put option that requires a third party to purchase its receivables. Debts can also be sold individually or in groups by one party to another. In this chapter, we discuss the accounting for these and other arrangements, as well as the extensive disclosure requirements associated with certain types of receivables.

> **Note**: The information contained within this chapter relates to the existing GAAP standard for receivables. A new standard in GAAP codification area 326 has been released and will have a significant impact on this chapter. However, the new standard is not effective until 2019, so it is not yet included in this chapter.

Related Chapter

See the Interest chapter for discussions of issues related to imputing interest on receivables.

Notes Receivable

One of the key aspects of notes receivable is how to recognize them in the accounting records. The following points describe the major issues to consider when initially accounting for a receivable of this type:

- *Notes acquired for cash.* When a note is received in exchange for cash, record the note at the amount of the cash paid.
- *Notes acquired for noncash consideration.* When a note is received in exchange for any type of consideration other than cash, the present value of the note is the fair value of the consideration paid. Alternatively, if similar notes are exchanged in an open market, market prices can provide evidence of the present value of the note. If neither option is available and the interest rate on the note does not match the market rate, use an imputed interest rate to arrive at the discounted present value of the note (subsequent changes in prevailing interest rates can be ignored).

Subsequent to the initial recordation of a note receivable, the following issues may arise that require accounting treatment:

- *Loan impairment.* A loan is considered to be impaired when it is probable that not all of the related principal and interest payments will be collected.
- *Impairment documentation.* Any allowance for loan impairments should be fully documented with the appropriate analysis, and updated consistently from period to period.
- *Impairment allowance.* An impairment allowance can be based on the examination of individual receivables, or groups of similar types of receivables. The creditor can use any impairment measurement method that is practical for the creditor's circumstances. When loans are aggregated for analysis purposes, use historical statistics to derive the estimated amount of impairment. The amount of impairment to recognize should be based on the present value of expected future cash flows, though a loan's market price or the fair value of the related collateral can also be used.
- *Impairment accounting.* The offset to the impairment allowance should be the bad debt expense account. Once actual credit losses are identified, subtract them from the impairment allowance, along with the related loan balance. If loans are subsequently recovered, the previous charge-off transaction should be reversed.

Tip: It is possible that there is no need to establish a reserve for an impaired loan if the value of the related collateral is at least as much as the recorded value of the loan.

As a result of impairment accounting, it is possible that the recorded investment in a loan judged to be impaired may be less than its present value, because the creditor has elected to charge off part of the loan.

In the following bullet points, we note several more specialized recognition practices for several types of receivables:

- *Delinquency fees.* Recognize delinquency fees when the fees are chargeable, as long as the collectability of the fees is reasonably assured.
- *Factoring arrangements.* When receivables are transferred to a factor, the factor should account for them as a purchase of receivables.
- *Interest income on receivables.* It may be necessary to impute interest on receivables, even if there is no stated interest rate associated with those receivables (see the Interest chapter).
- *Loan syndications.* When there are several lenders involved in a loan syndication, each lender separately accounts for the sums owed to it by the borrower. In cases where the lead lender is collecting repayments from the borrower, the lead lender's role is that of a loan servicer, so it would be inappropriate for the lead lender to recognize the aggregate loan as an asset.

- *Loans not previously held for sale.* When the decision is made to sell loans that had not previously been classified as held for sale, report these loans at the lower of cost or fair value. If the loan cost exceeds value at the time of the transfer to the held for sale classification, record the difference in a valuation allowance.
- *Loans receivable held to maturity.* If management intends to hold loans receivable until their maturity, report these loans at their outstanding principal, adjusted for charge-offs, allowances for loan losses, deferred costs, and unamortized premiums or discounts.
- *Nonmortgage loans held for sale.* Report nonmortgage loans that are being held for sale at the lower of their cost or fair value.
- *Prepayment fees.* Do not recognize prepayment penalties until the related loans or receivables are prepaid.
- *Purchase of credit card portfolio.* If a portfolio is purchased for an amount greater than the sum of receivables due, allocate the premium between the loans acquired and the cardholder relationships acquired (which is an intangible asset). Amortize this premium over the life of the loans.
- *Rebates on accrued interest income.* There is no impact on the accrual of interest income on installment loans or trade receivables when there is a prospect of issuing rebates. Any impact is recognized in income when the loans or receivables are paid or renewed.
- *Standby commitment to purchase loan.* When there is a standby commitment to purchase a loan where the settlement date is not within a reasonable period, or the business cannot accept delivery without selling assets, account for the commitment as a written put option, where the fee received is a liability (value the liability at the greater of the initial fee or the fair value of the put option). Otherwise, it is considered part of the normal production of loans, where the fee received is recorded as an offset to loans purchased.

Acquisition, Development, and Construction Arrangements

The guidance in this section only applies to situations where a lender participates in the expected residual profits or cash flows of a property transaction for which the lender is providing funding, either through profit sharing or above-market interest rates or fees. The following characteristics suggest the presence of such an arrangement where the lender takes on the role of an investor:

- *Delinquency.* The debt is structured to avoid foreclosure by not requiring payments until project completion.
- *Fees.* The lender pays for the commitment or origination fees by including them in the loan.
- *Funding.* The lender provides substantially all of the required funding.
- *Interest.* The lender rolls substantially all of the interest and fees during the loan term back into the loan balance.

- *Recourse*. The lender only has recourse to the acquisition, development, and construction project.
- *Repayment*. The lender will only be repaid if the property is sold, re-financed, or begins to generate enough cash flow to service the loan.

Conversely, there are situations where the lender has not taken on the role of an investor, and is merely financing property. The following characteristics suggest the presence of a simple lending arrangement:

- *Borrower investment*. The borrower has a substantial equity investment in the project that is not funded by the lender. The value of the borrower's efforts (sweat equity) in the property development is not to be considered when evaluating the borrower's investment.
- *Collateral*. The lender has recourse to significant other assets of the borrower besides the project, and which are not also pledged as collateral elsewhere, or the lender has an irrevocable letter of credit from a third party for a substantial amount of the loan.
- *Net cash flow*. There are sufficient noncancelable sale or lease contracts from third parties to provide the cash flow needed to service the debt.
- *Profit participation*. The profit participation of the lender is less than half of the expected residual profit.
- *Take-out commitment*. The lender has obtained a take-out commitment for the full amount of its lending arrangement from a third party.

The existence of a personal guarantee is not usually considered sufficient for classifying a lending arrangement as not being an investment. However, this may be the case if the guarantee covers a large part of the loan, the payment ability of the guarantor can be reliably measured (as represented by assets placed in escrow, an irrevocable letter of credit, or financial results), enforcing the guarantee is possible, and there is a demonstrated intent to enforce the guarantee.

When judging the financial statements of a guarantor, place particular emphasis on the presence of sufficient liquidity to fulfill the guarantee, and whether the guarantor has other contingent liabilities.

Also, the initial determination of investment or loan status for the lender may change over time, if the underlying terms of an arrangement are altered. Consequently, reassess the accounting treatment whenever loan terms are altered. The following situations that alter a lending scenario can impact how a lending arrangement is classified:

- *Risk reduction*. If the lender's risk diminishes significantly, an initial classification as an investment or joint venture might be reclassified as a loan.
- *Risk increase*. If the lender's risk increases (such as by releasing collateral) or the lender assumes a greater percentage of expected profits, an initial classification as a loan might be reclassified as an investment.

The initial accounting by a lender in an acquisition, development, and construction project is to be accounted for in one of two ways:

- *As an investment*. If the lender expects to receive more than 50% of the expected residual profit from a project, any income or loss from the arrangement is to be accounted for by the lender as a real estate investment.
- *As a loan*. If the lender expects to receive 50% or less of the expected residual profit from a project and there is a qualifying personal guarantee (as just described), the arrangement is to be accounted for as a loan. If the guarantee is not present, account for the arrangement as a real estate joint venture.

If a lender were to subsequently sell its share of any expected residual profits, there are two ways to account for the sale:

- *As an investment*. If the arrangement has been accounted for as an investment, the lender can account for the sale as a gain.
- *As a loan*. If the arrangement has been accounted for as a loan, the lender should recognize the proceeds from the sale as additional interest over the remaining term of the loan.

Nonrefundable Fees and Other Costs

This topic relates to the nonrefundable fees, origination costs, and acquisition costs relating to lending activities. The fees addressed by this topic have many names, including points, placement fees, commitment fees, application fees, and annual credit card fees; to save space, we will refer to them all as loan origination fees.

The accounting for nonrefundable fees and other costs and revenues is as follows:

- *Loan origination fees*. Defer the recognition of all loan origination fees, and recognize them over the life of the loan as interest income or expense. These costs can include labor, travel costs, phone calls, and mileage reimbursement. Examples of activities considered to relate to loan origination are loan counseling, application processing and credit analysis, asset appraisals, loan approval processing, and loan closing.
- *Loan origination labor*. The direct costs of loan origination can be deferred, which includes the labor associated with the successful production of loans. The cost of bonuses may be deferred if they directly relate to the successful production of loans.
- *Other lending-related costs*. Charge all other lending-related costs to expense as incurred. This includes advertising and solicitations, loan servicing, unsuccessful loan origination activities, idle time, service bureau fees, and administrative costs.

- *Commitment fees*. If the lender receives a commitment fee to originate or purchase a loan, defer recognition of the fee, and offset against it against the related loan origination costs. The following scenarios may apply:
    - o *Net cost, no exercise*. If the result is a net cost and the likelihood of the commitment being exercised is remote, charge the net amount to expense at once.
    - o *Net cost, exercised*. If the result is a net cost and the commitment is likely to be exercised, recognize it over the life of the loan as a reduction in loan yield.
    - o *Net revenue, no exercise*. If the result is net revenue and the likelihood of the commitment being exercised is remote, amortize recognition of the net amount on a straight-line basis over the period covered by the commitment as service fee income. If some amount remains unamortized when the commitment expires, recognize it in income as of the expiration date.
    - o *Net revenue, exercised*. If the result is net revenue and the commitment is likely to be exercised, recognize it over the life of the loan as an increase in loan yield.
- *Credit card fees*. Fees charged to the holders of credit cards should be deferred, and recognized on a straight-line basis over the period that the card fee entitles the card user to use the card. If there are any credit card origination costs, net them against credit card fees, which are then amortized as just noted. If the business pays a fee to acquire credit card accounts, net this payment against any credit card fees.
- *Lending fees unrelated to loans*. A lender may charge a fee for lending transactions apart from loan originations. Examples of such transactions are for the extension of the maturity date on a loan, or switching a variable-rate loan to a fixed-rate loan. Account for these fees as a yield adjustment over the remaining life of the loan with which the fee is associated.
- *Loan syndication fees*. The entity that constructs a loan syndication should recognize the loan syndication fees earned by it when the syndication is complete. However, if the syndicator retains a portion of the loan, it should defer a portion of the fees and recognize that portion over the term of the retained loan. The amount deferred should result in a loan yield that is not less than the average yield on the loans issued by the other participants in the syndication.
- *Loan purchase*. Defer the cost of fees paid to the seller of a loan or group of loans, and account for it as a yield adjustment over the life of the loan; if prepayments occur or some of the purchased loans are then sold, recognize a proportional amount of the deferred fees in income. Charge all other costs to expense that are incurred in connection with purchased loans or commitments to purchase such loans; these costs are not origination fees, since the loan has already been originated by the seller of the loan.

- *Loan refinancing or restructuring.* Account for a loan refinancing or restructuring as a new loan if the terms are at least as favorable for the lender as the terms associated with comparable loans where there is no refinancing or restructuring (such as when the effective yield on the new loan is similar to the same yield on comparable loans). If there are any unamortized fees or costs associated with the original loan, recognize them within interest income at this time. If the restructuring or refinancing does not meet these conditions or the modifications are minor, carry forward any unamortized fees or costs to the new loan.
- *Revolving line of credit.* When there is a revolving line of credit, recognize the associated net fees or costs in income on a straight-line basis over the period of the line of credit. If the borrower cannot reborrow from the line of credit upon paying off the line, recognize all remaining net fees and costs as of the payment date. If the line of credit includes a payment schedule, then account for the remaining net fees and costs as a yield adjustment over the remaining life of the loan.

EXAMPLE

Currency Bank enters into a one-year line of credit arrangement with a borrower, where the borrower can elect to convert the line of credit into a three-year term loan. Currency amortizes the net fees and costs associated with the line of credit over the combined period of the line of credit and term loan. The borrower elects to let the line of credit expire and pays off the remaining balance, without converting to a term loan, so Currency then recognizes the remaining unamortized net fees and costs as of the expiration date.

- *Third party fees.* Fees paid to a third party in regard to portfolio management, investment consultation, or loan origination activities are charged to expense as incurred.

Any loan origination costs related to a loan in process can be deferred until such time as the loan is closed or declared unsuccessful, at which point it is accounted for based on the loan outcome.

If there is a period during which the interest income on a loan is not being recognized due to concerns about the ability of the borrower to pay, do not amortize any deferred net fees or costs during that period.

> **Tip:** It may be more efficient to defer loan origination fees based on a standard costing system, rather than compiling actual loan origination costs during every accounting period.

Whenever GAAP requires that fees or costs be amortized using the effective interest method, the intent is to use an interest rate that creates an interest differential from the stated interest rate on a loan that recognizes the fees or costs over the life of the loan. The following example illustrates the concept.

EXAMPLE

Currency Bank purchases a loan that had been issued by another bank, at a stated principal amount of $100,000, which the debtor will repay in three years, with three annual interest payments of $5,000 and a balloon payment of $100,000 upon the maturity date of the loan.

Currency acquired the loan for $90,000, which is a discount of $10,000 from the principal amount of the loan. Based on this information, Currency calculates an effective interest rate of 8.95%, which is shown in the following amortization table:

Year	(A) Beginning Amortized Cost	(B) Interest and Principal Payments	(C) Interest Income (A × 8.95%)	(D) Debt Discount Amortization (C − B)	Ending Amortized Cost (A + D)
1	90,000	5,000	8,055	3,055	93,055
2	93,055	5,000	8,328	3,328	96,383
3	96,383	105,000	8,617	3,617	100,000

In a situation where the lender can demand payment of a loan at any time, recognize any remaining net fees or costs as an adjustment of yield on a straight-line basis under the remaining period as agreed to by the lender and borrower, or (if there is no agreement), the lender's estimate of this period. Review the remaining duration at regular intervals, and alter the adjustment of yield if the estimated duration varies.

If the lender has a number of similar loans, considers prepayments of those loans to be probable, and can estimate the timing and amounts of prepayments, it can incorporate prepayment information into its effective yield calculations. If so, and there turns out to be a difference between actual and anticipated prepayments, recalculate the effective yield to take into account the actual amount of prepayments, and adjust the net investment in loans accordingly. Prepayment tracking can be used for a group of loans, or for individual loans; whichever approach is used must be maintained through the life of the loans.

Loans and Debt Securities Acquired with Deteriorated Credit Quality

There are cases where a company will acquire loans that have already displayed evidence of deterioration in their credit quality prior to being acquired. The acquirer presumably pays less for this batch of loans, in expectation of being unable to collect all of the payments associated with the loans. The accounting for loans and debt securities acquired with deteriorated credit quality is as follows:

- *Interest income.* The loan acquirer should recognize the excess of cash flows expected from acquired loans at the acquisition date from the initial investment as interest income over the life of the loans, which is called *accretable yield*; it will result in a higher effective interest rate. Do not recognize interest income if the resulting net loan investment increases above the loan payoff amount. Subsequently, if the expected cash flows increase further, recalculate the accretable yield for the remaining life of the loan, which is a change in estimate. Alternatively, if the loan acquirer is not accounting for the loan as a debt security and expected cash flows increase further, first reduce any remaining valuation allowance and then recalculate the accretable yield for any remaining excess cash flows.

- *Income measurement.* Continue to estimate expected cash flows over the life of each loan or group of loans. If the fair value falls below its amortized cost and the decline is other than temporary, treat the loan as an impaired security (see the Investments – Debt and Equity Securities chapter).

- *Valuation allowances.* Any valuation allowance created for purchased loans should be based on only those losses incurred *after* acquisition. This is the difference between the present value of cash flows expected at the acquisition date and expectations at later dates of what will actually be received.

- *Pool of multiple loans.* Only remove a loan from a pool of loans if the loan is written off, paid off, foreclosed, or sold. Do not remove a loan from a pool of loans if the loan is refinanced.

- *Loans acquired for collateral ownership.* If the loan acquirer purchases loans with the intent of using the acquired collateral in its own operations or improving the collateral for resale, do not accrue any income related to the loans.

- *Variable rate loans.* If the interest rate upon which loan payments are calculated changes over time, calculate the contractually required payments on the interest rate as the rate changes over the life of the loan. The result is a change in yield over time. Do not project future changes in the interest rate.

EXAMPLE

Currency Bank acquires a loan with a principal balance of $10,000,000 and accrued delinquent interest of $600,000. Currency acquires the loan at a discount, due to concerns that the credit quality of the debtor has declined since the origination of the loan. Currency Bank pays $7,500,000 for the loan on December 31, 20X1. The contractual interest rate is 7% per year. In addition to the delinquent interest, annual payments of $2,300,000 are due in each of the five remaining years to maturity. Currency Bank's analysis staff concludes that it is probable that the bank will not collect the full amounts due, but rather $1,928,193 per year for five years. Based on this information, Currency Bank initially records the acquired loan at a net carrying amount of $7,500,000, and constructs the following table to document the remaining cash flows and interest income.

Year	(A) Beginning Carrying Amount	(B) Cash Flows Expected to be Collected	(C) Interest Income*	(B – C) Reduction of Carrying Amount	(A – D) Ending Carrying Amount
20X2	$7,500,000	$1,928,193	$675,000	$1,253,193	$6,246,807
20X3	6,246,807	1,928,193	562,213	1,365,980	4,880,827
20X4	4,880,827	1,928,193	439,274	1,488,919	3,391,908
20X5	3,391,908	1,928,123	305,272	1,622,921	1,768,987
20X6	1,768,987	1,928,123	159,209	1,768,984	3
		$9,640,965	$2,140,968	$7,499,997	

Calculation of nonaccretable difference:

Contractually required payments receivable (including delinquent interest)	$12,100,000
Less: Cash flows expected to be collected	-9,640,965
= Nonaccretable difference	$2,459,035

Initial calculation of accretable yield:

Cash flows expected to be collected	$9,640,965
Less: Initial investment	-7,500,000
= Accretable yield	$2,140,965

* Note: the effective interest rate for all of the years in this example is 9%, which is the rate that equates all cash flows expected to be collected with the purchase price of the loan.

Troubled Debt Restructurings by Creditors

When a creditor grants a concession under the terms of a debt agreement or receivable because of the financial difficulties of a debtor, the debt may be classified as a troubled debt restructuring. Examples of troubled debt restructurings are payment in the equity of the debtor, reducing the stated interest rate, and reducing the face amount of the debt. In essence, a concession has been granted when the creditor no longer expects to collect all amounts due, and any additional guarantees or collateral received do not offset the amount of the expected loss. When a restructuring results in an insignificant payment delay, this is not considered a concession.

The accounting for troubled debt restructurings is as follows:

- *Restructuring.* Account for a restructured loan as an asset impairment. When calculating the present value of the cash flows expected from a restructured loan, base the effective interest rate used for discounting present values on the original contractual rate, not the rate stated in the restructuring agreement.

- *Receipt of assets.* If the debtor transfers assets to the creditor as partial satisfaction of a debt, reduce the recorded amount of the receivable by the fair value of the assets received. If the assets received are in full satisfaction of the debt, record a loss in the amount of the remaining balance of the loan.
- *Foreclosure.* When the creditor forecloses on a loan and takes possession of the debtor's assets, it should record the possessed property at the lower of the net amount of the receivable or the fair value of the property.
- *Legal fees.* When the creditor incurs legal fees as part of a troubled debt restructuring, charge them to expense as incurred.

If the foreclosure involves residential real estate, foreclosure is considered to have occurred when the creditor obtains legal title to the property, or the borrower conveys all interest in the property using a deed in lieu of foreclosure.

Classification of Government-Guaranteed Loans

There are several government agencies, such as the Federal Housing Administration, that guarantee the repayment of the unpaid principal balance on certain mortgage loans. When a lender forecloses such a loan, it should derecognize the loan and recognize a separate receivable for the government guarantee. This accounting treatment only applies if the following conditions are present:

- There is a government guarantee associated with the loan that cannot be separated from the loan;
- The lender intends to convey the property to the guaranteeing government entity and make a claim under the terms of the guarantee, and has the ability to make a recovery under the claim; and
- The amount of the claim is fixed as of the foreclosure date.

The amount of the receivable recognized for the government guarantee should be based on the principal and interest expected to be recovered from the guarantor.

Receivables Presentation

There are a number of requirements regarding the proper presentation of receivables information in the financial statements. Given the number of these requirements, we are stating them separately from the disclosures in the following section, which are usually included in the notes that accompany the financial statements. The presentation requirements are:

- *Acquisition, development, and construction arrangements.* Separately report arrangements in the balance sheet that are classified as investments from those that are classified as loans.
- *Allowances.* Always pair asset valuation allowances with the assets to which they relate on the balance sheet.

- *Bad debt expense.* Report any changes in the observable market price or the fair value of collateral for an impaired loan as a change in bad debt expense.
- *Commitment fees.* Classify loan commitment fees as deferred income in the balance sheet. Report amortized commitment fees as service income in the income statement.
- *Foreclosed or repossessed assets.* It is permissible to either separately state foreclosed or repossessed assets on the balance sheet, or include them in other asset classifications and then disclose them in the accompanying notes. If there is an intent to use repossessed assets in the business, do not classify them separately as foreclosed or repossessed assets.
- *Loan fees.* Include the unamortized balance of loan fees and costs in the balance sheet as part of the loan balances with which these items are paired.
- *Loans or trade receivables.* Present loans or trade receivables in the balance sheet in aggregate. If any of these receivables are classified as held for sale, aggregate them into a separate line item. If there are major categories of loans or trade receivables, separate presentation is encouraged.
- *Receivables classified as current assets.* Trade receivables are classified within the current assets section of the balance sheet, as long as they are expected to be realized in cash during the operating cycle of the business or one year.
- *Receivables from officers, employees, or affiliates.* Separately state all notes or accounts receivable from officers, employees, or affiliates. Do not aggregate them with other notes receivable or accounts receivable.
- *Unearned discounts.* Report unearned discounts, finance charges, and interest stated on receivables as a deduction from the paired receivables line item.
- *Yield adjustments.* Include all interest yield adjustments for loan-related fees and costs as part of interest income.

Receivables Disclosures

There are quite a number of disclosures related to receivables, but many relate to very specialized topics that may not relate to a company's line of business. Consequently, be mindful of which of the following disclosure requirements actually apply to one's business, and ignore the rest. The disclosures are:

- *Policies.* State the following policies related to receivables, if applicable:
  - The basis for accounting for loans, lease financings, and trade receivables
  - The policy for charging off uncollectible trade receivables that have a maturity of less than one year, and which arose from the sale of goods or services
  - The policy for charging off financing receivables that cannot be collected
  - The policy for deciding upon past due or delinquency status

- o The policy for discontinuing the accrual of interest on receivables, and the policy for resuming the accrual of interest
- o The policy for recognizing interest income on impaired loans, as well as how cash receipts are recorded
- o The policy for recording payments received against nonaccrual loans and trade receivables
- o The policy for recognizing interest income on loan and trade receivables, related fees and costs, and for amortizing net deferred fees and costs
- o The policy for incorporating prepayments into the interest method for determining loan yield, as well as related assumptions
- o The policy for accounting for credit card fees and costs, both for originated and purchased credit cards

- *Allowance for credit losses related to loans.* Disclose the following information by portfolio segment, relating to the allowance for credit losses related to loans:
  - o The methodology used to estimate the allowance for credit losses, including a discussion of the historical losses and existing economic conditions that influenced management's judgment
  - o The risk characteristics of each portfolio
  - o Any changes in accounting policies from the prior period, the rationale for the change, and the effect of these changes on the current period provision
  - o The activity in the allowance for credit losses, including provisions, write-downs, and recoveries during the period
  - o The amount paid for significant purchases of financing receivables, by reporting period
  - o The amount of significant sales of financing receivables or reclassifications into the held for sale category, by reporting period
  - o A breakdown of the ending balance in the allowance for credit losses, by impairment method
  - o Match the ending investment in financing receivables to the allowance for credit losses, subdivided by impairment methodology used

- *Allowances.* Disclose the amount of all allowances related to credit losses, as well as unearned income and unamortized premiums and discounts. Also disclose the methodology used to estimate the allowance for losses on the various types of receivables; this may include a discussion of the risk elements relevant to certain categories of financial instruments.
- *Asset basis.* Describe the method used to determine the lower of cost or fair value for any nonmortgage loans held for sale.
- *Credit card fees and costs.* Disclose the net amount of credit card fees and costs capitalized, and the amortization period for these items.

- *Credit quality information.* Provide sufficient information for readers to understand how the company monitors the credit quality of its financing receivables, and the risks arising from the credit quality of those receivables. This information should include the credit quality indicator for each class of receivables, as well as the investment in these receivables by credit quality indicator, and the date range when the information was updated for each credit quality indicator.
- *Debt securities.* State the outstanding balance of debt securities at the beginning and end of the reporting period, and a reconciliation of accretable yield during the period.
- *Financing receivables.* Separately disclose the investment in financing receivables for those receivables on nonaccrual status, and for those receivables that are past due by 90 days or more and still accruing.
- *Impaired loans.* Disclose the accounting for and amount of impaired loans for each class of financing receivable, as well as the amount of related allowances. Also note the amount of the recorded investment for which there is no related allowance for credit losses. Further, disclose the average investment in impaired loans during each presented period, the related amount of interest income recognized, and the related amount of interest income recognized under the cash basis of accounting (if practicable to do so).
- *Interest income.* Describe the method for recognizing interest income on loans and trade receivables, as well as related fees and costs, and how net deferred fees are amortized.
- *Internal risk ratings.* If the business uses internal risk ratings regarding credit quality, discuss how the ratings relate to the likelihood of loss.
- *Loan fees and costs.* Report unamortized net loan fees and costs within the relevant loan categories on the balance sheet.
- *Loans acquired.* Disclose the contractually required payments receivable, expected cash flows, and fair value (at the acquisition date) of loans acquired during the period.
- *Loans not accounted for as debt securities.* If there are any loans not accounted for as debt securities, disclose the impairment losses, any reductions in the associated valuation allowance, and the amount of the allowance for uncollectible accounts at the beginning and end of the period.
- *Non-recovery situations.* Clarify the classification and method of accounting for assets that may be settled such that the holder may not recover its investment.
- *Off-balance-sheet exposures.* State the procedures used to determine the company's off-balance-sheet credit exposures (such as for standby letters of credit and guarantees) and the charges related to those exposures, including a description of risks and those factors influencing management's judgment.
- *Prepayments.* Describe how prepayments are factored into the calculation of loan-related contractual and expected cash flows.

- *Receivables analysis.* Disclose an analysis of the age of past due financing receivables as of the end of the reporting period.
- *Residential real estate holdings.* Disclose the amount of any foreclosed residential real estate property held by the creditor, as well as the recorded investment in consumer mortgage loans collateralized by such property that are being foreclosed.
- *Troubled debt restructurings.* Disclose how each class of financing receivable was modified as part of troubled debt restructurings, and the financial effects of those modifications. Also note for each portfolio segment how these modifications were incorporated into the calculation of the allowance for credit losses. Further, disclose the amount of any commitments to lend additional funds to debtors that currently owe receivables to the creditor that have been modified through troubled debt restructurings.

EXAMPLE

Currency Bank provides the following disclosure about its credit quality indicators:

Currency Bank
Credit Quality Indicators
As of December 31, 20X5 and 20X4

Corporate Credit Exposure
Credit Risk Profile by Creditworthiness Category

	Commercial		Commercial Real Estate	
(000s)	20X5	20X4	20X5	20X4
AAA – A	$15,400	$14,200	$9,100	$8,900
BBB – B	3,900	3,600	2,300	2,200
CCC – C	1,000	900	600	500
D	200	200	100	100
Total	$20,500	$18,900	$12,100	$11,700

Consumer Credit Exposure
Credit Risk Profile by Internally Assigned Grade

	Residential (Prime)		Residential (Subprime)	
(000s)	20X5	20X4	20X5	20X4
Grade:				
Pass	$83,000	$74,000	$25,000	$20,000
Watch list	17,000	15,000	13,000	10,000
Substandard	9,000	8,000	7,000	5,000
Total	$109,000	$97,000	$45,000	$35,000

Consumer Credit Exposure
Credit Risk Profile Based on Payment Activity

(000s)	Finance Leases		Consumer Auto	
	20X5	20X4	20X5	20X4
Performing	$35,000	$24,000	$60,000	$52,000
Nonperforming	5,000	3,000	10,000	8,000
Total	$40,000	$27,000	$70,000	$60,000

EXAMPLE

Armenian Consumer Finance (ACF) extends loans to the Armenian immigrant community. ACF provides the following disclosure about its impaired loans:

Armenian Consumer Finance
Impaired Loans
For the Year Ended December 31, 20X5

(000s)	Recorded Investment	Unpaid Principal Balance	Related Allowance	Average Recorded Investment	Interest Income Recognized
With no related allowance recorded:					
Consumer – Credit cards	$110,000	$116,000	$0	$125,000	$19,000
Consumer – Auto	180,000	189,000	0	193,000	15,000
Consumer – Other	40,000	42,000	0	46,000	7,000
With an allowance recorded:					
Commercial – Real estate	190,000	205,000	18,000	180,000	14,000
Residential – Prime	261,000	263,000	2,000	270,000	22,000
Residential – Subprime	156,000	130,000	26,000	145,000	11,000
Total:					
Consumer	$330,000	$347,000	$0	$364,000	$41,000
Commercial	190,000	205,000	18,000	180,000	14,000
Residential	417,000	393,000	28,000	415,000	33,000

EXAMPLE

Currency Bank provides the following disclosure about its troubled debt restructurings:

Currency Bank
Debt Modifications
As of December 31, 20X2

	Number of Contracts	Pre-Modification Outstanding Recorded Investment (000s)	Post-Modification Outstanding Recorded Investment (000s)
Troubled debt restructurings:			
Consumer – Auto	140	$4,000	$3,200
Commercial – Real estate	15	71,000	53,000
Residential – Prime	180	38,000	30,000
Residential – Subprime	48	6,000	3,000

	Number of Contracts	Recorded Investment (000s)
Troubled debt restructurings that subsequently defaulted		
Consumer – Auto	28	$1,000
Commercial – Real estate	4	12,000
Residential – Prime	54	10,000
Residential – Subprime	32	2,000

EXAMPLE

Currency Bank provides the following disclosures concerning loans acquired with deteriorated credit quality:

Currency Bank has acquired loans that it accounts for as debt securities, for which there was evidence of deterioration of credit quality prior to their acquisition. As of the acquisition date, it was probable that not all contractually required payments for these loans would be collected.

The carrying amounts of these loans are included in the balance sheet at December 31. The outstanding balance and carrying amounts of these loans are as follows, where the outstanding balance represents amounts owed to the company:

(000s)	20X5	20X4
Held-to-maturity debt securities:		
Outstanding balance	$29,400	$30,900
Carrying amount, net	23,100	27,200
Available-for-sale debt securities:		
Outstanding balance	$37,700	$39,800
Carrying amount, net	31,500	33,300

(000s)	Held-to-Maturity Securities	Available-for-Sale Debt Securities
Accretable yield:		
Balance at December 31, 20X3	$5,050	$6,130
Additions	520	730
Accretion	-,910	-1,380
Balance at December 31, 20X4	4,660	5,480
Additions	790	1,340
Accretion	-870	-1,250
Balance at December 31, 20X5	$4,580	$5,570

Summary

The bulk of the material in this chapter was concerned with the accounting for loan-related activities, and so may not apply to many businesses that do not extend long-term credit to other parties. However, some of the information in this chapter is more generally applicable when accounting for debt securities purchased as an investment, and when dealing with trade receivables that must be restructured due to financial problems afflicting a business partner.

Chapter 15
Investments – Debt and Equity Securities

320 = GAAP codification area for investments – debt securities
321= GAAP codification area for investments – equity securities
325 = GAAP codification area of investments – other

Introduction

The guidance in this chapter is almost entirely concerned with the proper classification of various kinds of investments, and how to initially and subsequently account for them. This includes the treatment of valuation impairment.

The guidance in this chapter applies to all entities, except those in such specialized industries as brokers, dealers, defined benefit pension plans, investment companies, and not-for-profits.

Related Chapters

See the following chapters for discussions of issues related to investments:

- *Debt.* Covers the classification of debt, as well as the accounting for debt conversion features, troubled debt restructurings, and other topics.
- *Financial Instruments.* Covers the disclosure of fair value, credit risk accounting, and registration payment arrangements.

Overview of Investments – Debt and Equity Securities

When a business acquires debt or equity securities for investment purposes, it must be cognizant of how these investments are to be classified, since the classification drives the accounting treatment. In this section, we address not only investment classifications and the related accounting, but also how to deal with investment impairment, and several related issues.

Accounting for Investments

When a business acquires an investment, it must classify the investment into one of the following categories:

- *Trading securities.* This is a security acquired with the intent of selling it in the short-term for a profit.
- *Held-to-maturity securities.* This is a debt security acquired with the intent of holding it to maturity, and where the holder has the ability to do so. This determination should be based not only on intent, but also on a history of

being able to do so. Do not classify convertible securities as held-to-maturity.

- *Available-for-sale securities.* This is an investment in a debt security that is not classified as a trading security or a held-to-maturity security.

Once these investments have been acquired, the subsequent accounting for them is as follows:

- *Trading securities.* Measure debt trading securities at their fair value on the balance sheet, and include all unrealized gains and losses on these holdings in earnings.
- *Held-to-maturity securities.* Measure all held-to-maturity debt securities at their amortized cost in the balance sheet. Thus, there is no adjustment to fair value.
- *Available-for-sale securities.* Measure available-for-sale debt securities at their fair value on the balance sheet, and include all unrealized gains and losses on these holdings in other comprehensive income until realized (i.e., when the securities are sold). However, if these gains or losses are being offset with a fair value hedge, include the amounts in earnings.

EXAMPLE

Armadillo Industries buys $150,000 of debt securities that it classifies as available-for-sale. After six months pass, the quoted market price of these securities declines to $130,000. Armadillo records the decline in value with the following entry:

	Debit	Credit
Loss on available-for-sale securities (recorded in other comprehensive income)	20,000	
Investments – Available-for-sale		20,000

Three months later, the securities have regained $6,000 of value, which results in the following entry:

	Debit	Credit
Investments – Available-for-sale	6,000	
Gain on available-for-sale securities (recorded in other comprehensive income)		6,000

GAAP mandates that an entity review the appropriateness of how each investment is classified and to then alter the classification (and related accounting) as necessary. Whenever there is a transfer between classifications, the investment is recorded at its fair value. If there is an unrealized holding gain or loss on the date of reclassification, use the following table to determine the appropriate accounting.

Accounting for Holding Gains and Losses on Reclassified Investments

Event	Related Accounting
Transfer out of trading classification	All unrealized gains and losses have already been recognized in earnings; do not change
Transfer into trading classification	Recognize all unrealized gains and losses in earnings
Transfer into available-for-sale classification from held-to-maturity	Recognize all unrealized gains and losses in other comprehensive income
Transfer into held-to-maturity from available-for-sale classification	Retain all unrealized gains and losses in other comprehensive income, but amortize it over the remaining life of the security as a yield adjustment

Impairment of Investments

If a security is classified as either available-for-sale or held-to-maturity and there is a decline in its market value below its amortized cost, determine whether the decline is other than temporary. This analysis must be performed in every reporting period. If market value is not readily determinable, evaluate if there have been any events or circumstances that might impact the fair value of an investment (such as a deterioration in the operating performance of the issuer of a security). Several rules regarding the determination of other-than-temporary impairment are:

- *Debt security.* If the business plans to sell a debt security, an other-than-temporary impairment is assumed to have occurred. The same rule applies if it is more likely than not that the company will have to sell the security before its amortized cost basis has been recovered; this is based on a comparison of the present value of cash flows expected to be collected from the security to its amortized cost.
- *Equity security.* If the business plans to sell an equity security and does not expect the fair value of the security to recover by the time of the sale, consider its impairment to be other-than-temporary when the decision to sell is made, not when the security is sold.

If an impairment loss on an equity security is considered to be other-than-temporary, recognize a loss in the amount of the difference between the cost and fair value of the security. Once the impairment is recorded, this becomes the new cost basis of the equity security, and cannot be adjusted upward if there is a subsequent recovery in the fair value of the security.

If an impairment loss on a debt security is considered to be other-than-temporary, recognize a loss based on the following criteria:

- If the business intends to sell the security or it is more likely than not that it will be forced to do so before there has been a recovery of the amortized cost of the security, recognize a loss in earnings in the amount of the difference between the amortized cost and fair value of the security.
- If the business does not intend to sell the security and it is more likely than not that it will not have to do so before there has been a recovery of the amortized cost of the security, separate the impairment into the amount representing a credit loss, and the amount relating to all other causes. Then recognize that portion of the impairment representing a credit loss in earnings. Recognize the remaining portion of the impairment in other comprehensive income, net of taxes.

EXAMPLE

Armadillo Industries buys $250,000 of the equity securities of Currency Bank. A national liquidity crisis causes a downturn in Currency's business, so a major credit rating agency lowers its rating for the bank's securities. These events cause the quoted price of Armadillo's holdings to decline by $50,000. The CFO of Armadillo believes that the liquidity crisis will end soon, resulting in a rebound of the fortunes of Currency Bank, and so authorizes the recordation of the $50,000 valuation decline in other comprehensive income. The following entry records the transaction:

	Debit	Credit
Loss on available-for-sale securities (recorded in other comprehensive income)	50,000	
Investments – Available-for-sale		50,000

In the following year, the prognostication abilities of the CFO are unfortunately not justified, as the liquidity crisis continues. Accordingly, the CFO authorizes shifting the $50,000 loss from other comprehensive income to earnings.

Once the impairment is recorded, this becomes the new amortized cost basis of the debt security, and cannot be adjusted upward if there is a significant recovery in the fair value of the security.

Once an impairment has been recorded for a debt security, account for the difference between its new amortized cost basis and the cash flows expected to be collected from it as interest income.

If any portion of the other-than-temporary impairment of a debt security classified as held-to-maturity is recorded in other comprehensive income, use accretion to gradually increase the carrying amount of the security until it matures or is sold.

If there is a subsequent change in the fair value of available-for-sale debt securities, include these changes in other comprehensive income.

It is not acceptable under GAAP to create a general allowance for unidentified impairments in the value of an investment portfolio. Instead, impairments must be determined at the level of each individual security.

Equity Securities without Readily Determinable Fair Values

An entity may own an equity security that does not have a readily determinable fair value. If so, it can elect to measure the security at its cost minus any impairment, with adjustments for any price changes observed under the following conditions:

- It is an orderly transaction; and
- It involves an identical or similar investment of the same issuer.

The preceding modifier condition is unlikely, since this type of security probably has a poor distribution.

This election is applied to each individual security held by the entity. Once the election is made to measure a security in this manner, the entity must continue to do so until the security no longer matches the measurement criteria.

When the fair value of this type of investment is less than its carrying value, the entity must write down the difference as an impairment adjustment. This analysis is based on impairment indicators that can include, but are not limited to, the following:

- A significant deterioration of the business prospects of the issuer
- A significant adverse change in the business environment of the issuer
- A significant adverse change in general market conditions of the issuer's geographic region or industry
- The receipt of an offer from the issuer to buy back the security for an amount less than its carrying amount
- Factors that raise valid concerns about the issuer's ability to continue as a going concern

Dividend and Interest Income

If there is any dividend, interest income, or amortization of premium or discount associated with investments, recognize these amounts in earnings.

Investment Disclosures

Any investments in available-for-sale and trading securities must be separately reported in the balance sheet. This can be done either by stating their fair value and non-fair-value carrying amounts on two separate lines, or by stating their aggregate amount in a single line, plus a parenthetical disclosure of the fair value amount included in the line.

For those securities classified as available-for-sale, disclose the following information by major type of security:

- Amortized cost basis
- Aggregate fair value
- The security-related total other-than-temporary impairments, total gains, and total losses reported in accumulated other comprehensive income
- The contractual maturities of the securities, which may be presented by group

For those securities classified as held-for-sale, disclose the following information by major type of security:

- Amortized cost basis
- Aggregate fair value
- Gross unrecognized holding gains and losses
- Net carrying amount
- The total amount of other-than-temporary impairment reported in accumulated other comprehensive income
- The gross gains and losses reported in accumulated other comprehensive income for any hedges of the forecasted acquisition of held-to-maturity securities
- The contractual maturities of the securities, which may be presented by group

For those equity securities without readily determinable fair values that have been measured at their carrying amounts less any impairments, disclose the following:

- The carrying amount of these investments
- The amount of any annual and cumulative impairment and other downward adjustments
- The amount of any annual and cumulative upward adjustments
- A discussion of the information used to determine carrying amounts and any valuation adjustments

If there are any other-than-temporary impairments of investments that have not yet been recognized in earnings, disclose the following information:

- Present in tabular form the aggregate fair value of investments with unrealized losses and the aggregate amount of the unrealized losses. Segregate this information for investments that have been in continuous unrealized loss positions for less than 12 months, and for 12 months or longer.

EXAMPLE

Armadillo Industries presents its impaired investment information in the following tabular format:

(000s) Securities Description	Less than 12 Months		12 Months or Greater		Total	
	Fair Value	Unrealized Losses	Fair Value	Unrealized Losses	Fair Value	Unrealized Losses
Corporate bonds	$500	$6	$200	--	$700	$6
Mortgage-backed securities	600	20	300	$10	900	30
U.S. Treasury obligations	2,010	5	1,400	3	3,410	8
Total	$3,110	$31	$1,900	$13	$5,010	$44

- Discuss the reasoning behind the conclusion that impairments were not other-than-temporary, which could include the nature of the impairments, the number of applicable unrealized loss positions, the severity and duration of the impairments, performance indicators, guarantees, sector credit ratings, and so forth.
- If only the portion of an impairment related to a credit loss was recognized, disclose (by major type of security) the reasoning and information used to measure the amount of the credit loss.
- Present a roll forward of the recognized amount of credit losses in the following format:

=	Beginning balance of credit losses on debt securities for which a portion of the other-than-temporary impairment is recognized in other comprehensive income
+	Amount of credit losses for which other-than-temporary impairments were not previously recognized
-	Reductions related to securities sold during the period
-	Reductions related to securities for which impairment recognized was shifted from other comprehensive income to earnings because of an intention to sell or likelihood of selling
+	Additional increases in the amount of credit losses, where there is no intent to sell the security or likelihood of doing so
-	Reductions related to increased cash flows expected to be collected
=	Ending balance of credit losses on debt securities for which a portion of the other-than-temporary impairment is recognized in other comprehensive income

If there were any sales or transfers of investments during the period, disclose the following information:

For all investments sold or reclassified	The basis on which investment costs or the amounts shifted from other comprehensive income to earnings were derived (such as by specific identification or an averaging method)
For available-for-sale securities	The proceeds from any sales, as well as the related amount of gross realized gains and gross realized losses recorded in earnings
For available-for-sale securities	The net unrealized holding gain or loss included in accumulated other comprehensive income, as well as the amount of gains and losses shifted from accumulated other comprehensive income and into earnings during the period
For trading securities	The amount of trading gains and losses for securities still held at the reporting date
For transfers from available-for-sale to trading classification	The amount of gross gains and gross losses recorded in earnings as a result of the transfer
From the held-to-maturity classification	The net carrying amount sold or transferred, the net gain or loss in accumulated other comprehensive income for hedges of the forecasted acquisition of held-to-maturity securities, the realized or unrealized gain or loss, and a discussion of the circumstances causing the decision to sell or transfer the securities

Summary

The accounting for and disclosure of the three types of investments clearly differ, and so it would initially appear that a considerable amount of detailed investment monitoring is required to ensure that the related accounting will be correct. However, the situation can be made considerably less complex as long as the need to transfer investments between classifications is minimized and the accountant develops a clear procedure for the treatment of each class of investment. The situation can be further clarified by restricting all investments to just one or two of the three allowed classifications. Following these rules can result in greatly simplified accounting for debt and equity investments.

Chapter 16
Investments – Equity Method and Joint Ventures

323 = GAAP codification area for investments – equity method and joint ventures

Introduction

This chapter is tightly focused on the applicability, accounting for, and disclosure of the equity method of accounting for investments, which is used when an investor has significant influence over an investee that is not a subsidiary. A highly-specific additional GAAP topic on qualified affordable housing project investments is not included. The guidance in this chapter applies to all entities.

The Equity Method

When a company owns an interest in another business that it does not control (such as a corporate joint venture), it may use the equity method to account for its ownership interest. The equity method is designed to measure changes in the economic results of the investee, by requiring the investor to recognize its share of the profits or losses recorded by the investee. The equity method is a more complex technique of accounting for ownership, and so is typically used only when there is a significant ownership interest that enables an investor to have influence over the decision-making of the investee.

The key determining factor in the use of the equity method is having significant influence over the operating and financial decisions of the investee. The primary determinant of this level of control is owning at least 20% of the voting shares of the investee, though this measurement can be repudiated by evidence that the investee opposes the influence of the investor. Other types of evidence of significant influence are controlling a seat on the board of directors, active participation in the decisions of the investee, or swapping management personnel with the investee.

The investor can avoid using the equity method if it cannot obtain the financial information it needs from the investee in order to correctly account for its ownership interest under the equity method.

The essential accounting under the equity method is to initially recognize an investment in an investee at cost, and then adjust the carrying amount of the investment by recognizing its share of the earnings or losses of the investee in earnings over time. The following additional guidance applies to these basic points:

- *Dividends.* The investor should subtract any dividends received from the investee from the carrying amount of the investor's investment in the investee.

- *Financial statement issuance.* The investor can only account for its share of the earnings or losses of the investee if the investee issues financial statements. This may result in occasional lags in reporting.
- *Funding of prior losses.* If the investor pays the investee with the intent of offsetting prior investee losses, and the carrying amount of the investor's interest in the investee has already been reduced to zero, then the investor's share of any additional losses can be applied against the additional funds paid to the investee.
- *Intra-entity profits and losses.* Eliminate all intra-entity profits and losses as part of the equity method accounting, as would be the case if financial statements were being consolidated.
- *Investee losses.* It is possible that the investor's share of the losses of an investee will exceed the carrying amount of its investment in the investee. If so, the investor should report losses up to its carrying amount, as well as any additional financial support given to the investee, and then discontinue use of the equity method. However, additional losses can be recorded if it appears assured that the investee will shortly return to profitability. If there is a return to profitability, the investor can return to the equity method only after its share of the profits has been offset by those losses not recognized when use of the equity method was halted.
- *Other comprehensive income.* The investor should record its proportionate share of the investee's equity adjustments related to other comprehensive income. The entry is an adjustment to the investment account, with an offsetting adjustment in equity. If the investor discontinues its use of the equity method, offset the existing proportionate share of these equity adjustments against the carrying value of the investment. If the result of this netting is a value in the carrying amount of less than zero, charge the excess amount to income. Also, stop recording the investor's proportionate share of the equity adjustments related to other comprehensive income in future periods.
- *Other write-downs.* If an investor's investment in an investee has been written down to zero, but it has other investments in the investee, the investor should continue to report its share of any additional investee losses, and offset them against the other investments, in sequence of the seniority of those investments (with offsets against the most junior items first). If the investee generates income at a later date, the investor should apply its share of these profits to the other investments in order, with application going against the most senior items first.
- *Share calculation.* The proportion of the investee's earnings or losses to be recognized by the investor is based on the investor's holdings of common stock and in-substance common stock.
- *Share issuances.* If the investee issues shares, the investor should account for the transaction as if a proportionate share of its own investment in the investee had been sold. If there is a gain or loss resulting from the stock sale, recognize it in earnings.

- *Ownership decrease.* If an investor decreases its ownership in an investee, this may drop its level of control below the 20% to 25% threshold, in which case the investor may no longer be qualified to use the equity method. If so, the investor should retain the carrying amount of the investment as of the date when the equity method no longer applies, so there is no retroactive adjustment.

EXAMPLE

Armadillo Industries purchases 30% of the common stock of Titanium Barriers, Inc. Armadillo controls two seats on the board of directors of Titanium as a result of this investment, so it uses the equity method to account for the investment. In the next year, Titanium earns $400,000. Armadillo records its 30% share of the profit with the following entry:

	Debit	Credit
Investment in Titanium Barriers	120,000	
Equity in Titanium Barriers income		120,000

A few months later, Titanium issues a $50,000 cash dividend to Armadillo, which the company records with the following entry:

	Debit	Credit
Cash	50,000	
Investment in Titanium Barriers		50,000

EXAMPLE

Armadillo Industries has a 35% ownership interest in the common stock of Arlington Research. The carrying amount of this investment has been reduced to zero because of previous losses. To keep Arlington solvent, Armadillo has purchased $250,000 of Arlington's preferred stock, and extended a long-term unsecured loan of $500,000.

During the next year, Arlington incurs a $1,200,000 loss, of which Armadillo's share is 35%, or $420,000. Since the next most senior level of Arlington's capital after common stock is its preferred stock, Armadillo first offsets its share of the loss against its preferred stock investment. Doing so reduces the carrying amount of the preferred stock to zero, leaving $170,000 to be applied against the carrying amount of the loan. This results in the following entry by Armadillo:

	Debit	Credit
Equity method loss	420,000	
Preferred stock investment		250,000
Loan		170,000

In the following year, Arlington records $800,000 of profits, of which Armadillo's share is $280,000. Armadillo applies the $280,000 first against the loan write-down, and then against the preferred stock write-down with the following entry:

	Debit	Credit
Preferred stock investment	110,000	
Loan	170,000	
Equity method income		280,000

The result is that the carrying amount of the loan is fully restored, while the carrying amount of the preferred stock investment is still reduced by $140,000 from its original level.

There may be situations in which an organization has a smaller investment in an investee that it is accounting for using some other method than the equity method. The level of ownership then increases, requiring the organization to account for its investment using the equity method. To initially do so, the firm adds the cost of acquiring the additional equity interest in the investee to the current basis of the previously held interest in the investee. This combined amount is now treated as the beginning investment for use of the equity method, which begins as of the day when the investment became qualified for use of the equity method. If the investment had previously been classified as an available-for-sale security, the firm should recognize in earnings any unrealized gain or loss stated in accumulated other comprehensive income.

Partnerships, Joint Ventures, and Limited Liability Entities

This section addresses the application of the equity method (noted in the preceding section) to investments in partnerships, unincorporated joint ventures, and limited liability companies. In essence, the equity method can be applied by the investor in any situation where it exercises significant influence over these types of investees.

The primary differences in usage of the equity method for the types of investee entities noted in this section are as follows:

- *Limited liability companies.* If a limited liability company maintains an ownership account for each investor, this account can be used as the basis for determining whether a significant influence exists for purposes of applying the equity method.
- *Limited partnerships.* The Securities and Exchange Commission (SEC) mandates use of the equity method for all investors, unless the investor interest is so minor as to preclude any influence over the partnership, which the SEC generally construes as being an ownership interest of less than 3% to 5%. This accounting only applies to publicly-held companies.

- *Partnerships.* Income taxes must be recorded on the profits accrued by investor-partners, irrespective of the tax basis used in the partnership tax return.

Investment Disclosures

When an investor uses the equity method to account for an investment, it should state the investment as a single line item in the balance sheet. Similarly, the investor should report its share of any investee gains or losses as a single line item in the income statement. The only exceptions to reporting investment information on a separate line are:

- Accounting changes
- Other comprehensive income items (to be combined with the investor's own other comprehensive income items)

An investor using the equity method to account for an investment should disclose the following information:

- *Identification.* The name of each investee and the investor's ownership percentage in it.
- *Market value.* The value of each investment at its quoted market price (if such a price is available).
- *Policies.* The investor's policies regarding its investments in common stock, including cases where the investor owns a 20% or more interest in a business but does not use the equity method. Also describe any situations where the investor uses the equity method despite owning less than 20% of an investee. Further, note any difference between the carrying amount of an investment and the amount of underlying equity in net assets.
- *Change in ownership.* If there is a potentially material impact on the investor's share of reported investee earnings from the conversion of convertible securities, the conversion of warrants, or similar transactions, disclose this information.

If equity method investments in corporate joint ventures and other entities are material (in aggregate) to the financial statements of the investor, consider disclosing summarized information about the assets, liabilities, and operational results of the investees.

Summary

From the perspective of the accountant, the equity method can safely be described as time-consuming, since it requires significantly more tracking work than the vastly simpler accounting for an investment at its cost (which can be used if there is no significant influence over the investee). Consequently, if there is any question about the existence of significant influence, it is best to present an argument that does not favor use of the equity method.

Chapter 17
Inventory

330 = GAAP codification area for inventory

Introduction

Inventory is one of the most important asset classifications, for it may represent the largest asset investment by a manufacturer or seller of goods. As a major asset, it is imperative that inventory be properly valued, as well as those goods designated as having been sold. This chapter discusses the surprisingly brief GAAP requirements for inventory, and then expands upon them with discussions of inventory tracking systems, costing methodologies, and a variety of related topics.

Related Podcast Episodes: Episodes 56, 66, 119, and 200 of the Accounting Best Practices Podcast discuss inventory record accuracy, obsolete inventory, overhead allocation, and the lower of cost or market rule, respectively. They are available at: **www.accountingtools.com/podcasts** or **iTunes**

Overview of Inventory

In general, inventory is to be accounted for at cost, which is considered to be the sum of those expenditures required to bring an inventory item to its present condition and location. There are three types of costs to apply to inventory, which are:

- *Direct costs.* If a cost was directly incurred to produce or acquire a specific unit of inventory, this is called a direct cost, and is recorded as a cost of inventory.
- *Variable overhead costs.* If there are any factory costs that are not direct, but which vary with production volume, they are assigned to inventory based on actual usage of a company's production facilities. There are usually not many variable overhead costs.
- *Fixed overhead costs.* If there are any factory costs that are not direct, and which do not vary with production volume, they are assigned to inventory based on the normal capacity of a company's production facilities.

The accounting for fixed overhead costs is particularly critical, given the large amount of fixed costs that are allocated in many production facilities. The basic GAAP rules for fixed overhead allocation are:

- *High production*. During periods of abnormally high production, the overhead allocation per unit should be reduced in order to keep from recording inventory above its actual cost.
- *Low production*. During periods of abnormally low production, the overhead allocation per unit is *not* increased.
- *Overhead expense recognition*. If there is any residual fixed overhead that is not allocated to inventory, the unallocated amount is recognized as expense in the period incurred; there is no delay in expense recognition to a later period.

GAAP specifically requires that overhead costs must be allocated to inventory, and that the allocation must be consistently performed from period to period.

Tip: Though GAAP requires that overhead be allocated to inventory, this does not mean that an inordinate amount of time should be spent compiling an exquisitely designed allocation system. Instead, focus on a simple and efficient allocation methodology that allows the books to be closed quickly.

Several other rules have been developed regarding inventory costs, most of which are designed to keep certain costs from being allocated to inventory. They are:

- *Abnormal expenses*. If unusually high costs are incurred, such as abnormal freight, spoilage, or scrap charges, they are to be charged to expense in the period incurred.
- *General and administrative expenses*. General and administrative costs can only be allocated to inventory when they are clearly related to production. In nearly all cases, these costs are charged to expense as incurred.
- *Selling expenses*. All costs related to selling are charged to expense as incurred; they are never allocated to inventory.
- *Stating inventory above cost*. Inventories can only be stated above cost in exceptional situations. In all cases where the cost is stated at the sale price, the cost is to be reduced by any expected disposal costs. Stating inventory above cost is specifically allowed by GAAP in the following situations:
  - Gold and silver, where there is a government-controlled market at a fixed price
  - Inventories of agricultural, mineral, and similar products that have the following criteria:
    - Immediate marketability at a quoted market price
    - Units are interchangeable
    - An inability to determine an appropriate per-unit cost

Once costs have initially been apportioned to inventory, GAAP requires that any decline in the utility of goods below their cost result in the recognition of a loss in the current period. This decline in utility is most commonly caused by the deterioration or obsolescence of inventory items. The Accounting for Obsolete Inventory section describes how to account for this type of loss. A decline in utility may also be caused by a decline in the price of inventory items. The Lower of Cost or Market Rule section describes how to calculate and account for this type of loss. In addition, if a company has a firm purchase commitment to acquire goods and the utility of the items to be acquired has declined, the company should recognize a loss in the current period for these future purchases; loss recognition is not required when the items to be purchased are also protected by firm sales contracts or similar arrangements.

The *inventory cost flow* assumption is the concept that the cost of an inventory item changes between the time it is acquired or built and the time when it is sold. Because of this cost differential, a company needs to adopt a cost flow assumption regarding how it treats the cost of goods as they move through the company.

For example, a company buys a widget on January 1 for $50. On July 1, it buys an identical widget for $70, and on November 1 it buys yet another identical widget for $90. The products are completely interchangeable. On December 1, the company sells one of the widgets. It bought the widgets at three different prices, so what cost should it report for its cost of goods sold? There are many possible ways to interpret the cost flow assumption. For example:

- *FIFO cost flow assumption.* Under the first in, first out method, assume that the first item purchased is also the first one sold. Thus, the cost of goods sold would be $50. Since this is the lowest-cost item in the example, profits would be highest under FIFO.
- *LIFO cost flow assumption.* Under the last in, first out method, assume that the last item purchased is also the first one sold. Thus, the cost of goods sold would be $90. Since this is the highest-cost item in the example, profits would be lowest under LIFO.
- *Weighted average cost flow assumption.* Under the weighted average method, the cost of goods sold is the average cost of all three units, or $70. This cost flow assumption tends to yield a mid-range cost, and therefore also a mid-range profit.

The cost flow assumption does not necessarily match the actual flow of goods (if that were the case, most companies would use the FIFO method). Instead, use a cost flow assumption that varies from actual usage. For this reason, companies tend to select a cost flow assumption that either minimizes profits (in order to minimize income taxes) or maximizes profits (in order to increase share value).

In periods of rising materials prices, the LIFO method results in a higher cost of goods sold, lower profits, and therefore lower income taxes. In periods of declining materials prices, the FIFO method yields the same results.

The cost flow assumption is a minor item when inventory costs are relatively stable over the long term, since there will be no particular difference in the cost of goods sold, no matter which cost flow assumption is used. Conversely, dramatic changes in inventory costs over time will yield a notable difference in reported profit levels, depending on the cost flow assumption used. Therefore, be especially aware of the financial impact of the inventory cost flow assumption in periods of fluctuating costs.

In the following sections, we describe the more commonly-used methods for inventory costing, several of which are based on cost flow assumptions. First, however, we address the two main record-keeping systems needed to accurately track inventory, which are the periodic inventory system and the perpetual inventory system.

The Periodic Inventory System

The periodic inventory system only updates the ending inventory balance when a physical inventory count is conducted. Since physical inventory counts are time-consuming, few companies do them more than once a quarter or year. In the meantime, the inventory account continues to show the cost of the inventory that was recorded as of the last physical inventory count.

Under the periodic inventory system, all purchases made between physical inventory counts are recorded in a purchases account. When a physical inventory count is done, shift the balance in the purchases account into the inventory account, which in turn is adjusted to match the cost of the ending inventory.

The calculation of the cost of goods sold under the periodic inventory system is:

Beginning inventory + Purchases = Cost of goods available for sale

Cost of goods available for sale – Ending inventory = Cost of goods sold

---

EXAMPLE

Milagro Corporation has beginning inventory of $100,000, has paid $170,000 for purchases, and its physical inventory count reveals an ending inventory cost of $80,000. The calculation of its cost of goods sold is:

$100,000 Beginning inventory + $170,000 Purchases - $80,000 Ending inventory

= $190,000 Cost of goods sold

The periodic inventory system is most useful for smaller businesses that maintain minimal amounts of inventory. For them, a physical inventory count is easy to complete, and they can estimate cost of goods sold figures for interim periods. However, there are several problems with the system:

- It does not yield any information about the cost of goods sold or ending inventory balances during interim periods when there has been no physical inventory count.
- The cost of goods sold must be estimated during interim periods, which will likely result in a significant adjustment to the actual cost of goods whenever a physical inventory count is eventually completed.

- There is no way to adjust for obsolete inventory or scrap losses during interim periods, so there tends to be a significant (and expensive) adjustment for these issues when a physical inventory count is eventually completed.

A more up-to-date and accurate alternative to the periodic inventory system is the perpetual inventory system, which is described in the next section.

The Perpetual Inventory System

Under the perpetual inventory system, an entity continually updates its inventory records to account for additions to and subtractions from inventory for such activities as received inventory items, goods sold from stock, and items picked from inventory for use in the production process. Thus, a perpetual inventory system has the advantages of both providing up-to-date inventory balance information and requiring a reduced level of physical inventory counts. However, the calculated inventory levels derived by a perpetual inventory system may gradually diverge from actual inventory levels, due to unrecorded transactions or theft, so periodically compare book balances to actual on-hand quantities.

EXAMPLE

This example contains several journal entries used to account for transactions in a perpetual inventory system. Milagro Corporation records a purchase of $1,000 of widgets that are stored in inventory:

	Debit	Credit
Inventory	1,000	
Accounts payable		1,000

Milagro records $250 of inbound freight cost associated with the delivery of widgets:

	Debit	Credit
Inventory	250	
Accounts payable		250

Milagro records the sale of widgets on credit from inventory for $2,000, for which the associated inventory cost is $1,200:

	Debit	Credit
Accounts receivable	2,000	
Revenue		2,000
Cost of goods sold	1,200	
Inventory		1,200

Milagro records a downward inventory adjustment of $500, caused by inventory theft, and detected during an inventory count:

	Debit	Credit
Inventory shrinkage expense	500	
Inventory		500

Inventory Costing

Several methods for calculating the cost of inventory are shown in this section. Of the methods presented, only the first in, first out method and the weighted average method have gained worldwide recognition. The last in, first out method cannot realistically be justified based on the actual flow of inventory, and is only used in the United States under the sanction of the Internal Revenue Service; it is specifically banned under international financial reporting standards. Standard costing is an acceptable alternative to cost layering, as long as any associated variances are properly accounted for. The retail inventory method and gross profit method should be used only to derive an approximation of the ending inventory cost, and so should be limited to interim reporting periods when a company does not intend to issue any financial results to outside parties.

The First In, First Out Method

The first in, first out (FIFO) method of inventory valuation operates under the assumption that the first goods purchased are also the first goods sold. In most companies, this accounting assumption closely matches the actual flow of goods, and so is considered the most theoretically correct inventory valuation method.

Under the FIFO method, the earliest goods purchased are the first ones removed from the inventory account. This results in the remaining items in inventory being accounted for at the most recently incurred costs, so that the inventory asset recorded on the balance sheet contains costs quite close to the most recent costs that could be obtained in the marketplace. Conversely, this method also results in older historical costs being matched against current revenues and recorded in the cost of goods sold, so the gross margin does not necessarily reflect a proper matching of revenues and costs.

EXAMPLE

Milagro Corporation decides to use the FIFO method for the month of January. During that month, it records the following transactions:

	Quantity Change	Actual Unit Cost	Actual Total Cost
Beginning inventory (layer 1)	+100	$210	$21,000
Sale	-75		
Purchase (layer 2)	+150	280	42,000
Sale	-100		
Purchase (layer 3)	+50	300	15,000
Ending inventory	= 125		

The cost of goods sold in units is calculated as:

100 Beginning inventory + 200 Purchased – 125 Ending inventory = 175 Units

Milagro's controller uses the information in the preceding table to calculate the cost of goods sold for January, as well as the cost of the inventory balance as of the end of January. The calculations appear in the following table:

	Units	Unit Cost	Total Cost
Cost of goods sold			
FIFO layer 1	100	$210	$21,000
FIFO layer 2	75	280	21,000
Total cost of goods sold	175		$42,000
Ending inventory			
FIFO layer 2	75	280	$21,000
FIFO layer 3	50	300	15,000
Total ending inventory	125		$36,000

Thus, the first FIFO layer, which was the beginning inventory layer, is completely used up during the month, as well as half of Layer 2, leaving half of Layer 2 and all of Layer 3 to be the sole components of the ending inventory.

Note that the $42,000 cost of goods sold and $36,000 ending inventory equals the $78,000 combined total of beginning inventory and purchases during the month.

The Last In, First Out Method

The last in, first out (LIFO) method operates under the assumption that the last item of inventory purchased is the first one sold. Picture a store shelf where a clerk adds items from the front, and customers also take their selections from the front; the remaining items of inventory that are located further from the front of the shelf are rarely picked, and so remain on the shelf – that is a LIFO scenario.

The trouble with the LIFO scenario is that it is rarely encountered in practice. If a company were to use the process flow embodied by LIFO, a significant part of its inventory would be very old, and likely obsolete. Nonetheless, a company does not actually have to experience the LIFO process flow in order to use the method to calculate its inventory valuation.

The reason why companies use LIFO is the assumption that the cost of inventory increases over time, which is reasonable in inflationary periods. If LIFO were to be used in such a situation, the cost of the most recently acquired inventory will always be higher than the cost of earlier purchases, so the ending inventory balance will be valued at earlier costs, while the most recent costs appear in the cost of goods sold. By shifting high-cost inventory into the cost of goods sold, a company can reduce its reported level of profitability, and thereby defer its recognition of income taxes. Since income tax deferral is the only justification for LIFO in most situations, it is banned under international financial reporting standards (though it is still allowed in the United States under the approval of the Internal Revenue Service).

EXAMPLE

Milagro Corporation decides to use the LIFO method for the month of March. The following table shows the various purchasing transactions for the company's Elite Roasters product. The quantity purchased on March 1 actually reflects the inventory beginning balance.

Date Purchased	Quantity Purchased	Cost per Unit	Units Sold	Cost of Layer #1	Cost of Layer #2	Total Cost
March 1	150	$210	95	(55 × $210)		$11,550
March 7	100	235	110	(45 × $210)		9,450
March 11	200	250	180	(45 × $210)	(20 × $250)	14,450
March 17	125	240	125	(45 × $210)	(20 × $250)	14,450
March 25	80	260	120	(25 × $210)		5,250

The following bullet points describe the transactions noted in the preceding table:

- *March 1.* Milagro has a beginning inventory balance of 150 units, and sells 95 of these units between March 1 and March 7. This leaves one inventory layer of 55 units at a cost of $210 each.
- *March 7.* Milagro buys 100 additional units on March 7, and sells 110 units between March 7 and March 11. Under LIFO, we assume that the latest purchase was sold first, so there is still just one inventory layer, which has now been reduced to 45 units.

- *March 11.* Milagro buys 200 additional units on March 11, and sells 180 units between March 11 and March 17, which creates a new inventory layer that is comprised of 20 units at a cost of $250. This new layer appears in the table in the "Cost of Layer #2" column.
- *March 17.* Milagro buys 125 additional units on March 17, and sells 125 units between March 17 and March 25, so there is no change in the inventory layers.
- *March 25.* Milagro buys 80 additional units on March 25, and sells 120 units between March 25 and the end of the month. Sales exceed purchases during this period, so the second inventory layer is eliminated, as well as part of the first layer. The result is an ending inventory balance of $5,250, which is derived from 25 units of ending inventory, multiplied by the $210 cost in the first layer that existed at the beginning of the month.

Before a LIFO system is implemented, consider the following points:

- *Consistent usage.* The Internal Revenue Service states that a company using LIFO for its tax reporting must also use LIFO for its financial reporting. Thus, a company wanting to defer tax recognition through early expense recognition must show those same low profit numbers to the outside users of its financial statements.
- *Layering.* Since the LIFO system is intended to use the most recent layers of inventory, earlier layers may never be accessed, which can result in an administrative problem if there are many layers to document.
- *Profit fluctuations.* If early layers contain inventory costs that depart substantially from current market prices, a company could experience sharp changes in its profitability if those layers are ever used.

In summary, LIFO is only useful for deferring income tax payments in periods of cost inflation. It does not reflect the actual flow of inventory in most situations, and may even yield unusual financial results that differ markedly from reality.

The Weighted Average Method

When using the weighted average method, divide the cost of goods available for sale by the number of units available for sale, which yields the weighted-average cost per unit. In this calculation, the cost of goods available for sale is the sum of beginning inventory and net purchases. This weighted-average figure is then used to assign a cost to both ending inventory and the cost of goods sold.

The singular advantage of the weighted average method is the complete absence of any inventory layers, which avoids the record keeping problems that would be encountered with either the FIFO or LIFO methods that were described earlier.

EXAMPLE

Milagro Corporation elects to use the weighted-average method for the month of May. During that month, it records the following transactions:

	Quantity Change	Actual Unit Cost	Actual Total Cost
Beginning inventory	+150	$220	$33,000
Sale	-125		
Purchase	+200	270	54,000
Sale	-150		
Purchase	+100	290	29,000
Ending inventory	= 175		

The actual total cost of all purchased or beginning inventory units in the preceding table is $116,000 ($33,000 + $54,000 + $29,000). The total of all purchased or beginning inventory units is 450 (150 beginning inventory + 300 purchased). The weighted average cost per unit is therefore $257.78 ($116,000 ÷ 450 units.)

The ending inventory valuation is $45,112 (175 units × $257.78 weighted average cost), while the cost of goods sold valuation is $70,890 (275 units × $257.78 weighted average cost). The sum of these two amounts (less a rounding error) equals the $116,000 total actual cost of all purchases and beginning inventory.

In the preceding example, if Milagro used a perpetual inventory system to record its inventory transactions, it would have to recompute the weighted average after every purchase. The following table uses the same information in the preceding example to show the recomputations:

	Units on Hand	Purchases	Cost of Sales	Inventory Total Cost	Inventory Moving Average Unit Cost
Beginning inventory	150	$--	$--	$33,000	$220.00
Sale (125 units @ $220.00)	25	--	27,500	5,500	220.00
Purchase (200 units @ $270.00)	225	54,000	--	59,500	264.44
Sale (150 units @ $264.44)	75	--	39,666	19,834	264.44
Purchase (100 units @ $290.00)	175	29,000	--	48,834	279.05
Total			$67,166		

Note that the cost of goods sold of $67,166 and the ending inventory balance of $48,834 equal $116,000, which matches the total of the costs in the original example. Thus, the totals are the same, but the moving weighted average calculation results in slight differences in the apportionment of costs between the cost of goods sold and ending inventory.

Standard Costing

The preceding methods (FIFO, LIFO, and weighted average) have all operated under the assumption that some sort of cost layering is used, even if that layering results in nothing more than a single weighted-average layer. The standard costing methodology arrives at inventory valuation from an entirely different direction, which is to set a standard cost for each item and to then value those items at the standard cost – not the actual cost at which the items were purchased.

Standard costing is clearly more efficient than any cost layering system, simply because there are no layers to keep track of. However, its primary failing is that the resulting inventory valuation may not equate to the actual cost. The difference is handled through several types of variance calculations, which may be charged to the cost of goods sold (if minor) or allocated between inventory and the cost of goods sold (if material).

At the most basic level, a standard cost can be created simply by calculating the average of the most recent actual costs for the past few months. An additional factor to consider when deriving a standard cost is whether to set it at a historical actual cost level that has been proven to be attainable, or at a rate that should be attainable, or one that can only be reached if all operations work perfectly. Here are some considerations:

- *Historical basis*. This is an average of the costs that a company has already experienced in the recent past, possibly weighted towards just the past few months. Though clearly an attainable cost, a standard based on historical results contains all of the operational inefficiencies of the existing production operation.
- *Attainable basis*. This is a cost that is more difficult to reach than a historical cost. This basis assumes some improvement in operating and purchasing efficiencies, which employees have a good chance of achieving in the short term.
- *Theoretical basis*. This is the ultimate, lowest cost that the facility can attain if it functions perfectly, with no scrap, highly efficient employees, and machines that never break down. This can be a frustrating basis to use for a standard cost, because the production facility can never attain it, and so always produces unfavorable variances.

Of the three types of standards noted here, use the attainable basis, because it gives employees a reasonable cost target to pursue. If standards are continually updated on this basis, a production facility will have an incentive to continually drive down its costs over the long term.

Standard costs are stored separately from all other accounting records, usually in a bill of materials for finished goods, and in the item master file for raw materials.

At the end of a reporting period, the following steps show how to integrate standard costs into the accounting system (assuming the use of a periodic inventory system):

1. *Cost verification.* Review the standard cost database for errors and correct as necessary. Also, if it is time to do so, update the standard costs to more accurately reflect actual costs.
2. *Inventory valuation.* Multiply the number of units in ending inventory by their standard costs to derive the ending inventory valuation.
3. *Calculate the cost of goods sold.* Add purchases during the month to the beginning inventory and subtract the ending inventory to determine the cost of goods sold.
4. *Enter updated balances.* Create a journal entry that reduces the purchases account to zero and which also adjusts the inventory asset account balance to the ending total standard cost, with the offset to the cost of goods sold account.

EXAMPLE

A division of the Milagro Corporation is using a standard costing system to calculate its inventory balances and cost of goods sold. The company conducts a month-end physical inventory count that results in a reasonably accurate set of unit quantities for all inventory items. The controller multiplies each of these unit quantities by their standard costs to derive the ending inventory valuation. This ending balance is $2,500,000.

The beginning balance in the inventory account is $2,750,000 and purchases during the month were $1,000,000, so the calculation of the cost of goods sold is:

Beginning inventory	$2,750,000
+ Purchases	1,000,000
- Ending inventory	(2,500,000)
= Cost of goods sold	$1,250,000

To record the correct ending inventory balance and cost of goods sold, the controller records the following entry, which clears out the purchases asset account and adjusts the ending inventory balance to $2,500,000:

	Debit	Credit
Cost of goods sold	1,250,000	
Purchases		1,000,000
Inventory		250,000

The Retail Inventory Method

The retail inventory method is sometimes used by retailers that resell merchandise to estimate their ending inventory balances. This method is based on the relationship between the cost of merchandise and its retail price. To calculate the cost of ending inventory using the retail inventory method, follow these steps:

1. Calculate the cost-to-retail percentage, for which the formula is (Cost ÷ Retail price).
2. Calculate the cost of goods available for sale, for which the formula is (Cost of beginning inventory + Cost of purchases).
3. Calculate the cost of sales during the period, for which the formula is (Sales × Cost-to-retail percentage).
4. Calculate ending inventory, for which the formula is (Cost of goods available for sale - Cost of sales during the period).

EXAMPLE

Milagro Corporation sells home coffee roasters for an average of $200, and which cost it $140. This is a cost-to-retail percentage of 70%. Milagro's beginning inventory has a cost of $1,000,000, it paid $1,800,000 for purchases during the month, and it had sales of $2,400,000. The calculation of its ending inventory is:

Beginning inventory	$1,000,000	(at cost)
Purchases	+ 1,800,000	(at cost)
Goods available for sale	= 2,800,000	
Sales	- 1,680,000	(sales of $2,400,000 × 70%)
Ending inventory	= $1,120,000	

The retail inventory method is a quick and easy way to determine an approximate ending inventory balance. However, there are also several issues with it:

- The retail inventory method is only an estimate. Do not rely upon it too heavily to yield results that will compare with those of a physical inventory count.
- The retail inventory method only works if there is a consistent mark-up across all products sold. If not, the actual ending inventory cost may vary wildly from what was derived using this method.
- The method assumes that the historical basis for the mark-up percentage continues into the current period. If the mark-up was different (as may be caused by an after-holidays sale), then the results of the calculation will be incorrect.

The Gross Profit Method

The gross profit method can be used to estimate the amount of ending inventory. This is useful for interim periods between physical inventory counts, or when inventory was destroyed and there is a need to back into the ending inventory balance for the purpose of filing a claim for insurance reimbursement. Follow these steps to estimate ending inventory using the gross profit method:

1. Add together the cost of beginning inventory and the cost of purchases during the period to arrive at the cost of goods available for sale.
2. Multiply (1 - expected gross profit percentage) by sales during the period to arrive at the estimated cost of goods sold.
3. Subtract the estimated cost of goods sold (step #2) from the cost of goods available for sale (step #1) to arrive at the ending inventory.

The gross profit method is not an acceptable method for determining the year-end inventory balance, since it only estimates what the ending inventory balance may be. It is not sufficiently precise to be reliable for audited financial statements.

EXAMPLE

Mulligan Imports is calculating its month-end golf club inventory for March. Its beginning inventory was $175,000 and its purchases during the month were $225,000. Thus, its cost of goods available for sale is:

$$\$175,000 \text{ beginning inventory} + \$225,000 \text{ purchases}$$

$$= \$400,000 \text{ cost of goods available for sale}$$

Mulligan's gross margin percentage for all of the past 12 months was 35%, which is considered a reliable long-term margin. Its sales during March were $500,000. Thus, its estimated cost of goods sold is:

$$(1 - 35\%) \times \$500,000 = \$325,000 \text{ cost of goods sold}$$

By subtracting the estimated cost of goods sold from the cost of goods available for sale, Mulligan arrives at an estimated ending inventory balance of $75,000.

There are several issues with the gross profit method that make it unreliable as the sole method for determining the value of inventory, which are:

- *Applicability*. The calculation is most useful in retail situations where a company is simply buying and reselling merchandise. If a company is instead manufacturing goods, then the components of inventory must also include labor and overhead, which make the gross profit method too simplistic to yield reliable results.

- *Historical basis.* The gross profit percentage is a key component of the calculation, but the percentage is based on a company's historical experience. If the current situation yields a different percentage (as may be caused by a special sale at reduced prices), then the gross profit percentage used in the calculation will be incorrect.
- *Inventory losses.* The calculation assumes that the long-term rate of losses due to theft, obsolescence, and other causes is included in the historical gross profit percentage. If not, or if these losses have not previously been recognized, then the calculation will likely result in an inaccurate estimated ending inventory (and probably one that is too high).

Overhead Allocation

The preceding section was concerned with charging the direct costs of production to inventory, but what about overhead expenses? In many businesses, the cost of overhead is substantially greater than direct costs, so extra attention must be expended on the proper method of allocating overhead to inventory.

There are two types of overhead, which are administrative overhead and manufacturing overhead. *Administrative overhead* includes those costs not involved in the development or production of goods or services, such as the costs of front office administration and sales; this is essentially all overhead that is *not* included in manufacturing overhead. *Manufacturing overhead* is all of the costs that a factory incurs, other than direct costs.

The costs of manufacturing overhead should be allocated to any inventory items that are classified as work-in-process or finished goods. Overhead is not allocated to raw materials inventory, since the operations giving rise to overhead costs only impact work-in-process and finished goods inventory.

The following items are usually included in manufacturing overhead:

Depreciation of factory equipment	Quality control and inspection
Factory administration expenses	Rent, facility and equipment
Indirect labor and production supervisory wages	Repair expenses
Indirect materials and supplies	Rework labor, scrap and spoilage
Maintenance, factory and production equipment	Taxes related to production assets
Officer salaries related to production	Uncapitalized tools and equipment
Production employees' benefits	Utilities

The typical procedure for allocating overhead is to accumulate all manufacturing overhead costs into one or more cost pools, and to then use an activity measure to apportion the overhead costs in the cost pools to inventory. Thus, the overhead allocation formula is:

Cost pool ÷ Total activity measure = Overhead allocation per unit

EXAMPLE

Mulligan Imports has a small production operation for an in-house line of golf clubs. During April, it incurs costs for the following items:

Cost Type	Amount
Building rent	$65,000
Building utilities	12,000
Factory equipment depreciation	8,000
Production equipment maintenance	7,000
Total	$92,000

All of these items are classified as manufacturing overhead, so Mulligan creates the following journal entry to shift these costs into an overhead cost pool:

	Debit	Credit
Overhead cost pool	92,000	
Depreciation expense		8,000
Maintenance expense		7,000
Rent expense		65,000
Utilities expense		12,000

Overhead costs can be allocated by any reasonable measure, as long as it is consistently applied across reporting periods. Common bases of allocation are direct labor hours charged against a product, or the amount of machine hours used during the production of a product. The amount of allocation charged per unit is known as the *overhead rate*.

The overhead rate can be expressed as a proportion, if both the numerator and denominator are in dollars. For example, Armadillo Industries has total indirect costs of $100,000 and it decides to use the cost of its direct labor as the allocation measure. Armadillo incurs $50,000 of direct labor costs, so the overhead rate is calculated as:

$$\frac{\$100,000 \text{ Indirect costs}}{\$50,000 \text{ Direct labor}}$$

The result is an overhead rate of 2.0.

Alternatively, if the denominator is not in dollars, then the overhead rate is expressed as a cost per allocation unit. For example, Armadillo decides to change its allocation measure to hours of machine time used. The company has 10,000 hours of machine time usage, so the overhead rate is now calculated as:

$100,000 Indirect costs
10,000 Machine hours

The result is an overhead rate of $10.00 per machine hour.

EXAMPLE

Mulligan Imports has a small golf shaft production line, which manufactures a titanium shaft and an aluminum shaft. Considerable machining is required for both shafts, so Mulligan concludes that it should allocate overhead to these products based on the total hours of machine time used. In May, production of the titanium shaft requires 5,400 hours of machine time, while the aluminum shaft needs 2,600 hours. Thus, 67.5% of the overhead cost pool is allocated to the titanium shafts and 32.5% to the aluminum shafts.

In May, Mulligan accumulates $100,000 of costs in its overhead cost pool, and allocates it between the two product lines with the following journal entry:

	Debit	Credit
Finished goods – Titanium shafts	67,500	
Finished goods – Aluminum shafts	32,500	
Overhead cost pool		100,000

This entry clears out the balance in the overhead cost pool, readying it to accumulate overhead costs in the next reporting period.

If the basis of allocation does not appear correct for certain types of overhead costs, it may make more sense to split the overhead into two or more overhead cost pools, and allocate each cost pool using a different basis of allocation. For example, if warehouse costs are more appropriately allocated based on the square footage consumed by various products, then store warehouse costs in a warehouse overhead cost pool, and allocate these costs based on square footage used.

Thus far, we have assumed that only actual overhead costs incurred are allocated. However, it is also possible to set up a standard overhead rate that is used for multiple reporting periods, based on long-term expectations regarding how much overhead will be incurred and how many units will be produced. If the difference between actual overhead costs incurred and overhead allocated is small, charge the difference to the cost of goods sold. If the amount is material, allocate the difference to both the cost of goods sold and inventory.

EXAMPLE

Mulligan Imports incurs overhead of $93,000, which it stores in an overhead cost pool. Mulligan uses a standard overhead rate of $20 per unit, which approximates its long-term experience with the relationship between overhead costs and production volumes. In September, it produces 4,500 golf club shafts, to which it allocates $90,000 (allocation rate of $20 × 4,500 units). This leaves a difference between overhead incurred and overhead absorbed of $3,000. Given the small size of the variance, Mulligan charges the $3,000 difference to the cost of goods sold, thereby clearing out the overhead cost pool.

A key issue is that overhead allocation is not a precisely-defined science – there is plenty of latitude in how one can go about allocating overhead. The amount of allowable diversity in practice can result in slipshod accounting, so be sure to use a standardized and well-documented method to allocate overhead using the same calculation in every reporting period. This allows for great consistency, which auditors appreciate when they validate the supporting calculations.

The Lower of Cost or Market Rule

The lower of cost or market rule (LCM) states that a business should record the cost of inventory at whichever cost is lower – the original cost or its current market price (hence the name of the rule). More specifically, the rule mandates that the recognized cost of an inventory item should be reduced to a level that does not exceed its replacement cost as derived in an open market. This replacement cost is subject to the following two conditions:

- The recognized cost cannot be greater than the likely selling price minus costs of disposal (known as net realizable value).
- The recognized cost cannot be lower than the net realizable value minus a normal profit percentage.

This situation typically arises when inventory has deteriorated, or has become obsolete, or market prices have declined. The following example illustrates the concept.

EXAMPLE

Mulligan Imports resells five major brands of golf clubs, which are noted in the following table. At the end of its reporting year, Mulligan calculates the upper and lower price boundaries of the LCM rule for each of the products, as noted in the table:

Product	Selling Price	-	Completion/ Selling Cost	=	Upper Price Boundary	-	Normal Profit	=	Lower Price Boundary
Free Swing	$250		$25		$225		$75		$150
Golf Elite	190		19		171		57		114
Hi-Flight	150		15		135		45		90
Iridescent	1,000		100		900		300		600
Titanium	700		70		630		210		420

The normal profit associated with these products is a 30% margin on the original selling price.

The information in the preceding table for the upper and lower price boundaries is then included in the following table, which completes the LCM calculation:

Product	Upper Price Boundary	Lower Price Boundary	Existing Recognized Cost	Replacement Cost*	Market Value**	Lower of Cost or Market
Free Swing	$225	$150	$140	$260	$225	$140
Golf Elite	171	114	180	175	171	171
Hi-Flight	135	90	125	110	110	110
Iridescent	900	600	850	550	600	600
Titanium	630	420	450	390	420	420

* The cost at which the item could be acquired on the open market
** The replacement cost, as limited by the upper and lower pricing boundaries

The LCM decisions noted in the last table are explained as follows:

- *Free Swing clubs.* It would cost Mulligan $260 to replace these clubs, which is above the upper price boundary of $225. This means the market value for the purposes of this calculation is $225. Since the market price is higher than the existing recognized cost, the LCM decision is to leave the recognized cost at $140 each.
- *Golf Elite clubs.* The replacement cost of these clubs has declined to a level below the existing recognized cost, so the LCM decision is to revise the recognized cost to $171. This amount is a small reduction from the unadjusted replacement cost of $175 to the upper price boundary of $171.
- *Hi-Flight clubs.* The replacement cost is less than the recognized cost, and is between the price boundaries. Consequently, there is no need to revise the replacement cost. The LCM decision is to revise the recognized cost to $110.
- *Iridescent clubs.* The replacement cost of these clubs is below the existing recognized cost, but is below the lower price boundary. Thus, the LCM decision is to set the market price at the lower price boundary, which will be the revised cost of the clubs.
- *Titanium clubs.* The replacement cost is much less than the existing recognized cost, but also well below the lower price boundary. The LCM decision is therefore to set the market price at the lower price boundary, which is also the new product cost.

A variation on the LCM rule simplifies matters somewhat, but only if a business is *not* using the last in, first out method or the retail method. The variation states that the measurement can be restricted to just the lower of cost and net realizable value.

If the amount of a write-down caused by the LCM analysis is minor, charge the expense to the cost of goods sold, since there is no reason to separately track the information. If the loss is material, track it in a separate account (especially if such losses are recurring), such as "Loss on LCM adjustment." A sample journal entry for a large adjustment is:

	Debit	Credit
Loss on LCM adjustment	147,000	
Finished goods inventory		147,000

Additional factors to consider when applying the LCM rule are:

- *Analysis by category.* The LCM rule is normally applied to a specific inventory item, but it can be applied to entire inventory categories. In the latter case, an LCM adjustment can be avoided if there is a balance within an inventory category of items having market below cost and in excess of cost.
- *Hedges.* If inventory is being hedged by a fair value hedge, add the effects of the hedge to the cost of the inventory, which frequently eliminates the need for an LCM adjustment.
- *Last in, first out layer recovery.* A write-down to the lower of cost or market can be avoided in an interim period if there is substantial evidence that inventory amounts will be restored by year end, thereby avoiding recognition of an earlier inventory layer.
- *Raw materials.* Do not write down the cost of raw materials if the finished goods in which they are used are expected to sell either at or above their costs.
- *Recovery.* A write-down to the lower of cost or market can be avoided if there is substantial evidence that market prices will increase before the inventory is sold.
- *Sales incentives.* If there are unexpired sales incentives that will result in a loss on the sale of a specific item, this is a strong indicator that there may be an LCM problem with that item.

Tip: When there is an LCM adjustment, it must be taken at once – the expense cannot be recognized over multiple reporting periods.

Work in Process Accounting

Work in process (WIP) is goods in production that have not yet been completed. It typically involves the full amount of raw materials needed for a product, since that is usually included in the product at the beginning of the manufacturing process. During production, the cost of direct labor and overhead is added in proportion to the amount of work done.

In prolonged production operations, there may be a large investment in work in process. Conversely, the production of some products occupies such a brief period of time that the accounting staff does not bother to track it at all; instead, the items in production are considered to still be in the raw materials inventory. In this latter case, inventory essentially shifts directly from the raw materials inventory to the finished goods inventory, with no separate work in process tracking.

Work in process accounting involves tracking the amount of WIP in inventory at the end of an accounting period and assigning a cost to it for inventory valuation purposes, based on the percentage of completion of the WIP items.

In situations where there are many similar products in process, it is more common to follow these steps to account for work in process inventory:

1. *Assign raw materials.* We assume that all raw materials have been assigned to work in process as soon as the work begins. This is reasonable, since many types of production involve kitting all of the materials needed to construct a product and delivering them to the manufacturing area at one time.

2. *Compile labor costs.* The production staff can track the time it works on each product, which is then assigned to the work in process. However, this is painfully time-consuming, so a better approach is to determine the stage of completion of each item in production, and assign a standard labor cost to it based on the stage of completion. This information comes from labor routings that detail the standard amount of labor needed at each stage of the production process.

3. *Assign overhead.* If overhead is assigned based on labor hours, then it is assigned based on the labor information compiled in the preceding step. If overhead is assigned based on some other allocation methodology, then the basis of allocation (such as machine hours used) must first be compiled.

4. *Record the entry.* This journal entry involves shifting raw materials from the raw materials inventory account to the work in process inventory account, shifting direct labor expense into the work in process inventory account, and shifting factory overhead from the overhead cost pool to the WIP inventory account.

It is much easier to use standard costs for work in process accounting. Actual costs are difficult to trace to individual units of production.

The general theme of WIP accounting is to always use the simplest method that the company can convince its auditors to accept, on the grounds that a complex costing methodology will require an inordinate amount of time by the accounting staff, which in turn interferes with the time required to close the books at the end of each month.

Accounting for Obsolete Inventory

Related Podcast Episodes: Episode 225 of the Accounting Best Practices Podcast discusses the reserve for obsolete inventory. It is available at: **www.accountingtools.com/podcasts** or **iTunes**

A materials review board should be used to locate obsolete inventory items. This group reviews inventory usage reports or physically examines the inventory to determine which items should be disposed of. Then review the findings of this group to determine the most likely disposition price of the obsolete items, subtract this projected amount from the book value of the obsolete items, and set aside the difference as a reserve. As the company later disposes of the items, or the estimated amounts to be received from disposition change, adjust the reserve account to reflect these events.

EXAMPLE

Milagro Corporation has $100,000 of excess home coffee roasters it cannot sell. However, it believes there is a market for the roasters through a reseller in China, but only at a sale price of $20,000. Accordingly, the controller recognizes a reserve of $80,000 with the following journal entry:

	Debit	Credit
Cost of goods sold	80,000	
Reserve for obsolete inventory		80,000

After finalizing the arrangement with the Chinese reseller, the actual sale price is only $19,000, so the controller completes the transaction with the following entry, recognizing an additional $1,000 of expense:

	Debit	Credit
Reserve for obsolete inventory	80,000	
Cost of goods sold	1,000	
Inventory		81,000

The example makes inventory obsolescence accounting look simple enough, but it is not. The issues are:

- *Timing.* A company's reported financial results can be improperly altered by changing the timing of the actual dispositions. As an example, if a supervisor knows that he can receive a higher-than-estimated price on the disposition of obsolete inventory, he can either accelerate or delay the sale in order to shift gains into whichever reporting period needs the extra profit.
- *Expense recognition.* Management may be reluctant to suddenly drop a large expense reserve into the financial statements, preferring instead to recognize small incremental amounts which make inventory obsolescence appear to be a minor problem. Since GAAP mandates immediate recognition of any obsolescence as soon as it is detected, the accountant may have a struggle enforcing immediate recognition over the objections of management.
- *Timely reviews.* Inventory obsolescence is a minor issue as long as management reviews inventory on a regular basis, so that the incremental amount of obsolescence detected is small in any given period. However, if

management does not conduct a review for a long time, this allows obsolete inventory to build up to quite impressive proportions, along with an equally impressive amount of expense recognition. To avoid this issue, conduct frequent obsolescence reviews, and maintain a reserve based on historical or expected obsolescence, even if the specific inventory items have not yet been identified.

EXAMPLE

Milagro Corporation sets aside an obsolescence reserve of $25,000 for obsolete roasters. However, in January the purchasing manager knows that the resale price for obsolete roasters has plummeted, so the real reserve should be closer to $35,000, which would call for the immediate recognition of an additional $10,000 of expense. Since this would result in an overall reported loss in Milagro's financial results in January, he waits until April, when Milagro has a very profitable month, and completes the sale at that time, thereby incorrectly delaying the additional obsolescence loss until the point of sale.

Consignment Accounting

Consignment occurs when goods are sent by their owner (the consignor) to an agent (the consignee), who undertakes to sell the goods. The consignor continues to own the goods until they are sold, so the goods appear as inventory in the accounting records of the consignor, not the consignee.

When the consignor sends goods to the consignee, there is no need to create an accounting entry related to the physical movement of goods. It is usually sufficient to record the change in location within the inventory record keeping system of the consignor. In addition, the consignor should consider the following maintenance activities:

- Periodically send a statement to the consignee, stating the inventory that should be on the consignee's premises. The consignee can use this statement to conduct a periodic reconciliation of the actual amount on hand to the consignor's records.
- Request from the consignee a statement of on-hand inventory at the end of each accounting period when the consignor is conducting a physical inventory count. The consignor incorporates this information into its inventory records to arrive at a fully valued ending inventory balance.

From the consignee's perspective, there is no need to record the consigned inventory, since it is owned by the consignor. It may be useful to keep a separate record of all consigned inventory, for reconciliation and insurance purposes.

When the consignee eventually sells the consigned goods, it pays the consignor a pre-arranged sale amount. The consignor records this prearranged amount with a debit to cash and a credit to sales. It also purges the related amount of inventory from its records with a debit to cost of goods sold and a credit to inventory. A profit or loss on the sale transaction will arise from these two entries.

Depending upon the arrangement with the consignee, the consignor may pay a commission to the consignee for making the sale. If so, this is a debit to commission expense and a credit to accounts payable.

From the consignee's perspective, a sale transaction triggers a payment to the consignor for the consigned goods that were sold. There will also be a sale transaction to record the sale of goods to the third party, which is a debit to cash or accounts receivable and a credit to sales.

Goods in Transit

Goods in transit are merchandise and other types of inventory that have left the shipping dock of the seller, but not yet reached the receiving dock of the buyer. Ideally, either the seller or the buyer should record goods in transit in its accounting records. The rule for doing so is based on the shipping terms associated with the goods, which are:

- *FOB shipping point.* If the shipment is designated as freight on board (FOB) shipping point, ownership transfers to the buyer as soon as the shipment departs the seller.
- *FOB destination.* If the shipment is designated as freight on board (FOB) destination, ownership transfers to the buyer as soon as the shipment arrives at the buyer.

EXAMPLE

Armadillo Industries ships $10,000 of merchandise to Antalya Clothiers on November 28. The terms of the delivery are FOB shipping point. Since these terms mean that Antalya takes on ownership of the merchandise as soon as they leave Armadillo's shipping dock, Armadillo should record a sale transaction on November 28, and Antalya should record an inventory receipt on the same date.

Assume the same scenario, but the terms of delivery are now FOB destination, and the shipment does not arrive at Antalya's receiving dock until December 2. In this case, the same transactions occur, but on December 2 instead of November 28. Thus, under the FOB destination shipping scenario, Armadillo does not record a sale transaction until December.

From a practical perspective, the buyer may not have a procedure in place to record inventory until it arrives at the receiving dock. This causes a problem under FOB shipping point terms, because the shipping entity records the transaction at the point of shipment, and the receiving company does not record receipt until the transaction is recorded at its receiving dock - thus, no one records the inventory while it is in transit.

Inventory Disclosures

The following information should be disclosed about a company's inventory practices in its financial statements:

- *Basis*. The basis on which inventories are stated. If there is a significant change in the basis of accounting, the nature of the change and the effect on income (if material) shall be stated.
- *LCM losses*. If there are substantial and unusual losses caused by the lower of cost or market rule, disclose this amount separately in the income statement. This is not a requirement.
- *Goods above cost*. Disclose the particulars concerning any inventory items that have been stated above cost.
- *Goods at sales prices*. Disclose the particulars concerning any inventory items that have been stated at their sales prices.
- *Firm purchase commitments*. Separately state in the income statement the amounts of any net losses that have been accrued on firm purchase commitments.
- *Estimate*. Disclose any significant estimates related to inventory.

Summary

When designing systems that will properly account for inventory, the key consideration is the sheer volume of transactions that must be tracked. It can be extremely difficult to consistently record these transactions with a minimal error rate, so tailor the accounting system to reduce the record keeping work load while still producing results that are in accordance with GAAP. In particular, be watchful for any additional accounting procedures that only refine the inventory information to a small degree, and eliminate or streamline them whenever possible. In essence, this is *the* accounting area in which having a cost-effective recordkeeping system is of some importance.

Chapter 18
Other Assets and Deferred Costs

340 = GAAP codification area for other assets and deferred costs

Introduction

This chapter contains guidance on a number of completely unrelated topics that are not large enough to justify their own subject areas, which may be the reason why they are aggregated into the "other assets" topic within GAAP. In this chapter, we address the accounting for prepaid assets, preproduction costs for long-term supply arrangements, capitalized advertising costs, and insurance contracts that do not transfer risk. Also, note the accounting for advertising reimbursements that is located within the discussion of capitalized advertising costs. The guidance in this chapter applies to all entities.

Related Chapters

See the following chapters for discussions of issues related to other assets and deferred costs:

- *Other Expenses*. Covers the accounting treatment for most types of advertising expenditures.
- *Research and Development*. Covers the treatment of research and development costs related to the development of tools and similar items.

Overview of Other Assets and Deferred Costs

Since the component parts of this chapter are so unrelated to each other, we have separated the discussion of each one into a different sub-section, as noted below.

Prepaid Expenses

There is a brief discussion of prepaid expenses in GAAP that appears more concerned with which items to treat as prepaid expenses than the proper accounting for these items. Common practice is to defer recognition of these items until consumed, at which point they are charged to expense. The following items are specifically noted as potentially being treated as prepaid expenses, as long as they are paid in advance.

Advertising service not yet received	Interest	Taxes
Insurance	Operating supplies	Unused royalties
	Rents	

Preproduction Costs for Long-Term Supply Arrangements

A business may incur preproduction costs to tool up for what are expected to be long-term supply arrangements with their customers. These costs may include the design and development of tools, molds, production processes, and other items. There are two situations in this area that call for differing accounting treatments:

- *Supplier ownership.* Preproduction costs for long-term supply arrangements that are incurred by the supplier should be charged to expense as incurred, including any related research and development costs. However, if costs are incurred to create or acquire fixed assets that will be used for long-term supply arrangements, capitalize these expenditures and depreciate them over the useful lives of the assets.
- *Customer ownership.* If the supplier expends funds to design and develop molds, dies, and other tools that will be owned by the customer, capitalize the cost only if the arrangement gives the supplier the noncancelable right to use the items over the term of the supply arrangement (in which case the cost is depreciated). If there is no noncancelable right, charge these costs to expense as incurred.

EXAMPLE

Armadillo Industries enters into a long-term arrangement with a supplier of titanium parts, in which Armadillo agrees to pay the supplier $1,000 per part for the first 1,000 parts produced and $250 for every part thereafter. The contract also states that if fewer than 1,000 parts are produced, Armadillo will reimburse the supplier for all development costs incurred, up to a maximum of $750,000 that is reduced by $750 for each part produced under the arrangement.

After six months, the supplier has delivered 800 parts and the arrangement is terminated. This means that Armadillo still owes $150,000 to the supplier for development costs not yet reimbursed. Since the amount of reimbursement can be easily measured under this arrangement, the supplier can initially recognize a maximum of $750,000 of its costs incurred as an asset.

Capitalized Advertising Costs

There are cases when a business engages in direct-response advertising, where the recognition of some costs can be deferred. Examples of costs that may be eligible for deferral are the third-party billings and in-house labor costs associated with idea development, writing ad copy, artwork, printing magazine space, and mailing.

This situation arises when there is a reliable and demonstrated relationship between costs incurred and future benefits achieved. For example, a company may have a history of obtaining a 1% response rate on all direct mail pieces mailed out. Thus, the cost of obtaining that 1% response rate can be associated with the total cost of the mailing.

The expense recognition for direct-response advertising can be deferred if both of the following conditions are met:

- The advertising is intended to generate sales for which customers can be shown to have responded specifically to the advertising by tracking the names of respondents and the specific advertising that triggered their response, such as a coupon or response card; and
- The advertising results in probable future benefits, which requires persuasive evidence of historical patterns of similar results for the business (historical patterns for the industry as a whole are not allowed). Test market results can be used.

To defer expenses related to direct-response advertising, create a separate cost pool for each significant advertising effort, so that costs can be recognized in direct proportion to the receipt of related customer sales. The costs in each pool are then recognized based on the proportion of actual revenues generated by the campaign to the total revenues expected from the campaign. The estimated amount of total revenues to be received may change over time, which can alter the remaining amortization calculation; prior period results are not altered if there is a subsequent change in the estimated amount of total revenues to be received.

If the carrying amount of advertising costs exceeds the associated amount of remaining net revenues yet to be realized, charge the excess amount of advertising costs to expense in the current period.

This guidance is only relevant to those situations where advertising is directed at an audience that can be shown to have responded specifically to the advertising. For all other types of advertising, see the Other Expenses chapter.

Tip: Though GAAP allows for the deferral of direct-response advertising costs, these costs can still be charged to expense as incurred, which is much easier than complying with the onerous GAAP requirements associated with delayed expense recognition.

There may also be situations where a company reimburses other parties (usually its distributors) for some or all of their advertising expenditures related to the products or services of the company. This means that the company may be recognizing the revenues associated with the advertising reimbursements prior to the reimbursements (since there is a timing delay between when the expenditures are made by other parties and when the company reimburses them). The proper accounting in these situations is to accrue the reimbursements in the periods when the associated revenues are generated.

There may be situations where a company invests in tangible assets that will be used for multiple advertising campaigns, such as a show booth or a billboard. In these instances, it is acceptable to capitalize the cost of the assets and depreciate them over their expected useful lives.

Insurance Contracts that Do Not Transfer Insurance Risk

The underlying premise of an insurance contract is that it transfers risk from one party to another. The transfer of risk must encompass both timing risk and underwriting risk. If these types of risk are not shifted from one party to the other, then payments made under the contract are accounted for as deposits. Examples of situations where risk is not transferred include:

- When an insurance contract provides for experience adjustments
- When the insurer can delay the reimbursement of losses

Under deposit accounting, record a deposit or liability based on the amount of consideration paid or received, minus any premiums or fees to be retained by the insurer. This accounting ignores any experience under the insurance contract. Subsequent accounting can follow one of the two following paths, depending upon the nature of the underlying insurance contract:

- *Transfers only timing risk or no risk.* Adjust the amount of the deposit with an effective yield calculation that reflects payments to date and expected future payments to date. On an ongoing basis, adjust the deposit amount to be the amount that would have been stated on the balance sheet date if the latest effective yield had been applied since the inception of the contract. If there is a significant change in actual or expected cash flows, it could mean that the contract should actually be accounted for using the following method (since it may contain underwriting risk).
- *Transfers only underwriting risk.* Measure the deposit based on the unexpired portion of the insurance coverage. Once there is a reimbursable loss, measure the deposit based on the present value of expected future cash flows, plus the unexpired portion of the coverage.

For these calculations, the insured entity should use as a discount rate the current interest rate on U.S. government obligations with similar cash flow characteristics, adjusted for default risk. The insuring entity should use as a discount rate the current interest rate on U.S. government obligations with similar cash flow characteristics. Establish these rates as of the date of each loss incurred, and do not alter them for the remaining life of the contract. However, if there are numerous losses, it is permissible to establish an average rate.

EXAMPLE

Armadillo Industries enters into an insurance contract that does not transfer timing risk or underwriting risk. The company pays a premium of $1,000 for a coverage period of one year, and expects to make recoveries under the contract of $263.80 at the end of each year for five years. The implicit interest rate is 10%. As shown in the following table, cash receipts reduce the carrying amount of the deposit, while interest income increases the deposit balance.

Description	10% Interest Income	Cash Recoveries*	Deposit Balance
Initial payment			$1,000
Year 1	$100		1,100
End of year 1		-$264	836
Year 2	84		920
End of year 2		-264	656
Year 3	66		722
End of year 3		-264	458
Year 4	46		504
End of year 4		-264	240
Year 5	24		264
End of year 5		-264	0
	$319	-$1,319	

* Rounded up from $263.80 to $264

Other Assets and Deferred Costs Disclosures

The presentation of other assets and deferred costs in the financial statements, as well as any additional disclosures, are broken out in this section by topic.

Preproduction Costs for Long-Term Supply Arrangements

The Securities and Exchange Commission requires that publicly-held companies disclose their accounting policy for pre-production design and development costs. In addition, they must disclose the aggregate amount of the following:

- Assets recognized for which there is contractual reimbursement
- Assets recognized by the supplier that are molds, dies, and other tools
- Assets recognized but not owned by the supplier that are molds, dies, and other tools

Capitalized Advertising Costs

If costs associated with direct-mail campaigns are capitalized, report them in the balance sheet as assets, net of any accumulated amortization.

Disclose the following information about capitalized advertising costs in the notes accompanying the financial statements:

- The amount of direct-response advertising reported as assets
- The accounting policy related to the treatment of direct-response advertising
- The period over which capitalized direct-response advertising is amortized
- The total amount of advertising expense recognized in each period, as well as any write-down to net realizable value
- The total amount of advertising classified as assets in the balance sheet

---

EXAMPLE

Armadillo Industries discloses the following information about its advertising:

Armadillo capitalizes its direct-response advertising and amortizes this cost over the expected period of future benefits.

Armadillo's direct-response advertising consists of targeted mailings that include order coupons for the company's products. The capitalized cost of the advertising is amortized over the two-month period following issuance of each mailing.

At December 31, 20X5, $250,000 of advertising was reported as assets. The advertising expense for the year ended December 31, 20X5 was $1,000,000, including $100,000 for amounts written down to net realizable value.

Insurance Contracts that Do Not Transfer Insurance Risk

There are three issues related to insurance contracts that impact the presentation of information in the financial statements, which are:

- *Deposits*. Report deposit assets and liabilities separately in the balance sheet. Netting of the amounts is not permitted, unless there is an explicit right of offset.
- *Deposit carrying amount*. Report changes in the carrying amount of the deposit as interest income or expense, when the underlying contract only transfers timing risk, or no risk at all.
- *Loss offset*. Record changes in the carrying amount of the deposit as an offset against the recorded loss that will be reimbursed under a contract that only transfers underwriting risk. This treatment does not include changes in the deposit caused by the unexpired portion of the coverage provided, which is accounted for as an adjustment to incurred losses by the insurer, and as an expense by the insured.

If insurance contracts are accounted for as deposits, describe the contracts accounted for in this manner, as well as the separate amounts of deposit assets and deposit liabilities reported in the balance sheet.

If an insurer has insurance contracts that only transfer underwriting risk, it should disclose the following information about these contracts:

- The present value of expected recoveries to be reimbursed under contracts recorded as an adjustment to incurred losses.
- Adjustments of amounts previously recognized for expected recoveries. Separately disclose all elements of these adjustments.
- The amortization expense caused by the expiration of contract coverage.

Summary

Realistically, none of the topics in this chapter will find broad application, other than the discussion of prepaid expenses. Instead, the topics are designed for very specific circumstances that the typical accountant may never see. In the case of capitalized advertising, the accounting associated with doing so is sufficiently time-consuming to keep any reasonably efficient accountant from wanting to engage in it; the result is that few organizations will want to capitalize their advertising costs. The only practical guidance given in any of the subject areas concerns preproduction costs for long-term supply arrangements, since it allows for the efficient deferral of costs in a manner that is easily managed.

Chapter 19
Intangibles – Goodwill and Other

Introduction

A business may record goodwill as part of a business combination, to account for the difference between the fair value of all other assets and liabilities and the purchase price. The initial recognition of goodwill is addressed in the Business Combinations chapter. In this chapter, we deal with the subsequent accounting for goodwill, and also address the accounting for and disclosure of the costs of internally developed goodwill, other intangible assets, internal-use software, and website development costs. The guidance provided in this chapter applies to all entities.

Related Podcast Episodes: Episodes 136, 146, and 175 of the Accounting Best Practices Podcast discuss goodwill impairment testing, intangible asset impairment testing, and goodwill amortization, respectively. They are available at: **www.accountingtools.com/podcasts** or **iTunes**

Related Chapters

See the following chapters for discussions of issues related to intangibles:

- *Business Combinations*. Describes the initial accounting for goodwill that is generated by an acquisition.
- *Property, Plant, and Equipment*. Provides a comparative view of fixed asset accounting, which is useful if an entity is accounting for intangible assets.
- *Segment Reporting*. Describes how segments are determined for reporting purposes.

Goodwill

Goodwill is a common byproduct of a business combination, where the purchase price paid for the acquiree is higher than the fair values of the identifiable assets acquired. After goodwill has initially been recorded as an asset, do not amortize it. Instead, test it for impairment at the reporting unit level. Impairment exists when the carrying amount of the goodwill is greater than its implied fair value.

A reporting unit is defined as an operating segment or one level below an operating segment. At a more practical level, a reporting unit is a separate business for which the parent compiles financial information, and for which management reviews the results. If several components of an operating segment have similar economic characteristics, they can be combined into a reporting unit. In a smaller business, it is entirely possible that one reporting unit could be an entire operating segment, or even the entire entity.

The examination of goodwill for the possible existence of impairment involves a multi-step process, which is:

1. *Assess qualitative factors.* Review the situation to see if it is necessary to conduct further impairment testing, which is considered to be a likelihood of more than 50% that impairment has occurred, based on an assessment of relevant events and circumstances. Examples of relevant events and circumstances that make it more likely that impairment is present are the deterioration of macroeconomic conditions, increased costs, declining cash flows, possible bankruptcy, a change in management, and a sustained decrease in share price. If impairment appears to be likely, continue with the impairment testing process. The accountant can choose to bypass this step and proceed straight to the next step.

2. *Identify potential impairment.* Compare the fair value of the reporting unit to its carrying amount. If the fair value is greater than the carrying amount of the reporting unit, there is no goodwill impairment, and there is no need to proceed to the next step. If the carrying amount exceeds the fair value of the reporting unit, recognize an impairment loss in the amount of the difference, up to a maximum of the entire carrying amount (i.e., the carrying amount of goodwill can only be reduced to zero). One should consider the income tax effect from any tax deductible goodwill on the carrying amount of the entity (or the reporting unit), if applicable, when measuring the goodwill impairment loss.

These steps are illustrated in the following flowchart.

Goodwill Impairment Decision Steps

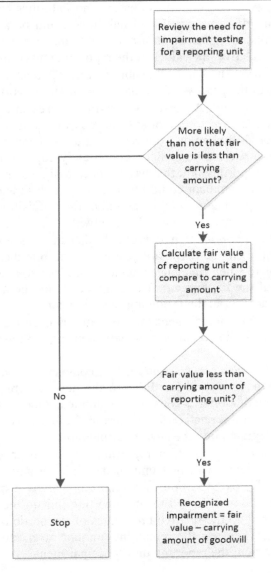

The fair value of the reporting unit is assumed to be the price that the company would receive if it were to sell the unit in an orderly transaction (i.e., not a rushed sale) between market participants. Other alternatives to the quoted market price for a reporting unit may be acceptable, such as a valuation based on multiples of earnings or revenue.

The following additional issues are associated with goodwill impairment testing:

- *Asset and liability assignment.* Assign acquired assets and liabilities to a reporting unit if they relate to the operations of the unit *and* they will be considered in the determination of reporting unit fair value. If these criteria can be met, even corporate-level assets and liabilities can be assigned to a reporting unit. If some assets and liabilities could be assigned to multiple reporting units, assign them in a reasonable manner (such as an allocation based on the relative fair values of the reporting units), consistently applied.

- *Asset recognition*. It is not allowable to recognize an additional intangible asset as part of the process of evaluating goodwill impairment.
- *Goodwill assignment*. All of the goodwill acquired in a business combination must be assigned to one or several reporting units as of the acquisition date, and not shifted among the reporting units thereafter. The assignment should be in a reasonable manner, consistently applied. If goodwill is to be assigned to a reporting unit that has not been assigned any acquired assets or liabilities, the assignment could be based on the difference between the fair value of the reporting unit before and after the acquisition, which represents the improvement in value caused by goodwill.
- *Impairment estimation*. If it is probable that there is goodwill impairment and the amount can be reasonably estimated, despite the testing process not being complete when financial statements are issued, recognize the estimated amount of the impairment. The estimate should be adjusted to the final impairment amount in the following reporting period.
- *No reversal*. Once impairment of goodwill has been recorded, it cannot be reversed, even if the condition originally causing the impairment is no longer present.
- *Reporting structure reorganization*. If a company reorganizes its reporting units, reassign assets and liabilities to the new reporting units based on a reasonable methodology, consistently applied. Goodwill should be reassigned based on the relative fair values of the portions of the old reporting unit to be integrated into the new reporting units.
- *Reporting unit disposal*. If a reporting unit is disposed of, include the goodwill associated with that unit in determining any gain or loss on the transaction. If only a portion of a reporting unit is disposed of, associate some of the goodwill linked to the reporting unit to the portion being disposed of, based on the relative fair values of the portions being disposed of and retained. Then test the remaining amount of goodwill assigned to the residual portion of the reporting unit for impairment.

EXAMPLE

Armadillo Industries is selling off a portion of a reporting unit for $500,000. The remaining portion of the unit, which Armadillo is retaining, has a fair value of $1,500,000. Based on these values, 25% of the goodwill associated with the reporting unit should be included in the carrying amount of the portion being sold.

- *Reporting unit disposal, minority owner.* If a company has less than complete ownership of a reporting unit, attribute any impairment losses to the parent entity and the noncontrolling interest in the reporting unit on a rational basis. However, if the reporting unit includes goodwill that is attributable to the parent entity, then attribute the loss entirely to the parent, not the noncontrolling interest.
- *Subsidiary goodwill impairment testing.* Any goodwill recognized by a corporate subsidiary should be dealt with in the same manner described elsewhere in this section for the impairment of goodwill. If there is a goodwill impairment loss at the subsidiary level, then also test the reporting unit of which that subsidiary is a part for goodwill impairment, if the triggering event is more likely than not to have also reduced the fair value of that reporting unit below its carrying amount.
- *Taxable transaction.* As part of the fair value estimation, determine whether the reporting unit could be bought or sold in a taxable or non-taxable transaction, since this affects its fair value.

Tip: From a practical perspective, it is almost always easier to estimate the fair value of the reporting unit based on a multiple of its earnings or revenues, though this should only be done when there are comparable operations whose fair values and related multiples are known, and which can therefore be used as the basis for a fair value estimate of the reporting unit.

Impairment testing is to be conducted at annual intervals. The impairment test may be conducted at any time of the year, provided that the test is conducted thereafter at the same time of the year. If the company is comprised of different reporting units, there is no need to test them all at the same time.

Tip: Each reporting unit is probably subject to a certain amount of seasonal activity. If so, select a period when activity levels are at their lowest to conduct impairment testing, so it does not conflict with other activities. Impairment testing should not coincide with the annual audit.

It may be necessary to conduct more frequent impairment testing if there is an event that makes it more likely than not that the fair value of a reporting unit has been reduced below its carrying amount. Examples of triggering events are a lawsuit, regulatory changes, the loss of key employees, and the expectation that a reporting unit will be sold.

The information used for an impairment test can be quite detailed. To improve the efficiency of the testing process, it is permissible to carry forward this information to the next year, as long as the following criteria have been met:

- There has been no significant change in the assets and liabilities comprising the reporting unit.

- There was a substantial excess of fair value over the carrying amount in the last impairment test.
- The likelihood of the fair value being less than the carrying amount is remote.

As an additional note for publicly-held companies that report segment information, the asset, liability, and goodwill allocations used for goodwill impairment testing do not have to be the same as the amounts stated in segment reports. However, aligning the two sets of information will make it easier to conduct both impairment testing and segment reporting.

Goodwill Amortization

The effort required to monitor the goodwill asset is considered to be excessive for private companies, while the usefulness of goodwill information is also considered to be limited. Consequently, a private company is allowed to amortize goodwill on a straight-line basis over a ten-year useful life. The entity may amortize goodwill over a shorter period if it can demonstrate that a shorter useful life is more appropriate. If an organization chooses to amortize goodwill, it must still test the goodwill asset for impairment at either the entity or reporting unit level. This test is triggered when there is an event that indicates a possible decline in the entity's or reporting unit's fair value to a point below its carrying amount. If an impairment loss is recognized, then any remaining carrying amount is to be amortized over its remaining useful life.

The amortization of goodwill will eventually reduce the carrying amount of an organization's goodwill asset so much that goodwill impairment will be quite unlikely, thereby reducing the need to spend time on such testing.

General Intangibles Other than Goodwill

In general, costs should be recognized as incurred when they are related to internally developing, maintaining, or restoring intangible assets that have any of the following characteristics:

- There is no specifically identifiable asset
- The useful life is indeterminate
- The cost is inherent in the continuing operation of the business

Conversely, it is possible to recognize an acquired intangible item as an asset. If a group of assets is acquired in a transaction that is not defined as a business combination, the acquisition cost should be entirely allocated to the individual acquired assets, based on their relative fair values. In such an arrangement, goodwill is not recognized.

If a business acquires an intangible asset specifically to deny its use to others (a *defensive intangible asset*), treat the asset as a separate unit of accounting. Assign the asset a useful life that reflects the period over which the company will benefit from the denial of use of the asset to others; this period is essentially the period over which the fair value of the asset will decline.

The general accounting for an intangible asset is to record the asset as a long-term asset and amortize the asset over its useful life, along with regular impairment reviews. The accounting is essentially the same as for other types of fixed assets (see the Property, Plant and Equipment chapter). The key differences between the accounting for tangible and intangible fixed assets are:

- *Amortization*. If an intangible asset has a useful life, amortize the cost of the asset over that useful life, less any residual value. Amortization is the same as depreciation, except that amortization is applied only to intangible assets. In this context, useful life refers to the time period over which an asset is expected to enhance future cash flows.
- *Asset combinations*. If several intangible assets are operated as a single asset, combine them for the purposes of impairment testing. This treatment is probably not suitable if they independently generate cash flows, would be sold separately, or are used by different asset groups.
- *Residual value*. If any residual value is expected following the useful life of an intangible asset, subtract it from the carrying amount of the asset for the purposes of calculating amortization. Assume that the residual value will always be zero for intangible assets, unless there is a commitment from another party to acquire the asset at the end of its useful life *and* the residual value can be determined by reference to transactions in an existing market *and* that market is expected to be in existence when the useful life of the asset ends.

EXAMPLE

Armadillo Industries purchases a patent from a third party. The remaining life of the patent's coverage of a key piece of production technology is eight years. Armadillo obtains a written commitment from a supplier to buy the patent in two years for 75% of the $100,000 price paid by Armadillo for the patent. Armadillo intends to sell the patent to the supplier in two years.

Based on this information, Armadillo should amortize $25,000 of the purchase price over the two years that the company expects to retain ownership of the patent.

- *Useful life*. An intangible asset may have an indefinite useful life. If so, do not initially amortize it, but review the asset at regular intervals to see if a useful life can then be determined. If so, test the asset for impairment and begin amortizing it. The reverse can also occur, where an asset with a useful life is judged to now have an indefinite useful life; if so, stop amortizing the asset and test it for impairment. Examples of intangible assets that have indefinite useful lives are taxicab licenses, broadcasting rights, and trademarks.

EXAMPLE

Milford Sound acquires a license to broadcast in the Milwaukee area for five years. The license is automatically renewable every five years, unless Milford violates a number of Federal Communications Commission rules. There is no limit to the number of renewals that Milford can obtain to the license period, and Milford intends to renew the license in perpetuity. Despite the impact of music streaming over the Internet, the cash flows associated with the license are not expected to decline appreciably in the foreseeable future. Thus, the cash flows that Milford expects to realize from the license should continue indefinitely. The license can be treated as an intangible asset having an indefinite useful life.

- *Useful life revisions.* The duration of the remaining useful lives of all intangible assets should be regularly reviewed, and adjusted if circumstances warrant the change. This will require a change in the remaining amount of amortization recognized per period.
- *Life extensions.* It is possible that the life of some intangible assets may be extended a considerable amount, usually based on contract extensions. If so, estimate the useful life of an asset based on the full duration of expected useful life extensions. These presumed extensions may result in an asset having an indefinite useful life, which avoids amortization.

EXAMPLE

Milford Sound entered into a license for noise cancelling technology three years ago, and plans to renew the license for an additional three-year period. However, management is aware of the development of a new technology that will probably render the current noise cancelling technology obsolete in two years. Milford had previously been amortizing the cost of the license over each three-year licensing period. Given the expected change in technology, management elects to amortize the cost of the license extension over just two years.

- *Straight-line amortization.* Use the straight-line basis of amortization to reduce the carrying amount of an intangible asset, unless the pattern of benefit usage associated with the asset suggests a different form of amortization.
- *Impairment testing.* An intangible asset is subject to impairment testing in the same manner as tangible assets. In short, recognize impairment if the carrying amount of the asset is greater than its fair value, and the amount is not recoverable. Once recognized, the impairment cannot be reversed.
- *Research and development assets.* If intangible assets are acquired through a business combination for use in research and development activities, initially treat them as having indefinite useful lives, and regularly test them for impairment. Once the related research and development activities have been completed or abandoned, charge them to expense.

> **Tip:** The usage pattern of nearly all intangible assets will suggest the use of straight-line amortization. Since this is also the simplest amortization method, use it unless the underlying usage pattern of an asset is substantially different.

Internal-Use Software

Companies routinely develop software for internal use, and want to understand how these development costs are to be accounted for. Software is considered to be for internal use when it has been acquired or developed *only* for the internal needs of a business. Examples of situations where software is considered to be developed for internal use are:

- Accounting systems
- Cash management tracking systems
- Membership tracking systems
- Production automation systems

Further, there can be no reasonably possible plan to market the software outside of the company. A market feasibility study is not considered a reasonably possible marketing plan. However, a history of selling software that had initially been developed for internal use creates a reasonable assumption that the latest internal-use product will also be marketed for sale outside of the company.

The accounting for internal-use software varies, depending upon the stage of completion of the project. The relevant accounting is:

- *Stage 1: Preliminary*. All costs incurred during the preliminary stage of a development project should be charged to expense as incurred. This stage is considered to include making decisions about the allocation of resources, determining performance requirements, conducting supplier demonstrations, evaluating technology, and supplier selection.
- *Stage 2: Application development*. Capitalize the costs incurred to develop internal-use software, which may include coding, hardware installation, and testing. Any costs related to data conversion, user training, administration, and overhead should be charged to expense as incurred. Only the following costs can be capitalized:
  - Materials and services consumed in the development effort, such as third party development fees, software purchase costs, and travel costs related to development work.
  - The payroll costs of those employees directly associated with software development.
  - The capitalization of interest costs incurred to fund the project.
- *Stage 3. Post-implementation*. Charge all post-implementation costs to expense as incurred. Samples of these costs are training and maintenance costs.

Any allowable capitalization of costs should begin *after* the preliminary stage has been completed, management commits to funding the project, it is probable that the project will be completed, and the software will be used for its intended function.

The capitalization of costs should end when all substantial testing has been completed. If it is no longer probable that a project will be completed, stop capitalizing the costs associated with it, and conduct impairment testing on the costs already capitalized. The cost at which the asset should then be carried is the lower of its carrying amount or fair value (less costs to sell). Unless there is evidence to the contrary, the usual assumption is that uncompleted software has no fair value.

A business may purchase software for internal use. If the purchase price of this software includes other elements, such as training and maintenance fees, only capitalize that portion of the purchase price that relates to the software itself.

In addition, any later upgrades of the software can be capitalized, but only if it is probable that extra system functionality will result from the upgrade. The costs of maintaining the system should be charged to expense as incurred. If the maintenance is provided by a third party and payment is made in advance for the services of that party, amortize the cost of the maintenance over the service period.

Once costs have been capitalized, amortize them over the expected useful life of the software. This is typically done on a straight-line basis, unless another method more clearly reflects the expected usage pattern of the software. Amortization should begin when a software module is ready for its intended use, which is considered to be when all substantial system testing has been completed. If a software module cannot function unless other modules are also completed, do not begin amortization until the related modules are complete.

It may be necessary to regularly reassess the useful life of the software for amortization purposes, since technological obsolescence tends to shorten it.

The capitalized cost of internal-use software should be routinely reviewed for impairment, as described in the Property, Plant, and Equipment chapter. The following are all indicators of the possible presence of asset impairment:

- The software is not expected to be of substantive use
- The manner in which the software was originally intended to be used has now changed
- The software is to be significantly altered
- The development cost of the software significantly exceeded original expectations

Once a business has developed software for internal use, management may decide to market it for external use by third parties. If so, the proceeds from software licensing, net of selling costs, should be applied against the carrying amount of the software asset. For the purposes of this topic, selling costs are considered to include commissions, software reproduction costs, servicing obligations, warranty costs, and installation costs. The business should not recognize a profit on sales of the software until the application of net sales to the carrying amount of the software asset have reduced the carrying amount to zero. The business can recognize all further proceeds as revenue.

Website Development Costs

A company may allocate funds to the development of a company website, in such areas as coding, graphics design, the addition of content, and site operation. The accounting for website development varies, depending upon the stage of completion of the project. The relevant accounting is:

- *Stage 1: Preliminary*. Charge all site planning costs to expense as incurred. This stage is considered to include project planning, the determination of site functionality, hardware identification, technology usability, alternatives analysis, supplier demonstrations, and legal considerations.
- *Stage 2: Application development and infrastructure*. The accounting matches what was just described in the last section for internal-use software. In essence, capitalize these costs. More specifically, capitalize the cost of obtaining and registering an Internet domain, as well as the procurement of software tools, code customization, web page development, related hardware, hypertext link creation, and site testing. Also, if a site upgrade provides new functions or features to the website, capitalize these costs.
- *Stage 3: Graphics development*. For the purposes of this topic, graphics are considered to be software, and so are capitalized, unless they are to be marketed externally. Graphics development includes site page design and layout.
- *Stage 4: Content development*. Charge data conversion costs to expense as incurred, as well as the costs to input content into a website.
- *Stage 5: Site operation*. The costs to operate a website are the same as any other operating costs, and so should be charged to expense as incurred. The treatment of selected operating costs associated with a website are:
  - o Charge website hosting fees to expense over the period benefited by the hosting
  - o Charge search engine registration fees to expense as incurred, since they are advertising costs

Intangibles Disclosures

A company that has recognized goodwill as an asset should disclose the following information in its financial statements:

- *Estimated impairment*. If a company recognizes an estimated amount of impairment in its financial statements, disclose the fact that the amount recognized is an estimate. In later periods, disclose the nature and amount of any significant adjustments made to the initial estimate.
- *Goodwill carrying amount*. Disclose a reconciliation of changes in the carrying amount of goodwill during the period, showing the beginning gross

amount and accumulated impairment losses, additional goodwill recognition, adjustments for deferred tax assets, goodwill related to assets held for sale, impairment losses, other changes, and the ending gross amount and accumulated impairment losses.

- *Goodwill by segment.* If a company is reporting segment information (which is required for publicly-held companies), disclose the amount of goodwill in total, and for each reportable segment, as well as significant changes in the allocation of goodwill by segment.
- *Goodwill impairment activity.* If there has been goodwill impairment, present the related losses in a separate line item in the income statement, positioned before the subtotal of income from continuing operations. If the goodwill is associated with a discontinued operation, then present the loss, net of taxes, in a line item in the discontinued operations section of the income statement.
- *Goodwill impairment loss.* If there is a goodwill impairment loss, disclose the facts and circumstances associated with the loss, the amount of the loss, and how the fair value of the related reporting unit was determined.
- *Goodwill presentation.* State the aggregate amount of goodwill in a separate line item in the balance sheet. If goodwill is being amortized, then this amount should be presented net of the amortization.
- *Unallocated goodwill.* If any goodwill has not been allocated to a reporting unit, disclose the unallocated amount and the reasons why no allocation has been made.

EXAMPLE

Armadillo Industries discloses the following information about changes in the carrying amount of its goodwill for the year ended December 31, 20X4:

(000s)	Body Armor Segment	High Pressure Container Segment	Total
Balance as of January 1, 20X4			
Goodwill	$5,700	$4,200	$9,900
Accumulated impairment losses	-400	-170	-570
	5,300	4,030	9,330
Goodwill acquired during year	360	1,080	1,440
Impairment losses	-250	--	-250
Goodwill written off related to disposal of business unit	--	-200	-200
Balance as of December 31, 20X4			
Goodwill	6,060	5,080	11,140
Accumulated impairment losses	-650	-170	-820
	$5,410	$4,910	$10,320

The company tests the body armor segment in the second quarter of each year, which is the low point in the company's sales cycle. Due to an increase in lower-priced competition from Asian manufacturers, management revised its estimate of future cash flows likely to be generated by the body armor segment, and concluded that a goodwill impairment of $250,000 should be recognized. The fair value of the body armor reporting unit was derived using the expected present value of future cash flows.

A company that has recognized other intangible assets should disclose the following information in its financial statements:

- *Intangible presentation.* Aggregate all recognized intangible assets into one line in the balance sheet (though the breakdown of this information into additional lines is allowed).
- *Amortization expense.* Report amortization expense within the continuing operations section of the income statement.
- *Impairment losses.* Report intangible asset impairment losses within the continuing operations section of the income statement.
- *Acquired intangibles.* If intangible assets are acquired, disclose the following:
  - The amount assigned to the major intangible asset classes
  - The amount of any residual value (if significant) by asset class and in total
  - The weighted average amortization period by asset class
  - The total amount of intangible assets with indefinite lives, by asset class
  - The research and development asset cost acquired and written off (other than through a business combination), and the income statement line item where this information is located
  - The weighted-average period before the next terms extension, by asset class, for those assets having renewal terms

When a company presents a balance sheet as part of its financial statements, it should also disclose the following information:

- *Amortization expense.* Note the total amortization expense for the period.
- *Assets with indefinite lives.* List the total carrying amount of all intangible assets that are not subject to amortization, as well as the same information by asset class.
- *Extended assets.* For those assets whose lives have been renewed or extended in the period, state the amount of renewal costs capitalized by asset class, as well as the weighted-average period before the next renewal, by asset class.
- *Future amortization.* State the estimated amount of amortization expense in each of the next five fiscal years.

- *Goodwill amortization.* If the organization engages in goodwill amortization, disclose the gross carrying amounts of goodwill, accumulated amortization, and accumulated impairment losses, as well as the aggregate amortization expense for the period. Additional disclosure is required for held-for-sale assets.
- *Impairment losses.* For each impairment loss recognized, disclose the period of recognition, the nature of the asset, the reasons for impairment, the amount of the loss, the method used to determine fair value, the income statement line item into which the loss is aggregated, and the segment in which the impaired asset is reported (only applicable to publicly-held companies).
- *Intangible asset totals.* State the gross carrying amount and related accumulated amortization for all intangible assets, and for each major asset class.
- *Life extension policy.* Describe the company policy for how it treats any costs incurred to renew the life of an intangible asset.
- *Renewal impact on cash flows.* Provide sufficient information for users to judge how cash flows will be affected by the ability of the business to renew the contractual life of an asset.

EXAMPLE

Armadillo Industries discloses the following information related to its acquisition of intangible assets:

Note X: Acquired Intangible Assets

(000s)	As of December 31, 20X1	
	Gross Carrying Amount	Accumulated Amortization
Amortized intangible assets		
Customer list	$2,130	-$720
Internet domain names	1,600	-870
Trademarks	420	-380
Total	$4,150	-$1,970
Unamortized intangible assets		
Trade secrets	$4,350	
Trademarks	1,880	
Total	$6,230	

Aggregate amortization expense:	
For the year ended 12/31/20X1	$395
Estimated amortization expense:	
For the year ended 12/31/20X2	580
For the year ended 12/31/20X3	520
For the year ended 12/31/20X4	490
For the year ended 12/31/20X5	370

Summary

The testing for goodwill impairment can be both time-consuming and expensive, so take full advantage of the option to avoid testing by reviewing qualitative factors to see if there is a low likelihood of impairment.

The accountant should be aware of how the capitalization of software for internal use or for the development of a website can skew the results reported by a business. If a company is developing a massive in-house system, the amount of costs capitalized may represent a significant proportion of all expenditures, resulting in financial statements that may reveal a profit, even while the business is hemorrhaging cash to pay for the development effort. If this is the case, consider full disclosure of the situation in the company's financial statements, as well as a narrow interpretation of the accounting standards to charge as much of these expenditures as possible to expense as incurred.

Chapter 20
Property, Plant, and Equipment

360 = GAAP codification area for property, plant, and equipment

Introduction

The accounting for property, plant, and equipment is not especially difficult in most respects, but does require a number of separate accounting transactions over the life of an asset, including acquisition, depreciation, and disposal. It is also necessary to be aware of other concepts that arise less frequently, including interest capitalization, asset retirement obligations (AROs), and impairment. The interest capitalization and ARO concepts are large enough to be treated separately in other chapters. All other concepts are addressed in the following sections.

Related Podcast Episodes: Episodes 122 and 139 of the Accounting Best Practices Podcast discuss fixed asset disposals and a lean system for fixed assets, respectively. They are available at: **www.accountingtools.com/podcasts** or **iTunes**

The "fixed asset" name is used in this chapter to describe the group of assets that generate economic benefits over a long period of time. The GAAP codification uses a somewhat longer name for the same assets, which is "property, plant, and equipment" (PP&E). The PP&E term is not used in this book for two reasons:

- The name describes a subset of all fixed assets, since it only implies the existence of land, buildings, and machinery.
- The PP&E name is simply too long.

Thus, we are using the more all-encompassing "fixed assets" term throughout the chapter.

Related Chapters

See the following chapters for discussions of issues related to fixed assets:

- *Asset Retirement and Environmental Obligations.* Covers the liabilities associated with the retirement of assets.
- *Interest.* Covers the capitalization of interest expense.
- *Leases.* Covers the treatment of fixed assets recorded under capital leases.

Overview of Fixed Assets

The vast majority of the expenditures that a company makes are for consumables, such as office supplies, wages, or products that it sells to customers. The effects of these items pass through a company quickly – they are used or sold and converted to cash, and they are recorded as expenses immediately, or with a slight delay (if they involve inventory). Thus, the benefits they generate are short-lived.

Fixed assets are entirely different. These are items that generate economic benefits over a long period of time. Because of the long period of usefulness of a fixed asset, it is not justifiable to charge its entire cost to expense when incurred. Instead, the *matching principle* comes into play. Under the matching principle, recognize both the benefits and expenses associated with a transaction (or, in this case, an asset) at the same time. To do so, we convert an expenditure into an asset, and use depreciation to gradually charge it to expense.

By designating an expenditure as a fixed asset, we are shifting the expenditure away from the income statement, where expenditures normally go, and instead place it in the balance sheet. As we gradually reduce its recorded cost through depreciation, the expenditure slowly flows from the balance sheet to the income statement. Thus, the main difference between a normal expenditure and a fixed asset is that the fixed asset is charged to expense over a longer period of time.

The process of identifying fixed assets, recording them as assets, and depreciating them is time-consuming, so it is customary to build some limitations into the process that will route most expenditures directly to expense. One such limitation is to charge an expenditure to expense immediately unless it has a useful life of at least one year. Another limitation is to only recognize an expenditure as a fixed asset if it exceeds a certain dollar amount, known as the *capitalization limit*. These limits keep the vast majority of expenditures from being classified as fixed assets, which reduces the work of the accounting department.

EXAMPLE

Armadillo Industries incurs expenditures for three items, and must decide whether it should classify them as fixed assets. Armadillo's capitalization limit is $2,500. The expenditures are:

- It buys a used mold for its plastic injection molding operation for $5,000. Armadillo expects that the mold only has two months of useful life left, after which it should be scrapped. Since the useful life is so short, the controller elects to charge the expenditure to expense immediately.
- It buys a laptop computer for $1,500, which has a useful life of three years. This expenditure is less than the capitalization limit, so the controller charges it to expense.
- It buys a 10-ton injection molding machine for $50,000, which has a useful life of 10 years. Since this expenditure has a useful life of longer than one year and a cost greater than the capitalization limit, the controller records it as a fixed asset, and will depreciate it over its 10-year useful life.

An alternative treatment of the $5,000 mold in the preceding example would be to record it under the Other Assets account in the balance sheet, and charge the cost to expense over two months. This is a useful alternative for expenditures that have useful lives of greater than one accounting period, but less than one year. It is a less time-consuming alternative for the accounting staff, which does not have to create a fixed asset record or engage in any depreciation calculations.

There are several key points in the life of a fixed asset that require recognition in the accounting records; these are the initial recordation of the asset, the recognition of any asset retirement obligations, depreciation, impairment, and the eventual derecognition of the asset. We describe these general concepts below, and include a reference to the more comprehensive treatment in later sections and chapters:

- *Initial recognition*. There are a number of factors to consider when initially recording a fixed asset, such as which costs to include, and when to stop capitalizing costs. These issues are dealt with in the Initial Fixed Asset Recognition section.
- *Interest capitalization*. If an asset is being constructed, or it is requiring some time to bring a fixed asset to the condition and location intended for its use, then it may be possible to capitalize the cost of the interest associated with the purchase. There are very specific rules for the use of interest capitalization, which are covered in the Interest chapter.
- *Asset retirement obligations*. There are situations where one can reasonably calculate the costs associated with retiring an asset, such as environmental remediation for a strip mine. These costs are known as asset retirement obligations, and the accountant is required to recognize their costs as part of the initial recordation of an asset. The Asset Retirement and Environmental Obligations chapter addresses this topic.
- *Depreciation*. The cost of a fixed asset should be gradually charged to expense over time, using depreciation. There are a variety of depreciation methods available, which are described further in the Depreciation and Amortization section.
- *Impairment*. If the fair value of a fixed asset falls below its recorded cost at any point during its useful life, the accountant is required to reduce its recorded cost to its fair value and recognize a loss for the difference between the two amounts. The Fixed Asset Impairment section delves into this accounting.
- *Disposal*. When an asset comes to the end of its useful life, a company will likely sell or otherwise dispose of it. At this time, remove it from the accounting records and record a gain or loss (if any) on the final disposal transaction. This issue is discussed in the Fixed Asset Disposal section.

Initial Fixed Asset Recognition

A fixed asset should be initially recorded at the historical cost of acquiring it, which includes the costs to bring it to the condition and location necessary for its intended use. If these preparatory activities will occupy a period of time, it is possible to include in the cost of the asset the interest costs related to the cost of the asset during the preparation period (see the Interest chapter for more information).

The activities involved in bringing a fixed asset to the condition and location necessary for its intended purpose include the following:

- Physical construction of the asset
- Demolition of any preexisting structures
- Renovating a preexisting structure to alter it for use by the buyer
- Administrative and technical activities during preconstruction for such activities as designing the asset and obtaining permits
- Administrative and technical work after construction commences for such activities as litigation, labor disputes, and technical problems

---

EXAMPLE

Nascent Corporation constructs a solar observatory. The project costs $10 million to construct. Also, Nascent takes out a loan for the entire $10 million amount of the project, and pays $250,000 in interest costs during the six-month construction period. Further, the company incurs $500,000 in architectural fees and permit costs before work begins.

All of these costs can be capitalized into the cost of the building asset, so Nascent records $10.75 million as the cost of the building asset.

Fixed Assets Acquired through a Business Combination

If a company acquires fixed assets as part of a business combination, it should recognize all identifiable assets, including such identifiable intangible assets as a patent, customer relationship, or a brand. Record these fixed assets at their fair values as of the acquisition date.

EXAMPLE

Nascent Corporation acquires Stellar Designs for $40 million. It allocates $10 million of the purchase price among current assets and liabilities at their book values, which approximate their fair values. Nascent also assigns $22 million to identifiable fixed assets and $4 million to a customer relationships intangible asset. This leaves $4 million that cannot be allocated, and which is therefore assigned to a goodwill asset.

Nonmonetary Exchanges

What if a fixed asset is acquired through an exchange of assets? Follow this sequence of decisions to decide upon the correct cost at which to record the asset received:

1. Measure the asset acquired at the fair value of the asset surrendered to the other party.
2. If the fair value of the asset received is more clearly evident than the fair value of the asset surrendered, measure the acquired asset at its own fair value.

In either case, recognize a gain or loss on the difference between the recorded cost of the asset transferred to the other party and the recorded cost of the asset that has been acquired.

If it is not possible to determine the fair value of either asset, record the asset received at the cost of the asset that was relinquished in order to obtain it. Use this latter approach under any of the following circumstances:

- It is not possible to determine the fair value of either asset within reasonable limits;
- The transaction is intended to facilitate a sale to a customer other than the parties to the asset exchange; or
- The transaction does not have commercial substance.

EXAMPLE

Nascent Corporation exchanges a color copier with a carrying amount of $18,000 with Declining Company for a print-on-demand publishing station. The color copier had an original cost of $30,000, and had incurred $12,000 of accumulated depreciation as of the transaction date. No cash is transferred as part of the exchange, and Nascent cannot determine the fair value of the color copier. The fair value of the publishing station is $20,000.

Nascent can record a gain of $2,000 on the exchange, which is derived from the fair value of the publishing station that it acquired, less the carrying amount of the color copier that it gave up. Nascent uses the following journal entry to record the transaction:

	Debit	Credit
Publishing equipment	20,000	
Accumulated depreciation	12,000	
Copier equipment		30,000
Gain on asset exchange		2,000

EXAMPLE

Nascent Corporation and Starlight Inc. swap spectroscopes, since the two devices have different features that the two companies need. The spectroscope given up by Nascent has a carrying amount of $25,000, which is comprised of an original cost of $40,000 and accumulated depreciation of $15,000. Both spectroscopes have identical fair values of $27,000.

Nascent's controller tests for commercial substance in the transaction. She finds that there is no difference in the fair values of the assets exchanged, and that Nascent's cash flows will not change significantly as a result of the swap. Thus, she concludes that the transaction has no commercial value, and so should account for it at book value, which means that Nascent cannot recognize a gain of $2,000 on the transaction, which is the difference between the $27,000 fair value of the spectroscope and the $25,000 carrying amount of the asset given up. Instead, she uses the following journal entry to record the transaction, which does not contain a gain or loss:

	Debit	Credit
Spectroscope (asset received)	25,000	
Accumulated depreciation	15,000	
Spectroscope (asset given up)		40,000

What if there is an exchange of cash between the two parties, in addition to a non-monetary exchange? The accounting varies if the amount of cash, or *boot*, paid as part of the asset exchange is relatively small (which is defined under GAAP as less than 25 percent of the fair value of the exchange), or if it is larger.

In the case of a small amount of boot, the recipient of the cash records a gain to the extent that the amount of cash received exceeds a proportionate share of the cost of the surrendered asset. This proportionate share is calculated as the ratio of the cash paid to the total consideration received (which is the cash received plus the fair value of the asset received); if the amount of the consideration received is not clearly evident, then instead use the fair value of the asset surrendered to the other party. The calculation is:

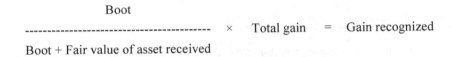

$$\frac{\text{Boot}}{\text{Boot} + \text{Fair value of asset received}} \times \text{Total gain} = \text{Gain recognized}$$

What is the accounting from the perspective of the party paying cash as part of the transaction? This entity records the asset received as the sum of the cash paid to the other party plus the recorded amount of the asset surrendered. If the transaction results in a loss, then record the entire amount of the loss at once. Under no circumstances is it allowable to record a gain on such a transaction.

EXAMPLE

Nascent Corporation is contemplating the exchange of one of its heliographs for a catadioptric telescope owned by Aphelion Corporation. The two companies have recorded these assets in their accounting records as follows:

	Nascent (Heliograph)	Aphelion (Catadioptric)
Cost	$82,000	$97,000
Accumulated depreciation	22,000	27,000
Net book value	$60,000	$70,000
Fair value	$55,000	$72,000

Under the terms of the proposed asset exchange, Nascent must pay cash (boot) to Aphelion of $17,000. The boot amount is 24 percent of the fair value of the exchange, which is calculated as:

$17,000 Boot ÷ ($55,000 Fair value of heliograph + $17,000 Boot) = 24%

The parties elect to go forward with the exchange. The amount of boot is less than 25 percent of the total fair value of the exchange, so Aphelion should recognize a pro rata portion of the $2,000 gain (calculated as the $72,000 total fair value of the asset received - $70,000 net book value of the asset received) on the exchange using the following calculation:

24% Portion of boot to total fair value received × $2,000 Gain = $480 Recognized gain

Nascent uses the following journal entry to record the exchange transaction:

	Debit	Credit
Telescope (asset received)	72,000	
Accumulated depreciation	22,000	
Loss on asset exchange	5,000	
Cash		17,000
Heliograph (asset given up)		82,000

Nascent's journal entry includes a $5,000 loss; the loss is essentially the difference between the book value and fair value of the heliograph on the transaction date.

Aphelion uses the following journal entry to record the exchange transaction:

	Debit	Credit
Heliograph (asset received)	53,480	
Accumulated depreciation	27,000	
Cash	17,000	
Gain on asset exchange		480
Telescope (asset given up)		97,000

Aphelion is not allowed to recognize the full value of the heliograph at the acquisition date because of the boot rule for small amounts of cash consideration; this leaves the heliograph undervalued by $1,520 (since its fair value is actually $55,000).

The accounting is different if the amount of boot is 25 percent or more of the fair value of the exchange. In this situation, both parties should record the transaction at its fair value.

EXAMPLE

Nascent Corporation exchanges a wide field CCD camera for a Schmidt-Cassegrain telescope owned by Aphelion Corporation. The two companies record these assets in their accounting records as follows:

	Nascent (Camera)	Aphelion (Schmidt-Cassegrain)
Cost	$50,000	$93,000
Accumulated depreciation	(30,000)	(40,000)
Net book value	$20,000	$53,000
Fair value	$24,000	$58,000

Under the terms of the agreement, Nascent pays $34,000 cash (boot) to Aphelion. This boot amount is well in excess of the 25 percent boot level, so both parties can now treat the deal as a monetary transaction.

Nascent uses the following journal entry to record the exchange transaction, which measures the telescope acquired at the fair value of the camera and cash surrendered:

	Debit	Credit
Telescope (asset received)	58,000	
Accumulated depreciation	30,000	
Gain on asset exchange		4,000
Cash		34,000
CCD camera (asset given up)		50,000

The gain recorded by Nascent is the difference between the $24,000 fair value of the camera surrendered and its $20,000 book value.

Aphelion uses the following journal entry to record the exchange transaction, which measures the camera acquired at the fair value of the telescope surrendered less cash received:

	Debit	Credit
Camera (asset received)	24,000	
Accumulated depreciation	40,000	
Cash	34,000	
Gain on asset exchange		5,000
Telescope (asset given up)		93,000

The gain recorded by Aphelion is the difference between the $58,000 fair value of the telescope surrendered and its $53,000 book value.

Depreciation and Amortization

The purpose of depreciation is to charge to expense a portion of an asset that relates to the revenue generated by that asset. This is called the matching principle, where revenues and expenses both appear in the income statement in the same reporting period, which gives the best view of how well a company has performed in a given accounting period.

There are three factors to consider in the calculation of depreciation, which are:

- *Useful life.* This is the time period over which it is expected that the asset will be productive, or the number of units of production expected to be generated from it. Past its useful life, it is no longer cost-effective to continue operating the asset, so one would dispose of it or stop using it. Depreciation is recognized over the useful life of an asset.

Tip: Rather than recording a different useful life for every asset, it is easier to assign each asset to an asset class, where every asset in that asset class has the same useful life. This approach may not work for very high-cost assets, where a greater degree of precision may be needed.

- *Salvage value.* When a company eventually disposes of an asset, it may be able to sell the asset for some reduced amount, which is the salvage value. Depreciation is calculated based on the asset cost, less any estimated salvage value. If salvage value is expected to be quite small, then it is generally ignored for the purpose of calculating depreciation. Salvage value is not discounted to its present value.

Tip: If the amount of salvage value associated with an asset is expected to be minor, it is easier from a calculation perspective to not reduce the depreciable amount of the asset by the salvage value. Instead, assume that the salvage value is zero.

EXAMPLE

Pensive Corporation buys an asset for $100,000, and estimates that its salvage value will be $10,000 in five years, when it plans to dispose of the asset. This means that Pensive will depreciate $90,000 of the asset cost over five years, leaving $10,000 of the cost remaining at the end of that time. Pensive expects to then sell the asset for $10,000, which will eliminate the asset from its accounting records.

- *Depreciation method.* Depreciation expense can be calculated using an accelerated depreciation method, or evenly over the useful life of the asset.

Property, Plant, and Equipment

The advantage of using an accelerated method is that more depreciation can be recognized early in the life of a fixed asset, which defers some income tax expense recognition into a later period. The advantage of using a steady depreciation rate is the ease of calculation. Examples of accelerated depreciation methods are the double declining balance and sum-of-the-years' digits methods. The primary method for steady depreciation is the straight-line method.

The *mid-month convention* states that, no matter when a fixed asset was purchased within a month, it is assumed to have been purchased in the middle of the month for depreciation purposes. Thus, if a fixed asset was bought on January 5th, assume that it was bought on January 15th; or, if it was bought on January 28, still assume that it was bought on January 15th. By doing so, it is easier to calculate a standard half-month of depreciation for that first month of ownership.

If the mid-month convention is used, this also means that a half-month of depreciation should be recorded for the *last* month of the asset's useful life. By doing so, the two-half month depreciation calculations equal one full month of depreciation.

Many companies prefer to use full-month depreciation in the first month of ownership, irrespective of the actual date of purchase within the month, so that they can slightly accelerate their recognition of depreciation, which in turn reduces their taxable income in the near term.

Straight-Line Method

Under the straight-line method of depreciation, depreciation expense is recognized evenly over the estimated useful life of an asset. The straight-line calculation steps are:

1. Subtract the estimated salvage value of the asset from the amount at which it is recorded on the books.
2. Determine the estimated useful life of the asset. It is easiest to use a standard useful life for each class of assets.
3. Divide the estimated useful life (in years) into 1 to arrive at the straight-line depreciation rate.
4. Multiply the depreciation rate by the asset cost (less salvage value).

EXAMPLE

Pensive Corporation purchases the Procrastinator Deluxe machine for $60,000. It has an estimated salvage value of $10,000 and a useful life of five years. Pensive calculates the annual straight-line depreciation for the machine as:

1. Purchase cost of $60,000 – estimated salvage value of $10,000 = Depreciable asset cost of $50,000
2. 1 / 5-year useful life = 20% depreciation rate per year

3. 20% depreciation rate × $50,000 depreciable asset cost = $10,000 annual depreciation

---

Sum-of-the-Years' Digits Method

The sum of the years' digits (SYD) method is more appropriate than straight-line depreciation if the asset depreciates more quickly or has greater production capacity in earlier years than it does as it ages. Use the following formula to calculate it:

$$\text{Depreciation percentage} = \frac{\text{Number of estimated years of life as of beginning of the year}}{\text{Sum of the years' digits}}$$

The following table contains examples of the sum of the years' digits noted in the denominator of the preceding formula:

Total Depreciation Period	Initial Sum of the Years' Digits	Calculation
2 years	3	1 + 2
3 years	6	1 + 2 + 3
4 years	10	1 + 2 + 3 + 4
5 years	15	1 + 2 + 3 + 4 + 5

The concept is most easily illustrated with the following example:

EXAMPLE

Pensive Corporation buys a Procrastinator Elite machine for $100,000. The machine has no estimated salvage value, and a useful life of five years. Pensive calculates the annual sum of the years' digits depreciation for this machine as:

Year	Number of estimated years of life as of beginning of the year	SYD Calculation	Depreciation Percentage	Annual Depreciation
1	5	5/15	33.33%	$33,333
2	4	4/15	26.67%	26,667
3	3	3/15	20.00%	20,000
4	2	2/15	13.33%	13,333
5	1	1/15	6.67%	6,667
Totals	15		100.00%	$100,000

The sum of the years' digits method is clearly more complex than the straight-line method, which tends to limit its use unless software is employed to automatically track the calculations for each asset.

Double-Declining Balance Method

The double declining balance (DDB) method is a form of accelerated depreciation. It may be more appropriate than the straight-line method if an asset experiences an inordinately high level of usage during the first few years of its useful life.

To calculate the double-declining balance depreciation rate, divide the number of years of useful life of an asset into 100 percent, and multiply the result by two. The formula is:

$$(100\%/\text{Years of useful life}) \times 2$$

The DDB calculation proceeds until the asset's salvage value is reached, after which depreciation ends.

EXAMPLE

Pensive Corporation purchases a machine for $50,000. It has an estimated salvage value of $5,000 and a useful life of five years. The calculation of the double declining balance depreciation rate is:

$$(100\%/\text{Years of useful life}) \times 2 = 40\%$$

By applying the 40% rate, Pensive arrives at the following table of depreciation charges per year:

Year	Book Value at Beginning of Year	Depreciation Percentage	DDB Depreciation	Book Value Net of Depreciation
1	$50,000	40%	$20,000	$30,000
2	30,000	40%	12,000	18,000
3	18,000	40%	7,200	10,800
4	10,800	40%	4,320	6,480
5	6,480	40%	1,480	5,000
Total			$45,000	

Note that the depreciation in the fifth and final year is only for $1,480, rather than the $3,240 that would be indicated by the 40% depreciation rate. The reason for the smaller depreciation charge is that Pensive stops any further depreciation once the remaining book value declines to the amount of the estimated salvage value.

An alternative form of double declining balance depreciation is 150% declining balance depreciation. It is a less aggressive form of depreciation, since it is calculated as 1.5 times the straight-line rate, rather than the 2x multiple that is used for the double declining balance method. Thus, if it were to be used, the formula would be:

$$(100\%/\text{Years of useful life}) \times 1.5$$

EXAMPLE

[Note: We are repeating the preceding example, but using 150% declining balance depreciation instead of double declining balance depreciation]

Pensive Corporation purchases a machine for $50,000. It has an estimated salvage value of $5,000 and a useful life of five years. The calculation of the 150% declining balance depreciation rate is:

$$(100\%/\text{Years of useful life}) \times 1.5 = 30\%$$

By applying the 30% rate, Pensive arrives at the following table of depreciation charges per year:

Year	Book Value at Beginning of Year	Depreciation Percentage	DDB Depreciation	Book Value Net of Depreciation
1	$50,000	30%	$15,000	$35,000
2	35,000	30%	10,500	24,500
3	24,500	30%	7,350	17,150
4	17,150	30%	5,145	12,005
5	12,005	30%	7,005	5,000
Total			$45,000	

In this case, the depreciation expense in the fifth and final year of $3,602 ($12,005 × 30%) results in a net book value that is somewhat higher than the estimated salvage value of $5,000, so Pensive instead records $7,005 of depreciation in order to arrive at a net book value that equals the estimated salvage value.

Depletion Method

Depletion is a periodic charge to expense for the use of natural resources. Thus, it is employed in situations where a company has recorded an asset for such items as oil reserves, coal deposits, or gravel pits. The calculation of depletion involves these steps:

1. Compute a depletion base.
2. Compute a unit depletion rate.
3. Charge depletion based on units of usage.

The depletion base is the asset that is to be depleted. It is comprised of the following four types of costs:

- *Acquisition costs*. The cost to either buy or lease property.
- *Exploration costs*. The cost to locate assets that may then be depleted. In most cases, these costs are charged to expense as incurred.
- *Development costs*. The cost to prepare the property for asset extraction, which includes the cost of such items as tunnels and wells.
- *Restoration costs*. The cost to restore property to its original condition after depletion activities have been concluded.

To compute a unit depletion rate, subtract the salvage value of the asset from the depletion base and divide it by the total number of measurement units expected to be recovered. The formula for the unit depletion rate is:

$$\text{Unit depletion rate} = \frac{\text{Depletion base} - \text{Salvage value}}{\text{Total units to be recovered}}$$

The depletion charge is then created based on actual units of usage. Thus, if 500 barrels of oil are extracted and the unit depletion rate is $5.00 per barrel, then charge $2,500 to depletion expense.

The estimated amount of a natural resource that can be recovered will change constantly as assets are gradually extracted from a property. As the estimates of the remaining amount of extractable natural resource are revised, incorporate these estimates into the unit depletion rate for the remaining amount to be extracted. This is not a retrospective calculation.

EXAMPLE

Pensive Corporation's subsidiary Pensive Oil drills a well with the intention of extracting oil from a known reservoir. It incurs the following costs related to the acquisition of property and development of the site:

Land purchase	$280,000
Road construction	23,000
Drill pad construction	48,000
Drilling fees	192,000
Total	$543,000

In addition, Pensive Oil estimates that it will incur a site restoration cost of $57,000 once extraction is complete, so the total depletion base of the property is $600,000.

Pensive's geologists estimate that the proven oil reserves that are accessed by the well are 400,000 barrels, so the unit depletion charge will be $1.50 per barrel of oil extracted ($600,000 depletion base ÷ 400,000 barrels).

In the first year, Pensive Oil extracts 100,000 barrels of oil from the well, which results in a depletion charge of $150,000 (100,000 barrels × $1.50 unit depletion charge).

At the beginning of the second year of operations, Pensive's geologists issue a revised estimate of the remaining amount of proven reserves, with the new estimate of 280,000 barrels being 20,000 barrels lower than the original estimate (less extractions already completed). This means that the unit depletion charge will increase to $1.61 ($450,000 remaining depletion base ÷ 280,000 barrels).

During the second year, Pensive Oil extracts 80,000 barrels of oil from the well, which results in a depletion charge of $128,800 (80,000 barrels × $1.61 unit depletion charge).

At the end of the second year, there is still a depletion base of $321,200 that must be charged to expense in proportion to the amount of any remaining extractions.

Units of Production Method

Under the units of production method, the amount of depreciation charged to expense varies in direct proportion to the amount of asset usage. Thus, more depreciation is charged in periods when there is more asset usage, and less depreciation in periods when there is less asset usage. It is the most accurate method for charging depreciation, since it links closely to the wear and tear on assets. However, it also requires the accountant to track asset usage, which means that its use is generally limited to more expensive assets. Also, it is necessary to estimate total usage over the life of the asset.

Tip: Do not use the units of production method if there is not a significant difference in asset usage from period to period. Otherwise, the accountant will spend a great deal of time tracking asset usage, and will be rewarded with a depreciation expense that varies little from the results that would have been seen with the straight-line method (which is far easier to calculate).

Follow these steps to calculate depreciation under the units of production method:

1. Estimate the total number of hours of usage of the asset, or the total number of units to be produced by it over its useful life.
2. Subtract any estimated salvage value from the capitalized cost of the asset, and divide the total estimated usage or production from this net depreciable cost. This yields the depreciation cost per hour of usage or unit of production.
3. Multiply the number of hours of usage or units of actual production by the depreciation cost per hour or unit, which results in the total depreciation expense for the accounting period.

If the estimated number of hours of usage or units of production changes over time, then incorporate these changes into the calculation of the depreciation cost per hour or unit of production. This will alter the depreciation expense on a go-forward basis.

EXAMPLE

Pensive Corporation's gravel pit operation, Pensive Dirt, builds a conveyor system to extract gravel from a gravel pit at a cost of $400,000. Pensive expects to use the conveyor to extract 1,000,000 tons of gravel, which results in a depreciation rate of $0.40 per ton (1,000,000 tons ÷ $400,000 cost). During the first quarter of activity, Pensive Dirt extracts 10,000 tons of gravel, which results in the following depreciation expense:

= $0.40 depreciation cost per ton × 10,000 tons of gravel

= $4,000 depreciation expense

Land Depreciation

Nearly all fixed assets have a useful life, after which they no longer contribute to the operations of a company or they stop generating revenue. During this useful life, they are depreciated, which reduces their cost to what they are supposed to be worth at the end of their useful lives. Land, however, has no definitive useful life, so there is no way to depreciate it.

The one exception is when some aspect of the land is actually used up, such as when a mine is emptied of its ore reserves. In this case, depreciate the natural resources in the land using the depletion method as described earlier in this chapter.

Land Improvement Depreciation

Land improvements are enhancements to a plot of land to make it more usable. If these improvements have a useful life, depreciate them. If there is no way to estimate a useful life, do not depreciate the cost of the improvements.

If land is being prepared for its intended purpose, then include these costs in the cost of the land asset. They are not depreciated. Examples of such costs are:

- Demolishing an existing building
- Clearing and leveling the land

If functionality is being added to the land and the expenditures have a useful life, then record them in a separate land improvements account. Examples of land improvements are:

- Drainage and irrigation systems
- Fencing
- Landscaping
- Parking lots and walkways

A special item is the ongoing cost of landscaping. This is a period cost, not a fixed asset, and so should be charged to expense as incurred.

EXAMPLE

Pensive Corporation buys a parcel of land for $1,000,000. Since it is a purchase of land, Pensive cannot depreciate the cost. Pensive then razes a building that was located on the property at a cost of $25,000, fills in the old foundation for $5,000, and levels the land for $50,000. All of these costs are to prepare the land for its intended purpose, so they are all added to the cost of the land. Pensive cannot depreciate these costs.

Pensive intends to use the land as a parking lot, so it spends $400,000 to pave the land, and adds walkways and fences. It estimates that the parking lot has a useful life of 20 years. The company should record this cost in the land improvements account, and depreciate it over 20 years.

Depreciation Accounting Entries

The basic depreciation entry is to debit the depreciation expense account (which appears in the income statement) and credit the accumulated depreciation account (which appears in the balance sheet as a contra account that reduces the amount of fixed assets). Over time, the accumulated depreciation balance will continue to increase as more depreciation is added to it, until such time as it equals the original cost of the asset. At that time, stop recording any depreciation expense, since the cost of the asset has now been reduced to zero.

The journal entry for depreciation can be a simple two-line entry designed to accommodate all types of fixed assets, or it may be subdivided into separate entries for each type of fixed asset.

EXAMPLE

Pensive Corporation calculates that it should have $25,000 of depreciation expense in the current month. The entry is:

	Debit	Credit
Depreciation expense	25,000	
Accumulated depreciation		25,000

In the following month, Pensive's controller decides to show a higher level of precision at the expense account level, and instead elects to apportion the $25,000 of depreciation among different expense accounts, so that each class of asset has a separate depreciation charge. The entry is:

	Debit	Credit
Depreciation expense - Automobiles	4,000	
Depreciation expense – Computer equipment	8,000	
Depreciation expense – Furniture and fixtures	6,000	
Depreciation expense – Office equipment	5,000	
Depreciation expense – Software	2,000	
Accumulated depreciation		25,000

The journal entry to record the amortization of intangible assets is fundamentally the same as the entry for depreciation, except that the accounts used substitute the word "amortization" for depreciation.

EXAMPLE

Pensive Corporation calculates that it should have $4,000 of amortization expense in the current month that is related to intangible assets. The entry is:

	Debit	Credit
Amortization expense	4,000	
Accumulated amortization		4,000

When an asset is sold or otherwise disposed of, remove all related accumulated depreciation from the accounting records at the same time. Otherwise, an unusually large amount of accumulated depreciation will build up on the balance sheet.

EXAMPLE

Pensive Corporate has $1,000,000 of fixed assets, for which it has charged $380,000 of accumulated depreciation. This results in the following presentation on Pensive's balance sheet:

Fixed assets	$1,000,000
Less: Accumulated depreciation	(380,000)
Net fixed assets	$620,000

Pensive then sells a machine for $80,000 that had an original cost of $140,000, and for which it had already recorded accumulated depreciation of $50,000. It records the sale with this journal entry:

	Debit	Credit
Cash	80,000	
Accumulated depreciation	50,000	
Loss on asset sale	10,000	
Fixed assets		140,000

As a result of this entry, Pensive's balance sheet presentation of fixed assets has changed, so that fixed assets before accumulated depreciation have declined to $860,000, and accumulated depreciation has declined to $330,000. The new presentation is:

Fixed assets	$860,000
Less: Accumulated depreciation	(330,000)
Net fixed assets	$530,000

The amount of net fixed assets declined by $90,000 as a result of the asset sale, which is the sum of the $80,000 cash proceeds and the $10,000 loss resulting from the asset sale.

Fixed Asset Impairment

There are rules under GAAP for periodically testing fixed assets to see if they are still as valuable as the costs at which they were recorded in the accounting records. If not, reduce the recorded cost of these assets by recognizing a loss. Also, under no circumstances should an impairment loss be reversed under GAAP.

An impairment loss should be recognized on a fixed asset if its carrying amount is not recoverable and exceeds its fair value. Recognize this loss within income from continuing operations on the income statement.

The carrying amount of an asset is not recoverable if it exceeds the sum of the undiscounted cash flows expected to result from the use of the asset over its remaining useful life and the final disposition of the asset. These cash flow estimates should incorporate assumptions that are reasonable in relation to the assumptions the entity uses for its budgets, forecasts, and so forth. If there are a range of possible cash flow outcomes, consider using a probability-weighted cash flow analysis.

> **Tip:** Impairment analysis is supposed to be based on the cash flows to be expected over the remaining useful life of an asset. If impairment for a group of assets (as discussed below) is being measured, then the remaining useful life is based on the useful life of the primary asset in the group. It is not allowable to skew the results by including in the group an asset with a theoretically unlimited life, such as land or an intangible asset that is not being amortized.

The amount of an impairment loss is the difference between an asset's carrying amount and its fair value. Once an impairment loss is recognized, this reduces the carrying amount of the asset, so it may be necessary to alter the amount of periodic depreciation being charged against the asset to adjust for this lower carrying amount (otherwise, an excessively large depreciation expense will be incurred over the remaining useful life of the asset).

If an asset has been designated as held for sale, then periodically test it for a possible loss on the expected disposal of the asset. Recognize a loss in the amount by which the fair value less costs to sell of the asset is lower than its carrying amount, and state it within income from continuing operations on the income statement.

Assets should be tested for impairment at the lowest level at which there are identifiable cash flows that are largely independent of the cash flows of other assets. In cases where there are no identifiable cash flows at all (as is common with corporate-level assets), place these assets in an asset group that encompasses the entire entity, and test for impairment at the entity level.

Only add goodwill to an asset group for impairment testing when the asset group is a reporting unit, or includes a reporting unit. Thus, do not include goodwill in any asset groups below the reporting unit level.

Only test for the recoverability of an asset whenever the circumstances indicate that its carrying amount may not be recoverable. Examples of such situations are:

- *Cash flow*. There are historical and projected operating or cash flow losses associated with the asset.
- *Costs*. There are excessive costs incurred to acquire or construct the asset.
- *Disposal*. The asset is more than 50% likely to be sold or otherwise disposed of significantly before the end of its previously estimated useful life.
- *Legal*. There is a significant adverse change in legal factors or the business climate that could affect the asset's value.
- *Market price*. There is a significant decrease in the asset's market price.
- *Usage*. There is a significant adverse change in the asset's manner of use, or in its physical condition.

If there is an impairment at the level of an asset group, allocate the impairment among the assets in the group on a pro rata basis, based on the carrying amounts of the assets in the group. However, the impairment loss cannot reduce the carrying amount of an asset below its fair value.

Tip: It is only necessary to determine the fair value of an asset for this test if it is "determinable without undue cost and effort." Thus, if an outside appraisal would be required to determine fair value, the accountant can likely dispense with this requirement and simply allocate the impairment loss to all of the assets in the group.

EXAMPLE

Luminescence Corporation operates a small floodlight manufacturing facility. Luminescence considers the entire facility to be a reporting unit, so it conducts an impairment test on the entire operation. The test reveals that a continuing decline in the market for floodlights (caused by the surge in LED lights in the market) has caused a $2 million impairment charge. Luminescence allocates the charge to the four assets in the facility as follows:

Asset	Carrying Amount	Proportion of Carrying Amounts	Impairment Allocation	Revised Carrying Amount
Ribbon machine	$8,000,000	67%	$1,340,000	$6,660,000
Conveyors	1,500,000	13%	260,000	1,240,000
Gas injector	2,000,000	16%	320,000	1,680,000
Filament inserter	500,000	4%	80,000	420,000
Totals	$12,000,000	100%	$2,000,000	$10,000,000

It is allowable under GAAP to recognize a gain on any increase in the fair value less costs to sell of a fixed asset that is designated as held for sale. The amount of this gain is capped at the amount of any cumulative disposal loss that has already been recognized for the asset. This gain will increase the carrying amount of the asset.

EXAMPLE

Luminescence Corporation has designated one of its fluorescent bulb factories as held for sale. The asset group comprising the factory has a carrying amount of $18 million. After six months, Luminescence determines that the fair value less costs to sell for the factory is $16 million, due to falling prices for similar factories, so it recognizes a disposal loss of $2 million. A few months later, the market for such factories rebounds, and the company finds that the factory now has a fair value less costs to sell of $19 million, which is an increase of $3 million.

Luminescence can only recognize a $2 million gain, which reverses the prior disposal loss.

Fixed Asset Disposal

An asset is derecognized upon its disposal, or when no future economic benefits can be expected from its use or disposal. Derecognition can arise from a variety of events, such as an asset's sale, scrapping, or donation.

The net effect of asset derecognition is to remove an asset and its associated accumulated depreciation from the balance sheet, as well as to recognize any related gain or loss. A gain on derecognition cannot be recorded as revenue. The gain or loss on derecognition is calculated as the net disposal proceeds, minus the asset's carrying amount.

Assets Held for Sale

There is a special asset classification under GAAP that is called *held-for-sale*. This classification is important for two reasons:

- All assets classified as held for sale are presented separately on the balance sheet.
- There is no depreciation or amortization of assets classified as held for sale.

Under GAAP, classify a fixed asset or a disposal group as held for sale if all of the following criteria are met:

- Management commits to a plan to sell the assets.
- The asset is available for sale immediately in its present condition.
- There is an active program to sell the asset.
- It is unlikely that the plan to sell the asset will be changed or withdrawn.
- Sale of the asset is likely to occur, and should be completed within one year.
- The asset is being marketed at a price that is considered reasonable in comparison to its current fair value.

EXAMPLE

Ambivalence Corporation plans to sell its existing headquarters facility and build a new corporate headquarters building. It will remain in its existing quarters until the new facility is complete, and will transfer ownership of the building to a buyer only after it has moved out. Since the company's continuing presence in the existing building means that it cannot be available for sale immediately, the situation fails the held-for-sale criteria, and Ambivalence should not reclassify its existing headquarters building as held-for-sale. This would be the case even if Ambivalence had a firm purchase commitment to buy the building, since the actual transfer of ownership will still be delayed.

The one-year limitation noted in the preceding criteria can be circumvented in any of the following situations:

- *Expected conditions imposed.* An entity other than the buyer is likely to impose conditions that will extend the sale period beyond one year, and the seller cannot respond to those conditions until after it receives a firm purchase commitment, and it expects that commitment within one year.

EXAMPLE

Ambivalence Corporation has a geothermal electricity-generating plant on the site of its Brew Master production facility. It plans to sell the geothermal plant to a local electric utility. The sale is subject to the approval of the state regulatory commission, which will likely require more than one year to issue its opinion. Ambivalence cannot begin to obtain the commission's approval until after it has obtained a firm purchase commitment from the local utility, but expects to receive the commitment within one year. The situation meets the criteria for maintaining an asset in the held-for-sale classification for more than one year.

- *Unexpected conditions imposed.* The seller obtains a firm purchase commitment, but the buyer or others then impose conditions on the sale that are not expected, and the seller is responding to these conditions, and the seller expects a favorable resolution of the conditions.

EXAMPLE

Ambivalence Corporation enters into a firm purchase commitment to sell its potions plant, but the buyer's inspection team finds that some potions have leaked into the local water table. The buyer demands that Ambivalence mitigate this environmental damage before the sale is concluded, which will require more than one year to complete. Ambivalence initiates these activities, and expects to mitigate the damage. The situation meets the criteria for maintaining an asset in the held-for-sale classification for more than one year.

- *Unlikely circumstances.* An unlikely situation arises that delays the sale, and the seller is responding to the change in circumstances, and is continuing to market the asset at a price that is reasonable in relation to its current fair value.

EXAMPLE

Ambivalence Corporation is attempting to sell its charm bracelet manufacturing line, but market conditions deteriorate, and it is unable to sell the line at the price point that it wants. Management believes that the market will rebound, so it leaves the same price in place, even though the market price is probably 20% lower. Given that the price now exceeds the current fair value of the manufacturing line, the company is no longer marketing it at a reasonable price, and so should no longer list the asset in the held-for-sale classification.

If a company acquires an asset as part of a business combination and wants to immediately classify it as held for sale, the asset must meet these requirements:

- Sale of the asset is likely to occur, and should be completed within one year.
- If any of the other criteria noted above are not met as of the acquisition date, it is probable that they will be met shortly after the acquisition has been completed.

Tip: The GAAP codification states that three months is "usually" the amount of time allowed for the buyer to meet the held-for-sale criteria. Given the wording of this pronouncement, there is probably some leeway in the actual amount of time allowed.

If assets are classified as held-for-sale, measure them at the lower of their carrying amount or their fair value minus any cost to sell. If it is necessary to write down the carrying amount of an asset to its fair value minus any cost to sell, then recognize a loss in the amount of the write down. One may also recognize a gain on an increase in the fair value minus any cost to sell, but only up to the amount of any cumulative losses previously recognized.

When an asset is classified as held-for-sale, do not also accrue any expected future losses associated with operating it while it is so classified. Instead, recognize these costs only as incurred.

EXAMPLE

Ambivalence Corporation sells its Brew Master product line in 20X1, recognizing a gain of $100,000 prior to applicable taxes of $35,000. During the final year of operations of the Brew Master line, Ambivalence lost $50,000 on its operation of the line; it lost $80,000 during the preceding year. The applicable amount of tax reductions related to these losses were $(17,000) and $(28,000), respectively. It reports these results in the income statement as follows:

	20X0	20X1
Discontinued operations:		
Loss from operation of the Brew Master product line (net of applicable taxes of $28,000 and $17,000)	$(52,000)	$(33,000)
Gain on disposal of Brew Master product line (net of applicable taxes of $35,000)	--	$65,000

Part of the sale agreement requires that Ambivalence reimburse the buyer for any outstanding warranty claims. In the following year, the amount of these claims is $31,000, prior to an applicable tax reduction of $(11,000). Ambivalence reports this update to the discontinued operation in the following year with this disclosure in the income statement:

	20X0	20X1	20X2
Discontinued operations:			
Loss from operation of the Brew Master product line (net of applicable taxes of $28,000 and $17,000)	$(52,000)	$(33,000)	--
Gain on disposal of Brew Master product line (net of applicable taxes of $35,000)	--	$65,000	--
Adjustment to gain on disposal of Brew Master product line (net of applicable taxes of $11,000)	--	--	$(20,000)

When the assets and liabilities of discontinued operations are itemized in the balance sheet, do not present them as a combined net figure. Instead, present them separately as assets and liabilities.

What if, despite initial expectations, an asset that has been classified as held for sale is not sold? If an asset no longer meets any one of the preceding six criteria for classification, remove it from the held-for-sale classification. At the time of reclassification, measure it at the lower of:

- The carrying amount of the asset prior to its classification as held-for-sale, minus any depreciation or amortization that would have been charged to it during the period when it was classified as held-for-sale, or
- The fair value of the asset when the decision was made not to sell it.

This measurement requirement effectively keeps a company from shifting assets into the held for sale classification in order to fraudulently avoid incurring any related depreciation expense.

Note: The GAAP codification states that an asset being reclassified *from* the held-for-sale designation should now be classified as held and used. Since there does not appear to be any distinction between the held and used classification and the normal accounting for fixed assets that are in use, we will assume that these assets are actually returned to their normal fixed asset accounting designations.

When the accounting records are adjusted for this measurement, record the transaction as an expense that is included in income from continuing operations and record the entry in the period when the decision is made not to sell the asset. Charge the expense to the income statement classification to which depreciation would normally be charged for the asset in question. Thus, the adjustment for a production machine would likely be charged to the cost of goods sold, while the adjustment for office equipment would likely be charged to general and administrative expense.

EXAMPLE

Ambivalence Corporation intends to sell its potion brewing factory, and so classifies the related assets into a disposal group and reports the group as held for sale, in the amount of $1,000,000. The journal entry is:

	Debit	Credit
Equipment held-for-sale	1,000,000	
Production machinery		1,000,000

After six months, the controller determines that the fair value of the disposal group has declined to $950,000, and so writes down the equipment cost with this entry:

	Debit	Credit
Loss on decline of fair value of held-for-sale equipment	50,000	
Equipment held-for-sale		50,000

The carrying value of the disposal group is now $950,000. After three more months, an independent appraiser determines that the fair value of the disposal group has increased to

$1,010,000. The controller can only record a gain up to the amount of any previously recorded losses, so he records the gain with this entry:

	Debit	Credit
Equipment held-for-sale	50,000	
Recovery of fair value of held-for-sale equipment		50,000

The carrying value of the disposal group is now $1,000,000.

After one full year has passed, management concludes that it cannot sell the disposal group, and decides to continue operating the potion brewing factory. The controller reclassifies the disposal group out of the held-for-sale classification with this entry:

	Debit	Credit
Production machinery	1,000,000	
Equipment held-for-sale		1,000,000

During the period when Ambivalence classified the disposal group as held for sale, it would have incurred a depreciation expense on the group of $50,000. The fair value of the group has now been re-appraised at $975,000. Since the carrying amount less depreciation of $950,000 is lower than the fair value of $975,000, Ambivalence records a charge of $50,000 to reduce the carrying amount of the group to $950,000 with the following entry:

	Debit	Credit
Depreciation – Production machinery	50,000	
Accumulated depreciation – Production machinery		50,000

Tip: The reclassification of assets into and out of the held-for-sale classification requires additional accounting effort to track. To minimize this effort, maintain a high capitalization limit, so that most assets are charged to expense when purchased. Also, if there is an expectation that an asset will be sold within a very short time period, it is easier to not shift the asset into the held-for-sale classification and then almost immediately sell it; instead, depreciate the asset up until the point of sale. Clearly, some judgment is needed to follow the intent of the held-for-sale rules without engaging in an excessive amount of unnecessary accounting work.

Abandoned Assets

If a company abandons an asset, consider the asset to be disposed of, and account for it as such (even if it remains on the premises). However, if the asset is only temporarily idle, do not consider it to be abandoned, and continue to depreciate it in a normal manner.

If an asset has been abandoned, reduce its carrying amount down to any remaining salvage value on the date when the decision is made to abandon the asset.

Idle Assets

Some fixed assets will be idle from time to time. There is no specific consideration of idle assets in GAAP, so continue to depreciate them in a normal manner. However, here are additional considerations regarding what an idle asset may indicate:

- *Asset impairment*. If an asset is idle, it may be an indicator that the value of the asset has declined, which may call for an impairment review.
- *Disclosure*. Identify idle assets separately on the balance sheet, and disclose why they are idle.
- *Useful life*. If an asset is idle, this may indicate that its useful life is shorter than the amount currently used to calculate its depreciation. This may call for a re-evaluation of its useful life.

Fixed Asset Disposal Accounting

There are two scenarios under which one may dispose of a fixed asset. The first situation arises when a fixed asset is being eliminated without receiving any payment in return. This is a common situation when a fixed asset is being scrapped because it is obsolete or no longer in use, and there is no resale market for it. In this case, reverse any accumulated depreciation and reverse the original asset cost. If the asset is fully depreciated, then that is the extent of the entry.

EXAMPLE

Ambivalence Corporation buys a machine for $100,000 and recognizes $10,000 of depreciation per year over the following ten years. At that time, the machine is not only fully depreciated, but also ready for the scrap heap. Ambivalence gives away the machine for free, and records the following entry.

	Debit	Credit
Accumulated Depreciation	100,000	
Machine asset		100,000

A variation on this situation is to write off a fixed asset that has not yet been completely depreciated. In this case, write off the remaining undepreciated amount of the asset to a loss account.

EXAMPLE

To use the same example, Ambivalence Corporation gives away the machine after eight years, when it has not yet depreciated $20,000 of the asset's original $100,000 cost. In this case, Ambivalence records the following entry:

	Debit	Credit
Loss on asset disposal	20,000	
Accumulated depreciation	80,000	
Machine asset		100,000

The second scenario arises when an asset is sold, so that cash is received (or some other asset) in exchange for the fixed asset being sold. Depending upon the price paid and the remaining amount of depreciation that has not yet been charged to expense, this can result in either a gain or a loss on sale of the asset.

EXAMPLE

Ambivalence Corporation still disposes of its $100,000 machine, but does so after seven years, and sells it for $35,000 in cash. In this case, it has already recorded $70,000 of depreciation expense. The entry is:

	Debit	Credit
Cash	35,000	
Accumulated depreciation	70,000	
Gain on asset disposal		5,000
Machine asset		100,000

What if Ambivalence had sold the machine for $25,000 instead of $35,000? Then there would be a loss of $5,000 on the sale. The entry would be:

	Debit	Credit
Cash	25,000	
Accumulated depreciation	70,000	
Loss on asset disposal	5,000	
Machine asset		100,000

If there is a gain or loss on disposal of a fixed asset, include it in income from continuing operations before income taxes on the income statement.

Fixed Asset Disclosures

This section contains the disclosures for various aspects of fixed assets that are required under GAAP. At the end of each set of requirements is a sample disclosure containing the more common elements of the requirements.

General Fixed Asset Disclosures

The financial statements should disclose the following information about a company's fixed assets:

- *Accumulated depreciation*. The balances in each of the major classes of fixed assets as of the end of the reporting period.
- *Asset aggregation*. The balances in each of the major classes of fixed assets as of the end of the reporting period.
- *Depreciation expense*. The amount of depreciation charged to expense in the reporting period.
- *Depreciation methods*. A description of the methods used to depreciate assets in the major asset classifications.

EXAMPLE

Suture Corporation gives a general description of its fixed asset recordation and depreciation as follows:

The company states its fixed assets at cost. For all fixed assets, the company calculates depreciation utilizing the straight-line method over the estimated useful lives for owned assets or, where appropriate, over the related lease terms for leasehold improvements. Useful lives range from 1 to 7 years.

Our fixed assets include the following approximate amounts:

	December 31,	
	20X2	20X1
Computer equipment	$9,770,000	$8,410,000
Computer software	2,800,000	1,950,000
Furniture and fixtures	860,000	780,000
Intangible assets	1,750,000	4,500,000
Leasehold improvements	400,000	360,000
Less: Accumulated depreciation and amortization	(5,400,000)	(4,800,000)
Totals	$10,180,000	$11,200,000

Change in Estimate Disclosures

It is relatively common to have changes in estimates related to fixed assets, since there are a variety of situations in which you may conclude that it is necessary to alter an asset's useful life, salvage value, or depreciation method – all of which are considered changes in estimate. If so, disclose the effect of a change in estimate on income from continuing operations, net income, and any per-share amounts for the reporting period. This disclosure is required only if the change is material.

EXAMPLE

Suture Corporation reports the following change in estimate within the notes accompanying its financial statements:

> During 20X4, management assessed its estimates of the residual values and useful lives of the company's fixed assets. Management revised its original estimates and now estimates that the medical production equipment that it had acquired in 20X1 and initially estimated to have a useful life of 8 years and salvage value of $100,000 will instead have a useful life of 12 years and salvage value of $80,000. The effects of this change in accounting estimate on the company's 20X4 financial statements are:
>
> Increase in:

Income from continuing operations and net income	$250,000
Earnings per share	$0.03

Intangible Asset Impairment Disclosures

If you have recognized an impairment loss for an intangible asset, disclose the following information for each such impairment:

- *Amount*. Note the amount of the impairment loss and the method used to determine fair value.
- *Description*. Describe the asset and the circumstances causing the impairment.
- *Location*. Note the line item in the income statement in which the loss is reported.
- *Segment*. State the segment in which the impaired asset is reported.

EXAMPLE

Suture Corporation determines that the values of several acquired patents have declined, which it discloses as follows:

> The company has written down the value of its patents related to the electronic remediation of cancer, on the grounds that subsequent testing of this equipment has

not resulted in the levels of cancer remission that management had anticipated. The company employed an appraiser to derive a new value that was based on anticipated cash flows. The resulting loss of $4.5 million was charged to the cancer treatment segment of the company, and is contained within the "Other Gains and Losses" line item on the income statement. The remaining value ascribed to these intangible assets as of the balance sheet date is $1.75 million. Management does not plan to sell the patents.

Intangible Asset Disclosures

If individual intangible assets have been acquired or the assets are part of a group, disclose the following information about them:

For Assets Subject to Amortization

- *Amortization expense.* Disclose the amortization charged to expense in the reporting period, as well as the estimated aggregate amortization expense for each of the next five fiscal years.
- *Amortization period.* Note the weighted-average amortization period, both for all intangible assets and by major intangible asset class.
- *Carrying amount.* Disclose the total amount of intangible assets, as well as the amount assigned to any major class of intangible asset. Also disclose accumulated amortization, both in total and by class of intangible asset.
- *Residual value.* If there is any significant residual value, disclose it in total and by major intangible asset class.

For Assets Not Subject to Amortization

- *Carrying amount.* Disclose the total amount of intangible assets, as well as the amount assigned to any major class of intangible asset.
- *Policy.* Describe the company's accounting policy for the treatment of any costs incurred in the renewal of an intangible asset's term.
- *Renewal costs.* If renewal costs are capitalized, disclose by major intangible asset class the total costs incurred during the reporting period to renew the term of an intangible asset.
- *Renewal period.* If these assets have renewal terms, state the weighted-average period before the next renewal for each major class of intangible asset.

EXAMPLE

Suture Corporation discloses the following information about its intangible assets:

	As of December 31, 20X1	
	Gross Carrying Amount	Accumulated Amortization
Amortized intangible assets		
Patents	$4,000,000	$1,450,000
Trademarks	1,200,000	400,000
Unpatented technology	800,000	650,000
Total	$6,000,000	$2,500,000
Unamortized intangible assets		
Distribution license	$500,000	
Trademark	450,000	
Total	$950,000	

Aggregate amortization expense:	
For the year ended 12/31/X1	$560,000
Estimated amortization expense:	
For the year ended 12/31/X2	$560,000
For the year ended 12/31/X3	420,000
For the year ended 12/31/X4	420,000
For the year ended 12/31/X5	380,000
For the year ended 12/31/X6	380,000

Not-for-Profit Fixed Asset Accounting

A not-for-profit entity is defined under GAAP as one possessing the following characteristics to some degree:

- *Contributions.* It receives significant contributions from other parties who do not expect any return compensation.
- *Purpose.* It does not exist primarily to earn a profit.
- *Ownership.* It does not have the ownership structure common in a business enterprise.

Thus, a not-for-profit entity is not one that is owned by investors, or which provides special benefits to its owners, members, or participants. Examples of not-for-profit organizations are associations, libraries, museums, and universities.

The accounting for fixed assets in a not-for-profit organization can be different from the accounting normally used by for-profit entities, *if the assets are donated*. In this section, we will review when to capitalize a contributed asset, what value to assign to it, and whether to depreciate it.

Initial Recognition of Fixed Assets

When a not-for-profit entity receives a contribution of any kind (not just a fixed asset), it records the asset with an offsetting entry to a revenue or gain account. Record a contribution as revenue if it is part of the entity's ongoing major activities, or record it as a gain if the contribution is part of peripheral or incidental activities.

If the contributor places a restriction on the use of a fixed asset, this does not impact the underlying value of the donation, so record the same amount for such a contributed asset as would be done for one without a restriction, with no change in the timing of recognition.

If a not-for-profit entity receives a contributed asset for which there is a major uncertainty about its value, it is not necessary to recognize it in the accounting records. Examples of such assets are those of historical value, photographs, or items that may be of use solely for scientific research.

Conversely, the accountant should record an asset that has a future economic benefit or service potential (usually by exchanging it for cash or using it to generate goods or services).

EXAMPLE

Newton Enterprises provides free science classes to high school students. It receives the following contributions:

- A philosopher's stone. The stone is of historical significance, but probably does not transmute lead into gold. Since there is considerable uncertainty about its value, Newton does not record the asset.
- A used lawn mower. The lawn mower is of no direct use to Newton's primary operations, and will be sold. Newton accordingly records the lawn mower as a gain.
- An electron microscope. The microscope is of direct use in Newton's primary operations, so Newton records it as revenue.

As an example of the journal entries to be used for a donated asset, if the microscope in the preceding example were to be valued at $50,000, the journal entry might be:

	Debit	Credit
Scientific devices	50,000	
Revenue		50,000

If the lawn mower in the preceding example were to be valued at $1,000, the journal entry might be:

	Debit	Credit
Maintenance equipment	1,000	
Gain on contributed assets		1,000

Restrictions on Contributed Assets

If a donor makes a contribution that is an *unconditional promise to give*, recognize the contribution when received. This calls for sufficient verifiable documentation that the promise was both made and received. The promise should be legally enforceable. If a contributor is able to rescind the promise to give, do not recognize the asset being contributed.

If a contributor makes a contribution that is a conditional promise to give, only recognize the asset when the underlying conditions have been substantially met (e.g., at the point when the promise becomes unconditional).

EXAMPLE

Newton Enterprises receives an offer from a contributor to pay $2 million for a new classroom building, but only if Newton can raise matching funds from other contributors within one year. Given the conditional nature of this offer, Newton cannot record the asset until the matching funds have been raised within the specified time period.

A conditional promise to give may be considered essentially unconditional if there is only a remote possibility that the condition will not be met.

EXAMPLE

Newton Enterprises receives a promise of multi-year funding for new schools, but only if Newton supplies its financial statements to the contributor at the end of each fiscal year. There is only a remote possibility that Newton will not comply with this requirement, so Newton can treat the contribution as an unconditional promise to give.

What if a donor contributes a fixed asset, but attaches a conditional promise to the contribution? The fixed asset is now on the premises, but can it be recorded as a fixed asset? No. Until the condition has been met or the donor has waived it, record the received asset as a refundable advance from the donor.

Valuation of Contributed Assets

A donated asset should be recognized at its fair value as of the receipt date. The following techniques are available for deriving fair value:

- *Market approach.* Use information from actual market transactions to arrive at an estimated fair value. Ideally, this information is based on quoted prices in an active market for identical items, but may also use information from transactions for similar items, or just the best available information.
- *Income approach.* Use discounted cash flows to derive the present value of an asset.
- *Cost approach.* Use an asset's current replacement cost. This is essentially the cost of acquiring or building a substitute asset that has comparable utility.

If the income approach is to be used and the asset being contributed will not be received for at least a year, it is possible to use the projected fair value of the asset as of the date when it is expected to be received, discounted back to its present value. Where it is impossible to determine fair value as of a future date, use the fair value of the asset at the initial recognition date, though without any discounting to present value.

EXAMPLE

Newton Enterprises is given an office building for use as a training center by a city government that has no use for the building. The city is suffering through a severe downturn, and the government was unable to find a buyer for the building. In general, there is very little market information available for the valuation of similar buildings, given the paucity of sale transactions. Newton also has trouble using the income approach to derive a value for the building, since it gives science classes for free. Thus, Newton elects to use the cost approach to value the building, under which it determines that the cost to create a substitute building of comparable utility would be $700,000.

Valuation of Contributed Services

What if volunteers donate their time to construct a fixed asset? Record the value of these services in either of the following situations:

- The services create or enhance non-financial assets; or
- The services require specialized skills, are provided by persons with those skills, and would otherwise need to be purchased.

Value these services at either their fair value or at the fair value of the fixed asset created or the change in value of the fixed asset being improved.

EXAMPLE

Newton Enterprises constructs a science school, using the services of a large group of volunteers, which include architects, carpenters, electricians, and plumbers. Newton spends $800,000 on materials for the building project. Once the asset is placed in service, a third-party appraiser estimates that the fair value of the building is now $1.2 million. Newton can therefore record the building asset at a cost of $1.2 million, of which $400,000 is the value of contributed services.

Valuation of Art, Historical Treasures, and Similar Items

If a donor contributes works of art, historical treasures, or similar items, it is possible to recognize them as assets, with offsetting revenue or gains. This only applies if the items contributed are not part of a collection. If such contributions are part of a collection, use any of the following alternatives for reporting them:

- Record them as fixed assets.; or
- Record only as fixed assets only those items received after a specific date; or
- Do not record them.

It is not allowed to record only *selected* collections or items as fixed assets; instead, the accountant must consistently apply any recordation policy selected for *all* collections or items.

Capitalize the cost of major preservation or restoration projects and assign them useful lives that extend until the next expected preservation or restoration project for the same asset.

EXAMPLE

Newton Enterprises maintains a small science museum, to which a donor contributes an original quadruplex telegraph built by Thomas Edison. An independent appraisal establishes that the device has a fair value of $150,000. Newton adds the telegraph to its Edison collection and records it as a fixed asset. This results in revenue of $150,000, as well as a new fixed asset.

Depreciation of Fixed Assets

A not-for-profit entity should depreciate any contributed assets that it has recorded as fixed assets, if they have a useful life. If an asset's useful life is extremely long (as would be the case for a work of art), it is allowable to not recognize depreciation for it. Only avoid depreciation in this manner if both of the following conditions exist:

- The asset should be preserved perpetually, due to its cultural, aesthetic, or historical value; and

- The entity has the ability to preserve the asset (such as by preserving it in a protected environment), and is currently doing so.

Art collections should be depreciated, on the grounds that they experience wear and tear during their intended uses that requires periodic major restoration efforts.

If the cost of a major restoration project has been capitalized, depreciate this cost over the expected period before the next restoration project is expected. Do this even if the asset being restored or preserved is not depreciated.

Summary

Even a brief perusal of this chapter will make it clear that the accounting for fixed assets is one of the more time-consuming accounting activities, simply because the related accounting records must be monitored (and possibly adjusted) for years. Accordingly, the efficient accountant will do anything possible to charge expenditures to expense at once, rather than recording them as fixed assets. The best options for reducing the number of fixed assets are to maintain a high capitalization limit, and to adopt a skeptical attitude when anyone wants to add subsequent expenditures to a fixed asset. The result should be a considerably reduced number of high-value fixed assets.

Chapter 21
Liabilities

Introduction

With the exception of brief discussions of liability extinguishments and joint and several liabilities, the GAAP treatment of the liabilities topic is really about how to account for and disclose insurance-related assessments. This topic is primarily targeted at insurers, but can apply to businesses that self-insure their workers' compensation claims.

Related Chapters

See the following chapters for discussions of issues related to liabilities:

- Asset Retirement and Environmental Obligations
- Exit or Disposal Cost Obligations
- Commitments
- Contingencies
- Guarantees
- Debt

Extinguishments of Liabilities

A business may extinguish a liability through the transfer of assets to a creditor, by obtaining a release from the creditor, or by setting aside assets that will be used to settle the liability. A liability is considered to have been extinguished under either of the following circumstances:

- *Payment*. The debtor pays the creditor.
- *Release*. The creditor or a court releases the debtor from its obligation. This situation can arise when the collateral for a debt is sold in conjunction with the assumption of the related debt by a third party. If the debtor then becomes secondarily liable, this is still considered a release, though the debtor now becomes a guarantor (see the Guarantees chapter), and should value the guarantee at its fair value.

Joint and Several Liability Arrangements

A joint and several liability situation typically arises when two or more entities are found liable as a result of a lawsuit judgment. The plaintiff can collect the entire judgment from any of the parties. This usually means that the plaintiff will keep collecting from the various liable parties until paid in full. A joint and several liability can also result from a loan agreement where debt and interest payments are due, or under a variety of receivable arrangements.

When the reporting entity is one of the liable parties, and the full amount of the liability has been fixed as of the reporting date, measure the amount of the liability as the sum of the following two items:

1. The portion of the total liability that the entity agreed with its co-obligors to pay; and
2. The additional amount (if any) that the entity expects to pay on behalf of the co-obligors, due to their inability to pay their shares of the obligation. If there is a range of possible additional payment amounts, use the most likely figure. If there is no most likely figure, use the minimum liability in the range of estimates.

Insurance-Related Assessments

An insurance entity may be subjected to a variety of assessments that relate to its insurance activities. For example, a state government may impose an assessment on an insurance company that is used to pay for the covered claims of other insurance companies that are now insolvent. Four of the more common assessment methods are:

*   *Historical premiums basis*. Assessments are based on an average of the premiums written or received in prior periods before an insolvency occurs. This approach is commonly used to cover the benefit payments of insolvent annuity, life, and health insurance companies.
*   *Future premiums basis*. Assessments are based on a percentage of the premiums written in the years following an insolvency. This approach is commonly used to cover the claims of insolvent property and casualty insurance companies.
*   *Prefunded premiums basis*. Assessments are based on the current level of written premiums, and are intended to cover the costs of insolvencies that have not yet occurred. This approach may be used to cover the claims of insolvent property and casualty insurance companies.
*   *Administrative basis*. This is a flat fee per insurer, which is used to fund the operations of a state's insurance guaranty association.

It may be possible for an insurer to recover a portion of these assessments through various redemption methods.

There are other insurance-related assessments that either cover the administrative costs of the applicable state governments, or fund certain types of injuries that would otherwise be excessively burdensome for employers. These assessments may be based on a percentage of an insurer's written premiums, or the insurer's proportion of incurred losses or paid losses in relation to these figures for all insurers subject to the assessments.

If an insurer is subject to an assessment that is related to its insurance activities, it should recognize a liability only when all of the following conditions are present:

- *Estimate*. It is reasonably possible to estimate the amount of the assessment within a range of amounts.
- *Obligation*. The underlying cause of the assessment has occurred before or prior to the date of the financial statements.
- *Probable assessment*. It is probable that a premium-based assessment will be imposed on the insurer, based on whether an insolvency has occurred, as per the state's definition of an insolvent insurer. Alternatively, it is probable that a prefunded assessment or administrative assessment will be imposed, based on the existence of the premiums on which the assessments will be based.

There are five possible ways to account for these assessments, which are:

- *Historical premiums basis*. Since assessments are based on premiums already written, recognize a liability for the full amount of the future assessment that is associated with a particular insolvency.
- *Future premiums basis*. Since the assessment is based on premiums written after the insolvency, there are two ways to account for the assessment. Either recognize a liability for the full amount of the future assessment that cannot be avoided, or recognize a liability when the insurer writes the related premiums (thereby deferring expense recognition until a later date).
- *Prefunded premiums basis*. Recognize a liability as premiums are written.
- *Administrative basis*. Record assessments related to administrative fees in the period assessed by the government.
- *Loss basis*. Recognize a liability when the related losses occur.

If the estimate of an assessment amount is a range of possible values, record the assessment based on that amount in the range that appears most likely to occur. If there is no such value, record the minimum value in the estimated range.

It is allowable, but not required, to discount the resulting assessment liability based on expected future cash flows, and only record the present value of the liability. There are no GAAP instructions regarding the interest rate to be used for the discounting calculation, other than that the rate should be "appropriate."

There may be situations where a portion of an insurance assessment will be recoverable through policy surcharges or other methods. If so, record an asset when the recovery is probable and the amount can be reasonably estimated. This accounting also applies to recoveries that will occur in the future from business currently in force (not including renewals of short-duration contracts) or which the insurer is obligated to write, but not to recoveries that are dependent upon future premium rate structures. It may be necessary to create an offsetting valuation allowance if it appears that some portion of this asset will not be realized in the future.

If a policy surcharge is essentially a pass-through that is then paid to the government, do not record the surcharge receipts as revenue or the pass-through payments as expense; instead, the accounting is similar to what is used for sales taxes, where the company is essentially a collection agent for the government.

A noninsurance entity may be the subject of an assessment when it self-insures (usually for workers' compensation claims) and the government uses an assessment to create a fund for additional employee claims made. There are several calculation methods available to a noninsurance entity for calculating the amount of an assessment accrual. Possible calculation options are:

- The assessment ratio used by the government in prior periods
- The total amount assessed in prior periods
- Changes in the current period that would alter the expected assessment amount

---

EXAMPLE

Armadillo Industries uses self-insurance to pay for its government-mandated workers' compensation obligations. The company is required to participate in the state government's second injury fund, from which it can recover indemnity claims from previously injured workers. The government obtains cash for this fund by assessing self-insurers. In the prior year, the amount of the assessment was 0.55% of the company's loss payouts; the government is limited by law to a 0.80% assessment.

Based on this information, Armadillo should recognize an assessment liability for 0.55% of its loss payouts, unless there is better information available regarding a different percentage. Also, the company could consider disclosing that the liability could reach the 0.80% maximum percentage allowed by law.

Prepaid Stored-Value Products

A prepaid stored-value product is a product that is intended to be accepted as a form of payment, such as a prepaid gift card or a traveler's check. When an organization sells a prepaid stored-value product, it expects some amount of breakage, which is that portion of the dollar value of the product that is not redeemed for cash or used to make a purchase. When a firm anticipates breakage on a liability associated with one of these products, it should derecognize the liability related to the expected breakage. The amount of the derecognition should be in proportion to the pattern of rights that the firm expects the product holder to exercise, and only to the extent that it is probable that a significant reversal of the recognized breakage amount will not occur thereafter. At the end of each period, the business should update its estimated breakage amounts to best represent the current circumstances. These updates are treated as changes in accounting estimate.

Note: This guidance does not apply when breakage must be remitted to a government entity in order to be in compliance with unclaimed property laws (which cover most prepaid stored-value products).

Liabilities Disclosures

If discounting has been used to record the present value of assessment-related assets or liabilities, disclose the undiscounted amount of the asset or liability, as well as the discount rate used.

If there is a joint and several liability situation, disclose the following information:

- The nature of the liability situation, including how the liability originated, the terms of the arrangement, and the entity's relationship with the other liable parties
- The grand total liability due under the arrangement from all parties
- The carrying amount that the entity has recognized for the liability
- The amount of any receivables due from co-obligors for amounts the entity has paid on their behalf
- The nature of any recourse provisions that the entity against third parties to collect on amounts paid out, as well as any limitations on these provisions
- The line items in which the liability (and any subsequent changes to it) was presented in the financial statements

If the undiscounted amounts of assessment-related assets and liabilities were recorded, disclose the following:

- The amount of the asset and liability
- The period over which it is expected that the assessment will be paid
- The period over which the recorded assessment asset should be realized

If an entity sells prepaid stored-value products and recognizes a breakage amount, it must disclose its method for recognizing breakage, as well as the significant judgments made in applying the method.

Summary

Only a small number of liability-related issues were addressed in this chapter, which does not mean that GAAP ignores liabilities – far from it. See the Related Chapters section for a listing of other GAAP areas in which more specialized issues related to liabilities are addressed.

Chapter 22
Asset Retirement and Environmental Obligations

410 = GAAP codification area for asset retirement and environmental obligations

Introduction

An asset retirement obligation (ARO) is a liability associated with the retirement of a fixed asset, such as a legal requirement to return a site to its previous condition. The concept of an ARO is dealt with in detail within GAAP. An example near the end of the chapter illustrates many of the concepts noted below. In addition, this chapter addresses when to record a liability associated with an environmental obligation, how to determine the amount of the liability and the types of costs that should be included in it.

Overview of Asset Retirement Obligations

A company usually incurs an ARO due to a legal obligation. It may also incur an ARO if a company promises a third party (even the public at large) that it will engage in ARO activities; the circumstances of this promise will drive the determination of whether there is an actual liability. This liability may exist even if there has been no formal action against the company. When making the determination of liability, base the evaluation on current laws, not on projections of what laws there may be in the future, when the asset retirement occurs.

EXAMPLE

Glow Atomic operates an atomic power generation facility, and is required by law to bring the property back to its original condition when the plant is eventually decertified. The company has come under some pressure by various environmental organizations to take the remediation one step further and create a public park on the premises. Because of the significant negative publicity generated by these groups, the company issues a press release in which it commits to create the park. There is no legal requirement for the company to incur this additional expense, so the company's legal counsel should evaluate the facts to determine if there is a legal obligation.

A business should recognize the fair value of an ARO when it incurs the liability, and if it can make a reasonable estimate of the fair value of the ARO.

EXAMPLE

Glow Atomic has completed the construction of an atomic power generation facility, but has not yet taken delivery of fuel rods or undergone certification tests. It will incur an ARO for decontamination, but since it has not yet begun operations, it has not begun to contaminate, and therefore should not yet record an ARO liability.

If a fair value is not initially obtainable, recognize the ARO at a later date, when the fair value becomes available. If a company acquires a fixed asset to which an ARO is attached, recognize a liability for the ARO as of the fixed asset acquisition date.

If there is not sufficient information available to reasonably estimate the fair value of an ARO, it may be possible to use an expected present value technique that assigns probabilities to cash flows, thereby creating an estimate of the fair value of the ARO. Use an expected present value technique under either of the following scenarios:

- Other parties have specified the settlement date and method of settlement, so that the only uncertainty is whether the obligation will be enforced.
- There is information available from which to estimate the range of possible settlement dates and possible methods of settlement, as well as the probabilities associated with them.

Examples of the sources from which to obtain the information needed for the preceding estimation requirements are past practice within the company, industry practice, the stated intentions of management, or the estimated useful life of the asset (which indicates a likely ARO settlement date at the end of the useful life).

> **Tip:** The ARO settlement date may be quite a bit further in the future than the useful life of an asset may initially indicate, if the company intends to prolong the useful life with asset upgrades, or has a history of doing so.

If there is an unambiguous requirement that causes an ARO, but there is a low likelihood of a performance requirement, a liability must still be recognized. When a low probability of performance is incorporated into the expected present value calculation for the ARO liability, this will likely reduce the amount of the ARO to be recognized. Even if there has been a history of non-enforcement of prior AROs for which there was an unambiguous obligation, do not defer the recognition of a liability.

The Initial Measurement of an Asset Retirement Obligation

In most cases, the only way to determine the fair value of an ARO is to use an expected present value technique. When constructing an expected present value of future cash flows, incorporate the following points into the calculation:

- *Discount rate*. Use a credit-adjusted risk-free rate to discount cash flows to their present value. Thus, the credit standing of a business may impact the discount rate used.
- *Probability distribution*. When calculating the expected present value of an ARO, and there are only two possible outcomes, assign a 50 percent probability to each one until there is additional information that alters the initial probability distribution. Otherwise, spread the probability across the full set of possible scenarios.

EXAMPLE

Glow Atomic is compiling the cost of a decontamination ARO several years in the future. It is uncertain of the cost, since supplier fees fluctuate considerably. It arrives at an expected weighted average cash flow based on the following probability analysis:

Cash Flow Estimates	Probability Assessment	Expected Cash Flows
$12,500,000	10%	$1,250,000
15,000,000	15%	2,250,000
16,000,000	50%	8,000,000
22,500,000	25%	5,625,000
Weighted average cash flows		$17,125,000

Follow these steps in calculating the expected present value of an ARO:

1. Estimate the timing and amount of the cash flows associated with the retirement activities.
2. Determine the credit-adjusted risk-free rate.
3. Recognize any period-to-period increase in the carrying amount of the ARO liability as *accretion expense*. To do so, multiply the beginning liability by the credit-adjusted risk-free rate derived when the liability was first measured.
4. Recognize upward liability revisions as a new liability layer, and discount them at the current credit-adjusted risk-free rate.
5. Recognize downward liability revisions by reducing the appropriate liability layer, and discount the reduction at the rate used for the initial recognition of the related liability layer.

When an ARO liability is initially recognized, also capitalize the related asset retirement cost by adding it to the carrying amount of the related fixed asset.

Subsequent Measurement of an Asset Retirement Obligation

It is possible that an ARO liability will not remain static over the life of the related fixed asset. Instead, the liability may change over time. If the liability increases, consider the incremental increase in each period to be an additional layer of liability, in addition to any previous liability layers. The following points will assist in the recognition of these additional layers:

- Initially recognize each layer at its fair value.

EXAMPLE

Glow Atomic has been operating an atomic power plant for three years. It initially recognized an ARO of $250 million for the eventual dismantling of the plant after its useful life has ended. In the fifth year, Glow detects groundwater contamination, and recognizes an additional layer of ARO liability for $20 million to deal with it. In the seventh year, a leak in the sodium cooling lines causes overheating and a significant release of radioactive steam that impacts 50 square miles of land downwind from the facility. Glow recognizes an additional layer of ARO liability of $150 million to address this issue.

- Systematically allocate the ARO liability to expense over the useful life of the underlying asset.
- Measure changes in the liability due to the passage of time, using the credit-adjusted risk-free rate when each layer of liability was first recognized. Recognize this cost as an increase in the liability. When charged to expense, this is classified as accretion expense (which is not the same as interest expense).
- As the time period shortens before an ARO is realized, the assessment of the timing, amount, and probabilities associated with cash flows will improve. It will likely be necessary to alter the ARO liability based on these changes in estimate. If an upward revision is made in the ARO liability, then discount it using the current credit-adjusted risk-free rate. If a downward revision is made in the ARO liability, discount it using the original credit-adjusted risk-free rate when the liability layer was first recognized. If the liability layer to which the downward adjustment relates cannot be identified, use a weighted-average credit-adjusted risk-free rate to discount it.

Settlement of an Asset Retirement Obligation

An ARO is normally settled only when the underlying fixed asset is retired, though it is possible that some portion of an ARO will be settled prior to asset retirement.

If it becomes apparent that no expenses will be required as part of the retirement of an asset, reverse any remaining unamortized ARO to zero.

> **Tip:** If a company cannot fulfill its ARO responsibilities and a third party does so instead, this does not relieve the company from recording an ARO liability, on the grounds that it may now have an obligation to pay the third party instead.

EXAMPLE

Glow Atomic operates an atomic power generation facility, and is legally required to decontaminate the facility when it is decommissioned in five years. Glow uses the following assumptions about the ARO:

- The decontamination cost is $90 million.
- The risk-free rate is 5%, to which Glow adds 3% to reflect the effect of its credit standing.
- The assumed rate of inflation over the five-year period is four percent.

With an average inflation rate of 4% per year for the next five years, the current decontamination cost of $90 million increases to approximately $109.5 million by the end of the fifth year. The expected present value of the $109.5 million payout, using the 8% credit-adjusted risk-free rate, is $74,524,000 (calculated as $109.5 million × 0.68058 discount rate).

Glow then calculates the amount of annual accretion using the 8% rate, as shown in the following table:

Year	Beginning Liability	Accretion	Ending Liability
1	$74,524,000	$5,962,000	$80,486,000
2	80,486,000	6,439,000	86,925,000
3	86,925,000	6,954,000	93,879,000
4	93,879,000	7,510,000	101,389,000
5	101,389,000	8,111,000	109,500,000

Glow then combines the accretion expense with the straight-line depreciation expense noted in the following table to show how all components of the ARO are charged to expense over the next five years. Note that the accretion expense is carried forward from the preceding table. The depreciation is based on the $74,524,000 present value of the ARO, spread evenly over five years.

Asset Retirement and Environmental Obligations

Year	Accretion Expense	Depreciation Expense	Total Expense
1	$5,962,000	$14,904,800	$20,866,800
2	6,439,000	14,904,800	21,343,800
3	6,954,000	14,904,800	21,858,800
4	7,510,000	14,904,800	22,414,800
5	8,111,000	14,904,800	23,015,800
			$109,500,000

After the plant is closed, Glow commences its decontamination activities. The actual cost is $115 million.

Here is a selection of the journal entries that Glow recorded over the term of the ARO:

	Debit	Credit
Facility decontamination asset	90,000,000	
Asset retirement obligation liability		90,000,000
To record the initial fair value of the asset retirement obligation		

	Debit	Credit
Depreciation expense	14,904,800	
Accumulated depreciation		14,904,800
To record the annual depreciation on the asset retirement obligation		

	Debit	Credit
Accretion expense	As noted in schedule	
Asset retirement obligation liability		As noted in schedule
To record the annual accretion expense on the asset retirement obligation liability		

	Debit	Credit
Loss on ARO settlement	5,500,000	
Remediation expense		5,500,000
To record settlement of the excess asset retirement obligation		

Overview of Environmental Obligations

There are a number of federal laws that impose an obligation on a business to remediate sites that contain environmentally hazardous conditions, as well as to control or prevent pollution. Remediation can include feasibility studies, cleanup costs, legal fees, government oversight costs, and restoration costs.

In total, these laws can create a serious liability for a business, to the extent of causing the business to go bankrupt. Consider, for example, the extent of liability associated with a Superfund site, where liability can be associated with:

- The current owner or operator of the site
- Previous owners or operators of the site at the time of disposal of hazardous substances
- Parties that arranged for the disposal of hazardous substances found at the site
- Parties that transported hazardous substances to the site

The level of liability imposed by other environmental laws may not be as all-encompassing as the Superfund liability, but the level of liability imposed can still be crushing. Accordingly, the accounting for environmental obligations must be well documented, in order to convey the full scope of the liability.

In general, a liability for an environmental obligation should be accrued if both of the following circumstances are present:

- It is probable that an asset has been impaired or a liability has been incurred. This is based on both of the following criteria:

  o An assertion has been made that the business bears responsibility for a past event; and
  o It is probable that the outcome of the assertion will be unfavorable to the business.

- The amount of the loss or a range of loss can be reasonably estimated.

It is recognized that the liability associated with environmental obligations can change dramatically over time, depending on the number and type of hazardous substances involved, the financial condition of other responsible parties, and other factors. Accordingly, the recorded liability associated with environmental obligations can change. Further, it may not be possible to initially estimate some components of the liability, which does not prevent other components of the liability from being recognized as soon as possible.

EXAMPLE

Glow Atomics has been notified by the government that it must conduct a remedial investigation and feasibility study for a Superfund site to which it sent uranium waste products in the past. There is sufficient information to estimate the cost of the study, for which Glow records an accrued liability. However, there is no way to initially determine the extent of any additional liabilities associated with the site until the study has at least commenced. Accordingly, Glow continually reviews the preliminary findings of the study, and updates the liability for its environmental obligation based on changes in that information.

Once there is information available regarding the extent of an environmental obligation, a business should record its best estimate of the liability. If it is not possible to create a best estimate, then at least a minimum estimate of the liability should be recorded. The estimate is refined as better information becomes available.

In some cases, it is possible to derive a reasonable estimate of liability quite early in the remediation process, because it is similar to the remediation that a business has encountered at other sites. In these instances, the full amount of the liability should be recognized at once.

The costs associated with the treatment of environmental contamination costs should be charged to expense in nearly all cases. The sole exceptions are:

- The costs incurred will increase the capacity of the property, or extend its life, or improve its safety or efficiency
- The costs incurred are needed to prepare a property for sale that is currently classified as held for sale
- The costs improve the property, as well as mitigate or prevent environmental contamination that has yet to occur and that might otherwise arise from future operations

---

EXAMPLE

Armadillo Industries spends $250,000 to construct a concrete pad that is designed to prevent fluid leaks from causing groundwater contamination. Making this investment improves the safety of the property, while also preventing future environmental contamination. Consequently, Armadillo can capitalize the $250,000 cost of the concrete pad, and should depreciate it over the remaining useful life of the property.

Measurement of Environmental Obligations

In order to determine the extent of the liability associated with an environmental obligation, follow these steps:

1. Identify those parties likely to be considered responsible for the site requiring remediation. These potentially responsible parties may include the following:

    - Participating parties
    - Recalcitrant parties
    - Unproven parties
    - Unknown parties
    - Orphan share parties

2. Determine the likelihood that those parties will pay their share of the liability associated with site remediation, based primarily on their financial condition. There is a presumption that costs will only be allocated among the participating responsible parties, since the other parties are less likely to pay their shares of the liability.

3. Based on the preceding steps, calculate the percentage of the total liability that the company should record. The sources for this information can include the liability percentages that the responsible parties have agreed to, or which have been assigned by a consultant, or which have been assigned by the Environmental Protection Agency (EPA). If the company chooses to record the liability in a different amount, it should be based on objective, verifiable information, examples of which are:

- Existing data about the types and amounts of waste at the site
- Prior experience with liability allocations in comparable situations
- Reports issued by environmental specialists
- Internal data that refutes EPA allegations

EXAMPLE

Armadillo Industries has been notified by the EPA that it is a potentially responsible party in a groundwater contamination case. The EPA has identified three companies as being potentially responsible. The three parties employ an arbitrator to allocate the responsibility for costs among the companies. The arbitrator derives the following allocations:

	Allocation Percentage
Armadillo Industries	40%
Boxcar Munitions	20%
Chelsea Chemicals	20%
	80%
Recalcitrant share (nonparticipating parties)	15%
Orphan share (no party can be identified)	5%
Total	100%

The total estimated remediation cost is estimated to be $5 million. Armadillo's direct share of this amount is $2 million (calculated as $5 million total remediation × 40% share). Also, Armadillo should record a liability for its share of those amounts allocated to other parties who are not expected to pay their shares, which is $500,000 (calculated as half of the total allocation for responsible parties × the cost allocated to the recalcitrant and orphan shares).

The costs that should be included in a company's liability for environmental obligations include the following:

- Direct remediation activity costs, such as investigations, risk assessments, remedial actions, activities related to government oversight, and post-remediation monitoring.
- The compensation and related benefit costs for those employees expected to spend a significant amount of their time on remediation activities.

When measuring these costs, do so for the estimated time periods during which activities will occur, which means that an inflation factor should be included for periods further in the future. It may also be possible to include a productivity factor that is caused by gaining experience with remediation efforts over time, and which may reduce mitigation costs. When it is not possible to estimate the costs of inflation, perhaps due to uncertainties about the timing of expenditures, it is acceptable to initially record costs at their current-cost estimates, and adjust them later, as more precise information becomes available.

Any costs related to routine environmental compliance activities, as well as any litigation costs associated with potential recoveries, are not considered part of the remediation effort, and so are not included in the environmental obligation liability. These costs are to be charged to expense as incurred.

Changes in the environmental liability are especially likely when there are multiple parties involved, since additional parties may be added over time, or the apportionment of liability between parties may change. Also, estimates of the exact amount of cost incurred will change continually. For these reasons, the amount of liability recorded for environmental obligations will almost certainly not be the exact amount that is eventually incurred, and so will have to be updated at regular intervals. If so, each update is treated as a change in estimate, which means that there is no retroactive change in the liability reported by a business; instead, the change is recorded only on a go-forward basis.

Recoveries Related to Environmental Obligations

It is possible that a business may contact other entities concerning the recovery of funds expended on environmental remediation, on the grounds that the other entities are liable for the remediation (or are liable because they are insurers).

The recognition of an asset related to the recovery of an environmental obligation should not be made unless recovery of the claimed amount is considered probable and the amount can be reasonably estimated. If a claim is currently the subject of litigation, it is reasonable to assume that recovery of the claim is not probable, and so should not be recognized.

A recovery can be recorded at its undiscounted amount if the liability is not discounted, and the timing of the recovery is dependent on the timing of the liability payment. This will be the case in most situations, so the recovery will generally be recorded at its undiscounted amount.

Asset Retirement and Environmental Obligations Disclosures

This section contains the disclosures for various aspects of asset retirement and environmental obligations that are required under GAAP. At the end of each set of requirements is a sample disclosure containing the more common elements of the requirements.

Asset Retirement Obligations

If a company's assets are subject to asset retirement obligations, disclose the following information:

- *Description.* Describe any asset retirement obligations, as well as fixed assets with which they are associated.
- *Fair values.* Disclose the fair values of any assets that are legally restricted for purposes of setting asset retirement obligations. If it is not possible to reasonably estimate the fair value of an asset retirement obligation, state the reasons for this estimation difficulty.
- *Reconciliation.* Present a reconciliation of the beginning and ending carrying amounts of all asset retirement obligations, in aggregate, showing the changes attributable to the following items:
  - o Accretion expense
  - o Liabilities incurred in the reporting period
  - o Liabilities settled in the reporting period
  - o Revisions to estimated cash flows

EXAMPLE

Suture Corporation discloses the following information about its asset retirement obligations:

The company records the fair value of a liability for an asset retirement obligation (ARO) that is recorded when there is a legal obligation associated with the retirement of a tangible long-lived asset and the liability can be reasonably estimated. The recording of ARO primarily affects the company's accounting for its mining of properties in Nevada for various substances used in its medical research. The company performs periodic reviews of its assets for any changes in the facts and circumstances that might require recognition of a retirement obligation.

The following table indicates the changes to the company's before-tax asset retirement obligations in 20X3, 20X2, and 20X1:

(000s)	20X3	20X2	20X1
Balance at January 1	$5,350	$4,450	$2,900
Liabilities assumed in ABC acquisition	--	--	1,200
Liabilities incurred	200	250	100
Liabilities settled	(1,000)	(400)	(200)
Accretion expense	270	250	300
Revisions in estimated cash flows	1,320	800	150
Balance at December 31	$6,140	$5,350	$4,450

In the table above, the amounts for 20X2 and 20X3 associated with "Revisions in estimated cash flows" reflect increased cost estimates to abandon the Harkness Mine in Nevada, due to increased regulatory requirements.

Environmental Obligations

The expenses associated with environmental obligations are to be recorded within operating expenses, on the grounds that environmental remediation is considered a regular cost of doing business. Credits from the recovery of environmental costs are also to be recorded within operating expenses.

If a business has recorded environmental obligations, disclose the following information:

- *Discounting.* Note whether the liability is measured on a discounted basis, the undiscounted amount, and the discount rate used. This is the only disclosure required for environmental obligations.
- *Obligation description.* Companies are encouraged to disclose the circumstances triggering a liability, as well as any policy related to the timing of recognition of recoveries.
- *Loss contingencies.* Disclosure of environmental remediation loss contingencies is encouraged.
- *Liability detail.* Companies are encouraged to disclose additional information about their environmental liabilities, including:
    - The time frame of disbursements
    - The time frame for realization of recognized probable recoveries
    - The reasons why losses cannot be estimated
    - If information about a specific remediation obligation is relevant to understanding the financial statements, note the amount accrued for that site, the nature of any reasonably possible loss contingency and an estimate of the possible loss, whether other potentially responsible parties are involved and the company's share of the obligation, the status of regulatory proceedings, and the time period during which the contingency is likely to be resolved.
    - The expense related to environmental remediation loss contingencies, the amount of any expense reduction caused by recoveries from third parties, and the income statement caption in which these costs and reductions are included.

- *Impact of laws and regulations.* Companies are encouraged to provide a description of the applicability and financial impact of environmental laws and regulations on their business, as well as how this may cause loss contingencies related to the remediation of environmental issues in the future.

EXAMPLE

Armadillo Industries has been notified of its liability to decontaminate the soil at one of its facilities, for which it provides the following disclosure in its financial statements:

Armadillo has begun a decontamination project related to the soil near its Central City facility. The company estimates that the cost of the project will be at least $1.8

million, and has accrued the entire amount of this expense as an operating expense. The total cost of the project will depend on the amount of soil contamination found as the project progresses, and may be as much as $3.2 million. The company expects that all remediation activities will have been completed within two years.

Summary

The accounting for an asset retirement obligation can be complex, especially if there are multiple liability layers and changes to those layers occur with some frequency. Because of the additional accounting effort required to track AROs, it makes sense to use every effort to avoid the recognition of an ARO within the boundaries set by GAAP. In many cases, the amount of an ARO will likely be so minimal as to not require recognition. However, in such industries as mining, chemicals, and power generation, the concept of the ARO is of great concern, and forms a significant proportion of a company's total liabilities.

Environmental obligations can strike any company, large or small, and can result in a massive liability. The accounting for this liability is not especially difficult. However, given its considerable impact on a company's financial results, it is necessary to thoroughly document the calculation of all recorded environmental liabilities, as well as the justification for *not* recording any additional liabilities.

Chapter 23
Exit or Disposal Cost Obligations

420 = GAAP codification area for exit or disposal cost obligations

Introduction

A business may find that it must sometimes exit or dispose of certain segments of its operations. When doing so, it may incur costs that are directly related to the exit or disposal activities. In this chapter, we address how to account for and disclose the results of these activities. The guidance in this chapter applies to all entities.

Overview of Exit or Disposal Cost Obligations

There are specific accounting and disclosure requirements when a business engages in exit or disposal activities (which can include restructurings). The costs addressed by this topic can include:

- Employee terminations
- Contract termination costs
- Facility closing costs
- Employee relocation costs

A business should recognize a liability for exit or disposal activities when it incurs the liability and it can reasonably estimate the fair value of the liability. A liability is incurred when there is little or no discretion to avoid the liability. It is not acceptable to record a liability as soon as an exit or disposal plan has been created.

A liability for employee termination costs can be recorded as soon as all of the following criteria have been met:

- The plan has been communicated to employees
- Management commits to the plan
- The plan states the number of terminations, the expected completion date, and the job classifications or locations that will be affected
- The plan states the specific benefits to be paid upon termination
- It is unlikely that the plan will be withdrawn or that significant changes will be made to it

The accounting period in which employee termination costs should be recognized will depend upon the existence of any intervening time periods during which employees are required to render services before they can receive termination benefits. The minimum retention period should not exceed the legal notification period. If there is no legal notification period, the minimum retention period should not exceed 60 days.

There are several variations on how termination benefits should be accounted for by the employer, which are:

- *No additional services required.* If there is no requirement for employees to render services prior to receiving termination benefits, recognize a liability for the termination costs at the communication date.
- *Extended services required.* If employees must first render services before they can qualify for termination benefits, and will continue to work for the company after the minimum retention period, record a liability for the termination costs at the communication date, using the fair value of the liability on the termination date, and then recognize the cost ratably over the future service period.
- *Mixed benefit package.* If termination benefits include benefits offered in exchange for voluntary termination of service, recognize a separate liability for that portion of the benefits relating to involuntary termination, and a separate liability for those benefits relating to the voluntary termination of service.

EXAMPLE

Armadillo Industries decides to close its Des Moines facility, and to terminate the employment of the 200 employees who work there. The company notifies the employees that each one will receive a $12,000 cash payment, to be paid in 60 days, when employees will stop rendering services to the business. Armadillo should recognize the full $2,400,000 liability on the communication date. Since there is only a short interval between the communication date and the payment date, the $2,400,000 is not likely to be materially different from the fair value of the liability.

There may also be costs associated with the termination of a contract. These costs can be either the cost to prematurely terminate the contract, or the costs that the business will continue to incur through its remaining term without receiving any economic benefit. A business should recognize the termination cost to prematurely cancel a contract when it terminates the contract. If costs will continue to be incurred under a contract, the business should recognize a liability for those costs at the cease-use date, based on the remaining payments due under the contract.

EXAMPLE

Armadillo Industries has two years remaining on its lease of a facility in Kansas City, which it plans to vacate as part of a corporate-wide consolidation of facilities. The remaining payments under the lease are $18,000 per month, or $432,000 in total. It is unlikely that the facility can be subleased. These cash flows are discounted at the current credit-adjusted risk-free rate to arrive at a fair value of $418,000 as of the cease-use date, which Armadillo records as a liability at that time.

Exit or disposal costs are supposed to be measured at their fair value, for which quoted market prices are the preferred source of information. If this information is not available, consider using the present value of future cash flows associated with these liabilities. Other estimation methods may be used, as long as they yield results approximating fair value.

Following the initial recognition of liabilities associated with exit or disposal cost obligations, it is possible that a variety of factors will change. If so, the following accounting applies:

- *Cost estimates change*. Recognize any change in the period of the change.
- *Retention period changes*. Employees may be retained past their original termination dates. If so, associate some of the original liability with their additional service period, and amortize the cost over that service period.
- *Passage of time*. If the termination period takes longer than expected, the costs that were originally recorded based on the present value of future cash flows should be increased to reflect the additional passage of time.
- *Reversals*. Some liabilities may be eliminated or reduced as part of the termination activities. If so, reverse the liabilities through the same income statement line item in which they were originally recognized.

Exit or Disposal Cost Obligation Disclosures

The following information related to exit or disposal cost obligations should be disclosed in the financial statements:

- *Discontinued operations classification*. Report costs related to a discontinued operation in the discontinued operations section of the income statement.
- *Income from continuing operations*. Report costs not related to discontinued operations in the income from continuing operations section of the income statement.
- *Description*. Describe the activity and the expected completion date.
- *Cost estimation*. If it is not possible to estimate the fair value of a liability, describe why this is the case.

- *Cost types.* Describe the total cost to be incurred, the cost incurred in the period, and the cumulative cost to date, as well as a liability reconciliation for each major type of cost.
- *Income statement location.* Note the line item(s) in the income statement in which the costs are reported.
- *Segment reporting.* Describe the total exit or disposal cost to be incurred, the cost incurred in the period, the cumulative cost to date, and liability adjustments for each reportable business segment (only applies to publicly-held companies that report segment information).

The Securities and Exchange Commission (SEC) has expressed an interest in having the following additional information disclosed in the financial statements that pertain to the exit or disposal costs of an acquired business:

- *Costs.* State the types and amounts of these costs included in the acquisition cost allocation.
- *Timing.* Disclose the date when the company began formulating exit plans.
- *Unresolved issues.* Describe any unresolved contingencies or purchase price allocation problems, as well as the amount of the liabilities that may result from their resolution.

The SEC also requires that a company disclose the effects of its exit or disposal plans on its future earnings and cash flows, the first period in which these effects should be seen, and whether the plans will be offset by increased expenses or reduced revenues elsewhere in the business. The SEC also requires a discussion of any plan targets that are not achieved, as well as the resulting impact on future operating results and liquidity.

Note that these SEC requirements are only applicable to the financial reporting of publicly-held companies.

Summary

The accounting and related disclosures described in this chapter are relatively uncommon issues for a smaller business to deal with, but are likely to be a common and ongoing topic for larger organizations that are routinely acquiring and disposing of various business segments. Consequently, this chapter is of most concern to larger organizations, and especially those that are publicly-held and therefore subject to additional SEC reporting requirements.

Chapter 24
Commitments

440 = GAAP codification area for commitments

Introduction

In some industries, a business may find it necessary to enter into a long-term commitment, where it is legally required to make a series of fixed or minimum payments. Depending upon the terms of the arrangement, GAAP requires that certain information be disclosed. This chapter details the circumstances under which these arrangements must be disclosed, and the information to be reported. The information provided in this chapter applies to all entities.

Overview of Commitments

GAAP requires that certain types of commitments containing unconditional long-term payment obligations be disclosed. An example of such a commitment is a *throughput agreement*, under which the shipper of goods commits to pay a shipping or manufacturing entity a certain minimum or fixed amount for shipping or processing services, even if it does not deliver any goods. Another example is a take-or-pay contract, under which the buyer agrees to periodically acquire goods or services from a seller at a minimum payment amount, even if it does not take delivery. In both cases, there is a long-term payment obligation that the readers of a company's financial statements should be aware of.

A business may have entered into an unconditional purchase obligation if the transaction has all of the following characteristics:

- *Noncancelable.* The contract cannot be cancelled, or only if a remote contingency arises, or with the permission of the other party, or if the contract is replaced with another agreement, or if there is a cancellation penalty so large that continuation of the contract is essentially assured; and
- *Nature.* The contract was negotiated to finance the costs of the goods or services to be purchased, or to assist in the financing of the facilities required to provide the goods or services; and
- *Term.* The term of the contract still has at least one year to run.

There are two alternative sets of disclosures for an unconditional purchase obligation, depending upon whether the obligation has been recorded on the purchaser's balance sheet. If it has *not* been recorded on the balance sheet, the following disclosures are required:

- The nature and duration of the obligation
- The aggregate amount of the fixed and determinable obligation as of the balance sheet date, and for each of the next five fiscal years
- The nature of any variable elements of the arrangement
- For each period for which an income statement is presented, the amounts purchased under the contract

> **Tip:** If the aggregate commitment for all unconditional purchase obligations is immaterial, it is not necessary to disclose any information about them.

In addition, GAAP encourages the disclosure of the amount of imputed interest required to reduce the obligation to its present value. The interest rate used should be the initial interest rate on the borrowed funds used to pay for the facility that will provide the contracted goods or services; if this information is not available, use the purchaser's incremental borrowing rate as of the date when the purchase obligation began. The disclosure of this information is *not* required.

If a business has recognized an unconditional purchase obligation on its balance sheet, it must disclose the aggregate amount of payments for unconditional purchase obligations for each of the next five fiscal years following the balance sheet date.

EXAMPLE

Armadillo Industries enters into a throughput contract with a local barge firm, under which Armadillo will provide sufficient goods to fill one barge per week for transport from Memphis to Baton Rouge. Under the terms of the eight-year contract, Armadillo will pay a minimum of $25,000 for this service, even if it has no goods available to be shipped during any given week. Armadillo must also pay a portion of the fuel costs incurred by the barge company. After one year under the contract, Armadillo discloses the following information:

> To secure access to reliable transport, Armadillo has signed a throughput contract with a barge service to provide guaranteed transport on a weekly basis for eight years, of which one year has been completed. Under the terms of the agreement, the company will pay a minimum of $25,000 per week for the duration of the contract. The aggregate amount of required payments at December 31, 20X1 is as follows:

20x2	$1,300,000
20x3	1,300,000
20x4	1,300,000
20x5	1,300,000
20x6	1,300,000
Later years	2,600,000
	$9,100,000

In addition, Armadillo is required to pay a share of the fuel costs incurred during transport. The company's total share of these fuel costs during the first year of the agreement, plus the minimum weekly fee, was $1,600,000.

Summary

Realistically, the disclosures noted in this chapter are unlikely to arise in most situations, unless the structure of a company's industry, transport, or manufacturing arrangements necessitate the use of long-term contracts of the type outlined in this chapter. If there are such contracts, the accounting staff should retain a copy of each one, so they can more easily derive the disclosure information required by GAAP.

Chapter 25
Contingencies

450 = GAAP codification area for contingencies

Introduction

A company may sometimes find it necessary to record a loss in anticipation of a future event that has not yet been settled. Or, it may want to record a gain in relation to a future event. While the first event is all too common, the latter event is essentially prohibited. In this chapter, we discuss when and how to account for and disclose contingencies. The guidance in this chapter applies to all entities.

Loss Contingencies

A loss contingency arises when there is a situation for which the outcome is uncertain, and which should be resolved in the future, possibly creating a loss. Examples of contingent loss situations are:

- Injuries that may be caused by a company's products, such as when it is discovered that lead-based paint has been used on toys sold by the business
- The threat of asset expropriation by a foreign government, where compensation will be less than the carrying amount of the assets that will probably be expropriated
- A threatened lawsuit

When deciding whether to account for a loss contingency, the basic concept is to only record a loss that is probable, and for which the amount of the loss can be reasonably estimated. If the best estimate of the amount of the loss is within a range, accrue whichever amount appears to be a better estimate than the other estimates in the range. If there is no "better estimate" in the range, accrue a loss for the minimum amount in the range.

If it is not possible to arrive at a reasonable estimate of the loss associated with an event, only disclose the existence of the contingency in the notes accompanying the financial statements. Or, if it is not probable that a loss will be incurred, even if it is possible to estimate the amount of a loss, only disclose the circumstances of the contingency, without accruing a loss.

EXAMPLE

Armadillo Industries has been notified by the local zoning commission that it must remediate abandoned property on which chemicals had been stored in the past. Armadillo has hired a consulting firm to estimate the cost of remediation, which has been documented at $10 million. Since the amount of the loss has been reasonably estimated and it is probable that the loss will occur, the company can record the $10 million as a contingent loss. If the zoning commission had not indicated the company's liability, it may have been more appropriate to only mention the loss in the disclosures accompanying the financial statements.

EXAMPLE

Armadillo Industries has been notified that a third party may begin legal proceedings against it, based on a situation involving environmental damage to a site once owned by Armadillo. Based on the experience of other companies who have been subjected to this type of litigation, it is probable that Armadillo will have to pay $8 million to settle the litigation. A separate aspect of the litigation is still open to interpretation, but could potentially require an additional $12 million to settle. Given the current situation, Armadillo should accrue a loss in the amount of $8 million for that portion of the situation for which the outcome is probable, and for which the amount of the loss can be reasonably estimated.

If the conditions for recording a loss contingency are initially not met, but then are met during a later accounting period, the loss should be accrued in the later period. Do not make a retroactive adjustment to an earlier period to record a loss contingency.

Gain Contingencies

GAAP does not allow the recognition of a gain contingency, since doing so might result in the recognition of revenue before the contingent event has been settled.

Contingency Disclosures

When a loss accrual is made that relates to a loss contingency, it may be necessary to disclose the nature of the accrual and the amount accrued, in order to keep the financial statements from being misleading. GAAP does not allow the word "reserve" to be used when describing a loss contingency, since it implies that a business has set aside funds to deal with a contingency – which may not be the case.

If it is not possible to estimate the amount of a loss contingency, but there is a reasonable possibility that a loss has been incurred, disclose the following:

- The nature of the contingency
- A statement that a loss estimate cannot be made, or the range of the possible loss

If a claim or assessment has not yet been asserted against a business, there is no need to disclose a loss contingency. However, disclosure must be made if it is probable that a claim will be asserted, and that there is a reasonable possibility of an unfavorable outcome.

In those rare cases where a reasonably-estimated loss contingency arises after the date of the financial statements, it may make sense to add pro forma financial information to the financial statements, showing the effect on the business if the loss had arisen during the reporting period.

EXAMPLE

Armadillo Industries is engaged in settlement discussions with a plaintiff regarding an environmental damages lawsuit. Armadillo makes the following disclosure:

> Armadillo is currently engaged in settlement discussions with a plaintiff in a lawsuit involving the amount of environmental mitigation activities needed for a property that Armadillo recently sold to the plaintiff. The company's current settlement offer is $10 million, while the plaintiff's offer is $30 million. Armadillo's estimate of this liability is a range between the two offers, with no amount in the range considered a better estimate than any other amount. Accordingly, the company has accrued a $10 million loss.

If a contingency may result in a gain, it is allowable to disclose the nature of the contingency. However, the disclosure should not make any potentially misleading statements about the likelihood of realization of the contingent gain.

Summary

The accounting for contingencies is rarely completely clear. Instead, the probability associated with a future event is gradually clarified over time, as is the amount of the associated loss. Accordingly, the accountant will likely have to monitor the circumstances of each contingent event over time, and make decisions regarding when to begin disclosing a contingency, and then later the amount to accrue if the event becomes more probable. The result may well be continuing revisions to the amount of a loss contingency, until such time as the exact amount is settled and paid out.

Chapter 26
Guarantees

Introduction

A business may find it necessary to guarantee a variety of occurrences in order to conduct operations with its business partners. The standards and related disclosures described in this chapter relate to these guarantees – when to accrue a liability, how much to accrue, and how to report it. The guidance in this chapter applies to all entities.

Overview of Guarantees

When an entity makes certain guarantees, it takes on an obligation to perform if certain future triggering events occur. The guarantee involves a payment or action. The guarantor may need to account for and disclose these guarantees. This recognition is likely to occur at the inception of a guarantee, and may require continuing disclosure of the existence of the guarantee until it has expired.

The situations in which guarantees must be recognized are when there is a contingent requirement for the guarantor to make payments based on either a change in an underlying, the failure of another entity to perform, or an indirect guarantee of indebtedness of other parties. A recognizable guarantee can also involve product warranties and extended warranties issued by a guarantor.

EXAMPLE

Armadillo Industries issues a written guarantee to a local health clinic to locate its new facility close to Armadillo's production facility, under which Armadillo will compensate the clinic for any revenue shortfalls that drop below a minimum stated amount.

Armadillo guarantees a standby letter of credit for a key supplier, so that the supplier can order parts from a foreign supplier that would otherwise demand cash in advance for a delivery.

Armadillo sells a subsidiary to a private equity firm, and issues a guarantee that it will indemnify the buyer if property taxes exceed an amount stated in the sale contract.

The accounting for guarantees encompasses the following points:

- *Initial guarantee (general)*. At the inception of a guarantee, recognize a liability for the guarantee, based on its fair value.
- *Initial guarantee (sale of)*. If there is a specific sale of a guarantee to a third party, recognize a liability in the amount of the payment received.
- *Initial guarantee (multiple elements)*. If a guarantee is included in a sales arrangement that includes other elements, record a liability for the guarantee at its estimated fair value. In the absence of fair value information, estimate the amount the company would charge for the guarantee, by itself, in an arm's length transaction.
- *Initial guarantee (contribution)*. If a business issues a guarantee to a third party in the form of a contribution, record a liability for the guarantee at its estimated fair value.
- *Product warranties*. Accrue a reserve for product warranty claims based on the prior experience of the business. In the absence of such experience, the company can instead rely upon the experience of other entities in the same business. If there is uncertainty in regard to the amount of projected product warranties, it may not be possible to record a product sale until the warranty period has expired or more experience has been gained with customer claims.

Once the guarantee period expires, and if a guarantee was not activated during that time, eliminate the associated liability with a credit to earnings. Also, if the fair value of a guarantee changes over time, adjust the related liability accordingly in the financial statements (if justified under the applicable GAAP standards).

Guarantee Disclosures

The following bullet points describe the various disclosures associated with guarantees. Not all items may be applicable.

- *Loss contingencies*. Disclose loss contingencies even if there is a remote possibility of occurrence, as long as the guarantor has the right to proceed against another party if the guarantor must satisfy a claim. Examples of reportable loss contingencies are guarantees of indebtedness and standby letters of credit. The disclosure should include the type and amount of the guarantee.
- *Guarantee information*. Disclose the following information about guarantees, even if there is a remote likelihood of occurrence:
  - What caused the guarantee
  - The term of the guarantee
  - The circumstances that would trigger the guarantee
  - The current payment and performance risk associated with the guarantee

- o The maximum undiscounted amount of future payments under the guarantee, or why this information cannot be estimated
- o Whether there is no limitation on the amount of future payments
- o The carrying amount of the liability associated with the guarantee
- o Any recourse provisions under which the guarantor can pursue payment from other parties
- o Any assets held by other parties that the guarantor can liquidate in order to recover payments made under the guarantee, as well as the extent to which these asset liquidations can offset the maximum guarantee liability

---

EXAMPLE

Armadillo Industries issues a written guarantee to a supplier to locate its new warehouse close to Armadillo's production facility, under which Armadillo will compensate the supplier for any revenue shortfalls that drop below a minimum stated amount. Its disclosure is:

> In 20X3, Armadillo issued a revenue guarantee to Rhino Warehousing, which operates a warehouse adjacent to the Armadillo production facility. The guarantee is a 100% gross margin reimbursement for any revenue shortfall below $5,000,000 per year, which expires in 20X8. In 20X5, this arrangement resulted in a payment of $210,000 to Rhino. The company expects that payments of a similar size will be paid through the remaining term of the guarantee. The associated liability has been recorded in the company's financial statements. The maximum amount of annual payments remaining under this guarantee should not exceed $1,000,000.

- • *Product warranties*. Disclose the following information about product warranties:
    - o The accounting policy used to calculate the liability for product warranties
    - o A reconciliation of changes in the warranty liability for the reporting period, including beginning and ending balances, the aggregate reduction for payments made, the aggregate increase in liability from new warranties issued, and the aggregate change in liability relating to pre-existing warranties
    - o The same information just noted for guarantees, except for the discussion of the maximum potential amount of future payments

Summary

Many organizations actively avoid all forms of guarantees, and so may believe that the provisions of this chapter do not apply to them. However, many companies that sell products or services have an implicit or explicit guarantee that their products will perform as advertised. The resulting product warranty is a form of guarantee, which falls under the guidance expressed in this chapter. Therefore, be sure to peruse the information in this chapter before dismissing the topic as not being applicable to one's operations.

Chapter 27
Debt

470 = GAAP codification area for debt

Introduction

Nearly every business will eventually become a debtor, and so must be aware of the accounting for an arrangement in which it owes funds to a creditor. This chapter discusses the accounting for 15 possible variations on the basic concept of borrowing money. These variations range from the issuance of warrants alongside a debt instrument to several permutations on a troubled debt restructuring, as well as transactions involving convertible securities, interest forfeiture, debt modifications, and more. As usual, the related disclosures for the debt scenarios are noted at the end of the chapter. The guidance in this chapter applies to all topics.

Related Chapter

See the Liabilities chapter for a discussion of short-term liability issues, as well as guidance that can be broadly applied to any liability topic.

General Debt Topics

The following sub-sections address two relatively minor debt topics that are not commonly encountered.

Sales of Future Revenues

A company may accept a payment from an investor in exchange for paying back a percentage of company revenues or income in the future. In this situation, the payment from the investor to the company should probably be recorded as debt if any of the following factors are present:

- *Cancellation terms*. The arrangement can be cancelled if the recipient pays the investor.
- *Form*. The form of the transaction is a debt arrangement.
- *Impact on rate of return*. Changes in the recipient's revenue or income have a minor impact on the investor's rate of return.
- *Involvement*. The recipient has significant continuing involvement in creating the cash flows to be paid to the investor.

- *Rate of return limitation*. The terms of the deal limit the investor's rate of return.
- *Recourse*. The investor has some kind of recourse associated with the payments due to it.

If the payment is recorded as debt, amortize the debt under the interest method. If the payment is recorded as deferred income, amortize it using the units-of-revenue method.

Increasing Rate Debt

A borrower may have a debt instrument that allows it to extend the maturity date in exchange for a predetermined increase in the interest rate at each extension. In order to calculate the interest cost in each period for this type of debt, use the estimated total duration of the instrument, based on the borrower's debt planning and intent to service the debt. The related accounting then addresses the following two issues:

- *Debt service costs*. Amortize the debt issuance cost over the expected term of the debt.
- *Interest costs*. Calculate the total amount of interest to be incurred over the expected term of the debt, and recognize it over the full term of the debt. This will result in the recognition of a larger amount of interest expense earlier in the term of the debt than would otherwise be the case, when the actual amount of interest expense being paid is lower.

Debt with Conversion and Other Options

Debt that converts into the equity of the issuing entity presents a number of challenges from an accounting perspective, based on the variety of ways in which the conversion can take place. Each of the following sub-sections addresses a different variation on the convertible debt concept.

Debt Instruments with Detachable Warrants

A debt instrument may be issued with warrants that allow an investor to acquire shares in the issuing company. Typically, the warrants exist independently from the debt, which may allow investors to sell the warrants to third parties. Investors have the right to use the warrants to buy company stock, or to let the warrants expire unused.

When a company issues a combination of debt and warrants, investors are willing to accept a lower interest rate, since they are also obtaining a valuable right to buy company stock at a fixed price at some future date.

Debt

When a company sells a debt instrument with attached warrants, it should account for the transaction by allocating funds received to the two elements of the instrument based on their relative fair values as of the issuance date. The allocated funds are then accounted for as follows:

- *Warrants*. Record the funds assigned to the warrants in the paid-in capital account.
- *Debt*. Record the remaining funds as debt. This will probably also result in a discount on the debt, which is the difference between the value assigned to the debt instrument and its face amount.

EXAMPLE

Armadillo Industries issues $500,000 of convertible debt that has 50,000 detachable warrants associated with it. The convertible debt is convertible at $18, which is also the fair value of the company's stock. The ratio of the fair values of the convertible debt and the warrants is 90:10. The company records the transaction by allocating 90% of the proceeds, or $450,000, to the convertible debt liability and 10% of the proceeds, or $50,000, to the detached warrants (which is recorded in the paid-in capital account).

Convertible Securities

A convertible security is a debt instrument that gives the holder the right to convert it into a certain number of shares of the stock of the issuing entity. This type of security has value to the investor, who can either receive interest payments on the debt or elect to acquire stock that may have increased in value. Because of this added value, the issuing company can achieve a lower interest rate on its debt than would normally be the case.

The accounting for a debt instrument that is converted into a company's equity under an inducement offer is to recognize an expense in the amount of:

(Fair value of all securities and other consideration transferred) – (Fair value of securities issued)

The fair value in this calculation is based on the fair values of the securities when a conversion inducement offer is accepted.

If there is no inducement offer, and instead the conversion of a debt instrument into a company's equity is based on the original conversion privileges stated in the debt instrument, do not recognize a gain or loss on the transaction.

EXAMPLE

Armadillo Industries issues a $1,000 face amount convertible bond that sells for $1,000. The bond is convertible into Armadillo stock at a conversion price of $20. To induce holders of the bonds to convert them into company stock, Armadillo issues an offer to reduce the conversion price to $10, if the conversion takes place within the next 30 days.

Debt

A number of investors accept the new conversion terms and convert their bonds into company stock. The market price of Armadillo's stock on the conversion date is $30. Based on this information, the calculation of the incremental consideration paid by Armadillo to effect the conversion is:

Value of securities issued to debt holders (using inducement):		
Face amount	$1,000	
÷ New conversion price	÷ $10	Per share
= Number of shares issued upon conversion	= 100	Shares
× Market price per common share	× $30	Per share
= Value of securities issued	$3,000	

Value of securities issued to debt holders (prior to inducement):		
Face amount	$1,000	
÷ Old conversion price	÷ $20	Per share
= Number of shares issued upon conversion	= 50	Shares
× Market price per common share	× $30	Per share
= Value of securities issued	$1,500	

By subtracting the value of the equity securities prior to the inducement price from the value of the securities including the inducement price, we arrive at the following fair value of the incremental consideration:

$3,000 Value of securities with inducement - $1,500 Value of securities prior to inducement

= $1,500 Fair value of incremental consideration

Based on this information, Armadillo records the following entry to document the conversion of a bond to company stock:

	Debit	Credit
Convertible debt	1,000	
Debt conversion expense	1,500	
Common stock		2,500

Beneficial Conversion Features

When a business issues a convertible security, it can include a beneficial conversion feature in the agreement. This feature allows for conversion into the common stock of the issuer at the lower of a fixed conversion rate or a fixed discount to the market price of the stock on the conversion date. This conversion feature may even be adjustable, depending on such future events as a change in control of the business or an initial public offering at a lower share price.

To account for an embedded beneficial conversion feature, record it separately from the convertible security at the issuance date. The amount to assign to the feature is its intrinsic value. Record the amount in the additional paid-in capital account. Do not recognize this feature in earnings until the contingent feature of the instrument has been resolved.

Use the following steps to determine the intrinsic value of a beneficial conversion feature:

1. Allocate the proceeds to the debt instrument and any detachable instruments based on their relative fair values.
2. Calculate an effective conversion price and use it to measure the intrinsic value of the conversion option. The *intrinsic value* is the difference between the conversion price and the fair value of the securities into which the instrument is convertible, multiplied by the number of shares into which the instrument converts.

EXAMPLE

Luminescence Corporation is a privately-held company. It issues a $5,000,000 convertible debt instrument that can be converted to the company's common stock in two years at a conversion price of $12 (which is also the current fair value of the stock). There is an additional provision in the debt agreement that the conversion price drops to $8 in 18 months if Luminescence does not complete an initial public offering by that date.

The intrinsic value of the conversion option is calculated as follows:

(Funding obtained ÷ Final conversion price) × Difference in conversion prices)

= ($5,000,000 ÷ $8) × ($12 - $8) = $2,500,000

Luminescence should recognize the intrinsic value of the conversion option when it issues the convertible instrument.

Additional issues related to the assignment of value to beneficial conversion features are as follows:

- *Not beneficial.* If an embedded feature is not beneficial to the debt holder, do not assign any of the proceeds to that feature.
- *Multi-step discount.* If there is a multi-step discount feature in the debt instrument, compute its intrinsic value based on those terms most beneficial to the instrument holder.

EXAMPLE

Armadillo Industries issues a convertible debt instrument that includes a multi-step discount that begins with a 20% discount from the market price of the company's stock if conversion is within the next year, to a 28% discount if conversion is between three and four years in the future. Since the computation of intrinsic value is based on the most beneficial terms to the investor, the 28% discount rate should be used.

- *Instrument paid in kind (mandatory).* If dividend or interest payments made to investors are with more of the convertible instrument on a mandatory basis, use the original commitment date for the instrument to determine the number of additional convertible instruments to issue, and value the intrinsic value of the conversion option at the fair value of the issuer's stock at the commitment date for the original issuance of the instrument.
- *Instrument paid in kind (not mandatory).* If an instrument is paid in kind, but the issuance of additional debt instruments in payment of dividends or interest is not mandatory, the commitment date moves forward to the date when the dividends or interest are accrued (see the preceding bullet for additional valuation information).
- *Instrument swapped for nonconvertible instrument.* If a convertible instrument is issued in exchange for a nonconvertible instrument, use the fair value of the new issuance as the redemption amount, if the original instrument has matured and this is not a troubled debt restructuring.
- *Discount accretion and amortization.* If a debt discount is recognized because a portion of the funds received are allocated to a beneficial conversion feature, the following accounting variations may apply:
  - If the instrument has a stated redemption date, discount amortization occurs between the dates of issuance and stated redemption, irrespective of when conversions actually occur.
  - If the instrument has a multiple-step discount and there is no stated redemption date, cumulative amortization should be the greater of the results of the effective yield method that is based on the conversion terms most beneficial to the investor, or the discount amount that the investor can realize at each interim date.
  - For all other convertible preferred securities, amortize from the date of issuance the discount using the effective yield method.
  - For all other convertible debt securities, use the effective yield method to recognize the discount as interest expense.
  - If the beneficial conversion feature terminates after a certain period of time and the instrument results in an equity share that must be redeemed when the conversion feature expires, treat the feature as a liability when the feature expires, measured at its fair value as of the expiration date. This will require an offsetting reduction in equity.

o If the beneficial conversion feature terminates after a certain period of time and must then be redeemed at a premium, amortize the resulting discount to the mandatory redemption amount.

In general, when a company issues a convertible instrument at a substantial premium, it is reasonable to assume that some portion of the funds received relate to a conversion feature, and so should be recorded within the paid-in capital account.

One or more accounting actions may be triggered when the holder of a convertible instrument exercises the related call option to convert the instrument into the equity of the issuer. The following options are possible outcomes:

- *Unamortized discount*. If a convertible instrument contains a beneficial conversion feature, and the holder of the instrument converts it, recognize the unamortized discount as of the conversion date. The amount recognized may be either interest expense or a dividend, depending upon the nature of the underlying instrument.
- *Substantive conversion feature*. If there is a substantive conversion feature, do not recognize a gain or loss on the issuance of equity securities.
- *No substantive conversion feature*. If there is no substantive conversion feature, account for the issuance of equity securities as a debt retirement. Thus, use the fair value of the equity securities to determine the cost of debt reacquisition.

Since the accounting for a conversion varies so much depending on whether there is a substantive conversion feature, it is of some importance to determine the nature of this feature. The key issue indicating a substantive conversion is when it is reasonably possible that the feature will be exercised. A high conversion price would make exercise less possible.

Interest Forfeiture

When a convertible debt instrument is converted into the equity of the issuer, the terms of the agreement may state that any accrued but unpaid interest as of the conversion date is retained by the issuer. This situation most commonly occurs when conversion happens between scheduled interest payment dates, but can also occur when zero-interest debt is converted. To account for interest forfeiture, charge the amount forfeited between the date of the last interest payment and the conversion date, net of any income tax effects to interest expense, with the offset to a capital account.

Induced Conversions

The issuer of a convertible debt instrument may have the right to alter the terms of the arrangement, such as by paying additional consideration to debt holders to convert their holdings to company stock.

Conversion by Exercise of Call Option

The issuer of a convertible debt instrument can exercise a call option that requires debt holders to convert their debt instruments into the company's equity.

Convertible Instruments Issued to Nonemployees as Payment

A company may issue a convertible instrument to a person or entity who is not an employee in exchange for the provision of goods or services by the third party. The accounting for this situation is to recognize a related expense for the cost of the goods or services received.

To measure the intrinsic value of the conversion option, compare the proceeds received to the fair value of the shares the counterparty would receive by exercising the conversion option. Use the following guidance to determine the fair value of the convertible instrument:

1. Use the fair value of the goods or services received, if this amount can be determined reliably and the company has not issued similar convertible instruments recently; or
2. Use the fair value of similar convertible instruments for cash to independent third parties that have been issued recently; or
3. Use as a minimum value the fair value of the equity shares into which the instrument can be converted, if the first two alternatives are not viable.

Contingent Conversion Option

The conversion terms associated with a convertible debt instrument may be altered in the future, based on future events that are not controlled by the issuing company. If so, do not recognize the intrinsic value of these conversion changes until a triggering event occurs, and then make the following computation:

1. Calculate the number of shares that would be issued to the recipient, based on the revised conversion price.
2. Compare the number of shares issued to the number that the counterparty would have received prior to the contingent event.
3. Multiply the excess number of shares by the stock price on the commitment date to arrive at the incremental intrinsic value resulting from resolution of the contingency.
4. Recognize this incremental amount when the triggering event occurs.

If there is recognition, the accounting entry is an increase in equity, with an offset to the discount for the convertible instrument.

Own-Share Lending Arrangements

A company may enter into a share lending arrangement with its investment bank that is connected to an offering of convertible debt. In this situation, the share lending arrangement is designed to enhance the ability of investors to hedge their option to convert the company's debt into its equity. The typical terms of such an arrangement require the company to loan shares to the investment bank in exchange for a small loan processing fee that equals the par value of the stock. Once the convertible instrument matures or is converted, the investment bank returns the loaned shares to the company. During the period when the investment bank is holding the company's shares, it is not allowed to vote the shares, and must return any dividends associated with the shares.

The accounting for an own-share lending arrangement is to be measured at its fair value and recognized as a cost of issuing the associated debt. The offset to this cost is the additional paid-in capital account.

If it is probable that the counterparty in such an arrangement will default, recognize an expense that equals the fair value of all shares not yet returned by the counterparty, less the amount of any probable recoveries. The offset to this expense is the additional paid-in capital account. Continue to remeasure the fair value of all shares that have not yet been returned until the amount of the eventual repayment (if any) has been settled. All of these subsequent remeasurements of the missing shares should be recognized in earnings.

Participating Mortgage Loans

A participating mortgage loan is one in which the lender can participate in the results of operations of the real estate operation being mortgaged, or in any appreciation in the market value of the real estate.

The borrower should account for a participating mortgage loan by recognizing a participation liability that is based on the fair value of the participation feature at the start of the loan. The offset to this liability is the debt discount account. Subsequently, account for the following issues related to the participating mortgage loan:

- *Interest.* Charge to expense any periodic interest expense amounts so designated in the mortgage agreement.
- *Amortization.* Amortize the amount of the debt discount related to the lender's participation in the profits of the real estate venture, using the interest method.
- *Participation payments.* Pay the lender for its share of profits of the real estate venture, and charge this amount to interest expense. The offset is to the participation liability account.
- *Participation adjustment.* At the end of each reporting period, adjust the participation liability to match the latest fair value of the participation feature.

If the mortgage loan is extinguished prior to its due date, recognize a debt extinguishment gain or loss on the difference between the recorded amount of the debt and the amount paid or exchanged to settle the debt liability.

EXAMPLE

Domicilio Corporation develops residential real estate in the Miami area. On April 1, 20X1, Domicilio buys a property for $20,000,000. Domicilio obtains the funding for this purchase primarily with a $15 million participating mortgage loan from Primero Bank. The loan agreement is for four years, and requires interest-only payments at a 6% interest rate, until a balloon payment is required at the end of the loan term. In addition, Primero will receive a 10% participation in the profits from the sale of each residential unit, payable at the maturity of the loan.

The initial estimate of the fair value of the participation feature is $60,000, so Domicilio records the following initial entry for the loan:

	Debit	Credit
Cash	15,000,000	
Loan discount	60,000	
Mortgage loan payable		15,000,000
Participation liability		60,000

At the end of one year, Domicilio records the following entry related to the interest expense paid on the mortgage, and the amortization of the discount on the mortgage (using straight-line amortization):

	Debit	Credit
Interest expense	915,000	
Cash		900,000
Loan discount		15,000

Midway through the next year, Domicilio adjusts its estimate of the fair value of the participation feature upward by $22,000. This results in the following entry:

	Debit	Credit
Loan discount	22,000	
Participation liability		22,000

Thus, 18 months into the participating mortgage loan, the participation liability recorded by Domicilio has increased to $82,000, while the balance in the loan discount account has increased to $67,000.

Product Financing Arrangements

There are cases where the sale of inventory is, in substance, actually a financing arrangement. A transaction is likely to be a financing arrangement in any of the following situations:

- The seller agrees to repurchase the item it has just sold, or an essentially identical unit.
- The seller commits to having a third party purchase the item, and then agrees to acquire the item from the third party.
- The seller controls how the item sold under either of the preceding situations is disposed of.

An option for the seller to reacquire inventory is the same as a commitment to repurchase items it has sold, if there is a penalty for not exercising the option. The same treatment applies for a put option that the reseller can exercise against the seller.

A product financing arrangement is more likely to exist when there is a resale price guarantee, whereby the original seller agrees to pay any shortfall between the price at which it sold to the reseller and the price at which the reseller sold to a third party.

The accounting for a product financing arrangement is to treat it as a borrowing arrangement and not a sale transaction. Thus, the "seller" continues to report its ownership of the asset "sold," as well as a liability for its repurchase obligation. There are two variations on the accounting for the repurchase obligation:

- *Primary repurchaser*. If the seller commits to repurchase the product, it records the repurchase obligation as soon as it receives the proceeds from the initial financing transaction.
- *Secondary repurchaser*. If a third party has committed to repurchase the product, the seller records the repurchase obligation as soon as the product is purchased by the third party.

In addition, the seller accrues any financing and holding costs incurred by the buyer. The following example illustrates the concept.

EXAMPLE

Armadillo Industries enters into a transaction where another entity is legally created under the name ArmaLoan, accepts inventory from Armadillo as its sole asset, and then uses the inventory as collateral to obtain a loan, the funds from which it then remits to Armadillo. As part of the arrangement, Armadillo pays inventory storage costs on behalf of ArmaLoan, as well as interest on the inventory that matches the interest charges incurred by ArmaLoan on the bank financing. Armadillo agrees to repurchase the inventory in one year, when the loan arrangement expires.

Debt Modifications and Extinguishments

When a borrower extinguishes a debt, the difference between the net carrying amount of the debt and the price at which the debt was settled is recorded separately in the current period in income as a gain or loss. The net carrying amount of the debt is considered to be the amount payable at maturity of the debt, netted against any unamortized discounts, premiums, and costs of issuance. If a settlement also involves an exchange of rights or privileges, assign a portion of the consideration received to these rights or privileges.

If debt is extinguished via an exchange of stock, calculate the reacquisition cost of the debt at the value of either the stock or the debt, whichever is more clearly discernible.

If there is an exchange or modification of debt that has substantially different terms, treat the exchange as a debt extinguishment. Such an exchange or modification is considered to have occurred when the present value of the cash flows of the new debt instrument vary by at least 10% from the present value of the original debt instrument. When determining present value for this calculation, the discount rate is the effective interest rate used for the original debt instrument. Substantially different terms have also been achieved when:

- The change in the fair value of an embedded conversion option is at least 10% of the carrying amount of the original debt instrument; or
- The debt modification either adds or eliminates a substantive conversion option

If the preceding testing concludes that the replacement and old debt instruments are substantially different, account for the replacement instrument at its fair value, which shall also be the basis for calculating any gain or loss on the debt modification.

If the preceding testing does *not* conclude that the replacement and old debt instruments are substantially different, use the following accounting instead:

- Calculate a new effective interest rate based on the carrying amount of the original debt instrument, adjusted for any increase in the fair value of any embedded conversion option. The fair value increase is based on any change in the fair value of the option before and after the modification. Do not adjust the effective interest rate based on any decline in the fair value of an embedded conversion option.
- If there is an increase in the fair value of an embedded conversion option, as just noted, use it to reduce the carrying amount of the debt instrument, with an offset to additional paid-in capital.
- Do not recognize a beneficial conversion feature.

If a debt modification or extinguishment involves the payment of fees between the debtor and creditor, the related accounting is:

- *If treated as a debt extinguishment.* Associate the fees with the extinguishment of the old debt instrument, so they are included in the calculation of any gains or losses from that extinguishment.
- *If not treated as a debt extinguishment.* Associate the fees with the replacement instrument, and amortize them as an interest expense adjustment over the remaining life of the instrument.

If the company incurs third party costs associated with the debt modification, the related accounting is:

- *If treated as a debt extinguishment.* Associate the third-party costs with the replacement instrument, and use the interest method to amortize them over the remaining life of the instrument.
- *If not treated as a debt extinguishment.* Charge the costs to expense as incurred.

If debt modifications involve a line of credit or a revolving debt arrangement, the debtor should account for the changes using the following decision tree:

1. Compare the maximum borrowing capacity of the old and new borrowing arrangements. Borrowing capacity is defined as the remaining term (in years) multiplied by the commitment amount.
2. If the borrowing capacity of the new arrangement is greater than the old arrangement, defer any unamortized costs associated with the old arrangement and instead amortize them over the term of the new arrangement.
3. If the borrowing capacity of the new arrangement is less than the old arrangement, defer any new fees incurred and amortize them over the term of the new arrangement. Also, write off any unamortized costs associated with the old arrangement in proportion to the reduction in borrowing capacity, and amortize the remaining amount over the term of the new arrangement.

EXAMPLE

Armadillo Industries revises the terms of its line of credit arrangement with Currency Bank. The terms of the original lending arrangement were a remaining term of two years and a $12,000,000 commitment. This results in a borrowing capacity of $24,000,000 (calculated as two years multiplied by $12,000,000).

The terms of the new lending arrangement are a $16,000,000 commitment over a three-year term. This results in a new borrowing capacity of $48,000,000 (calculated as three years multiplied by $16,000,000).

At the time of the conversion to the new line of credit, Armadillo has $40,000 of unamortized costs on its books related to the old line of credit. The company also incurs new costs of $75,000 related to the new arrangement. Armadillo can defer all of these costs and amortize them over the three-year term of the new lending arrangement.

Troubled Debt Restructurings by Debtors

When a debtor restructures its borrowing arrangements, the accounting for the resulting modified arrangements is based on the effect on cash flows, rather than how those cash flows are described in the revised borrowing arrangements. The adjustments most likely to affect cash flows are changes in the timing of payments, and the amounts designated as face amounts or interest.

A troubled debt restructuring is considered to have occurred when the creditor grants concessions that it would not normally consider, due to the financial difficulties of the debtor. A troubled debt restructuring is generally not considered to have occurred if the debtor can obtain funds from other sources than its existing creditor. The accounting for troubled debt restructuring spans a number of payment instruments, including accounts payable, notes, and bonds.

A troubled debt restructuring transaction can involve an array of possible settlement solutions, including the transfer of tangible or intangible assets, the granting of an equity interest in the debtor, an interest rate reduction, an extended maturity date at a below-market interest rate, a reduction in the face amount of the debt, and/or a reduction in the amount of accrued but unpaid interest. The accounting for these restructurings varies, depending upon the nature of the transaction, as noted below:

- *Full settlement with assets or equity*. If the debtor transfers receivables from third parties or other assets or equity to the creditor to fully settle a debt, it should recognize a gain on the transaction in the amount by which the carrying amount of the payable exceeds the fair value of the assets transferred. The fair value of the payable settled can be used instead of the fair value of the assets transferred, if this is more clearly evident.
- *Partial settlement with assets or equity*. If the debtor transfers receivables from third parties or other assets or equity to the creditor to partially settle a debt, it should only measure the transaction with the fair value of the assets transferred (not the fair value of the payable).
- *Change in terms*. If there is only a change in the terms of a debt instrument, only account for the change on a go-forward basis from the date of the restructuring. This means there is no need to change the carrying amount of the payable unless that amount exceeds the total amount of all remaining cash payments (including accrued interest) required under the new arrangement. This may result in the use of a new effective interest rate that equates the present value of the cash payments specified in the new arrangement with the current carrying amount of the liability. If the total future cash payments are less than the current carrying amount of the liability, reduce

the carrying amount to equal the total of all future cash payments, and recognize a gain on the difference; this means that no interest expense can be recognized in association with any remaining periods.

- *Partial settlement and change in terms.* If a portion of a debt is settled and the terms of the remaining amount are altered, first reduce the carrying amount of the payable by the total fair value of the assets transferred. Record a gain or loss on any difference between the fair value and carrying amount of the transferred assets. However, GAAP does not allow the recognition of a gain on the restructuring of payables unless the total future cash payments remaining are less than the remaining carrying amount of the liability.
- *Interest on contingent payments.* If there are contingent payments included in the restructuring arrangement, recognize interest expense for these payments only when the amount of the liability can be reasonably estimated and it is probable that the debtor has incurred the liability. However, only do so after deducting a sufficient amount of these payments from the carrying amount of the liability to eliminate any restructuring gain that would otherwise be recognized. If the interest rate on these payments is variable, estimate the amount of future payments based on the current interest rate on the date of the restructuring. Ongoing accounting for these contingent payments can be adjusted to reflect subsequent changes in interest rates.
- *Legal and other fees.* If there are legal or other fees associated with the granting of an equity interest in the debtor, offset them against the recorded amount of the equity interest. Any other such fees not related to granting an equity interest shall be used to reduce any gain recognized on the restructuring transaction; if there is no gain to offset, charge the fees to expense as incurred.

Debt Presentation

The following sub-sections address a variety of financial statement presentation issues related to debt.

Callable Debt

If the borrower has violated a provision of a long-term debt agreement that allows the lender to call the loan, classify the debt as a current liability. The only exception is in either of the following situations:

- The lender has waived its call rights under the debt agreement, or the borrower has cured the violation.
- There is a grace period in which the borrower can cure the violation, and it is probable that the borrower will cure the violation within that period.

Classification of Debt that Includes Covenants

There may be situations where a loan covenant must be met on a frequent basis, at intervals of less than one year. If such a covenant is violated and the lender waives its right to call the loan for at least the next year, classify the debt as noncurrent, except when both of the following issues are present:

- A violation of the covenant has occurred at the balance sheet date or would have occurred without a loan modification, and the lender now has the right to call the debt; and
- The borrower probably cannot comply with the covenant during the next 12 months.

Debt Issuance Costs

The debt issuance costs related to a note should be reported in the balance sheet as a direct deduction from the face amount of the note. Also, the ongoing amortization of debt issuance costs should be included in interest expense.

Due on Demand Loans

If a debt agreement allows the lender to demand payment at any time or within one year, classify the debt as a current liability, even if liquidation in the short term is not expected.

Increasing-Rate Debt

If a borrower has increasing-rate debt, the proper classification of this debt as current or long-term depends upon the expected source of debt repayment. For example, replacement with short-term debt would indicate classification of the increasing-rate debt as short-term, while replacement with long-term refinancing would indicate classification as long-term.

Revolving Debt Agreements

If a lending arrangement includes revolving credit, a subjective acceleration clause, and a lock-box arrangement, classify the debt as a short-term obligation. A lock-box arrangement is considered to be any situation where the cash receipts of the borrower are applied to reduce the amount of outstanding debt.

Short-Term Obligations to be Refinanced

A short-term obligation should be classified as a current liability. If the borrower expects to refinance a short-term obligation on a long-term basis and has the ability to do so, the obligation can be classified as a long-term obligation. The ability to refinance must be demonstrated in one of two ways:

- Long-term financing is secured after the balance sheet date, but before the balance sheet is issued or available to be issued; or

- The lender has committed to a financing agreement that funds the short-term obligation, and which does not expire within one year, cannot be cancelled within that period unless there is a terms violation, there is currently no terms violation, and the lender can honor the agreement.

The amount of the short-term obligation that can be classified as long-term cannot exceed the proceeds of the new long-term financing. Also, if the amount of funding available under the prospective long-term arrangement could fluctuate (typically due to changes in the underlying amount of collateral), the amount of the short-term obligation is restricted to a reasonable estimate of the minimum amount of long-term funding expected through the end of the fiscal year. If it is not possible to estimate the minimum amount of expected long-term funding, classify all of the related short-term obligations as current liabilities.

Thus, a short-term obligation will probably require classification as a current liability, unless longer-term financing is secured within a short interval after the balance sheet date.

Subjective Acceleration Clauses

If it appears probable that the subjective acceleration clause on long-term debt will be exercised, classify the debt as short-term. Otherwise, only disclose the existence of the clause. If the likelihood of acceleration is remote, there is no need to even disclose the existence of the clause.

In the rare case where a springing lock-box is used in conjunction with a subjective acceleration clause, related borrowings are considered long-term obligations. A springing lock-box is an arrangement where customer remittances are forwarded to the general bank account of the borrower, but are not forwarded to the lender unless it triggers a subjective acceleration clause.

EXAMPLE

Armadillo Industries obtained a five-year loan in 20X1, and it is now 20X2. The loan contains a covenant that requires Armadillo to maintain a 2:1 current ratio, which is tested on a quarterly basis. Due to reductions in its anticipated cash flow, Armadillo expects that it will fail to meet the covenant requirement at the next scheduled compliance date, which is three months in the future. Management does not believe it likely that the company can cure the projected violation. Based on this information, the company should assume that the lender will call the loan, which means that the loan should be classified as current.

Own-Share Lending Arrangements

If a company lends its shares to an investment bank as part of an own-share lending arrangement, exclude these shares from the calculation of basic and diluted earnings per share. However, if the investment bank defaults on the arrangement and retains the shares, include the shares in these earnings per share calculations.

If the dividends on loaned shares are not returned to the issuing company, include the dividend amounts in the calculation of income available to common shareholders in the earnings per share calculations.

Participating Mortgage Loans

Aggregate the amount of any debt discount associated with a mortgage participation liability into the interest expense line item in the income statement.

Troubled Debt Restructurings by Debtors

It may be necessary to reclassify a restructured debt between the current and long-term liability sections of the balance sheet, depending on the terms of the new arrangement.

Debt Disclosures

The following sub-sections address a variety of financial statement disclosure issues related to debt.

Long-Term Obligations

If a company has long-term debt obligations, disclose the aggregate amount of the maturities and sinking fund requirements for these borrowings for each of the five years after the balance sheet date. If there is a debt violation for a long-term debt agreement, and the borrower has continued to classify the debt on the grounds that it is probable that the violation can be cured in a timely manner, disclose the circumstances.

EXAMPLE

Armadillo Industries discloses the following information about its long-term debt obligations, which are divided into bonds and preferred stock. One bond has a sinking fund requirement that calls for continuing debt reductions in each year, while another bond is to be paid off in its entirety in five years. There is also preferred stock outstanding that is subject to a 10% annual buyback. The disclosure of this information follows:

The maturities and ongoing sinking fund requirements for the company's long-term debt obligations and outstanding preferred stock for the next five years are as follows:

(000s)	Long-Term Debt	Preferred Stock
20X2	$15,000	$3,275
20X3	15,000	3,275
20X4	15,000	3,275
20X5	15,000	3,275
20X6	175,000	--

Short-Term Obligations to be Refinanced

If a short-term obligation is classified as a long-term obligation due to its refinancing after the balance sheet date, disclose the general terms of the refinancing agreement, as well as the terms of the replacement debt or equity.

EXAMPLE

Armadillo Industries enters into a long-term financing arrangement that allows it to entirely refinance an obligation that is coming due within the current year. Its disclosure of the refinancing arrangement follows:

> The company has entered into a five-year financing arrangement with an industrial bank that allows the company to borrow up to $20,000,000 at the prime lending rate of the bank, plus 1%. Under the arrangement, the company must pay a ¼% commitment fee per year on any unused portion of the commitment, and also agrees to not issue dividends during the term of the agreement. The lender can terminate the agreement if the company's reported current ratio falls below 1.5 to 1. In July 20X3, the company borrowed $4,000,000 at a 6.5% interest rate and used the funds to liquidate a 5¼% current obligation.

Own-Share Lending Arrangements

If a company enters into a share-lending arrangement for its own shares, disclose the following information about the arrangement:

- Describe the share lending arrangement
- State all significant terms of the arrangement, including the number of shares loaned, the lending term, any circumstances requiring cash settlement, and any counterparty collateral provided
- The reason for entering into the arrangement
- The fair value of the shares loaned as of the balance sheet date
- How the arrangement is treated when calculating earnings per share
- Any unamortized issuance costs associated with the arrangement
- How any issuance costs are classified
- The interest cost recognized in the period for the amortization of any issuance costs
- The amount of any unreimbursed dividends paid on the loaned shares

If it is probable that the counterparty will default on its obligation to return shares to the company, disclose the expense related to the default. Also disclose in subsequent periods the amount of any material changes in this expense. If the anticipated default has not yet occurred, disclose the number of shares related to the lending arrangement that will be included in earnings per share calculations if the default occurs.

Participating Mortgage Loans

Disclose the following information in the financial statements that pertain to participating mortgage loans:

- The terms of the mortgage participation loans, addressing participations in market value appreciation or the results of operations.
- The aggregate amount of all participating mortgage obligations, along with separate disclosure of related debt discounts and participation liabilities.

Other Debt Disclosures

If a company has issued securities that are currently outstanding, disclose the rights and privileges of those securities.

If a company extinguishes its debt via an in-substance defeasance (see the Glossary), continue to describe the transaction and the related amount of extinguished debt in the financial statements for as long as any debt remains outstanding.

Troubled Debt Restructurings by Debtors

If there has been a troubled debt restructuring during the reporting period, the debtor should disclose the following information:

- *Terms change*. Describe the main changes in terms and/or the major features of the settlement. For reporting purposes, it is allowable to aggregate restructuring disclosures for similar payables.
- *Gain*. Note the aggregate amount of gain on all restructuring transactions.
- *Asset transfers*. State the aggregate gain or loss on assets transferred to creditors.
- *Per share impact*. Disclose the amount of the aggregate restructuring gain on a per-share basis.
- *Contingent payments*. If there are contingent payments associated with a restructuring, continue to disclose the extent of these payments in the carrying amounts of payables in future periods. Also disclose the conditions under which the contingent payments would be cancelled or become payable.

Summary

The discussion in this chapter addressed a large number of variations on the basic concept of borrowing funds, because so many alternatives to the basic debt scenario can be arranged. It is entirely possible that a particular real-life transaction will not slot perfectly into any of the debt-related rules laid out in this chapter. If so, it is best to pattern the accounting used for the transaction to the rules that most closely approximate the situation. Better yet, discuss the proposed accounting with the company's auditors before recording the transaction, which greatly reduces the risk of having to restate the financial statements with audit adjustments at year-end.

Debt

If a proposed debt issuance contains highly unusual features, it is best to take the proposed transaction straight to the auditors to determine the proper accounting before any agreements have been signed. By doing so, accounting issues may be spotted in advance that can be used to convince management that an alternative funding arrangement might yield better accounting results for the business.

Chapter 28
Equity

505 = GAAP codification area for equity

Introduction

This chapter addresses a variety of topics that are related to equity. The topics covered include equity appropriations, stock dividends, stock splits, stock repurchases, equity-based payments, spinoffs, and more. These topics are only related to each other in that they have an impact on the equity classification of transactions, and can otherwise be considered something of a smorgasbord of information. In this chapter, we deal with the concepts linked to each of these equity topics. The guidance in this chapter applies to all entities.

Related Chapters

See the following chapters for discussions of issues related to equity:

- *Compensation – Stock Compensation*. Discusses the issuance of shares in exchange for services rendered.
- *Presentation of Financial Statements*. Covers the presentation of information about discontinued operations, which applies to the spinoffs topic in this chapter.

Overview of Equity

Equity is the residual interest of owners in a business, once liabilities have been subtracted from assets. From the perspective of the accountant, key areas of concern are the issuance and repurchase of stock, though there are many lesser issues that can also impact equity.

The equity topics in this chapter are quite varied, and so cannot easily be combined into a single section. Instead, we have separated the larger topics into their own sections, and provide below only a few minor items related to equity:

- *Appropriations*. It is permissible to appropriate retained earnings for specific purposes, such as acquisitions, debt reductions, new construction, stock buybacks, and so forth. If there is an appropriation, disclose the amount in the equity section of the balance sheet. It is not permissible to charge expenses or losses against an appropriation. It is also not permissible to transfer an appropriation to income.
- *Note paid for equity*. There may be cases where an investor issues a note to a business in exchange for an equity position in the company (as opposed to

the usual cash payment). If there is not clear evidence that the investor intends to pay and has the ability to do so within a short period of time, do not record the note as an asset. Instead, offset the note against the corresponding equity line item in the equity section of the balance sheet.

The Sale of Stock

A common fund raising activity for a publicly-held entity is to sell stock – usually its common stock. The structure of the journal entry to record the sale of stock depends upon the existence and size of any par value associated with the stock. Par value is the legal capital per share, and the amount is printed on the face of each stock certificate. A portion of the price at which each share is sold is recorded in either the common stock or preferred stock account (depending on the type of share sold) in the amount of the par value, with the remainder being recorded in the additional paid-in capital account. Both entries are credits. The offsetting debit is to the cash account.

EXAMPLE

Arlington Motors sells 10,000 shares of its common stock for $8 per share. The stock has a par value of $0.01. Arlington records the share issuance with the following entry:

	Debit	Credit
Cash	80,000	
Common stock ($0.01 par value)		100
Additional paid-in capital		79,900

If Arlington were to only sell the stock for an amount equal to the par value, the entire credit would be to the common stock account; there would be no entry to the additional paid-in capital account. If the company were to sell preferred stock instead of common stock, the entry would be the same, except that the accounts in which the entries are made would be identified as preferred stock accounts, not common stock accounts.

Dividend Payments

The cash dividend is by far the most common of the dividend types used. On the date of declaration, the board of directors resolves to pay a certain dividend amount in cash to those investors holding the company's stock on a specific date. The date of record is the date on which dividends are assigned to the holders of the company's stock. On the date of payment, the company issues dividend payments.

EXAMPLE

On February 1, Milagro Corporation's board of directors declares a cash dividend of $0.50 per share on the company's 2,000,000 outstanding shares, to be paid on June 1 to all shareholders of record on April 1. On February 1, the company records this entry:

	Debit	Credit
Retained earnings	1,000,000	
Dividends payable		1,000,000

On June 1, Milagro pays the dividends and records the transaction with this entry:

	Debit	Credit
Dividends payable	1,000,000	
Cash		1,000,000

Stock Dividends and Stock Splits

A company may issue additional shares to its shareholders, which is called a stock dividend. This type of dividend does not involve the reduction of any company assets, nor does it increase the cash inflow to the recipient, so it can be considered a neutral event that has no impact on either party. However, the sheer volume of shares issued can have an effect on the value of the shareholdings of the recipient, which calls for different types of accounting. The two volume-based accounting treatments are:

- *Low-volume stock issuance.* If a stock issuance is for less than 20% to 25% of the number of shares outstanding prior to the issuance, account for the transaction as a stock dividend.
- *High-volume stock issuance.* If a stock issuance is for more than 20% to 25% of the number of shares outstanding prior to the issuance, account for the transaction as a stock split.

The dividing line between these two treatments is an estimate provided in GAAP, based on the assumption that a relatively small stock issuance will not appreciably alter the price of a share, which therefore creates value for the recipient of these shares. A larger share issuance is presumed to reduce the market price of shares outstanding, so that share recipients do not experience a net increase in the value of their shares.

If there are an ongoing series of stock issuances that would individually be accounted for as stock dividends, consider aggregating these issuances to see if the result would instead trigger treatment as a stock split.

Stock Dividend

When there is a stock dividend, transfer from retained earnings to the capital stock and additional paid-in capital accounts an amount equal to the fair value of the additional shares issued. The fair value of the additional shares issued is based on their market value after the dividend is declared. A stock dividend is never treated as a liability, since it does not reduce assets.

EXAMPLE

Davidson Motors declares a stock dividend to its shareholders of 10,000 shares. The fair value of the stock is $5.00, and its par value is $1.00. Davidson's controller records the following entry:

	Debit	Credit
Retained earnings	50,000	
Common stock, $1 par value		10,000
Additional paid-in capital		40,000

Stock Split

When a stock issuance is sufficiently large to be classified as a stock split, the only accounting is to ensure that the legally-required amount of par value has been properly designated as such in the accounting records. If a company's stock has no par value, then no reallocation of funds into the par value account is required.

EXAMPLE

Davidson Motors declares a stock dividend to its shareholders of 1,000,000 shares, which represents a doubling of the prior number of shares outstanding. Davidson's stock has a par value of $1, so the controller records the following entry to ensure that the correct amount of capital is apportioned to the par value account:

	Debit	Credit
Additional paid-in capital	1,000,000	
Common stock, $1 par value		1,000,000

Treasury Stock

A company may elect to buy back its own shares. These repurchased shares are called treasury stock. Management may intend to permanently retire these shares, or it could intend to hold them for resale or reissuance at a later date. Common reasons for the repurchase of stock include the following:

- A stock buyback program that is intended to reduce the overall number of shares and thereby increase earnings per share
- When a company is forced to buy back shares from someone who is attempting to gain control of the business
- When a company has the right of first refusal to reacquire shares
- When management wants to take a publicly-held company private, and needs to reduce the number of shareholders in order to do so

Stock that has been repurchased does not qualify for voting purposes, nor should it be included in the earnings per share calculation.

The two aspects of accounting for treasury stock are the purchase of stock by a company, and its resale of those shares. We deal with these issues next.

Purchase of Treasury Stock

When a company buys back its stock, the circumstances of the repurchase arrangement may indicate that the amount paid incorporates a larger payment than would be justified by the current market price of the stock. Indicators of this situation are a repurchase from only a small group of shareholders, or when the price is higher than the current market price. For example, a company may buy back the shares of a suitor at a high price, in exchange for an agreement by the suitor not to acquire additional shares in the company. In these cases, separate the excess amount of the payment, and charge it to expense as incurred.

EXAMPLE

Armadillo Industries settles a lawsuit with a former employee regarding payouts under his employment contract, under which the company agrees to pay $150,000 to buy back his 10,000 shares and settle all other claims under the contract. On the date when the agreement is reached, the market price of Armadillo's stock was $9. Based on this information, the company allocates $90,000 to treasury stock and $60,000 to compensation expense.

When treasury stock is acquired by the issuing business, the most common treatment of the transaction is to record it as a contra account, where the treasury stock appears as a deduction from the other equity items in the balance sheet.

Resale of Treasury Stock

If a company elects to resell shares that it had previously purchased, do not include any aspect of the sale in the income statement, since this is not a profit-generating activity; rather, it is a means of acquiring funds.

Cost Method

The simplest and most widely-used method for accounting for the repurchase of stock is the cost method. The accounting is:

- *Repurchase*. To record a repurchase, simply record the entire amount of the purchase in the treasury stock account.
- *Resale*. If the treasury stock is resold at a later date, offset the sale price against the treasury stock account, and credit any sales exceeding the repurchase cost to the additional paid-in capital account. If the sale price is less than the repurchase cost, charge the differential to any additional paid-in capital remaining from prior treasury stock transactions, and any residual amount to retained earnings if there is no remaining balance in the additional paid-in capital account.
- *Retirement*. If management decides to permanently retire stock that it has already accounted for under the cost method, it reverses the par value and additional paid-in capital associated with the original stock sale, with any remaining amount being charged to retained earnings.

EXAMPLE

The board of directors of Armadillo Industries authorizes the repurchase of 50,000 shares of its stock, which has a $1 par value. The company originally sold the sales for $12 each, or $600,000 in total. It repurchases the shares for the same amount. The controller records the transaction with this entry:

	Debit	Credit
Treasury stock	600,000	
Cash		600,000

Later, the company has a choice of either selling the shares to investors again, or of permanently retiring the shares. If the board were to resell the shares at a price of $13 per share, the entry would be:

	Debit	Credit
Cash	650,000	
Additional paid-in capital		50,000
Treasury stock		600,000

Alternatively, the board may elect to retire the shares. If it were to do so, the entry would be:

	Debit	Credit
Common stock, $1 par value	50,000	
Additional paid-in capital	550,000	
Treasury stock		600,000

Constructive Retirement Method

An alternative method of accounting for treasury stock is the constructive retirement method, which is used under the assumption that repurchased stock will not be reissued in the future. Under this approach, the amount of the original price at which the stock was sold is essentially being reversed. The remainder of the purchase price is debited to the retained earnings account.

EXAMPLE

The board of directors of Armadillo Industries authorizes the repurchase of 100,000 shares of its stock, which has a $1 par value. The company originally sold the shares for $12 each, or $1,200,000 in total. Armadillo pays $1,500,000 to repurchase the shares. The controller records the transaction with this journal entry:

	Debit	Credit
Common stock, $1 par value	100,000	
Additional paid-in capital	1,100,000	
Retained earnings	300,000	
Cash		1,500,000

In the journal entry, the controller is eliminating the $100,000 originally credited to the common stock account and associated with its par value. There is also an elimination from the additional paid-in capital account of the $1,100,000 originally paid into that account. The excess expenditure over the original proceeds is charged to the retained earnings account.

We do not show an example for the resale of treasury stock that was accounted for under the constructive retirement method, since these shares were recorded under the assumption that they would not be resold.

Equity-Based Payments to Non-Employees

An equity-based payment is one in which a business pays a provider of goods or services with its equity, such as shares or warrants. The accounting for equity-based payments depends upon the definition of the recipient, since the accounting for a payment to an employee differs from the accounting when payment is made to anyone else. In this section, we deal with the accounting for equity-based payments to non-employees. See the Compensation – Stock Compensation chapter for the accounting treatment of equity-based payments to employees. In the following subsections, we will deal with a number of variations on the concept of equity-based payments to non-employees.

Initial Recognition

The two main rules for equity-based payments are as follows:

- Recognize the fair value of the equity instruments issued or the fair value of the consideration received, whichever can be more reliably measured; and
- Recognize the asset or expense related to the provided goods or services at the same time.

The following additional conditions apply to more specific circumstances:

- *Fully vested equity issued.* If fully vested, nonforfeitable equity instruments are issued, the grantor should recognize the equity on the date of issuance. The offset to this recognition may be a prepaid asset, if the grantee has not yet delivered on its obligations.
- *Option expiration.* If the grantor recognizes an asset or expense based on its issuance of stock options to a grantee, and the grantee does not exercise the options, do not reverse the asset or expense.
- *Sales incentives.* If sales incentives are paid with equity instruments, measure them at the fair value of the equity instruments or the sales incentive, whichever can be more reliably measured.
- *Equity recipient.* If a business is the recipient of an equity instrument in exchange for goods or services, it should recognize revenue in the normal manner, as per the rules stated in the Revenue Recognition chapter.

The grantor usually recognizes an equity-based payment as of a measurement date. The measurement date is the earlier of:

- The date when the grantee's performance is complete; or
- The date when the grantee's commitment to complete is probable, given the presence of large disincentives related to nonperformance. Note that forfeiture of the equity instrument is not considered a sufficient disincentive to trigger this clause.

It is also possible to reach the measurement date when the grantor issues fully vested, nonforfeitable equity instruments to the grantee, since the grantee does not have an obligation to perform in order to receive payment.

If the grantor issues a fully vested, nonforfeitable equity instrument that can be exercised early if a performance target is reached, the grantor measures the fair value of the instrument at the date of grant. If early exercise is granted, then measure and record the incremental change in fair value as of the date of revision to the terms of the instrument. Also, recognize the cost of the transaction in the same period as if the company had paid cash, instead of using the equity instrument as payment.

EXAMPLE

Armadillo Industries issues fully vested warrants to a grantee. The option agreement contains a provision that the exercise price will be reduced if a project on which the grantee is working is completed to the satisfaction of Armadillo management by a certain date.

In another arrangement, Armadillo issues warrants that vest in five years. The option agreement contains a provision that the vesting period will be reduced to six months if a project on which the grantee is working is accepted by an Armadillo client by a certain date.

In both cases, the company should record the fair value of the instruments when granted, and then adjust the recorded fair values when the remaining provisions of the agreements have been settled.

In rare cases, it may be necessary for the grantor to recognize the cost of an equity payment before the measurement date. If so, measure the fair value of the equity instrument at each successive interim period until the measurement date is reached. If some terms of the equity instrument have not yet been settled during these interim periods (as is the case when the amount of equity paid will vary based on market conditions or counterparty performance), measure the instrument at its lowest aggregate fair value during each interim period, until all terms have been settled.

The grantee must also record payments made to it with equity instruments. The grantee should recognize the fair value of the equity instruments paid using the same rules applied to the grantor. If there is a performance condition, the grantee may have to alter the amount of revenue recognized, once the condition has been settled.

EXAMPLE

Gatekeeper Corporation operates a private toll road. It contracts with International Bridge Development (IBD) to build a bridge along the toll way. Gatekeeper agrees to pay IBD $10,000,000 for the work, as well as an additional 1,000,000 warrants if the bridge is completed by a certain date. IBD agrees to forfeit $2,000,000 of its fee if the bridge has not been completed by that date. The forfeiture clause is sufficiently large to classify the arrangement as a performance commitment.

Gatekeeper should measure the 1,000,000 warrants at the performance commitment date, which have a fair value of $500,000. Gatekeeper should then charge the $500,000 to expense over the normal course of the bridge construction project, based on milestone and completion payments.

EXAMPLE

Archaic Corporation hires a writer to create a series of books about ancient Greece. The terms of the deal are that Archaic will pay the writer $20,000 and 10,000 warrants per book completed. There is no penalty associated with the writer declining to continue writing books for the series. The writer completes work on the first book in the series on October 31, and then refuses to continue writing books for Archaic.

Archaic should recognize the fair value of the 10,000 warrants associated with the writer's completion of the first book when the writer completes the manuscript on October 31. On that date, the warrants have a fair value of $5,000, so Archaic should recognize a total expense of $25,000, which is comprised of the cash and warrant portions of the payment.

Spinoffs and Reverse Spinoffs

A company (the spinnor) may spin off a portion of its operations to shareholders, typically by transferring assets into a separate legal entity (the spinnee) and distributing shares in the spinnee to existing shareholders. This transaction is called a spinoff. In rare cases, the legal form of the transaction is that the spinnee is the surviving entity, in which case the event is called a reverse spinoff.

In general, the accounting for a spinoff is to record the assets of the spinnee at their carrying value. The transaction is not to be accounted for as a combination sale of the spinnee and subsequent distribution of the proceeds to shareholders.

If there is a reverse spinoff, treat the spinnee (which is the surviving entity) for accounting purposes as the spinnor. This approach bases the accounting on the substance of the transaction, not on its legal form. The proper treatment of a reverse spinoff as a spinoff for accounting purposes is based on the facts and circumstances of each individual situation. The following flags indicate that a spinoff could actually be a reverse spinoff:

- *Fair value*. The fair value of the legal spinnee is larger than the fair value of the legal spinnor.
- *Management*. The legal spinnee retains the senior management team.
- *Size*. The legal spinnee is larger than the legal spinnor, based on a comparison of assets, revenues, and earnings.
- *Time held*. The legal spinnee has been held for a longer period of time than the legal spinnor.

EXAMPLE

Armadillo Industries has a small division that produces films. Since this division is entirely unrelated to Armadillo's core business of manufacturing protective plating, senior management wants to shift the assets associated with the film division into a new entity, and distribute shares in the entity to shareholders on a pro rata basis. This is a spinoff.

Henderson Industrial is comprised of two subsidiaries, of which one produces milk cartons and the other manufactures conveyor systems. The milk carton unit is three times the size of the conveyor division. Henderson shareholders believe that the milk carton business has better prospects, and so want to dispose of the conveyor division. To do so, the company distributes shares in the milk carton subsidiary to shareholders and then sells all shares in the conveyor division to a third party. This is a reverse spinoff.

Equity Disclosures

There are a large number of disclosures related to the equity topic, so the disclosures related to each topic are addressed separately within the following sub-sections.

Rights and Privileges

Disclose a summary of the rights and privileges accorded to the holders of the various securities outstanding during the presented accounting periods. This may include the following items, or other rights and privileges:

- Conversion rights to other securities (and the associated prices and dates)
- Dividends
- Liquidation rights
- Participation rights
- Special voting rights

Preferred Stock

If there is preferred stock outstanding and those shares have a liquidation preference that significantly exceeds their par value, disclose the aggregate liquidation preference on the balance sheet. Also disclose the following information anywhere in the financial statements:

- *Arrearages.* The amount by which there are cumulative preferred dividends in arrears, both in aggregate and on a per-share basis.
- *Redemption.* The amounts of preferred stock subject to redemption, both in aggregate and on a per-share basis.

Contingently Convertible Securities

Disclose the significant conversion terms associated with contingently convertible securities. There must be sufficient information for readers to understand the contingent conversion option and what the impact of the conversion would be. The following disclosures would be helpful for gaining this understanding:

- Events that would alter the terms of the contingency
- Events that would trigger the contingency
- The conversion price
- The number of shares into which a security can be converted
- The timing of conversion rights
- The type of settlement (such as in cash or shares)

EXAMPLE

Armadillo Industries includes the following disclosure in the notes that accompany its financial statements, regarding the issuance of shares related to a recent acquisition:

> The company issued 2,000,000 shares of its common stock to the shareholders of Susquehanna Plating when it acquired that entity. If the market price of Armadillo's stock declines below $10 per share before December 31, 20X4, the company will be obligated to issue an additional 500,000 shares of its common stock to those shareholders.

Also disclose the excess amount by which the aggregate fair value of the securities to be issued at conversion exceeds the proceeds received, as well as the time period over which the discount would be amortized.

Redeemable Securities

If a business issues redeemable securities, disclose the redemption requirements in each of the five years following the date of the last balance sheet presented. The disclosure can be in aggregate or separately for each issuance of these securities.

Treasury Stock

If the company repurchases its stock at a price significantly in excess of the market price, disclose how the price is allocated between other items and the repurchase of stock, and how the transaction is accounted for.

If the company is organized in a state which has stock repurchase laws that restrict the availability of retained earnings for distributions, disclose this situation.

Changes in Shareholders' Equity

If both the income statement and balance sheet are presented, disclose the changes in the shareholders' equity accounts, as well as any changes in shares outstanding during at least the most recent fiscal year and subsequent interim periods. A sample statement, not including changes in shares outstanding, is shown in the following exhibit.

Statement of Retained Earnings

	Common Stock, $1 Par	Additional Paid-In Capital	Retained Earnings	Total Shareholders' Equity
Retained earnings at December 31, 20X2	$10,000	$40,000	$100,000	$150,000
Net income for the year ended 12/31/X3			40,000	40,000
Dividends paid to shareholders			-25,000	-25,000
Retained earnings at December 31, 20X3	$10,000	$40,000	$115,000	$165,000

The Securities and Exchange Commission also requires disclosure of adjustments to the beginning balance in this reconciliation for items that were retroactively applied to prior periods.

Equity-Based Payments to Non-Employees

There may be situations where a company issues fully vested, non-forfeitable equity instruments in exchange for goods or services. A likely outcome of this arrangement is that the goods or services have not yet been provided or performed, and so are recorded as a prepaid asset. This prepaid asset should be included within the assets section of the balance sheet, not as a deduction from equity.

An entity that has received an equity instrument should disclose the amount of gross operating revenue attributable to the instrument, since this is a nonmonetary transaction.

Spinoffs and Reverse Spinoffs

Classify the accounting spinnee as a discontinued operation if it meets the criteria for a discontinued operation (see the Presentation of Financial Statements chapter).

Summary

Many equity-related topics were addressed in this chapter. An accountant may not see most of these topics for years, or only have to deal with a few minor disclosures. However, the repurchase of shares is a relatively common event, so be familiar with the accounting for and presentation of treasury stock transactions. We recommend the cost method of accounting for treasury stock, since it is the easiest of the available accounting methods.

It is also relatively common to pay for goods and services with equity instruments, so be familiar with the concepts related to how these instruments are recognized. The level of judgment and accounting complexity increases when a business enters into arrangements where the issuance of equity instruments is subject to several variables. Consequently, it is best to provide advice on these arrangements before the business is contractually committed to them, in order to have commitments that require the least accounting effort and measurement uncertainty.

Chapter 29
Revenue Recognition

---

606 = GAAP codification area for revenue from contracts with customers

---

Introduction

Historically, the accounting standards related to the recognition of revenue have built up in a piecemeal manner, with guidance being established separately for certain industries and types of transactions. The result has been an inconsistent set of standards that, while workable, have not resulted in revenue recognition principles that could be applied consistently across many industries.

The accounting for revenue has been streamlined to a considerable extent with the release of Topic 606 in GAAP. Now, the overall intent of revenue recognition is to do so in a manner that reasonably depicts the transfer of goods or services to customers, for which consideration is paid that reflects the amount to which the seller expects to be entitled. The following sections describe the five-step process of revenue recognition, as well as a number of ancillary topics.

The Nature of a Customer

Revenue recognition only occurs if the third party involved is a customer. A customer is an entity that has contracted to obtain goods or services from the seller's ordinary activities in exchange for payment.

In some situations, it may require a complete examination of the facts and circumstances to determine whether the other party can be classified as a customer. For example, it can be difficult to discern whether there is a customer in collaborative research and development activities between pharmaceutical entities. Another difficult area is payments between oil and gas partners to settle differences between their entitlements to the output from a producing field.

EXAMPLE

The Red Herring Fish Company contracts with Lethal Sushi to co-develop a fish farm off the coast of Iceland, where the two entities share equally in any future profits. Lethal Sushi is primarily in the restaurant business, so developing a fish farm is not one of its ordinary activities. Also, there is no clear consideration being paid to Lethal. Based on the circumstances, Red Herring is not a customer of Lethal Sushi.

Steps in Revenue Recognition

Topic 606 establishes a series of actions that an entity takes to determine the amount and timing of revenue to be recognized. The main steps are:

1. Link the contract with a specific customer.
2. Note the performance obligations required by the contract.
3. Determine the price of the underlying transaction.
4. Match this price to the performance obligations through an allocation process.
5. Recognize revenue as the various obligations are fulfilled.

We will expand upon each of these steps in the following sections.

Step One: Link Contract to Customer

The contract is used as a central aspect of revenue recognition, because revenue recognition is closely associated with it. In many instances, revenue is recognized at multiple points in time over the duration of a contract, so linking contracts with revenue recognition provides a reasonable framework for establishing the timing and amounts of revenue recognition.

A contract only exists if there is an agreement between the parties that establishes enforceable rights and obligations. It is not necessary for an agreement to be in writing for it to be considered a contract. More specifically, a contract only exists if the following conditions are present:

- *Approval.* All parties to the contract have approved the document and substantially committed to its contents (based on all relevant facts and circumstances). The parties can be considered to be committed to a contract despite occasional lapses, such as not enforcing prompt payment or sometimes shipping late. Approval can be in writing or orally.
- *Rights.* The document clearly identifies the rights of the parties.
- *Payment.* The payment terms are clearly stated. It is acceptable to recognize revenue related to unpriced change orders if the seller expects that the price will be approved and the scope of work has been approved.
- *Substance.* The agreement has commercial substance; that is, the cash flows of the seller will change as a result of the contract, either in terms of their amount, timing, or risk of receipt. Otherwise, organizations could swap goods or services to artificially boost their revenue.
- *Probability.* It is probable that the organization will collect the amount stated in the contract in exchange for the goods or services that it commits to provide to the other party. In this context, "probable" means "likely to occur." This evaluation is based on the customer's ability and intention to pay when due. The evaluation can incorporate a consideration of the past practice of the customer in question, or of the class of customers to which that customer belongs.

If these criteria are not initially met, the seller can continue to evaluate the situation to see if the criteria are met at a later date.

> **Note:** These criteria do not *have* to be re-evaluated at a later date, unless the seller notes a significant change in the relevant facts and circumstances.

EXAMPLE

Prickly Corporation has entered into an arrangement to sell a large quantity of rose thorns to Ambivalence Corporation, which manufactures a number of potions for the amateur witch brewing market. The contract specifies monthly deliveries over the course of the next year.

Prior to the first shipment, Prickly's collections manager learns through her contacts that Ambivalence has just lost its line of credit and has conducted a large layoff. It appears that the customer's ability to pay has deteriorated significantly, which calls into question the probability of collecting the amount stated in the contract. In this case, there may no longer be a contract for the purposes of revenue recognition.

EXAMPLE

Domicilio Corporation, which develops commercial real estate, enters into a contract with Cupertino Beanery to sell a building to Cupertino to be used as a coffee shop. This is Cupertino's first foray into the coffee shop business, having previously only been a distributor of coffee beans to shops within the region. Also, there are a massive number of coffee shops already established in the area.

Domicilio receives a $100,000 deposit from Cupertino when the contract is signed. The contract also states that Cupertino will pay Domicilio an additional $900,000 for the rest of the property over the next three years, with interest. This financing arrangement is nonrecourse, meaning that Domicilio can repossess the building in the event of default, but cannot obtain further cash from Cupertino. Cupertino expects to pay Domicilio from the cash flows to be generated by the coffee shop operation.

Domicilio's management concludes that it is not probable that Cupertino will pay the remaining contractual amount, since its source of funds is a high-risk venture in which Cupertino has no experience. In addition, the loan is nonrecourse, so Cupertino can easily walk away from the arrangement. Accordingly, Domicilio accounts for the initial deposit and future payments as a deposit liability, and continues to recognize the building asset. If it later becomes probable that Cupertino will pay the full contractual amount, Domicilio can then recognize revenue and an offsetting receivable.

Whether a contract exists can depend upon standard industry practice, or vary by legal jurisdiction, or even vary by business segment.

There may be instances in which the preceding criteria are not met, and yet the customer is paying consideration to the seller. If so, revenue can be recognized only when one of the following events has occurred:

- The contract has been terminated and the consideration received by the seller is not refundable; or
- The seller has no remaining obligations to the customer, substantially all of the consideration has been received, and the payment is not refundable.

These alternatives focus on whether the contract has been concluded in all respects. If so, there is little risk that any revenue recognized will be reversed in a later period, and so is a highly conservative approach to recognizing revenue.

If the seller receives consideration from a customer and the preceding conditions do not exist, then the payment is to be recorded as a liability until such time as the sale criteria have been met.

A contract is not considered to exist when each party to the contract has a unilateral right to terminate a contract that has not been performed, and without compensating the other party. An unperformed contract is one in which no goods or services have been transferred to the customer, nor has the seller received any consideration from the customer in exchange for any promised goods or services.

In certain situations, it can make sense to combine several contracts into one for the purposes of revenue recognition. For example, if there is a portfolio of contracts that have similar characteristics, and the entity expects that treating the portfolio as a single unit will have no appreciable impact on the financial statements, it is acceptable to combine the contracts for accounting purposes. This approach may be particularly valuable in industries where there are a large number of similar contracts, and where applying the model to each individual contract could be impractical.

> **Tip:** When accounting for a portfolio of contracts, adjust the accompanying estimates and assumptions to reflect the greater size of the portfolio.

If the seller enters into two or more contracts with a customer at approximately the same time, these contracts can be accounted for as a single contract if any of the following criteria are met:

- *Basis of negotiation.* The contracts were negotiated as a package, with the goal of attaining a single commercial objective.
- *Interlinking consideration.* The consideration that will be paid under the terms of one contract is dependent upon the price or performance noted in the other contract.
- *Performance obligation.* There is essentially one performance obligation inherent in the two contracts.

EXAMPLE

Domicilio Corporation enters into three contracts with Milford Sound to construct a concert arena. These contracts involve construction of the concrete building shell, installation of seating, and the construction of a staging system. The three contracts are all needed in order to arrive at a functioning concert arena. Final payment on all three contracts shall be made once the final customer (a local municipality) approves the entire project.

Domicilio should account for these contracts as a single contract, since they are all directed toward the same commercial goal, payment is dependent on all three contracts being completed, and the performance obligation is essentially the same for all of the contracts.

Step Two: Note Performance Obligations

A performance obligation is essentially the unit of account for the goods or services contractually promised to a customer. The performance obligations in the contract must be clearly identified. This is of considerable importance in recognizing revenue, since revenue is considered to be recognizable when goods or services are transferred to the customer. Examples of goods or services are:

Item Sold	Example of the Seller
Arranging for another party to transfer goods or services	Travel agent selling airline tickets
Asset construction on behalf of a customer	Building construction company
Grant of a license	Software company issuing licenses to use its software
Grant of options to purchase additional goods or services	Airline granting frequent flier points
Manufactured goods	Manufacturer
Performance of contractually-mandated tasks	Consultant
Readiness to provide goods or services as needed	Snow plow operator, alarm system monitoring
Resale of merchandise	Retailer
Resale of rights to goods or services	Selling a priority for a new-model car delivery
Rights to future goods or services that can be resold	Wholesaler gives additional services to retailer buying a particular product

Note: If goods or services are immaterial in relation to a specific contract, it is not necessary to assess whether they are performance obligations.

There may also be an implicit promise to deliver goods or services that is not stated in a contract, as implied by the customary business practices of the seller. If there is a valid expectation by the customer to receive these implicitly-promised goods or services, they should be considered a performance obligation. Otherwise, the seller might recognize the entire transaction price as revenue when in fact there are still goods or services yet to be provided.

If there is no performance obligation, then there is no revenue to be recognized. For example, a company could continually build up its inventory through ongoing production activities, but just because it has more sellable assets does not mean that it can report an incremental increase in the revenue in its income statement. If such an activity-based revenue recognition model were allowed, organizations could increase their revenues simply by increasing their rate of activity.

If there is more than one good or service to be transferred under the contract terms, only break it out as a separate performance obligation if it is a distinct obligation or there are a series of transfers to the customer of a distinct good or service. In the latter case, a separate performance obligation is assumed if there is a consistent pattern of transfer to the customer.

The "distinct" label can be applied to a good or service only if it meets both of the following criteria:

- *Capable of being distinct.* The customer can benefit from the good or service as delivered, or in combination with other resources that the customer can readily find; and
- *Distinct within the context of the contract.* The promised delivery of the good or service is separately identified within the contract.

Goods or services are more likely to be considered distinct when:

- The seller does not use the goods or services as a component of an integrated bundle of goods or services.
- The items do not significantly modify any other goods or services listed in the contract.
- The items are not highly interrelated with other goods or services listed in the contract.

The intent of these evaluative factors is to place a focus on how to determine whether goods or services are truly distinct within a contract. There is no need to assess the customer's intended use of any goods or services when making this determination.

EXAMPLE

Aphelion Corporation sells a package of goods and services to Nova Corporation. The goods include a deep field telescope, an observatory to house the telescope, and calibration services for the telescope.

The observatory building can be considered distinct from the telescope and calibration services, because Nova could have the telescope installed in an existing facility instead. However, the telescope and calibration services are linked, since the telescope will not function properly unless it has been properly calibrated. Thus, one performance obligation can be considered the observatory, while the telescope and associated calibration can be stated as a separate obligation.

EXAMPLE

Norrona Software enters into a contract with a Scandinavian clothing manufacturer to transfer a software license for its clothing design software. The contract also states that Norrona will install the software and provide technical support for a two-year period. The installation process involves adjusting the data entry screens to match the needs of the clothing designers who will use the software. The software can be used without these installation changes. The technical support assistance is intended to provide advice to users regarding advanced features, and is not considered a key requirement for software users.

Since the software is functional without the installation process or the technical support, Norrona concludes that the items are not highly interrelated. Since these goods and services are distinct, the company should identify separate performance obligations for the software license, installation work, and technical support.

In the event that a good or service is not classified as distinct, aggregate it with other goods or services promised in the contract, until such time as a cluster of goods or services have been accumulated that can be considered distinct.

Note: If a different GAAP topic describes how to separate out the elements of a contract or initially measure it, follow that guidance before the requirements of Topic 606.

The administrative tasks needed to fulfill a contract are not considered to be performance obligations, since they do not involve the transfer of goods or services to customers. For example, setting up information about a new contract in the seller's contract management software is not considered a performance obligation.

Step Three: Determine Prices

This step involves the determination of the transaction price built into the contract. The transaction price is the amount of consideration to be paid by the customer in exchange for its receipt of goods or services. The transaction price does not include any amounts collected on behalf of third parties.

EXAMPLE

The Twister Vacuum Company sells its vacuum cleaners to individuals through its chain of retail stores. In the most recent period, Twister generated $3,800,000 of receipts, of which $200,000 was sales taxes collected on behalf of local governments. Since the $200,000 was collected on behalf of third parties, it cannot be recognized as revenue.

The transaction price may be difficult to determine, since it involves consideration of the effects noted in the following subsections.

Variable Consideration

The terms of some contracts may result in a price that can vary, depending on the circumstances. For example, there may be discounts, rebates, penalties, or performance bonuses in the contract. Or, the customer may have a reasonable expectation that the seller will offer a price concession, based on the seller's customary business practices, policies, or statements. Another example is when the seller intends to accept lower prices from a new customer in order to develop a strong customer relationship. If so, set the transaction price based on either the most likely amount or the probability-weighted expected value, using whichever method yields that amount of consideration most likely to be paid. In more detail, these methods are:

- *Most likely.* The seller develops a range of possible payment amounts, and selects the amount most likely to be paid. This approach works best when there are only two possible amounts that will be paid.
- *Expected value.* The seller develops a range of possible payment amounts, and assigns a probability to each one. The sum of these probability-weighted amounts is the expected value of the variable consideration. This approach works best when there are a large number of possible payment amounts. However, the outcome may be an expected value that does not exactly align with any amount that could actually be paid.

EXAMPLE

Grissom Granaries operates grain storage facilities along the Mississippi River. Its accounting staff is reviewing a contract that has just been signed with a major farming co-operative, and concludes that the contract could have four possible outcomes, which are noted in the following expected value table:

Price Scenario	Transaction Price	Probability	Probability-Weighted Price
1	$1,500,000	20%	$300,000
2	1,700,000	35%	595,000
3	2,000,000	40%	800,000
4	2,400,000	5%	120,000
		Expected Value	$1,815,000

The expected value derived from the four possible pricing outcomes is $1,815,000, even though this amount does not match any one of the four pricing outcomes.

Whichever method is chosen, be sure to use it consistently throughout the contract, as well as for similar contracts. However, it is not necessary to use the same measurement method to measure each uncertainty contained within a contract; different methods can be applied to different uncertainties.

Also, review the circumstances of each contract at the end of each reporting period, and update the estimated transaction price to reflect any changes in the circumstances.

EXAMPLE

Cantilever Construction has entered into a contract to tear down and replace five bridges along Interstate 70. The state government (which owns and maintains this section of the highway) is extremely concerned about how the work will interfere with traffic on the highway. Accordingly, the government includes in the contract a clause that penalizes Cantilever $10,000 for every hour over the budgeted amount that each bridge demolition and construction project shuts down the interstate, and a $15,000 bonus for every hour saved from the budgeted amount.

Cantilever has extensive experience with this type of work, having torn down and replaced 42 other bridges along the interstate highway system in the past five years. Based on the company's experience with these other projects and an examination of the budgeted hours allowed for shutting down the interstate, the company concludes that the most likely outcome is $120,000 of variable consideration associated with the project. Cantilever accordingly adds this amount to the transaction price.

Possibility of Reversal

Do not include in the transaction price an estimate of variable consideration if, when the uncertainty associated with the variable amount is settled, it is probable that there will be a significant reversal of cumulative revenue recognized. The assessment of a possible reversal of revenue could include the following factors, all of which might increase the probability of a revenue reversal:

- *Beyond seller's influence.* The amount of consideration paid is strongly influenced by factors outside of the control of the seller. For example, goods sold may be subject to obsolescence (as is common in the technology industry), or weather conditions could impede the availability of goods (as is common in the production of farm products).
- *Historical practice.* The seller has a history of accepting a broad range of price concessions, or of changing the terms of similar contracts.
- *Inherent range of outcomes.* The terms of the contract contain a broad range of possible consideration amounts that might be paid.

- *Limited experience.* The seller does not have much experience with the type of contract in question. Alternatively, the seller's prior experience cannot be translated into a prediction of the amount of consideration paid.
- *Long duration.* A considerable period of time may have to pass before the uncertainty can be resolved.

> **Note:** The probability of a significant reversal of cumulative revenue recognized places a conservative bias on the recognition of revenue, rather than a neutral bias, so there will be a tendency for recognized revenue levels to initially be too low. However, this approach is reasonable when considering that revenue information is more relevant when it is not subject to future reversals.

If management expects that a retroactive discount will be applied to sales transactions, the seller should recognize a refund liability as part of the revenue recognition when each performance obligation is satisfied. For example, if the seller is currently selling goods for $100 but expects that a 20% volume discount will be retroactively applied at the end of the year, the resulting entry should be:

	Debit	Credit
Accounts receivable	100	
Revenue		80
Refund liability		20

EXAMPLE

Medusa Medical sells a well-known snake oil therapy through a number of retail store customers. In the most recent month, Medusa sells $100,000 of its potent Copperhead Plus combination healing balm and sunscreen lotion. The therapy is most effective within one month of manufacture and then degrades rapidly, so that Medusa must accept increasingly large price concessions in order to ensure that the goods are sold. Historically, this means that the range of price concessions varies from zero (in the first month) to 80% (after four months). Of this range of outcomes, Medusa estimates that the expected value of the transactions is likely to be revenue of $65,000. However, since the risk of obsolescence is so high, Medusa cannot conclude that it is probable that there will not be a significant reversal in the amount of cumulative revenue recognized. Accordingly, management concludes that the price point at which it is probable that there will not be a significant reversal in the cumulative amount of revenue recognized is actually closer to $45,000 (representing a 55% price concession). Based on this conclusion, the controller initially recognizes $45,000 of revenue when the goods are shipped to retailers, and continues to monitor the situation at the end of each reporting period, to see if the recognized amount should be adjusted.

EXAMPLE

Iceland Cod enters into a contract with Lethal Sushi to provide Lethal with 10,000 pounds of cod per year, at $15 per pound. If Lethal purchases more than 10,000 pounds within one calendar year, then a 12% retroactive price reduction will be applied to all of Lethal's purchases for the year.

Iceland has dealt with Lethal for a number of years, and knows that Lethal has never attained the 10,000 pound level of purchases. Accordingly, through the first half of the year, Iceland records its sales to Lethal at their full price, which is $30,000 for 2,000 pounds of cod.

In July, Lethal acquires Wimpy Fish Company, along with its large chain of seafood restaurants. With a much larger need for fish to supply the additional restaurants, Lethal now places several large orders that make it quite clear that passing the 10,000 pound threshold will be no problem at all. Accordingly, Iceland's controller records a cumulative revenue reversal of $3,600 to account for Lethal's probable attainment of the volume purchase discount.

EXAMPLE

Armadillo Industries is a new company that has developed a unique type of ceramic-based body armor that is extremely light. To encourage sales, the company is offering a 90-day money back guarantee. Since the company is new to the industry and cannot predict the level of returns, there is no way of knowing if a sudden influx of returns might trigger a significant reversal in the amount of cumulative revenue recognized. Accordingly, the company must wait for the money back guarantee to expire before it can recognize any revenue.

Sales Taxes

An organization can elect to create an accounting policy that allows it to exclude sales tax amounts collected from customers from the transaction price.

Time Value of Money

If the transaction price is to be paid over a period of time, this implies that the seller is including a financing component in the contract. If this financing component is a significant financing benefit for the customer and provides financing for more than one year, adjust the transaction price for the time value of money. In cases where there is a financing component to a contract, the seller will earn interest income over the term of the contract.

A contract may contain a financing component, even if there is no explicit reference to it in the contract. When adjusting the transaction price for the time value of money, consider the following factors:

- *Standalone price.* The amount of revenue recognized should reflect the price that a customer would have paid if it had paid in cash.
- *Significance.* In order to be recognized, the financing component should be significant. This means evaluating the amount of the difference between the consideration to be paid and the cash selling price. Also note the combined effect of prevailing interest rates and the time difference between when delivery is made and when the customer pays.

Revenue Recognition

If it is necessary to adjust the compensation paid for the time value of money, use as a discount rate the rate that would be employed in a separate financing transaction between the parties as of the beginning date of the contract. The rate used should reflect the credit characteristics of the customer, including the presence of any collateral provided. This discount rate is not to be updated after the commencement of the contract, irrespective of any changes in the credit markets or in the credit standing of the customer.

EXAMPLE

Hammer Industries sells a large piece of construction equipment to Eskimo Construction, under generous terms that allow Eskimo to pay Hammer the full amount of the $119,990 receivable in 24 months. The cash selling price of the equipment is $105,000. The contract contains an implicit interest rate of 6.9%, which is the interest rate that discounts the purchase price of $119,990 down to the cash selling price over the two year period. The controller examines this rate and concludes that it approximates the rate that Hammer and Eskimo would use if there had been a separate financing transaction between them as of the contract inception date. Consequently, Hammer recognizes interest income during the two-year period prior to the payment due date, using the following calculation:

Year	Beginning Balance	Interest (at 6.9% Rate)	Ending Balance
1	$105,000	$7,245	$112,245
2	112,245	7,745	$119,990

As of the shipment date, Hammer records the following entry:

	Debit	Credit
Loan receivable	105,000	
Revenue		105,000

At the end of the first year, Hammer recognizes the interest associated with the transaction for the first year, using the following entry:

	Debit	Credit
Loan receivable	7,245	
Interest income		7,245

At the end of the second year, Hammer recognizes the interest associated with the transaction for the second year, using the following entry:

	Debit	Credit
Loan receivable	7,745	
Interest income		7,745

These entries increase the size of the loan receivable until it reaches the original sale price of $119,990. Eskimo then pays the full amount of the receivable, at which point Hammer records the following final entry:

	Debit	Credit
Cash	119,990	
Loan receivable		119,990

Also, note that the financing concept can be employed in reverse; that is, if a customer makes a deposit that the seller expects to retain for more than one year, the financing component of this arrangement should be recognized by the seller. Doing so properly reflects the economics of the arrangement, where the seller is using the cash of the customer to fund its purchase of materials and equipment for a project; if the seller had not provided the deposit, the seller would instead have needed to obtain financing.

There is assumed *not* to be a significant financing component to a contract in the presence of any of the following factors:

- *Advance payment.* The customer paid in advance, and the customer can specify when goods and services are to be delivered.
- *Variable component.* A large part of the consideration to be paid is variable, and payment timing will vary based on a future event that is not under the control of either party.
- *Non-financing reason.* The reason for the difference between the contractual consideration and the cash selling price exists for a reason other than financing, and the amount of the difference is proportional to the alternative reason.

EXAMPLE

Spinner Maintenance offers global technical support to the owners of rooftop solar power systems in exchange for a $400 fee. The fee pays for service that spans the first five years of the life of the power systems, and is purchased as part of the package of solar panels and initial installation work. This maintenance is intended to provide phone support to homeowners who are researching why their power systems are malfunctioning. The support does not include any replacement of solar panels for hail damage.

The support period is quite extensive, but Spinner concludes that there is no financing component to these sales, for the following reasons:

- The administrative cost of a monthly billing would be prohibitive, since the amount billed on a monthly basis would be paltry.
- Those more technologically proficient customers would be less likely to renew if they could pay on a more frequent basis, leaving Spinner with the highest-maintenance customers who require the most support.

- Customers are more likely to make use of the service if they are reminded of it by the arrival of monthly invoices.

In short, Spinner has several excellent reasons for structuring the payment plan to require an advance payment, all of which are centered on maintaining a reasonable level of profitability. The intent is not to provide financing to customers.

EXAMPLE

Glow Atomic sells a nuclear power plant to a French provincial government. The certification process for the plant is extensive, spanning a six-month test period. Accordingly, the local government builds into the contract a provision to withhold 20% of the contract price until completion of the test period. The rest of the payments are made on a milestone schedule, as the construction work progresses. Based on the circumstances and the amount of the withholding, the arrangement is considered to be non-financing, so Glow Atomic does not break out a financing component from the total consideration paid.

Noncash Consideration

If the customer will be paying with some form of noncash consideration, measure the consideration at its fair value as of the contract inception date. If it is not possible to measure the payment at its fair value, instead use the standalone selling price of the goods or services to be delivered to the customer. This approach also applies to payments made with equity instruments. In rare cases, the customer may supply the seller with goods or services that are intended to assist the seller in its fulfillment of the related contract. If the seller gains control of these assets or services, it should consider them to be noncash consideration paid by the customer.

EXAMPLE

Industrial Landscaping is hired by Pensive Corporation to mow the lawns and trim shrubbery at Pensive's corporate headquarters on a weekly basis throughout the year. Essentially the same service is provided each week. Pensive is a startup company with little excess cash, so it promises to pay Industrial with 25 shares of Pensive stock at the end of each week.

Industrial considers itself to have satisfied its performance obligation at the end of each week. Industrial should determine the transaction price as being the fair value of the shares at the end of each week, and recognizes this amount as revenue. There is no subsequent change in the amount of revenue recognized, irrespective of any changes in the fair value of the shares.

Payments to Customers

The contract may require the seller to pay consideration to the customer, perhaps in the form of credits or coupons that the customer can apply against the amounts it owes to the seller. This may also involve payments to third parties that have purchased the seller's goods or services from the original customer. If so, treat this consideration as a reduction of the transaction price. The following special situations may apply:

- *Customer supplies a good or service.* The customer may provide the seller with a distinct good or service; if so, the seller treats the payment as it would a payment to any supplier.
- *Supplier payment exceeds customer delivery.* If the customer provides a good or service to the seller, but the amount paid by the seller to the customer exceeds the fair value of the goods or services it receives in exchange, the excess of the payment is considered a reduction of the transaction price. If the fair value of the goods or services cannot be determined, then consider the entire amount paid by the seller to the customer to be a reduction of the transaction price.

If it is necessary to account for consideration paid to the customer as a reduction of the transaction price, do so when the later of the following two events have occurred:

- When the seller recognizes revenue related to its provision of goods or services to the customer; or
- When the seller either pays or promises to pay the consideration to the customer. The timing of this event could be derived from the customary business practices of the seller.

EXAMPLE

Dillinger Designs manufactures many types of hunting rifles. Dillinger enters into a one-year contract with Backwoods Survival, which has not previously engaged in rifle sales. Backwoods commits to purchase at least $240,000 of rifles from Dillinger during the contract period. Also, due to the considerable government-mandated safety requirements associated with the sale of rifles, Dillinger commits to pay $60,000 to Backwoods at the inception of the contract; these funds are intended to pay for a locking gun safe to be kept at each Backwoods store, as per firearms laws pertaining to retailers.

Dillinger determines that the $60,000 payment is to be treated as a reduction of the $240,000 sale price. Consequently, whenever Dillinger fulfills a performance obligation by shipping goods under the contract, it reduces the amount of revenue it would otherwise recognize by 25%, which reflects the proportion of the $60,000 payment related to locking gun safes of the $240,000 that Dillinger will be paid by Backwoods.

Refund Liabilities

In some situations, a seller may receive consideration from a customer, with the likelihood that the payment will be refunded. If so, the seller records a refund liability in the amount that the seller expects to refund back to the customer. The seller should review the amount of this liability at the end of each reporting period, to see if the amount should be altered.

Step Four: Allocate Prices to Obligations

Once the performance obligations and transaction prices associated with a contract have been identified, the next step is to allocate the transaction prices to the obligations. The basic rule is to allocate that price to a performance obligation that best reflects that amount of consideration to which the seller expects to be entitled when it satisfies each performance obligation. To determine this allocation, it is first necessary to estimate the standalone selling price of those distinct goods or services as of the inception date of the contract. If it is not possible to derive a standalone selling price, the seller must estimate it. This estimation should involve all relevant information that is reasonably available, such as:

- Competitive pressure on prices
- Costs incurred to manufacture or provide the item
- Item profit margins
- Pricing of other items in the same contract
- Standalone selling price of the item
- Supply and demand for the items in the market
- The seller's pricing strategy and practices
- The type of customer, distribution channel, or geographic region
- Third-party pricing

The following three approaches are acceptable ways in which to estimate a standalone selling price:

- *Adjusted market assessment.* This involves reviewing the market to estimate the price at which a customer in that market would be willing to pay for the goods and services in question. This can involve an examination of the prices of competitors for similar items and adjusting them to incorporate the seller's costs and margins.
- *Expected cost plus a margin.* This requires the seller to estimate the costs required to fulfill a performance obligation, and then add a margin to it to derive the estimated price.
- *Residual approach.* This involves subtracting all of the observable standalone selling prices from the total transaction price to arrive at the residual price remaining for allocation to any non-observable selling prices. This method can only be used if one of the following situations applies:
  - The seller sells the good or service to other customers for a wide range of prices; or
  - No price has yet been established for that item, and it has not yet been sold on a standalone basis.

The residual approach can be difficult to use when there are several goods or services with uncertain standalone selling prices. If so, it may be necessary to use a combination of methods to derive standalone selling prices, which should be used in the following order:

1. Estimate the aggregate amount of the standalone selling prices for all items having uncertain standalone selling prices, using the residual method.
2. Use another method to develop standalone selling prices for each item in this group, to allocate the aggregate amount of the standalone selling prices.

Once all standalone selling prices have been determined, allocate the transaction price amongst these distinct goods or services based on their relative standalone selling prices.

> **Tip:** Appropriate evidence of a standalone selling price is the observable price of a good or service when the seller sells it to a similar customer under similar circumstances.

Once the seller derives an approach for estimating a standalone selling price, it should consistently apply that method to the derivation of the standalone selling prices for other goods or services with similar characteristics.

EXAMPLE

Luminescence Corporation manufactures a wide range of light bulbs, and mostly sells into the wholesaler market. The company receives an order from the federal government for two million fluorescent bulbs, as well as for 100,000 units of a new bulb that operates outdoors at very low temperatures. Luminescence has not yet sold these new bulbs to anyone. The total price of the order is $7,000,000. Luminescence assigns $6,000,000 of the total price to the fluorescent bulbs, based on its own sales of comparable orders. This leaves $1,000,000 of the total price that is allocable to the low temperature bulbs. Since Luminescence has not yet established a price for these bulbs and has not sold them on a standalone basis, it is acceptable to allocate $1,000,000 to the low temperature bulbs under the residual approach.

If there is a subsequent change in the transaction price, allocate that change amongst the distinct goods or services based on the original allocation that was used at the inception of the contract. If this subsequent allocation is to a performance obligation that has already been completed and for which revenue has already been recognized, the result can be an increase or reduction in the amount of revenue recognized. This change in recognition should occur as soon as the subsequent change in the transaction price occurs.

Allocation of Price Discounts

It is assumed that a customer has received a discount on a bundled purchase of goods or services when the sum of the standalone prices for these items is greater than the consideration to be paid under the terms of a contract. The discount can be allocated to a specific item within the bundled purchase, if there is observable evidence that the discount was intended for that item. In order to do so, all of the following criteria must apply:

1. Each distinct item in the bundle is regularly sold on a standalone basis;
2. A bundle of some of these distinct items is regularly sold at a discount to their standalone selling prices; and
3. The discount noted in the second point is essentially the same as the discount in the contract, and there is observable evidence linking the entire contract discount to that bundle of distinct items.

If this allocation system is used, the seller must employ it before using the residual approach noted earlier in this section. Doing so ensures that the discount is not applied to the other performance obligations in the contract to which prices have not yet been allocated.

In all other cases, the discount is to be allocated amongst all of the items in the bundle. In this latter situation, the allocation is to be made based on the standalone selling prices of all of the performance obligations in the contract.

EXAMPLE

The Hegemony Toy Company sells board games that re-enact famous battles. Hegemony regularly sells the following three board games:

Product	Standalone Selling Price
Hastings Battle Game	$120
Stalingrad Battle Game	100
Waterloo Battle Game	80
Total	$300

Hegemony routinely sells the Stalingrad and Waterloo products as a bundle for $120.

Hegemony enters into a contract with the War Games International website to sell War Games the set of three games for $240, which is a 20% discount from the standard price. Deliveries of these games to War Games will be at different times, so the related performance obligations will be settled on different dates.

The $60 discount would normally be apportioned among all three products based on their standalone selling prices. However, because Hegemony routinely sells the Stalingrad/Waterloo bundle for a $60 discount, it is evident that the entire discount should be allocated to these two products.

If Hegemony later delivers the Stalingrad and Waterloo games to War Games on different dates, it should allocate the $60 discount between the two products based on their standalone selling prices. Thus, $33.33 should be allocated to the Stalingrad game and $26.67 to the Waterloo game. The allocation calculation is:

Game	Allocation
Stalingrad	($100 individual game price ÷ $180 combined price) × $60 discount = $33.33
Waterloo	($80 individual game price ÷ $180 combined price) × $60 discount = $26.67

If the two games are instead delivered at the same time, there is no need to conduct the preceding allocation. Instead, the discount can be assigned to them both as part of a single performance obligation.

Allocation of Variable Consideration

There may be a variable amount of consideration associated with a contract. This consideration may apply to the contract as a whole, or to just a portion of it. For example, a bonus payment may be tied to the completion of a specific performance obligation. It is allowable to allocate variable consideration to a specific performance obligation or a distinct good or service within a contract when the variable payment terms are specifically tied to the seller's efforts to satisfy the performance obligation.

EXAMPLE

Nova Corporation contracts with the Deep Field Scanning Authority to construct two three-meter telescopes that will operate in tandem in the low-humidity Atacama Desert in Chile. The terms of the contract include a provision that can increase the allowable price charged, if the commodity cost of the titanium required to build the telescope frames increases. Based on the prices stated in forward contracts at the contract inception date, it is likely that this variable cost element will increase the transaction price by $250,000. The variable component of the price is allocated to each of the telescopes equally.

Subsequent Price Changes

There are a number of reasons why the transaction price could change after a contract has begun, such as the resolution of uncertain events that were in need of clarification at the contract inception date. When there is a price change, the amount of the change is to be allocated to the performance obligations on the same basis used for the original price allocation at the inception of the contract. This has the following ramifications:

- Do not re-allocate prices based on subsequent changes in the standalone selling prices of goods or services.

- When there is a price change and that price is allocated, the result may be the recognition of additional or reduced revenue that is to be recognized in the period when the transaction price changes.
- When there has been a contract modification prior to a price change, the price allocation is conducted in two steps. First, allocate the price change to those performance obligations identified prior to the modification if the price change is associated with variable consideration promised before modification. In all other cases, allocate the price change to those performance obligations still remaining to be settled as of the modification date.

The result should be a reported level of cumulative revenue that matches the amount of revenue an organization would have recognized if it had the most recent information at the inception date of the contract.

Step Five: Recognize Revenue

Revenue is to be recognized as goods or services are transferred to the customer. This transference is considered to occur when the customer gains control over the good or service. Indicators of this date include the following:

- When the seller has the right to receive payment.
- When the customer has legal title to the transferred asset. This can still be the case even when the seller retains title to protect it against the customer's failure to pay.
- When physical possession of the asset has been transferred by the seller. Possession can be inferred even when goods are held elsewhere on consignment, or by the seller under a bill-and-hold arrangement. Under a bill-and-hold arrangement, the seller retains goods on behalf of the customer, but still recognizes revenue.
- When the customer has taken on the significant risks and rewards of ownership related to the asset transferred by the seller. For example, the customer can now sell, pledge, or exchange the asset.
- When the customer accepts the asset.
- When the customer can prevent other entities from using or obtaining benefits from the asset.

It is possible that a performance obligation will be transferred over time, rather than as of a specific point in time. If so, revenue recognition occurs when any one of the following criteria are met:

- *Immediate use*. The customer both receives and consumes the benefit provided by the seller as performance occurs. This situation arises if another entity would not need to re-perform work completed to date if the other entity were to take over the remaining performance obligation. Routine and recurring services typically fall into this classification.

EXAMPLE

Long-Haul Freight contracts to deliver a load of goods from Los Angeles to Boston. This service should be considered a performance obligation that is transferred over time, despite the fact that the customer only benefits from the goods once they are delivered. The reason for the designation as a transference over time is that, if a different trucking firm were to take over partway through the journey, the replacement firm would not have to re-perform the freight hauling that has already been completed to date.

EXAMPLE

Maid Marian is a nationwide home cleaning service run by friars within the Franciscan Order. Its customers both receive and simultaneously consume the cleaning services provided by its staff. Consequently, the services provided by Maid Marian are considered to be performance obligations satisfied over time.

- *Immediate enhancement.* The seller creates or enhances an asset controlled by the customer as performance occurs. This asset can be tangible or intangible.
- *No alternative use.* The seller's performance does not create an asset for which there is an alternative use to the seller (such as selling it to a different customer). In addition, the contract gives the seller an enforceable right to payment for the performance that has been completed to date. A lack of alternative use happens when a contract restricts the seller from directing the asset to another use, or when there are practical limitations on doing so, such as the incurrence of significant economic losses to direct the asset elsewhere. The determination of whether an asset has an alternative use is made at the inception of the contract, and cannot be subsequently altered unless both parties to the contract approve a modification that results in a substantive change in the performance obligation.

Construction contracts are likely to be designated as being performance obligations that are transferred over time. Under this approach, they can use the percentage-of-completion method to recognize revenue, rather than the completed contract method. This means that they can recognize revenue as a construction project progresses, rather than waiting until the end of the project to recognize any revenue.

EXAMPLE

Oberlin Acoustics is contractually obligated to deliver a highly-customized version of its Rhino brand electric guitar to a diva-grade European rock star. The contract clearly states that this customized version can only be delivered to the designated customer, and it is likely that this individual would pursue legal action if Oberlin were to attempt to sell it elsewhere (such as to the lead guitarist of a rival band). Also, Oberlin might have to incur significant costs to reconfigure the guitar for sale to a different customer. In this situation, there is no alternative use.

However, if Oberlin had instead contracted to deliver one of its standard Rhino brand guitars, the company could easily transfer the asset to a different customer, since the products are essentially interchangeable. In this case, there would be a clear alternative use.

EXAMPLE

Tesla Power Company is hired by a local government to construct one of its new, compact fusion power plants in the remote hinterlands of Malawi. There is clearly no alternative use for the power plant, since Tesla would have to incur major costs to dismantle the facility and truck it out of the remote area before it could be sold to a different customer. However, the contract states that 50% of the price will be paid at the end of the contract period, and there is no enforceable right to any payment; this means that Tesla must consider its performance obligation to be satisfied as of a point in time, rather than over time.

EXAMPLE

Hassle Corporation is in talks with a potential acquirer. The acquirer insists that Hassle have soil tests conducted in the area around its main production facility, to see if there has been any leakage of pollutants. Hassle engages Wilson Environmental to conduct these tests, which is a three-month process. The contract includes a clause that Wilson will be paid for its costs plus a 20% profit if Hassle cancels the contract. The acquisition talks break off after two months, so Hassle notifies Wilson that it no longer needs the environmental report. Since Wilson cannot possibly sell the information it has collected to a different customer, there is no alternative use. Also, since Wilson has an enforceable right to payment for all work completed to date, the company can recognize revenue over time by measuring its progress toward satisfying the performance obligation.

Measurement of Progress Completion

When a performance obligation is being completed over a period of time, the seller recognizes revenue through the application of a progress completion method. The goal of this method is to determine the progress of the seller in achieving complete satisfaction of its performance obligation. This method is to be consistently applied over time, and shall be re-measured at the end of each reporting period.

> **Note:** The method used to measure progress should be applied consistently for a particular performance obligation, as well as across multiple contracts that have obligations with similar characteristics. Otherwise, reported revenue will not be comparable across different reporting periods.

Both output methods and input methods are considered acceptable for determining progress completion. The method chosen should incorporate due consideration of the nature of the goods or services being provided to the customer. The following sub-sections address the use of output and input methods.

Output Methods

An output method recognizes revenue based on a comparison of the value to the customer of goods and services transferred to date to the remaining goods and services not yet transferred. There are numerous ways to measure output, including:

- Surveys of performance to date
- Milestones reached
- The passage of time
- The number of units delivered
- The number of units produced

Another output method that may be acceptable is the amount of consideration that the seller has the right to invoice, such as billable hours. This approach works when the seller has a right to invoice an amount that matches the amount of performance completed to date.

The number of units delivered or produced may not be an appropriate output method in situations where there is a large amount of work-in-process, since the value associated with unfinished goods may be so substantial that revenue could be materially under-reported.

The method picked should closely adhere to the concept of matching the seller's progress toward satisfying the performance obligation. It is not always possible to use an output method, since the cost of collecting the necessary information can be prohibitive, or progress may not be directly observable.

EXAMPLE

Viking Fitness operates a regional chain of fitness clubs that are oriented toward younger, very athletic people. Members pay a $1,200 annual fee, which gives them access to all of the clubs in the chain during all operating hours. In effect, Viking's performance obligation is to keep its facilities open for use by members, irrespective of whether they actually use the facilities. Clearly, this situation calls for measurement of progress completion based on the passage of time. Accordingly, Viking recognizes revenue from its annual customer payments at the rate of $100 per member per month.

Input Methods

An input method derives the amount of revenue to be recognized based on the to-date effort required by the seller to satisfy a performance obligation relative to the total estimated amount of effort required. Examples of possible inputs are costs incurred, labor hours expended, and machine hours used. If there are situations where the effort expended does not directly relate to the transfer of goods or services to a customer, do not use that input. The following are situations where the input used could lead to incorrect revenue recognition:

- The costs incurred are higher than expected, due to seller inefficiencies. For example, the seller may have wasted a higher-than-expected amount of raw materials in the performance of its obligations under a contract.
- The costs incurred are not in proportion to the progress of the seller toward satisfying the performance obligation. For example, the seller might purchase a large amount of materials at the inception of a contract, which comprise a significant part of the total price.

> **Tip:** If the effort expended to satisfy performance obligations occur evenly through the performance period, consider recognizing revenue on the straight-line basis through the performance period.

EXAMPLE

Eskimo Construction is hired to build a weather observatory in Barrow, Alaska, which is estimated to be a six-month project. Utilities are a major concern, especially since the facility is too far away from town for a power line to be run out to it. Accordingly, a large part of the construction cost is a diesel-powered turbine generator. The total cost that Eskimo intends to incur for the project is:

Turbine cost	$1,250,000
All other costs	2,750,000
Total costs	$4,000,000

The turbine is to be delivered and paid for at the beginning of the construction project, but will not be incorporated into the facility until late summer, when the building is scheduled to be nearly complete.

Eskimo intends to use an input method to derive the amount of revenue, using costs incurred. However, this approach runs afoul of the turbine cost, since the immediate expenditure for the turbine gives the appearance of the project being 31.25% complete before work has even begun. Accordingly, Eskimo excludes the cost of the turbine from its input method calculations, only using the other costs as the basis for deriving revenue.

The situation described in the preceding example is quite common, since materials are typically procured at the inception of a contract, rather than being purchased in equal quantities over the duration of the contract. Consequently, the accountant should be particularly mindful of this issue and incorporate it into any revenue recognition calculations based on an input method.

A method based on output is preferred, since it most faithfully depicts the performance of the seller under the terms of a contract. However, an input-based method is certainly allowable if using it would be less costly for the seller, while still providing a reasonable proxy for the ongoing measurement of progress.

Change in Estimate

Whichever method is used, be sure to update it over time to reflect changes in the seller's performance to date. If there is a change in the measurement of progress, treat the change as a change in accounting estimate.

A change in accounting estimate occurs when there is an adjustment to the carrying amount of an asset or liability, or the subsequent accounting for it. Changes in accounting estimate occur relatively frequently, and so would require a considerable amount of effort to make an ongoing series of retroactive changes to prior financial statements. Instead, GAAP only requires that changes in accounting estimate be accounted for in the period of change and thereafter. Thus, no retrospective change is required or allowed.

Progress Measurement

It is only possible to recognize the revenue associated with progress completion if it is possible for the seller to measure the seller's progress. If the seller lacks reliable progress information, it will not be possible to recognize the revenue associated with a contract over time. There may be cases where the measurement of progress completion is more difficult during the early stages of a contract. If so, it is allowable for the seller to instead recognize just enough revenue to recover its costs in satisfying its performance obligations, thereby deferring the recognition of other revenue until such time as the measurement system yields more accurate results.

Right of Return

A common right granted to customers is to allow them to return goods to the seller within a certain period of time following the customer's receipt of the goods. This return may take the form of a refund of any amounts paid, a general credit that can be applied against other billings from the seller, or an exchange for a different unit. The proper accounting for this right of return involves three components, which are:

1. Recognize the net amount of revenue to which the seller expects to be entitled after all product returns have been factored into the sale.
2. A refund liability that encompasses the number of units that the seller expects to have returned to it.
3. An asset based on the right to recover products from customers who have demanded refunds. This asset represents a reduction in the cost of goods sold. The amount is initially based on the former carrying amount of the inventory, less recovery costs and expected reductions in the value of the returned products.

This accounting requires the seller to update its assessment of future product returns at the end of each reporting period, both for the refund liability and the recovery asset. This update may result in a change in the amount of revenue recognized.

> **Note:** When a customer exchanges one product for another product with the same characteristics (such as an exchange of one size shirt for another), this is not considered a return.

EXAMPLE

Ninja Cutlery sells high-end ceramic knife sets through its on-line store and through select retailers. All customers pay up-front in cash. In the most recent month, Ninja sold 5,000 knife sets, which sold for an average price of $250 each ($1,250,000 in total). The unit cost is $150. Based on the history of actual returns over the preceding 12-month period, Ninja can expect that 200 of the sets (4% of the total) will be returned under the company's returns policy. Recovery costs are immaterial, and Ninja expects to be able to repackage and sell all returned products for a profit. Based on this information, Ninja records the following transactions when the knife sets are originally delivered:

	Debit	Credit
Cash	1,250,000	
Revenue		1,200,000
Refund liability		50,000

	Debit	Credit
Cost of goods sold	720,000	
Recovery asset	30,000	
Inventory		750,000

In these entries, the refund liability is calculated as the 200 units expected to be returned, multiplied by the average price of $250 each. The recovery asset is calculated as the 200 units expected to be returned, multiplied by the unit cost of $150.

Consistency

The preceding five steps must be applied consistently to all customer contracts that have similar characteristics, and under similar circumstances. The intent is to create a system of revenue recognition that can be relied upon to yield consistent results.

Contract Modifications

A contract modification occurs when there is a scope or price change to the contract, and the change is approved by both signatories to the contract. Other terms may be used for a contract modification, such as a change order. It is possible that a contract modification exists, despite the presence of a dispute between the parties concerning scope or price. All of the relevant facts and circumstances must be considered when determining whether there is an enforceable contract modification that can impact revenue recognition.

If a change in contract scope has already been approved, but the corresponding change in price to reflect the scope change is still under discussion, the seller must estimate the change in price. This estimate is based on the criteria used to determine variable consideration.

Treatment as Separate Contract

There are circumstances under which a contract modification might be accounted for as a separate contract. For this to be the case, the following two conditions must both be present:

- *Distinct change*. The scope has increased, to encompass new goods or services that are distinct from those offered in the original contract.
- *Price change*. The price has increased enough to encompass the standalone prices of the additional goods and services, adjusted for the circumstances related to that specific contract.

When these circumstances are met, there is an economic difference between a modified contract for the additional goods or services and a situation where an entirely new contract has been created.

EXAMPLE

Blitz Communications is buying one million cell phone batteries from Creekside Industrial. The parties decide to alter the contract to add the purchase of 200,000 battery chargers for a price increase of $2.8 million. The associated price increase includes a 30% discount, which Creekside was already offering to Blitz under the terms of the original contract. This contract change reflects a distinct change that adds new goods to the contract, and includes an associated price change that has been adjusted for the discount terms of the contract. This contract modification can be accounted for as a separate contract.

Treatment as Continuing Contract

It may not be possible to treat a contract modification as a separate contract. If so, there are likely to be goods or services not yet transferred to the customer as of the modification date. The seller can account for these residual deliveries using one of the following methods:

- *Remainder is distinct*. If the remaining goods or services to be delivered are distinct from those already delivered under the contract, account for the modification as a cancellation of the old contract and creation of a new one. In this case, the consideration that should be allocated to the remaining performance obligations is the sum total of:
  - The original consideration promised by the customer but not yet received; and
  - The new consideration associated with the modification.

321

EXAMPLE

Grizzly Golf Carts, maker of sturdy golf carts for overweight golfers, contracts with a local suburban golf course to deliver two golf carts for a total price of $12,000. The carts are different models, but have the same standalone price, so Grizzly allocates $6,000 of the transaction price to each cart. One cart is delivered immediately, so Grizzly recognizes $6,000 of revenue. Before the second cart can be delivered, the golf course customer requests that a third cart be added to the contract; this is a heftier cart that has a built-in barbecue grill. The contract price is increased by $8,000, which is less than the $10,000 standalone price of this model.

Since the second and third carts are distinct from the first cart model, there is a distinct change in the contract, which necessitates treating the change as a new contract. Accordingly, the second and third carts are treated as though they are part of a new contract, with the remaining $14,000 of the transaction price totally allocated to the new contract.

EXAMPLE

As noted in an earlier example, Nova Corporation contracted with the Deep Field Scanning Authority to construct two three-meter telescopes. The terms of the contract included a provision that could increase the allowable price charged by $250,000, with this price being apportioned equally between the two telescopes. One month into the contract period, Deep Field completely alters the configuration of the second telescope, from a reflector to a catadioptric model. The change is so significant that this telescope can now be considered a separate contract. However, since the variable price was already apportioned at the inception of the original contract, the $125,000 allocated to each telescope will continue. This is because the variable consideration was promised prior to the contract modification.

- *Remainder is not distinct.* If the remaining goods or services to be delivered are not distinct from those already delivered under the contract, account for the modification as part of the existing contract. This results in an adjustment to the recognized amount of revenue (up or down) as of the modification date. Thus, the adjustment involves calculating a change in the amount of revenue recognized on a cumulative catch-up basis.

EXAMPLE

Domicilio Corporation enters into a contract to construct the world headquarters building of the International Mushroom Farmers' Cooperative. Mushroom requires its architects to be true to the name of the organization, with the result being a design for a squat, dark building with no windows, high humidity, and a unique waste recycling system. Domicilio has not encountered such a design before, and so incorporates a cautious stance into its assumptions regarding the contract terms.

The contract terms state that Domicilio will be paid a total of $12,000,000, broken into a number of milestone payments. There is also a $100,000 on-time completion bonus. At the inception of the contract, Domicilio expects the following financial results:

Transaction price	$12,000,000
Expected costs	9,000,000
Expected profit (25%)	$3,000,000

The project manager anticipates trouble with several parts of the construction project, and advises strongly against including any part of the completion bonus in the transaction price.

At the end of seven months, the project manager is surprised to find that Domicilio is on target to complete the work on time. Also, the company has completed 65% of its performance obligation, based on the $5,850,000 of costs incurred to date relative to the total amount of expected costs. Through this point, the company has recognized the following revenues and costs:

Revenue	$7,800,000
Costs	5,850,000
Gross profit	$1,950,000

The project manager is still uncomfortable with recognizing any part of the completion bonus.

With one month to go on the project, the project manager finally allows that Domicilio will likely complete the project one week early, though he has completely lost all interest in eating mushrooms. At this point, the company has completed 92.5% of its performance obligation (based on costs incurred), so the controller recognizes an additional $92,500 for that portion of the $100,000 on-time completion bonus that has already been earned.

- *Mix of elements.* If the remaining goods or services to be delivered are comprised of a mix of distinct and not-distinct elements, separately identify the different elements and account for them as per the dictates of the preceding two methods.

Entitlement to Payment

At all points over the duration of a contract, the seller should have the right to payment for the performance completed to date, if the customer were to cancel the contract for reasons other than the seller's failure to perform. The amount of this payment should approximate the selling price of the goods or services transferred to the customer to date; this means that costs are recovered, plus a reasonable profit margin. This reasonable profit margin should be one of the following:

- A reasonable proportion of the expected profit margin, based on the extent of the total performance completed prior to contract termination; or
- A reasonable return on the cost of capital that the seller has experienced on its cost of capital for similar contracts, if the margin on this particular con-

tract is higher than the return the seller typically generates from this type of contract.

An entitlement to payment depends on contractual factors, such as only being paid when certain milestones are reached or when the customer is completely satisfied with a deliverable. There may not be an entitlement to payment if one of these contractual factors is present. Further, there may be legal precedents or legislation that may interfere with or bolster an entitlement to payment. For example:

- There may be a legal precedent that gives the seller the right to payment for all performance to date, even though this right is not clarified within the contract terms.
- Legal precedent may reveal that other sellers having similar rights to payment in their contracts have not succeeded in obtaining payment.
- The seller may not have attempted to enforce its right to payment in the past, which may have rendered its rights legally unenforceable.

Conversely, the terms of a contract may not legally allow a customer to terminate a contract. If so, and the customer still attempts to terminate the contract, the seller may be entitled to continue to provide goods or services to the customer, and require the customer to pay the amounts stated in the contract. In this type of situation, the seller has an enforceable right to payment.

An enforceable right to payment may not match the payment schedule stated in a contract. The payment schedule does not necessarily sync with the seller's right to payment for performance. For example, the customer could have insisted upon delayed payment dates in the payment schedule in order to more closely match its ability to make payments to the seller.

EXAMPLE

A customer of Hodgson Industrial Design pays a $50,000 nonrefundable upfront payment to Hodgson at the inception of a contract to overhaul the design of the customer's main product. The customer does not like Hodgson's initial set of design prototypes, and cancels the contract. On the cancellation date, Hodgson's billable hours on the project sum to $65,000. Hodgson has an enforceable right to retain the $50,000 it has already been paid. The right to be paid for the remaining $15,000 depends on the contract terms and legal precedents.

Bill-and-Hold Arrangements

There is a bill-and-hold arrangement between a seller and customer when the seller bills the customer, but initially retains physical possession of the goods that were sold; the goods are transferred to the customer at a later date. This situation may arise if a customer does not initially have the storage space available for the goods it has ordered.

In a bill-and-hold arrangement, the seller must determine when the customer gains control of the goods, since this point in time indicates when the seller can recognize revenue. Customer control can be difficult to discern when the goods are still located on the premises of the seller. The following are indicators of customer control:

- The customer can direct the use of the goods, no matter where they are located
- The customer can obtain substantially all of the remaining benefits of the goods

Further, the following conditions must all be present for the seller to recognize revenue under a bill-and-hold arrangement:

- *Adequate reason.* There must be a substantive reason why the seller is continuing to store the goods, such as at the direct request of the customer.
- *Alternate use.* The seller must not be able to redirect the goods, either to other customers or for internal use.
- *Complete.* The product must be complete in all respects and ready for transfer to the customer.
- *Identification.* The goods must have been identified specifically as belonging to the customer.

Under a bill-and-hold arrangement, the seller may have a performance obligation to act as the custodian for the goods being held at its facility. If so, the seller may need to allocate a portion of the transaction price to the custodial function, and recognize this revenue over the course of the custodial period.

EXAMPLE

Micron Metallic operates stamping machines that produce parts for washing machines. Micron's general manager has recently decided to implement the just-in-time philosophy throughout the company, which includes sourcing goods with suppliers who are located as close to Micron as possible. One of these suppliers is Horton Corporation, which designs and builds stamping machines for Micron. In a recent contract, Micron buys a customized stamping machine and a set of spare parts intended for that machine. Since Micron is implementing just-in-time concepts, it does not want to store the spare parts on its premises, and instead asks Horton to store the parts in its facility, which is just down the street from the Micron factory.

Micron's receiving staff travels to the Horton facility to inspect the parts and formally accepts them. Horton also sets them aside in a separate storage area, and flags them as belonging to Micron. Since the parts are customized, they cannot be used to fulfill any other customer orders. Under the just-in-time system, Horton commits to having the parts ready for delivery to Micron within ten minutes of receiving a shipping order.

The arrangement can clearly be defined as a bill-and-hold situation. Consequently, Horton should apportion the transaction price between the stamping machine, the spare parts, and the custodial service involved in storing the parts on behalf of Micron. The revenue associated with the machine and parts can be recognized at once, while the revenue associated with the custodial service can be recognized with the passage of time.

Consideration Received from a Supplier

A supplier may pay consideration to its customer, which may be in the form of cash, credits, coupons, and so forth. The customer can then apply this consideration to payments that it owes to the supplier, thereby reducing its net accounts payable.

The proper accounting for this type of consideration is to reduce the purchase price of the goods or services that the customer is acquiring from the supplier in the amount of the consideration received. If the consideration received relates to the customer attaining a certain amount of purchasing volume with the supplier (i.e., a volume discount), recognize the consideration as a reduction of the purchase price of the underlying transactions. This recognition can be made if attainment of the consideration is both probable and can be reasonably estimated. If these criteria cannot be met, then wait for the triggering milestones, and recognize them as the milestones are reached. Factors that can make it more difficult to determine whether this type of consideration is probable or reasonably estimated include:

- *Duration.* The relationship between the consideration to be received and purchase amounts spans a long period of time.
- *Experience.* The customer has no historical experience with similar products, or cannot apply its experience to changing circumstances.
- *External factors.* External factors can influence the underlying activity, such as changes in demand.
- *Prior adjustments.* It has been necessary to make significant adjustments to similar types of expected consideration in the past.

EXAMPLE

Puller Corporation manufactures plastic door knobs. Its primary raw material is polymer resin, which it purchases in pellet form from a regional chemical facility. Puller will receive a 2% volume discount if it purchases at least $500,000 of pellets from the supplier by the end of the calendar year. Puller has a long-term relationship with this supplier, has routinely earned the discount for the last five years, and plans to place orders in this year that will comfortably exceed the $500,000 mark. Accordingly, Puller accrues the 2% discount as a reduction of the purchase price of its pellet purchases throughout the year.

EXAMPLE

Puller has just entered into a new relationship with another supplier that will deliver black dye to the factory for inclusion in all of the company's black door knob products. This supplier offers a 5% discount if purchases exceed $50,000 for the calendar year. Puller has not sold this color of door knob before and so has no idea of what customer demand may be. Given the high level of uncertainty regarding the probability of being awarded the discount, Puller elects to record all purchases at their full price, and will re-evaluate the probability of attaining the discount as the year progresses.

The only exceptions to this accounting are:

- When the customer specifically transfers an asset to the supplier in exchange. If so, the customer treats the transaction as it would any sale to one of its customers in the normal course of business. If the amount paid by the supplier is higher than the standalone selling price of the item transferred to the supplier, the customer should account for the excess amount as a reduction of the purchase price of any goods or services received from the supplier.
- The supplier is reimbursing the customer for selling costs that the customer incurred to sell the supplier's products to third parties. If so, the amount of cash received is used to reduce the indicated selling costs. If the amount paid by the supplier is greater than the amount for which the customer applied for reimbursement, record the excess as a reduction of the cost of sales.
- The consideration is related to sales incentives offered by manufacturers who are selling through a reseller. When the reseller is receiving compensation in exchange for honoring incentives related to the manufacturer's products, the reseller records the amount received as a reduction of its cost of sales. This situation only arises when all of the following conditions apply:
  - The customer can tender the incentive to any reseller as part of its payment for the product;
  - The reseller receives reimbursement from the manufacturer based on the face amount of the incentive;
  - The reimbursement terms to the reseller are only determined from the incentive terms offered to consumers; they are not negotiated between the manufacturer and reseller; and
  - The reseller is an agent of the manufacturer in regard to the sales incentive transaction.

If only a few or none of these criteria are met for a sales incentive offered by a manufacturer, account for the transaction as a reduction of the purchase price of the goods or services that the reseller acquired from the manufacturer. If all of the criteria *are* met, consider the transaction to be a revenue-generating activity for the reseller.

Customer Acceptance

A customer may include an acceptance clause in a contract with a seller. An acceptance clause states that the customer has the right to inspect goods and reject them or demand proper remedial efforts before formal acceptance. Normally, customer control over goods occurs as soon as this acceptance step has been completed.

There are situations in which the seller can determine that control has passed to a customer, even if a formal acceptance review has not yet taken place. This typically occurs when customer acceptance is based upon a delivery meeting very specific qualifications, such as certain dimension or weight requirements. If the seller can determine in advance that these criteria have been met, it can recognize revenue prior to formal customer acceptance. If the seller cannot determine in advance that a customer will accept the delivered goods, it must wait for formal acceptance before it can confirm that the customer had taken control of the delivery, which then triggers revenue recognition.

EXAMPLE

Stout Tanks, Inc. manufactures scuba tanks, which it sells in bulk to a large customer in Bonaire, Drive-Thru Scuba. Drive-Thru insists upon a complete hydrostatic test of each tank before accepting delivery, since an exploding air tank is a decidedly terminal experience for a diver wearing the tank. Stout decides to conducts its own hydrostatic test of every tank leaving its factory. Since Stout is conducting the same test as Drive-Thru, Stout can reasonably establish that customer acceptance has occurred as soon as the scuba tanks leave its factory. As such, Stout can recognize revenue on the delivery date, and not wait for Drive-Thru to conduct its test.

Even if a customer recognizes revenue in advance of formal customer acceptance, it may still be necessary to determine whether there are any remaining performance obligations to which a portion of the transaction price should be allocated. For example, a seller may have an obligation to not only manufacture production equipment, but also to install it at the customer site. This later step could be considered a separate performance obligation.

A variation on the customer acceptance concept is when a seller delivers goods to a customer for evaluation purposes. In this case, the customer has no obligation to accept or pay for the goods until the end of a trial period, so control cannot be said to have passed to the customer until such time as the customer accepts the goods or the trial period ends.

Customer Options for Additional Purchases

A seller may offer customers a number of ways in which to obtain additional goods or services at reduced rates or even for free. For example, the seller may offer a discount on a contract renewal, award points to frequent buyers, host periodic sales events, and so on.

When a contract grants a customer the right to acquire additional goods or services at a discount, this can be considered a performance obligation if the amount is material and the customer is essentially paying in advance for future goods or services. In this case, the seller recognizes revenue associated with the customer option when:

- The option expires; or
- The future goods or services are transferred to the customer.

If revenue is to be recognized for such an option, allocate the transaction price to the option based on the relative standalone price of the option. In the likely event that the standalone selling price of the option is not directly observable, use an estimate of its price. The derivation of this estimate should include the discount that the customer would obtain by exercising the option, adjusted for the following two items:

- Reduced by the amount of any discount that the customer could have received without the option, such as a standard ongoing discount offered to all customers; and
- The probability that the customer will not exercise the option.

A material right to additional purchases of goods or services is not considered to have been passed to a customer if the option is at a price that reflects the standalone selling price of a good or service. In this case, there is no particular advantage being granted to the customer, since it could just as easily purchase the goods or services at the same price, even in the absence of the option.

EXAMPLE

Twister Vacuum Company sells its top-of-the-line F5 vacuum cleaner to 50 customers for $800 each. As part of each sale, Twister gives each customer a discount code that, if used, gives the customer a 50% discount on the purchase of Twister's F1 hand-held vacuum cleaner, which normally sells for $100. The discount expires in 60 days.

In order to determine the standalone selling price of the discount code, Twister estimates (based on past experience) that 30% of all customers will use the code to purchase the F1 model. This means that the standalone selling price of the discount code is $15, which is calculated as follows:

$100 F1 standalone price × 50% discount × 30% probability of code usage = $15

The combined standalone selling prices of the F5 vacuum and the discount code sum to $815. Twister uses this information to allocate the $800 transaction price between the product and the discount code, using the following calculation:

Performance Obligation	Allocated Price	Calculation
F5 vacuum cleaner	$785.28	($800 ÷ $815) × $800
Discount code	14.72	($15 ÷ $815) × $800
Total	$800.00	

This allocation means that Twister can recognize $785.28 of revenue whenever it completes a performance obligation related to the sale of the F5 units to the 50 customers. Twister also allocates $14.72 to the discount code and recognizes the revenue associated with this item either when it is redeemed by a customer in the purchase of an F1 vacuum cleaner, or when the code expires.

EXAMPLE

Sojourn Hotel has a customer loyalty program that grants customers one loyalty point for each night that they stay in a Sojourn-affiliated hotel. Each loyalty point can be redeemed to reduce another stay at a Sojourn hotel by $5. If not used, the points expire after 24 months. During the most recent reporting period, customers earn 60,000 loyalty points on $2,000,000 of customer purchases. Based on past experience, Sojourn expects 60% of the points to be redeemed. Based on the likelihood of redemption, each point is worth $3 (calculated as $5 redemption value × 60% probability of redemption), so all of the points awarded are worth $180,000 (calculated as $3/ point × 60,000 points issued).

The loyalty points program gives a material right to customers that they would not otherwise have had if they had not stayed at a Sojourn hotel (i.e., entered into a contract with Sojourn). Thus, Sojourn concludes that the issued points constitute a performance obligation. Sojourn then allocates the $2,000,000 of customer purchases for hotel rooms to the hotel room product and the points awarded based on their standalone selling prices, based on the following calculations:

Performance Obligation	Allocated Price	Calculation
Hotel rooms	$1,834,862	($2,000,000 ÷ $2,180,000) × $2,000,000
Loyalty points	165,138	($180,000 ÷ $2,180,000) × $2,000,000
Total	$2,000,000	

The $165,138 allocated to loyalty points is initially recorded as a contract liability. The $1,834,862 allocated to hotel rooms is recognized as revenue, since Sojourn has completed its performance obligation related to these overnight stays.

As of the end of the next quarterly period, Sojourn finds that 8,000 of the loyalty points have been redeemed, so it recognizes revenue related to the loyalty points of $22,018 (calculated as 8,000 points ÷ 60,000 points × $165,138).

Licensing

A seller may offer a license to use intellectual property owned by the seller. Examples of licensing arrangements are:

- Licensing to use software
- Licensing to listen to music
- Licensing to view a movie
- Franchising the name and processes of a restaurant
- Licensing of a book copyright to republish the book
- Licensing to use a patent within a product

If a contract contains both a licensing agreement and a provision to provide goods or services to the customer, the seller must identify each performance obligation within the contract and allocate the transaction price to each one.

If the licensing agreement can be separated from the other elements of a contract, the seller must decide whether the license is being transferred to the customer over a period of time, or as of a point in time. A key point in making this determination is whether the license is intended to give the customer access to the intellectual property of the seller only as of the point in time when the license is granted, or over the duration of the license period. The first case would indicate that the revenue associated with the license is recognized as of a point in time, while the second case would indicate that the revenue is recognized over a period of time.

A license is more likely to have been granted as of a point in time when a customer can direct the use of a license and obtain substantially all of the remaining benefits from the license on the date when the license is granted to it. This will not be the case if the intellectual property to which the customer has rights continues to change throughout the license period, which occurs when the seller continues to engage in activities that significantly affect its intellectual property.

The intent of the seller of a license is to provide the customer with the right to access its intellectual property when the seller commits to update the property, the customer will be exposed to the effects of those updates, and the updates do not result in the transfer of a good or service to the customer. These conditions may not be stated in a contract, but could be inferred from the seller's customary business practices. For example, if the customer pays the seller a royalty based on its sales of products derived from intellectual property provided by the seller, this implies that the seller will be updating the underlying intellectual property. If these conditions are present, the associated revenue should be recognized over time, rather than as of a point in time.

Some licensing arrangements involve symbolic intellectual property, which is intellectual property that lacks any significant standalone functionality, such as a brand name, a logo, or franchise rights. The licensor is assumed to be maintaining this intellectual property during the license period. Given the maintenance issue, a license to symbolic intellectual property is recognized over time.

If the facts and circumstances of a contract indicate that the revenue associated with a contract should be recognized as of a point in time, this does not mean that the revenue can be recognized prior to the point in time when the customer can use and benefit from the license. This date may be later than the commencement date of the underlying contract. For example, the license to use intellectual property may be granted, but the actual property may not yet have been delivered to the customer or activated.

If it is not possible to separate the licensing agreement from the other components of a contract, account for them as a single performance obligation. An example of when this situation arises is when a license is integrated into a tangible product to such an extent that the product cannot be used without the license.

> **Note:** A guarantee by the seller that it will defend a patent from unauthorized use is not considered a performance obligation.

A contract under which there is a right to use a license may include the payment of a royalty to the seller. This arrangement may occur, for example, when the customer is acting as a distributor to re-sell the licensed intellectual property to other parties. In this situation, the seller may only recognize the royalty as revenue as of the later of these two events:

- The subsequent sale to or usage by the third party has occurred; or
- The underlying performance obligation associated with the royalty has been satisfied.

EXAMPLE

Territorial Lease Corporation (TLC) has spent years accumulating a massive database of oil and gas leases throughout the United States and Canada. It sells this information to oil and gas exploration companies, which use it to derive the prices at which they are willing to bid for oil and gas leases. TLC sells the information in three ways, which are:

- It sells a CD that contains lease information that is current as of the ship date. TLC does not issue any further updates to customers. Since TLC does not update the intellectual property, the associated revenue recognition can be considered to occur as of a point in time, which is the delivery date of the CD.
- The company also sells subscriptions to an on-line database of lease information, which it updates every day. Since TLC is continually upgrading the database, the recognition of revenue is considered to take place over time. Accordingly, TLC recognizes revenue over the term of the subscriptions it sells.
- TLC sells its lease information to another company, Enviro Consultants, which repurposes the information for the environmental remediation industry. The information is billed to the customers of Enviro, and Enviro pays TLC a 50% royalty once Enviro receives payment from its customers. Since the subsequent sale of the information has occurred by the time TLC receives royalty payments, it can recognize the payments as revenue upon receipt.

Nonrefundable Upfront Fees

In some types of contracts, it is customary for the seller to charge a customer a nonrefundable upfront fee. Examples of these fees are:

- Health club member ship fee
- Phone service activation fee
- Long-term contract setup fee

There may be a performance obligation associated with these fees. In some cases, it could actually relate to an activity that the seller completes at the beginning of a contract. However, this activity rarely relates to the fulfillment of a performance obligation by the seller, and simply represents an expenditure. Consequently, the most appropriate treatment of this fee is to recognize it as revenue when the goods or services stated in the contract are provided to the customer. Several additional issues to consider are:

- *Recognition period.* If the seller grants the customer a material option to renew the contract, the revenue recognition period associated with the up-front fee is extended over the additional contract term.
- *Setup costs.* It is possible that the costs incurred to set up a contract are an asset, which should be charged to expense over the course of the contract.

EXAMPLE

Providence Alarm Systems offers its customers a home monitoring system that includes a $200 setup fee and a monthly $35 charge to monitor their homes through an alarm system, for a minimum one-year period. Providence does not charge the setup fee again if a customer chooses to renew.

The setup activities that Providence engages in do not transfer a good or service to customers, and so do not create a performance obligation. Thus, the upfront fee can be considered an advance payment relating to the company's monthly monitoring activities. Providence should recognize the $200 fee over the initial one-year monitoring period, as services are provided.

Principal versus Agent

There are situations where the party providing goods or services to a customer is actually arranging to have another party provide the goods and services. In this case, the party is an agent, not the principal party acting as seller. Use the following rules to differentiate between the two concepts of principal and agent:

Criterion	Principal	Agent
Controls the good or service before transfer to customer	Yes	No
Obtains legal title just prior to transfer to seller	Either	Either
Hires a subcontractor to fulfill some performance obligations	Yes	No
Arranges for the provision of goods or services by another party	No	Yes
Does not have inventory risk before or after the customer orders goods, including the absence of risk related to product returns	No	Yes
Does not have discretion in establishing prices	No	Yes

The most critical rule in the preceding list is that the seller must have control over the goods or services being provided. This rule is not necessarily satisfied if the seller momentarily gains title to goods just prior to the transfer of title to the customer.

The seller should determine whether it is the principal or an agent for each product or service being provided to a customer.

The differentiation between principal and agent is of some importance, for a principal recognizes the gross amount of a sale, while an agent only recognizes the fee or commission it earns in exchange for its participation in the transaction. This fee or commission may be the net amount remaining after the agent has paid the principal the amount billed for its goods or services provided to the customer.

In a situation where the seller is initially the principal in a transaction but then hands off the performance obligation to a third party, the seller should not recognize the revenue associated with the performance obligation. Instead, the seller may have assumed the role of an agent.

EXAMPLE

High Country Vacations operates a website that puts prospective vacationers in touch with resorts located in ski towns around the world. When a vacationer purchases a hotel room on the website, High Country takes a 15% commission from the resort where the hotel room is located. The resort sets the prices for hotel rooms. High Country is not responsible for the actual provision of hotel rooms to vacationers.

Since High Country does not control the hotel rooms being provided, is arranging for the provision of services by a third party, does not maintain an inventory of rooms and cannot establish prices, the company is clearly an agent in these transactions. Consequently, High Country should only recognize revenue in the amount of the commissions paid to it, not the amount paid by vacationers for their hotel rooms.

EXAMPLE

Dirt Cheap Tickets sells discounted tickets for cruises with several prominent cruise lines. The company purchases tickets in bulk from cruise lines and must pay for them, irrespective of its ability to re-sell the tickets to the public. Dirt Cheap can alter the prices of the tickets that it purchases, which typically means that the company gradually lowers prices as cruise dates approach, in order to ensure that its excess inventory of tickets is sold. If customers have issues with the cruise lines, Dirt Cheap will intercede on their behalf, but generally encourages them to go directly to the cruise lines with their complaints.

Based on its business model, Dirt Cheap is acting as the principal. It controls the goods being sold, has inventory risk, and actively alters prices. Consequently, Dirt Cheap can recognize revenue in the gross amount of the tickets sold.

Repurchase Agreements

A repurchase agreement is a contract in which the seller agrees to sell an asset and either promises or has the option to repurchase the asset. The asset that the seller repurchases can be the original asset sold, a substantially similar asset, or an asset of which the original unit is a part. There are three variations on the repurchase agreement:

- *Forward*. The seller has an obligation to repurchase the asset.
- *Call option*. The seller has the right to repurchase the asset.
- *Put option*. The seller has an obligation to repurchase the asset if required to by the customer.

If the contract is essentially a forward or call option, the customer never gains control of the asset, since the seller can or will take it back. Given the circumstances, revenue recognition can vary as follows:

- *Reduced repurchase price*. If the seller either can or must repurchase the asset for an amount less than the original selling price (considering the time value of money), the seller accounts for the transaction as a lease.
- *Same or higher repurchase price*. If the seller either can or must repurchase the asset for an amount equal to or greater than the original selling price (considering the time value of money), the seller accounts for the transaction as a financing arrangement.
- *Sale-leaseback*. If the transaction is a sale-leaseback arrangement, the seller accounts for the transaction as a financing arrangement.

When a customer has a put option, the proper accounting depends upon the market price of the asset and the existence of a sale-leaseback arrangement. The alternatives are:

- *Incentive to exercise option*. If the customer has a significant economic incentive to exercise the option, the seller accounts for the transaction as a lease. Such an incentive would exist, for example, when the repurchase price exceeds the expected market value of an asset through the period when the put option can be exercised (considering the time value of money).

- *No incentive to exercise option.* If the customer does not have an economic incentive to exercise a put option, the seller accounts for the agreement as a sale of a product with a right of return.
- *Sale-leaseback.* Even if the seller has a significant economic incentive, as noted in the last bullet point, if the arrangement is a sale-leaseback arrangement, the seller accounts for it as a financing arrangement.
- *Higher repurchase price.* If the repurchase price is equal to or higher than the selling price and is more than the asset's expected market value (considering the time value of money), the seller accounts for it as a financing arrangement.
- *Higher repurchase price with no incentive.* In the rare case where the repurchase price is equal to or higher than the original purchase price, but is less than or equal to the expected market value of the asset (considering the time value of money), this indicates that the customer has no economic incentive to exercise the option. In this case, the seller accounts for the transaction as a sale of a product with a right of return.

When the seller accounts for a transaction as a financing arrangement, the seller continues to recognize the asset, as well as a liability for any consideration it has received from the customer. The difference between the amount of consideration paid by and due to the customer is to be recognized as interest and processing (or related) costs.

If a call option or put option expires without being exercised, the seller can derecognize the repurchase liability and recognize revenue instead.

EXAMPLE

Domicilio Corporation sells a commercial property to Mole Industries for $3,000,000 on March 1, but retains the right to repurchase the property for $3,050,000 on or before December 31 of the same year. This transaction is a call option.

Control over the property does not pass to Mole Industries until after the December 31 termination date of the call option, since Domicilio can repurchase the asset. In the meantime, Domicilio accounts for the arrangement as a financing transaction, since the exercise price exceeds the amount of Mole's purchase price. This means that Domicilio retains the asset in its accounting records, records the $3,000,000 of cash received as a liability, and recognizes interest expense of $50,000 over the intervening months, which gradually increases the amount of the liability to $3,050,000.

On December 31, Domicilio lets the call option lapse; it can now derecognize the liability and recognize $3,050,000 of revenue.

EXAMPLE

Assume the same transaction, except that the option is a requirement for Domicilio to repurchase the property for $2,900,000 at the behest of the customer, Mole Industries. This is a put option. The market value by the end of the year is expected to be lower than $2,900,000.

At the inception of the contract, it is apparent that Mole will have an economic incentive to exercise the put option, since it can earn more from exercising the option than from retaining the property. This means that control over the property does not really pass to Mole. In essence, then, the transaction is to be considered a lease.

Unexercised Rights of Customers

A customer may prepay for goods or services to be delivered at a later date, which the seller initially records as a liability, and later as revenue when the goods or services are delivered. However, what if the customer does not exercise all of its rights to have goods or services delivered? The unexercised amount of this prepayment may be referred to as *breakage*.

The amount of breakage associated with a customer prepayment should be recognized as revenue. The question is, when should the recognition occur? There are two possible scenarios:

- *Existing pattern*. If there is a historical pattern of how a customer exercises the rights associated with its prepayments, the seller can estimate the amount of breakage likely to occur, and recognize it in proportion to the pattern of rights exercised by the customer.
- *No expectation*. If there is no expectation that the seller will be entitled to any breakage, the seller recognizes revenue associated with breakage only when there is a remote likelihood that the customer will exercise any remaining rights.

No revenue related to breakage should be recognized if it is probable that such recognition will result in a significant revenue reversal at a later date.

In a situation where there are unclaimed property laws, the seller is legally required to remit breakage to the applicable government entity. In this case, the breakage is recorded as a liability (rather than revenue), which is cleared from the seller's books when the funds are remitted to the government.

EXAMPLE

Clyde Shotguns receives a $10,000 deposit from a customer, to be used for the construction of a custom-made shotgun. Clyde completes the weapon and delivers it to the customer, recognizing $9,800 of revenue based on the number of billable hours expended. Clyde notifies the customer of the residual deposit amount, but the customer does not respond, despite repeated attempts at communication. Under the escheatment laws of the local state government, Clyde is required to remit these residual funds to the state if they have not been claimed within three years. Accordingly, Clyde initially records the $200 as an escheatment liability, and pays over the funds to the government once three years have passed.

Warranties

A warranty is a guarantee related to the performance of delivered goods or services. If related to a product, the seller typically guarantees the replacement or repair of the delivered goods. If related to a service, the warranty may involve replacement services, or a full or partial refund.

If a customer has the option to separately purchase a warranty, this is to be considered a distinct service to be provided by the seller. As such, the warranty is to be considered a separate performance obligation, with a portion of the transaction price allocated to it. If there is no option for the customer to separately purchase a warranty, the warranty is instead considered an obligation of the seller, in which case the following accounting applies:

- Accrue a reserve for product warranty claims based on the prior experience of the business. In the absence of such experience, the company can instead rely upon the experience of other entities in the same industry. If there is considerable uncertainty in regard to the amount of projected product warranties, it may not be possible to record a product sale until the warranty period has expired or more experience has been gained with customer claims.
- Adjust the reserve over time to reflect changes in prior and expected experience with warranty claims. This can involve a credit to earnings if the amount of the reserve is too large, and should be reduced.
- If there is a history of minimal warranty expenditures, there is no need to accrue a reserve for product warranty claims.

A warranty may provide a customer with a service, as well as a guarantee that provided goods or services will function as claimed. Consider the following items when determining whether a service exists:

- *Duration*. The time period needed to discover whether goods or services are faulty is relatively short, so a long warranty period is indicative of an additional service being offered.
- *Legal requirement*. There is a legal requirement to provide a warranty, in which case the seller is more likely to just be offering the mandated warranty without an additional service.
- *Tasks*. If the warranty requires the seller to perform specific tasks that are identifiable with the remediation of faulty goods or services, there is unlikely to be any additional identifiable service being offered.

If an additional service is being offered through a warranty, consider this service to be a performance obligation, and allocate a portion of the transaction price to that service. If the seller cannot reasonably account for this service separately, instead account for both the assurance and service aspects of the warranty as a bundled performance obligation.

There may be a legal obligation for the seller to compensate its customers if its goods or services cause harm. If so, this is not considered a performance obligation. Instead, this legal obligation is considered a loss contingency. A loss contingency arises when there is a situation for which the outcome is uncertain, and which should be resolved in the future, possibly creating a loss. For example, there may be injuries caused by a company's products when it is discovered that lead-based paint has been used on toys sold by the business.

When deciding whether to account for a loss contingency, the basic concept is to only record a loss that is probable and for which the amount of the loss can be reasonably estimated. If the best estimate of the amount of the loss is within a range, accrue whichever amount appears to be a better estimate than the other estimates in the range. If there is no "better estimate" in the range, accrue a loss for the minimum amount in the range.

If it is not possible to arrive at a reasonable estimate of the loss associated with an event, only disclose the existence of the contingency in the notes accompanying the financial statements. Or, if it is not probable that a loss will be incurred, even if it is possible to estimate the amount of a loss, only disclose the circumstances of the contingency without accruing a loss.

If the conditions for recording a loss contingency are initially not met, but then *are* met during a later accounting period, the loss should be accrued in the later period. Do not make a retroactive adjustment to an earlier period to record a loss contingency.

Contract-Related Costs

Thus far, the discussion has centered on the recognition of revenue – but what about the costs that an organization incurs to fulfill a contract? In this section, we separately address the accounting for the costs incurred to initially obtain a contract, costs incurred during a contract, and how these costs are to be charged to expense.

Costs to Obtain a Contract

An organization may incur certain costs to obtain a contract. If so, it is allowable to record these costs as an asset, and amortize them over the life of the contract. The following conditions apply:

- The costs must be incremental; that is, they would not have been incurred if the organization had not obtained the contract.
- If the amortization period will be one year or some lesser period, it is allowable to simply charge these costs to expense as incurred.
- There is an expectation that the costs will be recovered.

An example of a contract-related cost that could be recorded as an asset and amortized is the sales commission associated with a sale, though as a practical expedient it is usually charged to expense as incurred.

EXAMPLE

A water engineering firm bids on a contract to investigate the level of silt accumulation in the Oswego Canal in New York, and wins the bid. The firm incurs the following costs as part of its bidding process.

Staff time to prepare proposal	$18,000
Printing fees	2,500
Travel costs	5,000
Commissions paid to sales staff	15,000
	$40,500

The firm must charge the staff time, printing fees, and travel costs to expense as incurred, since it would have incurred these expenses even if the bid had failed. Only the commissions paid to the sales staff can be considered a contract asset, since that cost should be recovered through its future billings for consulting services.

Costs to Fulfill a Contract

In general, any costs required to fulfill a contract should be recognized as assets, as long as they meet all of these criteria:

- The costs are tied to a specific contract;
- The costs will be used to satisfy future performance obligations; and
- There is an expectation that the costs will be recovered.

Costs that are considered to relate directly to a contract include the following:

- *Direct labor*. Includes the wages of those employees directly engaged in providing services to the customer.
- *Direct materials*. Includes the supplies consumed in the provision of services to the customer.
- *Cost allocations*. Includes those costs that relate directly to the contract, such as the cost of managing the contract, project supervision, and depreciation of the equipment used to fulfill the contract.
- *Chargeable costs*. Includes those costs that the contract explicitly states can be charged to the customer.
- *Other costs*. Includes costs that would only be incurred because the seller entered into the contract, such as payments to subcontractors providing services to the customer.

Other costs are to be charged to expense as incurred, rather than being classified as contract assets. These costs include:

- *Administration*. General and administrative costs, unless the contract terms explicitly state that they can be charged to the contract.

- *Indistinguishable*. Costs for which it is not possible to determine whether they relate to unsatisfied or satisfied performance obligations. In this case, the default assumption is that they relate to satisfied performance obligations.
- *Past performance costs*. Any costs incurred that relate to performance obligations that have already been fulfilled.
- *Waste*. The costs of resources wasted in the contract fulfillment process, which were not included in the contract price.

EXAMPLE

Tele-Service International enters into a contract to take over the phone customer service function of Artisan's Delight, a manufacturer of hand-woven wool shopping bags. Tele-Service incurs a cost of $50,000 to construct an interface between the inventory and customer service systems of Artisan's Delight and its own call database. This cost relates to activities needed to fulfill the requirements of the contract, but does not result in the provision of any services to Artisan's Delight. This cost should be amortized over the term of the contract.

Tele-Service assigns four of its employees on a full-time basis to handle incoming customer calls from Artisan's customers. Though this group is providing services to the customer, it is not generating or enhancing the resources of Tele-Service, and so its cost cannot be recognized as an asset. Instead, the cost of these employees is charged to expense as incurred.

Amortization of Costs

When contract-related costs have been recognized as assets, they should be amortized on a systematic basis that reflects the timing of the transfer of related goods and services to the customer. If there is a change in the anticipated timing of the transfer of goods and services to the customer, update the amortization to reflect this change. This is considered a change in accounting estimate.

Impairment of Costs

The seller should recognize an impairment loss in the current period when the carrying amount of an asset associated with a contract is greater than the remaining payments to be received from the customer. The calculation is:

Remaining consideration to be received – Costs not yet recognized as expenses

= Impairment amount (if result is a negative figure)

Note: When calculating possible impairment, adjust the amount of the remaining consideration to be received for the effects of the customer's credit risk.

It is not allowable to reverse an impairment loss on contract assets that has already been recognized.

Exclusions

The revenue recognition rules contained within Topic 606 do not apply to the following areas, for which more specific recognition standards apply:

- Lease contracts
- Insurance contracts
- Financial instruments involving receivables, investments, liabilities, debt, derivatives, hedging, or transfers and servicing
- Guarantees, not including product or service warranties
- Nonmonetary exchanges between entities in the same line of business, where the intent is to facilitate sales transactions to existing or potential customers

---

EXAMPLE

Two distributors of heating oil swap stocks of different grades of heating oil, so that they can better meet the forecasted demand of their customers. No revenue recognition occurs in this situation, since the two parties are in the same line of business and the intent of the transaction is to facilitate sales to potential customers.

Since Topic 606 only applies to contracts with customers, there are a number of transactions that do not incorporate these elements, and so are not covered by the provisions of this Topic. Consequently, the following transactions and events are not covered:

- Dividends received
- Non-exchange transactions, such as donations received
- Changes in regulatory assets and liabilities caused by alternative revenue programs for rate-regulated entities

Revenue Disclosures

There are a number of disclosures related to revenue. As a general overview, the intent of the disclosures is to reveal enough information so that readers will understand the nature of the revenue, the amount being recognized, the timing associated with its recognition, and the uncertainty of the related cash flows. More specifically, disclosures are required in the following three areas for both annual and interim financial statements:

- *Contracts.* Disclose the amount of revenue recognized, any revenue impairments, the disaggregation of revenue, performance obligations, contract balances, and the amount of the transaction price allocated to the remaining performance obligations. Contract balances should include beginning and ending balances of receivables, contract assets, and contract liabilities. In particular:
  - *Revenue.* Separately disclose the revenue recognized from contracts with customers.
  - *Impairment losses.* Separately disclose any impairment losses on receivables or contract assets that arose from contracts with customers. These disclosures must be separated from the disclosure of losses from other types of contracts.
  - *Disaggregation.* Disaggregate the reported amount of revenue recognized into categories that reflect the nature, amount, timing, and uncertainty of cash flows and revenue. Examples are:
    - By contract type (such as by cost-plus versus fixed-price contract)
    - By country or region
    - By customer type (such as by retail versus government customer)
    - By duration of contract
    - By major product line
    - By market
    - By sales channels (such as by Internet store, retail chain, or wholesaler)
    - By transfer timing (such as sales as of a point in time versus over time)

  The nature of this disaggregation may be derived from how the organization discloses information about revenue in other venues, such as within annual reports, in presentations to investors, or when being evaluated for financial performance or resource allocation judgments. If the entity is publicly-held and therefore reports segment information, consider how the reporting of disaggregated revenue information might relate to the revenue information reported for segments of the business. It is also allowable for certain non-public entities to *not* disaggregate revenue information, but only if this disclosure is replaced by the disclosure of revenue by the timing of transfers to customers, and with a discussion of how economic factors (such as contract types or customer types) impact the nature, amount, timing, and uncertainty of cash flows and revenue.

EXAMPLE

Lowry Locomotion operates a number of business segments generally related to different types of trains. It compiles the following information for its disaggregation disclosure:

(000s) Segments	Freight Trains	Passenger Trains	Railbus	Total
Primary Geographical Markets				
Europe	$53,000	$41,000	$14,000	$108,000
North America	91,000	190,000	---	281,000
	$144,000	$231,000	$14,000	$389,000
Major Product Lines				
Diesel	$106,000	$---	$---	$106,000
Electric	38,000	190,000	14,000	242,000
Trolleys	---	41,000	---	41,000
	$144,000	$231,000	$14,000	$389,000
Timing of Revenue Recognition				
Goods transferred at a point in time	$129,000	$189,000	$11,000	$329,000
Services transferred over time	15,000	42,000	3,000	60,000
	$144,000	$231,000	$14,000	$389,000

o *Contract-related.* The disclosure of contract balances for all entities shall include the opening and closing balances of receivables, contract assets, and contract liabilities. Publicly-held and certain other entities must provide considerably more information. This includes:

- Revenue recognized in the period that was included in the contract liability at the beginning of the period, and revenue recognized in the period from performance obligations at least partially satisfied in previous periods (such as from changes in transaction prices).
- How the timing of the completion of performance obligations relates to the timing of payments from customers and the impact this has on the balances of contract assets and contract liabilities.

- Explain significant changes in the balances of contract assets and contract liabilities in the period. Possible causes to discuss might include changes caused by business combinations, impairments, or cumulative catch-up adjustments.

o *Performance obligations.* Describe the performance obligations related to contracts with customers, which should include the timing of when these obligations are typically satisfied (such as upon delivery), significant payment terms, the presence of any significant financing components, whether consideration is variable, and whether the consideration may be constrained. Also note the nature of the goods or services being transferred, and describe any obligations to have a third party transfer goods or services to customers (as is the case in an agent relationship). Finally, describe any obligations related to returns, refunds, and warranties.

o *Price allocations.* If there are remaining performance obligations to which transaction prices are to be allocated, disclose the aggregate transaction price allocated to those unsatisfied obligations. Also note when this remaining revenue is likely to be recognized, either in a qualitative discussion or by breaking down the amounts to be recognized by time band. None of these disclosures are needed if the original expected duration of a contract's performance obligation is for less than one year. Also, certain non-public entities can elect to not disclose any of this information.

EXAMPLE

Franklin Oilfield Support provides gas field maintenance to gas exploration companies in North America. Franklin discloses the following information related to the allocation of transaction prices to remaining performance obligations:

Franklin provides gas field maintenance services to several of the larger gas exploration firms in the Bakken field in North Dakota. The company typically enters into two-year maintenance service agreements. Currently, the remaining performance obligations are for $77,485,000, which are expected to be satisfied within the next 24 months. These obligations are noted in the following table, which also states the year in which revenue recognition is expected:

(000s)	20X1	20X2	Totals
Revenue expected to be recognized:			
Gates contract	$14,250	$7,090	$21,340
Hollander contract	23,825	17,900	41,725
Ives contract	9,070	5,350	14,420
Totals	$47,145	$30,340	$77,485

- *Judgments.* Note the timing associated with when performance obligations are satisfied, as well as how the transaction price was determined and how it was allocated to the various performance obligations. In particular:
  - o *Recognition methods.* When performance obligations are to be satisfied over time, describe the methods used to recognize revenue, and explain why these methods constitute a faithful depiction of the transfer of goods or services to customers.
  - o *Transfer of control.* When performance obligations are satisfied as of a point in time, disclose the judgments made to determine when a customer gains control of the goods or services promised under contracts.
  - o *Methods, inputs and assumptions.* Disclose sufficient information about the methods, inputs, and assumptions used to determine transaction prices, the constraints on any variable consideration, allocation of transaction prices, and measurement of obligations for returns, refunds, and so forth. The discussion of transaction prices should include how variable consideration is estimated, how noncash consideration is measured, and how the time value of money is used to adjust prices.
  - o *Disclosure avoidance.* Certain non-public entities can elect not to disclose information about the following items pertaining to judgments:
    - Why revenue recognition methods constitute a faithful depiction of the transfer of goods or services to customers.
    - The judgments made to determine when a customer gains control of the goods or services promised under contracts.
    - All methods, inputs, and assumptions used, though this information must still be supplied in regard to the determination of whether variable consideration is constrained.

- *Asset recognition.* Note the recognized assets associated with obtaining or completing the terms of the contract. This shall include the closing balances of contract-related assets by main category of asset, such as for setup costs and the costs to obtain contracts. The disclosure should also include the amount of amortization expenses and impairment losses recognized in the period. Also describe:
  - o *Judgments.* The judgments involved in determining the amount of costs incurred to obtain or fulfill a customer contract.
  - o *Amortization.* The amortization method used to charge contract-related costs to expense in each reporting period.

A non-public entity can elect not to make the disclosures just noted for asset recognition.

It may be necessary to aggregate or disaggregate these disclosures to clarify the information presented. In particular, do not obscure information by adding large amounts of insignificant detail, or by combining items whose characteristics are substantially different.

There may be a change in estimate related to the measurement of progress toward completion of a performance obligation. If the change in estimate will affect several future periods, disclose the effect on income from continuing operations, net income, and any related per-share amounts (if the entity is publicly held). This disclosure is only required if the change is material. If there is not an immediate material effect, but a material effect is expected in later periods, provide a description of the change in estimate.

Summary

A key benefit of Topic 606 is that the recognition of revenue from contracts with customers will now be quite consistent across a number of contract types and industries. Previously, industry-specific standards did not always treat essentially the same types of transactions in a similar manner. This may mean that some industries, such as software, may experience significant recognition changes, since they were previously governed by highly specific recognition rules. Some entities, irrespective of their industry, may find that their recognition accounting will also change to a considerable extent if they had previously been using an interpretation of the existing standards that is no longer valid. For many industries, however, especially those involving retail transactions, the net effect of this standard is minimal.

Chapter 30
Compensation – General

710 = GAAP codification area for compensation – general

Introduction

This chapter addresses a small number of compensation issues, of which several are routinely addressed by most organizations – compensated absences and deferred compensation. There is also brief coverage of a minor issue relating to lump sum payments made under a union contract. The guidance in this chapter applies to all entities.

Related Chapters

See the following chapters for discussions of issues related to compensation:

- *Compensation – Retirement Benefits*. Covers defined benefit plans, defined contribution plans, and multi-employer plans.
- *Compensation – Stock Compensation*. Covers different types of payments made with stock, employee stock ownership plans, and employee share purchase plans.

Overview of Compensation

In this section, we address the accounting for compensated absences, deferred compensation, and lump-sum payments made under union contracts.

Compensated Absences

A business should accrue an expense for employee compensation related to future absences if all of the following conditions are present:

- *Estimation*. It is possible to reasonably estimate the amount of the compensation.
- *Probable payment*. It is probable that the compensation will be paid.
- *Service basis*. The future obligation is based on employee services already rendered to the company.
- *Vesting or accumulation*. Employee rights that vest or accumulate over time are the basis for the obligation.

The accrual should account for anticipated forfeitures, which will reduce the amount of the accrual. Also, the accrual should be recognized in the year in which employees earn the compensated absence, not when they take the absence.

EXAMPLE

A new employee receives a vested right to one month of paid vacation at the beginning of the second year of her employment. The employer does not grant any pro rata payout if she is terminated prior to the vesting date.

The compensated absence is considered to be earned in the first year of the person's employment, so the employer should accrue an expense for the vacation pay during her first year of employment, reduced by an allowance for expected forfeitures that are caused by employee departures.

If the right to a compensated absence expires (as commonly occurs when a company grants "use it or lose it" vacation time), do not accrue a liability for future absences in the period prior to when the right expires. This is because any later payout cannot be attributed to employee services from prior periods. However, if compensated absences are cumulative, accrue a liability in an amount that is reasonably probable that employees will be paid in later periods, and if the amount can be reasonably estimated.

EXAMPLE

There is already an existing accrued balance of 40 hours of unused vacation time for Fred Smith on the books of Armadillo Industries. In the most recent month, Fred accrued an additional five hours of vacation time (since he is entitled to 60 hours of accrued vacation time per year, and 60 ÷ 12 = five hours per month). He also used three hours of vacation time during the month. This means that, as of the end of the month, Armadillo should have accrued a total of 42 hours of vacation time for him, which is calculated as:

40 Hours existing balance + 5 Hours additional accrual – 3 Hours used

Mr. Smith is paid $30 per hour, so his total vacation accrual should be $1,260 (42 hours × $30/hour). The beginning liability balance for him is $1,200 (40 hours × $30/hour), so Armadillo accrues an additional $60 of vacation liability.

There may be situations where a sabbatical leave is granted so that an employee can perform public service or research that benefits the employer in some manner. In this situation, the compensation paid to the employee is not related to prior services rendered, and so should not be accrued in advance. In the more likely event that a sabbatical is based on prior services rendered, the employer should accrue the cost of the sabbatical during the required service period.

If an employer pays its employees for sick time off, the accounting should follow actual sick time payment practices, rather than what is stated in the company's employee manual. The general rule of sick pay benefits is that it is not necessary to accrue an expense for nonvesting accumulating sick pay rights, unless all four of the preceding requirements for compensated absences are met.

Deferred Compensation Arrangements

If a deferred compensation arrangement is based on employee performance during a specific time period, accrue the cost of the deferred compensation in that performance period. If the deferred compensation is based on both current and future service, only accrue an expense for that portion of the compensation attributable to current service. As of the full eligibility date for the deferred compensation, the employer should have accrued the present value of those benefits expected to be paid in the future. Depending on the terms of the arrangement, it may be necessary to record an accrual based on the life expectancy of the employee, as supported by mortality tables, or on the estimated cost of an annuity contract.

EXAMPLE

Armadillo Industries creates a deferred compensation agreement for its CEO, under which he will become eligible for the benefits stated in the contract after five years have passed. The terms of the agreement indicate that the CEO will render services for five years in order to earn the deferred compensation, so Armadillo accrues the cost of the contract over the intervening five years.

In some types of deferred compensation arrangements, employee compensation is invested in the stock of the employer and placed in a rabbi trust. The accounting for these plans varies, depending upon how the trusts are structured. The options are:

- *No diversification and stock settlement.* If the plan does not permit diversification and can only be settled through the delivery of a fixed number of shares of company stock, the deferred compensation in the trust is classified as an equity instrument. The employer stock held in the trust is accounted for in a manner similar to treasury stock. Do not record subsequent changes in the fair value of the employer's stock, nor any changes in the fair value of the amount owed to the employee.
- *No diversification and settlement options.* If the plan does not permit diversification and can be settled in company stock or cash, the deferred compensation in the trust is classified as a liability. The employer stock held in the trust is accounted for in a manner similar to treasury stock. Do not record subsequent changes in the fair value of the employer's stock, but record subsequent changes in the fair value of the amount owed, with an offsetting charge to compensation expense.

- *Diversification allowed but not used.* If the plan permits diversification but the employee has not done so, the deferred compensation in the trust is classified as a liability. The employer stock held in the trust is accounted for in a manner similar to treasury stock. Do not record subsequent changes in the fair value of the employer's stock, but record subsequent changes in the fair value of the amount owed, with an offsetting charge to compensation expense.
- *Diversification allowed and used.* If the plan permits diversification and the employee has done so, the deferred compensation in the trust is classified as a liability. The assets held in the trust are accounted for using the GAAP that applies to those assets. Record subsequent changes in the fair value of the amount owed, with an offsetting charge to compensation expense.

Lump-Sum Payments under Union Contracts

There may be a clause in a new union contract, under which union members accept a lump-sum payment in exchange for a wage rate increase. If it is clear that the lump-sum payment will result in a lower base wage than would otherwise be the case in future periods, defer recognition of the lump-sum payments and recognize them ratably over the future periods being benefited (not to exceed the termination date of the union contract).

Compensation Disclosures

There are several issues related to rabbi trusts that can impact the presentation of certain information in the financial statements. The issues are:

- Consolidate the accounts used by all rabbi trusts with those of the employer.
- If a deferred compensation obligation will be settled by the delivery of company shares, include these shares in the calculation of basic and diluted earnings per share. If the obligation can be settled through multiple payment options, do not include the company shares in the calculation of basic earnings per share, but *do* include them in the calculation of diluted earnings per share.
- If diversification is allowed and used in a rabbi trust, do not record changes in the fair value of the deferred compensation obligation in other comprehensive income.

If there is no accrual for compensated absences because the amount cannot be reasonably estimated, though all other conditions for recognizing compensated absences are present, disclose this situation.

Summary

This chapter provided guidance regarding compensation for just a few specific kinds of arrangements (though they occur frequently). For more detailed discussions of other compensation issues, see the following two chapters, which deal with retirement benefits and stock compensation, respectively.

Chapter 31
Compensation – Retirement Benefits

715 = GAAP codification area for compensation – retirement benefits

Introduction

This chapter addresses the accounting for two types of pension plans, called defined benefit plans and defined contribution plans. Nearly all of the discussion is concentrated on defined benefit plans, which require ongoing estimations of and accounting for future costs that may be incurred, as well as changes to existing benefits.

Some of the complexity of this topic is caused by a rare circumstance in GAAP – where provisions are made to allow a business to defer costs and recognize them in later periods through amortization. This approach contravenes the vastly more common approach of charging all costs to expense as incurred. While this type of modified accounting undoubtedly allows a business to defer expense recognition, it causes ongoing headaches for accountants, and likely increases the profits of the actuarial industry.

The guidance in this chapter applies to all entities.

Related Chapters

See the following chapters for discussions of issues related to retirement benefits:

- Compensation – General
- Compensation – Stock Compensation

Overview of Retirement Benefits

A retirement benefit is one in which the employer promises to deliver a fixed benefit to its employees at some point in the future. Examples of these benefits are pensions and health benefits to be paid following the retirement of employees. Employees qualify for retirement benefits either through the passage of time, by attaining a certain age, or a combination of both. Retirement benefits paid to employees may begin as soon as they retire, or the benefits may be delayed until a certain age is reached, or even when employees elect to begin accepting benefits.

Retirement benefits are a form of deferred compensation, so the employer must estimate the amount of future expenditure that will be made, and recognize a portion of it in the current period. Expense recognition occurs before the benefits are paid, because employees are earning these future benefits via their services in earlier periods.

It is possible that some of the costs associated with retirement benefits will be capitalized into inventory as part of the application of factory overhead to inventory. These costs can also be capitalized into fixed assets, if they relate to employee labor in constructing fixed assets.

Defined Benefit Plans

In a defined benefit retirement plan, the employer provides a pre-determined periodic payment to employees after they retire. The amount of this future payment depends upon a number of future events, such as estimates of employee lifespan, how long current employees will continue to work for the company, and the pay level of employees just prior to their retirement. In essence, the accounting for defined benefit plans revolves around the estimation of the future payments to be made, and recognizing the related expense in the periods in which employees are rendering the services that qualify them to receive payments in the future under the terms of the plan.

There are a number of costs associated with defined benefit plans that may at first appear arcane. Here is a summary of the relevant costs, which sum to the net periodic pension cost that is recognized in each accounting period:

Cost	Explanation
+ Service cost	This is the actuarial present value of benefits related to services rendered during the current reporting period. The cost includes an estimate of the future compensation levels of employees from which benefit payments will be derived.
+ Interest cost	This is the interest on the projected benefit obligation. It is a financial item, rather than a cost related to employee compensation.
+ Actual return on plan assets	This is the difference between the fair values of beginning and ending plan assets, adjusted for contributions and benefit payments. It is a financial item, rather than a cost related to employee compensation.
+ Amortization of prior service costs	When an employer issues a plan amendment, it may contain increases in benefits that are based on services rendered by employees in prior periods. If so, the cost of these additional benefits is amortized over the future periods in which those employees active on the amendment date are expected to receive benefits.
+ Gain or loss	This is the gain or loss resulting from a change in the value of a projected benefit obligation from changes in assumptions, or changes in the value of plan assets.
= Net periodic pension cost	

The accounting for the relevant defined benefit plan costs is as follows:

- *Service cost.* The amount of service cost recognized in earnings in each period is the incremental change in the actuarial present value of benefits related to services rendered during the current reporting period.
- *Interest cost.* The interest cost associated with the projected benefit obligation is recognized as incurred.
- *Amortization of prior service costs.* These costs are charged to other comprehensive income on the date of the amendment, and then amortized to earnings over time. The amount to be amortized is derived by assigning an equal amount of expense to each future period of service for each employee who is expected to receive benefits. If most of the employees are inactive, the amortization period is instead the remaining life expectancy of the employees. Straight-line amortization of the cost over the average remaining service period is also acceptable. Once established, this amortization schedule is not usually revised, unless there is a plan curtailment or if events indicate that a shorter amortization period is warranted.

EXAMPLE

Armadillo Industries creates a pension plan amendment that grants $90,000 of prior service costs to the 200 employees in its Mississippi facility. The company expects the employees at this location to retire in accordance with the following schedule:

Group	Number of Staff	Expected Year of Retirement
A	20	Year 1
B	40	Year 2
C	80	Year 3
D	40	Year 4
E	20	Year 5
Total	200	

The company uses the following grid to calculate the service years for each of the employee groups:

| | Service Years | | | | | |
Year	Group A	Group B	Group C	Group D	Group E	Total
1	20	40	80	40	20	200
2		40	80	40	20	180
3			80	40	20	140
4				40	20	60
5					20	20
Totals	20	80	240	160	100	600

There are 600 service years listed in the preceding table, over which the $90,000 prior service cost is to be allocated, which is $150 of cost per service year. Armadillo inserts the $150 per year figure into the following table to determine the amount of prior service cost amortization to recognize in each year.

Year	Total of Service Years	×	Cost per Service Year	=	Amortization per Year
1	200		$150		$30,000
2	180		150		27,000
3	140		150		21,000
4	60		150		9,000
5	20		150		3,000
Totals	600				$90,000

- *Prior service credits.* If a plan amendment reduces plan benefits, record it in other comprehensive income on the date of the amendment. This amount is then offset against any prior service cost remaining in accumulated other comprehensive income. Any residual amount of the credit is then amortized using the same methodology just noted for prior service costs.
- *Gains and losses.* Gains and losses can be recognized immediately if the method is applied consistently. If the election is not made to recognize them immediately, it is also possible to account for them as changes in other comprehensive income as they occur. If there is a gain or loss on the difference between the expected and actual amount of return on plan assets, recognize the difference in other comprehensive income in the period in which it occurs, and amortize it to earnings using the following calculation:
    1. Include the gain or loss in net pension cost for a year in which, as of the beginning of that year, the gain or loss is greater than 10% of the

greater of the projected benefit obligation or the market-related value of plan assets.

2. If this test is positive, amortize the excess just noted over the average remaining service period of those active employees who are expected to receive benefits. If most of the plan participants are inactive, amortize the excess over their remaining life expectancy.

A key additional term that arises in the accounting for defined benefit plans is the *projected benefit obligation*. This is the actuarial present value of future benefits attributed to service already rendered by employees. The "actuarial" part of the definition refers to *expected* payments, since some payments will never be made, due to the turnover of employees before they vest, the death of employees who would otherwise have been entitled to payments, and so forth. The projected benefit obligation also incorporates assumptions regarding the future pay levels and service periods of existing employees, which tends to increase the amount of the benefit obligation in comparison to what the obligation would be based on current employee compensation levels and periods of service.

When a business incurs obligations for future pension payments, it should presumably begin accumulating assets into a pension plan that will be available to pay the pension benefits in the future. If the projected benefit obligation is greater than the fair value of the plan assets on the balance sheet date, the employer should recognize a liability for the difference (known as the *unfunded projected benefit obligation*). In those rare cases where plan assets exceed the projected benefit obligation, the employer recognizes an asset in the amount of the difference. If there are multiple plans, all overfunded plans should be aggregated for reporting purposes, and all underfunded plans should be aggregated for reporting purposes.

It is possible that the unfunded or overfunded projected benefit obligation will result in a temporary difference for income tax purposes. If so, recognize the deferred tax effects of the temporary difference within the year.

If there are adjustments to the funded status of a pension plan, net gains or losses, prior service costs, and so forth, the offset to these entries is other comprehensive income.

When the employer buys annuity contracts to cover the cost of future employee benefits, the cost of the benefits should be the same as the cost of acquiring the annuity contracts.

Expense Attribution for Delayed Vesting

There are a number of methods available for assigning benefits to employees, usually with the intent of delaying the vesting of benefits. For example, a plan may provide no benefits after nine years of service, and then vests employees in a future benefit payment following the tenth year of service (known as *cliff vesting*). In these situations, do not defer the recognition of a benefit expense until the delayed vesting occurs. Instead, assume that the benefit accumulates over time in proportion to the number of completed periods of service, which means that there should be an ongoing accrual of the related benefit expense over time.

EXAMPLE

Uncanny Corporation has a defined benefit pension plan, under which it pays a pension benefit of $60 per month for the remainder of each employee's life for each year of service completed, up to a maximum of ten years of service. The actuary employed by Uncanny calculates that the average employee will have 210 months of life expectancy following their retirement from Uncanny, and will have the full 10 years of service completed as of their retirement. The actuarial present value discount is set at 0.35. Based on this information, the actuary calculates the following pension benefits attributable to each of Uncanny's employees:

Years of service period completed	10
× Pension benefit per month	× $60
= Payment to be made per month to each employee	= $600
× Average life expectancy (in months)	× 210
= Gross pension payment	= $126,000
× Actuarial present value discount rate	× 0.35
= Present value of pension benefit	$44,100

Discount Rates

Service costs are based on the actuarial present value of benefits to be paid in the future. A discount rate must be employed to arrive at this actuarial present value. The discount rate should be one that reflects the rate at which benefits can actually be settled. A good source of information for this discount rate is the rate implicit in the current prices of annuity contracts that an employer could purchase to settle a future benefit obligation. Another source of information is the rate of return on high-quality fixed income investments that are expected to be available through the period during which the pension benefits will be paid.

Interest rates vary, depending upon the time period of investments. Thus, the discount rate used for benefits to be paid to a group of 50-year old employees will likely be different from the discount rate used for benefits to be paid to a group of 30-year olds.

Settlements and Curtailments

A benefit plan may be adjusted or terminated at some point. Variations that may be encountered include:

- *Curtailments*. Employee services or the benefit plan itself may be terminated earlier than expected, which reduces or eliminates the accrual of additional benefits.
- *Settlements*. Lump-sum cash payments may be made to plan participants in exchange for their rights to receive pension benefits.

When benefit obligations are settled, curtailed, or terminated, net gains or losses and prior service costs are shifted from accumulated other comprehensive income to earnings. This transfer occurs in the period in which all pension obligations are settled, benefits are no longer accrued, no plan assets remain, employees are terminated, *and* the plan ceases to exist. Also, the plan cannot be replaced by another plan.

If only a portion of the projected benefit obligation is settled, recognize in earnings that portion of the settlement that represents the reduction in the projected benefit obligation.

If the cost of the settlements completed in a year is greater than the sum of the service and interest cost components of the net periodic pension cost for that period, record a gain or loss in the amount of the difference. If the cost is lower than the sum of the service and interest cost components, recognition in earnings is permitted, but not required. The manner in which management chooses to deal with a lower-cost situation should be followed consistently.

If an employer purchases an annuity contract in order to settle a benefit plan, and the annuity was purchased from an entity that the employer controls, settlement accounting cannot be used to record the transaction. Similarly, if the employer retains the risks and rewards associated with a benefit obligation, despite purchasing an annuity contract, settlement accounting cannot be used.

If there is a curtailment of a benefit plan, the associated amount of prior service cost already recorded in accumulated other comprehensive income that is related to future years of service should be recognized in earnings as a loss. Also, the projected benefit obligation may be increased or decreased by a curtailment. This is a curtailment gain in the amount by which it exceeds any loss included in accumulated other comprehensive income. This is a curtailment loss in the amount by which it exceeds any net gain included in accumulated other comprehensive income. A curtailment loss should be recognized in earnings when the amount can be reasonably estimated and the curtailment is probable. A curtailment gain should be recognized in earnings when the plan is formally suspended or the impacted employees are terminated.

EXAMPLE

Following the devastation of a major earthquake, Armadillo Industries closes down its California facility. The employees located there will no longer earn any benefits. As of the plan curtailment date, the actuarial assumptions associated with the plan are:

- Defined benefit obligation = $300,000
- Plan assets fair value = $275,000
- Net cumulative unrecognized actuarial gains = $15,000

The curtailment event shrinks the present value of the benefit obligation by $20,000, to $280,000. Also, 20% of the net cumulative unrecognized actuarial gains are associated with that portion of the obligation that was eliminated by the curtailment. These alterations are incorporated into the following table:

	Before Curtailment	Gain on Curtailment	After Curtailment
Present value of obligation	$300,000	-$20,000	$280,000
Fair value of plan assets	-275,000	--	-275,000
	25,000	-20,000	5,000
Unrecognized actuarial gains	15,000	3,000	18,000
Net liability	$40,000	-$17,000	$23,000

Based on the preceding information, Armadillo's controller records the following entry to record the gain on curtailment:

	Debit	Credit
Accrued pension cost	17,000	
Curtailment gain		17,000

Termination Benefits

An employer may provide a certain set of benefits to employees that it terminates. Examples of termination benefits are lump-sum cash payments and a series of periodic payments in the future. The employer should recognize a liability and expense for the full amount of these benefits as soon as terminated employees accept the termination offer to which the benefits are linked. This expense should include the present value of any future payments to be made. To determine the amount of termination expense to recognize, use the following calculation:

+	Actuarial present value of accumulated pension benefits, including termination benefits
+	Actuarial present value of accumulated pension benefits, without termination benefits
=	Termination benefits to charge to expense

Combined Pension Plans

A company may elect to combine several of its pension plans, which means that the assets of each predecessor plan can now be used to satisfy the obligations of the combined plan. The company should create a single amortization schedule for each of the pension costs that must be amortized. The amortization periods incorporated into these schedules shall be based on a weighted average of the remaining amortization periods used by the individual pension plans before they were combined. However, the prior service cost associated with each individual pension plan shall continue to be amortized under the old amortization schedules formulated prior to the combination of plans.

Defined Contribution Plans

Under a defined contribution plan, the employer's entire obligation is complete once it has made a contribution payment into the plan, as long as no associated costs are being deferred for recognition in later periods. Thus, the employer commits to pay a specific amount of funds into a plan, but does not commit to the amount of benefits subsequently distributed by that plan.

The accounting for a defined contribution plan is simplicity itself (as opposed to the accounting just described for a defined benefit plan). The employer charges its contributions to expense as incurred. If such a plan calls for additional payments to be made after an employee leaves the company, the estimated cost of these additional payments shall be accrued during the service period of the applicable employee.

In those cases where an employer terminates a defined benefit plan and shifts the assets in the plan to a defined contribution plan that is a replacement plan, there may be an excess of assets in the replacement plan over the required annual contribution to the plan. If so, the employer should maintain the excess assets in a suspense account until such time as they are needed to fund the replacement account. Until the assets in the suspense account are used to fund the replacement account, the employer continues to retain the risks and rewards of ownership associated with those assets, and so shall account for the assets within its own balance sheet.

Presentation of Retirement Benefit Information

If an employer has a defined benefit pension or other postretirement plan, it should provide line items in the financial statements for the following information:

- State the service cost component of net periodic pension cost and net periodic postretirement benefit cost in the same line item or items in the income statement as other compensation costs caused by services rendered by employees during the period.[1]
- Separately state the funding status of each plan in the financial statements.
- The recognized amounts of related assets, current liabilities, and noncurrent liabilities.
- Classify any underfunded plan liabilities as being current or noncurrent liabilities, or both. For the purposes of this classification, a current plan liability is the excess amount of the actuarial present value of the longer of the benefits payable in the next 12 months or the operating cycle, over the fair value of plan assets.
- If a plan is overfunded, classify the overfunding as a noncurrent asset.

---

[1] Not including the amount of these costs that is being capitalized in connection with the manufacture or construction of an asset, such as inventory or a building.

Retirement Benefit Disclosures

The disclosures related to defined benefit plans vary for publicly-held and privately-held companies, so the requirements are stated separately for each type of business. There is also a discussion of the much more abbreviated disclosures for defined contribution plans.

Defined Benefit Plan Disclosures for Public Companies

The following disclosures related to retirement benefits are required for a publicly-held business, and are to be provided separately for pension plans and other postretirement plans:

- *Benefit obligation reconciliation*. The beginning and ending balances of the benefit obligation, showing the reconciling effects of service cost, interest cost, participant contributions, actuarial gains and losses, exchange rate effects, benefits paid, plan amendments, business combinations, divestitures, curtailments, settlements, and termination benefits.
- *Assets reconciliation*. A reconciliation of the beginning and ending balances of the fair value of plan assets, showing the reconciling effects of the return on plan assets, exchange rate changes, employer contributions, participant contributions, benefits paid, business combinations, divestitures, and settlements.
- *Funded status*. The funded status of each plan, with the related assets, current liabilities, and noncurrent liabilities.
- *Plan asset information*. Investment policies and strategies, target allocation percentages, the fair value of each class of plan assets as of each balance sheet date, the approach used to estimate the long-term rate of return on assets, and enough information for users to assess the inputs and valuation techniques needed to develop fair value measurements (including a discussion of how the fair value hierarchy was used).
- *Accumulated benefit obligation*
- *Benefit payments*. The expected benefits to be paid in each of the next five years, and in aggregate for the five years thereafter.
- *Contributions paid*. The estimated amount of contribution payments expected during the next fiscal year, aggregating required, discretionary, and noncash contributions.
- *Net benefit cost*. The net benefit cost recognized, separately stating the service cost, interest cost, expected return on plan assets, gain or loss, prior service cost, transition asset, and gain or loss caused by settlements or curtailments.
- *Other comprehensive income*. The net gain or loss, the net prior service cost or credit, and reclassification adjustments recognized for the period in other comprehensive income.
- *Accumulated other comprehensive income*. Any amounts in accumulated other comprehensive income that have not been recognized in net periodic

benefit cost, along with the net gain or loss, net prior service cost or credit, and net transition asset or obligation.

- *Assumptions.* In tabular format, the assumptions for assumed discount rates, rates of compensation increase, and expected long-term rates of return on plan assets that were used to calculate the benefit obligation and net benefit cost.
- *Cost trends.* The projected trends in health care costs for the next year, as well as the pattern of change thereafter, the ultimate trend rate, and when the ultimate rate is expected.
- *Change effects.* The effect of a one-percent increase and decrease in the health care cost trend rate on service and interest cost components of net periodic postretirement health care benefit costs and the accumulated benefit obligation.
- *Asset contents.* The types and amounts of securities issued by the employer and related parties that are part of plan assets, significant transactions between the plan and the employer and related parties in the period, and the amount of future annual benefits covered by insurance contracts.
- *Amortization.* The method used to amortize prior service amounts or net gains and losses.
- *Commitments.* Any significant commitment incorporated into the benefit obligation, such as a history of granting benefit increases.
- *Termination benefits.* The cost of providing termination benefits during the period, and the nature of these benefits.
- *Other changes.* The nature of any other significant changes in the benefit obligation or plan assets.
- *Assets returned to employer.* The amount of any plan assets to be returned to the employer in the next year, and the timing of the return.
- *Expected recognition.* The accumulated other comprehensive income amounts to be recognized as part of net periodic benefit cost in the next year, stating the net gain or loss, net prior service cost or credit, and the net transition asset or obligation.

EXAMPLE

Armadillo Industries discloses the following information about its retirement plans in the notes accompanying its financial statements:

The company has a funded defined benefit pension plan that covers substantially all of its employees. The plan provides defined benefits based on years of service and the average salary of employees over their final five years of service.

Obligations and Funded Status of Pension Benefits

(000s)	20X3	20X2
Change in benefit obligation:		
Benefit obligation at beginning of year	$2,190	$2,200
Service cost	110	120
Interest cost	65	50
Amendments	25	10
Actuarial loss	15	
Benefits paid	-205	-190
Benefit obligation at end of year	$2,200	$2,190

Change in Plan Assets

(000s)	20X3	20X2
Change in plan assets:		
Fair value of plan assets at beginning of year	$1,845	$1,860
Actual return on plan assets	65	50
Employer contributions	180	125
Benefits paid	-205	-190
Fair value of plan assets at end of year	$1,885	$1,845
Funded status at end of year	-$315	-$345

Components of Net Periodic Benefit Cost and Other Amounts Recognized in Accumulated Other Comprehensive Income

(000s)	20X3	20X2
Net periodic benefit cost:		
Service cost	$110	$120
Interest cost	65	50
Expected return on plan assets	45	40
Amortization of prior service cost	15	10
Net periodic benefit cost	$235	$220

Other Changes in Plan Assets and Benefit Obligations Recognized in Other Comprehensive Income

(000s)	20X3	20X2
Net loss (gain)	$30	-$20
Prior service cost	50	--
Amortization of prior service cost	-15	-10
Total recognized in other comprehensive income	65	-30
Total recognized in net periodic benefit cost and other comprehensive income	$300	$190

The estimated net loss and prior service cost that will be amortized from accumulated other comprehensive income into net periodic benefit cost over the next fiscal year are $3,000 and $12,000, respectively.

Weighted-Average Assumptions used to Determine Pension Obligations at December 31

	20X3	20X2
Discount rate	4.50%	3.75%
Rate of compensation increase	4.25%	4.00%

Weighted-Average Assumptions used to Determine Net Periodic Benefit Cost at December 31

	20X3	20X2
Discount rate	4.75%	4.00%
Expected long-term return on plan assets	5.50%	5.00%
Rate of compensation increase	4.75%	4.25%

Plan Assets

The company follows an investment strategy of 60 percent in long-term growth investments and 40 percent in short-term investments from which benefits can be paid. Target allocations are 70 percent in large cap equities and 20 percent in corporate bonds, in all cases with issuers located in the United States and Europe. Ten percent of the target allocation is to other investments approved in advance by the board of directors. The fair value of Armadillo's pension plan assets at December 31, 20X3 is as follows:

Fair Value of Pension Plan Assets

| (000s) | Total | Fair Value Measurements at 12/31/X3 | | |
		Quoted Prices in Active Markets for Identical Assets (Level 1)	Significant Observable Inputs (Level 2)	Significant Unobservable Inputs (Level 3)
Cash	$90	$90		
Equity securities				
U.S. large-cap	750	750		
Europe large-cap	480	480		
Corporate bonds	375		$375	
Hedge funds	120			$120
Real estate	70			70
	$1,885	$1,320	$375	$190

The company expects to contribute $200,000 to its pension plan in 20X4.

Defined Benefit Plan Disclosures for Private Companies

The following disclosures related to retirement benefits are required for a privately-held business:

- *Benefit obligation.* The benefit obligation, funded status, and fair value of plan assets.
- *Contributions.* Employer and participant contributions, and the amount of benefits paid.
- *Plan asset information.* Investment policies and strategies, target allocation percentages, the fair value of each class of plan assets as of each balance sheet date, the approach used to estimate the long-term rate of return on assets assumption, and enough information for users to assess the inputs and valuation techniques used to develop fair value measurements (including a discussion of how the fair value hierarchy was used).
- *Accumulated benefit obligation*
- *Benefit payments.* The expected benefits to be paid in each of the next five years, and in aggregate for the five years thereafter.
- *Contributions paid.* The estimated amount of contribution payments expected during the next fiscal year, aggregating required, discretionary, and noncash contributions.
- *Assets and liabilities.* The postretirement benefit assets, and both current and noncurrent postretirement benefit liabilities.
- *Other comprehensive income.* The net gain or loss, the net prior service cost or credit, and reclassification adjustments recognized for the period in other comprehensive income.

- *Accumulated other comprehensive income.* Any amounts in accumulated other comprehensive income that have not been recognized in net periodic benefit cost, along with the net gain or loss, net prior service cost or credit, and net transition asset or obligation.
- *Assumptions.* In tabular format, the assumptions for assumed discount rates, rates of compensation increase, and expected long-term rates of return on plan assets that were used to calculate the benefit obligation and net benefit cost.
- *Cost trends.* The projected trends in health care costs for the next year, as well as the pattern of change thereafter, the ultimate trend rate, and when the ultimate rate is expected.
- *Asset contents.* The types and amounts of securities issued by the employer and related parties that are part of plan assets, significant transactions between the plan and the employer and related parties in the period, and the amount of future annual benefits covered by insurance contracts.
- *Nonroutine events.* The nature of significant nonroutine events, including divestitures, combinations, amendments, curtailments, and settlements.
- *Recognition of accumulated other comprehensive income.* Any amounts in accumulated other comprehensive income to be recognized in the next year as net periodic benefit cost, showing the net gain or loss, net prior service cost or credit, and net transition asset or obligation.
- *Assets returned to employer.* The amount of any plan assets to be returned to the employer in the next year, and the timing of the return.
- *Net periodic benefit.* The amount of net periodic benefit cost recognized in the period.

Disclosures for Defined Benefit Plans in Interim Periods

The disclosures for retirement benefits in interim financial statements are greatly reduced from the requirements to be listed in annual financial statements. Only the following disclosures are required in the interim statements of a publicly-held company:

- *Net benefit cost.* The net benefit cost for the period, separately stating service cost, interest cost, the expected return on plan assets, gain or loss, prior service cost or credit, the transition asset or obligation, and any gains or losses due to a settlement or curtailment.
- *Contributions.* The total contributions paid by the employer, if significantly different from the amount disclosed in the preceding annual financial statements.

A privately-held company has even fewer required disclosures in an interim period, which are:

- *Contributions.* The total contributions paid by the employer, if significantly different from the amount disclosed in the preceding annual financial statements.

Disclosures for Defined Contribution Plans

If a company has one or more defined contribution plans, it should disclose the amount of cost recognized for these plans for all periods presented in the financial statements. These costs should be disclosed separately from the costs disclosed for any defined benefit plans. Also, describe the nature of any significant changes during the presented periods that affect the comparability of the information from period to period. Examples of such comparability events are the effects of an acquisition or divestiture.

Summary

When a company has a defined benefit plan, the number of variables impacting the amount of future payments makes it extremely difficult to recognize expenses that actually approximate the amounts that are later paid. In many cases, the variance between actual and estimated pension costs can have a profound impact on the financial results reported by a business, to the extent that users of this information may decide that the financial statements cannot be relied upon to reveal the actual results and condition of the business. The result can be additional analysis by investors, who use their own estimates of future pension liabilities to adjust the company's financial statements, and make investment decisions based on their own estimates.

The level of confusion engendered by defined benefit plans bolsters the case for not entering into such plans. As an alternative, the accounting for defined contribution plans is neat, simple, and highly predictable, and results in more reliable financial statements. While the complaints of accountants are hardly likely to convince management to avoid using defined benefit plans, these issues can be considered alongside other factors, such as the massive long-term liabilities associated with defined benefit plans, to hopefully reduce their use.

Chapter 32
Compensation – Stock Compensation

Introduction

A company may issue shares to its employees that are intended to be compensation for past or future services rendered. These payments can take many forms, such as stock grants, stock options, and discounted employee stock purchase plans. In this chapter, we address how to account for each of these types of stock compensation, as well as similar arrangements. The guidance in this chapter applies to all entities.

Related Chapters

See the following chapters for discussions of issues related to stock compensation:

- *Earnings per Share.* Covers how the shares issued as part of stock option plans are treated in the calculation of earnings per share.
- *Compensation – General.* Addresses a number of topics related to employee compensation.

Overview of Stock Compensation

A company may issue payments to its employees in the form of shares in the business. When these payments are made, the essential accounting is to recognize the cost of the related services as they are received by the company, at their fair value. The offset to this expense recognition is either an increase in an equity or liability account, depending on the nature of the transaction. In rare cases, the cost of the services received by the company may be capitalized into a fixed asset, if the services are related to the acquisition or construction of the asset.

The following issues relate to the measurement and recognition of stock-based compensation:

- *Employee designation.* The accounting for stock compensation noted in this chapter only applies to employees. It also applies to the board of directors, as long as they were elected by company shareholders. However, the accounting only applies to stock grants issued in compensation for their services as directors, not for other services provided.
- *Employee payments.* If an employee pays the issuer an amount in connection with an award, the fair value attributable to employee service is net of the amount paid. For example, if a stock option has a fair value on the grant date

of $100, and the recipient pays $20 for the option, the award amount attributable to employee service is $80.

EXAMPLE

Armadillo Industries issues 1,000 shares of common stock to Mr. Jones, the vice president of sales, at a large discount from the market price. On the grant date, the fair value of these shares is $20,000. Mr. Jones pays $1,000 to the company for these shares. Thus, the amount that can be attributed to Mr. Jones' services to the company is $19,000 (calculated as $20,000 fair value - $1,000 payment).

- *Expense accrual.* When the service component related to a stock issuance spans several reporting periods, accrue the related service expense based on the probable outcome of the performance condition. Thus, always accrue the expense when it is probable that the condition will be achieved. Also, accrue the expense over the initial best estimate of the employee service period, which is usually the service period required in the arrangement related to the stock issuance.

EXAMPLE

The board of directors of Armadillo Industries grants stock options to its president that have a fair value of $80,000, which will vest in the earlier of four years or when the company achieves a 20% market share in a new market that the company wants to enter. Since there is not sufficient historical information about the company's ability to succeed in the new market, the controller elects to set the service period at four years, and accordingly accrues $20,000 of compensation in each of the next four years.

If both performance conditions had been required before the stock options would be awarded, and there was no way of determining the probability of achieving the 20% market share condition, the controller would only begin to accrue any compensation expense after it became probable that the market share condition could be achieved. In this latter case, compensation expense would be recognized at once for all of the earlier periods during which no compensation expense had been accrued.

- *Expired stock options.* If stock option grants expire unused, do not reverse the related amount of compensation expense.
- *Fair value determination.* Stock-based compensation is measured at the fair value of the instruments issued as of the grant date, even though the stock may not be issued until a much later date. Fair value is based on the share price at the grant date, though this information is not typically available for the shares of a privately-held company. The fair value of a stock option is estimated with a valuation method, such as an option-pricing model.
- *Fair value of nonvested shares.* The fair value of a nonvested share is based on its value as though it were vested on the grant date.

- *Fair value of restricted shares.* The fair value of a restricted share is based on its value as a restricted share, which is likely to be less than the fair value of an unrestricted share.
- *Fair value restrictions.* If a restriction is imposed on awarded equity instruments that continue after the required service period, such as being unable to sell shares for a period of time, this restriction is considered in determining the fair value of the stock award.
- *Forfeitures.* A business can set a company-wide policy to either estimate the number of awards that are expected to vest or to account for forfeitures when they occur. In the latter case, the company reverses any compensation cost previously recognized in the period when the forfeiture occurs.
- *Grant date.* The date on which a stock-based award is granted is assumed to be the date when the award is approved under the corporate governance requirements. The grant date can also be considered the date on which an employee initially begins to benefit from or be affected by subsequent changes in the price of a company's stock, as long as subsequent approval of the grant is considered perfunctory.
- *Non-compete agreement.* If a share-based award contains a non-compete agreement, the facts and circumstances of the situation may indicate that the non-compete is a significant service condition. If so, accrue the related amount of compensation expense over the period covered by the non-compete agreement.

EXAMPLE

Armadillo Industries grants 200,000 restricted stock units (RSUs) to its chief high-pressure module design engineer, which are vested on the grant date. The fair value of the grant is $500,000, which is triple his compensation for the past year. Under the terms of the arrangement, the RSUs will only be transferred to the engineer ratably over the next five years if he complies with the terms of the non-compete agreement.

Since the RSUs are essentially linked to the noncompete agreement, and the amount of the future payouts are quite large, it is evident that the arrangement is really intended to be compensation for future services yet to be rendered to the company. Consequently, the appropriate accounting treatment is not to recognize the expense at once, but rather to recognize it ratably over the remaining term of the noncompete agreement.

- *Payroll taxes.* Accrue an expense for the payroll taxes associated with stock-based compensation at the same time as the related compensation expense.
- *Reload valuation.* A compensation instrument may have a reload feature, which automatically grants additional options to an employee once that person exercises existing options that use company shares to pay the exercise price. Do not include the value of the reload feature in the fair value of an award. Instead, measure reload options as separate awards when they are granted.

- *Service not rendered.* If an employee does not render the service required for an award, any related amount of compensation expense that had previously been recognized may then be reversed.

EXAMPLE

Uncanny Corporation grants 5,000 restricted stock units (RSUs) to its vice president of sales, with a three-year cliff vesting provision. The fair value of the RSUs on the grant date is $60,000, so the company accrues $20,000 of compensation expense per year for three years.

One week prior to the cliff vesting date, the vice president of sales unexpectedly resigns. Since the award has not yet vested, the company reverses all of the accrued compensation expense.

- *Service period.* The service period associated with a stock-based award is considered to be the vesting period, but the facts and circumstances of the arrangement can result in a different service period for the purpose of determining the number of periods over which to accrue compensation expense. This is called the *implicit service period.*

EXPENSE

Mrs. Smith is granted 10,000 stock options by the board of directors of Uncanny Corporation, which vest over 24 months. There is no service specified under the arrangement, so the service period is assumed to be the 24-month vesting period. Thus, the fair value of the award should be recognized ratably over the vesting period.

- *Service rendered prior to grant date.* If some or all of the requisite service associated with stock-based compensation occurs prior to the grant date, accrue the compensation expense during these earlier reporting periods, based on the fair value of the award at each reporting date. When the grant date is reached, adjust the compensation accrued to date based on the per-unit fair value assigned on the grant date. Thus, the initial recordation is a best guess of what the eventual fair value will be.
- *Service rendered prior to performance target completion.* An employee may complete the required amount of service prior to the date when the associated performance target has been achieved. If so, recognize the compensation expense when it becomes probable that the target will be achieved. This recognition reflects the service already rendered by the employee.
- *Subsequent changes.* If the circumstances later indicate that the number of instruments to be granted has changed, recognize the change in compensation cost in the period in which the change in estimate occurs. Also, if the initial estimate of the service period turns out to be incorrect, adjust the expense accrual to match the updated estimate.

EXAMPLE

The board of directors of Armadillo Industries initially grants 5,000 stock options to the engineering manager, with a vesting period of four years. The shares are worth $100,000 at the grant date, so the controller plans to recognize $25,000 of compensation expense in each of the next four years. After two years, the board is so pleased with the performance of the engineering manager that they accelerate the vesting schedule to the current date. The controller must therefore accelerate the remaining $50,000 of compensation expense that had not yet been recognized to the current date.

If the offsetting increase to stock-based compensation is equity, it should be to the paid-in capital account, as noted in the following example.

EXAMPLE

Armadillo Industries issues stock options with 10-year terms to its employees. All of these options vest at the end of four years (known as *cliff vesting*). The company uses a lattice-based valuation model to arrive at an option fair value of $15.00. The company grants 100,000 stock options. On the grant date, it assumes that 10% of the options will be forfeited. The exercise price of the options is $25.

Given this information, Armadillo charges $28,125 to expense in each month. The calculation of this compensation expense accrual is:

($15 Option fair value × 100,000 Options × 90% Exercise probability) ÷ 48 Months = $28,125

The monthly journal entry to recognize the compensation expense is:

	Debit	Credit
Compensation expense	28,125	
Additional paid-in capital		28,125

Armadillo is subject to a 35% income tax rate, and expects to have sufficient future taxable income to offset the deferred tax benefits of the share-based compensation arrangements. Accordingly, the company records the following monthly entry to recognize the deferred tax benefit:

	Debit	Credit
Deferred tax asset	9,844	
Deferred tax benefit		9,844

Thus, the net after-tax effect of the monthly compensation expense recognition is $18,281 (calculated as $28,125 compensation expense - $9,844 deferred tax benefit).

At the end of the vesting period, the actual number of forfeitures matches the originally estimated amount, leaving 90,000 options. All of the 90,000 options are exercised once they have vested, which results in the following entry to record the conversion of options to shares:

	Debit	Credit
Cash (90,000 shares × $25/share)	2,250,000	
Additional paid-in capital	1,350,000	
Common stock		3,600,000

The Volatility Concept

A key component of the value of a company's stock is its volatility, which is the range over which the price varies over time, or is expected to vary. Since an employee holding a stock option can wait for the highest possible stock price before exercising the option, that person will presumably wait for the stock price to peak before exercising the option. Therefore, a stock that has a history or expectation of high volatility is worth more from the perspective of an option holder than one that has little volatility. The result is that a company with high stock price volatility will likely charge more employee compensation to expense for a given number of shares than a company whose stock experiences low volatility.

Tip: It is useful for a publicly-held company to engage in a high level of investor relations activity in order to manage stock price expectations and thereby reduce the volatility of the stock price. Doing so reduces the cost of stock-based compensation, which is based on the level of price volatility.

Stock price volatility is partially driven by the amount of leverage that a company employs in its financing. Thus, if a business uses a large amount of debt to fund its operations, its profit will fluctuate in a wider range than a business that uses less debt, since the extra debt can be used to generate more sales, but the associated interest expense will reduce net profits if revenues decline.

Fair Value Calculation Alternatives

When a publicly-held company issues stock compensation, it can derive fair value from the current market price of its stock, which is readily available. This information is not available to a privately-held organization, for which there is no ready market for its stock. The alternative is to estimate share value based on the historical volatility of a related industry sector index, which is comprised of companies that are similar to the entity conducting the measurement in terms of size, leverage, industry, and so forth. This latter approach is called the *calculated value method*. If a nonpublic company operates in several markets, it is permissible to model its stock price volatility on a weighted average of several related industry sector indexes that approximately mirror the structure of the company, or simply rely upon that industry sector that is most representative of its operations. Broad-based market indexes are not acceptable, since they are not sufficiently closely-related to a specific industry.

EXAMPLE

Abbreviated Corporation is a privately-held company that produces short versions of famous literature. The company grants 60,000 stock options to its editorial staff. The company controller elects to use the calculated value method to derive a valuation for the stock options. She locates an industry stock price index for publicly-held publishing companies, from which she derives historical stock price volatility of 27%. She plugs this information and other factors into the Black-Scholes-Merton formula to derive a fair value of $3.18 per share. When multiplied by the 60,000 options granted, the result is total compensation expense of $190,800. Forfeitures are expected to be 20%, so the net compensation expense is $152,640. Since the vesting period of the options is three years, the controller recognizes the net expense at the rate of $50,880 per year, through the vesting period.

When it is not possible to estimate the fair value of an equity instrument, it is permissible to use an alternative valuation technique, as long as it is applied consistently, reflects the key characteristics of the instrument, and is based on accepted standards of financial economic theory. Models that are commonly used to derive fair value are the Black-Scholes-Merton formula and the lattice model. Key characteristics of these models are:

- *Black-Scholes-Merton formula.* Assumes that options are exercised at the end of the arrangement period, and that price volatility, dividends, and interest rates are constant through the term of the option being measured.
- *Lattice model.* Can incorporate ongoing changes in price volatility and dividends over successive time periods in the term of an option. The model assumes that at least two price movements are possible in each measured time period.

EXAMPLE

Armadillo Industries grants an option on $25 stock that will expire in 12 months. The exercise price of the option matches the $25 stock price. Management believes there is a 40% chance that the stock price will increase by 25% during the upcoming year, a 40% chance that the price will decline by 10%, and a 20% chance that the price will decline by 50%. The risk-free interest rate is 5%. The steps required to develop a fair value for the stock option using the lattice model are:

1. Chart the estimated stock price variations.
2. Convert the price variations into the future value of options.
3. Discount the options to their present values.

The following lattice model shows the range and probability of stock prices for the upcoming year:

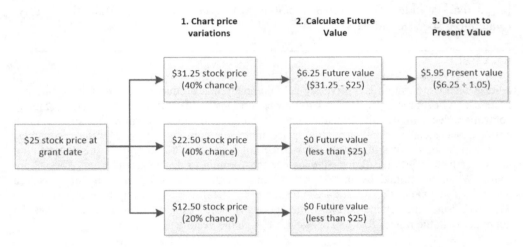

In short, the option will expire unexercised unless the stock price increases. Since there is only a 40% chance of the stock price increasing, the present value of the stock option associated with that scenario can be assigned the following expected present value for purposes of assigning a fair value to the option at the grant date:

$5.95 Option present value × 40% Probability = $2.38 Option value at grant date

---

It is acceptable to employ a different valuation model to develop the fair value of different equity instruments. It is also permissible to switch valuation methods if the replacement method can yield a better estimate of fair value.

Whatever valuation method is used, it must take into account the exercise price and expected term of the option being measured, the risk-free interest rate over the expected term of the option, and the expected dividends and volatility of the underlying shares. Accounting notes related to these inclusions are:

- *Interest-free rate.* Use the implied yield on U.S. Treasury zero-coupon issuances over the term of the option.
- *Expected term.* The expected term of an option is generally shorter than its contractual term, and can be based on historical experience. Another choice is to estimate the term based upon expected future price points of the underlying stock.
- *Volatility.* A reasonable way to estimate volatility is the historical pattern of changes in the price of a company's stock, adjusted for anticipated future issues that may impact volatility.
- *Dividends.* Include the historical pattern of changes in dividend payments in the estimation of future dividends.

When developing estimates for these inputs to the valuation model, select the amount that is the most likely; if no value appears to be the most likely, use an average of the range of possible outcomes.

> **Tip:** From an accounting efficiency perspective, it is useful to aggregate individual awards into homogeneous groups for valuation purposes.

Awards Classified as Equity

In this section, we address a number of variations on how to account for awards that are classified as equity arrangements (that is, the offset to compensation expense is an increase in equity). The bulk of these issues relate to subsequent modifications of existing stock-based awards.

Award Measurement Problems

When it is not possible to reasonably estimate the fair value of a stock-based award at its grant date, continue to remeasure the award at each successive reporting date until the award has been settled. Once the award has been settled, adjust the compensation-to-date associated with the award to the intrinsic value of the award. Intrinsic value is the excess amount of the fair value of a share over the exercise price of an underlying stock option.

Contingent Features

If there is a contingent feature in a stock-based award that allows the recipient to return equity instruments earned or to pay for equity instruments at less than their fair value when sold, account for the feature only if it is actually used.

Award Modifications

When adjustments are made to an award, it is considered to have been modified unless *all* of the following conditions have been met:

- The vesting conditions have not changed;
- The award's classification as an equity or liability instrument has not changed; and
- The fair value of the award has not changed.

If a stock-based award has been modified, treat the modification as an exchange of the original award for an entirely new award. Thus, the company is assumed to buy back the original award and exchange it for an award of equal or greater value. The accounting for a modified award includes the following points:

- *Fair value basis*. If there is an incremental change in value between the "old" and "new" awards, this is treated as additional compensation expense. The amount of expense is calculated by determining the fair value of the "old" award immediately prior to the terms modification, and subtracting it from the fair value of the modified award.

- *Intrinsic value basis.* If intrinsic value is being used instead of fair value to calculate the associated cost of compensation, measure the incremental change in value by comparing the intrinsic value of the award just prior to modification with the intrinsic value of the modified award.
- *Short-term inducements.* If the company offers short-term inducements to convince employees to accept an alteration of their stock-based compensation plans, only treat these inducements as modifications if they are accepted by employees.
- *Equity restructuring.* If there is an equity restructuring and awards are replaced with new ones that have the same fair values, do not alter the existing accounting. However, if the fair values have changed, treat the effects of the equity restructuring as a modification.
- *Repurchase of award.* If the company repurchases an award, it should charge the amount of the payment to equity, up to the amount of the fair value of the instruments repurchased. If the amount paid exceeds the fair value of the instruments repurchased, charge the difference to compensation expense.
- *Cancellation and replacement.* If the company cancels a stock-based award and concurrently grants a replacement award or other form of payment, treat these two events as the modification of terms of the original award.
- *Award cancellation.* If the company cancels an award outright, without any offer to replace the award, accelerate the recognition of any remaining unrecognized compensation expense to the cancellation date.

EXAMPLE

Armadillo Industries issues 10,000 stock options to various employees in 20X1. The designated exercise price of the options is $25, and the vesting period is four years. The total fair value of these options is $20,000, which the company charges to expense ratably over four years, which is $5,000 per year.

One year later, the market price of the stock has declined to $15, so the board of directors decides to modify the options to have an exercise price of $15.

Armadillo incurs additional compensation expense of $30,000 for the amount by which the fair value of the modified options exceeds the fair value of the original options as of the date of the modification. The accounting department adds this additional expense to the remaining $15,000 of compensation expense associated with the original stock options, which is a total unrecognized compensation expense of $45,000. The company recognizes this amount ratably over the remaining three years of vesting, which is $15,000 per year.

Income Tax Effects

If there is a compensation cost associated with the issuance of equity instruments that would normally result in a tax deduction at a future date, it is considered a deductible temporary difference for income tax purposes. If some portion of this compensation cost is capitalized into the cost of an asset (such as inventory or a fixed asset), the capitalized cost is considered part of the tax basis of the asset.

If there is a compensation cost that does not result in a tax deduction, do not treat it as a deductible temporary difference. If a future event will change the treatment of such an item to a tax deduction, wait until the future event occurs before treating the item as a tax deduction.

Awards Classified as Liabilities

A key element of stock-based compensation arrangements is whether these arrangements result in an offsetting increase in equity or liabilities. The following situations indicate the presence of a liability:

- *Cash settlement.* An employee can require the issuing company to settle an option by paying in cash or other assets, rather than stock.
- *Indexing.* An award is indexed to some additional factor, such as the market price of a commodity.
- *Puttable shares.* An employee has the right to require the issuing company to repurchase shares at their fair value, where the put feature essentially allows the employee to avoid the risks associated with owning stock.
- *Share classification.* Certain types of share-based payments, such as mandatorily-redeemable shares, are themselves classified as liabilities.

If an award is classified as a liability, the offsetting expense should be remeasured at its fair value as of the end of each reporting period, until the related service has been completed. Any change in value is to be recognized in the measurement period, adjusted for the percentage of required service rendered through the reporting period. Thus, the measurement date for a liability is the settlement date, not the grant date.

If a company is privately-held, management should make a policy decision to either measure the liabilities incurred under share-based payment arrangements at their fair value or their intrinsic value. Further, if the company is unable to estimate the volatility of its share price, the policy decision is to measure the liabilities based on either the calculated value or intrinsic value of the arrangements.

If an award is modified, treat it as the exchange of the "old" award for a "new" award. However, since the accounting for awards classified as liabilities already provides for the ongoing remeasurement of a liability, there is no need for any additional accounting for a modified award.

EXAMPLE

Uncanny Corporation grants 20,000 stock appreciation rights (SARs) to its chief executive officer (CEO). Each SAR entitles the CEO to receive a cash payment that equates to the increase in value of one share of company stock above a baseline value of $25. The award cliff vests after two years. The fair value of each SAR is calculated to be $11.50 as of the grant date. The entry to record the associated amount of compensation expense for the first year, along with the company's deferred tax asset at its 35% income tax rate, is:

	Debit	Credit
Compensation expense	115,000	
Share-based compensation liability		115,000

	Debit	Credit
Deferred tax asset	40,250	
Deferred tax benefit		40,250

At the end of the first year of vesting, the fair value of each SAR has increased to $12.75, so an additional entry is needed to adjust the vested amount of compensation expense and deferred tax asset for the $12,500 incremental increase in the value of the award over the first year (calculated as $1.25 increase in SAR fair value × 20,000 SARs × 0.5 service period).

At end of the vesting period, the fair value of each SAR has increased again, to $13.00, which increases the total two-year vested compensation expense for the CEO to $260,000. Since $127,500 of compensation expense has already been recognized at the end of the first year, the company must recognize an additional $132,500 of compensation expense, along with the related amount of deferred tax asset. When the cash payment is made to the CEO, the entry is:

	Debit	Credit
Share-based compensation liability	260,000	
Cash		260,000

Employee Share Purchase Plans

A company may offer its employees the opportunity to directly purchase shares in the business through an employee share purchase plan (ESPP). These plans frequently offer sales without any brokerage charge, and possibly also at a price somewhat below the market rate.

From an accounting perspective, the main issue with an ESPP is whether it represents a form of compensation to employees. An ESPP is not considered compensatory if it meets all of the following criteria:

- *Employee qualification.* Essentially all employees meeting a limited set of employment qualifications can participate in the plan.

- *Favorable terms.* The terms offered under the plan are no more favorable than those available to investors at large, or does not offer a purchase discount of greater than five percent (which is considered the per-share cost that would otherwise be required to raise funds through a public offering). It is possible to justify a percentage greater than five percent, but the justification must be reassessed on an annual basis.
- *Option features.* The plan only allows a maximum 31-day notice period to enroll in the plan after the share price has been fixed, the share price is based only on the market price on the purchase date, and employees can cancel their participation before the purchase date.

Under the following circumstances, an ESPP is considered to be compensatory, which means that the company must record the difference between the market price of the stock and the lower price at which employees purchase the shares as compensation expense:

- The purchase discount offered under the plan is greater than five percent.
- The purchase price is the lesser of the market price on the grant date or the market price on the purchase date.

EXAMPLE

Armadillo Industries has an employee stock purchase plan, under which employees can purchase shares for a 10% discount from the market price of the company's stock. In the most recent quarter, employees authorized the deduction of $90,000 from their pay, which was used to purchase $100,000 of company stock. Since the discount exceeds the 5% threshold, Armadillo must record the $10,000 discount as compensation expense.

Stock-Based Compensation Disclosures

A company that issues stock-based compensation should disclose sufficient information to ensure that users of its financial statements are aware of the nature of these arrangements, the effect of the resulting compensation cost on the income statement, how the fair value of the services received or instruments granted is derived, and the cash flow effects of these arrangements. Disclosure at this level of detail is not required for interim financial statements.

The following disclosures are considered to be the minimum level of information required to meet the preceding disclosure requirements:

- *General description.* The general terms of the arrangements, including service periods, the maximum term of stock options, and the number of shares authorized for awards.
- *Cash payments.* The cash paid by the company to settle equity instruments that were granted under share-based compensation arrangements.

- *Cash receipts*. The cash paid to the company for the exercise of stock options, and the tax benefit from the exercised stock options.
- *Compensation cost not recognized*. As of the latest balance sheet date, the total cost of compensation related to unvested awards not yet recognized, and the weighted-average period over which this cost will be recognized.
- *Compensation cost*. For each year in which an income statement is presented, the aggregate compensation cost recognized that was related to share-based payment arrangements, net of taxes, as well as any amount capitalized. Also, the terms of any modifications and the related change in cost, and the number of employees affected by the modifications.
- *Fair value assumptions*. For each year for which an income statement is presented, the method used to estimate fair value, and the assumptions incorporated into these estimations, including expected option terms (which includes expected employee behavior), expected volatility and how it is estimated, expected dividends, the risk-free rate, and the discount for post-vesting restrictions. A privately-held company should also disclose the industry sector index and how it calculates volatility from that index.
- *Fair values*. For the most recent year, the number and weighted-average grant-date fair values of those stock options nonvested at the beginning and end of the year, and for those granted, vested, and forfeited during the year.
- *Measurement*. The method used to measure compensation cost from these stock-based payment arrangements.
- *Multi-year information*. For each year for which an income statement is presented, the weighted-average grant date fair values of stock options granted, the intrinsic value of options exercised, share-based liabilities paid, and the aggregate fair value of shares vested.
- *Option information*. For the most recent year, the number and weighted-average exercise prices of those stock options at the beginning and end of the year, as well as for those exercisable at year-end, and for those granted, exercised, forfeited, and expired during the year.
- *Policy*. The company policy for issuing shares related to exercised stock options, including the source of the shares (such as treasury stock). If this policy will result in the repurchase of shares in a later period, state the range or estimated amount of shares that will be repurchased. Also note the policy for estimating expected forfeitures or recognizing forfeitures as they occur.
- *Vested information*. For stock options that have vested or are expected to vest by the balance sheet date, the number of options outstanding, as well as their weighted-average exercise price, aggregate intrinsic value, and weighted-average remaining option term, stated both for options outstanding and options currently exercisable.

EXAMPLE

Armadillo Industries discloses the following information about its stock options as part of its year-end financial statements:

The company's 20X2 employee stock option plan permits the granting of stock options to its employees for up to 2,000,000 shares of common stock. All option awards are granted with an exercise price equal to the market price of Armadillo's stock on the grant date. Option awards vest after four years of service and have 10-year terms. All awards issued thus far vest on an accelerated basis if there is a change in control of the company.

The fair values of all option awards are estimated using a lattice-based model that uses as inputs the assumptions noted in the following table:

	20X2	20X1
Expected dividends	2%	0%
Expected term (years)	4.8 – 7.7	4.3 – 7.2
Expected volatility	30% - 55%	35% - 60%
Weighted-average volatility	45%	47%
Risk-free rate	2.3% - 3.0%	2.5% - 3.2%

The expected term of options granted is based on historical experience; expected volatility ranges are based on the implied volatilities of an industry index of stocks; the risk-free rate is based on the U.S. Treasury yield curve on the grant dates.

Option activity under the Armadillo stock option plan as of December 31, 20X2, and changes during that year are noted in the following table:

Options	Shares (000s)	Weighted-Average Exercise Price	Weighted-Average Remaining Contractual Term	Aggregate Intrinsic Value ($000s)
Outstanding at 1/1/X2	985	$18		
Granted	420	25		
Exercised	-570	17		
Expired or forfeited	-120	23		
Outstanding at 12/31/X2	715	20	5.3	$2,860
Exercisable at 12/31/X2	405	18	4.9	$1,620

The weighted-average grant-date fair value of stock options granted during the years 20X2 and 20X1 were $10.15 and $9.68, respectively. The total intrinsic value of options exercised during the years ended 20X2 and 20X1 were $953,000 and $802,000, respectively.

Nonvested share activity as of December 31, 20X2 and changes during that year are noted in the following table:

Nonvested Shares	Shares (000s)	Weighted-Average Grant-Date Fair Value
Nonvested at 1/1/X1	500	$19.80
Granted	75	24.17
Vested	-120	18.25
Forfeited	-20	23.50
Nonvested at 12/31/X2	435	20.52

As of December 31, 20X2, $8,900,000 of compensation cost related to nonvested share-based compensation arrangements had not yet been recognized. We estimate that this cost will be recognized over a weighted-average period of 4.2 years. The total fair value of shares vested in 20X2 and 20X1 was $2,190,000 and $1,990,000, respectively.

Summary

The measurement of stock-based compensation can be complex, but is not inordinately so, as long as the accounting staff develops a standard procedure for dealing with these arrangements and follows it consistently. It is also useful to gain the cooperation of the human resources department in formulating compensation arrangements that consistently include the same terms, so that the pre-existing accounting procedures can be readily applied to them. The worst-case scenario is when stock-based compensation plans are issued with substantially different terms, which forces the accounting department to adopt unique and detailed accounting plans to deal with each one. In short, a consistently-applied pay system greatly reduces the effort of accounting for stock-based compensation.

Chapter 33
Other Expenses

720 = GAAP codification area for other expenses

Introduction

There are a few sections of GAAP that are a dumping ground for a wide array of topics. In the expenses area, the Other Expenses topic is such a place. It contains relatively brief treatment of a number of completely unrelated expenses, including startup costs, insurance, contributions, property taxes, advertising costs, electronic equipment waste obligations, and reengineering costs. In this chapter, we address the accounting and disclosure requirements for each of these expenses.

Related Chapter

See the Other Assets and Deferred Costs chapter for a discussion of the accounting for direct-response advertising.

Startup Costs

Startup activities are those activities required to organize a new business, introduce a new product, and so forth. Essentially, the accounting for startup activities is to expense them as incurred. While the guidance is simple enough, the key issue is not to assume that other costs similar to start-up costs should be treated in the same way. Thus, it is necessary to review other elements of GAAP to find the proper treatment of other costs, such as customer acquisition costs, loan origination costs, research and development costs, and the cost of internally developed assets.

EXAMPLE

Armadillo Industries is opening a new subsidiary in Argentina that will produce and sell its police body armor products within South America. Armadillo incurs the following expenses, all of which are subject to the guidance in this section:

Accounting and legal startup costs	Feasibility studies
Depreciation of new equipment	Nonrecurring operating losses
Employee salary-related costs	Recruiting costs
Employee training	Travel costs

Insurance Costs

The following sub-sections describe the differing accounting treatment required for certain types of insurance contracts.

Retroactive Contracts

This topic addresses how an insured business accounts for the purchase of a retroactive insurance policy. Any amounts paid by an insured business for retroactive insurance should be charged to expense as incurred. Also, the insured should record a receivable immediately for the recoveries expected under the policy.

If the receivable related to expected recoveries exceeds the amount of insurance premium paid, defer the resulting gain. Amortize the gain over the estimated period when recovery is expected under the contract terms, using the interest method. If it is not possible to estimate the amounts and/or timing of recoveries, recognize the gain based on the proportion of actual to total estimated recoveries.

Claims-Made Contracts

A claims-made insurance policy provides coverage only for those claims reported during the term of a policy. These claims may relate to situations arising prior to the policy period. Also, situations may arise during the coverage period for which no claims are made, and which therefore fall outside of the scope of this insurance.

A claims-made contract may provide coverage for known claims that were reportable prior to the coverage period. If such coverage is part of the contract, the insured should separately account for the retroactive and prospective portions of the contract.

If there is a retroactive portion of the contract, but it is not practicable to separately account for the retroactive and prospective portions, account for the entire contract as a retroactive contract.

EXAMPLE

Armadillo Industries has a claims-made policy for product liability coverage. Prior to extending the insurance coverage with its existing carrier into the new year, Armadillo discusses with its insurer a product-based liability lawsuit that has just been filed against the company. The insurer then alters the contract price from $5 million for the prior year's coverage to $25 million for the next year's coverage.

Because the large increase in the price of the product liability coverage occurs in response to a known incident that was reported to the insurer, Armadillo should assume that the insurance premium contains a large retroactive element.

If the insured business has incurred but not reported liabilities that are insurable under tail coverage (which protects against claims that have not yet been discovered or reported) for which the premium will not exceed a maximum amount, the insured should:

- Record a receivable for expected insurance recoveries; and
- Record the cost of the expected insurance premium

Under this scenario, it may still be necessary to accrue a liability if there are policy limits associated with the insurance.

If the insured company's policy year and fiscal year happen to coincide, any of the following methods, or a combination thereof, can be used to recognize insurance expense:

- Amortize the insurance premium over the year
- Accrue a liability for incurred but not reported costs (which may approximate historical experience)
- Accrue an expected increase in amounts recoverable through insurance

The result should be an annual expense that is the sum of the premium paid, the net change in incurred but not reported liabilities, and the net change in the amount of recoverable insurance. Recognize this annual expense in interim periods based on a method that reflects how insurance costs are actually incurred.

If the insured company's policy year and fiscal year do not coincide, take the following steps to account for claims-made contracts at the *end* of the fiscal year:

- Base the insurance premium component of the amount recognized in interim periods on the estimated premium that will be paid in the later portion of the fiscal year
- Recognize all incurred but not reported claims liabilities
- Recognize insurance recoveries that are to be recovered under the current policy
- Recognize prepaid insurance

If the insured company's policy year and fiscal year do not coincide, take the following steps to account for claims-made contracts during accounting periods *within* the fiscal year:

At the beginning of the fiscal year

1. Estimate the future premium cost of the policy that the insured expects to purchase later in the fiscal year.
2. Estimate that portion of the future premium cost that will carry forward as prepaid insurance after the current fiscal year.
3. Estimate the incurred but not reported liability at the end of the fiscal year, which probably approximates the same amount as of the beginning of the fiscal year, adjusted for historical results.
4. Compute an estimated insurance expense based on the total of the premium cost expiring in the current year, the estimated future premium cost, the

change in incurred but not reported liabilities during the year, and the change in insurance receivables during the year.

5. Recognize the estimated insurance expense ratably over the year, based on how the insurance asset is consumed.

<u>During the fiscal year</u>

*   Review the estimated incurred but not reported liability during interim periods, and adjust the related liability and insurance expense as necessary.
*   If there are unusual claims and incidents during the fiscal year, immediately adjust the estimated year-end liability for incurred but not reported liabilities.

If there are any liabilities for unusual claims that arise during an interim period and/or related amounts recoverable through insurance, recognize them in the interim period as soon as they become evident. If there are expected changes in incurred but not reported liabilities and/or recoverable amounts that do not relate to specific events, recognize these items over the full year, rather than within a specific interim period.

Multiple-Year Retrospectively Rated Contracts

A multiple-year retrospectively rated contract typically provides coverage of liability risks. These contracts include a retrospective provision that allows for changes in the future coverage of the contract, and/or adjustments to the premium, settlements, or refunds. For this type of contract, the insured entity should either:

*   Record a liability in an amount matching any obligation to pay consideration to the insurer that would not have been required if there had been no experience under the contract; or
*   Record an asset in an amount matching the consideration payable to the insured, based on the experience to date under the contract.

There may also be a second part of these contracts that is related to prospective activity, rather than retroactive (historical) experience. For this element of the insurance, the insured should recognize an expense in each accounting period based on the *with-and-without method*; this is the difference between the total contract cost before and after factoring in the experience under the contract for such costs as premium and settlement adjustments, as well as coverage impairments.

If the insured business can terminate the insurance contract prior to the contract termination date, and if doing so would alter the amounts paid, there are two scenarios for measuring the contract liability:

*   *Termination decision made.* If the decision to terminate the contract has been made, base the liability measurement on experience to date.
*   *Termination decision not made.* If the decision to terminate has not yet been made, measure the liability on the lesser of:

   o The incremental amount that would be paid, assuming experience to
     date and contract termination; or
   o The incremental amount that would be paid, assuming experience to
     date and no contract termination.

Contributions Made

The guidance in this section is intended for those businesses that make cash and
other types of contributions, as well as promises to give at some point in the future.
The accounting for contributions by the contributor is as follows:

- *General.* Any contributions made shall be charged to expense as incurred,
  usually with an offset to the asset account from which a contribution is being made, or to the liability account from which a liability is being reduced
  or eliminated.
- *Unconditional promises to give.* If the promise to give is unconditional,
  recognize a contribution expense and offsetting payable.
- *Conditional promises to give.* Do not recognize a contribution expense and
  offsetting payable until such time as the promise becomes unconditional.

If the fair value of an asset transferred to a third party (or a cancelled liability) as a
contribution varies from its carrying amount, recognize a gain or loss on the
difference between the fair value and the carrying amount.

It is acceptable to measure an unconditional promise to give at its net settlement
value (rather than fair value) if the related asset payment or liability cancellation is
to be completed within one year.

Real and Personal Property Taxes

The GAAP treatment of real and personal property taxes is remarkably vague, likely
because the dates on which an expense is assigned to a property owner and the
methods for its calculation are so varied. In essence, a business should accrue a tax
expense on a monthly basis throughout the period when the taxes are to be levied.
The key points are to create a consistently-applied accrual in every accounting
period, and to regularly adjust the accrual to reflect the latest information about the
company's tax liability.

Advertising Costs

Advertising is the promotion of a business or its products, with the intent of creating a positive image or stimulating customer purchases. The costs incurred for advertising can be aggregated into two areas, which are the production of advertisements and their dissemination. The accounting for advertising costs is as follows:

- *Production costs*. Charge advertising production costs to expense as incurred or when the related advertising first takes place.
- *Dissemination costs*. Charge advertising costs to expense as used. For example, charge the cost to air a television advertisement to expense as the airtime is used.

This treatment is based on the belief that the beneficial effects of advertising are short-lived, and because it is difficult to determine the number of periods over which the resulting benefits can be measured. This guidance does not apply to direct-response advertising.

Tip: Sales materials can be accounted for as prepaid supplies, which spreads recognition of the related expense over the usage period until the on-hand supply is used up.

Electronic Equipment Waste Obligations

This is a specialized topic, dealing with the accounting for electronic equipment waste held by private households, as outlined in the European Union's Directive 2002/96/EC. The directive states that historical waste equipment is comprised of all products put on the market on or before August 13, 2005, while all other products are considered to be new waste. Costs relating to new waste are borne solely by the producers of that equipment.

The remediation of historical waste equipment held by private households is to be paid for collectively by the producers selling in the market during the measurement period, with liabilities being proportional to each producer's participation in the market by equipment type.

Given the requirements of the directive, the accounting for historical waste obligations is to record a liability for the obligation, as well as an offsetting expense, which is to be recognized over the measurement period. A producer should alter this liability over time as there are changes in its market share, and as the costs of the program change.

Business and Technology Reengineering

A business may engage in a variety of process reengineering activities to streamline its operations or make those operations more efficient. The cost of business process reengineering activities should be charged to expense as incurred. The same accounting rule holds true even if the reengineering activities are part of a project to acquire or build software for internal use. Examples of the costs that should be charged to expense as incurred are the preparation of requests for proposal, conducting an assessment of current processes, reengineering those processes, and restructuring the workforce.

If a supplier bills the company for services provided, and only some of the services relate to process reengineering, allocate the billed cost to each billed activity based on the relative fair values of the activities. When making this allocation, use objective evidence of fair value, which may not correspond to the prices listed in the supplier's invoice.

This guidance excludes expenditures for any fixed assets associated with business and technology reengineering projects.

Other Expenses Disclosures

There are a relatively small number of disclosures associated with the other expenses topic, which are noted below under separate headings.

Insurance Cost Disclosures

It is not appropriate to net offsetting prepaid insurance and receivables for expected recoveries against insurance liabilities. Instead, they should be reported separately on the balance sheet.

Disclose a change from occurrence-based insurance to claims-made insurance, or when there is a significant reduction in insurance coverage, and it is reasonably possible that a loss was incurred.

Real and Personal Property Tax Disclosures

Include any accrual for real and personal property taxes in the current liabilities section of the balance sheet. When there is a substantial amount of uncertainty about the amount to accrue, describe the accrual as an estimate.

Real and personal property taxes may be stated in the income statement as a separate line item, as a part of the aggregate amount of operating expenses, or distributed among those line items to which the taxes apply.

Advertising Cost Disclosures

Disclose the method used to charge advertising costs to expense, as well as the total advertising cost charged to expense during the accounting period.

EXAMPLE

Armadillo Industries discloses the following information about its advertising expenditures:

Armadillo expenses the production costs of advertising as incurred. For the year ended December 31, 20X5, advertising expense was $4,200,000.

Summary

The topics listed in this section of GAAP represent a smorgasbord of expenses. The only unifying element is that every item listed is some form of expense. Other than that, there is no common treatment that spans multiple topics. Instead, review each topic individually and model the entity's accounting procedures accordingly. Despite the lack of cohesion, this is a chapter that the reader may return to with some frequency, since it addresses several areas that are of concern to most businesses, such as advertising, property taxes, and insurance costs.

Chapter 34
Research and Development

> 730 = GAAP codification area for research and development

Introduction

Many companies invest considerable amounts in their research and development activities. In this chapter, we describe how most of these expenditures must be charged to expense as incurred, as well as the minority of situations where expense deferral is allowed. The guidance in this chapter applies to all entities.

Related Chapters

See the following chapters for discussions of issues related to research and development:

- *Business Combinations*. Covers the accounting for acquired research and development assets.
- *Intangibles*. Covers the accounting for acquired intangible assets.

Overview of Research and Development

Research and development involves those activities that create or improve products or processes. Examples of activities typically considered to fall within the research and development functional area include the following:

Research to discover new knowledge	Modifying formulas, products, or processes
Applying new research findings	Designing and testing prototypes
Formulating product and process designs	Designing tools that involve new technology
Testing products and processes	Designing and operating a pilot plant

The basic problem with research and development expenditures is that the future benefits associated with these expenditures are sufficiently uncertain that it is difficult to record the expenditures as an asset. Given these uncertainties, GAAP mandates that all research and development expenditures be charged to expense as incurred. The chief variance from this guidance is in a business combination, where the acquirer can recognize the fair value of research and development assets.

The basic rule of charging all research and development expenditures to expense is not entirely pervasive, since there are exceptions, as noted below:

- *Assets.* If materials or fixed assets have been acquired that have alternative future uses, record them as assets. The materials should be charged to expense as consumed, while depreciation should be used to gradually reduce the carrying amount of the fixed assets. Conversely, if there are no alternative future uses, charge these costs to expense as incurred.
- *Computer software.* If computer software is acquired for use in a research and development project, charge the cost to expense as incurred. However, if there are future alternative uses for the software, capitalize its cost and depreciate the software over its useful life.
- *Contracted services.* If the company is billed by third parties for research work conducted on behalf of the company, charge these invoices to expense.
- *Indirect costs.* A reasonable amount of overhead expenses should be allocated to research and development activities.
- *Purchased intangibles.* If intangible assets are acquired from third parties and these assets have alternative uses, they are to be accounted for as intangible assets. However, if the intangibles are purchased for a specific research project and there are no alternative future uses, charge them to expense as incurred.
- *Software development.* If software is developed for use in research and development activities, charge the associated costs to expense as incurred, without exception.
- *Wages.* Charge the costs of salaries, wages, and related costs to expense as incurred.

Tip: *Alternative future uses* can include other research and development projects, or other uses.

There may also be research and development arrangements where a third party (a sponsor) provides funding for the research and development activities of a business. The arrangements may be designed to shift licensing rights, intellectual property ownership, an equity stake, or a share in the profits to the sponsors. The business conducting the research and development activities may be paid a fixed fee or some form of cost reimbursement arrangement by the sponsors.

These arrangements are frequently constructed as limited partnerships, where a related party fulfills the role of general partner. The general partner may be authorized to obtain additional funding by selling limited-partner interests, or extending loans or advances to the partnership that may be repaid from future royalties.

When an entity is a party to a research and development arrangement, several accounting issues must be resolved, which are:

- *Loans or advances issued.* If the business lends or advances funds to third parties, and repayment is based entirely on whether there are economic benefits associated with the research and development work, charge these amounts to expense.

- *Nonrefundable advances.* Defer the recognition of any nonrefundable advance payments that will be used for research and development activities, and recognize them as expenses when the related goods are delivered or services performed. If at any point it is not expected that the goods will be delivered or services performed, charge the remaining deferred amount to expense.
- *Obligation to perform services.* If repayment of the funds provided by the funding parties is solely dependent upon the results of the related research and development activities, account for the repayment obligation as a contract to perform work for others.
- *Repayment obligation.* If there is an obligation to repay the funding parties or the business has indicated an intent to do so, no matter what the outcome of the research and development may be, recognize a liability for the amount of the repayment, and charge research and development costs to expense as incurred. This accounting is also required if there is a significant related party relationship between the business and the funding entities. This scenario also applies if the funding parties can require the business to purchase their interest in the partnership, or if the funding parties automatically receive securities from the business upon termination of the arrangement.
- *Warrants issuance.* If the business issues warrants as part of a funding arrangement, allocate a portion of paid-in funds to paid-in capital. The amount allocated to warrants should be their fair value as of the date of the arrangement.

Research and Development Disclosures

When there are research and development expenditures, disclose the total amount charged to expense for every period in which an income statement is presented. Also disclose the research and development costs incurred relating to computer software to be marketed outside of the company.

If a company has a contractual arrangement to perform research and development activities for other parties, it must disclose the following information:

- *Financial results.* State the compensation earned and costs incurred under the contractual arrangements for each accounting period presented.
- *Terms.* Describe the terms of each research and development arrangement.

Aggregation of the financial results for more than one research and development contract is acceptable, unless separate disclosure is needed to better show their impact on the financial statements.

Summary

Much of the GAAP guidance concerning research and development relates to the use of partnerships to funnel cash to research-specific operations that may or may not pay off with usable results. However, most organizations conduct all of their research and development activities in-house, where the accounting rule is a simple one – charge all expenditures to expense as incurred.

Chapter 35
Income Taxes

740 = GAAP codification area for income taxes

Introduction

If a company generates a profit, it will probably be necessary to record income tax expense that is a percentage of the profit. However, the calculation of income tax is not so simple, since it may be based on a number of adjustments to net income that are allowed by the taxing authorities. The result can be remarkably complex tax measurements. In this chapter, we describe the general concepts of income tax accounting, as well as the calculation of the appropriate tax rate, the evaluation of tax positions, how to treat deferred taxes, the taxation of undistributed earnings, how to record taxes in interim periods, and other related topics.

Related Chapters

See the following chapters for discussions of issues related to income taxes:

- *Business Combinations*. Covers how the structure of business combinations is impacted by tax considerations.
- *Compensation – Stock Compensation*. Discusses the impact of taxes on payments made in stock.

Overview of Income Taxes

Before delving into the income taxes topic, we must clarify several concepts that are essential to understanding the related accounting. The concepts are:

- *Temporary differences*. A company may record an asset or liability at one value for financial reporting purposes, while maintaining a separate record of a different value for tax purposes. The difference is caused by the tax recognition policies of taxing authorities, who may require the deferral or acceleration of certain items for tax reporting purposes. These differences are temporary, since the assets will eventually be recovered and the liabilities settled, at which point the differences will be terminated. A difference that results in a taxable amount in a later period is called a *taxable temporary difference*, while a difference that results in a deductible amount in a later period is called a *deductible temporary difference*. Examples of temporary differences are:

- o Revenues or gains that are taxable either prior to or after they are recognized in the financial statements. For example, an allowance for doubtful accounts may not be immediately tax deductible, but instead must be deferred until specific receivables are declared bad debts.
- o Expenses or losses that are tax deductible either prior to or after they are recognized in the financial statements. For example, some fixed assets are tax deductible at once, but can only be recognized through long-term depreciation in the financial statements.
- o Assets whose tax basis is reduced by investment tax credits.

EXAMPLE

In its most recent year of operations, Table Furniture earns $250,000. Table also has $30,000 of taxable temporary differences and $80,000 of deductible temporary differences. Based on this information, Table's taxable income in the current year is calculated as:

$250,000 Profit - $30,000 Taxable temporary differences + $80,000 Deductible temporary differences

= $300,000 Taxable profit

- • *Carrybacks and carryforwards.* A company may find that it has more tax deductions or tax credits (from an operating loss) than it can use in the current year's tax return. If so, it has the option of offsetting these amounts against the taxable income or tax liabilities (respectively) of the tax returns in earlier periods, or in future periods. Carrying these amounts back to the tax returns of prior periods is always more valuable, since the company can apply for a tax refund at once. Thus, these excess tax deductions or tax credits are carried back first, with any remaining amounts being reserved for use in future periods. Carryforwards eventually expire, if not used within a certain number of years. A company should recognize a receivable for the amount of taxes paid in prior years that are refundable due to a carryback. A deferred tax asset can be realized for a carryforward, but possibly with an offsetting valuation allowance that is based on the probability that some portion of the carryforward will not be realized.

EXAMPLE

Spastic Corporation has created $100,000 of deferred tax assets through the diligent generation of losses for the past five years. Based on the company's poor competitive stance, management believes it is more likely than not that there will be inadequate profits (if any) against which the deferred tax assets can be offset. Accordingly, Spastic recognizes a valuation allowance in the amount of $100,000 that fully offsets the deferred tax assets.

- *Deferred tax liabilities and assets.* When there are temporary differences, the result can be deferred tax assets and deferred tax liabilities, which represent the change in taxes payable or refundable in future periods.

EXAMPLE

Armadillo Industries elects to account for a government contract on the percentage of completion method for financial reporting purposes, and on the completed contract method for tax reporting purposes. By doing so, the company recognizes income in its financial statements throughout the term of the contract, but does not do so for tax reporting purposes until the end of the contract.

EXAMPLE

Uncanny Corporation has recorded the following carrying amount and tax basis information for certain of its assets and liabilities:

(000s)	Carrying Amount	Tax Basis	Temporary Difference
Accounts receivable	$12,000	$12,250	-$250
Prepaid expenses	350	350	0
Inventory	8,000	8,400	-400
Fixed assets	17,300	14,900	2,400
Accounts payable	3,700	3,700	0
Totals	$41,350	$39,600	$1,750

In the table, Uncanny has included a reserve for bad debts in its accounts receivable figure and for obsolete inventory in its inventory number, neither of which are allowed for tax purposes. Also, the company applied an accelerated form of depreciation to its fixed assets for tax purposes and straight-line depreciation for its financial reporting. These three items account for the total temporary difference between the carrying amount and tax basis of the items shown in the table.

All of these factors can result in complex calculations to arrive at the appropriate income tax information to recognize and report in the financial statements.

Accounting for Income Taxes

Despite the complexity inherent in income taxes, the essential accounting in this area is derived from the need to recognize two items, which are:

- *Current year.* The recognition of a tax liability or tax asset, based on the estimated amount of income taxes payable or refundable for the current year.

- *Future years*. The recognition of a deferred tax liability or tax asset, based on the estimated effects in future years of carryforwards and temporary differences.

Based on the preceding points, the general accounting for income taxes is:

+/-	Create a tax liability for estimated taxes payable, and/or create a tax asset for tax refunds, that relate to the current or prior years
+/-	Create a deferred tax liability for estimated future taxes payable, and/or create a deferred tax asset for estimated future tax refunds, that can be attributed to temporary differences and carryforwards
=	Total income tax expense in the period

Tax Positions

A tax position is a stance taken by a company in its tax return that measures tax assets and liabilities, and which results in the permanent reduction or temporary deferral of income taxes. When constructing the proper accounting for a tax position, the accountant follows these steps:

1. Evaluate whether the tax position taken has merit, based on the tax regulations.
2. If the tax position has merit, measure the amount that can be recognized in the financial statements.
3. Determine the probability and amount of settlement with the taxing authorities. Recognition should only be made when it is more likely than not (i.e., more than 50% probability) that the company's tax position will be sustained once it has been examined by the governing tax authorities.
4. Recognize the tax position, if warranted.

Tip: Given the large financial impact of some tax positions, it makes sense to obtain an outside opinion of a proposed position by a tax expert, and document the results of that review thoroughly. This is helpful not only if the position is reviewed by the taxing authorities, but also when it is reviewed by the company's outside auditors.

EXAMPLE

Armadillo Industries takes a tax position on an issue and determines that the position qualifies for recognition, and so should be recognized. The following table shows the estimated possible outcomes of the tax position, along with their associated probabilities:

Possible Outcome	Probability of Occurrence	Cumulative Probability
$250,000	5%	5%
200,000	20%	25%
150,000	40%	65%
100,000	20%	85%
50,000	10%	95%
0	5%	100%

Since the benefit amount just beyond the 50% threshold level is $150,000, Armadillo should recognize a tax benefit of $150,000.

If a company initially concludes that the probability of a tax position being sustained is less than 50%, it should not initially recognize the tax position. However, it can recognize the position at a later date if the probability increases to be in excess of 50%, or if the tax position is settled through interaction with the taxing authorities, or the statute of limitations keeps the taxing authorities from challenging the tax position. If a company subsequently concludes that it will change a tax position previously taken, it should recognize the effect of the change in the period in which it alters its tax position. An entity can also derecognize a tax position that it had previously recognized if the probability of the tax position being sustained drops below 50%.

EXAMPLE

Armadillo Industries takes a tax position under which it accelerates the depreciation of certain production equipment well beyond the normally-allowed taxable rate, resulting in a deferred tax liability after three years of $120,000.

After three years, a tax court ruling convinces Armadillo management that its tax position is untenable. Consequently, the company recognizes a tax liability for the $120,000 temporary difference. At the company's current 35% tax rate, this results in increased taxes of $42,000 and the elimination of the temporary difference.

If there is a change in the tax laws or tax rates, a business cannot recognize alterations in its income tax liability in advance of the enactment of these laws and rates. Instead, the company must wait until enactment has been completed, and can then recognize the changes on the enactment date.

Deferred Tax Expense

Deferred tax expense is the net change in the deferred tax liabilities and assets of a business during a period of time. The amount of deferred taxes should be compiled for each tax-paying component of a business that provides a consolidated tax return. Doing so requires that the business complete the following steps:

1. Identify the existing temporary differences and carryforwards.
2. Determine the deferred tax liability amount for those temporary differences that are taxable, using the applicable tax rate.
3. Determine the deferred tax asset amount for those temporary differences that are deductible, as well as any operating loss carryforwards, using the applicable tax rate.
4. Determine the deferred tax asset amount for any carryforwards involving tax credits.
5. Create a valuation allowance for the deferred tax assets if there is a more than 50% probability that the company will not realize some portion of these assets. Any changes to this allowance are to be recorded within income from continuing operations on the income statement. The need for a valuation allowance is especially likely if a business has a history of letting various carryforwards expire unused, or it expects to incur losses in the next few years.

Applicable Tax Rate

In general, when measuring a deferred tax liability or asset, a business should use the tax rate that it expects to apply to the taxable income that results from the realization of deferred tax assets or settlement of deferred tax liabilities. Also consider the following issues:

- *Alternative minimum tax*. The alternative minimum tax may increase the effective tax rate used. It may be necessary to reduce the deferred tax asset for the alternative minimum tax credit carryforward with a valuation allowance, if it is more than 50% probable that the asset will not be realized.
- *Discounting*. Deferred taxes are not to be discounted to their present value when they are recognized.
- *Graduated tax rates*. If the applicable tax law has graduated tax rates, and the graduated rates significantly affect the average tax rate paid, use the average tax rate that applies to the estimated annual taxable income in those periods when deferred tax liabilities are settled or deferred tax assets are realized. If a company earns such a large amount of income that the graduated rate is not significantly different from the top-tier tax rate, use the top-tier rate for the estimation of annual taxable income.

- *New tax laws or rates.* A company should adjust the amount of its deferred tax liabilities and assets for the effect of any changes in tax laws or tax rates, which shall be recorded within income from continuing operations. Doing so may also call for an adjustment to the related valuation allowance.

Interest and Penalties

When there is a requirement in the tax law that interest be paid when income taxes are not fully paid, a company should begin recognizing the amount of this interest expense as soon as the expense would be scheduled to begin accruing under the tax law.

If a company takes a tax position that will incur penalties, it should recognize the related penalty expense as soon as the company takes the position in a tax return. Whether penalties should be recognized may depend on management's judgment of whether a tax position exceeds the minimum statutory threshold required to avoid the payment of a penalty.

If a tax position is eventually sustained, reverse in the current period any related interest and penalties that had been accrued in previous periods under the expectation that the position would not be sustained.

Intraperiod Tax Allocation

Intraperiod tax allocation is the allocation of income taxes to different parts of the results appearing in the income statement of a business, so that some items are stated net of tax. Income taxes are allocated among the following items:

- Continuing operations
- Discontinued operations
- Other comprehensive income
- Items assigned directly to shareholders' equity

The intraperiod tax allocation concept is used to reveal the "true" results of certain transactions net of all effects, rather than disaggregating them from income taxes. For example, a company records a gain of $1 million. Its tax rate is 35%, so the company reports the gain net of taxes, at $650,000.

When allocating income taxes among the various income statement items just noted, allocate the taxes using either of the following methodologies:

- *One allocation target.* First assign income taxes to continuing operations, and then assign all remaining income taxes to the remaining allocation target.
- *Multiple allocation targets.* First assign income taxes to continuing operations, and then assign the remaining income taxes to the other items in proportion to their individual impact on the amount of remaining income taxes.

Note that, though the income tax included in these net calculations is usually an expense, it may also be a credit, so that any of the preceding items presented net of tax would include the tax credit.

Most elements of the income statement are not presented net of the intraperiod tax allocation. For example, revenue, the cost of goods sold, and administrative expenses are not presented net of income taxes.

EXAMPLE

Uncanny Corporation earns $500,000 of income from continuing operations, and experiences a loss of $150,000 from a discontinued operation. At the beginning of the year, Uncanny had a $600,000 tax loss carryforward. Uncanny applies the tax loss carryforward against the $500,000 income from continuing operations. Since the offset eliminates the $500,000 of income from operations, no income tax is applied to it. The company then applies the remaining $100,000 of tax loss carryforward against the loss from a discontinued operation, leaving $50,000 of taxable loss to be reported for the discontinued operation.

Taxes Related to Undistributed Earnings

There are a few instances where a business is not required to engage in the standard accounting and disclosure of deferred income taxes for temporary differences. These exceptions relate to investments in subsidiaries and corporate joint ventures, and whether they remit earnings to the corporate parent or investors, respectively.

A corporate subsidiary typically remits earnings to the parent entity only after a number of issues have been considered, such as the need for cash by the subsidiary and parent, tax issues, and creditor and government restrictions. Funds may be remitted from a corporate joint venture based on the payout clauses in the original joint venture agreement, or with the agreement of the investing parties. In many situations, no funds are remitted, or only a small portion of the full amount of earnings.

Generally, the accounting for these undistributed earnings is to include them in the earnings of the parent entity, which results in a temporary difference, unless there is a means by which an investment in a domestic subsidiary can be recovered, free of tax. The same accounting approach applies to the pretax income of corporate joint ventures that are unlikely to be remitted to investors, and where the investors account for their investments in the joint ventures with the equity method.

A corporate joint venture may have a limited life span that will likely trigger the release of undistributed earnings to investors at the end of that lifespan. If so, investors should record deferred taxes when the profits or losses of the venture are recorded in its financial statements.

An investor entity should record a deferred tax liability when there is an excess of the reported taxable temporary difference over the tax basis:

- Of an investment in a domestic subsidiary
- In an investee that is $\leq 50\%$ owned

A temporary difference is not considered a taxable temporary difference when there is a method permitted under the tax law for recovering the amount of an investment tax-free, *and* the investing entity expects to use that method. For example, it is possible to do so under certain types of acquisition structures, such as when a subsidiary is merged into the parent company, with noncontrolling shareholders receiving the stock of the parent company in exchange for their shares in the subsidiary.

When there is an excess of tax basis for an investment in a subsidiary or joint venture over the amount recorded in the financial statements, and the temporary difference will reverse in the foreseeable future, the corporate parent or investor should recognize a deferred tax asset in the amount of the difference. For example, the decision to sell a subsidiary would make it likely that a temporary difference will reverse in the near future.

The tax benefit associated with a deferred tax asset should be recognized when it is more than 50% probable that the temporary difference will reverse in the foreseeable future. Similarly, a tax expense should be recognized when it is more than 50% probable that a deferred tax liability will reverse in the foreseeable future.

It may be necessary to create a valuation allowance that will offset a deferred tax asset. The amount of this allowance (if any) shall be based on a periodic assessment of the allowance.

The parent entity should *not* accrue income taxes for unremitted earnings only in those situations where a subsidiary will permanently retain its earnings (which requires a reinvestment plan), or where the remittance will involve a tax-free liquidation. If circumstances change, and it appears that some portion of a subsidiary's undistributed earnings will be remitted, the parent should accrue income taxes related to the amount that will be remitted. If the reverse situation arises, where it no longer appears likely that earnings will be remitted, reduce the amount of income tax expense that had been previously recognized.

Interim Reporting

If a business reports its financial results during interim reporting periods (such as monthly or quarterly financial statements), it must report income taxes in those interim reports. In general, the proper accounting is to report income taxes using an estimated effective tax rate in all of the interim periods. However, the application of this general principle varies somewhat as noted below:

- *Ordinary income.* Calculate the income tax on ordinary income at the estimated annual effective tax rate.
- *Other items.* Calculate and recognize the income tax on all items other than ordinary income at the rates that are applicable when the items occur. This means that the related tax effect is recognized in the period in which the underlying items occur.

The following factors apply to the determination of the estimated annual effective tax rate:

- The tax benefit associated with any applicable operating loss carryforward
- The tax effect of any valuation allowance used to offset the deferred tax asset
- Anticipated investment tax credits (for the amount expected to be used within the year)
- Foreign tax rates
- Capital gains rates
- The effects of new tax legislation, though only after it has been passed
- Other applicable factors

EXAMPLE

In the current fiscal year, Armadillo Industries anticipates $1,000,000 of ordinary income, to which will be applied the statutory tax rate of 40%, which will result in an income tax expense of $400,000. Armadillo also expects to take advantage of a $100,000 investment tax credit. Thus, the effective tax rate for the year is expected to be 30%, which is calculated as $300,000 of net taxes, divided by $1,000,000 of ordinary income.

Do not include in the determination of the estimated annual effective tax rate the effect of taxes related to unusual or discontinued operations that are expected to be reported separately in the financial statements.

The estimated tax rate is to be reviewed at the end of each interim period and adjusted as necessary, based on the latest estimates of taxable income to be reported for the full year. If it is not possible to derive an estimated tax rate, it may be necessary to instead use the actual effective tax rate for the year to date.

If the estimated tax rate is revised in an interim period from the rate used in a prior period, use the new estimate to derive the year-to-date tax on ordinary income for all interim periods to date.

The tax benefit associated with a loss recorded in an earlier interim period may not be recognized, on the grounds that it is less than 50% probable that the benefit will be realized. If so, do not recognize any income tax for ordinary income reported in subsequent periods until the unrecognized tax benefit associated with the original loss has been offset with income.

EXAMPLE

Through its first two quarters, Uncanny Corporation has experienced losses of $400,000 and $600,000. Management concludes that it is more likely than not that the tax benefit associated with these losses will not be realized. The company then earns profits in the third and fourth quarters, resulting in the following application of taxes at the statutory 40% corporate rate:

(000s)	Ordinary Income		Income Tax		
	Current Period	Cumulative	Cumulative Tax (40%)	Less Previous Amount	Tax Provision
Quarter 1	-$400	-$400	--	---	--
Quarter 2	-600	-1,000	--	---	--
Quarter 3	1,100	100	$40	---	$40
Quarter 4	300	400	160	$40	120
Totals	$400				$160

If a company records a loss during an interim period, the company should only recognize the tax effects of the loss (i.e., a corresponding reduction in taxes) when there is an expectation that the tax reduction will be realized later in the year, or will be recognized as a deferred tax asset by year-end. This recognition may occur later in the year, if it later becomes more likely than not that the tax effects of the loss can be realized.

EXAMPLE

Uncanny Corporation has a history of recording losses in its first and second quarters, after which sales increase during the summer and winter holiday seasons. In the first half of the current year, Uncanny records a $1,000,000 loss, but expects a $2,000,000 profit in the final half of the year. Based on the company's history of seasonal sales, realization of the tax loss appears to be more likely than not, so Uncanny records the tax effect of the loss in the first half of the year.

If a business is subject to a variety of tax rates because of its operations in multiple tax jurisdictions, the estimated tax rate shall be based on a single tax rate for the entire company. When developing the single company-wide tax rate, exclude the effects of ordinary losses within jurisdictions, and develop a separate estimated tax rate for those jurisdictions. Also, if it is impossible to estimate a tax rate or ordinary income in a foreign jurisdiction, exclude that jurisdiction from the computation of the company-wide tax rate.

A company may decide to record a change in accounting principle (see the Accounting Changes and Error Corrections chapter). If so, the amount of the change included in retained earnings at the beginning of the fiscal year shall include the effect of the applicable amount of tax expense or benefit, employing the tax rate used for the full fiscal year. If the change in principle is made in an interim period other than the first interim period of a fiscal year, retrospectively apply the change to the preceding interim periods in the same year; when doing so, apply the estimated tax rate that originally applied to those periods, modified for the effects of the change in principle.

Income Taxes Presentation

The following income tax issues can affect the presentation of tax information in the financial statements:

- *Deferred tax accounts*. Classify deferred tax assets and deferred tax liabilities as noncurrent amounts.
- *Interest and penalties*. Any recognized interest expense related to tax positions can be classified within either the interest expense or income taxes line items. Any penalties expense related to tax positions can be classified within either the income taxes or some other expense line items.
- *Intraperiod tax allocation*. If income taxes are being allocated among income statement line items in an interim period, allocate taxes based on the estimated amount of annual ordinary income, plus other items that have occurred during the year to date.
- *Netting*. Within a tax jurisdiction for a single entity, it is permissible to net the noncurrent deferred tax assets and the noncurrent deferred tax liabilities. Do not net those deferred tax assets and deferred tax liabilities that are attributed to unrelated tax jurisdictions or components of the business.
- *Tax status*. If there is a change in the tax status of an entity, record the change within the income from continuing operations section of the income statement.
- *Undistributed earnings*. All changes in the income tax accruals related to undistributed earnings from subsidiaries and joint ventures should be recorded in the income tax expense line item.

Income Taxes Disclosure

A business should disclose the following information in its financial statements that relates to income taxes, broken down by where the information should be disclosed.

Balance Sheet

The following information about income taxes should be disclosed within the balance sheet or the accompany notes:

- *Carryforwards*. The amounts of all operating loss carryforwards and tax credit carryforwards, as well as their related expiration dates.
- *Deferrals*. The total of all deferred tax liabilities, the total of all deferred tax assets, and the total valuation allowance associated with the deferred tax assets. Also disclose the net change in the valuation allowance during the year.
- *Tax status*. A change in tax status, if the change occurred after the end of the reporting year but before the related financial statements have been issued or are available to be issued.

- *Temporary differences and carryforwards.* The types of significant temporary differences and carryforwards, if the company is not publicly-held. If the entity is publicly-held, it must also disclose the tax effect of each temporary difference and carryforward that causes a significant part of the reported deferred tax assets and liabilities.
- *Unrecognized tax benefits, offsetting of.* If there is an unrecognized tax benefit, present it as a reduction of any deferred tax assets for a tax credit carryforward, a net operating loss carryforward, or a similar tax loss. If there is no offset available, present the unrecognized tax benefit as a liability.
- *Valuation allowance.* That portion of the valuation allowance (if any) related to deferred tax assets for which recognized tax benefits are to be credited to contributed capital (such as a deductible expenditure that reduces the proceeds from a stock issuance).

EXAMPLE

Armadillo Industries discloses the following information about the realizability of its deferred tax assets:

The company has recorded a $10 million deferred tax asset, which reflects the $25 million benefit to be derived from loss carryforwards. These carryforwards expire during the period 20X5 to 20X9. The realization of this tax asset is dependent upon the company generating a sufficient amount of taxable income before the loss carryforwards expire. Management believes it is more likely than not that all $10 million of the deferred tax asset will be realized.

Income Statement

The following information about income taxes should be disclosed within the income statement or the accompanying notes:

- *Comparison to statutory rate.* The nature of significant reasons why the reported income tax differs from the statutory tax rate, for a privately-held company. Also, expand the discussion to a numerical reconciliation, if the entity is publicly-held.
- *Interest and penalties.* The amount of interest and penalties recognized in the period.
- *Tax allocations.* The income tax amount allocated to continuing operations and to other items.
- *Tax components.* The components of income taxes attributable to continuing operations, including the current tax expense, deferred tax expense, investment tax credits, government grants, benefits related to operating loss carryforwards, the tax expense resulting from the allocation of tax benefits to contributed capital, adjustments related to enacted tax laws or rates, adjustments from a change in tax status, and adjustments to the beginning valuation allowance.

EXAMPLE

Armadillo Industries discloses the following information about its income taxes in the notes accompanying its financial statements:

(000s)	
Current tax expense	$810
Deferred tax expense	1,240
Tax expense from continuing operations	$2,050
Tax expense at statutory rate	$2,250
Benefit of investment tax credits	-80
Benefit of operating loss carryforwards	-120
Tax expense from continuing operations	$2,050

Other

The following disclosures are not associated with a particular financial statement. They must be disclosed as part of the general set of financial statements.

- *Examination years*. The tax years remaining that are subject to examination by taxing authorities.
- *Impact on tax rate*. If the entity is publicly-held, the amount of unrecognized tax benefits that would impact the effective tax rate if they were recognized.
- *Interim period tax variations*. If the application of accounting standards for income taxes in interim periods results in a significant variation from the usual income tax percentage, the reasons for the variation.
- *Policies*. The policy for the classification of interest and penalty expenses. Also, the policy for the methods used to account for investment tax credits.
- *Tax holiday*. If the entity is publicly-held, the aggregate and per-share effect of a tax holiday, a description of the circumstances, and when the tax holiday will end.
- *Undistributed earnings*. Whenever a deferred tax liability is not recognized, disclose the following:
    - Description of the underlying temporary differences, and what would cause them to be taxable
    - The cumulative amount of each temporary difference
    - The amount related to permanent investments in foreign subsidiaries and foreign joint ventures, or a statement that the amount cannot be determined
    - The amount related to permanent investment in domestic subsidiaries and domestic joint ventures

- *Unrecognized tax benefits reconciliation.* If the entity is publicly-held, a tabular reconciliation of unrecognized tax changes during the period, including changes caused by tax positions taken in the current period and separately for the prior period, decreases based on settlements concluded, and any decreases caused by a lapse in the statute of limitations.

EXAMPLE

Uncanny Corporation discloses the following reconciliation of its unrecognized tax benefits:

(000s)	20X4	20X3
Balance at January 1	$5,170	$4,080
Additions based on tax positions related to the current year	880	1,530
Additions for tax positions of prior years	240	930
Reductions for tax positions of prior years	-390	-570
Settlements	-2,810	-800
Balance at December 31	$3,090	$5,170

- *Unrecognized tax benefits, changes to.* If unrecognized tax benefits are expected to change significantly within the next 12 months, the reason for the change, the type of event that will cause the change, and the estimated range of the change (or a statement that the range cannot be estimated).

Summary

Many accountants consider income tax accounting to be an area best left to a tax specialist, who churns through the information provided and creates a set of tax-related journal entries. While this approach should result in accurate tax accounting, it does not give management a good view of how its actions are affecting the taxes the company is paying – instead, the tax accounting function is treated as a black box whose contents are unknown to all, save the tax specialist who guards it.

A better approach is to engage the management team in tax planning by instructing them on the essential tax issues that can be impacted by strategic and tactical decisions. Even if management does not become conversant at a detailed level in how their actions impact income taxes, they will at least know when to call in a tax expert to advise them. Thus, a certain amount of transparency in the tax area can improve the results of a business.

Chapter 36
Business Combinations

805 = GAAP codification area for business combinations

Introduction

The business combination, or acquisition, is a relatively uncommon event that entails a considerable amount of detailed accounting. At its least-complex level, the accounting involves the allocation of the purchase price to the acquiree's assets and liabilities, with any overage assigned to a goodwill asset. However, there are a multitude of additional issues that may apply, such as noncontrolling interests, reverse acquisitions, asset purchases, pushdown accounting, income taxes, and more. This chapter deals with the accounting required for all of these issues.

Related Chapters

See the following chapters for discussions of the recognition of certain assets and liabilities, which overrides the fair value recognition basis used in this chapter:

- Income Taxes
- Intangibles – Goodwill and Other
- Compensation – Retirement Benefits
- Compensation – Stock Compensation
- Property, Plant, and Equipment

Overview of Business Combinations

A business combination has occurred when a group of assets acquired and liabilities assumed constitute a business. A business exists when processes are applied to inputs to create outputs. Examples of inputs are fixed assets, intellectual property, inventory, and employees. An output is considered to have the ability to generate a return to investors.

A business combination must be accounted for using the *acquisition method*. This method requires the following steps:

1. *Identify the acquirer.* The entity that gains control of the acquiree is the acquirer. This is typically the entity that pays assets or incurs liabilities as a result of a transaction, or whose owners receive the largest portion of the voting rights in the combined entity. If a variable interest entity is acquired, the main beneficiary of that entity is the acquirer. One of the combining entities must be the acquirer.

2. *Determine the acquisition date.* The acquisition date is when the acquirer gains control of the acquiree, which is typically the closing date.
3. *Recognize and measure all assets acquired and liabilities assumed.* These measurements should be at the fair values of the acquired assets and liabilities as of the acquisition date.
4. *Recognize any noncontrolling interest in the acquiree.* The amount recognized should be the fair value of the noncontrolling interest.
5. *Recognize and measure any goodwill or gain from a bargain purchase.* See the Goodwill or Gain from Bargain Purchase section for a discussion of goodwill and bargain purchases.

There are two types of business combinations that can result in some modification of the preceding accounting treatment. These types are:

- *Step acquisition.* A business may already own a minority interest in another entity, and then acquires an additional equity interest at a later date that results in an acquisition event. In this situation, the acquirer measures the fair value of its existing equity interest in the acquiree at the acquisition date, and recognizes a gain or loss in earnings at that time. If some of this gain or loss had previously been recognized in other comprehensive income, reclassify it into earnings.
- *No transfer of consideration.* There are rare cases where no consideration is paid while gaining control of an acquiree, such as when the acquiree repurchases enough of its own shares to raise an existing investor into a majority ownership position. In this situation, recognize and measure the noncontrolling interest(s) in the acquiree.

There are a number of additional issues that can affect the accounting for a business combination, as outlined below:

- *Contingent consideration.* Some portion of the consideration paid to the owners of the acquiree may be contingent upon future events or circumstances. If an event occurs after the acquisition date that alters the amount of consideration paid, such as meeting a profit or cash flow target, the accounting varies depending on the type of underlying consideration paid, as noted next:
  - *Asset or liability consideration.* If the consideration paid is with assets or liabilities, remeasure these items at their fair values until such time as the related consideration has been fully resolved, and recognize the related gains or losses in earnings.
  - *Equity consideration.* If the consideration paid is in equity, do not remeasure the amount of equity paid.

- *Provisional accounting.* If the accounting for a business combination is incomplete at the end of a reporting period, report provisional amounts, and

413

later adjust these amounts to reflect information that existed as of the acquisition date.

- *New information*. If new information becomes available about issues that existed at the acquisition date concerning the acquiree, adjust the recordation of assets and liabilities as appropriate.

EXAMPLE

Armadillo Industries acquires Cleveland Container on December 31, 20X3. Armadillo hires an independent appraiser to value Cleveland, but does not expect a valuation report for three months. In the meantime, Armadillo issues its December 31 financial statements with a provisional fair value of $4,500,000 for the acquisition. Three months later, the appraiser reports a valuation of $4,750,000 as of the acquisition date, based on an unexpectedly high valuation for a number of fixed assets.

In Armadillo's March 31 financial statements, it adjusts the asset records to increase the carrying amount of fixed assets by $250,000, as well as to reduce the amount of goodwill by the same amount.

Any changes to the initial accounting for an acquisition must be offset against the recorded amount of goodwill. These changes to the initial provisional amounts should be recorded in the period in which the adjustments were determined.

The measurement period during which the recordation of an acquisition may be adjusted ends as soon as the acquirer receives all remaining information concerning issues existing as of the acquisition date, not to exceed one year from the acquisition date.

The acquirer will probably incur a number of costs related to an acquisition, such as fees for valuations, legal advice, accounting services, and finder's fees. These costs are to be charged to expense as incurred.

Identifiable Assets and Liabilities, and Noncontrolling Interests

When the acquirer recognizes an acquisition transaction, it should recognize identifiable assets and liabilities separately from goodwill, and at their fair values as of the acquisition date. The following special situations also apply:

- No asset or liability is recognized in relation to an acquired operating lease in which the acquiree is the lessee, except to the extent of any favorable or unfavorable lease feature relative to market terms, or the willingness of third parties to acquire a lease even at market rates.
- Do not include any costs that the acquirer expects to incur in the future, but is not obligated to incur in relation to the acquiree, such as possible employee relocation costs.

It is entirely possible that the acquirer will recognize assets and liabilities that the acquiree had never recorded in its own accounting records. In particular, the acquirer will likely assign value to a variety of intangible assets that the acquiree may have developed internally, and so was constrained by GAAP from recognizing as assets. Examples of intangible assets are:

Broadcast rights	Internet domain names	Noncompetition agreements
Computer software	Lease agreements	Order backlog
Customer lists	Licensing agreements	Patented technology
Customer relationships	Literary works	Pictures
Employment contracts	Motion pictures	Service contracts
Franchise agreements	Musical works	Trademarks

A key intangible asset for which GAAP does not allow separate recognition is the concept of the assembled workforce, which is the collected knowledge and experience of company employees. This intangible must be included in the goodwill asset.

A special option only available to private companies is to not recognize separately from goodwill either of the following two types of intangible assets:

- Customer-related intangible assets, unless they are capable of being sold or licensed independently from other assets
- Noncompetition agreements

If a private company elects to not recognize these types of intangible assets, it must amortize goodwill, as described in the Intangibles – Goodwill and Other chapter.

The accounting treatment for special cases related to the recognition of assets and liabilities is as follows:

- *Contingency fair value not determinable*. It is quite common for a contingent asset or liability to not be measurable on the acquisition date, since these items have not yet been resolved. If so, only recognize them if the amount can be reasonably estimated, and events during the measurement period confirm that an asset or liability existed at the acquisition date.
- *Defined benefit pension plan*. If the acquiree sponsored a defined benefit pension plan, the acquirer should recognize an asset or liability that reflects the funding status of that plan.
- *Indemnification clause*. The seller of the acquiree may agree to an indemnification clause in the acquisition agreement, whereby it will indemnify the acquirer for changes in the value of certain assets or liabilities, such as for unusual bad debt losses from receivables in existence at the acquisition date. In these cases, the seller recognizes an indemnification asset when it recognizes a loss on an item to be indemnified; this should be retrospectively applied as of the acquisition date.

> **Tip:** Realistically, if there is still an attempt to establish a valuation for assets and liabilities more than a few months after an acquisition, they probably had no value at the acquisition date, and so should not be recognized as part of the acquisition.

Acquired assets and liabilities are supposed to be measured at their fair values as of the acquisition date. Fair value measurement can be quite difficult, and may call for different valuation approaches, as noted below:

- *Alternative use assets.* Even if the acquirer does not intend to apply an asset to its best use (or use the asset at all), the fair value of the asset should still be derived as though it were being applied to its best use. This guidance also applies to situations where an asset is acquired simply to prevent it from being used by competitors.
- *Assets where acquiree is the lessor.* If the acquiree owns assets that it leases to a third party (such as a building lease), derive fair values for these assets in the normal manner, irrespective of the existence of the lease.
- *Fair value exceptions.* There are exceptions to the general rule of recognizing acquired assets and liabilities at their fair values. The GAAP related to the recognition of income taxes, employee benefits, indemnification assets, reacquired rights, share-based awards, assets held for sale, and certain contingency situations overrides the use of fair value.
- *Noncontrolling interest.* The best way to measure the fair value of a noncontrolling interest is based on the market price of the acquiree's stock. However, this information is not available for privately-held companies, so alternative valuation methods are allowed. This valuation may differ from the valuation assigned to the acquirer, since the acquirer also benefits from gaining control over the entity, which results in a control premium.
- *Valuation allowances.* Some assets, such as receivables and inventory, are normally paired with a valuation allowance. The valuation allowance is not used when deriving fair values for these assets, since the fair value should already incorporate a valuation allowance.

A few assets and liabilities that are initially measured as part of an acquisition require special accounting during subsequent periods. These items are:

- *Contingencies.* If an asset or liability was originally recognized as part of an acquisition, derive a systematic and consistently-applied approach to measuring it in future periods.
- *Indemnifications.* Reassess all indemnification assets and the loss items with which they are paired in each subsequent reporting period, and adjust the recorded amounts as necessary until the indemnifications are resolved.
- *Reacquired rights.* An acquirer may regain control over a legal right that it had extended to the acquiree prior to the acquisition date. If these reacquired rights were initially recognized as an intangible asset as part of the acquisi-

tion accounting, amortize the asset over the remaining period of the contract that the acquiree had with the acquirer.

- *Leasehold improvements.* If the acquirer acquires leasehold improvement assets as part of an acquisition, amortize them over the lesser of the useful life of the assets or the remaining reasonably assured lease periods and renewals.

> **Tip:** The amortization period for leasehold improvements may be a significant issue for the acquirer, if it intends to shut down acquiree leases as soon as practicable. Doing so may accelerate the recognition of leasehold improvement assets.

The Securities and Exchange Commission (SEC) does not allow use of the residual method in deriving the value of intangible assets. The residual method is the two-step process of first assigning the purchase price to all identifiable assets, and then allocating the remaining residual amount to other intangible assets. This SEC guidance only applies to publicly-held companies.

Goodwill or Gain from Bargain Purchase

This section addresses the almost inevitable calculation of goodwill that is associated with most acquisitions. It also addresses the considerably less common recognition of a bargain purchase.

Goodwill Calculation

Goodwill is an intangible asset that represents the future benefits arising from assets acquired in a business combination that are not otherwise identified. Goodwill is a common element in most acquisition transactions, since the owners of acquirees generally do not part with their companies unless they are paid a premium.

The acquirer must recognize goodwill as an asset as of the acquisition date. The goodwill calculation is as follows:

$$\text{Goodwill} = (\text{Consideration paid} + \text{Fair value of noncontrolling interest}) - (\text{Assets acquired} - \text{Liabilities assumed})$$

If no consideration is transferred in an acquisition transaction, use a valuation method to determine the fair value of the acquirer's interest in the acquiree as a replacement value.

When calculating the total amount of consideration paid as part of the derivation of goodwill, consider the following additional factors:

- *Fair value of assets paid.* When the acquirer transfers its assets to the owners of the acquiree as payment for the acquiree, measure this consideration at its fair value. If there is a difference between the fair value and carrying amount of these assets as of the acquisition date, record a gain or loss in earnings to reflect the difference. However, if these assets are simply being transferred to the acquiree entity (which the acquirer now controls), do not restate these assets to their fair value; this means there is no recognition of a gain or loss.

- *Share-based payment awards.* The acquirer may agree to swap the share-based payment awards granted to employees of the acquiree for payment awards based on the shares of the acquirer. If the acquirer must replace awards made by the acquiree, include the fair value of these awards in the consideration paid by the acquirer, where the portion attributable to pre-acquisition employee service is considered consideration paid for the acquiree. If the acquirer is not obligated to replace these awards but does so anyways, record the cost of the replacement awards as compensation expense.

Bargain Purchase

When an acquirer gains control of an acquiree whose fair value is greater than the consideration paid for it, the acquirer is said to have completed a bargain purchase. A bargain purchase transaction most commonly arises when a business must be sold due to a liquidity crisis, where the short-term nature of the sale tends to result in a less-than-optimum sale price from the perspective of the owners of the acquiree. To account for a bargain purchase, follow these steps:

1. Record all assets and liabilities at their fair values.
2. Reassess whether all assets and liabilities have been recorded.
3. Determine and record the fair value of any contingent consideration to be paid to the owners of the acquiree.
4. Record any remaining difference between these fair values and the consideration paid as a gain in earnings. Record this gain as of the acquisition date.

EXAMPLE

The owners of Failsafe Containment have to rush the sale of the business in order to obtain funds for estate taxes, and so agree to a below-market sale to Armadillo Industries for $5,000,000 in cash of a 75% interest in Failsafe. Armadillo hires a valuation firm to analyze the assets and liabilities of Failsafe, and concludes that the fair value of its net assets is $7,000,000 (of which $8,000,000 is assets and $1,000,000 is liabilities), and the fair value of the 25% of Failsafe still retained by its original owners has a fair value of $1,500,000.

Since the fair value of the net assets of Failsafe exceeds the consideration paid and the fair value of the noncontrolling interest in the company, Armadillo must recognize a gain in earnings, which is calculated as follows:

$7,000,000 Net assets - $5,000,000 Consideration - $1,500,000 Noncontrolling interest

= $500,000 Gain on bargain purchase

Armadillo records the transaction with the following entry:

	Debit	Credit
Assets acquired	8,000,000	
Cash		5,000,000
Liabilities assumed		1,000,000
Gain on bargain purchase		500,000
Equity – noncontrolling interest in Failsafe		1,500,000

Reverse Acquisitions

A reverse acquisition occurs when the legal acquirer is actually the acquiree for accounting purposes. The reverse acquisition concept is most commonly used when a privately-held business buys a public shell company for the purposes of rolling itself into the shell and thereby becoming a publicly-held company. This approach is used to avoid the expense of engaging in an initial public offering.

To conduct a reverse acquisition, the legal acquirer issues its shares to the owners of the legal acquiree (which is the accounting acquirer). The fair value of this consideration is derived from the fair value amount of equity the legal acquiree would have had to issue to the legal acquirer to give the owners of the legal acquirer an equivalent percentage ownership in the combined entity.

When a reverse acquisition occurs, the legal acquiree may have owners who do not choose to exchange their shares in the legal acquiree for shares in the legal acquirer. These owners are considered a noncontrolling interest in the consolidated financial statements of the legal acquirer. The carrying amount of this noncontrolling interest is based on the proportionate interest of the noncontrolling shareholders in the net asset carrying amounts of the legal acquiree prior to the business combination.

EXAMPLE

The management of High Noon Armaments wants to take their company public through a reverse acquisition transaction with a public shell company, Peaceful Pottery. The transaction is completed on January 1, 20X4. The balance sheets of the two entities on the acquisition date are as follows:

	Peaceful (Legal Acquirer, Accounting Acquiree)	High Noon (Legal Subsidiary, Accounting Acquirer)
Total assets	$100	$8,000
Total liabilities	$0	$4,500
Shareholders' equity		
Retained earnings	10	3,000
Common stock		
100 shares	90	
1,000 shares		500
Total shareholders' equity	100	3,500
Total liabilities and shareholders' equity	$100	$8,000

On January 1, Peaceful issues 0.5 shares in exchange for each share of High Noon. All of High Noon's shareholders exchange their holdings in High Noon for the new Peaceful shares. Thus, Peaceful issues 500 shares in exchange for all of the outstanding shares in High Noon.

The quoted market price of Peaceful shares on January 1 is $10, while the fair value of each common share of High Noon shares is $20. The fair values of Peaceful's few assets and liabilities on January 1 are the same as their carrying amounts.

As a result of the stock issuance to High Noon investors, those investors now own 5/6ths of Peaceful shares, or 83.3% of the total number of shares. To arrive at the same ratio, High Noon would have had to issue 200 shares to the shareholders of Peaceful. Thus, the fair value of the consideration transferred is $4,000 (calculated as 200 shares × $20 fair value per share).

Goodwill for the acquisition is the excess of the consideration transferred over the amount of Peaceful's assets and liabilities, which is $3,900 (calculated as $4,000 consideration - $100 of Peaceful net assets).

Based on the preceding information, the consolidated balance sheet of the two companies immediately following the acquisition transaction is:

	Peaceful	High Noon	Adjustments	Consolidated
Total assets	$100	$8,000	$3,900	$12,000
Total liabilities	$0	$4,500	--	$4,500
Shareholders' equity				
Retained earnings	10	3,000	-10	3,000
Common stock				
100 shares	90		-90	--
1,000 shares		500		500
600 shares			4,000	4,000
Total shareholders' equity	100	3,500	3,900	7,500
Total liabilities and shareholders' equity	$100	$8,000	$3,900	$12,000

Related Issues

This section addresses several issues that are similar to business combinations, but which are not treated in the same manner.

Acquisition of Assets

A common form of acquisition is to acquire only selected assets and liabilities of an acquiree. This approach is used to avoid any undocumented liabilities that may be associated with the acquiree. See the author's *Mergers & Acquisitions* book for more information about why this type of acquisition is used. The accounting for asset acquisitions encompasses the following situations:

- *Cash consideration paid.* When cash is paid for assets, recognize the assets at the amount of cash paid for them.
- *Noncash assets paid.* Measure assets acquired at the fair value of the consideration paid or the fair value of the assets acquired, whichever is more reliably measurable. Do not recognize a gain or loss on an asset acquisition, unless the fair value of any noncash assets used by the acquirer to pay for the assets differs from the carrying amounts of these assets (see the Non-monetary Transactions chapter for more information).
- *Cost allocation.* If assets and liabilities are acquired in a group, allocate the cost of the entire group to the individual components of that group based on their relative fair values.

EXAMPLE

Armadillo Industries acquires the sheet metal stamping facility of a competitor, which includes production equipment, a manufacturing facility, and the real estate on which the facility is located. The total purchase price of this group of assets is $800,000. Armadillo allocates the purchase price to the individual assets in the following manner:

Asset	Fair Value	Percent of Total Fair Value		Purchase Price		Cost Allocation
Production equipment	$325,000	35%	×	$800,000	=	$280,000
Manufacturing facility	400,000	43%	×	800,000	=	344,000
Real estate	200,000	22%	×	800,000	=	176,000
	$925,000	100%				$800,000

Transactions between Entities under Control of Same Parent

When two or more entities are owned by a common parent, it is relatively common for them to enter into a variety of business transactions with each other, such as the transfer of assets or the sale of goods or services. Other examples of these transactions are shifting assets to a new entity, shifting assets into the parent, and the parent shifting its ownership interest in partially-owned subsidiaries into a new subsidiary.

When transferring assets or exchanging shares between entities under common control, the entity receiving the assets or equity interests should recognize the transferred items at their carrying amounts as stated in the records of the transferring entity on the transfer date. If these carrying amounts have been altered due to pushdown accounting (see next), the entity receiving the assets or equity interests should instead recognize the transferred items at the historical cost of the parent entity.

If the sending and receiving entities use different accounting methods to account for similar types of assets and liabilities, it is permissible to adjust the carrying amounts of transferred items to the accounting method used by the recipient, if doing so represents a preferable treatment. If there is a change in accounting method, it must be applied retrospectively to the transferred items for all prior periods for which financial statements are presented, unless it is impracticable to do so.

Pushdown Accounting

Pushdown accounting involves requiring the acquiree to adopt a new basis of accounting for its assets and liabilities. This approach is used when a master limited partnership is formed from the assets of existing businesses (though usage is restricted), as well as when there is a step-up in the tax basis of a subsidiary. The SEC has stated that it believes pushdown accounting should be used in purchase transactions where the acquiree becomes substantially wholly owned. Pushdown accounting is not required if a business is not publicly-held.

An acquired business has the option to apply pushdown accounting in its separate financial statements as of the point when an acquirer takes control. The acquired business also has the option to apply pushdown accounting in a subsequent reporting period. Once made, the election is irrevocable. If there is a change to pushdown accounting, this is considered a change in accounting principle. For any change in accounting principle, disclose all of the following items in the period in which the change takes place:

- *Nature of the change.* The nature of the change and why the new principle is preferable.
- *Application method.* State the method used to apply the change, including:
    o The information being adjusted
    o The effect of the change on income from continuing operations, net income, any other affected financial statement line items, and any affected per-share amounts
    o The cumulative effect of the change on retained earnings in the balance sheet as of the beginning of the earliest period presented
    o The reasons why retrospective application is impracticable (if this is the case), and the alternative method used to report the change

Thus, if the election is made to use pushdown accounting, the acquired entity should disclose sufficient information in the accompanying footnotes for users of the financial statements to evaluate the effect of the change.

Income Taxes

The nature of an acquisition transaction represents a balance of the taxation goals of the acquirer and the owners of the acquiree, as is described further in the author's *Mergers & Acquisitions* book. The likely result of the acquisition structure is that some deferred tax liabilities and deferred tax assets should be recognized. Specifically, the following tax-related accounting may be required:

- *Goodwill.* The amortization of goodwill is allowed as a tax deduction in some tax jurisdictions, but not in others. The result may be a difference in the book and tax basis for goodwill in future years, for which a deferred tax asset or liability should be recorded.
- *Replacement awards.* If the acquirer issues replacement awards to the employees of the acquiree, and those awards are classified as equity and eligible to be tax deductions, recognize a deferred tax asset for the deductible temporary difference relating to that portion of the award relating to the precombination service of the awardee. The deduction may exceed the fair value of the award; if so, record the excess as additional paid-in capital.

- *Tax allocation to acquired entity*. If the acquirer retains the historical basis for the financial reporting of an acquiree in conjunction with a step-up in the tax basis of acquired assets, it is allowable to use any of the following methods to allocate the consolidated tax provision:

  o Allocate taxes to the acquiree on a preacquisition tax basis
  o When realized, credit the tax benefit caused by the step-up in tax basis to the additional paid-in capital account of the acquiree
  o When realized, credit the tax benefit caused by the step-up in tax basis to the income of the acquiree

- *Temporary differences*. If there are temporary differences related to deferred tax liabilities or assets related to a business combination, recognize them at the acquisition date.

- *Valuation allowance or tax position change*. If there is a change in the valuation allowance or tax position of an acquiree that occurs during the post-acquisition measurement period, and which results from new information about issues in existence at the acquisition date, record the offset to the change as an adjustment to goodwill. If goodwill has been reduced to zero, the offset is then recorded as a bargain purchase. All other changes in the acquiree's allowance or tax position are recognized as a change in income tax expense.

- *Valuation allowance*. Assess the need for a valuation allowance that offsets any deferred tax asset for which there is uncertainty about the recoverability of the asset. If the acquirer has already established a valuation allowance, it may be necessary to alter the allowance based on tax laws that may restrict the future use of deductible temporary differences or carryforwards of either the acquirer or the acquiree.

Business Combination Disclosures

Business combinations are one of the areas in which GAAP requires unusually thorough disclosures. Disclosure topics are addressed under the following headers that describe different aspects of business combinations.

General Disclosures

If an acquirer enters into a business combination during the current reporting period or after the reporting date but before the financial statements are issued or available to be issued, disclose the following information:

- The name of the acquiree and its description
- The acquisition date
- The acquired percentage of voting equity interest in the acquiree
- The reason(s) for the combination
- How the acquirer gained control of the acquiree

In addition, there may be other transactions with an acquiree that are recognized separately from the acquisition transaction. If so, disclose the following information:

- The transaction and how it was accounted for
- The amounts recognized for each transaction, and the line item(s) in the financial statements where these amounts are located
- If the result is settlement of a preexisting relationship, describe how the settlement was determined
- The amount of costs related to the acquisition, the amount of these costs recognized as expense, any issuance costs not charged to expense, and how these costs were recognized

If a business combination was achieved in stages, disclose the following information:

- The fair value of the acquirer's equity interest in the acquiree just prior to the acquisition date
- Any gain or loss resulting from the remeasurement of the existing equity interest to fair value, and where that gain or loss is recorded in the income statement
- The valuation technique used to measure the fair value of the existing equity interest
- Additional information that assists users to assess the development of this fair value measurement

If the acquirer is a publicly-held company, disclose the following information:

- The amount of revenue and earnings attributable to the acquiree since the acquisition date and included in the results of the reporting period
- A pro forma statement of the revenue and earnings of the combined entity, as though the acquisition had been completed at the beginning of the year
- If there are comparative financial statements, a pro forma statement of the revenue and earnings of the combined entity, as though the acquisition had been completed at the beginning of all the periods presented
- The nature and amount of any nonrecurring pro forma adjustments attributable to a business combination that are material
- If it is impracticable to report any of the preceding items required for a publicly-held company, disclose why the reporting is impracticable

If the acquirer recognized adjustments in the current reporting period that relate to prior periods, disclose the following information:

- The reason(s) why the initial accounting for a business combination is incomplete
- The specific items for which the accounting is incomplete, including assets, liabilities, equity interests, and/or payments

- The amount and type of any adjustments recognized during the period. Separately state the adjustments made to income statement line items in the current period that relate to the income effects that would have been recognized in prior periods if the adjustments had instead been recognized as of the acquisition date.

It is allowable to aggregate the preceding disclosure information if there are several business combinations in a period that are individually immaterial, but material when reported as a group.

The preceding disclosures are still required if a business combination occurs after the reporting date of the financial statements, but before the statements are issued or available to be issued. The only exception is when the initial accounting for the combination is incomplete, in which case describe which disclosures were not made and why they were not made.

EXAMPLE

Armadillo Industries discloses the following information pertaining to its acquisition of High Pressure Designs:

On June 30, 20X1, Armadillo acquired 20% of the outstanding common stock of High Pressure Designs ("High Pressure"). On March 31, 20X3, Armadillo acquired 45% of the outstanding common stock of High Pressure. High Pressure designs the containment walls for deep-sea submersible devices, and typically sells its services to oceanographic and military customers. As a result of the acquisition, Armadillo expects to solidify its leading market position in the submersible construction market.

The fair value of Armadillo's equity holdings in High Pressure was $3,500,000 at the acquisition date, which represented a $200,000 gain. The valuation technique to derive the fair value was the discounted cash flows method, which incorporated an 8% discount rate. The gain is recorded in other income in the company's income statement for the quarter ended March 31, 20X3.

Armadillo paid $8,750,000 for its March 31 purchase of 45% of High Pressure's common stock. This payment was made with 437,500 shares of the company's common stock, which had a closing market price of $20 on the acquisition date.

Identifiable Assets and Liabilities, and any Noncontrolling Interest

If an acquirer completes a business combination, it should disclose the following information in the period in which the combination was completed:

- *Indemnification assets*. If there are indemnification assets, describe the arrangement, and state the amount recognized as of the acquisition date and the basis for determining it. Also estimate the range of undiscounted outcomes, the reasons why a range cannot be estimated, or if the maximum amount is unlimited.

- *Acquired receivables.* By major class of receivables, state the gross amount and fair value of the receivables, and estimate the contractual cash flow that is not expected to be collected.
- *Major asset and liability classes.* State the amount recognized for each major class of assets and liabilities.
- *Contingencies.* State the nature and amount of each asset or liability recognized in relation to a contingency, and how they were measured. Disclosures may be aggregated for similar assets and liabilities.
- *Noncontrolling interests.* If less than 100% ownership of the acquiree is held, state the fair value of the noncontrolling interest and the valuation method used to arrive at that figure.

If there were several acquisitions in the period that were individually immaterial but material when aggregated, disclose the preceding items in aggregate for the group of acquisitions.

If acquisitions are completed after the balance sheet date but before the financial statements have been issued or are available to be issued, still disclose all of the preceding information. However, if the initial accounting for the acquisitions is incomplete, describe the disclosures that could not be reported and why they could not be made.

Goodwill or Gain from Bargain Purchase

If the acquirer recognizes goodwill as part of an acquisition transaction, disclose the following information for each business combination completed in a reporting period:

- *Bargain purchase.* If the acquisition is a bargain purchase, disclose the resulting gain and the line item in which it is located in the income statement, as well as the reasons why the acquisition generated a gain.
- *Consideration paid.* State the fair value of all consideration paid, as well as by class of asset, liability, and equity item.
- *Contingent assets and liabilities.* In later periods, continue to report any changes in the fair values of unsettled contingent assets and liabilities, as well as changes in (and the reasons for) the range of possible outcomes.
- *Contingent consideration.* If there is consideration contingent upon future events or circumstances, state the amount of this consideration already recognized on the acquisition date, describe the arrangement, estimate the range of undiscounted outcomes or reasons why a range cannot be presented, and whether the maximum payment can be unlimited.
- *Goodwill content.* Describe the factors that comprise goodwill, such as expected synergies from combining the companies.

- *Reconciliation*. Present a reconciliation of the carrying amount of goodwill at the beginning and end of the reporting period.
- *Segment reporting*. If the acquirer is publicly-held, disclose the amount of goodwill assigned to each reportable segment. If this assignment has not yet been completed, disclose this point.
- *Tax deductibility*. Note the amount of resulting goodwill expected to be tax deductible.

If there were several acquisitions in the period that were individually immaterial but material when aggregated, disclose the preceding items in aggregate for the group of acquisitions.

If acquisitions are completed after the balance sheet date but before the financial statements have been issued or are available to be issued, still disclose all of the preceding information. However, if the initial accounting for the acquisitions is incomplete, describe the disclosures it was not possible to report and why they could not be made.

Reverse Acquisitions

When there is a reverse acquisition, consolidated financial statements are issued under the name of the legal acquirer (which is the accounting acquiree). The accompanying notes should clarify that the financial statements are actually a continuation of the financial statements formerly issued by the legal acquiree, with a retroactive adjustment to reflect the legal capital of the legal acquirer. If comparative information is presented for prior periods, this means that the presented amount of legal capital should also be adjusted in the prior periods. The following additional points apply to the presentation of the consolidated financial statements of the two entities:

- *Carrying amounts*. Assets and liabilities are stated at their precombination carrying amounts – there is no fair value restatement.
- *Equity structure*. The equity structure in the statements reflects the equity structure of the legal acquirer, which includes any equity changes resulting from the combination.
- *Earnings per share*. Assuming that the reverse acquisition was completed in order to take the legal acquiree public, it must now report earnings per share (see the Earnings per Share chapter). The earnings per share calculation requires the formulation of the weighted-average number of shares outstanding during each reporting period. To calculate the number of shares for the period in which the acquisition occurs, use the following guidance:
  - *Shares outstanding from beginning of period to acquisition date*. This is the weighted-average number of shares of the legal acquiree outstanding in the period, multiplied by the exchange ratio used to replace them with shares of the legal acquirer.

○ *Shares outstanding from acquisition date to end of period.* This is the actual weighted-average number of shares of the legal acquirer outstanding.

To calculate the basic earnings per share information for any comparative periods presented for periods prior to the date of a reverse acquisition, use the following formula:

$$\frac{\text{Income of legal acquiree attributable to common shareholders}}{(\text{Legal acquiree's weighted-average common shares outstanding} \times \text{Exchange ratio})}$$

Transactions between Entities under Control of Same Parent

When there is an exchange of assets or equity interests between entities under common control, the receiving entity records these transactions as though they occurred at the beginning of the reporting period. In addition, retrospectively adjust all comparative financial statements presented for previous reporting periods to reflect the amounts of these transactions. This prior-period adjustment is only required for those periods during which the entities had a common parent.

When there is a transfer of assets and/or liabilities, or an exchange of equity interests, disclose the following information:

- *Description.* State the name and description of the entity being included in the reporting entity.
- *Method of accounting.* Describe the method of accounting for the indicated transaction.

Income Taxes

If there is a change in the valuation allowance of the deferred tax assets of an acquirer that is caused by a business combination, disclose the adjustments to the beginning balance of the valuation.

Summary

A company controller may deal with acquisitions on only rare occasions, and so may be unfamiliar with the proper accounting to be used to recognize these transactions. While texts such as this one can certainly provide guidelines for how to structure these transactions, there is still a strong likelihood of incorrectly accounting for an acquisition. Given the high level of accounting complexity in this area, it is best to engage the services of an acquisition accounting expert, for whom a recommendation may be obtained from the company's certified public accountants. Either this person's work can be thoroughly documented and copied for use in later acquisitions, or the company can continue to engage his or her services whenever an acquisition is completed. The latter approach is recommended, since it reduces the risk of a reporting error.

Chapter 37
Financial Statement Consolidation

810 = GAAP codification area for consolidation

Introduction

There are a number of circumstances under which a business may need to report its financial results and financial position in combination with similar information for other entities over which it has control. In this chapter, we address the mechanics of this consolidation process, as well as the circumstances under which a business is considered to have control over another entity.

Related Chapter

See the Business Combinations chapter to review the accounting for an acquisition by the acquirer; this transaction precedes the consolidation discussion in this chapter.

Overview of Consolidations

A financial statement consolidation is intended to present the results and financial position of a parent entity and its subsidiaries, as though they were a single entity. It is also possible to have consolidated financial statements for a portion of a group of companies, such as for a subsidiary and those other entities owned by the subsidiary. Consolidated financial statements are useful for reviewing the financial position and results of an entire group of commonly-owned businesses. Otherwise, reviewing the results of individual businesses within the group does not give an indication of the financial health of the group as a whole.

A consolidation is performed under the assumption that this combined level of information is more useful to readers, who are likely to be the owners or creditors of the parent.

A consolidation is typically conducted when the parent entity has a controlling financial interest in other entities. A controlling financial interest is considered to be present when there is a direct or indirect majority voting interest of more than 50% of the outstanding voting shares. It is possible that a controlling financial interest is not present despite having more than 50% of the outstanding voting shares, when noncontrolling interests interfere with a financial interest.

A power of control may also exist when there is less than 50% ownership of the outstanding voting shares, which (for example) may occur by court order, contract, or an agreement to which other shareholders are parties. If so, the results and financial positions of the entities can be consolidated.

A consolidation may not be allowed in certain circumstances where there is not a clear indication of a controlling financial interest. For example:

- A subsidiary is engaged in a legal reorganization
- A subsidiary is in bankruptcy proceedings
- A foreign subsidiary is restricted to such an extent by government-imposed controls or restrictions that there is significant doubt about the ability of the parent to exercise control over the subsidiary
- A noncontrolling shareholder of a subsidiary has approval or veto rights that restrict the ability of the parent to exercise control over a subsidiary

Note: A broker-dealer temporarily holding the shares of an entity should not consolidate its results with those of the investee.

An excuse sometimes used to avoid consolidation is that the fiscal periods used by a parent and a subsidiary are different. Under GAAP, this reasoning is not considered valid, so results of such entities should be consolidated, assuming that a controlling financial interest exists.

Recognition of a Consolidation

A consolidation typically occurs when a reporting entity has a majority voting interest in another entity. It is possible to argue against a consolidation when a reporting entity has a majority voting interest in another entity; this is a matter of judgment that depends on the facts and circumstances of each individual case, and is supported when a noncontrolling shareholder is effectively participating in significant decisions of the other entity. Effective participation is occurring when a noncontrolling shareholder can veto the actions of the majority shareholder in certain situations. The following points clarify the issue:

- *Protective rights*. A noncontrolling shareholder may have rights that protect its investment, such as a veto over the liquidation of a business or the sale of major assets. These rights are not considered to interfere with the control of a majority voting interest.
- *Substantive participating rights*. A noncontrolling shareholder may have the right to select, terminate, or set the compensation of management, or to establish operating or capital decisions of the investee. If so, this can be considered to interfere with a majority voting interest.

EXAMPLE

A noncontrolling shareholder has the right to block the board of directors of Amalgamated Investments from issuing an extraordinary dividend distribution to shareholders. This is a protective right, since it prevents an excessive amount of funds from being removed from

Amalgamated. If the blocking right had instead applied to customary dividends, it might be construed as a substantive participating right.

EXAMPLE

The same noncontrolling shareholder has the right to block any long-term supplier agreements with a supplier of bauxite to Amalgamated. The total value of this agreement is minor, and there are alternative suppliers that Amalgamated can use. Given the minor impact on the organization of this blocking right, it is not considered a substantive participating right.

- *Other factors*. The following additional factors could be considered when deciding whether noncontrolling shareholders are interfering with the control of the majority voting interest:
    - *Percent ownership*. If the majority voting interest is substantially greater than 50%, the rights of other investors are more likely to be protective rights, and so do not keep the majority voting interest from engaging in consolidation accounting.
    - *Voting matters*. The extent to which matters can be put to a shareholder vote should be considered when determining whether a noncontrolling interest has substantive participating rights.
    - *Related parties*. If the noncontrolling interest is related to the controlling interest, this makes it more likely that the majority voting interest has control over the investee.
    - *Minor decisions*. A noncontrolling interest may have rights in regard to minor operating or capital decisions, such as the name of the investee, the selection of auditors, and the location of the investee's headquarters. These decisions do not interfere with the control of the majority voting interest.
    - *Rare decisions*. A noncontrolling interest may have the right to participate in significant decisions, but ones for which the probability is remote. These decisions do not interfere with the control of the majority voting interest.
    - *Buyout clause*. If the majority voting interest has a right to buy out the interest of a noncontrolling shareholder for fair value or less, and the buyout would be prudent and feasible, this negates the veto rights of the noncontrolling shareholder when deciding whether the majority voting interest has control.

Note: The participation of noncontrolling interests in an entity shall be reassessed whenever there are significant changes in the terms or rights of a noncontrolling shareholder.

Consolidation accounting is the process of combining the financial results of several subsidiary companies into the combined financial results of the parent company. Consolidated financial statements require considerable effort to construct, since they must exclude the impact of any transactions between the entities being reported on. Thus, if there is a sale of goods between the subsidiaries of a parent company, this intercompany sale must be eliminated from the consolidated financial statements. Another common intercompany elimination is when the parent company pays interest income to the subsidiaries whose cash it is using to make investments; this interest income must be eliminated from the consolidated financial statements. The following steps document the consolidation accounting process flow:

1. *Record intercompany loans.* If the parent company has been consolidating the cash balances of its subsidiaries into an investment account, record intercompany loans from the subsidiaries to the parent company. Also record an interest income allocation for the interest earned on consolidated investments from the parent company down to the subsidiaries.

2. *Charge corporate overhead.* If the parent company allocates its overhead costs to subsidiaries, calculate the amount of the allocation and charge it to the various subsidiaries.

3. *Charge payables.* If the parent company runs a consolidated payables operation, verify that all accounts payable recorded during the period have been appropriately charged to the various subsidiaries.

4. *Charge payroll expenses.* If the parent company has been using a common paymaster system to pay all employees throughout the company, ensure that the proper allocation of payroll expenses has been made to all subsidiaries.

5. *Complete adjusting entries.* At the subsidiary and corporate levels, record any adjusting entries needed to properly record revenue and expense transactions in the correct period.

6. *Investigate asset, liability, and equity account balances.* Verify that the contents of all asset, liability, and equity accounts for both the subsidiaries and the corporate parent are correct, and adjust as necessary.

7. *Review subsidiary financial statements.* Print and review the financial statements for each subsidiary, and investigate any items that appear to be unusual or incorrect. Make adjustments as necessary.

8. *Eliminate intercompany transactions.* If there have been any intercompany transactions, reverse them at the parent company level to eliminate their effects from the consolidated financial statements. Examples of intercompany transactions are:

   - Security holdings
   - Debt
   - Sales (with the reversal of related inventory amounts)
   - Purchases (with the reversal of related inventory amounts)
   - Interest
   - Dividends
   - Gains or losses on asset sales

9. *Eliminate subsidiary retained earnings*. Remove the retained earnings of each subsidiary as of its acquisition date from the consolidated financial statements.

10. *Eliminate LIFO liquidation profits*. If there were inventory transfers between the subsidiaries that caused inventory to be liquidated that was valued using the last-in, first-out (LIFO) method, eliminate the profit related to these transfers.

11. *Eliminate parent shares held by subsidiary*. If a subsidiary holds shares in the parent entity, these are not treated as outstanding shares in the consolidated balance sheet. Instead, they are considered to be treasury stock.

12. *Defer taxes on inter-company profits*. If income taxes have already been paid on inter-company profits, defer them in the consolidated financial statements. An alternative treatment is to reduce the amount of the inter-entity profits to be eliminated by the amount of the taxes.

13. *Review parent financial statements*. Print and review the financial statements for the parent company, and investigate any items that appear to be unusual or incorrect. Make adjustments as necessary.

14. *Close subsidiary books*. Depending upon the accounting software in use, it may be necessary to access the financial records of each subsidiary and flag them as closed. This prevents any additional transactions from being recorded in the accounting period being closed.

15. *Close parent company books*. Flag the parent company accounting period as closed, so that no additional transactions can be reported in the accounting period being closed.

16. *Issue financial statements*. Print and distribute the consolidated financial statements.

If a subsidiary uses a different currency as its operating currency, an additional consolidation accounting step is to convert its financial statements into the operating currency of the parent company.

Given the considerable number of steps, it is useful to convert them into a detailed procedure, which the accounting department should follow religiously as part of its closing process. Otherwise, a key step could be missed, which would throw off the financial statement results.

Consolidation Examples

This section contains a number of examples that clarify the consolidation outcome for different situations. Each situation is dealt with in a different sub-section.

Recognition of Noncontrolling Interest

A parent company may find it necessary to sell a share of its ownership interest in a subsidiary to a third party. This event can trigger the recognition of a gain or loss if the amount of the sale differs from the carrying amount of the equity. It will also result in the recognition of a noncontrolling interest, as noted in the following example.

EXAMPLE

Blitz Communications owns all 100,000 the outstanding shares of Prompt Installers. Blitz manufactures office phone systems, and the subsidiary installs phone systems at client locations. The carrying amount of the equity of Prompt is $1,000,000.

Blitz needs new financing for a production facility, and elects to sell 30,000 of its Prompt shares to a third party for $350,000 in cash. This transaction reduces the ownership of Blitz in Prompt to a 70% interest. This change in ownership is accounted for by recognizing a noncontrolling interest of $300,000, which is calculated as follows:

$$\$1,000,000 \text{ Carrying amount of equity} \times 30\% \text{ Interest} = \$300,000$$

The remaining $50,000 that Blitz received from the third party is recognized as an increase in additional paid-in capital for Blitz.

Sale of Shares by Subsidiary

The managers of a subsidiary may find it necessary to sell shares to third parties. Doing so will reduce the ownership interest of the parent entity. When this happens, multiply the newly-adjusted ownership interest of the parent by the carrying amount of the subsidiary's new equity balance to arrive at the revised investment of the parent in the subsidiary. This situation is addressed in the following example.

EXAMPLE

Hammer Industries has 50,000 shares of common stock outstanding. Of this amount, 40,000 shares are owned by its parent, Mole Industries, and the remaining shares are owned by unrelated third parties. The carrying amount of the equity of Hammer is $1,000,000. Of the $1,000,000, 80% (or $800,000) is attributed to Mole, and 20% (or $200,000) to the noncontrolling interest in Hammer.

Hammer is in need of additional funding, and elects to sell 10,000 shares to an unrelated third party for $220,000. This transaction reduces Mole's ownership interest in Hammer to 67%, which is calculated as:

$$40,000 \text{ Shares owned by Mole} \div 60,000 \text{ Total shares outstanding} = 66.67\%$$

As a result of the stock sale, Hammer's equity has increased from $1,000,000 to $1,220,000. Mole's share of this increased equity is 66.67%, which is $813,374. This means that Mole recognizes an increase of $13,374 in its Hammer investment, with a corresponding increase in its additional paid-in capital. The noncontrolling interest in Hammer is now $406,626, which is calculated as follows:

$1,220,000 Carrying amount of equity × 33.33% Ownership interest = $406,626

The combined ownership amounts of Mole and the noncontrolling interests equal $1,220,000, which matches the total carrying amount of Hammer's equity.

Share of Accumulated Other Comprehensive Income

A subsidiary may carry on its books an accumulated other comprehensive income balance. This account is used to accumulate unrealized gains and unrealized losses on those line items in the income statement that are classified within the other comprehensive income category. A transaction is unrealized when it has not yet been settled. Thus, if a subsidiary were to invest in a bond, it would record any gain or loss in its fair value in other comprehensive income until it sells the bond, at which time the gain or loss would be realized, and then shifted out of the accumulated other comprehensive income account.

A noncontrolling interest is assigned a proportional share of the balance in the accumulated other comprehensive income account. If the ownership percentages of the controlling and noncontrolling interests change, then the proportional assignment of the balance in this account must also change. The following example illustrates the concept.

EXAMPLE

Latham Lumber is a subsidiary of Camelot Construction. Latham has 25,000 shares of common stock outstanding, of which 20,000 shares are owned by Camelot and 5,000 by a third party that has a noncontrolling interest in Latham. The carrying amount of the noncontrolling interest is $40,000, which includes $10,000 of accumulated other comprehensive income.

Camelot pays $20,000 to acquire half of the noncontrolling interest. As a result of this transaction, Camelot has increased its ownership percentage of Latham to 90% from the prior 80% level. The accounting for the transaction is a reduction of the noncontrolling interest to $20,000 (half of the previous amount). Also, Camelot's share of the accumulated other comprehensive income that had been ascribed to the noncontrolling interest is $5,000 (half of the total). This transfer is accomplished with an offsetting decrease in the additional paid-in capital attributable to Camelot.

Full Consolidation Example

The following example combines a number of issues, including the sale and subsequent partial re-purchase of a noncontrolling interest, and the assignment of accumulated other comprehensive income.

EXAMPLE

Icelandic Cod has a subsidiary, Canadian Crab. During 20X2, Icelandic owns all of the 50,000 shares outstanding for Canadian, so its ownership interest in Canadian is 100%.

In February of 20X2, Canadian is flush with cash from the king crab season, for which the fishing season ended in January. Accordingly, Canadian purchases $250,000 of securities and classifies them as available for sale. By the end of the year, the carrying amount of these securities has increased to $260,000. For the full year, Canadian earned net profits of $300,000. As of year-end, the detail of Canadian's equity was as follows:

Common stock	50,000
Additional paid-in capital	100,000
Retained earnings	350,000
Accumulated other comprehensive income	10,000
Total equity	$510,000

On the first day of the new year, Icelandic elects to sell 10% of its interest in Canadian, so it sells 5,000 shares to a third party for $60,000. In the consolidated financial statements of the entities, the sale of stock is accounted for as follows:

- Recognize a noncontrolling interest of $51,000 (calculated as $510,000 total equity × 10%).
- Recognize an increase in the additional paid-in capital of Icelandic of $9,000, which is the difference between the $60,000 cash received from the third party and the $51,000 carrying amount of the noncontrolling interest.
- Recognize an increase in the additional paid-in capital of Icelandic of $1,000, and a matching reduction of its accumulated other comprehensive income. This change reflects the carrying amount of Canadian's $10,000 of accumulated other comprehensive income related to the available for sale securities, of which 10% is now assigned to the noncontrolling interest.
- These activities result in the following journal entry:

	Debit	Credit
Cash	60,000	
Accumulated other comprehensive income (Icelandic)	1,000	
Noncontrolling interest		51,000
Additional paid-in capital (Icelandic)		10,000

For the year ended 20X3, Canadian does not enjoy as large a profit, due to overfishing in the king crab fishing areas; its net profit is $100,000. At year-end, the carrying amount of the noncontrolling interest is $64,000, of which $3,000 is accumulated other comprehensive income.

Immediately following year-end, Icelandic thinks better of its earlier decision to sell Canadian shares to a third party, and negotiates to repurchase half of the shares (2,500 shares) for $40,000. This results in an increase in Icelandic's ownership of Canadian to 95%.

Icelandic accounts for this purchase of stock for the consolidated financial statements through the following steps:

- Recognize a reduction of the noncontrolling interest of $25,500 (calculated as $51,000 noncontrolling interest × 50%).
- Recognize a reduction in the additional paid-in capital of Icelandic of $14,500, which is the difference between the $40,000 paid to the third party and the $25,500 reduction in the carrying amount of the noncontrolling interest.
- Recognize a $1,500 reduction in the additional paid-in capital account of Icelandic, which is 50% of the carrying amount of the accumulated other comprehensive income formerly attributed to the third party, which has been repurchased by Icelandic. The offset to this transaction is an increase of $1,500 in the accumulated other comprehensive income attributable to Icelandic.
- These activities result in the following journal entry:

	Debit	Credit
Noncontrolling interest	25,500	
Additional paid-in capital (Icelandic)	16,000	
Accumulated other comprehensive income (Icelandic)		1,500
Cash		40,000

Consolidation of Variable Interest Entities

A variable interest entity (VIE) is an entity in which an investor has a noncontrolling interest, and which may be subject to consolidation in some situations. A VIE is subject to consolidation with another entity when it was designed so that any one of the following conditions would exist:

- *Equity at risk.* The total amount of the reporting entity's equity investment at risk in the VIE is not enough for the VIE to finance its own activities without additional subordinated financial support. Subordinated support requires that the supplier of the additional support absorb some portion of the VIE's expected losses. The total equity investment at risk should only include those investments that:
  - o Have a significant participation in profits or losses;

      o Does not include equity interests issued by the reporting entity in exchange for subordinated interests in other VIEs;

      o Does not include amounts given to an equity investor by the reporting entity or other parties involved with the VIE; and

      o Does not include amounts financed directly by the VIE or other parties related to the VIE, unless they are the parent or fellow subsidiaries.

- *Lack of controlling interest.* The holders of the equity investment, as a group, do not have any one of the following characteristics normally ascribed to a controlling financial interest:

      o The ability to use voting rights to make significant decisions about the VIE;

      o There is no obligation to absorb the expected losses of the VIE; or

      o There is no right to receive the expected residual returns of the VIE, such as when their return is capped under the terms of the VIE's governing documents.

Given the number of conditions that can arise when deciding whether consolidation should occur for a VIE, it is important to focus only on those decision factors that are substantive. Inconsequential transactions and arrangements not impacting VIE status, the reporting entity's power over the VIE, or the reporting entity's obligation to absorb losses of or receive benefits from the VIE should not influence the decision. The ultimate determination should be based on an analysis of the activities of the VIE, the terms of the contracts that it has entered into, and the terms under which investments were made in the VIE.

A reporting entity should consolidate its results with those of a VIE if the reporting entity and its related parties has a variable interest that will:

- Absorb a majority of the VIE's expected losses;
- Receive a majority of the VIE's expected residual returns; or both.

Related parties include officers, employees, or board members of the organization, or other entities with which the reporting entity has a close business relationship.

If one organization will absorb a majority of a VIE's expected losses and another organization will absorb a majority of the expected residual returns, the entity absorbing the losses should consolidate its results with those of the VIE.

It is possible that a VIE is not consolidated with any other entity. This situation arises when power is so distributed among multiple parties that no one party can direct the activities of a VIE. However, when power over similar activities is shared among multiple parties but one organization has power over a majority of the VIE activities, that entity should consolidate its results with those of the VIE. If an organization has power over activities that most significantly impact the economic performance of the VIE, that entity should consolidate.

The reporting entity that consolidates its results with those of a VIE is called the primary beneficiary. An entity should determine whether it is the primary beneficiary when it becomes involved with a VIE, and re-evaluate the situation whenever the contractual arrangement with the VIE changes to reallocate the expected losses and residual returns of the VIE. The primary beneficiary status should also be examined whenever the VIE issues additional variable interests to other parties, or the organization disposes of all or a portion of its interest in the VIE.

Note: If a reporting entity has a variable interest in specific assets of a VIE, this is considered a variable interest in the VIE when the fair value of the identified assets is more than half of the fair value of all the VIE assets.

Initial Consolidation

A key point when initially consolidating a new subsidiary is that the consolidated financial statements of the combined entity only include the revenues, expenses, gains, and losses of the subsidiary from the date of the initial consolidation. Any operating or financing results prior to the initial consolidation are not considered to belong to the corporate parent, and so are not included in the consolidated financial statements.

If the primary beneficiary of a VIE and the VIE are already under common control by a parent entity, the primary beneficiary initially measures the assets, liabilities, and noncontrolling interests of the VIE at the amounts at which they are carried in the accounting records of the reporting entity that has control over the VIE. If there is no parent entity and this is the initial consolidation of the two entities, then it is accounted for as a business combination, as described in the Business Combinations chapter.

If a VIE is not a business, the primary beneficiary does not recognize any goodwill as part of the initial consolidation. Instead, the primary beneficiary recognizes a gain or loss based on the following calculation:

| + Fair value of consideration received
+ Fair value of any noncontrolling interests
+ Reported amount of any previously held interests | - | Net amount of the VIE's identifiable assets and liabilities |

Subsequent Consolidation

Following the initial consolidation with a VIE, subsequent consolidations shall measure the assets, liabilities, and noncontrolling interests as though the VIE were consolidated based on the voting interests in the VIE. All other consolidation steps match those used for other entities, including the elimination of inter-company balances and transactions as described earlier in the Recognition of a Consolidation section.

Consolidation of Leasing Entities by Private Companies

The managers of a privately-held company may create a lessor entity that is separate from the main organization in order to take advantage of tax or estate-planning laws, or to reduce the legal liability of the main entity. They are not doing so in order to enter into off-balance sheet debt arrangements. In this situation, the reporting entity can elect not to apply VIE rules to the lessor entity. This option is only available when:

- Both entities are under common control;
- The private company has a lease arrangement with the lessor entity;
- Substantially all of the transactions between the entities relate to leasing activities; and
- If there is a private company guarantee of the obligations of the lessor, the beginning principal amount does not exceed the value of the asset leased by the private company.

Under this alternative, there is no need to provide VIE disclosures about the lessor entity. Instead, the private company only needs to disclose the following information:

- The amount and key terms of those lessor entity liabilities that expose the private company to an obligation to provide financial support; and
- A qualitative description of those circumstances that could expose the private company to providing financial support.

Consolidation of Contractually-Controlled Entities

A contractual management arrangement is one having both of the following characteristics:

- There is a relationship between two entities in the healthcare industry, where one entity is a physician practice and the other is a physician practice management entity; and
- The physician practice management entity does not own a majority of the voting equity of the physician practice.

Under this arrangement, the physician practice management entity can still establish a controlling financial interest in the physician practice via a contractual management arrangement where *all* of the following conditions exist:

- The term of the arrangement is for at least 10 years or the remaining life of the physician practice (based on the stated contract term and contract renewal provisions) and the agreement cannot be terminated by the physician practice except for cases of gross negligence or similar matters;

- The physician practice management entity has authority over decisions regarding the operations of the physician practice (except for medical services provided), including physician compensation; and
- The physician practice management entity has a significant financial interest in the physician practice that is saleable or transferable, and which gives it the right to receive income from the performance and changes in the fair value of the physician practice, as manifested when the practice is sold or liquidated. If the management arrangement ends before the liquidation or sale of the practice, the management entity must have the right to share in any change in fair value arising during the entity's relationship with the physician practice.

In the absence of a formal agreement, this controlling financial interest can still be established from the facts and circumstances of the situation.

EXAMPLE

Behemoth Medical enters into a practice management arrangement with Devonshire Medical Practice. The agreement has a contract term of four years, plus two three-year renewal options that can be unilaterally exercised by Behemoth. With the extensions included, this agreement is essentially a 10-year agreement, and so falls under the consolidation guidelines for a contractually-controlled entity.

If there is a binding arbitration clause in the management agreement, this does not necessarily mean that the physician practice management entity does not have authority over decisions regarding the operations of a physician practice, as long as the arbitration clause only applies to minor issues that do not override the authority of the management entity.

If the physician practice management entity cannot make decisions regarding the scope of services offered by a physician practice, this can preclude the assumption that the management entity can consolidate the physician practice. Examples of the scope of services offered are decisions about the range of urology, cardiology, or obstetrics services to provide.

A physician practice management entity is considered to have a controlling financial interest in a physician practice when both of the following conditions exist:

- The management entity owns a majority of the outstanding voting equity of the physician practice; and
- The management entity has the power to revise the terms of its financial interest in the physician practice, for little or no consideration.

Control of Partnerships

A reporting entity may be required to consolidate its investment in a partnership. No consolidation is required when the investment is as a limited partner in a partnership.

However, if the reporting entity is a general partner in a partnership, it is presumed to have control, and so should consolidate. If there are multiple general partners, determine which one has control by examining the relevant facts and circumstances of the arrangement.

In rare cases, additional rights given to limited partners overcome the assumption that a general partner has control of a partnership. This is the case when a simple majority (or less) vote of the limited partners can trigger one or more of the following events, without there being any significant barriers to doing so:

- Dissolve the partnership
- Remove the general partners without cause

EXAMPLE

There are 10 limited partners in the Altman Partnership, each holding an equal interest. Under the terms of the partnership agreement, a simple majority of the partners is required to remove the general partner, which therefore requires six favorable votes. If the partnership agreement had instead required at least seven votes in favor, this would be a supermajority requirement, and there would be no presumption that the limited partners control the partnership.

Barriers to such a vote that are considered significant include only being able to vote within a narrow time window, incurring a financial penalty, and the absence of a mechanism for the limited partners to conduct a vote.

The general partners may also not have control over a partnership when the limited partners have substantive participating rights. These rights allow limited partners to participate in certain decisions regarding the finances and operations of a partnership in the ordinary course of business. Examples of such decisions are setting management compensation, selecting or terminating managers, and establishing budgets. Examples of decisions that are *not* considered substantive are the right to select the name of the partnership, the location of its headquarters, and its outside auditors. The limited partners are not considered to have substantive participating rights when the general partners have the right to buy them out at fair value or less, and this option is prudent, feasible, and within the control of the general partners.

If the rights noted in this section are substantive, then the general partners are considered to not have control. In this situation, the general partners would not consolidate; instead, they should each use the equity method to account for their participation in the partnership.

Termination of a Consolidation

A parent entity should remove from its consolidated financial statements any subsidiary or group of assets as of the date when the parent no longer has a controlling financial interest in it. This means that the following items related to a subsidiary or group of assets are derecognized:

- Assets
- Liabilities
- Equity components, including noncontrolling interests, and amounts recognized in accumulated other comprehensive income

At the time of a deconsolidation, the parent entity recognizes a gain or loss based on the following calculation:

+ Fair value of consideration received		Carrying amount of the former
+ Fair value of any retained noncontrolling investment	-	subsidiary's assets and liabilities, or
+ Carrying amount of any noncontrolling interest		the carrying amount of the asset group

The control of a parent entity over a subsidiary may decline over time, through multiple transactions. It may be necessary to account for the effect of these transactions as a single event, depending on the terms of these arrangements or their effects. The following are indicators of situations where multiple transactions could be treated as a single transaction:

- The transactions occur at the same time
- One transaction contemplates the occurrence of another transaction at a later date
- They are designed to achieve an aggregated commercial effect
- One transaction is dependent on another transaction
- The outcome of the transactions net to a positive economic outcome, but not individually

The net effect of this analysis might be that a deconsolidation could occur sooner than might be indicated by a single underlying transaction.

Consolidation Presentation

It is sometimes necessary for a parent company to present just its own financial statements, without any consolidation with its subsidiaries. This information may be needed, for example, when the parent has issued bonds, and the security holders want to review the financial statements of just the entity that is committed to repay the bonds. In this situation, the general-purpose financial statements of the parent are considered to be its consolidated statements, not its individual statements. Thus, issuance of the statements for just the parent is considered to be a special-use situation.

It is possible that the fiscal year-ends of the parent and its subsidiary are different. If so, the subsidiary should prepare financial statements that match the fiscal year-end of the parent. It is also possible to use the existing fiscal year financial statements of the subsidiary, as long as the date difference is no more than "about" three months. In the latter case, be sure to disclose the effect of any intervening events that might materially affect the results or financial position of the subsidiary.

Note: For publicly-held entities, the Securities and Exchange Commission (SEC) allows a difference of not more than 93 days. When there is a difference, the SEC requires that the entity explain the necessity for using different closing dates, and also disclose any intervening events that materially affect the financial position or results of operations.

When there is a difference of more than 93 days, the SEC states that the financial statements for the latest fiscal be recast to dates that do not differ by more than 93 days, if practicable.

If there is a change in the previously existing difference between the reporting periods of a parent and a consolidated entity, disclose this change in the consolidated financial statements as a change in accounting principle. A typical cause of this change is that there has been a change in the previously-existing time lag related to the ability of the parent to obtain information for a reporting period that is the same as the one used by the parent.

There may be a noncontrolling interest in a subsidiary; this situation arises when there are other owners of a subsidiary than the parent. If so, this noncontrolling interest is considered to be part of the consolidated group's equity. This interest is reported in the consolidated balance sheet as part of equity, but separate from the equity of the parent. The noncontrolling interest should be clearly labeled as such. The following sample layout illustrates the concept. If an entity has a noncontrolling interest in several of the parent's subsidiaries, these interests can be aggregated for presentation in the consolidated balance sheet.

Sample Equity Layout within the Balance Sheet

Equity:	
Glow Atomic shareholders' equity	
Common stock, $0.01 par	$10,000
Paid-in capital	400,000
Retained earnings	2,300,000
Accumulated other comprehensive income	12,000
Total Glow Atomic shareholders' equity	$2,722,000
Noncontrolling interest	400,000
Total equity	$3,122,000

If there is a noncontrolling interest in a subsidiary, the amount of consolidated net income reported in the income statement should be separated into the amount attributable to the noncontrolling interest and the shareholders of the parent company. The following sample layout illustrates the concept.

Sample Net Income Layout within the Income Statement

Revenues	$10,000,000
Expenses	8,000,000
Net income	2,000,000
Less: Net income attributable to the noncontrolling interest	-400,000
Net income attributable to Dude Skis shareholders	$1,600,000

If there is a noncontrolling interest in a subsidiary, the reported amount of consolidated comprehensive income should be separated into the amount attributable to the noncontrolling interest and the shareholders of the parent company. The following sample layout illustrates the concept.

Net income	$400,000
Other comprehensive income:	
Unrealized holding gain on available for sale securities	20,000
Total other comprehensive income	20,000
Comprehensive income	420,000
Comprehensive income attributable to noncontrolling interest	-15,000
Comprehensive income attributable to Cud Farms shareholders	$405,000

If there is a noncontrolling interest in a subsidiary, it is also necessary to present a full-period reconciliation of the carrying amounts of total equity, and the equity portions attributable to the parent and the noncontrolling interest. The following sample layout illustrates the concept.

Financial Statement Consolidation

Franklin Drilling, Inc.
Consolidated Statement of Changes in Equity
Year Ended December 31, 20X4

(000s)	Total	Retained Earnings	Accumulated Other Comprehensive Income	Common Stock	Paid-in Capital	Noncontrolling Interest
			Franklin Drilling Shareholders			
Beginning balance	$1,000	$710	$50	$10	$150	$80
Purchase of subsidiary shares from noncontrolling interest	-60		-2		-18	-40
Net income	120	115				5
Other comprehensive income						
Unrealized gains on securities	30		28			2
Other comprehensive income	30					
Dividends paid on common stock	-40	-40				
Ending balance	$1,050	$785	$76	$10	$132	$47

Consolidation Disclosures

The following general disclosures should be made regarding consolidated financial statements:

- *Policy.* Note the consolidation policy being followed. For publicly-held companies, the SEC further requires that disclosure be made of the principles followed in consolidating financial statements, including the principles related to whether subsidiaries are included in the financial statements.
- *Partial ownership.* If a parent entity is consolidating with less than wholly-owned subsidiaries, it should disclose the following information:

  o The amounts of consolidated net income and consolidated comprehensive income, and the amount of each attributable to the parent and any noncontrolling interests.
  o The amounts of income from continuing operations and discontinued operations attributable to the parent.

447

- o   A reconciliation of the carrying amount of total equity, equity attributable to the parent, and equity attributable to the noncontrolling interest.
- o   A schedule stating the effects of any changes in the parent's ownership interest in a subsidiary on the equity attributed to the parent.

- *Deconsolidation*. When a subsidiary or a group of assets is deconsolidated, disclose the following information:

  - o   The amount of any gain or loss recognized, and the portion of this amount related to the remeasurement of any retained investment in the subsidiary or group of assets to its fair value.
  - o   A caption in the income statement that notes the nature of the gain or loss.
  - o   The valuation techniques used to measure the fair value of any retained investment in the subsidiary or group of assets, as well as information that can be used to assess the inputs used to develop this fair value amount.
  - o   The nature of any continuing involvement following deconsolidation.
  - o   Whether a related party was involved in the transaction resulting in the deconsolidation, and whether the former subsidiary or entity acquiring the asset group will now be a related party.

- *Change in reporting periods*. If there is a change in the previously existing difference between the reporting periods of a parent and a consolidated entity, disclose this change as a change in accounting principle.

The following additional disclosures are needed when consolidating with a VIE:

- *Primary beneficiary*. If the primary beneficiary of a VIE does not also hold a majority voting interest in the VIE, it should disclose the following information:

  - o   The size, purpose, nature, and activities of the VIE.
  - o   The carrying amount and classification of those consolidated assets that are designated as collateral for the VIE's obligations.
  - o   Whether there is no recourse for the creditors of a consolidated VIE to the credit of the primary beneficiary.
  - o   The terms of any arrangements with a consolidated VIE that might require the reporting entity to provide financial support to the VIE, and the circumstances under which this situation might arise.

- *Holder of a significant variable interest*. If a reporting entity is not the primary beneficiary of a VIE, but holds a significant variable interest in it, the entity should disclose the following information:

  - o   The nature of its involvement with the VIE.
  - o   When its involvement with the VIE began.

- o The size, purpose, nature, and activities of the VIE.
- o The maximum exposure to loss caused by the entity's involvement with the VIE, how this loss amount is determined, and the significant sources of exposure. If it is not possible to quantify the maximum loss, note this fact.
- o The carrying amount and classification of those assets and liabilities of the reporting entity relating to its variable interest in the VIE.
- o A tabular presentation of the asset and liability carrying amounts and maximum loss exposure previously noted. This should include a quantitative and qualitative discussion that allows users to understand the differences between these amounts. Included in the discussion should be the terms of any arrangements that could require the reporting entity to provide financial support, as well as the circumstances that could trigger a loss.
- o Information concerning any liquidity arrangements, guarantees, or other third-party commitments that could affect the fair value or risk of the variable interest of the reporting entity.
- o Any significant factors considered and judgments made in regard to the determination of which entity has the power to direct the activities of the VIE.

- *Involvement.* Either a reporting entity that is a primary beneficiary of a VIE or one that holds a variable interest in a VIE but is not the entity's primary beneficiary should disclose the following information:

  - o The method used to determine whether the reporting entity is the primary beneficiary of the VIE. This should include the significant judgments and assumptions made to arrive at the determination.
  - o If the decision to consolidate a VIE has changed, note the primary factors causing the change, as well as the effect on the financial statements of the reporting entity.
  - o The type and amount of any support provided to the VIE, and the reasons for doing so.
  - o A qualitative and quantitative discussion of the reporting entity's involvement with the VIE, including how the VIE is financed.

Summary

A large proportion of the text in this chapter was concerned with the control decision – does an organization have control over another entity or not? Examples of the situations in which this issue can arise are with VIEs, partnerships, and contractually-controlled entities. However, in most cases the establishment of control is clear, and will rarely change. Nonetheless, it makes sense to schedule a periodic review of the control situation for all business relationships, and to document the outcome of this review. The auditors may want to examine the thought process behind the determination of whether to consolidate, and so will want to examine this documentation.

Chapter 38
Derivatives and Hedging

---

815 = GAAP codification area for derivatives and hedging

Introduction

There are two key concepts in the accounting for derivatives and hedges. The first is that ongoing changes in the fair value of derivatives not used in hedging arrangements are generally recognized in earnings at once. The second is that ongoing changes in the fair value of derivatives and the hedged items with which they are paired may be parked in other comprehensive income for a period of time, thereby removing them from the basic earnings reported by a business. In the following sections, we build upon these concepts by addressing the nature of other comprehensive income, the details of the various types of derivative and hedge accounting, and related disclosure issues.

Other Comprehensive Income

In the following sections, we will refer to the recordation of certain hedging results in other comprehensive income. What is other comprehensive income?

The intent behind the concept of comprehensive income is to report on all changes in the equity of a business, other than those involving the owners of the business. Not all of these transactions appear in the income statement, so comprehensive income is needed to provide a broader view. Comprehensive income is comprised of net income and other comprehensive income. Other comprehensive income is comprised of the following items:

Foreign Currency Items

- Foreign currency translation adjustments
- Gains and losses on intra-company foreign currency transactions where settlement is not planned in the foreseeable future

Hedging Items

- Gains and losses on derivative instruments that are cash flow hedges
- Gains and losses on foreign currency translation adjustments that are net investment hedges in a foreign entity

Investment Items

- Unrealized holding gains and losses on available-for-sale debt securities
- Unrealized holding gains and losses resulting from the transfer of a debt security from the held-to-maturity classification to the available-for-sale classification
- Amounts recognized in other comprehensive income for debt securities classified as available-for-sale and held-to-maturity, if the impairment is not recognized in earnings
- Subsequent changes in the fair value of available-for-sale debt securities that had previously been written down as impaired

Postretirement Benefit Items

- Gains and losses from pension or postretirement benefits that have not been recognized as a component of net periodic benefit cost
- Prior service costs or credits associated with pension or postretirement benefits
- Transition assets or obligations linked to pension or postretirement benefits that have not been recognized as a component of net periodic benefit cost

If the items initially stated in other comprehensive income are later displayed as part of net income (typically because the transactions have been settled), this is essentially a reclassification out of the other comprehensive income classification. Otherwise, the items will be double-counted within comprehensive income. For example, an unrealized gain on an investment is initially recorded within other comprehensive income and is then sold, at which point the gain is realized and shifted from other comprehensive income to net income. In short, there is a continual shifting of items from other comprehensive income to net income over time.

Items of comprehensive income must be reported in a financial statement for the period in which they are recognized. If this information is presented within a single continuous income statement, the presentation encompasses the following:

- Net income and its components
- Other comprehensive income and its components
- Total comprehensive income

EXAMPLE

Armadillo Industries presents the following statement of income and comprehensive income.

Armadillo Industries
Statement of Income and Comprehensive Income
For the Year Ended December 31, 20X2

Revenues		$250,000
Expenses		-200,000
Other gains and losses		10,000
Gain on sale of securities		5,000
Income from operations before tax		$65,000
Income tax expense		-20,000
Net income		$45,000
Other comprehensive income, net of tax		
Foreign currency translation adjustments		2,000
Unrealized holding gains arising during period		11,000
Defined benefit pension plans:		
Prior period service cost arising during period	-$4,000	
Net loss arising during period	-1,000	-5,000
Other comprehensive income		8,000
Comprehensive income, net of tax		$53,000

In addition, the total of other comprehensive income for the reporting period must be stated in the balance sheet in a component of equity that is stated separately from retained earnings and additional paid-in capital.

EXAMPLE

Armadillo Industries reports accumulated other comprehensive income within the equity section of its balance sheet as follows:

Equity:	
Common stock	$1,000,000
Paid-in capital	850,000
Retained earnings	4,200,000
Accumulated other comprehensive income	270,000
Total equity	$6,320,000

Derivative Accounting

The essential accounting for a derivative instrument is outlined in the following bullet points:

- *Initial recognition.* When it is first acquired, recognize a derivative instrument in the balance sheet as an asset or liability at its fair value.
- *Subsequent recognition (hedging relationship).* Recognize all subsequent changes in the fair value of the derivative (known as *marked to market*). If the instrument has been paired with a hedged item, then recognize these fair value changes in other comprehensive income.
- *Subsequent recognition (speculation).* Recognize in earnings all subsequent changes in the fair value of the derivative. Speculative activities imply that a derivative has not been paired with a hedged item.

The following additional rules apply to the accounting for derivative instruments when specific types of investments are being hedged:

- *Held-to-maturity investments.* This is a debt instrument for which there is a commitment to hold the investment until its maturity date. When such an investment is being hedged, there may be a change in the fair value of the paired forward contract or purchased option. If so, only recognize a loss in earnings when there is an other-than-temporary decline in the hedging instrument's fair value.
- *Trading securities.* This can be either a debt or equity security, for which there is an intent to sell in the short term for a profit. When this investment is being hedged, recognize any changes in the fair value of the paired forward contract or purchased option in earnings.
- *Available-for-sale securities.* This is a debt security that does not fall into the held-to-maturity or trading classifications. When such an investment is being hedged, there may be a change in the fair value of the paired forward contract or purchased option. If so, only recognize a loss in earnings when there is an other-than-temporary decline in the hedging instrument's fair value. If the change is temporary, record it in other comprehensive income.

Hedge Accounting - General

The accounting for hedges involves matching a derivative instrument to a hedged item, and then recognizing gains and losses from both items in the same period. A derivative is always measured at its fair value. If the instrument is effective for a period of time, this may mean that incremental changes in its fair value are continually being recorded in the accounting records.

The intent behind hedge accounting is to allow a business to record changes in the value of a hedging relationship in other comprehensive income (except for fair value hedges), rather than in earnings. This is done in order to protect the core earnings of a business from periodic variations in the value of its financial instruments before they have been liquidated. Once a financial instrument has been liquidated, any accumulated gains or losses stored in other comprehensive income are shifted into earnings.

When a business uses a derivative as a hedge, it can elect to designate the derivative as belonging to one of the following three hedging classifications:

- *Fair value hedge*. The derivative is used to hedge the risk of changes in the fair value of an asset or liability, or of an unrecognized firm commitment.
- *Cash flow hedge*. The derivative is used to hedge variations in the cash flows associated with an asset or liability, or of a forecasted transaction.
- *Foreign currency hedge*. The derivative is used to hedge variations in the foreign currency exposure associated with a net investment in a foreign operation, a forecasted transaction, an available-for-sale security, or an unrecognized firm commitment.

If a derivative instrument is designated as belonging within one of these classifications, the gains or losses associated with the hedge are matched to any gains or losses incurred by the asset or liability with which the derivative is paired. However, the hedging relationship must first qualify for hedge accounting. To do so, the relationship must meet all of the following criteria:

- *Designation*. The hedging relationship must be designated as such at its inception. The documentation of the relationship must include the following:
  - The hedging relationship
  - The risk management objective and strategy, which includes identification of the hedging instrument and the hedged item, the nature of the risk being hedged, and the method used to determine hedge effectiveness and ineffectiveness.
  - If there is a fair value hedge of a firm commitment, a method for recognizing in earnings the asset or liability that represents the gain or loss on the hedged commitment.
  - If there is a cash flow hedge of a forecasted transaction, the period when the forecasted transaction will occur, the nature of the asset or liability involved, either the amount of foreign exchange being hedged or the number of items encompassed by the transaction, and the current price of the forecasted transaction.
- *Eligibility (hedged item)*. Only certain types of assets and liabilities can qualify for special accounting as a hedging relationship.
- *Eligibility (hedging item)*. Designate either all or a portion of the hedging instrument as such. Also, several derivative instruments can be jointly designated as the hedging instrument.
- *Effectiveness*. There is an expectation that the pairing will result in a highly effective hedge that offsets prospective changes in the cash flows or fair value associated with the hedged risk. A highly effective hedge is one in

which the change in fair value or cash flows of the hedge falls between 80% and 125% of the opposing change in the fair value or cash flows of the financial instrument that is being hedged. A regression analysis can be used instead of these percentage boundaries to determine hedge effectiveness. Over the life of a hedging relationship, the effectiveness of the pairing must be examined at least quarterly. A prospective analysis should also be made to estimate whether the relationship will be highly effective in future periods, typically using a probability-weighted analysis of changes in fair value or cash flows. If the relationship is no longer highly effective through the date of this assessment, then the pairing no longer qualifies for hedge accounting. It is possible to make a *qualitative* assessment of hedge effectiveness in these subsequent assessments; doing so requires the entity to verify and document in each quarter that the facts and circumstances related to the hedging relationship have not changed.

If a hedging relationship is not fully documented or is never documented at all, then all subsequent changes in fair value associated with these instruments must be immediately recorded as gains or losses in earnings.

Even if a hedge is considered to be effective, it is quite possible that some portion of the risk inherent in an underlying transaction will not be covered by a hedge. In this situation, gains and losses on the unhedged portion of a hedged pairing should be recorded in earnings.

EXAMPLE

Suture Corporation pays $1 million for an investment that is denominated in pounds. Suture's treasurer enters into a hedging transaction that is also denominated in pounds, and which is designed to be a hedge of the investment. One year later, Suture experiences a loss of $12,000 on the investment and a $9,000 gain on the hedging instrument. The full $9,000 gain on the hedging instrument is considered effective, so only the difference between the investment and its hedge - $3,000 – is recorded as a loss in earnings.

There may be cases in which a hedging instrument is being employed, where the third party is actually another entity under the umbrella of a parent company. In this case, risk is not being offloaded to a third party. Consequently, such a hedging instrument is not considered to be a hedge for the purposes of hedge accounting.

Hedge Accounting – Fair Value Hedges

The fair value of an asset or liability could change, which may affect the profits of a business. A fair value hedge is designed to hedge against this exposure to changes in fair value that are caused by a specific risk. It is possible to only hedge the risks associated with a portion of an asset or liability, as long as the effectiveness of the related hedge can be measured.

When a hedging relationship has been established for a fair value hedge, continually re-measure the fair value of the hedge and the item with which it is paired. The accounting for this re-measurement is as follows:

- *Hedging item.* Record a gain or loss in earnings for the change in fair value of the hedging instrument.
- *Hedged item.* Record a gain or loss in earnings for the change in fair value of the hedged item that can be attributed to the risk for which the hedge pairing was established. This also means that the carrying amount of the hedged item must be adjusted to reflect its change in fair value.

If the hedging relationship is fully effective, either the gain on the hedging instrument will exactly offset the loss on the hedged item that is associated with the hedged risk, or vice versa. The net result of a fully effective hedge is no change in earnings. If there is a net gain or loss appearing in earnings, it is due to hedge ineffectiveness, where the hedging relationship does not perfectly offset fair value changes in the hedged item.

EXAMPLE

Prickly Corporation buys ten bonds having an aggregate face value of $10,000. The bonds pay a 6% interest rate, which matches the current market rate. Prickly records the acquisition as an available-for-sale investment.

Prickly's treasurer reviews the investment, and concludes that an increase in the market rate of interest will reduce the value of the bonds. To hedge this risk, the treasurer enters into an interest rate swap whereby Prickly swaps the fixed 6% interest payments it is receiving from the bond issuer for payments from a third party that are based on a floating interest rate. The treasurer documents the interest rate swap as a hedge of the ten bonds.

Over the following months, the applicable market interest rate does indeed increase, which reduces the value of the bonds by an aggregate amount of $800. However, the interest rate swap yields an offsetting $800 gain, since the variable interest rate payments being received have increased to match the change in the market rate of interest. Prickly first records the following entry to document the loss in value of the bonds:

	Debit	Credit
Hedging loss	800	
Available-for-sale investment (asset)		800

Prickly also records the following entry to document the increased value of the interest rate swap:

	Debit	Credit
Swap asset (asset)	800	
Hedging gain		800

There is no net gain or loss arising from the increase in the market rate of interest, since the loss on the investment is exactly offset by the gain on the hedging instrument. This means the hedge pairing has been 100% effective.

Fair value hedge accounting should be terminated at once if any of the following situations arises:

- The hedging arrangement is no longer effective
- The hedging instrument expires or is sold or terminated
- The organization revokes the hedging designation

As noted in the preceding example, changes in the fair value of the hedged item are being used to adjust its carrying amount over time. Once the item is eventually disposed of, the adjusted carrying amount of the asset is recorded as the cost of the asset sold.

EXAMPLE

The treasurer of Prickly Corporation needs cash for operational requirements, and elects to sell the ten bonds that the company had acquired in the preceding example. In that example, the carrying amount of the bonds had been written down by $800 to reflect an increase in the market interest rate. The bonds are then sold for $9,200, resulting in the following entry:

	Debit	Credit
Cash	9,200	
Available-for-sale investment (asset)		9,200

Hedge Accounting – Cash Flow Hedges

There could be variations in the cash flows associated with an asset or liability or a forecasted transaction, which may affect the profits of a business. A cash flow hedge is designed to hedge against this exposure to changes in cash flows that are caused by a specific risk. It is possible to only hedge the risks associated with a portion of an asset, liability, or forecasted transaction, as long as the effectiveness of the related hedge can be measured. The entire change in the fair value of the hedging instrument included in the assessment of hedge effectiveness is to be initially recorded in other comprehensive income; this amount is then reclassified to earnings within the same income statement line item that is used to present the earnings effect of the item being hedged when that hedged item affects earnings.

There are several additional special situations involving cash flow hedges that require different accounting transactions. The following scenarios reveal the more likely accounting variations:

1. *Exclusions from strategy.* If the documented risk management strategy does not include a certain component of the gains or losses experienced by the hedged item, recognize this excluded amount in earnings. Doing so reduces the aggregate amount of gains or losses in other comprehensive income. Next;

2. *Adjust other comprehensive income.* Reduce the amount of accumulated other comprehensive income related to a hedging relationship to the lesser of:

    *   The cumulative gain or loss on the derivative from the date when the hedge began, less any gains or losses already reclassified into earnings; or
    *   The cumulative gain or loss on the derivative that will be needed to offset the cumulative change in expected future cash flows on the hedged transaction from the date when the hedge began, less any gains or losses already reclassified into earnings.

3. *Further gain or loss recognition.* Recognize in earnings any remaining gain or loss on the hedging derivative, or to revise the accumulated other comprehensive income amount to match the balance derived in step 2.

4. *Foreign currency adjustments.* If a foreign currency position is being hedged, and hedge effectiveness is based on the total changes in the cash flow of an option, then reclassify from other comprehensive income to earnings an amount sufficient to adjust earnings for the amortization of the option cost.

A key issue with cash flow hedges is when to recognize gains or losses in earnings when the hedging transaction relates to a forecasted transaction. These gains or losses should be reclassified from other comprehensive income to earnings when the hedged transaction affects earnings.

EXAMPLE

Suture Corporation has acquired equipment from a company in the United Kingdom, which Suture must pay for in 60 days in the amount of £150,000. Suture's functional currency is the U.S. Dollar. At the time of the purchase, Suture could settle this obligation for $240,000, based on the exchange rate then in effect.

To hedge against the risk of an unfavorable change in exchange rates during the intervening 60 days, Suture enters into a forward contract with its bank to buy £150,000 in 60 days, at the current exchange rate. Suture's controller designates the forward contract as a hedge of its exposure to adverse changes in the dollar to pounds exchange rate.

At the end of the next month, the pound has increased in value against the dollar, so that it would now require $242,000 to settle the obligation. Luckily, the value of the forward contract has also increased by $2,000, which results in the following entry:

	Debit	Credit
Forward asset (asset)	2,000	
Other comprehensive income		2,000

The exchange rate remains the same for the following month, after which the treasurer settles the forward contract and the controller records the following entry:

	Debit	Credit
Cash (asset)	2,000	
Forward asset (asset)		2,000

The payables staff then pays the $242,000 obligation to the United Kingdom supplier, as noted in the following entry. The transaction also includes a $2,000 reduction of the purchase price, which represents the deferred gain on the forward contract.

	Debit	Credit
Fixed assets – Equipment (asset)	240,000	
Other comprehensive income	2,000	
Cash (asset)		242,000

The net result of this hedging transaction is that Suture has used a hedging instrument to offset the risk of an adverse change in the applicable exchange rate, and so is able to pay for the equipment at the original purchase price.

EXAMPLE

Suture Corporation borrows $10 million on January 1, to be repaid with a balloon payment of $10 million on December 31 of the same year. The interest rate on the loan is LIBOR plus 2.0%, and is to be paid semi-annually. LIBOR on January 1 is 4.50%, so the initial interest rate on the loan is 6.50%. The treasurer of Suture is concerned that interest rates will increase during the borrowing period, and so enters into an interest rate swap with 3rd National Bank on the same day. Under the terms of the swap, Suture pays a fixed interest rate of 6.80% semi-annually for one year, while 3rd National takes over the variable interest payments of Suture. The notional amount of the swap arrangement is $10 million. Suture's cost of capital is 7%.

The swap arrangement qualifies as a cash flow hedge.

On June 30, the interest paid for the first six months of the loan is based on the initial 6.50% interest rate, so Suture records the following entry for a half-year of interest at 6.50% for a $10 million loan:

	Debit	Credit
Interest expense	325,000	
Cash (asset)		325,000

In addition, Suture also pays the net difference in the swapped interest rates of 0.3% on the notional contract amount of $10 million for the same six-month period. The entry is:

	Debit	Credit
Interest expense	15,000	
Cash (asset)		15,000

On June 30, the reference LIBOR rate adjusts upward to 5.50%, which means that the interest rate on Suture's loan will now be 7.50% for the remaining six months of the loan period. This also means that Suture will be paid the 0.7% difference between the new 7.50% variable interest rate and the 6.80% fixed-rate amount stated in the swap agreement, with this payment being made by 3rd National on the next (and final) payment date, which is December 31. The amount of this payment will be $35,000; when discounted to its present value at Suture's 7% cost of capital for six months, the amount is approximately $33,775. The entry to record this future payment on June 30 is:

	Debit	Credit
Swap contract	33,775	
Other comprehensive income		33,775

On the loan termination date of December 31, Suture makes the following interest expense payment to the lender, based on the 7.50% interest rate that applied to the preceding six-month period:

	Debit	Credit
Interest expense	375,000	
Cash (asset)		375,000

In addition, Suture reverses its accrual of the present value of the swap contract that it recorded on June 30, and replaces it with a recordation of the cash received from 3rd National in settlement of the swap contract. As calculated earlier, the amount of this payment is $35,000.

	Debit	Credit
Other comprehensive income	33,775	
Swap contract		33,775
Cash (asset)	35,000	
Interest expense		35,000

The net undiscounted effect of the interest rate swap is a net decline in Suture's interest expense of $20,000 over the full year covered by the loan, which represents a net decline of 0.2% in the interest rate paid.

Cash flow hedge accounting should be terminated at once if any of the following situations arises:

- The hedging arrangement is no longer effective
- The hedging instrument expires or is terminated
- The organization revokes the hedging designation

If it is probable that the hedged forecasted transaction will not occur within the originally-stated time period or within two months after this period, shift the derivative's gain or loss from accumulated other comprehensive income to earnings.

Hedge Accounting – Net Investment Hedges

A business may have an investment in operations in another country. If so, changes in the exchange rate between the functional currency of the parent entity and the currency of the foreign operations could create gains or losses. In this situation, it is possible to create a net investment hedge that is equal to or less than the carrying amount of the net assets of the foreign operation.

The accounting for such a hedge is to recognize the entire amount of any gains or losses on the hedge in the currency translation adjustment section of other comprehensive income. If the parent entity ever disposes of the foreign operations, shift the cumulative net amount of any gains or losses recognized in other comprehensive income as part of the hedging instrument into earnings.

EXAMPLE

Suture Corporation invests $20 million in a new subsidiary located in England. The functional currency of this subsidiary is the pound. The exchange rate on the investment date is $1 = £0.6463, so the initial investment is priced at £12,926,000. Suture takes out a loan in England in the amount of £9,695,000 (which translates to $15,000,000) and designates it as a hedge of its investment in the subsidiary. The stated strategy is that any change in the fair value of the loan attributed to foreign exchange risk will offset 75% of the translation gains or losses on the Suture investment.

One year later, the exchange rate has changed to $1 = £0.6600, which yields the following loss on the investment for Suture:

$$(£12,926,000 \div 0.6600 = \$19,585,000) - \$20,000,000$$

$$= \$(415,000) \text{ Investment translation loss}$$

Against this loss is set the following gain on the related loan:

$$(£9,695,000 \div 0.6600 = \$14,689,000) - \$15,000,000$$

$$= \$311,000 \text{ Loan translation gain}$$

Suture creates the following entry to record the reduction in value of its investment, as well as the translation gain related to its loan:

	Debit	Credit
Cumulative translation adjustment	415,000	
Investment in subsidiary		415,000
Pound-denominated debt	311,000	
Cumulative translation adjustment		311,000

Embedded Derivatives

An embedded derivative is an element of a financial instrument that has the characteristics of a derivative. Thus, the embedded derivative must require that some portion of the cash flows associated with the overall instrument be adjusted in relation to changes in an underlying, as noted earlier. To be an embedded derivative, it is not possible for this element of a financial instrument to be transferred separately from the rest of the contract.

When there is an embedded derivative within a financial instrument, the entire instrument is considered a hybrid financial instrument.

It is possible to separately account for an embedded derivative, but only when both of the following conditions are present:

- The economic characteristics and risks of the derivative element are not closely related to the economic characteristics and risks of the financial instrument in which it is embedded; and
- A separate instrument with the characteristics and risks of the embedded derivative would have been classified as a derivative instrument.

There are several alternatives available for accounting for an embedded derivative, including the following:

- *No separate measurement possible.* If it is not possible to reliably measure an embedded derivative, then measure the entire hybrid financial instrument at its fair value. Also, when there is a change in this fair value, recognize the change in earnings in the reporting period in which the change occurs.
- *Election to combine.* A one-time and irrevocable election can be made to measure the entire hybrid financial instrument at its fair value, with no breakout of the embedded derivative. When there is a change in this fair

value, recognize the change in earnings in the reporting period in which the change occurs.

- *Separate accounting.* If the preceding two conditions are present that allow for the separate accounting for an embedded derivative, then the derivative and the contract in which it is embedded are tracked and accounted for separately, based on their respective fair values. However, the sum of their fair values cannot exceed the overall fair value of the hybrid instrument.

EXAMPLE

Hubble Corporation purchases 50 convertible bonds that have been issued by Medusa Medical. Hubble acquires the bonds at face value, so the total amount paid is $50,000. The conversion terms incorporated into the bonds state that each bond contains an option to purchase two shares of Medusa common stock for $14 per share.

The economic characteristics and risks of the option feature are not closely related to the debt features of the bond to which it is attached, and a separate instrument with the option features would have been classified as a derivative instrument. The estimated fair value of the option feature, in aggregate for all 50 bonds, is $600.

Based on this information, Hubble's accountant elects to separately account for the option feature and the bonds. The result is the following initial entry:

	Debit	Credit
Investments (asset)	49,400	
Derivative asset (asset)	600	
Cash (asset)		50,000

Derivative and Hedging Disclosures

There are a number of specific disclosures related to derivatives and hedging, as well as more specific disclosure requirements for fair value hedges and cash flow hedges. As a general presentation rule, a business should present the earnings effect of the hedging instrument in the same line item in the income statement in which the earnings effect of the hedged item is reported. By doing so, a user of the income statement can more clearly see the results and costs of the hedging program.

In the following sub-sections, we separately address the disclosures required for fair value hedges and cash flow hedges. These disclosures are stated at a relatively high level – GAAP calls for exceedingly detailed disclosures for derivatives and hedges.

General Disclosures

The following information should be disclosed about the derivative positions and hedging activities of a business in the notes that accompany its financial statements;

the disclosures should be made separately for cash flow hedging instruments, fair value hedging instruments, foreign currency hedging instruments, and all other derivatives:

- *Overview*. The objectives and strategies of the entity's derivatives program, including how and why the business uses them. This information can be more meaningful to the reader if the discussion is in the context of overall risk exposures relating to risks for interest rates, foreign exchange, commodity prices, credit, and equity prices.
- *Accounting*. How the derivatives and hedged items are accounted for by the organization.
- *Impact*. The effect of the hedging activities on the financial position, financial results, and cash flows of the business.
- *Volume*. The volume of activity in the organization's derivatives program.

SAMPLE DISCLOSURE

As a matter of policy, we use derivatives for risk management purposes, and we do not use derivatives for speculative purposes. A key risk management objective for our leasing business is to mitigate interest rate and currency risk by seeking to ensure that the characteristics of the debt match the assets they are funding. If the form (fixed versus floating) and currency denomination of the debt we issue do not match the related assets, we typically execute derivatives to adjust the nature and tenor of funding to meet this objective within pre-defined limits. The determination of whether we enter into a derivative transaction or issue debt directly to achieve this objective depends on a number of factors, including market-related factors that affect the type of debt we can issue.

The notional amounts of derivative contracts represent the basis upon which interest and other payments are calculated and are reported gross, except for offsetting foreign currency forward contracts that are executed in order to manage our currency risk of net investment in foreign subsidiaries. Of the outstanding notional amount of $40 million, approximately 87%, or $28 million, is associated with reducing or eliminating the interest rate, currency or market risk between financial assets and liabilities in our leasing business. The remaining derivative activities primarily relate to hedging against adverse changes in currency exchange rates related to anticipated sales and purchases and contracts containing certain clauses that meet the accounting definition of a derivative. The instruments used in these activities are designated as hedges when practicable.

In addition, the following information should be disclosed by contract type:

- *Fair values*. The fair values of all derivatives recognized in the balance sheet, as well as the line items in which they are located.
- *Fair value hedge totals*. The gains or losses on derivatives and the hedged items with which they are paired for fair value hedges.
- *Cash flow hedge totals*. The gains or losses on derivatives and the hedged items with which they are paired for cash flow hedges.

- *All other hedge totals*. The gains or losses on derivatives and the hedged items with which they are paired for all other hedges.

SAMPLE DISCLOSURE

Fair Value of Derivative Instruments at December 31, 20X5:

(000s)	Derivative Assets Balance Sheet Location	Fair Value	Derivative Liabilities Balance Sheet Location	Fair Value
Hedging Instruments				
Interest rate contracts	Other assets	$13,000	Other liabilities	-$7,000
Foreign exchange contracts	Other assets	27,000	Other liabilities	-12,000
Commodity contracts	Other assets	3,000	Other liabilities	-2,000
Totals		$43,000		-$21,000
Non-Hedging Instruments				
Interest rate contracts	Other assets	$3,000	Other liabilities	-$2,000
Foreign exchange contracts	Other assets	9,000	Other liabilities	-4,000
Commodity contracts	Other assets	2,000	Other liabilities	-1,000
Total		$14,000		-$7,000
Total derivatives		$57,000		-$28,000

If there are disclosures related to derivatives in several footnotes, cross-reference the information across the footnotes.

Fair Value Hedge Disclosures

The following additional disclosure should be made when the organization engages in fair value hedging transactions:

- *Tabular disclosure*. When items qualify as being hedged in a fair value hedge, the following information should be presented in tabular format:
  o The carrying amount of the hedged assets and liabilities.
  o The cumulative amount of fair value hedging adjustments included in the carrying amount of the hedged assets and liabilities.
  o The balance sheet line item in which the hedged assets and liabilities are located.
  o The cumulative amount of fair value hedging adjustments remaining when hedge accounting has been discontinued.

- *Terminated qualification.* When a hedged firm commitment no longer qualifies as a fair value hedge, note the net gain or loss that was recognized in earnings.

Cash Flow Hedge Disclosures

The following additional disclosures should be made when the organization engages in cash flow hedging transactions:

- *Reclassifications.* The transactions that caused a reclassification of gains or losses from other comprehensive income to earnings.
- *Estimated reclassifications.* The estimated amount of gains or losses that are expected to be reclassified from other comprehensive income to earnings within the next 12 months.
- *Exposure duration.* The maximum period over which the organization is hedging its exposure to the future cash flows arising from forecasted trans- actions.
- *Discontinuance reclassifications.* The amount of the gains or losses that were reclassified from other comprehensive income to earnings, due to cash flow hedges being discontinued because it is no longer probable that fore- casted transactions will occur during the planned time period.
- *Net changes.* The beginning and ending accumulated gain or loss for derivatives, including for the current period the net changes caused by cur- rent period hedging activities and the net amount of all reclassifications into earnings.

In addition, note in a separate line item within the statement of comprehensive income the net gain or loss on derivative instruments that have been designated as cash flow hedges.

SAMPLE DISCLOSURE

For derivatives that are designated in a cash flow hedging relationship, the effective portion of the change in fair value of the derivative is reported as a component of other comprehensive income and reclassified into earnings contemporaneously and in the same caption with the earnings effects of the hedged transaction.

We expect to transfer $28 million to earnings as an expense in the next 12 months contemporaneously with the earnings effects of the related forecasted transactions.

At December 31, 20X3 and 20X2, the maximum term of derivative instruments that hedge forecasted transactions was 9 years and 10 years, respectively.

In 20X3, we recognized insignificant gains and losses related to hedged forecasted transactions and firm commitments that did not occur by the end of the originally specified period.

The following table provides information about the amounts recorded in other comprehensive income, as well as the gain (loss) recorded in earnings, when reclassified out of other comprehensive income, for the years ended December 31, 20X3 and 20X2, respectively.

(000s)	Gain (Loss) Recognized in Accumulated Other Comprehensive Income		Gain (Loss) Reclassified from Accumulated Other Comprehensive Income into Earnings	
	20X7	20X6	20X7	20X6
Interest rate contracts	-$114	-$73	-$342	-$210
Currency exchange contracts	582	389	436	291
Totals	$468	$316	$94	$81

Summary

The accounting for derivatives and hedges is among the most complex in all of accounting, especially for outlier situations where the circumstances must be closely examined to ensure that the proper accounting rules are followed. In many instances, and especially when the accountant is dealing with a new transaction, it can make sense to consult with the company's auditors regarding the proper accounting to use.

The payoff for this high level of accounting complexity is a delay in the recognition of gains or losses in earnings. If management is not concerned about more immediate recognition, or if the gains or losses are minor, it may make sense to ignore the multitude of compliance issues associated with hedge accounting. Instead, simply create hedges as needed and record gains or losses on foreign exchange holdings and hedges at once, without worrying about the proper documentation of each hedging relationship and having to repeatedly measure hedge effectiveness.

Chapter 39
Fair Value Measurement

Introduction

There is a growing emphasis within GAAP (and other accounting frameworks) to recognize assets and liabilities at their fair values, rather than the costs at which they were originally purchased or assumed. The techniques for determining fair values are described within this chapter, as well as fair value disclosure requirements and several related topics. Fair value is also mentioned in passing in a number of other chapters, for those assets and liabilities to which the concept applies.

The Fair Value Concept

A business may have certain assets or liabilities that are to be recorded at their fair values, rather than their historical costs. A classic example is marketable securities, for which the recognized costs of certain classes of securities are to be adjusted at the end of each reporting period. The adjustment to fair value is based on a theoretical price at which an asset may be sold or a liability settled – there is no need to actually sell off assets or obtain bids in order to derive fair value.

Fair value is the estimated price at which an asset can be sold or a liability settled in an orderly transaction to a third party under current market conditions. This definition includes the following concepts:

- *Current market conditions.* The derivation of fair value should be based on market conditions on the measurement date, rather than a transaction that occurred at some earlier date.
- *Intent.* The intention of the holder of an asset or liability to continue to hold it is irrelevant to the measurement of fair value. Such intent might otherwise alter the measured fair value. For example, if the intent is to immediately sell an asset, this could be inferred to trigger a rushed sale, which may result in a lower sale price.
- *Orderly transaction.* Fair value is to be derived based on an orderly transaction, which infers a transaction where there is no undue pressure to sell, as may be the case in a corporate liquidation.
- *Third party.* Fair value is to be derived based on a presumed sale to an entity that is not a corporate insider or related in any way to the seller. Otherwise, a related-party transaction might skew the price paid.

The ideal determination of fair value is based on prices offered in an active market. An active market is one in which there is a sufficiently high volume of transactions to provide ongoing pricing information. Also, the market from which a fair value is derived should be the principal market for the asset or liability, since the greater transaction volume associated with such a market should presumably lead to the best prices for the seller. The market in which a business normally sells the asset type in question or settles liabilities is assumed to be the principal market.

> **Tip:** If there is no principal market for the assets or liabilities being valued, the alternative is to obtain a fair value from the most advantageous market, which is the market in which the best price can be obtained, net of transaction costs.

It is possible to derive a price from a quote issued by a broker. In this case, the resulting price is considered more reliable when it is associated with a binding offer. Conversely, the mere issuance of an indicative price by a broker does not indicate much pricing research by the broker or a commitment to sell, and so is considered less reliable.

In addition, the determination of fair value should be based on the condition and location of the asset, as well as any restrictions on the use of the asset. For example, shares in a company that are restricted will have a substantially lower fair value than unrestricted shares. Also, machinery that has been used more than the average number of hours will have a lower fair value.

> **Tip:** If an asset or liability is location-dependent, include in the fair value determination the cost required to transport the item to the market in which its fair value is to be estimated.

An additional consideration when determining fair value is the concept of highest and best use. Under this concept, fair value is determined based on the price at which an asset could theoretically be employed in its highest and best use, rather than the use in which an asset is currently employed.

EXAMPLE

Creekside Industrial buys a patent for $1,000,000 that would allow the company to build a technologically-advanced lithium-ion battery. However, Creekside simply sits on the patent, thereby preventing any competitors from using the technology. The fair value of the patent should be based on licensing the patent to competitors, since doing so would yield substantially higher profits than simply parking the patent, as is currently the case.

Depending on the applicable GAAP standards, it may be necessary to update fair values in the accounting records at regular intervals. If so, account for these changes as changes in accounting estimate (see the Accounting Changes and Error Corrections chapter).

Fair Value Differences from Actual Prices Paid

There are a number of reasons why the price at which an asset is sold or a liability is settled can vary from its fair value. Consider the following situations:

- *Duress*. The seller may be in a position where it must liquidate assets at once, and so cannot engage in a more prolonged and detailed sales process to achieve a better price. The most common case is the seller's bankruptcy, but it is also possible that the seller was required to sell in order to meet new regulatory requirements.
- *Market*. The asset or liability may be sold or settled in a market that is not the most advantageous one in which to handle such a transaction, resulting in a less-than-favorable price. For example, securities may be sold in a local market, where there are fewer bidders than on a national exchange.
- *Related parties*. The buyer and seller may be related, which introduces the possibility that there are insider reasons for skewing the price paid.
- *Unusual elements*. The seller may be including additional warranties or bundling other products or services with the item being sold, which makes it difficult to compare prices.

In these situations, do not place reliance on the information for deriving fair values, for these results could vary significantly from actual fair market values. Conversely, if these factors are not present, *and* the volume of market transactions is large, *and* the comparison transactions are close to the measurement date, the derived fair values can probably be relied upon.

Fair Value Measurement Approaches

There are several general approaches that GAAP permits for deriving fair values. These approaches are outlined below:

- *Market approach*. Uses the prices associated with actual market transactions for similar or identical assets and liabilities to derive a fair value. For example, the prices of securities held can be obtained from a national exchange on which these securities are routinely bought and sold.
- *Income approach*. Uses estimated future cash flows or earnings, adjusted by a discount rate that represents the time value of money and the risk of cash flows not being achieved, to derive a discounted present value. An alternative way to incorporate risk into this approach is to develop a probability-weighted-average set of possible future cash flows. Option pricing models can also be used under the income approach.
- *Cost approach*. Uses the estimated cost to replace an asset (or the capabilities of the asset), adjusted for the obsolescence of the existing asset.

EXAMPLE

There are several possible cash flows expected from the use of an asset. Management assigns the following probabilities to each scenario:

Cash Flow Scenario	Probability	Probability-Weighted Cash Flows
$800,000	10%	$80,000
1,500,000	70%	1,050,000
3,000,000	20%	600,000
	100%	$1,730,000

The risk-free interest rate is 3%, and the estimated risk premium for the variability of cash flows is 4%, for a combined discount rate of 7%. The discounted cash flows of these probability-weighted cash flows are therefore $1,730,000 ÷ 1.07, or $1,616,822. This is the fair value of the asset, using the income approach.

EXAMPLE

A company recently purchased a machine and heavily customized it to meet the needs of the organization's unique production line. Since the machine has been so heavily customized, there are no comparable market transactions that relate to it. Also, since the machine is part of a production line, there is no way to associate any cash flows specifically to it. These concerns leave the business no alternative other than to use the cost approach to derive fair value. The company determines that it would require a $380,000 expenditure to replace the capabilities of this asset, adjusted for the amount of existing wear and tear on the equipment.

Ideally, the valuation method chosen should maximize the use of observable inputs to the valuation process. Observable inputs are derived from market data that properly reflect the assumptions that third parties would use when setting prices for assets and liabilities. Examples of markets that are considered to provide observable inputs are stock exchanges and dealer markets.

No matter which method is chosen, it may be necessary to include a risk adjustment in the formulation of fair value. This risk adjustment may be a premium that a counterparty would require in order to take on any uncertainties in the cash flows associated with an asset or liability.

The ideal conditions are not always available for obtaining the fair value of an asset or liability. Consequently, GAAP provides a hierarchy of information sources that range from Level 1 (best) to Level 3 (worst). The general intent of these levels of information is to step the accountant through a series of valuation alternatives, where solutions closer to Level 1 are preferred over Level 3. The characteristics of the three levels are as follows:

- *Level 1.* This is a quoted price for an identical item in an active market on the measurement date. This is the most reliable evidence of fair value, and should be used whenever this information is available. When there is a bid-ask price spread, use the price most representative of the fair value of the asset or liability. This may mean using a bid price for an asset valuation and an ask price for a liability. When a quoted Level 1 price is adjusted , doing so automatically shifts the result into a lower level. Also, do not alter a Level 1 price just because the company's holdings of a security are quite large in comparison to the normal daily trading volume of the relevant market.

- *Level 2*. This is directly or indirectly observable inputs other than quoted prices. An example of a Level 2 input is a valuation multiple for a business unit that is based on the sale of comparable entities. This definition includes prices for assets or liabilities that are (with key items noted in bold):
    - o For **similar** items in active markets; or
    - o For identical or similar items in **inactive** markets; or
    - o For inputs **other than** quoted prices, such as credit risks, default rates, and interest rates; or
    - o For inputs **derived from** correlation with observable market data.

It may be necessary to adjust the information derived from Level 2 inputs, since it does not exactly match the assets or liabilities for which fair values are being derived. Adjustments may be needed for such factors as the condition of assets and the transaction volume of the markets from which information is derived.

- *Level 3*. This is an unobservable input. It may include the company's own data, adjusted for other reasonably available information. Examples of a Level 3 input are an internally-generated financial forecast and the prices contained within an offered quote from a distributor.

These three levels are known as the *fair value hierarchy*. Please note that these three levels are only used to select inputs to valuation techniques (such as the market approach). The three levels are not used to directly create fair values.

A company may rely upon the prices obtained in a particular market to derive its fair value calculations. These prices can require significant adjustment if the volume of activity in the market has declined. Evidence of such a decline includes a reduced number of recent transactions, large swings in price quotations over time, wide bid-ask spreads, and a decline in new issuances.

If the accountant is using information in a higher category of the fair value hierarchy and adjusts it with information from a lower level of the hierarchy, it may be necessary to designate the outcome as being from the lower level of the hierarchy. This happens when the adjustment results in a significantly higher or lower fair value measurement.

When adjusting fair values from period to period, use the same valuation technique(s) each time. Doing so introduces consistency into the derivation process. However, it is permissible to switch to alternative valuation technique(s) if the resulting change will be equally or more representative of the fair value of the asset or liability in question. Such a change may be necessary, for example, when a new market develops for the sale of an asset that yields enhanced pricing. If there is a change in fair value that is triggered by a change in measurement method, account for the change as a change in accounting estimate (see the Accounting Changes and Error Corrections chapter).

The Net Asset Value Variation

An entity may be able to redeem an investment. For example, a partner in a business may be able to redeem shares held in the business at the net asset value of shares held. As a practical expedient, net asset value per share is not categorized within the fair value hierarchy.

Fair Value Measurements for Liabilities

It is much less common to derive a fair value for a liability than for an asset. When it is necessary to do so, it is possible that there will be few markets available on which similar liabilities are sold. If so, here are several alternatives for deriving fair value:

- *Offsetting asset in active market*. There may be a market in which other parties hold the same item, but as the counterparty. This means they are holding the item as an asset. If so, use the quoted price for sale of the asset.
- *Offsetting asset in inactive market*. A less-reliable source of information is the same as the last bullet point, but in an inactive market for the same asset.
- *Income approach*. In the absence of the first two alternatives, estimate the income that a counterparty can be expected to receive from holding the liability as an asset. Alternatively, estimate the cash flows that a market participant would likely incur to fulfill the requirements of the liability, including a premium for taking on the risk that the liability could be higher than expected.

When developing the fair value of a liability based on the value of an asset held by a counterparty, it may be necessary to adjust the fair value. For example, the characteristics of the related asset may vary somewhat from the characteristics of the liability in question, as may be the case with the credit quality of a receivable, or for a bundle of receivables.

Use of Multiple Measurements

It is allowable to estimate fair value using a number of valuation methods. This is especially common when deriving the fair value of a substantial asset, such as a reporting unit. The result is likely to be a fairly wide range of valuations. If so, it will be necessary to derive a single value from this information that will then be used as the fair value of the asset. The ideal result is one that best represents the asset's fair value. The designation of this fair value point should be the result of a careful evaluation of the inputs to the valuation methods, the nature of the valuation methods, the amount of subjective judgments made, and possibly a weighting of the various results. If there is still a wide range of valuations, this can indicate that additional analysis is required.

Ideally, the valuation chosen should maximize the use of observable inputs in the analysis process. Observable inputs are derived from market data that properly reflect the assumptions that third parties would use when setting prices for assets and liabilities.

Fair Value Disclosures

On an ongoing basis, a company should disclose information that allows readers of its financial statements to assess the valuation techniques and inputs used to develop fair values, as well as the impact on earnings and changes in net assets of Level 3 measurements. To meet these disclosure goals, a business should disclose the following items in each interim and annual reporting period for each class of assets and liabilities:

- *Measurement.* The amount of the fair value measurement as of the reporting date.
- *Fair value hierarchy.* The level within the fair value hierarchy associated with each fair value measurement.
- *Transfers.* The amounts of any transfers between Levels 1 and 2 that are significant, and the reasons for the transfers. State transfers in and out of each level separately.
- *Level 3.* For measurements based on Level 3 inputs, reconcile the beginning and ending balances, separately noting total gains and losses, gains and losses recognized in earnings, gains and losses recognized in other comprehensive income, and notations regarding the financial statement line items in which these gains and losses are located. Also separately state all purchases, sales, issuances, and settlements. State any transfers into or out of Level 3, and the reasons for these transfers. Finally, note the total gains and losses recognized in earnings that are caused by a change in unrealized gains or losses in assets and liabilities that are still held as of the reporting date, as well as where these gains and losses are stated in the income statement.
- *Techniques used.* For valuations using Level 2 or 3 inputs, describe the valuation techniques and inputs used to determine fair value. Disclose any changes in valuation techniques, and the reasons for these changes.
- *Sensitivity analysis.* For valuations using Level 3 inputs, describe the sensitivity of the valuations to changes in observable inputs.
- *Highest and best use.* Note those situations in which the highest and best use of a nonfinancial asset differs from its actual usage, and why this is the case.
- *Credit enhancement.* If a liability has an inseparable third-party credit enhancement and its fair value is being measured, note the existence of the credit enhancement.

There are also a number of disclosures associated with fair value measurements that occur on a non-recurring basis (such as for an impaired asset). These disclosures are:

- *Measurement*. The amount of the fair value measurement in the period, and the reason for the measurement.
- *Fair value hierarchy*. The level within the fair value hierarchy associated with the fair value measurement. This should include segregation of fair values by each level in the fair value hierarchy.
- *Techniques used*. For valuations using Level 2 or 3 inputs, describe the valuation techniques and inputs used to determine fair value. Disclose any changes in valuation techniques, and the reasons for these changes.
- *Highest and best use*. Note those situations in which the highest and best use of a nonfinancial asset differs from its actual usage, and why this is the case.

There are situations where assets are measured at the net asset value of shares held (see the Net Asset Value Variation section). In these cases, disclose the following information:

- *Measurement*. The fair values of the investments in this classification, as well as the investment strategies of the investees.
- *Liquidation period*. For those assets that cannot be redeemed, but for which there are liquidation distributions, the time period over which liquidation should occur.
- *Commitments*. The amount of any unfunded commitments for the designated investments.
- *Redemption terms*. The terms and conditions under which investment redemption can occur.
- *Restrictions*. The circumstances of any restrictions on investment redemption, as well as the time left until the restriction lapses. If the restriction does not lapse, note this fact, as well as how long the restriction has been imposed. Also note any other significant restrictions on the ability to sell these assets.

When presenting fair value information by classification, the classification of assets and liabilities should be based on the following factors:

- The nature of the underlying assets and liabilities, which includes their characteristics and risk profiles.
- The level of the fair value hierarchy in which the fair value measurements for the assets or liabilities are categorized.

There may be more classifications of assets and liabilities presented in the accompanying disclosures than are shown in the balance sheet. If so, present sufficient information in the disclosures so that readers of the financial statements can reconcile the disclosures back to the balance sheet.

When presenting the quantitative information for any of the preceding disclosures, the information must be disclosed in a tabular format. For example:

(000s) Description	Total as of 12/31/X2	Quoted Prices in Active Markets for Identical Assets (Level 1)	Significant Other Observable Inputs (Level 2)	Significant Unobservable Inputs (Level 3)
Trading securities	$1,390	$1,000	$390	
Available-for-sale securities	325	275	50	
Derivatives	480	100	200	$180
Private equity investments	150			150
Totals	$2,345	$1,375	$640	$330

Summary

A considerable amount of work can be required to devise the fair values of some assets and liabilities. Consequently, this is one area of GAAP that seems to require an inordinate amount of work. To lessen the burden, consider avoiding any transactions that will require the company to delve into Level 3 of the fair value hierarchy, where the murky nature of the information requires additional disclosure. Also, try to standardize transactions from period to period, so that the same valuation procedures can be copied forward over time, reducing the amount of original accounting effort that might otherwise be required.

Chapter 40
Financial Instruments

825 = GAAP codification area for financial instruments

Introduction

This chapter provides coverage of several general topics related to financial instruments, including off-balance sheet credit risk, disclosures related to the fair value option, and registration statement arrangements. References to more information about financial instruments are provided in the Related Chapters section. The guidance in this chapter applies to all entities.

Related Chapters

See the following chapters for discussions of issues related to financial instruments:

- *Debt*. Covers the classification of debt, as well as the accounting for debt conversion features, troubled debt restructurings, and other topics.
- *Investments – Debt and Equity Securities*. Covers the proper classification of debt and equity securities.

Off-Balance Sheet Credit Risk

Some financial instruments may have off-balance-sheet credit risk that relates to such items as loan commitments and standby letters of credit. If there are credit losses on these instruments, use the following accounting:

- Record an accrual for the credit loss separately from any valuation account that is paired with the financial instrument.
- Deduct credit losses from the liability for credit losses on the settlement date.

Fair Value Option

A business has the option to record its financial instruments at their fair values. GAAP allows this treatment for the following items:

- A financial asset or financial liability
- A firm commitment that only involves financial instruments
- A loan commitment

- An insurance contract where the insurer can pay a third party to provide goods or services in settlement, and where the contract is not a financial instrument (i.e., requires payment in goods or services)
- A warranty in which the warrantor can pay a third party to provide goods or services in settlement, and where the contract is not a financial instrument (i.e., requires payment in goods or services)

The fair value option cannot be applied to the following items:

- An investment in a subsidiary or variable interest entity that will be consolidated
- Deposit liabilities of depository institutions
- Financial assets or financial leases recognized under lease arrangements
- Financial instruments classified as an element of shareholders' equity
- Obligations or assets related to pension plans, postemployment benefits, stock option plans, and other types of deferred compensation

When the election is made to measure an item at its fair value, do so on an instrument-by-instrument basis. When the fair value option election is taken for an instrument, the change in reporting is irrevocable. The fair value election can be made on either of the following dates:

- The election date, which can be when an item is first recognized, when there is a firm commitment, when qualification for specialized accounting treatment ceases, or there is a change in the accounting treatment for an investment in another entity.
- In accordance with a company policy for certain types of eligible items.

It is acceptable not to apply the fair value option to eligible items when reporting the results of a subsidiary or consolidated variable interest entity, but to apply the fair value option to these items when reporting consolidated financial statements.

> **Tip:** It is much easier to apply the fair value option for both subsidiary-level and consolidated financial results, so do not attempt separate treatment, even though it is allowed by GAAP.

In most cases, it is acceptable to choose the fair value option for an eligible item, while not electing to use it for other items that are essentially identical.

If the fair value option is taken, report unrealized gains and losses on the elected items at each subsequent reporting date. If a portion of the change in the fair value of a financial liability results from a change in the instrument-specific credit risk, enter this element separately in other comprehensive income. This separate element is later shifted into net income when the financial liability is derecognized.

Registration Payment Arrangements

There are situations in which a company issues shares, warrants, and so forth, which are subject to a registration payment arrangement. Such an arrangement requires the issuer to accomplish one of the following:

- File a registration statement for the resale of certain financial instruments and have it be declared effective by the Securities and Exchange Commission (SEC) within a certain period of time; or
- Maintain the effectiveness of an existing registration statement.

In addition, the arrangement requires that the issuer pay the counterparty if one of the preceding conditions is not met. The form of payment may include a change in the price at which securities were issued, the issuance of additional securities, a cash payment, or some similar arrangement.

These registration payment arrangements are common, especially in situations where a company cannot otherwise raise sufficient capital for its needs, and must accept the registration requirement. Investors want their securities to be registered, so they can sell the securities to a third party.

When there is a registration payment arrangement, measure the arrangement as a separate unit of account from the financial instrument to which it is linked. There are three ways in which this arrangement can be measured:

- *At inception.* If it is probable that a payment will be made under this arrangement, and the amount of the payment can be reasonably estimated at the inception of the arrangement, include the contingent liability in the allocation of proceeds from issuance of the linked financial instrument.
- *Subsequent.* If it subsequently becomes probable that a payment will be made under the arrangement and the amount of the payment can be reasonably estimated, recognize the amount in earnings in the current period.
- *Subsequent change.* If the probable amount of the payment changes over time, recognize the amount of the change in earnings in the current period.

EXAMPLE

Armadillo Industries sells 1,000,000 shares of its common stock to investors for $10,000,000. As part of the sale, the company enters into a registration payment arrangement, under which it commits to have a registration statement for these shares be declared effective by the SEC within 180 days. If this cannot be achieved, the company must make a cash payment to the investors of 2% of their original investment per month, until such time as the registration statement is declared effective.

At the share sale date, the company considers the probability of a late registration to be remote. However, after 120 days, it becomes apparent that the SEC will not declare the statement effective by the target date. A reasonable estimate of the additional amount of time required beyond the original time limit is four more months. Accordingly, the company recognizes a liability in the amount of $800,000, which is a 2% penalty per month, for four months.

If this liability had been evident on the date when the shares were originally sold, the $10,000,000 sale price of the stock issuance would have been recorded as $9,200,000 of common stock proceeds and an $800,000 contingent liability.

Financial Instruments Disclosures

The disclosures noted in this section are required in interim periods for publicly-held companies. The disclosures are not required in annual reporting periods for companies that are not publicly-held. The exceptions are the disclosures for registration payment arrangements and the separate presentation of financial assets and financial liabilities, which are required for all entities.

Fair Value of Financial Instruments

Disclose the following fair value information:

- *Fair value.* The fair value of those financial instruments for which fair value can be derived.
- *Hierarchy placement.* The level of the fair value hierarchy used to categorize the fair value measurements (either Levels 1, 2, or 3).
- *Presentation.* The fair value together with the related carrying amount, showing whether these items are assets or liabilities.
- *Summary table.* Note in a summary table the fair values, carrying amounts, and cross-references to other disclosures for all financial instruments. This is only required if fair values are disclosed in multiple notes.

There is no requirement to disclose the fair value of trade receivables or payables due in one year or less, or deposit liabilities that have no defined or contractual maturities.

Concentrations of Credit Risk of Financial Instruments

Disclose the following information about the concentration of credit risk in the financial instruments held by the business:

- *Credit risk.* Disclose all significant concentrations of credit risk associated with the financial instruments. This information may be stated for groups of counterparties if their ability to meet contractual obligations will react in a similar manner to economic conditions.
- *Concentration description.* Note the economic characteristic, region, or other feature that describes a credit risk concentration.

- *Maximum risk.* State the maximum amount of credit risk that may be incurred if the parties in each risk concentration completely fail to perform, and any associated collateral has no value.
- *Collateral.* State the company's policy for requiring collateral, its access to collateral, and the nature of the collateral.
- *Netting arrangements.* State the company's policy for using master netting arrangements, describe the arrangements, and note the degree to which they reduce losses from credit risk.

Market Risk of Financial Instruments

It is not required that a company discloses information about market risk associated with its financial instruments, but the disclosure is encouraged. If the accountant elects to do so, consider any of the following:

- A quantitative analysis of market risks that may include the potential effect on income of changes in market prices
- The duration of the instruments
- Activity during the period
- The value at risk from derivatives

This presentation can vary, depending on the nature of the business and the financial instruments that it uses.

Fair Value Option

If the fair value option has been selected, report the associated assets and liabilities separately from the carrying amounts of other assets and liabilities for which the option was not selected. This can be achieved with separate disclosure in the notes to the financial statements, or by breaking out the information with separate line items in the financial statements.

Disclose the following information concerning the fair value option in both interim and annual financial statements:

- *Usage reason.* State management's reasons for using the fair value option.
- *Partial election reasons.* If the fair value option is selected only for some items within a group of similar items, describe the reason for partial election, as well as how the group relates to specific line items in the balance sheet.
- *Line item discussion.* For each line item in the balance sheet containing items stated at their fair values, state how the line item relates to the classes of items reported at their fair values, as well as the total carrying amount of items within each line item that are not stated at their fair values.
- *Unpaid principal balance.* Separately state the difference between the total fair value and unpaid principal balance for loans and long-term receivables, as well as for long-term debt instruments.

- *Loans held as assets.* If loans are held as assets and the fair value option has been selected for them, state the fair value of such loans that are over 90 days past due, the fair value of the loans for which interest income is not being accrued, and the difference between total fair value and the total unpaid principal balance of those loans that are over 90 days past due or in interest income nonaccrual status.
- *Gains and losses.* Disclose the amount of gains and losses caused by changes in fair value in the period, and the income statement line item in which this information is listed.
- *Interest and dividends.* State how interest and dividends are measured and where they are shown in the income statement.
- *Credit risk gains and losses.* Describe the estimated amount of changes attributable to instrument-specific credit risk. Also, if the liability was settled during the reporting period, state the amount of change recognized in other comprehensive income that is now recognized in net income.
- *Liability value changes.* Disclose the estimated gains and losses due to credit risk, the reasons for these changes, and how they were determined for liabilities whose fair values changed significantly during the reporting period.

Also, disclose in the annual financial statements the methods and assumptions used to estimate fair value when the fair value option has been selected.

EXAMPLE

Armadillo Industries discloses a selection of its fair value option information in the following tabular format, using separate columns to state how the fair value hierarchy was used to value items:

(000s)	Total Carrying Amount at 12/31/X3	Fair Value Estimate at 12/31/X3	Assets or Liabilities Measured at Fair Value at 12/31/X3	Fair Value Measurements at 12/31/X3		
				Quoted Prices in Active Markets for Identical Assets (Level 1)	Significant Other Observable Inputs (Level 2)	Significant Unobservable Inputs (Level 3)
Trading debt securities	$82,000	$82,000	$82,000	$75,000	$7,000	
Available-for-sale debt securities	60,000	60,000	60,000	60,000		
Loans, net	300,000	318,000	165,000		100,000	$65,000
Derivatives	25,000	25,000	25,000	10,000	10,000	5,000
Long-term debt	-250,000	-255,000	-75,000	-40,000	-20,000	-15,000

Registration Payment Arrangements

If there is a registration payment arrangement associated with the issuance of financial instruments, disclose the following information:

- *Term.* The term of the arrangement.
- *Financial instruments.* The financial instruments to which the arrangement is linked.
- *Payment triggers.* The circumstances under which payment would be triggered under the arrangement.
- *Alternatives.* The different payment alternatives available, and who controls the choice of alternatives.
- *Maximum payment.* The maximum amount of consideration that could be paid under the arrangement.
- *No limit.* If there is no limit to the maximum amount of consideration to be paid, disclose this issue.
- *Carrying amount.* The carrying amount of the liability relating to the arrangement.
- *Line item.* The line item in the income statement in which the company records any gains or losses relating to changes in the carrying amount of the liability associated with the arrangement.

These disclosures are required, even if there is a remote probability that payments will be made under the arrangement.

Separate Presentation of Financial Assets and Financial Liabilities

An organization must separately present its financial assets and financial liabilities by measurement category and form of financial asset in the balance sheet or the accompanying disclosures. Examples of a form of financial asset are securities or loans and receivables.

Summary

The topics in this chapter are only loosely tied to the general concept of financial instruments, and appear to have been aggregated within GAAP in this manner because there were no better topics within which to place these items. The bulk of the discussion was about the appropriate disclosure of information related to the fair value option, which a company can neatly avoid by not choosing to use the fair value option. Of more importance to those companies selling securities is the disclosure of registration payment arrangements. These arrangements are quite common, and can potentially result in the payment of substantial amounts of consideration, which the readers of a company's financial statements should certainly be made aware of.

Chapter 41
Foreign Currency Matters

> 830 = GAAP codification area for foreign currency matters

Introduction

A large number of businesses routinely engage in foreign currency transactions with their business partners, in which case they will probably deal with foreign currencies. Others have subsidiaries located in foreign countries, and need to convert the financial statements of these entities into the currency used by the parent for consolidation purposes. We deal with the accounting for and disclosure of these two situations in the following sections. The guidance in this chapter applies to all entities.

Related Chapters

See the following chapters for discussions of the financial statements that are impacted by foreign exchange translation activities:

- Presentation of Financial Statements
- Balance Sheet
- Comprehensive Income
- Income Statement
- Statement of Cash Flows
- Interim Reporting

Foreign Currency Transactions

A business may enter into a transaction where it is scheduled to receive a payment from a customer that is denominated in a foreign currency, or to make a payment to a supplier in a foreign currency. On the date of recognition of each such transaction, record it in the functional currency of the reporting entity, based on the exchange rate in effect on that date. If it is not possible to determine the market exchange rate on the date of recognition of a transaction, use the next available exchange rate.

If there is a change in the expected exchange rate between the functional currency of the entity and the currency in which a transaction is denominated, record a gain or loss in earnings in the period when the exchange rate changes. This can result in the recognition of a series of gains or losses over a number of accounting periods, if the settlement date of a transaction is sufficiently far in the future. This also means that the stated balances of the related receivables and payables will reflect the current exchange rate as of each subsequent balance sheet date.

The two situations in which a gain or loss on a foreign currency transaction should not be recognized are:

- When a foreign currency transaction is designed to be an economic hedge of a net investment in a foreign entity, and is effective as such; or
- When there is no expectation of settling a transaction between entities that are to be consolidated.

EXAMPLE

Armadillo Industries sells goods to a company in the United Kingdom, to be paid in pounds having a value at the booking date of $100,000. Armadillo records this transaction with the following entry:

	Debit	Credit
Accounts receivable	100,000	
Sales		100,000

Later, when the customer pays Armadillo, the exchange rate has changed, resulting in a payment in pounds that translates to a $95,000 sale. Thus, the foreign exchange rate change related to the transaction has created a $5,000 loss for Armadillo, which it records with the following entry:

	Debit	Credit
Cash	95,000	
Foreign currency exchange loss	5,000	
Accounts receivable		100,000

The following table shows the impact of transaction exposure on different scenarios.

Risk When Transactions Denominated in Foreign Currency

	Import Goods	Export Goods
Home currency weakens	Loss	Gain
Home currency strengthens	Gain	Loss

Financial Statement Translation

A company may have subsidiaries located in other countries, and creates financial statements for those subsidiaries that are denominated in the local currency. If so, the parent company will need to translate the results of these subsidiaries into the currency used by the parent company when it creates consolidated financial statements for the entire entity (called the *reporting currency*). The steps in this process are as follows:

1. Determine the functional currency of the foreign entity.
2. Remeasure the financial statements of the foreign entity into the reporting currency of the parent company.
3. Record gains and losses on the translation of currencies.

Determination of Functional Currency

The financial results and financial position of a company should be measured using its functional currency, which is the currency that the company uses in the majority of its business transactions.

If a foreign business entity operates primarily within one country and is not dependent upon the parent company, its functional currency is the currency of the country in which its operations are located. However, there are other foreign operations that are more closely tied to the operations of the parent company, and whose financing is mostly supplied by the parent or other sources that use the dollar. In this latter case, the functional currency of the foreign operation is probably the dollar. These two examples anchor the ends of a continuum on which foreign operations will be found. Unless an operation is clearly associated with one of the two examples provided, it is likely that the accountant must make a determination of functional currency based on the unique circumstances pertaining to each entity. For example, the functional currency may be difficult to determine if a business conducts an equal amount of business in two different countries. An examination of the following factors can assist in determining a functional currency:

Indicators	Indicates Use of Foreign Currency as Functional Currency	Indicates use of Reporting Currency as Functional Currency
Cash flow	The cash flows relating to an entity's assets and liabilities are primarily in the foreign currency, and have no direct impact on the cash flows of the parent	The cash flows relating to an entity's assets and liabilities directly affect the cash flows of the parent and are available for remittance to it
Expenses	The labor, material, and other costs of the entity are primarily obtained locally	The labor, material, and other costs of the entity are primarily obtained from the parent's country
Financing	Any financing obtained is primarily denominated in a foreign currency, and locally-generated funds should be able to service the entity's existing and expected debts	Financing is obtained from the parent or is in dollar-denominated obligations, or locally-generated funds are not sufficient for the servicing of existing and expected debts without a cash infusion
Intra-entity transactions	There are few intra-entity transactions, and operations are not tightly integrated with those of the parent	There are many intra-entity transactions, and operations are more likely to be tightly integrated with those of the parent

Indicators	Indicates Use of Foreign Currency as Functional Currency	Indicates use of Reporting Currency as Functional Currency
Sales market	There is an active local market for the products of the entity	The primary market for the entity's products is the country of the parent, or sales are denominated in the currency of the parent's country
Sales price	Sales prices are mostly based on local competition and regulations, rather than on exchange rate changes	Sales prices are mostly based on exchange rate changes, which can be driven by international price competition

The functional currency in which a business reports its financial results should rarely change. A shift to a different functional currency should be used only when there is a significant change in the economic facts and circumstances. If there is a change in functional currency, do not restate previously-issued financial statements into the new currency.

If there is a change in functional currency from the reporting currency of an entity (i.e., the functional currency of the parent company) to a foreign currency, report the adjustment associated with the current-rate translation of any nonmonetary assets in other comprehensive income. Conversely, if the functional currency changes from a foreign currency to the reporting currency, the translated amounts previously stated for nonmonetary assets as of the prior period become the cost basis for these assets going forward; also, do not remove any prior period translation adjustments from equity.

EXAMPLE

Armadillo Industries has a subsidiary in Australia, to which it ships its body armor products for sale to local police forces. The Australian subsidiary sells these products and then remits payments back to corporate headquarters. Armadillo should consider U.S. dollars to be the functional currency of this subsidiary.

Armadillo also owns a subsidiary in Russia, which manufactures its own body armor for local consumption, accumulates cash reserves, and borrows funds locally. This subsidiary rarely remits funds back to the parent company. In this case, the functional currency should be the Russian ruble.

Translation of Financial Statements

When translating the financial statements of an entity for consolidation purposes into the reporting currency of a business, translate the financial statements using the following rules:

- *Assets and liabilities*. Translate using the current exchange rate at the balance sheet date for assets and liabilities.

- *Income statement items*. Translate revenues, expenses, gains, and losses using the exchange rate as of the dates when those items were originally recognized.
- *Allocations*. Translate all cost and revenue allocations using the exchange rates in effect when those allocations are recorded. Examples of allocations are depreciation and the amortization of deferred revenues.
- *Different balance sheet date*. If the foreign entity being consolidated has a different balance sheet date than that of the reporting entity, use the exchange rate in effect as of the foreign entity's balance sheet date.
- *Profit eliminations*. If there are intra-entity profits to be eliminated as part of the consolidation, apply the exchange rate in effect on the dates when the underlying transactions took place.
- *Statement of cash flows*. In the statement of cash flows, state all foreign currency cash flows at their reporting currency equivalent using the exchange rates in effect when the cash flows occurred. A weighted average exchange rate may be used for this calculation.

If there are translation adjustments resulting from the implementation of these rules, record the adjustments in the equity section of the parent company's consolidated balance sheet.

EXAMPLE

Armadillo Industries has a subsidiary located in England, which has its net assets denominated in pounds. The functional currency of Armadillo is U.S. dollars. At year-end, when the parent company consolidates the financial statements of its subsidiaries, the U.S. dollar has depreciated in comparison to the pound, resulting in a decline in the value of the subsidiary's net assets.

The following table shows the impact of translation exposure on different scenarios.

Risk When Net Assets Denominated in Foreign Currency

	Assets	Liabilities
Reporting currency weakens	Gain	Loss
Reporting currency strengthens	Loss	Gain

If the process of converting the financial statements of a foreign entity into the reporting currency of the parent company results in a translation adjustment, report the related profit or loss in other comprehensive income.

EXAMPLE

A subsidiary of Armadillo Industries is located in Argentina, and its functional currency is the Argentine peso. The relevant peso exchange rates are:

- 0.20 to the dollar at the beginning of the year
- 0.24 to the dollar at the end of the year
- 0.22 to the dollar for the full-year weighted average rate

The subsidiary had no retained earnings at the beginning of the year. Based on this information, the financial statement conversion is as follows:

(000s)	Argentine Pesos	Exchange Rate	U.S. Dollars
Assets			
Cash	89,000	0.24	21,360
Accounts receivable	267,000	0.24	64,080
Inventory	412,000	0.24	98,880
Fixed assets, net	608,000	0.24	145,920
Total assets	1,376,000		330,240
Liabilities and Equity			
Accounts payable	320,000	0.24	76,800
Notes payable	500,000	0.24	120,000
Common stock	10,000	0.20	2,400
Additional paid-in capital	545,000	0.20	130,800
Retained earnings	1,000	(*)	220
Translation adjustments	0	--	20
Total liabilities and equity	1,376,000		330,240

* Reference from the following income statement

(000s)	Argentine Pesos	Exchange Rate	U.S. Dollars
Revenue	1,500,000	0.22	330,000
Expenses	1,499,000	0.22	329,780
Net income	1,000		220
Beginning retained earnings	0		0
Add: Net income	1,000	0.22	220
Ending retained earnings	1,000		220

Use of Average Exchange Rates

We have noted that the remeasurement of financial statements may require the use of historical exchange rate information. It can be burdensome to keep track of these exchange rates and the dates on which the rates are to be applied. To reduce the work involved, GAAP allows the use of an average exchange rate, or other labor-saving methods that reasonably approximate the exchange rates that were more frequently applied. If an average exchange rate is used, derive a weighted average based on the volume of currency transactions in the period. For example, a reasonably accurate result might be achieved by developing an average rate for each month of the year, to be applied to those transactions occurring within each month.

Hyperinflationary Effects

An entity may find itself operating in an environment that has cumulative inflation of 100% or more. If this level of inflation continues over a three-year period, a country is considered to have a highly inflationary economy. When this is the case, remeasure the financial statements of the entity operating in that environment as though the functional currency were the reporting currency.

If the economy is no longer considered to be hyperinflationary, restate the financial statements of the relevant entity so that the local currency is now the functional currency. This means translating the reporting currency amounts into the local currency amounts at the current exchange rate on the date of change; these translated amounts then become the new functional currency for the nonmonetary assets and liabilities of the entity.

EXAMPLE

A subsidiary of Armadillo Industries is operating in a highly inflationary economy. On March 31 of 20X3, it bought a machine for 50,000 units of the local currency. The exchange rate at that time was five units of the local currency to one U.S. dollar, so the equivalent cost of the machine in U.S. dollars was $10,000. Five years later, on March 31, 20X8, the machine's net book value on the subsidiary's books has declined to 25,000 units of the local currency, due to ongoing depreciation. On March 31 of 20X8, hyperinflation has altered the exchange rate to 25 to one U.S. dollar. During this time, the parent company has been using the historical exchange rate to account for the machine, so the recorded amount has declined to $5,000, based on the depreciation incurred during the intervening years.

On April 1 of 20X8, Armadillo's management no longer considers the local economy of the subsidiary to be highly inflationary, so it establishes a new cost basis for the equipment by translating the current $5,000 cost of the machine back into the local currency at the current exchange rate of 25:1. This means the functional accounting basis for the machine on April 1 of 20X8 would be 125,000 units of the local currency.

Derecognition of a Foreign Entity Investment

When a company sells or liquidates its investment in a foreign entity, complete the following steps to account for the situation:

- Remove the translation adjustment recorded in equity for the investment
- Report a gain or loss in the period in which the sale or liquidation occurs

If a company only sells a portion of its investment in a foreign entity, recognize only a pro rata portion of the accumulated translation adjustment recorded in equity.

Foreign Currency Disclosures

Disclose the following information related to transactions denominated in foreign currencies:

- *Gains and losses.* If there are transaction-based gains or losses during the period that are caused by changes in foreign exchange rates, disclose the aggregate amount in the financial statements or in the accompanying notes.
- *Subsequent rate changes.* If there is a foreign currency rate change after the date of the financial statements that has a significant effect on unsettled balances, disclose the impact of the rate on unsettled transactions between the date of the financial statements and the date of the rate change.
- *Rate change effects.* GAAP encourages a discussion of the effects of rate changes on the reported results of operations, but does not require it.

If translation adjustments have been reported in equity, disclose an analysis of the changes during the period in the financial statements. This information can be integrated into the statement of changes in equity. The analysis should state the following:

	Beginning balance of cumulative translation adjustments
+/-	The aggregate adjustment caused by translation adjustments, as well as from the gains and losses caused by certain hedges and intra-entity balances
+/-	The amount of income taxes allocated to translation adjustments
+/-	Transfers from cumulative translation adjustments as a result of the sale or liquidation of an investment in a foreign entity
=	Ending balance of cumulative translation adjustments

If there are income taxes associated with translation adjustments, report them in other comprehensive income.

Report in the statement of cash flows the effect of any changes in exchange rates on cash balances held in foreign currencies. This information should be stated in separate line items within the reconciliation of the change in cash and cash equivalents during the period.

493

Summary

The key factor to consider when translating financial statements into the reporting currency is the use of average exchange rates. Consider creating a standard procedure for calculating the weighted average exchange rate for each relevant currency for each reporting period, and then retain the calculation, to justify the exchange rate(s) for audit purposes. Using a weighted average is much more efficient from an accounting perspective than translating specific transactions at the associated exchange rate on a daily basis.

Chapter 42
Interest

Introduction

The interest topic addresses two items, which are the capitalization of interest into fixed assets, and the derivation of a different interest rate when the rate associated with a borrowing arrangement diverges from the market rate. The capitalization of interest is not a common issue to be concerned about, unless a business is spending multiple months constructing a fixed asset, and has incurred debt to build the asset. In all other cases, interest capitalization can be ignored. The use of imputed interest is somewhat more common, particularly in regard to situations where a note is issued at a below-market interest rate, or at no interest rate at all.

In this chapter, we describe the mechanics of interest capitalization and imputed interest, as well as the relevant accounting and disclosures associated with both topics.

Overview of Capitalized Interest

When a fixed asset is recorded, part of the cost that can be included is the costs incurred to bring it to the condition and location of its intended use. If these activities require some time to complete, capitalize the cost of the interest incurred during that period that relate to the asset. This chapter describes the assets for which interest capitalization is allowable (or not), how to determine the capitalization period and the capitalization rate, and how to calculate the amount of interest cost to be capitalized.

Interest is a cost of doing business, and if a company incurs an interest cost that is directly related to a fixed asset, it is reasonable to capitalize this cost, since it provides a truer picture of the total investment in the asset. Since a business would not otherwise have incurred the interest if it had not acquired the asset, the interest is essentially a direct cost of owning the asset.

Conversely, if this interest cost was not capitalized and it was instead charged to expense, the accountant would be unreasonably reducing the amount of reported earnings during the period when the company incurred the expense and increasing earnings during later periods, when the entity would otherwise have been charging the capitalized interest to expense through depreciation.

> **Tip:** If the amount of interest that may be applied to a fixed asset is minor, try to avoid capitalizing it. Otherwise, too much time will be spent documenting the capitalization, and the auditors will spend time investigating it – which may translate into higher audit fees.

The value of the information provided by capitalizing interest may not be worth the effort of the incremental accounting cost associated with it. Here are some issues to consider when deciding whether to capitalize interest:

- How many assets would be subject to interest capitalization?
- How easy is it to separately identify those assets that would be subject to interest capitalization?
- How significant would be the effect of interest capitalization on the company's reported resources and earnings?

Thus, only capitalize interest when the informational benefit derived from doing so exceeds the cost of accounting for it. The positive impact of doing so is greatest for construction projects, where:

- Costs are separately compiled
- Construction covers a long period of time
- Expenditures are large
- Interest costs are considerable

GAAP specifically does *not* allow for the capitalization of interest for inventory items that are routinely manufactured in large quantities on a repetitive basis.

Assets on Which to Capitalize Interest

Capitalize interest that is related to the following types of fixed assets:

- Assets that are constructed for the company's own use. This includes assets built for the company by suppliers, where the company makes progress payments or deposits.
- Assets that are constructed for sale or lease, and which are constructed as discrete projects.

EXAMPLE

Milford Sound builds a new corporate headquarters. The company hires a contractor to perform the work, and makes regular progress payments to the contractor. Milford should capitalize the interest expense related to this project.

Milford Sound creates a subsidiary, Milford Public Sound, which builds custom-designed outdoor sound staging for concerts and theatre activities. These projects require many months to complete, and are accounted for as discrete projects. Milford should capitalize the interest cost related to each of these projects.

If a company is undertaking activities to develop land for a specific use, capitalize interest related to the associated expenditures for as long as the development activities are in progress.

Assets on Which Interest is not Capitalized

Do not capitalize interest that is related to the following types of fixed assets:

- Assets that are already in use or ready for their intended use
- Assets not being used, and which are not being prepared for use
- Assets not included in the company's balance sheet
- Inventories that are routinely manufactured

The Interest Capitalization Period

Capitalize interest over the period when there are ongoing activities to prepare a fixed asset for its intended use, but only if expenditures are actually being made during that time, and interest costs are being incurred.

EXAMPLE

Milford Public Sound is constructing an in-house sound stage in which to test its products. It spent the first two months designing the stage, and then paid a contractor $30,000 per month for the next four months to build the stage. Milford incurred interest costs during the entire time period.

Since Milford was not making any expenditures related to the stage during the first two months, it cannot capitalize any interest cost for those two months. However, since it was making expenditures during the next four months, it can capitalize interest cost for those months.

If a company stops essentially all construction on a project, stop capitalizing interest during that period. However, continue to capitalize interest under any of the following circumstances:

- Brief construction interruptions
- Interruptions imposed by an outside entity
- Delays that are an inherent part of the asset acquisition process

EXAMPLE

Milford Public Sound is constructing a concert arena that it plans to lease to a local municipality upon completion. Midway through the project, the municipality orders a halt to all construction, when construction reveals that the arena is being built on an Indian burial ground. Two months later, after the burial site has been relocated, the municipality allows construction to begin again.

Since this interruption was imposed by an outside entity, Milford can capitalize interest during the two-month stoppage period.

A company should terminate interest capitalization as soon as an asset is substantially complete and ready for its intended use. Here are several scenarios showing when interest capitalization should be terminated:

- *Unit-level completion.* Parts of a project may be completed and usable before the entire project is complete. Stop capitalizing interest on each of these parts as soon as they are substantially complete and ready for use.
- *Entire-unit completion.* All aspects of an asset may need to be completed before any part of it can be used. Continue capitalizing interest on such assets until the entire project is substantially complete and ready for use.
- *Dependent completion.* An asset may not be usable until a separate project has also been completed. Continue capitalizing interest on such assets until not only the specific asset, but also the separate project is substantially complete and ready for use.

EXAMPLE

Milford Public Sound is building three arenas, all under different circumstances. They are:

1. *Arena A.* This is an entertainment complex, including a stage area, movie theatre, and restaurants. Milford should stop capitalizing interest on each component of the project as soon as it is substantially complete and ready for use, since each part of the complex can operate without the other parts being complete.
2. *Arena B.* This is a single outdoor stage with integrated multi-level parking garage. Even though the garage is completed first, Milford should continue to capitalize interest for it, since the garage is only intended to service patrons of the arena, and so will not be operational until the arena is complete.
3. *Arena C.* This an entertainment complex for which Milford is also constructing a highway off-ramp and road that leads to the complex. Since the complex is unusable until patrons can reach the complex, Milford should continue to capitalize interest expenses until the off-ramp and road are complete.

Do not continue to capitalize interest when completion is being deliberately delayed, since the cost of interest then changes from an asset acquisition cost to an asset holding cost.

EXAMPLE

The CEO of Milford Sound wants to report increased net income for the upcoming quarter, so he orders the delay of construction on an arena facility that would otherwise have been completed, so that the interest cost related to the project will be capitalized. He is in error, since this is now treated as a holding cost – the related interest expense should be recognized in the period incurred, rather than capitalized.

The Capitalization Rate

The amount of interest cost to capitalize for a fixed asset is that amount of interest that would have been avoided if the asset had not been acquired. To calculate the amount of interest cost to capitalize, multiply the capitalization rate by the average amount of expenditures that accumulate during the construction period.

The basis for the capitalization rate is the interest rates that are applicable to the company's borrowings that are outstanding during the construction period. If a specific borrowing is incurred in order to construct a specific asset, use the interest rate on that borrowing as the capitalization rate. If the amount of a specific borrowing that is incurred to construct a specific asset is less than the expenditures made for the asset, use a weighted average of the rates applicable to other company borrowings for any excess expenditures over the amount of the project-specific borrowing.

EXAMPLE

Milford Public Sound incurs an average expenditure over the construction period of an outdoor arena complex of $15,000,000. It has taken out a short-term loan of $12,000,000 at 9% interest specifically to cover the cost of this project. Milford can capitalize the interest cost of the entire amount of the $12,000,000 loan at 9% interest, but it still has $3,000,000 of average expenditures that exceed the amount of this project-specific loan.

Milford has two bonds outstanding at the time of the project, in the following amounts:

Bond Description	Principal Outstanding	Interest
8% Bond	$18,000,000	$1,440,000
10% Bond	12,000,000	1,200,000
Totals	$30,000,000	$2,640,000

The weighted-average interest rate on these two bond issuances is 8.8% ($2,640,000 interest ÷ $30,000,000 principal), which is the interest rate that Milford should use when capitalizing the remaining $3,000,000 of average expenditures.

These rules regarding the formulation of the capitalization rate are subject to some interpretation. The key guideline is to arrive at a *reasonable* measure of the cost of financing the acquisition of a fixed asset, particularly in regard to the interest cost that could have been avoided if the acquisition had not been made. Thus, it is possible to use a selection of outstanding borrowings as the basis for a weighted average calculation. This may result in the inclusion or exclusion of borrowings at the corporate level, or just at the level of the subsidiary where the asset is located.

EXAMPLE

Milford Public Sound (MPS) has issued several bonds and notes, totaling $50,000,000, that are used to fund both general corporate activities and construction projects. It also has access to a low-cost 4% internal line of credit that is extended to it by its corporate parent, Milford Sound. MPS regularly uses this line of credit for short-term activities, and typically draws the balance down to zero at least once a year. The average amount of this line that is outstanding is approximately $10,000,000 at any given time.

Since the corporate line of credit comprises a significant amount of MPS's ongoing borrowings, and there is no restriction that prevents these funds from being used for construction projects, it would be reasonable to include the interest cost of this line of credit in the calculation of the weighted-average cost of borrowings that is used to derive MPS's capitalization rate.

Calculating Interest Capitalization

Follow these steps to calculate the amount of interest to be capitalized for a specific project:

1. Construct a table itemizing the amounts of expenditures made and the dates on which the expenditures were made.
2. Determine the date on which interest capitalization ends.
3. Calculate the capitalization period for each expenditure, which is the number of days between the specific expenditure and the end of the interest capitalization period.
4. Divide each capitalization period by the total number of days elapsed between the date of the first expenditure and the end of the interest capitalization period to arrive at the capitalization multiplier for each line item.
5. Multiply each expenditure amount by its capitalization multiplier to arrive at the average expenditure for each line item over the capitalization measurement period.
6. Add up the average expenditures at the line item level to arrive at a grand total average expenditure.
7. If there is project-specific debt, multiply the grand total of the average expenditures by the interest rate on that debt to arrive at the capitalized interest related to that debt.
8. If the grand total of the average expenditures exceeds the amount of the project-specific debt, multiply the excess expenditure amount by the

weighted average of the company's other outstanding debt to arrive at the remaining amount of interest to be capitalized.

9. Add together both capitalized interest calculations. If the combined total is more than the total interest cost incurred by the company during the calculation period, reduce the amount of interest to be capitalized to the total interest cost incurred by the company during the calculation period.

10. Record the interest capitalization with a debit to the project's fixed asset account and a credit to the interest expense account.

EXAMPLE

Milford Public Sound is building a concert arena. Milford makes payments related to the project of $10,000,000 and $14,000,000 to a contractor on January 1 and July 1, respectively. The arena is completed on December 31.

For the 12-month period of construction, Milford can capitalize all of the interest on the $10,000,000 payment, since it was outstanding during the full period of construction. Milford can capitalize the interest on the $14,000,000 payment for half of the construction period, since it was outstanding during only the second half of the construction period. The average expenditure for which the interest cost can be capitalized is calculated in the following table:

Date of Payment	Expenditure Amount	Capitalization Period*	Capitalization Multiplier	Average Expenditure
January 1	$10,000,000	12 months	12/12 months = 100%	$10,000,000
July 1	14,000,000	6 months	6/12 months = 50%	7,000,000
				$17,000,000

* In the table, the capitalization period is defined as the number of months that elapse between the expenditure payment date and the end of the interest capitalization period.

The only debt that Milford has outstanding during this period is a line of credit, on which the interest rate is 8%. The maximum amount of interest that Milford can capitalize into the cost of this arena project is $1,360,000, which is calculated as:

8% Interest rate × $17,000,000 Average expenditure = $1,360,000

Milford records the following journal entry:

	Debit	Credit
Fixed assets – Arena	1,360,000	
Interest expense		1,360,000

Tip: There may be an inordinate number of expenditures related to a larger project, which could result in a large and unwieldy calculation of average expenditures. To reduce the workload, consider aggregating these expenses by month, and then assume that each expenditure was made in the middle of the month, thereby reducing all of the expenditures for each month to a single line item.

It is not allowable to capitalize more interest cost in an accounting period than the total amount of interest cost incurred by the business in that period. If there is a corporate parent, this rule means that the amount capitalized cannot exceed the total amount of interest cost incurred by the business on a consolidated basis.

Tip: The cost of asset retirement obligations cannot be included in the expenditure total on which the interest capitalization calculation is based, since there is no up-front expenditure associated with such an obligation (see the Asset Retirement and Environmental Obligations chapter for more information).

Overview of Imputed Interest

When two parties enter into a business transaction that involves payment with a note, the default assumption is that the interest rate associated with the note will be close to the market rate of interest. However, there are times when no interest rate is stated, or when the stated rate departs significantly from the market rate.

If the stated and market interest rates are substantially different, it is necessary to record the transaction using an interest rate that more closely accords with the market rate. The rate that should be used is one that approximates the rate that would have been used if an independent borrower and lender had entered into a similar arrangement under comparable terms and conditions. This guidance does not apply to the following situations:

- Receivables and payables using customary trade terms that do not exceed one year
- Advances, deposits, and security deposits
- Customer cash lending activities of a financial institution
- When interest rates are affected by a governmental agency (such as a tax-exempt bond)
- Transactions between commonly-owned entities (such as between subsidiaries)

If available, the preferred option for deriving imputed interest is to locate the established exchange price of the goods or services involved in the transaction, and use that as the basis for calculating the interest rate. The exchange price is presumed to be the price paid in a cash purchase. In essence, this means that goods or services shall be recorded at their fair value. Any difference between the present value of the note and the fair value of the goods or services shall then be accounted for as a change in interest expense (i.e., as a note discount or premium) over the life of the note.

If it is not possible to determine the established exchange price, an applicable interest rate must be derived at the time the note is issued. The rate selected should be the prevailing rate for similar borrowers with similar credit ratings, which may be further adjusted for the following factors:

- The credit standing of the borrower
- Restrictive covenants on the note
- Collateral on the note
- Tax consequences to the buyer and seller
- The rate at which the borrower can obtain similar financing from other sources

Any subsequent changes in the market interest rate shall be ignored for the purposes of this transaction.

Tip: Selecting a justifiable imputed interest rate is a matter of some importance, since an incorrect interest rate that is applied to a sufficiently large and long-term debt can result in the inaccurate acceleration or deferral of earnings.

Once the correct interest rate has been selected, use it to amortize the difference between the imputed interest rate and the rate on the note over the life of the note, with the difference being charged to the interest expense account. This is called the *interest method*. The following example illustrates the concept.

EXAMPLE

Armadillo Industries issues a $5,000,000 bond at a stated rate of 5% interest, where similar issuances are being purchased by investors at 8% interest. The bonds pay interest annually, and are to be redeemed in six years.

In order to earn the market rate of 8% interest, investors purchase the Armadillo bonds at a discount. The following calculation is used to derive the discount on the bond, which is comprised of the present values of a stream of interest payments and the present value of $5,000,000 payable in six years, with both calculations based on the 8% interest rate:

Present value of 6 payments of $250,000	= $250,000 × 4.62288	$1,155,720
Present value of $5,000,000	= $5,000,000 × 0.63017	3,150,850
	Total of present values	$4,306,570
	Less: Stated bond price	$5,000,000
	Bond discount	$693,430

The initial entry to record the sale of bonds is:

	Debit	Credit
Cash	4,306,570	
Discount on bonds payable	693,430	
Bonds payable		5,000,000

The controller of Armadillo creates the following table, which shows the derivation of how much of the discount should be charged to interest expense in each of the following years. In essence, the annual amortization of the discount is added back to the present value of the bond, so that the bond's present value matches its $5,000,000 stated value by the date when the bonds are scheduled for redemption from the bond holders.

Year	Beginning Present Value of Bond	Unamortized Discount	Interest Expense*	Cash Payment**	Discount Reduction***
1	$4,306,570	$693,430	$344,526	$250,000	$94,526
2	4,401,096	598,904	352,088	250,000	102,088
3	4,503,184	496,816	360,255	250,000	110,255
4	4,613,439	386,561	369,075	250,000	119,075
5	4,732,514	267,486	378,601	250,000	128,601
6	4,861,115	138,885	388,885	250,000	138,885
7	$5,000,000	$0			

* Bond present value at the beginning of the period, multiplied by the 8% market rate
** Scheduled annual interest payment for the bond
*** Interest expense, less the cash payment

As an example of the entries that the controller would derive from this table, the entry for the first annual interest payment would be:

	Debit	Credit
Interest expense	344,526	
Discount on bonds payable		94,526
Cash		250,000

The reasoning behind the entry is that Armadillo is only obligated to make a cash payment of $250,000 per year, despite the higher 8% implicit interest rate that its investors are earning on the issued bonds. The difference between the actual interest of $344,526 and the cash payment represents an increase in the amount of the bond that the company must eventually pay back to its investors. Thus, by the end of the first year, the present value of Armadillo's obligation to pay back the bond has increased from $4,306,570 to $4,401,096. By the end of the six-year period, the present value of the amount to be paid back will have increased to $5,000,000.

> **Tip:** GAAP requires that the interest method be used to amortize any discount or premium associated with a note. However, other methods can be used if the results do not differ materially from those of the interest method. Accordingly, we suggest using the simpler straight-line method if the results do not differ materially from those of the interest method.

Interest Disclosures

This section contains the disclosures for various aspects of interest that are required under GAAP. At the end of each set of requirements is a sample disclosure containing the more common elements of the requirements.

Capitalized Interest Disclosures

If a company has capitalized any of its interest expense, disclose the total amount of interest cost it incurred during the period, as well as the portion of it that has been capitalized.

EXAMPLE

Suture Corporation discloses the following information about the interest cost it has capitalized as part of the construction of a laboratory facility:

> The company incurred interest cost of $800,000 during the year. Of that amount, it charged $650,000 to expense and included the remaining $150,000 in the capitalized cost of its Dumont laboratory facility.

Imputed Interest Disclosures

Any discount or premium related to a note must be stated in the balance sheet as a deduction from or addition to the face amount of a note. The discount or premium is not to be stated as a deferred charge or deferred credit.

In addition, the description of the note in the financial statement disclosures shall include the effective interest rate.

EXAMPLE

Nascent Corporation discloses the following information in its balance sheet about a note receivable from the sale of property:

Note receivable from sale of property:	
Noninterest bearing note due December 31, 20x7	$3,000,000
Less unamortized discount based on imputed interest rate of 7%	450,000
Note receivable less unamortized discount	$2,550,000

Summary

The key issue with interest capitalization is whether to use it at all. It requires a certain amount of administrative effort to compile, and so is not recommended for lower-value fixed assets. Instead, reserve its use for larger projects where including the cost of interest in an asset will improve the quality of the financial information reported by the entity. It should *not* be used merely to delay the recognition of interest expense. If the choice is made to use interest capitalization, adopt a procedure for determining the amount to be capitalized and closely adhere to it, with appropriate documentation of the results. This will result in a standardized calculation methodology that auditors can more easily review.

If a situation arises where imputed interest must be used, the accounting staff must subsequently account for any associated discount or premium. To avoid this additional accounting, consider advising senior management to avoid notes that include unusual interest rates, or no interest rate at all.

Chapter 43
Leases

---

840 = GAAP codification area for leases

Introduction

This chapter addresses the core concepts surrounding the accounting for leases by all parties entering into these arrangements. There are several fundamental leasing issues that we will cover in the following pages, including the following:

- *Types of leases.* There are several possible designations that can be applied to a lease, depending upon the facts and circumstances associated with it. Each of these designations triggers a different set of accounting rules.
- *Balance sheet recognition.* One of the key aspects of the accounting for leases is that lease assets and lease liabilities are now recognized on the balance sheet. Under previous guidance, it was possible for lessees to keep certain leases off their balance sheets, which masked their true financial condition.
- *Elections.* There are several lease-related elections that an entity can take, which are generally designed to simplify the accounting for leases.
- *Disclosures.* The presentation and disclosure rules for leases are quite extensive, in order to provide the maximum amount of information to the readers of an organization's financial statements.

The Nature of a Lease

A lease is an arrangement under which a lessor agrees to allow a lessee to control the use of identified property, plant, and equipment for a stated period of time in exchange for one or more payments. A lease arrangement is quite a useful opportunity, for the following reasons:

- The lessee reduces its exposure to asset ownership
- The lessee obtains financing from the lessor in order to pay for the asset
- The lessee now has access to the leased asset

An arrangement is considered to give control over the use of an asset when both of these conditions are present:

- The lessee obtains the right to substantially all of the economic benefits from using an asset; and
- The lessee obtains the right to direct the uses to which an asset is put.

EXAMPLE

Blitz Communications obtains the rights to the entire output of an undersea cable for the next ten years, in order to benefit from an expected increase in traffic from new data centers in Sweden to users in the United States. Since Blitz has the right to substantially all of the economic benefits from using the cable, the underlying contract is considered a lease. If the arrangement had instead been for only a certain proportion of the total capacity of the cable, where the cable operator could choose which fibers within the cable would carry Blitz's data, the arrangement would not be considered a lease.

EXAMPLE

The Cupertino Beanery enters into a contract to operate a store from retail space. Part of the contract states that Cupertino must pay 10% of its revenues to the landlord. Cupertino still obtains the right to substantially all of the economic benefits from using the retail space – subsequent to obtaining the revenues, the company then pays 10% to the landlord. This contract clause does not prevent the contract from being designated as a lease.

The following additional points all apply to whether a lease exists:

- *Partial period*. If a leasing arrangement only lasts for a portion of the period spanned by a contract, a lease is still presumed to exist for the partial period specified within the contract.
- *Right of substitution*. If a contract allows the supplier to substitute an identified asset with another asset throughout the usage period, there is no lease. This situation only applies when the supplier has the practical ability to substitute alternative assets, and the supplier obtains a positive economic benefit from doing so. The evaluation of the ability to substitute assets does not include assets that are unlikely to occur.

EXAMPLE

Nova Corporation operates a deep field scanning telescope for sky survey work, which it leases from Alpha Centauri Leasing. If the contract language is interpreted in a certain way, it appears possible that Alpha could substitute the telescope at a later date. However, the telescope is located at Nova's observatory, and would be difficult to dismount and replace. The cost of substitution is therefore likely to be higher than any benefits that Alpha might gain from the substitution. In this case, it appears likely that there is a lease.

EXAMPLE

Grissom Granaries stores corn and wheat along the Mississippi River. It enters into an agreement with a local transport firm to transport crops up and down the river. The volume of transport services indicated in the contract translates into the ongoing use of 10 barges. The transport firm has several hundred barges that it can use to fulfill the contract. When not in use, the barges are stored at one of the transport firm's riverside facilities. No specific barges are described in the contract. Given these conditions, it is apparent that Grissom does not direct the use of the barges, nor does it have the right to obtain substantially all of the economic benefits from use of the barges. Consequently, this arrangement is not a lease.

Lease Components (Lessee)

Once it has been established that a contract contains a lease, it is necessary to separate the lease into its components (if any). This can result in a business tracking several different leases within one contract. A separate lease component exists when both of the following conditions are present:

- The lessee can benefit from the right of use of a single asset, or together with other readily available resources; and
- The right of use is separate from the rights to use other assets in the contract. This is not the case when the rights of use of the different assets significantly affect each other.

The right to use land is always considered a separate lease component, unless doing so would have an insignificant effect.

EXAMPLE

Treetops Telecommunications leases a cell phone tower, along with the land on which it is positioned and the building within which it is located. The building was designed specifically to house the cell phone tower and related equipment. In this case, the rights of use of the different assets significantly affect each other, so one lease arrangement encompasses all of the assets. The inclusion of the land component in the same lease is considered to have an insignificant effect.

There may also be non-lease components to a contract. These components will not meet the criteria just stated for a lease component, but will transfer a good or service to the lessee. There may also be other activities that do not qualify as non-lease components, since there is no transfer of goods or services; for example, the reimbursement of lessor costs falls into this category.

A common charge associated with a lease is common area maintenance. The lessor typically performs maintenance and cleaning services for all common areas in a building, and then charges a portion of these costs through to the building tenants. The lessee would otherwise have to perform these services itself or pay a third party to do so. Common area maintenance costs are considered a non-lease component.

The classifications of lease components are not reassessed after the commencement date of the lease, unless the contract is subsequently modified and the change is not treated as a separate contract. Lease classifications can also be revisited if the lease term changes or there is a change in the probability that an option will be exercised to purchase an underlying asset.

Once all lease and non-lease components have been identified, allocate the consideration in the contract to them. This allocation is derived as follows:

1. Determine the standalone price of each separate lease and non-lease component. This should be based on the observable standalone price. If this price is not available, it can be estimated.
2. Allocate the consideration in proportion to the standalone prices of the various components.
3. If there are any initial direct costs associated with the contract, allocate these costs on the same basis as the lease payments.

EXAMPLE

Micron Metallic leases a stamping machine and a CNC (computer numerical control) machine for its washing machine production facility, along with periodic maintenance and repair services. The total consideration that Micron will pay over the five-year term of the lease is $800,000.

Micron's controller concludes that there are two separate leases, since the stamping and CNC machines are to be used separately, in different parts of the factory. The controller also decides to account for the maintenance and repair services as non-lease components of the contract. Further, these services are considered to be distinct for each machine, and so are separate non-lease performance obligations.

The controller needs to allocate the $800,000 of consideration to the various lease and non-lease components. She notes that there are a number of local suppliers that provide similar maintenance and repair services for each of the machines, and that standalone prices can be found to separately lease the two machines. These standalone prices are noted in the following table:

	Lease	Maintenance	Totals
Stamping machine	$200,000	$30,000	$230,000
CNC machine	570,000	100,000	670,000
Totals	$770,000	$130,000	$900,000

The controller allocates the $800,000 consideration in the contract to the lease and non-lease components on a relative basis, employing their standalone prices. This results in the following allocation:

	Lease	Maintenance	Totals
Stamping machine	$177,778	$26,667	$204,445
CNC machine	506,667	88,888	595,555
Totals	$684,445	$115,555	$800,000

The consideration in a lease should be remeasured and reallocated when either of the following events occurs:

- The lease liability is remeasured. This could be triggered by a change in the term of the lease, or a revision to the assessment of whether a lease option will be exercised.
- There is a contract modification that is not being accounted for as a separate contract.

Lease Components (Lessor)

In general, a lessor allocates consideration to lease components in the same manner as the lessee. In addition, the lessor allocates any capitalized costs to the lease and non-lease components to which those costs relate. An example of a capitalized cost is the initial direct costs incurred to create a contract. Initial direct costs are discussed in the next section.

If a lessor receives a variable payment amount that relates to a lease component, it should recognize the payment as income in the same period as the one on which the variable payment was based.

EXAMPLE

Prickly Corporation leases space from Capital Inc., which it uses as a retail store to sell cacti and other thorny plants. Following the end of each month, Prickly is required to pay 2% of its revenue to Capital; this is the variable portion of the lease payment for the retail space. In early March, Prickly sends a payment of $540 to Capital, which is the variable portion of the payment, and which relates to its February sales. Capital should recognize this payment as income in its February income statement.

Prickly discloses in its financial statements the fixed amount of its operating lease cost, while separately disclosing the $540 as a variable lease cost.

Initial Direct Costs

Initial direct costs are those costs that are only incurred if a lease agreement occurs. This usually includes broker commissions and payments made to existing tenants to obtain a lease, because these costs are only incurred if a lease agreement is signed. Legal fees are usually not included, since the parties must pay their attorneys even if a lease arrangement falls through. Also, staff time spent working on a lease arrangement will be incurred irrespective of the lease agreement, and so is not considered part of initial direct costs.

Initial direct costs are capitalized at the inception of a lease, and are then amortized ratably over the term of the lease. Throughout the term of a lease, any unamortized initial direct costs are included in the measurement of the right-of-use asset (which is discussed later).

Lease Consideration

Consideration is defined as something of value that induces the parties to a contract to exchange mutual performances. The consideration in a leasing arrangement is most obviously the periodic fixed lease payments made by the lessee. Consideration can also include monthly service charges, as well as variable payments that are defined by an index or a rate. For example, a lease payment may be adjusted each year, based on changes in the consumer price index.

The Lease Term

One of the key components of a lease is the lease term. This is considered to be the noncancelable period of a lease, as well as the following additional periods that may apply:

- Lease extension options if it is reasonably certain that the lessee will exercise these options
- Lease termination options if it is reasonably certain that the lessee will not exercise these options
- Lease extension options where the lessor controls the options

An entity makes a judgment call as of the lease commencement date regarding which of the preceding factors will apply to the derivation of an estimated lease term. This judgment is based on those factors that create an economic incentive for the lessee. Examples of economic incentives are reduced lease payments in the optional period, the significance of any leasehold improvements, and the importance of the underlying asset to the lessee's operations.

EXAMPLE

Subatomic Research operates a laboratory in leased facilities. The laboratory has been designated as an airborne infection isolation room by the federal government, which is quite a difficult certification to obtain. The lease has an option for Subatomic to extend the lease term by five years. It is highly likely that Subatomic will renew the lease, given the high cost of moving elsewhere and then applying for recertification.

If the lessor provides a period of free rent, the lease term is considered to begin at the commencement date and to include all rent-free periods.

A lease term should not extend past the period when it is enforceable. A lease is no longer enforceable when both the lessee and the lessor can terminate the lease without permission from the other party, and by paying no more than an insignificant penalty.

A government entity that leases space may require that a fiscal funding clause be inserted into the lease. This clause allows the government to cancel a lease if it does not have sufficient funding. When this clause is present, the lease term should only include those periods for which there is a reasonable certainty of funding.

Initial Measurement of Lease Payments

There are a number of possible payments by a lessee that can be associated with a lease component. All of the following payments relate to the use of the underlying asset in a lease:

- Fixed payments, minus any lease incentives payable to the lessee
- Variable lease payments that depend on an index or a rate (such as the consumer price index)
- The exercise price of an option to purchase the underlying asset, if it is reasonably certain that the lessee will exercise the option
- Penalty payments associated with an assumed exercise of an option to terminate the lease
- Fees paid to the owners of a special-purpose entity for creating the transaction
- Residual value guarantees, if it is probable that these amounts will be owed. Note that a lease provision requiring the lessee to pay for any deficiency in residual value that is caused by damage or excessive usage is not considered a guarantee of the residual value.

At the commencement of a lease, a number of direct costs may also have been incurred. Examples of these costs are commissions and payments made to incentivize a tenant to terminate a lease. Costs that would have been incurred even in the absence of a lease (such as general overhead and salaries) are not direct costs.

A lessor might pay a third party for a guarantee of the residual value of an underlying asset. This payment is considered an executory cost of the contract; it is not considered part of the lease payments.

If there is a requirement in a lease agreement that the lessee dismantle and remove an underlying asset following the end of a lease, this cost is considered a lease payment.

Subsequent Measurement of Lease Payments

It is only necessary to reassess a lessee's option to purchase an underlying asset or the length of the lease term when one of the following events occurs subsequent to the initial measurement of a lease:

- *Contractual requirement.* An event occurs that was addressed in the contract, requiring the lessee to exercise (or not exercise) an option or terminate the lease.
- *No option exercise.* The lessee does not exercise an option despite a previous determination that it was reasonably certain for the lessee to do so.

- *Option exercise*. The lessee exercises an option despite a previous determination that it was reasonably certain that the lessee would not do so.
- *Significant event*. A significant event has occurred that is within the control of the lessee, and which directly affects the lessee's decision to exercise or not exercise an option, or to purchase the underlying asset. Examples of significant events are the construction of significant leasehold improvements that will be of value to the lessee during the option period, and making significant modifications to the underlying asset.

It is only necessary to remeasure the lease payments associated with a lease when one of the following events occurs:

- *Lease modification*. The initial lease is modified, and the modification is not accounted for as a separate contract.
- *Resolved contingency*. A contingency that had resulted in variable lease payments has now been resolved, so that the payments become fixed for the remainder of the lease term.
- *Other changes*. There is a change in the lease term, a change in the assessment of whether an option will be exercised, or a change in the probable amount that will be owed by the lessee under a residual value guarantee.

Types of Leases

There are several types of lease designations, which differ if an entity is the lessee or the lessor. It is critical to determine the type of a lease, since the accounting varies by lease type. The choices for a **lessee** are that a lease can be designated as either a finance lease or an operating lease. In essence, a *finance lease* designation implies that the lessee has purchased the underlying asset (even though this may not actually be the case) while an *operating lease* designation implies that the lessee has obtained the use of the underlying asset for only a period of time. A lessee should classify a lease as a finance lease when any of the following criteria are met:

- *Ownership transfer*. Ownership of the underlying asset is shifted to the lessee by the end of the lease term.
- *Ownership option*. The lessee has a purchase option to buy the leased asset, and is reasonably certain to use it.
- *Lease term*. The lease term covers the major part of the underlying asset's remaining economic life. This is considered to be 75% or more of the remaining economic life of the underlying asset. This criterion is not valid if the lease commencement date is near the end of the asset's economic life, which is considered to be a date that falls within the last 25% of the underlying asset's total economic life.
- *Present value*. The present value of the sum of all lease payments and any lessee-guaranteed residual value matches or exceeds the fair value of the underlying asset. The present value is based on the interest rate implicit in the lease.

- *Specialization*. The asset is so specialized that it has no alternative use for the lessor following the lease term. In this situation, there are essentially no remaining benefits that revert to the lessor.

When none of the preceding criteria are met, the lessee must classify a lease as an operating lease.

When the lessor is a government entity, the underlying asset may be a more substantial facility, such as an airport, where it is impossible to determine an economic life or the fair value of the asset. For these reasons, such leases should be considered operating leases. All of the following conditions should apply before a lease from a government entity is considered an operating lease:

- *Ownership*. The underlying asset is owned by a government entity, and ownership cannot be transferred to the lessee.
- *Nature of the asset*. The underlying asset is part of a larger facility, such as an airport, and is a permanent structure that cannot be moved.
- *Termination right*. The lessor has the right to terminate the lease at any time.

The choices for a **lessor** are that a lease can be designated as a *sales-type lease*, *direct finance lease*, or *operating lease*. If all of the preceding conditions just noted for a lessee's finance lease are met by a lease, then the lessor designates it as a sales-type lease (in effect, an asset is being sold to the lessee). If this is not the case, then the lessor has a choice of designating a lease as either a direct financing lease (in effect, the lessor earns interest income from its leasing activities) or an operating lease.

The lessor should designate any remaining lease as a direct financing lease when both of the following criteria are met:

- *Present value*. The present value of the lease payments and any residual asset value that is guaranteed by the lessee or any other party matches or exceeds substantially all of the fair value of the underlying asset. In this context, "substantially" means 90% or more of the fair value of the underlying asset. The present value is based on the rate implicit in the lease.
- *Collection probability*. The lessor will probably collect the lease payments, as well as any additional amount needed to satisfy the residual value guarantee.

When none of these additional criteria are met, the lessor classifies a lease as an operating lease.

Asset and Liability Recognition (Lessee)

A central concept of the accounting for leases is that the lessee should recognize the assets and liabilities that underlie each leasing arrangement. This concept results in the following recognition in the balance sheet of the lessee as of the lease commencement date:

- Recognize a liability to make lease payments to the lessor
- Recognize a right-of-use asset that represents the right of the lessee to use the leased asset during the lease term

There are a number of sub-topics related to asset and liability recognition, which are stated in the following sub-sections.

Initial Measurement

As of the commencement date of a lease, the lessee measures the liability and the right-of-use asset associated with the lease. These measurements are derived as follows:

- *Lease liability.* The present value of the lease payments, discounted at the discount rate for the lease. This rate is the rate implicit in the lease when that rate is readily determinable. If not, the lessee instead uses its incremental borrowing rate.
- *Right-of-use asset.* The initial amount of the lease liability, plus any lease payments made to the lessor before the lease commencement date, plus any initial direct costs incurred, minus any lease incentives received.

EXAMPLE

Inscrutable Corporation enters into a five-year lease, where the lease payments are $35,000 per year, payable at the end of each year. Inscrutable incurs initial direct costs of $8,000. The rate implicit in the lease is 8%.

At the commencement of the lease, the lease liability is $139,745, which is calculated as $35,000 multiplied by the 3.9927 rate for the five-period present value of an ordinary annuity. The right-of-use asset is calculated as the lease liability plus the amount of the initial direct costs, for a total of $147,745.

Short-Term Leases

When a lease has a term of 12 months or less, the lessee can elect not to recognize lease-related assets and liabilities in the balance sheet. This election is made by class of asset. When a lessee makes this election, it should usually recognize the expense related to a lease on a straight-line basis over the term of the lease.

If the lease term changes so that the remaining term now extends more than 12 months beyond the end of the previously determined lease term or the lessee will likely purchase the underlying asset, the arrangement is no longer considered a short-term lease. In this situation, account for the lease as a longer-term lease as of the date when there was a change in circumstances.

Finance Leases

When a lessee has designated a lease as a finance lease, it should recognize the following over the term of the lease:

- The ongoing amortization of the right-of-use asset
- The ongoing amortization of the interest on the lease liability
- Any variable lease payments that are not included in the lease liability
- Any impairment of the right-of-use asset

The amortization period for the right-of-use asset is from the lease commencement date to the earlier of the end of the lease term or the end of the useful life of the asset. An exception is when it is reasonably certain that the lessee will exercise an option to purchase the asset, in which case the amortization period is through the end of the asset's useful life.

After the commencement date, the lessee increases the carrying amount of the lease liability to include the interest expense on the lease liability, while reducing the carrying amount by the amount of all lease payments made during the period. The interest on the lease liability is the amount that generates a constant periodic discount rate on the remaining liability balance.

After the commencement date, the lessee reduces the right-of-use asset by the amount of accumulated amortization and accumulated impairment (if any).

EXAMPLE

Giro Cabinetry agrees to a five-year lease of equipment that requires an annual $20,000 payment, due at the end of each year. At the end of the lease period, Giro has the option to buy the equipment for $1,000. Since the expected residual value of the equipment at that time is expected to be $25,000, the large discount makes it reasonably certain that the purchase option will be exercised. At the commencement date of the lease, the fair value of the equipment is $120,000, with an economic life of eight years. The discount rate for the lease is 6%.

Giro classifies the lease as a finance lease, since it is reasonably certain to exercise the purchase option.

The lease liability at the commencement date is $84,995, which is calculated as the present value of five payments of $20,000, plus the present value of the $1,000 purchase option payment, discounted at 6%. Giro recognizes the right-of-use asset as the same amount, since there are no initial direct costs, lease incentives, or other types of payments made by Giro, either at or before the commencement date.

Giro amortizes the right-of-use asset over the eight-year expected useful life of the equipment, under the assumption that it will exercise the purchase option and therefore keep the equipment for the eight-year period.

As an example of the subsequent accounting for the lease, Giro recognizes a first-year interest expense of $5,100 (calculated as 6% × $84,995 lease liability), and recognizes the amortization of the right-of-use asset in the amount of $10,624 (calculated as $84,995 ÷ 8 years). This results in a lease liability at the end of Year 1 that has been reduced to $70,095 (calculated as $84,995 + $5,100 interest - $20,000 lease payment) and a right-of-use asset that has been reduced to $74,371 (calculated as $84,995 - $10,624 amortization).

By the end of Year 5, which is when the lease terminates, the lease liability has been reduced to $1,000, which is the amount of the purchase option. Giro exercises the option, which settles the remaining liability. At that time, the carrying amount of the right-of-use asset has declined to $31,875 (reflecting five years of amortization at $10,624 per year). Giro shifts this amount into a fixed asset account, and depreciates it over the remaining three years of its useful life.

Operating Leases

When a lessee has designated a lease as an operating lease, the lessee should recognize the following over the term of the lease:

- A lease cost in each period, where the total cost of the lease is allocated over the lease term on a straight-line basis. This can be altered if there is another systematic and rational basis of allocation that more closely follows the benefit usage pattern to be derived from the underlying asset.
- Any variable lease payments that are not included in the lease liability
- Any impairment of the right-of-use asset

EXAMPLE

Nuance Corporation enters into an operating lease in which the lease payment is $25,000 per year for the first five years and $30,000 per year for the next five years. These payments sum to $275,000 over ten years. Nuance will therefore recognize a lease expense of $27,500 per year for all of the years in the lease term.

At any point in the life of an operating lease, the remaining cost of the lease is considered to be the total lease payments, plus all initial direct costs associated with the lease, minus the lease cost already recognized in previous periods.

After the commencement date, the lessee measures the lease liability at the present value of the lease payments that have not yet been made, using the same discount rate that was established at the commencement date.

After the commencement date, the lessee measures the right-of-use asset at the amount of the lease liability, adjusted for the following items:

- Any impairment of the asset
- Prepaid or accrued lease payments
- Any remaining balance of lease incentives received
- Any unamortized initial direct costs

EXAMPLE

Hubble Corporation enters into a 10-year operating lease for its corporate offices. The annual lease payment is $40,000 to be paid at the end of each year. The company incurs initial direct costs of $8,000, and receives $15,000 from the lessor as a lease incentive. Hubble's incremental borrowing rate is 6%. The initial direct costs and lease incentive will be amortized over the 10 years of the lease term.

Hubble measures the lease liability as the present value of the 10 lease payments at a 6% discount rate, which is $294,404. The right-of-use asset is measured at $287,404, which is the initial $294,404 measurement, plus the initial direct costs of $8,000, minus the lease incentive of $15,000.

After one year, the carrying amount of the lease liability is $272,068, which is the present value of the remaining nine lease payments at a 6% discount rate. The carrying amount of the right-of-use asset is $265,768, which is the amount of the liability, plus the unamortized initial direct costs of $7,200, minus the remaining balance of the lease incentive of $13,500.

Optional Lease Payments

When there is an optional payment in a lease agreement that can be made by the lessee to purchase a leased asset, this optional payment is only included in the recognition of assets and liabilities if it is reasonably certain that the lessee will exercise the purchase option.

Right-of-Use Asset Impairment

If a right-of-use asset is determined to be impaired, the impairment is immediately recorded, thereby reducing the carrying amount of the asset. Its subsequent measurement is calculated as the carrying amount immediately after the impairment transaction, minus any subsequent accumulated amortization.

EXAMPLE

Horton Corporation enters into a five-year equipment lease that is classified as an operating lease. At the end of Year 2, when the carrying amount of the lease liability and the right-of-use asset are both $100,000, the controller determines that the asset is impaired, and recognizes an impairment loss of $70,000. This reduces the carrying amount of the asset to $30,000.

Beginning in Year 3 and continuing through the remainder of the lease term, Horton amortizes the right-of-use asset at a rate of $10,000 per year, which will bring the carrying amount of the asset to zero by the end of the lease term.

Leasehold Improvement Amortization

A leasehold improvement is a customization of rented property, such as the addition of carpeting, cabinetry, lighting, and walls. This asset should be amortized over the shorter of the remaining lease term and its useful life. The one exception is when it is reasonably certain that the lessee will take possession of the underlying asset at the end of the lease, in which case the amortization period is through the end of the asset's useful life.

Subleases

A sublease occurs when a lessee leases the underlying asset to a third party. A sublease agreement typically arises when the original tenant no longer needs to use leased space or can no longer afford to make the lease payments. This situation is most common for commercial properties, but can arise for residential properties as well. The following accounting can apply to this situation:

- *Operating lease*. If a lease is classified as an operating lease, the original lessee continues to account for it in the same manner that it did before the commencement of the sublease.
- *Conversion from finance lease*. If the original lease was classified as a finance lease and the sublease is classified as either a sales-type or direct financing lease, then the original lessee must derecognize the right-of-use asset on its books. The accounting for the original lease liability remains the same.
- *Conversion from operating lease*. If the original lease was classified as an operating lease and the sublease is classified as either a sales-type lease or a direct financing lease, then the original lessee must derecognize the right-of-use asset on its books, and account for the original lease liability as of the sublease commencement date as though it were a finance lease (see the preceding Finance Leases sub-section).

Maintenance Deposits

A lessee may be required to pay the lessor a maintenance deposit, which the lessor retains if the lessee damages the property during the lease term. If it is probable that the lessor will retain this deposit at the end of the lease, the lessee should recognize the payment as a variable lease expense.

Derecognition

At the termination of a lease, the right-of-use asset and associated lease liability are removed from the books. The difference between the two amounts is accounted for as a profit or loss at that time. If the lessee purchases the underlying asset at the termination of a lease, then any difference between the purchase price and the lease liability is recorded as an adjustment to the asset's carrying amount.

If a lessee subleases an underlying asset and the terms of the original agreement then relieve the lessee of the primary lease obligation, this is considered a termination of the original lease.

Lease Recognition Topics (Lessor)

The accounting for leases by lessors varies in several respects from the accounting by lessees. In particular, there are more classifications of leases for a lessor; there are sales-type leases, direct financing leases, and operating leases. The accounting for these leases is addressed in the following sub-sections.

Sales-Type Leases

In a sales-type lease, the lessor is assumed to actually be selling a product to the lessee, which calls for the recognition of a profit or loss on the sale. Consequently, this results in the following accounting at the commencement date of the lease:

- *Derecognize asset.* The lessor derecognizes the underlying asset, since it is assumed to have been sold to the lessee.
- *Recognize net investment.* The lessor recognizes a net investment in the lease. This investment includes the following:
    - The present value of lease payments not yet received
    - The present value of the guaranteed amount of the underlying asset's residual value at the end of the lease term
    - The present value of the unguaranteed amount of the underlying asset's residual value at the end of the lease term
- *Recognize profit or loss.* The lessor recognizes any selling profit or loss caused by the lease.
- *Recognize initial direct costs.* The lessor recognizes any initial direct costs as an expense, if there is a difference between the carrying amount of the underlying asset and its fair value. If the fair value of the underlying asset is

instead equal to its carrying amount, then defer the initial direct costs and include them in the measurement of the lessor's investment in the lease.

In addition, the lessor must account for the following items subsequent to the commencement date of the lease:

- *Interest income*. The ongoing amount of interest earned on the net investment in the lease.
- *Variable lease payments*. If there are any variable lease payments that were not included in the net investment in the lease, record them in profit or loss in the same reporting period as the events that triggered the payments.
- *Impairment*. Recognize any impairment of the net investment in the lease.
- *Net investment*. Adjust the balance of the net investment in the lease by adding interest income and subtracting any lease payments collected during the period.

However, if the collectability of the lease payments and payments related to a residual value guarantee are not probable as of the commencement date, the lessor should not derecognize the underlying asset. Instead, the lessor recognizes lease payments (including variable lease payments) as a deposit liability as they are received. This treatment continues until the earlier of either of these events:

- *Probable collectability*. It becomes probable that lease payments and payments related to a residual value guarantee will be collectible.
- *Contract termination*. Either of the following occurs:
  - The contract has been terminated *and* the lease payments received to date are not refundable; or
  - The lessor has repossessed the underlying asset, *and* has no further obligation to the lessee, *and* the lease payments received to date are not refundable.

When the collectability of payments from a lessee was initially considered to not be probable, but this assessment was later changed, the lessor should take the following steps as of the latter event:

- *Derecognize asset*. Derecognize the carrying amount of the underlying asset.
- *Derecognize liability*. If there is a deposit liability, derecognize it.
- *Recognize net investment*. Recognize a net investment in the lease. This amount is derived from the remaining lease payments, the remaining lease term, and the rate implicit in the lease at the commencement date.
- *Recognize profit or loss*. Recognize any selling profit or loss, which is calculated as the lease receivable plus the carrying amount of the deposit liability, minus the carrying amount of the underlying asset, net of the unguaranteed residual asset.

Leases

If this type of lease is terminated before the end of its lease term, the lessor must test the net investment in the lease for impairment and recognize an impairment loss if necessary. Then reclassify the net investment in the lease to the most appropriate fixed asset category. The reclassified asset is recorded at the sum of the carrying amounts of the lease receivable and the residual asset.

At the end of the lease term, the lessor reclassifies its net investment in the lease to the most appropriate fixed asset account.

EXAMPLE

Capital Inc. enters into an eight-year lease of equipment with a lessee. Under the terms of the agreement, Capital will receive an annual lease payment of $10,000, payable at the end of each year. The lessee also provides Capital with a residual value guarantee of $15,000. Upon reviewing the credit rating of the lessee, Capital's controller concludes that it is probable that Capital will collect the lease payments and any additional funding necessary to satisfy the lessee's residual value guarantee. Additional pertinent facts are:

- The equipment has a 10-year estimated economic life
- The equipment has a carrying amount of $60,000
- The equipment has a fair value of $71,509 at the commencement date
- The expected residual value of the equipment is $18,000 at the end of the lease term
- There is no transfer of equipment ownership to the lessee, nor is there a purchase option
- The rate implicit in the lease is 6%

The controller classifies the lease as a sales-type lease, because the combined present value of the lease payments and the residual value guaranteed by the lessee is $71,509, which is substantially all of the fair value of the underlying asset.

The controller measures the net investment in the lease at $73,391 at the commencement date of the lease; this equals the fair value of the equipment. This net investment consists of the following:

Present value of eight lease payments of $10,000 each	$62,098
Present value of $15,000 residual value guarantee	9,411
Present value of the $3,000 unguaranteed residual value	1,882
Net investment in the lease	$73,391

523

The selling profit on the lease is $13,391, which is the difference between the lease receivable (the present values of the lease payments and the guaranteed residual value) and the carrying amount of the equipment net of the unguaranteed residual asset. The calculation is:

Lease receivable (present values of lease payments and guaranteed residual value)	$71,509
- Carrying amount of the equipment net of the present value of the unguaranteed residual asset	58,118
Selling profit	$13,391

At the lease commencement date, the controller derecognizes the $60,000 carrying amount of the equipment, recognizes the net investment in the lease of $73,391, and recognizes the selling profit of $13,391.

At the end of the first year of the lease, Capital receives and recognizes the annual $10,000 lease payment. Capital also recognizes interest on the net investment in the lease, which is $4,403 (calculated as $73,391 net investment in the lease × 6% rate implicit in the lease). This results in a reduced balance of $67,794 in the net investment in the lease, which is calculated as the $73,391 beginning balance, plus the $4,403 interest income, minus the $10,000 lease payment.

Direct Financing Leases

In a direct financing lease, the lessor acquires assets and leases them to its customers, with the intent of generating revenue from the resulting interest payments. At the commencement date of a direct financing lease, the lessor engages in the following activities:

- Recognize the net investment in the lease. This includes the selling profit and any initial direct costs for which recognition is deferred.
- Recognize a selling loss caused by the lease arrangement, if this has occurred
- Derecognize the underlying asset

In addition, the lessor must account for the following items subsequent to the commencement date of the lease:

- *Interest income.* Record the ongoing amount of interest earned on the net investment in the lease.
- *Variable lease payments.* If there are any variable lease payments that were not included in the net investment in the lease, record them in profit or loss in the same reporting period as the events that triggered the payments.
- *Impairment.* Record any impairment of the net investment in the lease.

- *Net investment*. Adjust the balance of the net investment in the lease by adding interest income and subtracting any lease payments collected during the period.

If this type of lease is terminated before the end of its lease term, the lessor must test the net investment in the lease for impairment and recognize an impairment loss if necessary. Then reclassify the net investment in the lease to the most appropriate fixed asset category. The reclassified asset is recorded at the sum of the carrying amounts of the lease receivable and the residual asset.

At the end of the lease term, the lessor reclassifies its net investment in the lease to the most appropriate fixed asset account.

Operating Leases

An operating lease is any lease other than a sales-type lease or a direct financing lease. At the commencement date of an operating lease, the lessor shall defer all initial direct costs. In addition, the lessor must account for the following items subsequent to the commencement date of the lease:

- *Lease payments*. Lease payments are recognized in profit or loss over the term of the lease on a straight-line basis, unless another systematic and rational basis more clearly represents the benefit that the lessee is deriving from the underlying asset. Profits cannot be recognized at the beginning of an operating lease, since control of the underlying asset has not been transferred to the lessee.
- *Variable lease payments*. If there are any variable lease payments, record them in profit or loss in the same reporting period as the events that triggered the payments.
- *Initial direct costs*. Recognize initial direct costs as an expense over the term of the lease, using the same recognition basis that was used for the recognition of lease income.

If the collectability of the lease payments and payments related to a residual value guarantee are not probable as of the commencement date, the lessor limits the recognition of lease income to the lesser of the payments described in the immediately preceding bullet points or the actual lease payments (including variable lease payments) that have been received. If this assessment later changes, any difference between the income that should have been recognized and which had been recognized is recognized in the current period.

EXAMPLE

Scottish Colonial Leasing enters into a five-year lease where the annual lease payments begin at $5,000 and escalate by $500 for each of the next four years. There are initial direct costs of $2,000. The collectability of lease payments is not probable, so Scottish classifies the lease as an operating lease.

Since the lease is classified as an operating lease, Scottish continues to measure the underlying asset as a fixed asset. Due to the risk of nonpayment, Scottish only recognizes lease income when payments are received from the lessee, and in the amount of those payments. Thus, when the first year payment of $5,000 is received, Scottish recognizes lease income of $5,000.

Scottish recognizes 20% of the initial direct costs in each year, which is a $400 expense recognition per year.

Variable Lease Payments

Most variable lease payments should be excluded from the recognition of lease assets and liabilities. However, lease payments that depend on an index or a rate should be included in this recognition.

Any variable charges to a lessee that are essentially a reimbursement of the lessor's costs are not considered part of a lease. For example, a lessor may require a lessee to pay the real estate taxes on a leased property, or the associated building insurance. Neither variable payment is for the right to use the underlying asset and does not depend on an index or a rate, and so is not a component of the contract.

In addition, a payment that is called a variable payment, but which is in reality a fixed payment should be included in the recognition of a leased asset or liability.

Lease Modifications

When a contract is modified, the change is accounted for as a separate contract, but only when both of the following conditions are present:

- *Additional right of use*. The lessee is granted an additional right of use as part of the modification.
- *Incremental price*. There is an incremental increase in the lease price that is commensurate with the standalone price of the additional right of use that is being granted, adjusted for the contract-specific circumstances.

EXAMPLE

Grunge Motor Sports needs additional warehouse space for the storage of its dirt bike products. The lessor of its current warehouse has adjacent warehouse space, which is added onto the current lease. The lease price for this additional space is less than the current market rate in the area, because the lessor did not have to incur several additional charges that it normally would have paid for an entirely new client. It will be accounted for as a separate contract.

EXAMPLE

Monk Books currently leases 30,000 square feet of space for its scriptorium, and is in the 6th year of a 10-year lease. Given the increased demand for hand-illuminated books, Monk enters into a lease modification with the lessor, which adds 15,000 more square feet to the scriptorium as of the beginning of the 7th year at the then-current market rate.

Monk's controller accounts for the modification as a new contract, since Monk is being granted an additional right of use in excess of the original contract. The new contract only includes the incremental change noted in the lease modification.

If these two conditions are not present, then the existing lease classification is re-assessed as of the date of the contract modification. This reassessment encompasses the modified terms and conditions, as well as the facts and circumstances of the situation as of that date. For example, the fair value of the underlying asset might have changed between the initial contract date and the modification date.

Lessee Impact

When there is a contract modification, the lessee should reallocate the consideration remaining in the contract to the lease components, and also remeasure the lease liability with a discount rate for the lease that is derived as of the effective date of the contract modification. These changes should only be made when a contract modification causes any of the following to occur:

- An additional right of use is granted to the lessee. This adjusts the amount of the right-of-use asset.
- Alters the term of the lease. This adjusts the amount of the right-of-use asset.
- Either fully or partially terminates the existing lease. This decreases the carrying amount of the right-of-use asset proportionally, based on the amount of lease termination. If this causes a difference between the revised lease liability and the right-of-use asset, the difference is recognized as a gain or loss as of the effective date of the modification.
- Alters the amount of the consideration in the contract. This adjusts the amount of the right-of-use asset.

EXAMPLE

Country Fresh Produce enters into a 5-year lease for 20,000 square feet of office space. The lease payments are fixed at $100,000 per year. The original discount rate for the lease was 8%. The lease is classified as an operating lease. At the beginning of Year 3, Country Fresh and the lessor agree to modify the original lease for the remaining three years by reducing the lease payments by $10,000 per year. Since only the lease payments are being modified, this alteration cannot be accounted for as a separate contract, nor does the lease classification change.

These changes call for a remeasurement of the lease liability, based on the following information:

- Remaining lease term is three years
- Payments of $90,000 in each year, from Year 3 through Year 5
- Country Fresh's incremental borrowing rate is 6% as of the effective date of the modification

The remeasured lease liability is $240,570, which is $17,140 less than the $257,710 pre-modification lease liability. Country Fresh treats the $17,140 as a reduction in the right-of-use asset.

As of the date of the modification, the remaining lease cost for Country Fresh is $270,000, which is the sum of the remaining three payments of $90,000 each. The lease liability on Country Fresh's balance sheet in the following years will be as indicated in the following table:

Beginning of	Lease Liability	Derivation
Year 3	$240,570	[Ordinary annuity factor for 3 years] 2.6730 × $90,000
Year 4	165,006	[Ordinary annuity factor for 2 years] 1.8334 × $90,000
Year 5	84,906	[Ordinary annuity factor for 1 year] 0.9434 × $90,000

Lessor Impact

When there is a contract modification and it is not accounted for as a separate contract, the lessor accounts for the change as though the original lease was cancelled and replaced by a new lease as of the effective date of the modification. Those changes are as follows:

- *Operating lease treatment*. If a lease has been classified as an operating lease, any prepaid or accrued lease rentals associated with the original lease are now considered to be part of the payments associated with the modified lease.
- *Direct financing or sales-type lease*. If a lease has been classified as a direct financing or sales-type lease, derecognize the accrued rent asset or deferred rent liability; then adjust the selling profit or loss to match the amount of the derecognition.

EXAMPLE

Capital Inc. enters into a 5-year operating lease as the lessor. The lease is for 5,000 square feet of prime office space, for which the annual lease payment is $100,000. This amount increases by 5% in each subsequent year, which results in the following schedule of lease payments:

Year	Lease Payment
1	$100,000
2	105,000
3	110,250
4	115,763
5	121,551
Total	$552,564
Average	$110,513

At the beginning of Year 3, both parties agree to modify the lease for the remaining three years to include an additional 2,000 square feet of office space, which results in a new annual lease payment of $130,000, and which then increases by 5% in each subsequent year. The incremental increase in the lease payment represents a substantial reduction from the market rate for this type of property. Because the pricing of the modification is not commensurate with the standalone price, the modification is not treated as an entirely new lease. Instead, Capital Inc. accounts for the modified lease on a go-forward basis with the following inputs:

- Total lease payments yet to be made of $409,825 (calculated as $130,000 + $136,500 + $143,325)
- At the beginning of Year 3, Capital Inc. has an accrued lease rental asset of $16,026 (calculated as $110,513 annual average lease income × 2 years, minus lease payments of $100,000 and $105,000).

Capital Inc. subtracts the accrued lease rental asset of $16,026 from the $409,825 total lease payments yet to be made to arrive at $393,799 of lease income to be recognized over the remaining three years of the lease. This is recognized on a straight-line basis, at $131,266 per year.

If a modified lease was originally classified as a direct financing lease, and the modification is not accounted for as a separate contract, the modified lease is accounted for by the lessor as follows:

- *Continues as direct financing lease.* If the classification of the lease continues to be as a direct financing lease, the discount rate for the lease is adjusted in order to have the initial net investment in the modified lease equal the carrying amount of the net investment in the original lease just before the effective date of the lease modification. The same accounting applies if a sales-type lease is modified to be a direct financing lease.

EXAMPLE

Capital Inc. is the lessor in an existing leasing arrangement, which is about to be modified. The lease is classified as a direct financing lease, and will continue to be classified in that manner after the modification has been completed. The carrying amount of Capital's net investment in the lease is $62,000 just before the effective date of the lease modification. The modification will shorten the term of the lease, which increases the residual value of the underlying asset to $40,000. In order to have the $62,000 carrying amount of the investment equal its $40,000 residual value by the end of the lease period, Capital must calculate the interest rate that will generate interest income on the net investment over the remaining four-year term of the lease. Using a derived interest rate of 10.3775%, that calculation is:

Year	Beginning Balance	Interest Income	Ending Balance
1	$62,000	$6,434	$55,566
2	55,566	5,766	49,800
3	49,800	5,168	44,632
4	44,632	4,632	40,000

- *Reclassified as sales-type lease*. If the classification of the lease is altered to be a sales-type lease, it is subsequently accounted for as a sales-type lease. To calculate the selling profit or loss associated with the lease, the fair value of the underlying asset is derived as of the effective date of the lease modification, and the carrying amount of the net investment in the original lease is that value just prior to the effective date of the modification.

EXAMPLE

Capital Inc. is the lessor in a leasing arrangement that was originally classified as a direct financing lease, because the lease covered only a reduced portion of the economic life of the underlying asset. The lease is then modified to extend the lease term, which now encompasses such a large proportion of the economic life of the asset that the lease is reclassified as a sales-type lease. In effect, Capital is now assumed to be selling the asset to the lessee.

At the effective date of the modification, Capital derecognizes the carrying amount of the net investment in the original direct financing lease, which is $71,500. Capital then recognizes a net investment in the sales-type lease of $75,000, which is the fair value of the underlying asset on the effective date of the modification. The $3,500 difference between these two values is the selling profit earned by Capital on the modified lease.

- *Reclassified as operating lease*. If the classification of the lease is altered to an operating lease, the carrying amount of the underlying asset is the same as the net investment in the original lease just prior to the effective date of the modification. The same accounting applies if a sales-type lease is modified to be an operating lease.

EXAMPLE

Capital Inc. is the lessor in a leasing arrangement that had originally been classified as a direct financing lease. The lease is then modified, resulting in a reclassification to an operating lease. Just prior to the effective date of the modification, Capital's net investment in the lease is $132,000. Capital derecognizes this net investment, and recognizes the underlying asset as a fixed asset in the same amount. The lease payments are $20,000 annually for the next five years. Capital recognizes these payments on a straight-line basis over the remaining years of the lease. Capital also depreciates the underlying asset during those five years.

Elections

There are several elections that an organization can use to simplify the accounting for leases. One option is to use a risk-free discount rate for present value calculations, rather than having to justify some other rate. Another election is to include non-leasing components in a leasing arrangement, thereby reducing the number of elements within a contract to which costs may be assigned. These two options are explained within this section. In addition, a lessee can elect not to recognize lease-related assets and liabilities in the balance sheet when a lease has a term of 12 months or less. This option was explained earlier in the Asset and Liability Recognition section.

Discount Rate

A business that is not publicly-held can elect to use a risk-free discount rate when deriving the present value of a lease. If so, this discount rate should be determined using a period comparable to that of the lease term. This election will apply to all of the entity's leases; it is not available for just a single lease or class of asset.

Separation of Non-Lease Components

A leasing arrangement may contain non-leasing components. For example, a lease contract might include a maintenance contract under which the lessor provides ongoing servicing of the leased asset. In this case, the consideration stated in the contract is to be allocated by the lessee to these separate parts based on their relative standalone prices. The accounting for non-leasing contract components will vary depending on their nature; it is not covered by the leasing standard.

A lessee can choose to not separate non-lease components from lease components. Instead, it can account for a lease component and any non-lease components associated with that lease component as a single lease component. This election must be made by class of asset; it is not available for just a single lease.

Sale and Leaseback Transactions

A sale and leaseback transaction occurs when the seller transfers an asset to the buyer, and then leases the asset from the buyer. This arrangement most commonly occurs when the seller needs the funds associated with the asset being sold, despite still needing to occupy the space.

When such a transaction occurs, the first accounting step is to determine whether the transaction was at fair value. This can be judged from either of the following comparisons:

- Compare the difference between the sale price of the asset and its fair value.
- Compare the present value of the lease payments and the present value of market rental payments. This can include an estimation of any variable lease payments reasonably expected to be made.

If this comparison results in the determination that a sale and leaseback transaction is not at fair value, the entity must adjust the sale price on the same basis just used to determine whether the transaction was at fair value. This can result in the following adjustments:

- Any increase to the asset's sale price is accounted for as a rent prepayment
- Any reduction of the asset's sale price is accounted for as additional financing provided to the seller-lessee by the buyer-lessor. The seller-lessee should adjust the interest rate on this liability to ensure that:
    - Interest on the liability is not greater than the principal payments over the shorter of the lease term and the financing term; and
    - The carrying amount of the asset is not greater than the carrying amount of the liability at the earlier of the termination date of the lease or the date when asset control switches to the buyer-lessor.

In this arrangement, the consideration paid for the asset is accounted for as a financing transaction by both parties. However, if there is a repurchase option under which the seller can later buy back the asset, then the initial transaction cannot be considered a sale. The only exceptions are when:

- There are alternative assets readily available in the marketplace, and
- The price at which the option can be exercised is the fair value of the asset on the option exercise date.

If a sale and leaseback transaction is not considered a sale, then the seller-lessee cannot derecognize the asset, and accounts for any amounts received as a liability. Also, the buyer-lessor does not recognize the transferred asset, and accounts for any amount paid as a receivable.

EXAMPLE

Epic Rest Hotels sells one of its hotel properties to Capital Inc. The sale price is a cash payment of $7 million. At the same time as the sale, Epic Rest enters into a contract with Capital for the right to use the hotel for the next 10 years, in exchange for annual payments of $800,000, payable in arrears. Additional facts are:

- Immediately prior to the transaction, the hotel had a carrying amount on Epic's books of $6 million
- The fair value of the hotel is $7 million
- Capital obtains legal title to the property
- Capital has significant risks and rewards of ownership, such as the risk of loss if the property value declines
- The transaction is classified as an operating lease

As of the transaction commencement date, Epic Rest derecognizes the $6 million carrying amount of the hotel property, recognizes the $7 million cash receipt, and recognizes a $1 million gain on sale of the hotel. Also as of this date, Capital recognizes the hotel at a cost of $7 million.

Lease Presentation

The following presentation issues related to leases must be followed by the *lessee* in its financial statements:

Balance Sheet

- Right-of-use assets related to finance leases and operating leases are to be reported separately and not included with other assets. If these amounts are aggregated into other line items, disclose the line items in which they are located.
- Lease liabilities related to finance leases and operating leases are to be reported separately and not included with other assets. If these amounts are aggregated into other line items, disclose the line items in which they are located.
- Right-of-use assets for finance leases cannot be presented in the same line as right-of-use assets for operating leases
- Lease liabilities for finance leases cannot be presented in the same line as lease liabilities for operating leases.

Statement of Comprehensive Income

- The interest expense on the lease liability for finance leases does not have to be presented as a separate line item.
- The amortization expense for right-of-use assets does not have to be presented as a separate line item.

- The lease expense for operating leases should be included within the income from continuing operations section.

Statement of Cash Flows

- Repayments of the principal portion of the lease liability associated with financing leases are to be reported within the financing activities classification.
- Payments related to operating leases are to be reported within the operating activities classification.

The following presentation issues related to leases must be followed by the *lessor* in its financial statements:

Balance Sheet

- The aggregate amount of the lessor's net investment in sales-type leases and direct financing leases is presented separately from other assets.

Statement of Comprehensive Income

- Disclose the income arising from sales-type and direct financing leases (or do so in the accompanying footnotes). If this information is not separately presented in the statement of comprehensive income, note the line items in which it is located.
- There are several ways to present the profits or losses associated with the lessor's leasing activity for sales-type and direct financing leases. For example:
  - o If leases are used to provide financing to lessees (a direct finance lease), present the profit or loss in a single line item.
  - o If leases are used as a way to derive value from goods that would otherwise be sold (a sales-type lease), present in separate line items the revenue and cost of goods sold related to these leases. In this case, the amount of revenue recognized is the lesser of the fair value of the underlying asset at the commencement date and the sum of the lease receivable and any prepaid lease payments. The derivation of the cost of goods sold is the carrying amount of the underlying asset at the commencement date, minus the unguaranteed residual asset.

Statement of Cash Flows

- Cash receipts from all types of leases are classified by the lessor within operating activities.

Lease Disclosures

There are a considerable number of required disclosures for leases. In this section, we provide descriptions of these disclosures for the lessee and the lessor, as well as a few additional disclosures related to sale and leaseback transactions.

Lessee Disclosures

The following disclosure requirements related to leases must be followed by the *lessee* in its financial statements:

Nature of the Leases

- General description of the leases
- The basis upon which variable lease payments are calculated
- The nature of any lease extension or termination options
- The nature of any residual value guarantees
- The nature of any restrictions imposed by leases
- The nature of any leases that have not yet commenced, that will create significant rights and obligations for the lessee
- The significant assumptions and judgments made, including whether a lease exists, the allocation of consideration to leases, and the determination of the lease discount rate

Lease Costs

- The finance lease cost, separately reporting the amortization of right-of-use assets and the interest expense on lease liabilities
- The operating lease cost
- The short-term lease cost, not including leases with a term of one month or less
- The variable lease cost
- The income from subleases
- The net gain or loss on sale and leaseback transactions

Other Information

- Cash paid for items included in the measurement of lease liabilities
- Non-cash information regarding lease liabilities caused by securing right-of-use assets
- The weighted-average remaining lease term
- The weighted-average discount rate
- A maturity analysis of finance lease liabilities and operating lease liabilities, which reveals undiscounted cash flows for each of the first five years and the total for all subsequent years

- A reconciliation of undiscounted cash flows to the finance lease liabilities and operating lease liabilities recognized in the balance sheet
- All lease transactions between related parties
- Disclosure of a policy to account for short-term leases without the recognition of a lease liability or right-of-use asset
- Disclosure of a policy to not separate lease components from non-lease components, and the classes of underlying assets to which it applies

SAMPLE LESSEE DISCLOSURE

(000s)	Year Ending December 31,	
	20X4	20X3
Lease cost		
Finance lease cost:		
Amortization of right-of-use assets	$1,320	$1,295
Interest on lease liabilities	475	463
Operating lease cost	280	240
Short-term lease cost	72	65
Variable lease cost	11	9
Sublease income	40	10
Total lease cost	$2,198	$2,082
Other Information		
(Gains) and losses on sale and leaseback transactions	$--	$400
Cash paid for amounts included in the measurement of lease liabilities		
Operating cash flows from finance leases	810	615
Operating cash flows from operating leases	275	228
Financing cash flows from finance leases	460	420
Weighted-average remaining lease term – finance leases	4.7 years	4.3 years
Weighted-average remaining lease term – operating leases	3.0 years	2.9 years
Weighted-average discount rate – finance leases	6.9%	6.5%
Weighted-average discount rate – operating leases	7.2%	7.0%

Lessor Disclosures

The following disclosure requirements related to leases must be followed by the *lessor* in its financial statements:

Nature of the Leases

- General description of the leases
- The basis upon which variable lease payments are calculated
- The nature of any lease extension or termination options
- The nature of any options for a lessee to purchase an underlying asset
- The existence of any lease transactions between related parties

Significant Judgments Made

- The significant assumptions and judgments made, including whether a lease exists, the allocation of consideration to lease and non-lease components, and the determination of the amount the lessor expects to derive from the underlying asset at the end of the lease term
- How the lessor manages the risk associated with the residual value of its leased assets, including the following:
    - Its risk management strategy for residual assets
    - The carrying amount of the residual assets that are covered by residual value guarantees
    - Other means by which the lessor acts to reduce its residual asset risk

Financial Statement Recognition

- A tabulation of lease income for the annual and interim reporting period, which includes:
    - For sales-type and direct financing leases, the profit or loss recognized at the commencement date, as well as interest income
    - For operating leases, the lease income related to lease payments
    - Lease income related to variable lease payments that were not included in the measurement of the lease receivable
- The components of the aggregate net investment in sales-type and direct financing leases

Additional Disclosures for Sales-Type and Direct Financing Leases

- Explain any significant changes in the balance of the lessor's unguaranteed residual assets, as well as the deferred selling profit on its direct financing leases
- Provide a maturity analysis of the lessor's lease receivables, stating the undiscounted annual cash flows for each of the next five years and the total receivables remaining thereafter.

- Reconcile the undiscounted cash flows to the lease receivables stated in the balance sheet.

Additional Disclosures for Operating Leases

- Provide a maturity analysis of lease payments, stating the undiscounted annual cash flows for each of the next five years and the total amounts remaining thereafter. This analysis is to be stated separately from the analysis for sales-type and direct financing leases.
- Separately make all fixed asset-related disclosures for underlying assets from all other assets that are owned by the lessor.

Sale and Leaseback Transactions

A seller-lessee in a sale and leaseback transaction should disclose the primary terms and conditions of the transaction. In addition, it should separately disclose any gains or losses from the transaction, so that they are not aggregated into the gains or losses derived from the disposal of other assets.

Summary

A key element of the accounting for leases is that an organization must now recognize assets and liabilities for the rights and obligations created by leases that have terms of more than 12 months. This level of disclosure gives a substantial amount of transparency regarding a lessee's financial leverage and its leasing activities. Unfortunately, it also introduces a greater degree of complexity to the accounting for leases. Consequently, it may be useful to create a procedure for the leasing transactions that an entity engages in most frequently, along with accompanying examples, and rigidly adhere to that procedure when accounting for leases. It may also be useful to structure leasing transactions in the future so that the procedure can be applied to them. Doing so reduces the potential variability in the accounting that may be applied to leasing transactions, which in turn reduces the risk of having errors creep into the financial statements.

Chapter 44
Nonmonetary Transactions

845 = GAAP codification area for nonmonetary transactions

Introduction

There are times when a business does not use cash to settle its transactions. Instead, it may enter into an exchange of nonmonetary assets, or use cash for only a portion of the settlement. In this chapter, we review the accounting for several variations on the concept of the nonmonetary transaction.

Related Chapter

See the Other Assets and Deferred Costs chapter for a discussion of advertising barter transactions.

Overview of Nonmonetary Transactions

Nearly all transactions between parties involve the exchange of cash for goods or services. However, there are a few situations where primarily nonmonetary assets are exchanged. This latter situation is referred to as (predictably enough) a nonmonetary transaction. There are three possible types of nonmonetary transactions, which are:

- *Nonreciprocal transfers with owners.* This is typically a distribution to stockholders, such as the issuance of shares or tangible goods as a dividend.
- *Nonreciprocal transfers with other than owners.* This is a distribution to a third party, such as the contribution of assets to a charity.
- *Nonmonetary exchanges.* This is an asset exchange with another entity, such as the exchange of one real estate holding for another.

In general, a reciprocal transfer of a nonmonetary asset is considered an exchange only when each party gives up any continuing involvement in the asset that it has transferred to the other party.

The accounting for a nonmonetary transaction is based on the fair values of the assets transferred. This results in the following set of alternatives for determining the recorded cost of a nonmonetary asset acquired in an exchange, in declining order of preference:

1. At the fair value of the asset transferred in exchange for it. Record a gain or loss on the exchange.

2. At the fair value of the asset received, if the fair value of this asset is more evident than the fair value of the asset transferred in exchange for it.
3. At the recorded amount of the surrendered asset, if no fair values are determinable or the transaction has no commercial substance.

If there is a nonreciprocal asset transfer, the accounting by the two parties involved in the transaction is:

- *Recipient*. Record the cost of the asset received at its fair value.
- *Transferor*. Record the asset being surrendered at its fair value, which may result in the recognition of a gain or loss on the disposition.

There are some variations on the accounting for nonmonetary exchanges that may apply in limited circumstances, which are:

- *Reacquired stock*. When making a transfer of assets to shareholders to acquire treasury stock or retire stock, the value of the stock retired may represent the best evidence of the value of the surrendered assets.
- *Cash option*. If a party to a nonmonetary transaction had the option to receive cash instead, the amount of the cash alternative could represent the best evidence of the value of the assets exchanged.

EXAMPLE

Nascent Corporation exchanges a color copier with a carrying amount of $18,000 with Declining Company for a print-on-demand publishing station. The color copier had an original cost of $30,000, and had incurred $12,000 of accumulated depreciation as of the transaction date. No cash is transferred as part of the exchange, and Nascent cannot determine the fair value of the color copier. The fair value of the publishing station is $20,000.

Nascent can record a gain of $2,000 on the exchange, which is derived from the fair value of the publishing station that it acquired, less the carrying amount of the color copier that it gave up. Nascent uses the following journal entry to record the transaction:

	Debit	Credit
Publishing equipment	20,000	
Accumulated depreciation	12,000	
Copier equipment		30,000
Gain on asset exchange		2,000

EXAMPLE

Nascent Corporation and Starlight Inc. swap spectroscopes, since the two devices have different features that the two companies need. The spectroscope given up by Nascent has a carrying amount of $25,000, which is comprised of an original cost of $40,000 and accumulated depreciation of $15,000. Both spectroscopes have identical fair values of $27,000.

Nascent's controller tests for commercial substance in the transaction. She finds that there is no difference in the fair values of the assets exchanged, and that Nascent's cash flows will not change significantly as a result of the swap. Thus, she concludes that the transaction has no commercial value, and so should account for it at book value, which means that Nascent cannot recognize a gain of $2,000 on the transaction, which is the difference between the $27,000 fair value of the spectroscope and the $25,000 carrying amount of the asset given up. Instead, she uses the following journal entry to record the transaction, which does not contain a gain or loss:

	Debit	Credit
Spectroscope (asset received)	25,000	
Accumulated depreciation	15,000	
Spectroscope (asset given up)		40,000

Purchases and Sales of Inventory with the Same Counterparty

There are situations where a company may sell inventory to another entity, and also buys inventory from that same entity, with the inventory in both transactions being sold in the same line of business. In many cases, the intent behind these transactions is for each party to procure inventory from the counterparty in the most cost-efficient manner, rather than to record a sale. If there is no commercial substance to each individual sale, the exchanges are instead clustered together and treated as a nonmonetary exchange (even if individual invoices or other sale agreements are documented between the parties).

The following factors are indicators that these purchase and sale transactions are entered into as paired units, rather than individual transactions, and so may not have commercial substance:

- *Certainty of transfer*. It is relatively certain that the counterparty will initiate a reciprocal inventory transfer.
- *Off-market terms*. The transactions incorporate off-market terms. This is especially relevant for exchange-traded commodities.
- *Offset*. There is a right of offset of obligations between the parties. This is especially evident when the different purchase and sale transactions are specifically identified by both parties.
- *Simultaneous transactions*. The purchase and sale transactions are entered into simultaneously.

EXAMPLE

Exotic Cars Limited routinely has an excess number of Ferraris in its Florida dealership, and is not allocated enough Maserati cars to meet demand. High Speed Auto, located in Texas, finds itself in the reverse situation, given the differing demographics and consumer buying habits where it is located. The dealerships enter into an agreement to sell each other their excess cars at roughly equivalent wholesale prices. Each transaction is separately invoiced and settled in cash.

Despite the form of settlement, this is clearly a reciprocal arrangement, and so should be accounted for as a nonmonetary exchange.

EXAMPLE

Armadillo Industries and Texas Armor Plating have done business with each other for many years, and routinely buy components from each other at market prices. Purchase orders are used to initiate each transaction, purchases are made at irregular intervals, and there is no arrangement to predicate one purchase on the presence of an offsetting arrangement. Historically, Texas Armor Plating has sold substantially more inventory to Armadillo. Each transaction is paid separately in cash, with no netting of transactions.

Since there is no correlation between the inventory values being exchanged, nor in the timing of exchanges, this scenario is not treated as a nonmonetary exchange, but instead as an ongoing series of sale and purchase transactions.

Nonmonetary exchanges of inventory should be recognized at the carrying amount of the inventory transferred (not their fair values). This means that the following exchanges should be recorded at inventory carrying amounts:

Transferred Out	In Exchange For
Raw materials or work-in-process inventory	Raw materials, work-in-process, or finished goods
Finished goods	Finished goods

If there is a transfer of finished goods in exchange for raw materials or work-in-process inventory, the transferor of the finished goods should record the transaction at its fair value, if fair value is determinable and the transaction has commercial substance.

Barter Transactions

In a barter transaction, a company may enter into a transaction where it exchanges a nonmonetary asset for barter credits which can then be used to acquire a different type of asset. These transactions can be directly between two entities, or through an intermediary that acts as a central exchange for a number of businesses that engage in barter transactions.

It is assumed that the fair value of the nonmonetary asset surrendered is more readily evident than the fair value of the barter credits received, which means that the barter credits received should be recorded at the fair value of the asset surrendered, unless one of the following situations is present:

- The company can convert the credits into cash in the near term
- There are quoted market prices available for items that can be acquired with barter credits

A business may need to recognize an impairment loss on the receipt of barter credits if it later becomes apparent that either of the following conditions exists:

- The fair value of unused barter credits has declined below their carrying amount
- The business will not use some or all of its remaining barter credits

Exchanges Involving Monetary Consideration

There can be any number of variations on the nonmonetary exchange concept, including ones where some cash is exchanged, along with other nonmonetary assets. If there is a significant amount of monetary consideration paid (known as *boot*), the entire transaction is considered to be a monetary transaction. In GAAP, a significant amount of boot is considered to be 25% of the fair value of an exchange. Conversely, if the amount of boot is less than 25%, the following accounting applies:

- *Payer*. The party paying boot is not allowed to recognize a gain on the transaction (if any).
- *Recipient*. The receiver of the boot recognizes a gain to the extent that the monetary consideration is greater than a proportionate share of the carrying amount of the surrendered asset. This calculation is based on the percentage of monetary consideration received to either:
  - Total consideration received, or
  - The fair value of the nonmonetary asset received (if more clearly evident)

The recipient's gain calculation is:

$$\frac{\text{Boot}}{\text{Boot} + \text{Fair value of asset received}} \times \text{Total gain} = \text{Gain recognized}$$

If the terms of the transaction indicate that a loss has occurred, the entire amount of the loss is to be recognized at once.

EXAMPLE

Nascent Corporation is contemplating the exchange of one of its heliographs for a catadioptric telescope owned by Aphelion Corporation. The two companies have recorded these assets in their accounting records as follows:

	Nascent (Heliograph)	Aphelion (Catadioptric)
Cost	$82,000	$97,000
Accumulated depreciation	22,000	27,000
Net book value	$60,000	$70,000
Fair value	$55,000	$72,000

Under the terms of the proposed asset exchange, Nascent must pay cash (boot) to Aphelion of $17,000. The boot amount is 24 percent of the fair value of the exchange, which is calculated as:

$17,000 Boot ÷ ($55,000 Fair value of heliograph + $17,000 Boot) = 24%

The parties elect to go forward with the exchange. The amount of boot is less than 25 percent of the total fair value of the exchange, so Aphelion should recognize a pro rata portion of the $2,000 gain (calculated as the $72,000 total fair value of the asset received - $70,000 net book value of the asset received) on the exchange using the following calculation:

24% Portion of boot to total fair value received × $2,000 Gain = $480 Recognized gain

Nascent uses the following journal entry to record the exchange transaction:

	Debit	Credit
Telescope (asset received)	72,000	
Accumulated depreciation	22,000	
Loss on asset exchange	5,000	
Cash		17,000
Heliograph (asset given up)		82,000

Nascent's journal entry includes a $5,000 loss; the loss is essentially the difference between the book value and fair value of the heliograph on the transaction date.

Aphelion uses the following journal entry to record the exchange transaction:

	Debit	Credit
Heliograph (asset received)	53,480	
Accumulated depreciation	27,000	
Cash	17,000	
Gain on asset exchange		480
Telescope (asset given up)		97,000

Aphelion is not allowed to recognize the full value of the heliograph at the acquisition date because of the boot rule for small amounts of cash consideration; this leaves the heliograph undervalued by $1,520 (since its fair value is actually $55,000).

The accounting is different if the amount of boot is 25 percent or more of the fair value of the exchange. In this situation, both parties should record the transaction at its fair value.

EXAMPLE

Nascent Corporation exchanges a wide field CCD camera for a Schmidt-Cassegrain telescope owned by Aphelion Corporation. The two companies have recorded these assets in their accounting records as follows:

	Nascent (Camera)	Aphelion (Schmidt-Cassegrain)
Cost	$50,000	$93,000
Accumulated depreciation	(30,000)	(40,000)
Net book value	$20,000	$53,000
Fair value	$24,000	$58,000

Under the terms of the agreement, Nascent pays $34,000 cash (boot) to Aphelion. This boot amount is well in excess of the 25 percent boot level, so both parties can now treat the deal as a monetary transaction.

Nascent uses the following journal entry to record the exchange transaction, which measures the telescope acquired at the fair value of the camera and cash surrendered:

	Debit	Credit
Telescope (asset received)	58,000	
Accumulated depreciation	30,000	
Gain on asset exchange		4,000
Cash		34,000
CCD camera (asset given up)		50,000

The gain recorded by Nascent is the difference between the $24,000 fair value of the camera surrendered and its $20,000 book value.

Aphelion uses the following journal entry to record the exchange transaction, which measures the camera acquired at the fair value of the telescope surrendered less cash received:

	Debit	Credit
Camera (asset received)	24,000	
Accumulated depreciation	40,000	
Cash	34,000	
Gain on asset exchange		5,000
Telescope (asset given up)		93,000

The gain recorded by Aphelion is the difference between the $58,000 fair value of the telescope surrendered and its $53,000 book value.

Exchanges of a Nonfinancial Asset for a Noncontrolling Ownership Interest

There are certain types of nonmonetary exchanges where a business transfers nonfinancial assets to a second entity in exchange for a noncontrolling interest in the second entity. This requires the recognition of the surrendered assets at their fair value (or the fair value of the ownership interest received, if that figure is more readily determinable), and the recognition of a full or partial gain on the transaction.

If the fair value of the assets surrendered exceeds the amount of their carrying value, recognize a gain under either of the following options:

- *Cost method.* If the transferor accounts for the ownership interest received using the cost method, recognize a gain in the full amount of the difference.
- *Equity method.* If the transferor accounts for the ownership interest received using the equity method, recognize a partial gain. In this case, the gain is reduced by the company's portion of its economic interest in the other entity.

EXAMPLE

Armadillo Industries exchanges an asset with a carrying value of $1,000,000 and a fair value of $1,500,000 for a 25% economic interest in Armor International. Armadillo accounts for its interest in Armor using the cost method. Armadillo should recognize a gain of $375,000 on the transaction, which is calculated as follows:

($1,500,000 Fair value - $1,000,000 Carrying amount) × (1 - 25% Economic interest)

= $375,000 Gain

If the fair value of the assets surrendered is less than the amount of their carrying value, recognize the full amount of the loss at once.

The result of the transfer of a nonfinancial asset for a noncontrolling ownership interest might be the deconsolidation of the entity surrendering the asset, if the asset is a subsidiary or a group of assets that constitute a business.

Nonmonetary Transaction Disclosures

If a business engages in nonmonetary transactions, it should disclose the following information:

- *Description.* Disclose the nature of these transactions.
- *Basis.* Describe the basis of accounting for the transferred assets.
- *Gains or losses.* State the amount of any gains or losses recognized in relation to the nonmonetary transfers.
- *Revenue.* State the amount of gross operating revenue resulting from nonmonetary transfers.
- *Transfers.* If inventory is being exchanged, note the related amount of revenues and costs associated with the exchanges at their fair values.

Summary

Of the types of nonmonetary transactions described in this chapter, the most common one by far is exchanges using monetary consideration. These transactions arise when a business trades in old equipment for new equipment, and pays a significant sum for the difference between the fair values of the two assets being exchanged. The accountant may never encounter the other types of nonmonetary transactions noted in this chapter.

Chapter 45
Related Party Disclosures

850 = GAAP codification area for related party disclosures

Introduction

A separate area of the GAAP codification has been reserved for related party disclosures, which is somewhat unusual, because the related GAAP does not mandate any accounting recordation – only the disclosure of information involving related party transactions. This chapter describes the nature of a related party transaction, and then itemizes the required disclosures for these types of transactions. The guidance in this chapter applies to all entities.

Overview of Related Parties

A company may do business with a variety of parties with which it has a close association. These parties are known as related parties. Examples of related parties are:

- Affiliates
- Other subsidiaries under common control
- Owners of the business, its managers, and their families
- The parent entity
- Trusts for the benefit of employees

There are many types of transactions that can be conducted between related parties, such as sales, asset transfers, leases, lending arrangements, guarantees, allocations of common costs, and the filing of consolidated tax returns.

The disclosure of related party information is considered useful to the readers of a company's financial statements, particularly in regard to the examination of changes in the financial results and financial position over time, and in comparison to the same information for other businesses.

Related Party Disclosures

In general, any related party transaction should be disclosed that would impact the decision making of the users of a company's financial statements. This involves the following disclosures:

- *General*. Disclose all material related party transactions, including the nature of the relationship, the nature of the transactions, the dollar amounts of the transactions, the amounts due to or from related parties and the settlement terms (including tax-related balances), and the method by which any current and deferred tax expense is allocated to the members of a group. Do not include compensation arrangements, expense allowances, or any transactions that are eliminated in the consolidation of financial statements.

- *Control relationship.* Disclose the nature of any control relationship where the company and other entities are under common ownership or management control, and this control could yield results different from what would be the case if the other entities were not under similar control, even if there are no transactions between the businesses.
- *Receivables.* Separately disclose any receivables from officers, employees, or affiliated entities.

Depending on the transactions, it may be acceptable to aggregate some related party information by type of transaction. Also, it may be necessary to disclose the name of a related party, if doing so is required to understand the relationship.

When disclosing related party information, do not state or imply that the transactions were on an arm's-length basis, unless the claim can be substantiated.

Summary

Related party transactions are surprisingly common, especially when the owners of a company are continually propping up the business with additional funding or granting favorable financing terms. Accordingly, this is a topic worthy of regular review, since there can be an ongoing series of related party transactions that must be disclosed.

Chapter 46
Subsequent Events

855 = GAAP codification area for subsequent events

Introduction

There will always be a continuing series of events that can impact the information incorporated into a company's financial statements, and some of them will occur after the balance sheet date. This chapter sets forth the general principles needed to determine whether the recognition of these subsequent events can be safely delayed until the next set of financial statements, or if the statements relating to the last accounting period must be revised to incorporate them. The guidance in this chapter applies to all entities.

Overview of Subsequent Events

A subsequent event is an event that occurs after a reporting period, but before the financial statements for that period have been issued or are available to be issued. The two types of subsequent events are:

- *Additional information.* An event provides additional information about conditions in existence as of the balance sheet date, including estimates used to prepare the financial statements for that period.
- *New events.* An event provides new information about conditions that did not exist as of the balance sheet date.

GAAP states that the financial statements should include the effects of all subsequent events that provide additional information about conditions in existence as of the balance sheet date. This rule requires that all entities evaluate subsequent events through the date when financial statements are available to be issued, while a public company should continue to do so through the date when the financial statements are actually filed with the Securities and Exchange Commission. Examples of situations calling for the adjustment of financial statements are:

- *Lawsuit.* If events take place before the balance sheet date that trigger a lawsuit, and lawsuit settlement is a subsequent event, consider adjusting the amount of any contingent loss already recognized to match the amount of the actual settlement.
- *Bad debt.* If a company issues invoices to a customer before the balance sheet date, and the customer goes bankrupt as a subsequent event, consider adjusting the allowance for doubtful accounts to match the amount of receivables that will likely not be collected.

If there are subsequent events that provide new information about conditions that did not exist as of the balance sheet date, and for which the information arose before the financial statements were available to be issued or were issued, these events should not be recognized in the financial statements. Examples of situations that do not trigger an adjustment to the financial statements if they occur after the balance sheet date but before financial statements are issued or are available to be issued are:

- A business combination
- Changes in the value of assets due to changes in exchange rates
- Destruction of company assets
- Entering into a significant guarantee or commitment
- Sale of equity
- Settlement of a lawsuit where the events causing the lawsuit arose after the balance sheet date

Subsequent Event Disclosures

A company should disclose the date through which there has been an evaluation of subsequent events, as well as either the date when the financial statements were issued or when they were available to be issued.

There may be situations where the non-reporting of a subsequent event would result in misleading financial statements. If so, disclose the nature of the event and an estimate of its financial effect.

There may be situations where management believes it necessary to present pro forma financial statements (usually just the balance sheet) that incorporate the effects of subsequent events as if they had occurred on the balance sheet date. This is not a requirement.

If a business reissues its financial statements, disclose the dates through which it has evaluated subsequent events, both for the previously issued and revised financial statements.

Summary

The recognition of subsequent events in financial statements can be quite subjective in many instances. Given the amount of time required to revise financial statements at the last minute, it is worthwhile to strongly consider whether the circumstances of a subsequent event can be construed as *not* requiring the revision of financial statements.

There is a danger in inconsistently applying the subsequent event rules, so that similar events do not always result in the same treatment of the financial statements. Consequently, it is best to adopt internal rules regarding which events will always lead to the revision of financial statements; these rules will likely require continual updating, as the business encounters new subsequent events that had not previously been incorporated into its rules.

Glossary

A

Accounting change. A change in an accounting principle, accounting estimate, or reporting entity.

Accretable yield. The excess amount of cash flows from a loan expected to be received in excess of the initial investment in a loan.

Accretion expense. An expense arising from an increase in the carrying amount of the liability associated with an asset retirement obligation.

Accumulated benefit obligation. The actuarial present value of all benefits attributed to employee service rendered before a certain date.

Acquiree. A business that an acquirer gains control of via a business combination.

Acquirer. An entity that gains control of an acquiree.

Acquisition, development, and construction arrangement. An arrangement in which a lender participates in the expected residual profits generated by the sale or refinancing of property.

Actuarial present value. The value of a series of future payments, adjusted for the probability of payment.

Affiliate. A party that controls, is controlled by, or is under common control with an entity.

Amortization. The write-off of an intangible asset over its expected period of use.

Asset retirement obligation. A liability associated with the retirement of a fixed asset.

Available-for-sale securities. Investments that are not classified as held-to-maturity or trading securities.

Award. An instrument granted to one or more employees at the same time, all with the same terms and conditions.

B

Bargain purchase. A business combination in which the fair value received by the acquirer exceeds the consideration paid.

Bargain purchase option. A lease clause allowing the lessee to purchase leased property for an amount below its expected fair value.

Bargain renewal option. A lease clause allowing the lessee to renew a lease for an amount below its expected fair value.

Glossary

Basic earnings per share. The earnings for an accounting period divided by the common stock outstanding during that period.

Bill and hold. A situation where the seller recognizes revenue from a sale, despite not shipping the related goods to the buyer.

Book value. An asset's original cost, less any depreciation or impairment that has been subsequently incurred.

Boot. The cash paid as part of an exchange of assets between two parties.

Breakage. That portion of the dollar value of the product that is not redeemed for cash or used to make a purchase.

Business combination. A transaction that results in an acquirer gaining control of an acquiree.

Business interruption insurance. Insurance that reimburses for certain losses associated with the loss of use of a property or the equipment within it.

C

Capital lease. A lease agreement that either shifts ownership of the leased asset to the lessee, contains a bargain purchase option, represents a long-term lease, or for which the present value of all lease payments represent nearly all of the fair value of the asset.

Capitalization. When an expenditure is recorded as an asset, rather than an expense.

Capitalization limit. A minimum threshold, above which an expenditure is recorded as a long-term asset, and below which it is charged to expense.

Capitalization rate. The rate used to calculate the amount of interest to be capitalized.

Carryback. A tax deduction or a tax credit that cannot be used in the tax return for the current year, but which can be used in an earlier year to reduce the amount of taxable income or taxes payable. An operating loss carryback represents excess available tax deductions, while a tax credit carryback represents excess available tax credits.

Carryforward. A tax deduction or tax credit that cannot be used in the tax return for the current year, but which can be used in a future period to reduce the amount of taxable income or taxes payable. An operating loss carryforward represents excess available tax deductions, while a tax credit carryforward represents excess available tax credits.

Carrying amount. The recorded amount of an asset, net of any accumulated depreciation or accumulated impairment losses.

Cash equivalent. A short-term, very liquid investment that is easily convertible into a known amount of cash, and which is so near its maturity that it presents an insignificant risk of a change in value because of changes in interest rates.

Cease-use date. The date on which a business stops using the rights conveyed by a contract.

Change in accounting estimate. A change that adjusts the carrying amount of an asset or liability, or the subsequent accounting for it.

Change in accounting principle. A change from one generally accepted accounting principle to another, or a change in the method of applying it.

Change in reporting entity. A situation in which financial statements become those of a different entity, usually due to consolidation or altering the subsidiaries in consolidated results.

Chief operating decision maker. A person who is responsible for making decisions about resource allocations to the segments of a business, and for evaluating those segments.

Class. A group of fixed assets having common characteristics and usage.

Commercial substance. When a company expects that its future cash flows will change significantly as a result of a transaction. A cash flow change is considered significant if the risk, timing, or amount of future cash flows of the asset received differ significantly from those of the asset given up.

Commitment fee. A fee charged for entering into a loan agreement.

Communication date. The date on which the plan for employee termination benefits is communicated to employees, and meets a number of additional criteria.

Compensated absence. An employee absence for which the employee will be paid.

Component of an entity. Operations and cash flows that can be clearly distinguished from the rest of a business.

Comprehensive income. The change in equity of a business during a period, not including investments by or distributions to owners.

Conditional promise to give. A promise to contribute that is dependent upon the future occurrence of a specific future event whose occurrence is uncertain.

Consideration. Items used by a buyer to pay a seller, such as cash, credits, goods, and services.

Consolidated financial statements. Financial statements that present the results of a group of entities as though they were a single entity.

Contingency. An uncertain situation that will be resolved in the future, generating a possible gain or loss.

Contingent consideration. A payment obligation by the acquirer to the former owners of an acquiree if certain events occur or conditions are met.

Contractor. An entity that contracts to build facilities, construct goods, or provide services in accordance with the specifications of the buyer.

Contribution. The unconditional transfer of cash or other assets to a third party, or the cancellation of a liability owed by a third party.

Control. Having the power to direct the management and policies of an entity.

Corporate joint venture. A separate corporation owned by a small number of investors for the mutual benefit of the investors.

Cost-plus-fixed fee contract. A contract under which a contractor is reimbursed for costs incurred, plus a fixed fee.

Cost pool. A grouping of individual costs, typically by department or service center. Cost allocations are then made from the cost pool.

Cost to sell. The costs incurred in a sale transaction that would not have been incurred if there had been no sale. Examples of costs to sell are title transfer fees and brokerage commissions.

Credit default swap. A contract that transfers credit exposure between parties.

Credit quality indicator. A statistic that describes the credit quality of financing receivables, such as consumer credit risk scores, collection experience, and internal credit risk grades.

Credit rating. A published score relating to an entity's ability to repay a debt obligation.

Credit risk. The risk that a borrower will not pay back a loan, or that the counterparty to a contract will not pay.

Current assets. Cash and other assets that are expected to be converted into cash during the normal operating cycle of a business.

Current cost-constant purchasing power. Accounting based on measures of either current cost or lower recoverable amount.

Current liabilities. Those liabilities whose payment is expected to require the use of current assets or their replacement with other current liabilities.

Curtailment. An event that reduces the expected years of future service of current employees and/or eliminates defined benefits.

D

Debt. A contractual right to receive payment that is considered an asset by the lender and a liability by the borrower.

Debt security. A security that involves a creditor relationship with a borrower, such as bonds, commercial paper, and Treasury securities.

Deductible temporary difference. A temporary difference that yields a deductible amount when the underlying asset or liability is eventually recovered or settled.

Defensive intangible asset. An intangible asset acquired to keep it from being used by others.

Deferred tax asset. A tax reduction whose recognition is delayed due to deductible temporary differences and carryforwards.

Deferred tax expense. The net change in the deferred tax liabilities and assets of a business during a period of time.

Deferred tax liability. A tax whose payment is delayed due to taxable temporary differences.

Defined benefit plan. A payment plan that defines the amount of benefits to be provided.

Defined contribution plan. A payment plan that pays participants based on the original amounts contributed, and net of subsequent investment experience, forfeitures, and administrative costs.

Depreciation. The gradual charging to expense of an asset's cost over its expected useful life.

Derivative financial instrument. A financial contract whose value depends on the price of an underlying asset.

Diluted earnings per share. The earnings for an accounting period divided by the common stock outstanding during that period and all potential common stock.

Dilution. When earnings per share is reduced by the assumption that all potential common stock is converted to common stock.

Direct cash flows. Cash flows associated with the revenue-producing and cost-generating activities of a component.

Direct costs. Costs that can be clearly associated with specific activities or products, such as direct materials.

Direct method. A format of the statement of cash flows that presents specific cash flows in the operating activities section of the report.

Disposal group. A group of assets that are expected to be disposed of in a single transaction, along with any liabilities that might be transferred to another entity along with the assets.

E

Effective interest rate. The contractual interest rate of a loan, adjusted for discounts, premiums, and other costs.

Employee. A person over whom an employer has sufficient control to establish an employer-employee relationship.

Equity security. A security that represents an ownership interest in, or a right to acquire or dispose of an ownership interest in, an entity.

Exchange. A reciprocal transfer between two entities of assets and/or liabilities.

Exchange rate. The ratio at which a unit of one currency can be exchanged for another currency.

Expected residual profit. Any profit greater than a reasonable amount of interest and fees that a lender would be expected to earn.

Experience adjustment. An insurance contract provision that alters the premium, coverage, and/or commission based on loss experience.

Extended warranty. The provision of a warranty beyond the scope or term of the original manufacturer's warranty.

F

Fair value. The price paid for an asset or liability in an orderly transaction between market participants.

Fair value hedge. A hedge of the exposure to changes in the fair value of an asset or liability that is attributable to a specific risk.

Financial asset. Either cash or an ownership interest or contract that conveys the right to receive cash or another financial instrument.

Financial instrument. A document that has monetary value or which establishes an obligation to pay.

Financial liability. A contract that imposes an obligation to deliver cash or another financial instrument to another entity.

Financial risk. The risk that changes in the markets will have a negative impact on the profits of a business.

Financial statements available to be issued. When financial statements are complete, comply with GAAP, and have been approved for issuance.

Firm commitment. A legally binding agreement between two unrelated parties, that states all of the significant terms of a transaction, and which contains a large disincentive for nonperformance.

Firm fixed-price contract. A contract under which the price paid is not subject to adjustment.

Fiscal funding clause. A lease clause that allows the lessee to cancel a lease if a funding authority does not provide sufficient funding to make scheduled lease payments.

Forecasted transaction. A transaction that is expected to occur at a later date, but for which there is no firm commitment.

Foreign currency. A currency other than the functional currency being used by an entity.

Foreign currency translation. The process of converting amounts stated in a foreign currency into the reporting currency of the parent entity.

Foreign exchange rate. The price at which one currency can be converted into a different currency.

Foreign exchange risk. The risk that the value of an investment will be reduced by changes in the applicable foreign exchange rate.

Functional currency. The currency that an entity uses in the majority of its business transactions.

G

Gain contingency. An uncertain situation that will be resolved in the future, generating a possible gain.

Goodwill. An intangible asset that represents the future benefits arising from assets acquired in a business combination that are not otherwise identified.

Grant date. The date on which an employer agrees to become contingently obligated to issue a payment to an employee once that person renders a service.

Gross margin. Revenues less the cost of goods sold.

Gross profit method. The use of the historical gross margin to estimate the amount of ending inventory.

H

Hazardous waste. A type of waste that can cause an increase in mortality or illness, or be a hazard to the environment.

Hedge. An action taken to reduce an existing or expected risk.

Held for sale. A designation given to assets that an entity intends to sell to a third party within one year.

Held-to-maturity securities. A debt security that the holder intends to hold to maturity, and who has the ability to do so.

Historical cost. Costing based on measures of historical prices, without subsequent restatement.

Holding gain or loss. A change in the fair value of a security.

I

Impairment. A condition that arises when the carrying amount of an asset exceeds its fair value.

Implicit service period. A period of time or event that is not specifically stated in the terms of a share-based award, but which can be construed from the facts and circumstances.

Imputed interest rate. The estimated interest rate used instead of the established interest rate associated with a debt.

In-force policies. Insurance policies in effect prior to a designated date, and which have not yet terminated.

In-substance common stock. An investment that has the risk and reward characteristics of an entity's common stock.

In-substance defeasance. When a debtor places an amount equal to the principal, interest, and prepayment penalties for a debt instrument in a trust for the benefit of a creditor.

Income taxes. Taxes that are based on the reported amount of income.

Incurred losses. Losses for which an insuring entity has become liable during a period.

Indirect guarantee of indebtedness. An agreement requiring a payment by a guarantor to a debtor when certain events occur.

Indirect method. A format of the statement of cash flows that uses accrual-basis accounting as part of the presentation of cash flow information.

Intangible assets. Assets that have no physical substance.

Intercompany transaction. A transaction that occurs between different entities within a consolidated entity.

Interest method. The determination of a periodic interest cost that equates to a flat effective interest rate on the sum total of the face amount of a debt and any related unamortized discounts and premiums.

Interest rate. The rate charged for the use of money for a period of time.

Interim period. A financial reporting period that is shorter than a full fiscal year.

Intrinsic value. The excess amount of the fair value of a share over the exercise price of an underlying stock option.

Inventory. Tangible items held for routine sale, or which are being produced for sale, or which are consumed in the production of goods for sale. Depreciated assets are not considered inventory.

Investee. A business whose equity instruments are owned by an investor.

Investor. An entity that owns the voting stock of a business.

Item master. A record that lists the name, description, unit of measure, weight, dimensions, ordering quantity, and other key information for a component part.

L

Lease. An agreement that allows the lessee use of a fixed asset.

Legal notification period. The time period during which a business is legally required to provide notice to employees regarding a termination event.

Lessee. The entity allowed use of a fixed asset under a lease agreement.

Lessor. The entity allowing use of its fixed asset to a third party under a lease agreement.

LIFO layer. A cost per unit ascribed to certain units of stock under the last in, first out method of inventory costing.

Liquidation. The process of converting assets into cash and settling creditor claims, in expectation of ceasing operations.

Loan origination fee. A fee charged as prepaid interest or an interest rate adjustment, or to reimburse the lender for its costs.

Loan syndication. When several lenders share in the lending to a borrower.

Local currency. The legal currency being used within a country.

Lock-box arrangement. A debt repayment arrangement, where the customers of the borrower send their remittances to the lender, and these payments are applied against the debt.

Loss contingency. An uncertain situation that will be resolved in the future, generating a possible loss.

Lower of cost or market. The concept that inventory items should be recorded at the lower of their cost or the current market price.

M

Management. Those responsible for and with the authority to achieve the objectives of an entity. Usually considered to include the board of directors, the chief executive officer, chief operating officer, and those vice presidents operating key functional areas.

Market. The current replacement cost of an item, as long as it does not exceed net realizable value, and is not less than net realizable value minus a normal profit margin.

Milestone. An event about which there is uncertainty that a target will be achieved, and where achievement is based on vendor performance and a specific outcome, and from which additional payments will be due to the supplier. It is not contingent solely upon the passage of time or the result of counterparty performance.

Monetary assets. Money or the right to receive money, for which the amount is fixed or determinable.

Monetary liability. The obligation to pay money, for which the amount is fixed or determinable.

N

Near term. A period not exceeding one year following the date of the financial statements.

Net income. Revenues and gains, less expenses and losses, not including items of other comprehensive income.

Net periodic pension cost. The expense that an employer recognizes in a reporting period as the cost of a pension plan.

Net realizable value. The estimated selling price of an item in the ordinary course of business, not including any costs of completion and disposal.

Nonaccretable difference. Required loan payments in excess of the cash flows expected to be collected.

Noncontrolling interest. That portion of the equity of a subsidiary not owned by the parent entity.

Nonreciprocal transfer. The transfer of assets from one entity to another.

Nonvested shares. Shares not yet issued, because the consideration that earns the shares has not yet been completed.

Normal capacity. The production volume a business expects to achieve over a number of periods under normal circumstances.

Notional amount. The face value of a financial instrument, which is used to make calculations based on that amount.

O

Obligated to write. When an insurer cannot cancel a policy and is required to offer policies in a future period.

Operating cycle. The time period from the acquisition of goods and services to the receipt of cash from their sale.

Operating lease. Any lease not designated as a capital lease.

Operating segment. A component of a public entity.

Option. A contract that gives the holder the right, but not the obligation, to purchase or sell an asset at a specific price for a designated period of time.

Orphan share. The share of liability for environmental remediation costs attributable to other parties that exceeds the amount for which those parties have already settled their liability.

Other comprehensive income. Revenue, expense, gain, and loss items that are excluded from net income but included in comprehensive income.

Overhead absorbed. Manufacturing overhead that has been applied to products or other cost objects.

P

Parent. A business that has a controlling interest in a subsidiary.

Participation rights. The rights accorded to the holder of a security to receive payments associated with the profits, cash flows, or other results of a business.

Potential common stock. Securities that can be converted to common stock, such as options, warrants, and convertible securities.

Preferred stock. A security that receives preferential treatment in comparison to common stock.

Premiums written. The premiums on the policies issued by an insurer during a specific period of time.

Prepaid stored-value product. A product in physical or digital form with stored monetary value that is intended to be accepted as a form of payment.

Principal owners. Owners having more than 10% of the voting interests of a business.

Prior service cost. The cost of those benefits retroactively granted in an amendment to a benefit plan that apply to employee services provided in periods prior to the amendment.

Probable. When there is a likely chance of occurrence for a future event.

Product financing arrangement. A transaction in which the seller of inventory agrees to repurchase it at the original selling price.

Projected benefit obligation. The actuarial present value of the benefits to employee service prior to a measurement date.

Promise to give. An agreement to contribute assets to a third party.

Public entity. A business that is required to file financial statements with the Securities and Exchange Commission.

Purchasing power gain or loss. The net gain or loss derived from restating the beginning and ending balances of monetary assets and liabilities in units of constant purchasing power.

Pushdown accounting. When the acquirer's basis of accounting is used to prepare the financial statements of the acquiree.

R

Rabbi trust. A trust created for compensation paid to certain managers or highly paid executives, and whose contents are available to satisfy the claims of creditors if the employer goes bankrupt.

Glossary

Readily determinable fair value. A valuation for an equity security that is based on readily determinable or bid-and-ask quotations that are currently available on a securities exchange.

Reasonably possible. When the chance of occurrence for a future event is more than remote but less than likely.

Recorded investment. The stated amount that a lender records in its accounting records for a loan, net of any write-down adjustments.

Recourse. The right to receive payment from the transferor of receivables if there are collection issues with the receivables.

Recoverable amount. The amount of cash expected to be recoverable from the use or sale of an asset.

Registration payment arrangement. A requirement to register securities issued to investors, or to maintain the effectiveness of a registration statement, with penalty clauses if these objectives are not met.

Related parties. Includes the affiliates, principal owners, and management of a business, as well as equity method investors, trusts for the benefit of employees, family members of principal owners and managers, and other parties having influence over the business.

Reload feature. The automatic granting of additional options whenever previously granted options are exercised, in the amount used to exercise the previous option.

Remote. When there is a slight chance of occurrence for a future event.

Reporting currency. The currency in which a business prepares its financial statements.

Reporting entity. An organization whose financial statements are being referred to.

Reporting unit. An operating segment or one level below an operating segment. An operating segment is a component of a public entity that engages in business activities and whose results are reviewed by the chief operating decision maker, and for which discrete financial information is available.

Repurchase agreement. Assets sold under an agreement to repurchase the assets.

Research and development. Research is the search for new knowledge, while development is the translation of research findings into new products or process improvements.

Residual value. The estimated fair value of an intangible asset once an entity judges its useful life to be complete, minus disposal costs.

Restatement. The revision of prior financial statements to correct an error.

Restricted share. A share that cannot be sold for a certain period of time.

Restructuring. A program that materially changes the scope of a business or the manner in which it conducts business.

Retirement. The permanent removal of a long-lived asset from service.

Retrospective application. The application of a different accounting principle to prior financial statements or the balance sheet at the beginning of the current period.

Reverse acquisition. A business combination in which the legal acquirer is the acquiree for accounting purposes.

Reverse repurchase agreement. Assets purchased under an agreement to resell the assets.

Reverse spinoff. The transfer of a subsidiary to shareholders where the transferred entity is the continuing entity.

Right of setoff. A debtor's right to apply its debt owed to another party to a debt owed by the other party to the debtor.

S

Sabbatical leave. A compensated absence earned by working for an employer for a certain period of time.

Salvage value. The estimated value of an asset at the end of its useful life.

Security. An interest in an entity or an obligation of the issuer that is represented by an instrument that is a medium of investment, and which is divisible into a class of shares or other interests.

Segment. A distinct component of a business that produces revenue, and for which the business produces separate financial information that is regularly reviewed internally by a chief operating decision maker.

Service condition. A service rendered by an employee that affects the vesting, price, or other component of the fair value of an award.

Severe impact. A significant financial disruption to company operations.

Significant influence. The ability to exercise significant influence over the operations of an investee, such as through a board seat, voting control (considered to be at least 20% of the voting stock), or the interchange of management personnel.

Slotting fees. Consideration from a supplier to a reseller to obtain space for the supplier's products in the reseller's store.

Spinoff. The transfer of a business into a new entity, where shares in the new entity are distributed to shareholders, while the shareholders retain their holdings of the original entity.

Sponsor. A person or business that capitalizes the expenditures associated with a research and development arrangement.

Springing lock-box arrangement. When customer remittances are sent to the borrower's general bank account, and are then only used to reduce the amount of debt outstanding if the lender triggers a subjective acceleration clause.

Standby letter of credit. A letter of credit that can require the issuer to make a payment in the event of the default or indebtedness of the beneficiary.

Startup activities. Any activities related to opening a facility, introducing a product, entering a territory, commencing a new operation, and so forth.

Stock dividend. A common stock issuance to existing common shareholders that does not diminish corporate assets or increase the interests of shareholders.

Stock option. An instrument that gives the holder the right, but not the obligation, to buy or sell shares at a certain price, and for a certain period of time.

Stock split. A common stock issuance to existing common shareholders that causes a stock price reduction, with the intent of enhancing the marketability of the shares.

Subjective acceleration clause. A provision in a debt agreement that allows the lender to require payment acceleration based on conditions that cannot be objectively determined.

Sublease. An arrangement in which the lessee re-leases property to a third party, while the original lease agreement remains in effect.

Subsequent event. An event that occurs after the date of the balance sheet, but before financial statements have been issued or are available to be issued.

Subsidiary. A business in which a parent entity owns a controlling interest.

Substantive conversion feature. A conversion feature for which the probability of exercise is reasonably possible, if the issuer does not exercise a call option.

T

Take-or-pay contract. An agreement between a buyer and seller, under which the buyer is obligated to periodically pay specific amounts for goods or services, even if it does not take delivery of these items.

Tax position. A position taken in a tax return that measures tax assets and liabilities, and which results in the permanent reduction or temporary deferral of income taxes.

Taxable temporary difference. A temporary difference that yields a taxable amount when the underlying asset or liability is eventually recovered or settled.

Temporary difference. The difference between the tax and accounting bases of an asset or liability that will result in a taxable or deductible amount when recovery or settlement eventually occurs.

Throughput contract. An agreement between the shipper of goods and an entity providing transport or processing services, under which the shipper is obligated to periodically pay specific amounts in exchange for transport or processing services, even if the shipper does not ship any goods.

Time-and-materials contract. A contract under which the contractor is paid a fixed hourly rate for hours worked, as well as for the cost of materials.

Timing risk. Risk caused by uncertainties in the timing of cash flows from premiums, commissions, claims, and claim settlements under an insurance contract.

Trading securities. Securities acquired with the intent of selling them in the near term to generate a profit.

Translation adjustment. An adjustment resulting from the translation of financial statements into the reporting currency of an entity.

Treasury stock. A company's stock that it has reacquired.

Troubled debt restructuring. A debt restructuring where the creditor grants a concession that it would not normally consider.

U

Unconditional promise to give. A commitment that only requires the passage of time or a demand by the receiving entity for the commitment to be realized.

Unconditional purchase obligation. An obligation to make future payments at fixed or minimum prices in exchange for the delivery of goods or services.

Underlying. A variable, such as an interest rate, exchange rate, or commodity price, that is used to determine the settlement of a derivative instrument.

Underwriting risk. Risk caused by uncertainties in the amount of cash flows from premiums, commissions, claims, and claim settlements under an insurance contract.

Unit-price contract. A contract under which a contractor is paid a fixed price for every unit of work completed.

Units-of-revenue method. The amortization of deferred revenue, based on the ratio of proceeds received to total payments expected to be paid to the investor, as applied to the current period's cash payment.

Unrealized gain or loss. The difference between the carrying amount and market price of a financial instrument that has not yet been sold.

Useful life. The time period over which an asset is expected to be productive or enhance cash flows, or the number of units of production expected to be generated from it.

V

Value in use. The discounted future cash flows derived from the expected future use of an asset.

Variable interest entity. An entity in which an investor has a noncontrolling interest, and which may be subject to consolidation in some situations.

Vest. When rights have been earned, such as when the end of a service period required for the issuance of shares has been reached.

Vested right. An employee right for which an employer must make a payment, even if the person's employment is terminated.

Volatility. The amount by which a variable fluctuates over time.

W

Warranty. A guarantee related to the performance of nonfinancial assets owned by the guaranteed party.

Index

9 781938 910999